A Writer's Toolbox

For quick reference, below are key concepts referred to throughout *The Prentice Hall Guide for College Writers*. (For handbook references, see inside back cover.)

Eighth Edition

The Prentice Hall Guide for College Writers

Stephen Reid

Colorado State University

PEARSON

Prentice Hall

Upper Saddle River, New Jersey 07458

Library of Congress Cataloging-in-Publication Data

Reid, Stephen
The Prentice Hall guide for college writers / Stephen Reid. — 8th ed.
  p. cm.
Includes bibliographical references and index.
ISBN 978-0-13-601698-4
1. English language—Rhetoric—Handbooks, manuals, etc. 2. Report writing—Handbooks,
manuals, etc. 3. College readers. I. Title.
  PE1408.R424 2008
  808'.042—dc22   2007037760

Editorial Director: Leah Jewell
Editor-in-Chief: Craig Campanella
Senior Editor: Brad Potthoff
Editorial Assistant: Tracy Clough
Marketing Director: Brandy Dawson
Marketing Manager: Windley Morley
Marketing Assistant: Heather Halpern
Text Permission Specialist: Kathleen Karcher
Senior Operations Supervisor: Sherry Lewis
Production Manager: Maureen Benicasa
Senior Art Director: Nancy Wells

Interior & Cover Design: Laura Gardner
Director, Image Resource Center: Melinda Patelli
Manager, Cover Visual Research and Permissions: Karen Sanatar
Manager, Rights and Permissions: Zina Arabia
Manager, Visual Research: Beth Brenzel
Image Permission Coordinator: Silvana Attansio
Image Researcher: Sheila Norman
Full-Service Production and Composition: S4Carlisle
  Publishing Services
Full-Service Project Management: Lynn Steines
Printer/Binder: Courier Companies
Cover Printer: Courier Companies

This book was set in 10/13.5 ACaslon.

Credits and acknowledgments borrowed from other sources and reproduced, with permission, in this textbook appear
on appropriate page within text (or on page C-1).

Pearson Education Ltd., London
Pearson Education Singapore, Pte. Ltd.
Pearson Education, Canada, Ltd.
Pearson Education—Japan
Pearson Education Australia PTY, Limited

Pearson Education North Asia Ltd.
Pearson Educación de Mexico, S.A. de C.V.
Pearson Education Malaysia, Pte. Ltd.
Pearson Education, Upper Saddle River, New Jersey

10 9 8 7 6 5 4 3 2
ISBN-13: 978-0-13-601698-4
ISBN-10: 0-13-601698-7

Brief Contents

Contents

6 Analyzing and Designing Visuals 215

7 Investigating 279

8 Explaining 343

9 Evaluating   399

10 Problem Solving   455

11 Arguing   509

Techniques for Writing: Argument   510

WARMING UP: Journal Exercises   525

Multigenre Casebook on Immigration Reform   540

Arguing: The Writing Process   568

Choosing a Subject   569

Postscript on the Writing Process   582

12 Responding to Literature   600

Responding to a Short Story   604

Responding to a Poem   607

Techniques for Responding to Literature   608

WARMING UP: Journal Exercises   609

Purposes for Responding to Literature   610

Responding to Short Fiction   612

Responding to Poetry   631

Responding to Literature: The Writing Process   640

Postscript on the Writing Process   647

13 Writing a Research Paper   656

Thematic Contents

The Prentice Hall Guide for College Writers, eighth edition, contains selections from over 100 writers, artists, poets, and photographers. Thematic clusters of essays, articles, editorials, Web sites, cartoons, poems, short fiction, and images are indicated below. An asterisk (*) indicates a complete essay.

TECHNOLOGY AND THE INTERNET

ENVIRONMENTAL ISSUES

EDUCATION

LITERACY AND LANGUAGE

ADVERTISING AND THE MEDIA

SOCIAL ISSUES

CULTURAL EXPLORATIONS

Preface

Ready or not, teachers of writing today find themselves ushered or perhaps even beamed into a New Media world. In some cases, we have a technological head start on our students; in other cases, we are scrambling to catch up with our students' knowledge of and facility with hybrid texts. The Internet, with its proliferation of Web sites, databases, blogs, and Facebook pages, is quickly becoming the dominant medium, and it features an amazing array of genres, designs, images, photographs, video clips, sound bites, and other forms of digitized communication. The public and academic writing we prepare our students for is itself a rapidly evolving target. Academic writing is becoming more hypertextual, and public writing is more and more multimedia based. We need to think only of Al Gore's *An Inconvenient Truth* to realize how academic and scientific information can be combined with digital images in a performed script to achieve a socially transformative goal.

Like climate change, New Media is arriving with seemingly scary speed and inevitability, and like global warming, it has both its doomsday scenarios and its positive and constructive visions. First, the doomsday scenarios. Some teachers complain that when students turn to visual communication, two things happen and both of them are bad. First, because students focus most of their time and attention on selecting images, their critical thinking and critical reading suffer, and the organization, coherence, and readability of their prose decline. Second, students' choices of visuals are often ineffective because the images are not connected to the text or are not appropriate for the intended genre, purpose, or audience. On the positive side, however, if we treat visuals and digital texts in a rhetorical manner, we can reemphasize our overall rhetorical principles. Once students understand that readers expect visuals to function in context, just as examples, facts, or statistics should do, they can see how rhetorical goals should govern their entire text. They can learn that using images must follow the golden rule: *Visuals must be relevant to and appropriate for the rhetorical goals of their text.* Multimedia elements must add to rather than detract from the purpose of their text.

Incorporating visual and digital elements into our writing classes thus places even more importance on designing our courses with clear rhetorical goals and principles. The WPA Outcomes Statement for First-Year Composition (available at www.wpacouncil.org) outlines four key goals: building students' *rhetorical knowledge* of purpose, audience, genre, cultural context, voice, and tone; improving students' *critical thinking, reading, and writing* skills; developing students' strategies for *writing processes*; and helping students develop their *knowledge of conventions*. Clearly, the first of these goals—building rhetorical knowledge of purpose, audience, genre, and cultural context—is crucial to helping students create effective New Media texts.

The eighth edition of *The Prentice Hall Guide for College Writers* keeps rhetorical context in the forefront in its new chapter, "Analyzing and Designing Visuals." This chapter shows students how to think always about rhetorical goals, purposes, and contexts in analyzing the effectiveness of multimedia texts that they read and in designing their own hybrid texts. This new chapter will help students learn to analyze hybrid texts in a rhetorical context; once students are more proficient at analyzing and evaluating visuals, they will be better able to create effective multimedia texts of their own. In addition to Chapter 6, "Analyzing and Designing Visuals," the eighth edition has several other important new features.

NEW FEATURES

Because more and more teachers are assigning *multigenre projects*, a greater variety of genres are represented throughout the eighth edition of *The Prentice Hall Guide for College Writers*. In particular, Chapter 11, "Arguing," has a multigenre casebook focusing on immigration reform in the United States. This section contains samples from a variety of public genres including essays, editorials, newspaper articles, photographs, online news, blogs, letters to the editor, cartoons, and Web sites. Students are encouraged to see the great variety of perspectives on an important and complex social issue and then to consider which genres they might use as they enter the conversation.

Second, the principle of providing *multiple perspectives on social topics*—rather than the more traditional pro-con approach—is illustrated in several chapters in this eighth edition. In addition to the multigenre casebook on immigration, the eighth edition features collections of multiple points of view on climate change and organic food production and consumption. Additional thematic groups are listed in the thematic table of contents.

Third, the important principles of *critical thinking* and *critical reading* are continued and expanded to apply to images, advertisements, posters, photographs, and cartoons. Students are provided guidelines for reading these texts critically when they appear by themselves, when they appear with a text, and when the social or political context is important.

Fourth, Chapter 13, "Writing a Research Paper," has been updated in order to make students' research processes easier and more in line with contemporary documentation guidelines. New color visuals enable students to understand how to evaluate their sources and document accurately using the new MLA or APA guidelines.

Finally, this eighth edition features over *twenty-five new selections*, including student writing and essays by professional writers such as Michael Pollan, Eric Schlosser, Peter Singer, Suze Orman, Robin Williams and John Tollett, Ellen Goodman, Daniel "Nene" Alejandrez, Jonathan Alter, Tania Ralli, William K. Stevens, Robert J. Samuelson, and Ruben Navarrette, Jr.

CONTINUING KEY FEATURES

ANNOTATED INSTRUCTOR'S EDITION

The Annotated Instructor's Edition contains additional guidelines for teaching each chapter, including instructional tips on critical reading, critical thinking, responding to assignments, peer group activities, and ESL teaching tips designed to alert teachers to possible problems and solutions for ESL writers.

ALTERNATE THEMATIC TABLE OF CONTENTS

The essays, stories, poems, and images in the eighth edition combine to create thematic clusters of topics that recur throughout the text: Climate Change, Race and Cultural Diversity, Gender Roles, Immigration Reform, Technology and the Internet, Environmental Issues, Education, Literacy and Language, Advertising and the Media, Social Issues, and Cultural Explorations.

EMPHASIS ON STUDENT WRITING

The eighth edition continues to showcase student writing, featuring the work of more than forty student writers from several colleges and universities. The eighth edition contains twenty-five full-length student essays and eleven essays with sample prewriting materials, rough drafts, peer response sheets, and postscripts.

LOGICAL SEQUENCE OF PURPOSE-BASED CHAPTERS

Within the rhetorical situation, aims and purposes help guide the reader to select appropriate genres, organizational strategies, appeals to audience, and appropriate styles. Early chapters in *The Prentice Hall Guide for College Writers* focus on observing, remembering, critical reading, analyzing visuals, and investigating while later chapters emphasize exposition and argumentation (explaining, evaluating, problem solving, and arguing).

FOCUS ON WRITING PROCESSES

Every major chapter contains guidelines for writing, journal exercises, reading and writing activities, collaborative activities, peer response guidelines, revision suggestions, and professional and student samples to assist students with their work-in-progress within their rhetorical situation.

JOURNAL WRITING

Throughout the text, write-to-learn activities help writers improve their critical reading skills, warm up for each assignment, and practice a variety of invention and shaping strategies appropriate for understanding their purpose, audience, genre, and social context.

MARGINAL QUOTATIONS

Nearly a hundred short quotations by composition teachers, researchers, essayists, novelists, and poets personalize for the inexperienced writer a larger community of writers still struggling with the same problems that each student faces.

AN INTRODUCTION TO MYTHS AND RITUALS FOR WRITING

Chapter One, "Writing Myths and Rituals," discounts some common myths about college writing courses, introduces the notion of writing rituals, and outlines the variety of journal writing used throughout the text. Writing process rituals are crucial for all writers but especially so for novice writers. Illustrating a variety of possible writing rituals are testimonies from a dozen professional writers on the nature of writing. These quotations continue throughout the book, reminding students that writing is not some magical process, but rather a madness that has a method to it, a process born of reading, thinking, observing, remembering, discussing, and writing.

AN ORIENTATION TO RHETORICAL SITUATION AND TO WRITING PROCESSES

Chapter Two, "Situations, Purposes, and Processes for Writing," grounds the writing process in the rhetorical situation. It shows how audience, genre, subject, and context work together with the writer's purpose to achieve a rhetorical end. It demonstrates how meaning evolves from a variety of recursive, multidimensional, and hierarchical activities that we call the *writing process*. Finally, it reassures students that, because individual writing and learning styles differ, they will be encouraged to discover and articulate their own processes from a range of appropriate possibilities.

AIMS AND PURPOSES FOR WRITING

The text then turns to specific purposes and assignments for writing. Chapters Three through Seven ("Observing," "Remembering," "Reading," "Analyzing and Designing Visuals," and "Investigating") focus on invention and critical reading strategies. These chapters introduce genres and situations for writing that build students' rhetorical repertoires: observing people, places, objects, and images; remembering people, places, and events; developing critical reading and responding strategies; developing critical reading strategies for visuals and rhetorical principles for designing visuals; and investigating and reporting through genres such as interviews, profiles, and multiple-source articles.

Chapters Eight through Eleven ("Explaining," "Evaluating," "Problem Solving," and "Arguing") emphasize subject- and audience-based purposes and occasions for writing. The sequence in these chapters moves the student smoothly from exposition to argumentation (acknowledging the obvious overlapping), building on the strategies and repertoires of the previous chapters. The teacher may, in fact, use Chapters Eight through Eleven as a minicourse in argument, teaching students how to develop and argue claims of fact and definition, claims of cause and effect, claims about values, and claims about solutions or policies.

RESPONDING TO LITERATURE

Chapter Twelve, "Responding to Literature," guides students through the process of reading and responding to poetry and short fiction, using many of the critical reading strategies, invention techniques, and shaping strategies practiced in earlier chapters.

WRITING FROM SOURCES

Chapter Thirteen, "Writing a Research Paper," draws on all the reading, writing, and researching strategies presented in the first twelve chapters. Research papers are written for specific purposes, audiences, and contexts, but the invention, drafting, and revising processes are more extended. This chapter helps students select and plan their projects, find and critically evaluate library and Internet sources, record their progress in a research logs, and document their sources using MLA or APA styles.

HANDBOOK

A brief handbook includes a review of basic sentence elements, sentence structure and grammar, diction and style, and punctuation and mechanics.

SUPPLEMENTARY MATERIAL FOR INSTRUCTORS AND STUDENTS

ANNOTATED INSTRUCTOR'S EDITION (ISBN 0-13-601699-5)

The Annotated Instructor's Edition contains additional guidelines for each chapter, including teaching tips on critical reading, critical thinking, responding to assignments, and peer group activities. The AIE also offers teaching tips designed to alert instructors to problems commonly experienced by ESL writers and suggests solutions to those problems.

INSTRUCTOR'S MANUAL: TEACHING COMPOSITION WITH *THE PRENTICE HALL GUIDE FOR COLLEGE WRITERS* (ISBN 0-13-601701-0)

This instructor's manual, written by Stephen Reid, is designed to complement the AIE with additional classroom activities and ideas, as well as detailed discussion of effective strategies for the teaching of written expression skills. The manual also includes chapter commentaries, answers to discussion questions, and sections on composition theory, policy statements, lesson plans, collaborative writing, writing in a computer classroom, teaching ESL writers, small group learning, write-to-learn exercises, reading/writing exercise, journal assignments, suggestions for student conferences, and ideas for responding to and evaluating writing.

PRENTICE HALL POCKET READERS

Prentice Hall is pleased to offer additional collections of readings to accompany *The Prentice Hall Guide for College Writers,* as well as any of our composition textbooks.

Purposes: *A Prentice Hall Pocket Reader* (ISBN: 0-13-225069-1), compiled by Stephen Reid, features 23 additional readings by well-known writers and is an accompanying text to *The Prentice Hall Guide.* Contents are organized by purposes of writing, mirroring the format of the main text. This supplemental collection of readings may be packaged with the main text for a nominal charge.

Other Prentice Hall Pocket Readers include *Argument, Patterns, Themes, Writing Across the Curriculum,* and *Literature.* Consult your Pearson/Prentice Hall representative for details.

 *MyCompLab*® offers online writing support by composition instructors for composition instructors and their students.

MyCompLab (www.mycomplab.com), including an electronic and interactive version of *The Prentice Hall Guide for College Writers,* Eighth Edition, offers comprehensive online resources in grammar, writing, and research in one dynamic, accessible place:

- Grammar resources include *ExerciseZone,* with more than three thousand self-grading practice questions on sentences and paragraphs; and ESL *ExerciseZone,* with more than seven hundred self-grading questions.
- Writing resources include numerous writing activities involving videos, images, and Web sites; guided assistance through the writing process, with worksheets and exercises; and an extensive collection of sample papers from across the disciplines.
- Research resources include ResearchNavigator™, which provides help with the research process, the AutoCite™ bibliography maker, and access to ContentSelect™ by EBSCOhost and the subject-search archive of the New York Times. Also included is Avoiding Plagiarism, which offers tutorials in recognizing plagiarism, paraphrasing, documenting sources in MLA or APA style, and other topics.

MyCompLab includes an intelligent system called Grade Tracker that allows students to track their work, communicate with instructors, and monitor their improvement.

And more . . . *MyCompLab* includes even more resources to help students use this book and improve their writing. They can use the site independently, or their instructor may direct them to portions of it as part of their course assignments.

- Downloadable checklists and other materials from the book
- More than a thousand electronic exercises
- Video tutorials that supplement the book's explanations
- Hundreds of links to other Web sites providing additional help with the book's topics
- Sample research papers from various academic disciplines
- Usage flashcards on tricky words and phrases

PEARSON TUTOR SERVICES, POWERED BY SMARTHINKING

Students can submit their written work to Pearson Tutor Services for personalized and detailed feedback. Highly qualified writing tutors review the writing submitted and return it to the author with suggestions for improvement. Visit www.mycomplab.com for more detailed information.

ACKNOWLEDGMENTS

Because teaching writing is always a situated enterprise, I would like to thank the members of the composition faculty and staff at Colorado State University whose teaching expertise and enthusiasm have improved every page of the text: Kenneth Autrey, Francis Marion University; Dona Cady, Middlesex Community College; Joseph Rocky Colavito, Northwestern State University; Jennifer Pooler Courtney, University of North Carolina at Charlotte; Darin Cozzens, Surry Community College; Jessica Enoch, University of Pittsburgh; Beverly Fatherree, Hinds Community College; Dan Ferguson, Amarillo College; April Gentry, Savannah State University; Dawn Hayward, Delaware County Community College; Pamela Herring, Southwest Texas Junior College; Kim Jameson, Oklahoma City Community College; Gayle Larson, Dakota County Technical College; Juliet McDaniel, College of Lake County; Eileen Miller, Keiser College; Paralee Norman, Northwestern State University; Jarrod Patterson, Alabama A&M University; Althea Rhodes, University of Arkansas – Fort Smith; Rebekah Rios-Harris, Cedar Valley College; Christy Rishoi, Mott Community College; Carolee Ritter, Southeast Community College; Stephen Ruffus, Salt Lake Community College; Renee Rule, Ivy Tech; Karin Russell, Keiser College; Andrew Scott, Ball State University; Helen Szymanski, College of DuPage; Melissa Whiting, University of Arkansas – Fort Smith; Susan Whitlow, University of Arkansas – Fort Smith. Many of the innovative teaching strategies, resources, and syllabi developed by Colorado State University composition faculty members are available at http://writing.colostate.edu.

In addition, Stephen Ruffus expertly revised and updated the research strategies in Chapter 13, "Writing a Research Paper." Many of the other key suggestions for improvement came from the following teachers who offered excellent advice about changes and additions for the eighth edition: Pamela Herring, Southwest Texas Junior College; Gayle Larson, Dakota County Technical College; Jarrod Patterson, Alabama A&M University; Stephen Ruffus, Salt Lake Community College; Renee Rule, Ivy Tech; Helen Szymanski, College of DuPage. I wish to thank them for their thorough, honest, constructive, and professional advice.

For the expert crew at Prentice Hall, I am especially grateful. Phil Miller, a fine editor and friend, has enthusiastically supported this text from the first edition. Brad Potthoff provided an excellent vision for this revision, while Alexis Walker, Maureen Benicasa, and Lynn Steines gave invaluable developmental and production support.

Finally, I wish to thank my family for their continued personal and professional support.

—STEPHEN REID
Colorado State University

The
Prentice Hall
Guide for
College
Writers

Edouard Manet
Monet Painting in His Floating Studio (1874)
Bayerische Staatsgemäldesammlungen, Munich

This painting by Edouard Manet shows Monet's love of painting in the outdoors where he could capture the natural outdoor light. In this chapter, the journal exercise on page 12 invites you to consider on what occasions you enjoy reading, writing, or painting outdoors.

Writing Myths and Rituals

For me, the most effective writing ritual is to gather up all of my stuff—legal pad and pencil, notes, dictionary, and thesaurus—and get on my bike, ride to campus, and set myself up in the art lounge in the student center. During the week, I'll do this in the evening after dinner. On a weekend, I go any time from 10 A.M. to midnight. I don't write effectively at home because there are always distractions. Some people will be moving around and I'll go see who they are and what they're doing, or I'll go get a cup of coffee or a piece of toast, or I'll snap on the TV, ignoring that tiny voice inside saying, "Get busy—you have to get this done!" So what makes the art lounge better? Simple—no distractions. I can lay out all of my stuff, get a cup of coffee, and go to work. All around me people are doing the same thing, and somehow all of those hardworking people are an encouragement. The art lounge is always quiet, too—quieter than the library—and it doesn't smell like the library.

One myth about writing I have believed my whole life is that "good writers are born, not made." My attitude when beginning this writing course was one of apprehension and dread. I wondered if I *could* improve my writing, or if I was destined to receive Bs and Cs on every essay for the rest of my life. This writing class has given me concrete examples and suggestions for improvement—not just grammar or essay maps. The freewriting is such a great help that whenever I'm stuck, I immediately turn to my ten-minute freewriting to open up blocked passages. Once I get past my writer's block, I see that I can be a good writer.

> **A writer is someone who writes, that's all.**
> —GORE VIDAL, NOVELIST AND SOCIAL COMMENTATOR

> **I've always disliked words like *inspiration*. Writing is probably like a scientist thinking about some scientific problem or an engineer about an engineering problem.**
> —DORIS LESSING, AUTHOR OF ESSAYS AND FICTION, INCLUDING *THE GOLDEN NOTEBOOK*

> **I always worked until I had something done and I always stopped when I knew what was going to happen next. That way I could be sure of going on the next day.**
> —ERNEST HEMINGWAY, JOURNALIST AND NOVELIST, AUTHOR OF *THE OLD MAN AND THE SEA*

A S YOU BEGIN A COLLEGE WRITING COURSE, YOU NEED TO GET RID OF SOME MYTHS ABOUT WRITING THAT YOU MAY HAVE BEEN PACKING AROUND FOR SOME TIME. DON'T ALLOW MISCONCEP-TIONS TO RUIN A GOOD EXPERIENCE. HERE ARE A FEW COMMON myths about writing, followed by some facts compiled from the experiences of working writers.

MYTH: "Good writers are born, not made. A writing course really won't help my writing."

FACT: *Writers acquire their skills the same way athletes do—through practice and hard work.* There are very few "born" writers. Most writers—even professional writers and journalists—are not continually inspired to write. In fact, they often experience "writer's block," the stressful experience of staring helplessly at a piece of paper, unable to think or to put words down on paper. A writing course will teach you how to cope with your procrastination, anxiety, lack of "inspiration," and false starts by focusing directly on solving the problems that occur during the writing process.

MYTH: "Writing courses are just a review of boring grammar and punctuation. When teachers read your writing, the only thing they mark is that stuff, anyway."

FACT: *Learning and communicating—not grammar and punctuation—come first in college writing courses.* Knowledge of grammar, spelling, punctuation, and usage is essential to editing, but it is secondary to discovering ideas, thinking, learning, and communicating. In a writing course, students learn to revise and improve the content and organization of each other's writing. *Then* they help each other edit for grammar, punctuation, or spelling errors.

MYTH: "College writing courses are really 'creative writing,' which is not what my major requires. If I wanted to be another Shakespeare and write poetry, I'd change my major."

FACT: *Writing courses emphasize rhetoric, not poetry.* Rhetoric involves practicing the most effective means or strategies for informing or persuading an audience. All writing—even technical or business writing—is "creative." Deciding what to write, how to write it, how best to get your reader's attention, and how to inform or persuade your reader requires creativity and imagination. Every major requires the skills that writing courses teach: exploring new ideas, learning concepts and processes, communicating with others, and finding fresh or creative solutions to problems.

MYTH: "Writing courses are not important in college or the real world. I'll never have to write, anyway."

FACT: *Writing courses do have a significant effect on your success in college, on the job, and in life.* Even if you don't have frequent, formal writing assignments in other

> **"** I work at my writing as an athlete does at . . . training, taking it very seriously. What is important is the truth in it and the way that truth is expressed. **"**
> —EDNA O'BRIEN,
> NOVELIST AND PLAYWRIGHT

courses, writing improves your note-taking, reading comprehension, and thinking skills. When you do have other written tasks or assignments, a writing course teaches you to adapt your writing to a variety of different purposes and audiences—whether you are writing a lab report in biology, a letter to an editor, a complaint to the Better Business Bureau, or a memorandum to your boss. Taking a writing course helps you express yourself more clearly, confidently, and persuasively—a skill that comes in handy whether you're writing a philosophy essay, a job application, or a love letter.

The most important fact about writing is that you are already a writer. You have been writing for years. A writer is someone who writes, not someone who writes a nationally syndicated newspaper column, publishes a bestseller, or wins a Pulitzer Prize. To be an effective writer, you don't have to earn a million dollars; you just have to practice writing often enough to get acquainted with its personal benefits for you and its value for others.

▌ WARMING UP: Freewriting

Put this book aside—right now—and take out pencil or pen and a piece of paper. Use this free exercise (private, unjudged, ungraded) to remind yourself that you are already a writer. Time yourself for five minutes. Write on the first thing that comes to mind—*anything whatsoever*. Write nonstop. Keep writing even if you have to write, "I can't think of anything to say. This feels stupid!" When you get an idea, pursue it.

When five minutes are up, stop writing and reread what you have written. Whether you write about a genuinely interesting topic or about the weather, freewriting is an excellent way to warm up, to get into the habit of writing, and to establish a writing ritual.

> ❝ My idea of a prewriting ritual is getting the kids on the bus and sitting down. ❞
> —BARBARA KINGSOLVER
> AUTHOR OF *PRODIGAL SUMMER*

Writing Fitness: Rituals and Practice

Writing is no more magic or inspiration than any other human activity that you admire: figure skating at the Olympics, rebuilding a car engine, cooking a gourmet meal, or acting in a play. Behind every human achievement are many unglamorous hours of practice—working and sweating, falling flat on your face, and picking yourself up again. You can't learn to write just by reading some chapters in a textbook or

❝ Writing is [like] making a table. With both you are working with reality, a material just as hard as wood. Both are full of tricks and techniques. Basically very little magic and a lot of hard work are involved. . . . What is a privilege, however, is to do a job to your own satisfaction. **❞**

—GABRIEL GARCÍA MÁRQUEZ,
NOBEL PRIZE-WINNING AUTHOR OF *ONE HUNDRED YEARS OF SOLITUDE*

by memorizing other people's advice. You need help and advice, but you also need practice. Consider the following parable about a Chinese painter.

A rich patron once gave money to the painter Chu Ta, asking him to paint a picture of a fish. Three years later, when he still had not received the painting, the patron went to Chu Ta's house to ask why the picture was not done. Chu Ta did not answer but dipped a brush in ink and with a few strokes drew a splendid fish. "If it is so easy," asked the patron, "why didn't you give me the picture three years ago?" Again, Chu Ta did not answer. Instead, he opened the door of a large cabinet. Thousands of pictures of fish tumbled out.

Most writers develop little rituals that help them practice their writing. A ritual is a *repeated pattern of behavior* that provides structure, security, and a sense of progress to the one who practices it. Creating your own writing rituals and making them part of your regular routine will help reduce that dreaded initial panic and enable you to call upon your writing process with confidence when you need it.

PLACE / TIME / TOOLS	ENERGY / ATTITUDE	JOURNAL

PLACE, TIME, AND TOOLS

Some writers work best in pen and ink, sprawled on their beds in the afternoon while pets snooze on nearby blankets. Others start at 8 A.M. and rely on hard chairs, clean tables, and a handful of number 2 pencils sharpened to needle points. Still others are most comfortable with their keyboards and word processors at their desks or in the computer lab. Legal-sized pads help some writers produce, while others feel motivated by spiral notebooks with pictures of mountain streams on the covers. Only you can determine which place, time, and tools give you the best support as a writer.

The place where you write is also extremely important. If you are writing in a computer lab, you have to adapt to that place, but if you write a draft in long-hand or on your own word processor, you can choose the place yourself. In selecting a place, keep the following tips in mind.

- **Keep distractions minimal.** Some people simply can't write in the kitchen, where the refrigerator is distractingly close, or in a room that has a TV in it. On the other hand, a public place—a library, an empty classroom, a cafeteria—can be fine as long as the surrounding activity does not disturb you.

- **Control interruptions.** If you can close the door to your room and work without interruptions, fine. But even then, other people often assume that you want to take a break when they do. Choose a place where you can decide when it's time to take a break.

- **Have access to notes, journal, textbooks, sources, and other materials.** If the place is totally quiet but you don't have room to work or access to important notes or sources, you still may not make much progress. Whatever you need—a desk to spread your work out on, access to notes and sources, extra pens, or computer supplies—make sure your place has it.

The time of day you write and the tools you write with can also affect your attitude and efficiency. Some people like to write early in the morning, before their busy days start; others like to write in the evening, after classes or work. Whatever time you choose, try to write regularly—at least three days a week—at about the same time. If you're trying to get in shape by jogging, swimming, or doing aerobics, you wouldn't exercise for five straight hours on Monday and then take four days off. Like exercise, writing requires regular practice and conditioning.

Your writing tools—pen, pencil, paper, legal pads, four-by-six-inch notecards, notebooks, computer—should also be comfortable for you. Some writers like to make notes with pencil and paper and write drafts on computers; some like to do all composing on computers. As you try different combinations of tools, be aware of how you feel and whether your tools make you more effective. If you feel comfortable, it will be easier to establish rituals that lead to regular practice.

Rituals are important because they help you with the most difficult part of writing: getting started. So use your familiar place, time, and tools to trick yourself into getting some words down on paper. Your mind will devise clever schemes to avoid writing those first ten words—watching TV, balancing your checkbook, drinking some more coffee, or calling a friend and whining together about all the writing you have to do. But if your body has been through the ritual before, it will walk calmly to your favorite place, where all your tools are ready (perhaps bringing the mind kicking and screaming all the way). Then, after you get the first ten words down, the mind will say, "Hey, this isn't so bad— I've got something to say about that!" And off you'll go.

> " Writers are notorious for using any reason to keep from working: overresearching, retyping, going to meetings, waxing the floors—anything. "
> —GLORIA STEINEM, FORMER EDITOR OF *MS. MAGAZINE*

FRANK AND ERNEST ©by Bob Thaves

Copyright © 1987 by Bob Thaves. Reprinted with the permission of Bob Thaves.

Each time you perform your writing ritual, the *next* time you write will be that much easier. Soon, your ritual will let you know: "*This is where you write. This is when you write. This is what you write with.*" No fooling around. Just writing.

| PLACE / TIME / TOOLS | ENERGY / ATTITUDE | JOURNAL |

ENERGY AND ATTITUDE

Once you've tricked yourself into the first ten words, you need to keep your attitude positive and your energy high. When you see an intimidating wall starting to form in front of you, don't ram your head into it; figure out a way to sneak around it. Try these few tricks and techniques.

- **Start anywhere, quickly.** No law says that when you sit down to write a draft, you have to "begin at the beginning." If the first sentence is hard to write, begin with the first thoughts that come to mind. Or begin with a good example from your experience. Use that to get you going; then come back and rewrite your beginning after you've figured out what you want to say.

- **Write the easiest parts first.** Forcing yourself to start a piece of writing by working on the hardest part first is a sure way to make yourself hate writing. Take the path of least resistance. If you can't get your thesis to come out right, jot down more examples. If you can't think of examples, go back to brainstorming.

- **Keep moving.** Once you've plunged in, write as fast as you can—whether you are scribbling ideas out with a pencil or hitting the keys of a computer. Maintain your momentum. Reread if you need to, but then plunge ahead.

- **Quit when you know what comes next.** When you do have to quit for the day, stop at a place where you know what comes next. Don't drain the well dry; stop in the middle of something you know how to finish. Make a few notes about what you need to do next and circle them. Leave yourself an easy place to get started next time.

One of the most important strategies for every writer is to *give yourself a break from the past and begin with a fresh image.* In many fields—mathematics, athletics, art, engineering—some people are late bloomers. Don't let that C or D you got in English back in tenth grade hold you back now like a ball and chain. Imagine yourself cutting the chain and watching the ball roll away for good. Now you are free to start fresh with a clean slate. Your writing rituals should include only positive images about the writer you are right now and realistic expectations about what you can accomplish.

- **Visualize yourself writing.** Successful athletes know how to visualize a successful tennis swing, a basketball free throw, or a baseball swing. When you are planning your activities for the day, visualize yourself writing at your favorite place. Seeing yourself doing your writing will enable you to start writing more quickly and maintain a positive attitude.

- **Discover and emphasize the aspects of writing that are fun for you.** Emphasize whatever is enjoyable for you—discovering an idea, getting the organization of a paragraph to come out right, clearing the unnecessary words and junk out of your writing. Concentrating on the parts you enjoy will help you make it through the tougher parts.

- **Set modest goals for yourself.** Don't aim for the stars; just work on a sentence. Don't measure yourself against some great writer; be your own yardstick. Compare what you write to what *you* have written before.

- **Congratulate yourself for the writing you do.** Writing is hard work; you're using words to create ideas and meanings literally out of nothing. So pat yourself on the back occasionally. Keep in mind the immortal words of comedian and playwright Steve Martin: "I think I did pretty well, considering I started out with nothing but a bunch of blank paper."

> ❝I carry a journal with me almost all the time. . . . ❞
>
> —NTOZAKE SHANGE, AUTHOR OF THE PLAY *FOR COLORED GIRLS WHO HAVE CONSIDERED SUICIDE WHEN THE RAINBOW IS ENUF*

PLACE / TIME / TOOLS	ENERGY / ATTITUDE	JOURNAL

KEEPING A JOURNAL

Many writers keep some kind of notebook in which they write down their thoughts, ideas, plans, and important events. Some writers use a journal, a private place for their day-to-day thoughts. Other writers create weblogs, or "blogs," a more public place for their ideas. Both journals and blogs can be a "place for daily writing." If you choose a private, written journal, you can later select what you want others to read; if you use your blog, your thoughts and ideas are there for others to read and respond to. Whatever medium you choose, use it as part of your daily writing ritual. In it can go notes and ideas, bits and pieces of experience, or responses to essays or books you're reading. Sometimes journals or blogs are assigned as part of your class work. In that case, you may do in-class, write-to-learn entries, plans for your essays, postscripts for an essay, or reflections on a portfolio. Your journal or blog can be a place for formal assignments or just a place to practice, a room where all your "fish paintings" go.

As the following list indicates, there are many kinds of journal entries. They fall into three categories: *reading entries, write-to-learn entries,* and *writing entries.* Reading entries help you understand and actively respond to student or professional writing. Write-to-learn entries help you summarize, react to, or question ideas or

> ❝The most valuable writing tool I have is my daybook. . . . I write in my lap, in the living room or on the porch, in the car or an airplane, in meetings at the university, in bed, or sitting down on a rock wall during a walk. . . . It is always a form of talking to myself, a way of thinking on paper. ❞
>
> —DONALD MURRAY, JOURNALIST, AUTHOR OF BOOKS AND ESSAYS ABOUT WRITING

essays discussed in class. Writing entries help you warm up, test ideas, make writing plans, practice rhetorical strategies, or solve specific writing problems. All three kinds of journal writing, however, take advantage of the unique relationship between thinking, writing, and learning. Simply put, writing helps you learn what you know (and don't know) by shaping your thoughts into language.

READING ENTRIES

- **Prereading journal entries.** Before you read an essay, read the headnote and write for five minutes on the topic of the essay—what you know about the subject, what related experiences you have had, and what opinions you hold. After you write your entry, the class can discuss the topic before you read the essay. The result? Your reading will be more active, engaged, and responsive.

- **Double-entry logs.** Draw a line vertically down a sheet of paper. On the left-hand side, summarize key ideas as you reread an essay. On the right-hand side, write down your reactions, responses, and questions. Writing while you read helps you understand and respond more thoroughly.

- **Essay annotations.** Writing your comments in the margin as you read is sometimes more efficient than writing separate journal entries. Also, in a small group in class, you can share your annotations and collaboratively annotate a copy of the essay.

- **Vocabulary entries.** Looking up unfamiliar words in a dictionary and writing out definitions in your journal will make you a much more accurate reader. Often an essay's thesis, meaning, or tone hinges on the meanings of a few key words.

- **Summary/response entries.** Double-entry logs help you understand while you reread, but a short one-paragraph summary and one-paragraph response after you finish your rereading helps you focus on both the main ideas of a passage and your own key responses.

WRITE-TO-LEARN ENTRIES

- **Lecture/discussion entries.** At key points in a class lecture or discussion, your teacher may ask you to write for five minutes by responding to a few questions: What is the main idea of the discussion? What one question would you like to ask? How does the topic of discussion relate to the essay that you are currently writing?

- **Responses to essays.** Before discussing an essay, write for a few minutes to respond to the following questions: What is the main idea of this essay?

What do you like best about the essay? What is confusing, misleading, or wrong in this essay? What strategies illustrated in this essay will help you with your own writing?

- **Time-out responses.** During a controversial discussion or argument about an essay, your teacher may stop the class, take time out, and ask you to write for five minutes to respond to several questions: What key issue is the class debating? What are the main points of disagreement? What is your opinion? What evidence, either in the essay or in your experience, supports your opinion?

WRITING ENTRIES

- **Warming up.** Writing, like any other kind of activity, improves when you loosen up, stretch, get the kinks out, practice a few lines. Any daybook or journal entry gives you a chance to warm up.

- **Collecting and shaping exercises.** Some journal entries will help you collect information by observing, remembering, or investigating people, places, events, or objects. You can also record quotations or startling statistics for future writing topics. Other journal entries suggested in each chapter of this book will help you practice organizing your information. Strategies of development, such as comparison/contrast, definition, classification, or process analysis will help you discover and shape ideas.

- **Writing for a specific audience.** In some journal entries, you need to play a role, imagining that you are in a specific situation and writing for a defined audience. For example, you might write a letter of application for a job or letter to a friend explaining why you've chosen a certain major.

- **Revision plans and postscripts.** Your journal is also the place to keep a log—a running account of your writing plans, revision plans, problems, and solutions. Include your research notes, peer responses, and postscripts on your writing process in this log.

- **Imitating styles of writers.** Use your journal to copy passages from writers you like. Practice imitating their styles on different topics. Also, try simply transcribing a few paragraphs. Even copying effective writers' words will reveal some of their secrets for successful writing.

- **Writing free journal entries.** Use your journal to record ideas, reactions to people on campus, events in the news, reactions to controversial articles in the campus newspaper, conversations after class or work, or just your private thoughts.

> ❚ **WARMING UP: Journal Exercises**
>
> Choose three of the exercises below and write for ten minutes on each. Date and number each entry.
>
> 1. Make an "authority" list of activities, subjects, ideas, places, people, or events that you already know something about. List as many topics as you can. If your reaction is "I'm not really an *authority* on anything," then imagine you've met someone from another school, state, country, or historical period. With that person as your audience, what are you an "authority" on?
>
> 2. Choose one activity, sport, or hobby that you do well and that others might admire you for. In the form of a letter to a friend, describe the steps or stages of the process through which you acquired that skill or ability.
>
> 3. In two or three sentences, complete the following thought: "I have trouble writing because . . ."
>
> 4. In a few sentences, complete the following thought: "In my previous classes and from my own writing experience, I've learned that the three most important rules about writing are . . ."
>
> 5. Describe your own writing rituals. *When, where,* and *how* do you write best?
>
> 6. Write an open journal entry. Describe events from your day, images, impressions, bits of conversation—anything that catches your interest. For possible ideas for open journal entries, read the essay by Roy Hoffman reprinted here.
>
> 7. Look again at the chapter opening work of art by Edouard Manet, *Monet Painting in His Floating Studio.* If you have taken an art class, have you drawn or painted outdoors, as Monet is depicted? What are the advantages or disadvantages of painting outside versus in a studio? Similarly, as a writer or student, can you read or write effectively while sitting outside, or do you need to be inside, in a work environment? Does it depend on what you are reading or writing? Explain.

PROFESSIONAL WRITING

On Keeping a Journal

Roy Hoffman

In a Newsweek On Campus *essay, Roy Hoffman describes his own experience, recording events and trying out ideas just as an artist doodles on a sketch pad.*

Your own journal entries about events, images, descriptions of people, and bits of conversation will not only improve your writing but also become your own personal time capsule, to dig up and reread in the year 2030.

Wherever I go I carry a small notebook in my coat or back pocket for thoughts, observations and impressions. As a writer I use this notebook as an artist would a sketch pad, for stories and essays, and as a sporadic journal of my comings and goings. When I first started keeping notebooks, though, I was not yet a professional writer. I was still in college.   *1*

I made my first notebook entries . . . just after my freshman year, in what was actually a travel log. A buddy and I were setting out to trek from our Alabama hometown to the distant tundra of Alaska. With unbounded enthusiasm I began: "Wild, crazy ecstasy wants to wrench my head from my body." The log, written in a university composition book, goes on to chronicle our adventures in the land where the sun never sets, the bars never close and the prepipeline employment prospects were so bleak we ended up taking jobs as night janitors.   *2*

When I returned to college that fall I had a small revelation: the world around me of libraries, quadrangles, Frisbees and professors was as rich with material for my journals and notebooks as galumphing moose and garrulous fishermen.   *3*

These college notebooks, which built to a pitch my senior year, are gold mines to me now. Classrooms, girlfriends, cups of coffee and lines of poetry—from mine to John Keats's—float by like clouds. As I lie beneath these clouds again, they take on familiar and distinctive shapes.   *4*

Though I can remember the campus's main quadrangle, I see it more vividly when I read my description of school on a visit during summer break: "the muggy, lassitudinal air . . . the bird noises that cannot be pointed to, the summer emptiness that grows emptier with a few students squeaking by the library on poorly oiled bicycles." An economics professor I fondly remember returns with less fondness in my notebooks, "staring down at the class with his equine face." And a girl I had a crush on senior year, whom I now recall mistily, reappears with far more vitality as "the ample, slightly-gawky, whole-wheat, fractured object of my want gangling down the hall in spring heat today."   *5*

When, in reading over my notebooks, I am not peering out at quadrangles, midterm exams, professors or girlfriends, I see a portrait of my parents and hometown during holidays and occasional weekend breaks. Like a wheel, home revolves, each turn regarded differently depending on the novel or political essay I'd been most influenced by the previous semester.   *6*

... *continued* On Keeping a Journal, **Roy Hoffman**

Mostly, though, in wandering back through my notebooks, I meet 7 someone who could be my younger brother: the younger version of myself. The younger me seems moodier, more inquisitive, more fun-loving and surprisingly eager to stay up all night partying or figuring out electron orbitals for a 9 A.M. exam. The younger me wanders through a hall of mirrors of the self, writes of "seeing two or three of myself on every corner," and pens long meditations on God and society before scribbling in the margin, "what a child I am." The younger me also finds humor in trying to keep track of this hall of mirrors, commenting in ragged verse.

I hope that one day
Some grandson or cousin
Will read these books,
And know that I was
Once a youth
Sitting in drugstores with
Anguished looks.
And poring over coffee,
And should have poured
The coffee
Over these lines.

I believe that every college student should attempt to keep some form 8 of notebook, journal or diary. A notebook is a secret garden in which to dance, sing, muse, wander, perform handstands, even cry. In the privacy of this little book, you can make faces, curse, turn somersaults and ask yourself if you're really in love. A notebook or journal is one of the few places you can call just your own.

... Journal writing suffers when you let someone, in your mind, look 9 over your shoulder. Honesty wilts when a parent, teacher or friend looms up in your imagination to discourage you from putting your true thoughts on the page. Journal writing also runs a related hazard: the dizzying suspicion that one day your private thoughts, like those of Samuel Pepys or Virginia Woolf, will be published in several volumes and land up required reading for English 401. How can you write comfortably when the eyes of all future readers are upon you? Keep your notebooks with the abandon of one who knows his words will go up in smoke. Then you might really strike fire a hundred years or so from now if anyone cares to pry.

By keeping notebooks, you improve your writing ability, increasing *10* your capacity to communicate both with yourself and others. By keeping notebooks, you discover patterns in yourself, whether lazy ones that need to be broken or healthy ones that can use some nurturing. By keeping notebooks, you heighten some moments and give substance to others: even a journey to the washateria offers potential for some off-beat journal observations. And by keeping notebooks while still in college, you chart a terrain that, for many, is more dynamically charged with ideas and discussions than the practical, workaday world just beyond. Notebooks, I believe, not only help us remember this dynamic charge, but also help us sustain it.

Not long ago, while traveling with a friend in Yorktown, Va., I passed *11* by a time capsule buried in the ground in 1976, intended to be dug up in 2076. Keeping notebooks and journals is rather like burying time capsules into one's own life. There's no telling what old rock song, love note, philosophical complaint or rosy Saturday morning you'll unearth when you dig up these personal time capsules. You'll be able to piece together a remarkable picture of where you've come from, and may well get some important glimmers about where you're going.

■ ■ ■

Mona Lisa Barn
Cornell, Wisconsin
Layne Kennedy, Photographer

The picture above, taken by photographer Layne Kennedy, shows a famous Mona Lisa barn painting on a farm near Cornell, Wisconsin. Mona Lisa's shirt has been repainted to celebrate Wisconsin's victory in the 1994 Rose Bowl. A freewriting assignment on page 28 invites you to describe the purpose, audience, and genre of this image.

Situations, Purposes, and Processes for Writing

2

A veteran smoker, you have become increasingly irritated at the non-smoking regulations that have appeared in restaurants, businesses, and other public places. And it's not just the laws that are irritating, but the holier-than-thou attitude of people who presume that what's good for them should be good for you. Non-smoking laws seem to give people license to censure your behavior while totally ignoring their own offensive behavior: polluting the atmosphere with hydrocarbons, fouling the aquifers with fertilizers, and generally corrupting the social air with odors of false superiority. So after one particularly memorable experience, you write a letter to the editor of the local paper, intending not only to express your own frustration but also to satirize all those smug do-gooders.

As a Chinese-American woman growing up in America, you decide to write about the difficulty of living in two cultures. You recall how, during your childhood, you rebelled against your mother when she insisted that you learn about your Chinese heritage. You remember how much you hated your Chinese school and how embarrassed you were that your mother could not speak English properly. As you grew older, however, you realized the price you paid for your assimilation into American culture. After discussing this conflict with your friends, you decide to describe your experiences to others who share them or who may want to know what you learned. At that point, you write an autobiographical account of your experiences and send it to a metropolitan newspaper.

> **"** First and foremost I write for myself. Writing has been for a long time my major tool for self-instruction and self-development. **"**
> —TONI CADE BAMBARA,
> AUTHOR OF _THE SALT EATERS_

> **"** How do I know what I think until I see what I say? **"**
> —E. M. FORSTER,
> AUTHOR OF _A PASSAGE TO INDIA_

T HE WRITING FOR THIS COURSE (AND THE STRUCTURE OF THIS TEXT-BOOK) ASSUMES THAT WRITING IS VALUABLE FOR TWO RELATED REASONS. FIRST, WRITING ENABLES YOU TO LEARN ABOUT SOME-THING, TO HELP YOU OBSERVE YOUR SURROUNDINGS, TO REMEMBER important ideas and events, and to record and analyze what you see and read. Second, writing is an important means to communicate with your readers, to explain or evaluate an idea, to offer a solution, or to argue your point of view. These two reasons for writing are usually related. If you want to persuade others to agree with your point of view, you'll be more effective if you reflect on how your personal observations, memories, experiences, and things you've read and heard might help you convince your readers. Whatever you write, however, you are always writing in a particular situation or context. Understanding how your goals as a writer relate to the writing situation and to your own processes for writing is the focus of this chapter.

Rhetorical Situations

As you begin this writing course, consider how you and your writing fit into a larger context. Anytime you write an e-mail response, a letter to your friends, an essay for your English or history class, an application for a job, a letter to the editor, or an entry in your journal, you are in the middle of a rhetorical situation. If rhetoric is the "art of using language effectively or persuasively," then the rhetorical situation is the overall context in which your writing occurs. The key parts of the rhetorical situation are you, the writer; the immediate occasion that prompts you to write; your intended purpose and audience; your genre or type of writing; and the larger social context in which you are writing. Because these key terms are used repeatedly in this course, you need to know exactly what each term means and how it will help guide your writing.

THE WRITER   You are the writer. Sometimes you write in response to an assignment, but at other times, you choose to write because of something that happened or something that made you think or react. In college or on the job, you often have writing assignments, but in your life, you are often the one who decides to write when you need to remember something, plan, remind others, express your feelings, or solve a problem.

THE OCCASION   The occasion is whatever motivates you to write. Often you are motivated by an assignment that a teacher or a boss gives you. Sometimes, however, a particular event or incident makes you want to write. The cause may be a conversation you had with a friend, an article you read, or something that happened to you recently. The occasion is simply the immediate cause or the pressing need to write, whether assigned to you by someone else or just determined by you to be the reason for your desire to write.

PURPOSE   Your purpose in writing is the effect you wish to have on your intended audience. Major purposes for writing include **expressing** your feelings; investigating a subject and **reporting** your findings; **explaining** an idea or concept; **evaluating** some object, performance, or image; **proposing a solution** to a problem; and **arguing** for your position and responding to alternative or opposing positions.

AUDIENCE   Your knowledge about your intended audience should always guide and shape your writing. If you are writing for yourself, you can just list ideas, express your thoughts, or make informal notes. If you are writing to explain an idea or concept, you should think about who needs or wants to know about your idea. To whom do you want to explain this idea? Are they likely to be novices or experts on the topic? Similarly, if you are arguing your position, you need to consider the thoughts and feelings of readers who may have several different points of view. What do they believe about your topic? Do they agree or disagree with your position, or are they undecided?

GENRE   The genre you choose is simply the kind, type, or form of writing you select. Everyone is familiar with genres in literature, such as poems, novels, and plays. In nonfiction, typical genres are essays, memoirs, magazine articles, and editorials. In college, you may write in a variety of genres, including e-mail, personal essays, lab reports, summaries, reviews of research, analytical essays, argumentative essays, and even scientific or business reports. Sometimes, you may need to write multigenre or multimedia reports with graphic images or pictures. For community service learning or on the job, you may write reports, analyses, brochures, or flyers. As a citizen of the community, you may write letters to the editor, responses to an online discussion forum, or letters to your representative.

> **❝** Every genre positions those who participate in a text of that kind: as interviewer or interviewee, as listener or storyteller, as a reader or a writer, as a person interested in political matters, as someone to be instructed or as someone who instructs; each of these positionings implies different possibilities for response and for action. **❞**
> —GUNTHER KRESS, AUTHOR OF *LITERACY IN THE NEW MEDIA AGE*

> " A rhetorically sound definition of genre must be centered not on the substance or form of discourse but on the action it is used to accomplish. "
>
> —CAROLYN MILLER, TEACHER AND AUTHOR OF GENRE AS SOCIAL ACTION

The genre you choose helps create the intellectual, social, or cultural relationship between you and your reader. It helps you communicate your purpose to your reader or makes possible the social action you wish to achieve. If your purpose is to analyze or critique material you are reading in a class, an essay is a genre suitable to your purpose and your intended audience (your teacher and your peers in class). A lab report is a different genre, requiring your notes, observations, and hypothesis about your experiment, presented for members of a scientific community. Finally, the purpose of a one-page brochure for your community crisis center, for example, may be to advertise its services to a wide audience that includes college students and members of the community. The point is to learn what readers expect of each genre and then choose—or modify—a genre that is appropriate for your purpose and audience. Learning which genres are appropriate for each writing situation and learning about the formal features of each genre (such as introduction, presentation of information, paragraphing, and vocabulary) is a key part of each writing task. Remember, however, that genres have rules but are not rulebound. Every text should have recognizable features of a genre but also individual variation appropriate for that particular occasion.

CONTEXT   As both a reader and a writer, you must consider the rhetorical and social context. When you read an essay or other text, think about the **author,** the **place of publication,** the **ongoing conversation** about this topic, and the larger **social or cultural context**. First, consider who wrote an essay and where it appeared. Was the essay a citizen's editorial in the *New York Times,* a journalist's feature article in *Vogue,* a scientist's research report in the *New England Journal of Medicine,* or a personal essay on an individual's Web site? Often, who wrote the article, what his or her potential bias or point of view was, and the place of publication can be just as important as what the article says. Next, consider the ongoing conversation to which this essay contributes. What different viewpoints exist on this topic? Which perspectives does this essay address? Finally, the larger sense of culture, politics, and history in which the article appears may be crucial to your understanding.

Similarly, when you write an essay, think about where it might be read or published and what conversation already exists on the topic. What cultural or political points of view are represented in the conversation? How does that ongoing conversation affect what you think? How does your own cultural, political, ethnic, or personal background affect what you believe? Understanding and analyzing the larger rhetorical and social context helps you become a better reader and writer.

REVIEW OF THE RHETORICAL SITUATION

Now that you've finished reading about these terms, notice how they overlap. They are separate, yet they all function together. Go back and reread each of the definitions for *occasion, purpose, audience, genre, context,* but this time pay attention to how they are interconnected. It's silly, for example, to talk about purpose or about audience without talking about everything else in the writing situation: the writer, the occasion for writing, the purpose, audience, genre, and overall context.

WHY THE RHETORICAL SITUATION IS IMPORTANT

So, you understand each of the elements of the rhetorical situation, and you see how they are interconnected. But how does that knowledge help you as a writer? The answer is both easy and difficult. The easy part is that every decision you make as a writer—how to begin, how much evidence you include, how you organize, whether you can use "I" in your writing, what style or tone you should use—depends on the rhetorical situation. The style and organization of a lab report is different from an essay, which is different from a brochure. If you've ever asked your teacher, "Won't you just tell me what you want?" the answer to that question always is, "Well, it depends." It depends on what is appropriate for the purpose, audience, genre, and context. And that is where the difficult part of writing begins: learning which genres, styles, appeals to your readers, and methods of organization are appropriate for each writing situation. To learn the various approaches to writing and how they are most effectively used is the reason that you continually read and practice writing the major genres taught in your composition class.

FREEWRITING: INVENTORY OF YOUR WRITING

Before you read further in this chapter, take out a pen or open a computer file and make a list of what you have written in the last year or two. Brainstorm a list of all the genres you can think of: shopping lists for a trip, letters to family or friends, applications for jobs, school essays, personal or professional Web sites, science projects, or memos for your boss. Then,

Continued

for one of your longer writing projects, jot down several sentences describing the situation that called for that piece of writing—what was the occasion, purpose, and audience? What form or genre did your writing take? How did that genre help define a relationship between you and your reader? Where did you write it, and what was your writing process?

Purposes for Writing

Getting a good grade, sharing experiences with a friend, or contributing to society may be among your motives for writing. However, as a writer, you also have more specific rhetorical purposes for writing. These purposes help you make key decisions related to your audience and genre. When your main purpose is to express your feelings, you may write a private entry in your journal. When your main purpose is to explain how your sales promotion increased the number of your company's customers, you may write a formal sales report to your boss. When your main purpose is to persuade others to see a movie that you like, you may write a review for the local newspaper. In each case, the intended rhetorical purpose—your desire to create a certain effect on your audience—helps determine what you write and how you say it.

WRITER-BASED PURPOSES

Because writing is, or should be, for yourself first of all, everything you write involves at least some purpose that benefits you. Of course, expressing yourself is a fundamental purpose of all writing. Without the satisfaction of expressing your thoughts, feelings, reactions, knowledge, or questions, you might not make the effort to write in the first place.

A closely related purpose is learning: Writing helps you discover what you think or feel, simply by using language to identify and compose your thoughts. Writing not only helps you form ideas but actually promotes observing and remembering. If you write down what you observe about people, places, or things, you can actually "see" them more clearly. Similarly, if you write down facts, ideas, experiences, or reactions to your readings, you will remember them longer. Writing and rewriting facts, dates, definitions, impressions, or personal experiences will improve your powers of recall on such important occasions as examinations and job interviews.

SUBJECT- AND AUDIENCE-BASED PURPOSES

Although some writing is intended only for yourself—such as entries in a diary, lists, class notes, reminders—much of your writing will be read by others, by those readers who constitute your "audience."

- You may write to *inform* others about a particular subject—to tell them about the key facts, data, feelings, people, places, or events.
- You may write to *explain* to your readers what something means, how it works, or why it happens.
- You may write to *persuade* others to believe or do something—to convince others to agree with your judgment about a book, record, or restaurant, or to persuade them to take a certain class, vote for a certain candidate, or buy some product you are advertising.
- You may write to *explore* ideas and "truths," to examine how your ideas have changed, to ask questions that have no easy answers, and then to share your thoughts and reflections with others.
- You may write to *entertain*—as a primary purpose in itself or as a purpose combined with informing, explaining, persuading, or exploring. Whatever your purposes may be, good writing both teaches and pleases. Remember, too, that your readers will learn more, remember more, or be more convinced when your writing contains humor, wit, or imaginative language.

> **❝** I think writing is really a process of communication. . . . It's the sense of being in contact with people who are part of a particular audience that really makes a difference to me in writing. **❞**
> —SHERLEY ANN WILLIAMS, POET, CRITIC, AND NOVELIST

COMBINATIONS OF PURPOSES

In many cases, you write with more than one purpose in mind. Purposes may appear in combinations, connected in a sequence, or actually overlapping. Initially, you may take notes about a subject to learn and remember, but later you may want to inform others about what you have discovered. Similarly, you may begin by writing to express your feelings about a movie that you loved or that upset you; later, you may wish to persuade others to see it—or not to see it.

Purposes can also contain each other, like Chinese boxes, or overlap, blurring the distinctions. An explanation of how an automobile works will contain information about that vehicle. An attempt to persuade someone to buy an automobile may contain an explanation of how it handles and information about its body style or

> **❝** Writing, as a rhetorical act, is carried out within a web of purpose. **❞**
> —LINDA FLOWER, TEACHER AND RESEARCHER IN COMPOSITION

engine. Usually, writing to persuade others will contain explanations and basic information, but the reverse is not necessarily true; you can write simply to give information, without trying to persuade anyone to do anything.

SUBJECT, PURPOSE, AND THESIS

The *thesis, claim,* or *main idea* in a piece of writing is related to your purpose. As a writer, you usually have a purpose in mind that serves as a guide while you gather information about your subject and think about your audience. However, as you collect and record information, impressions, and ideas you gradually narrow your subject to a specific topic and thus clarify your purpose. You bring your purpose into sharper and sharper focus—as if progressing on a target from the outer circles to the bull's-eye—until you have narrowed your purpose down to a central thesis. The thesis is the dominant idea, explanation, evaluation, or recommendation that you want to impress upon your readers.

The following examples illustrate how a writer moves from a general subject, guided by purpose, to a specific thesis or claim.

SUBJECT	PURPOSE	THESIS, CLAIM, OR MAIN IDEA
Childhood experiences	To express your feelings and explain how one childhood experience was important.	The relentless competition between my sisters and me distorted my easygoing personality.
Heart disease	To inform readers about relationships between Type A personalities and heart attacks.	Type A personalities do not necessarily have an abnormally high risk of suffering heart attacks.
The death penalty	To persuade readers that the death penalty should be used.	Despite our belief that killing is wrong, a state-administered death penalty is fair, just, and humane.

Purpose and Audience

Writing for yourself is relatively easy; after all, you already know your audience and can make spontaneous judgments about what is essential and what is not.

However, when your purpose is to communicate to other readers, you need to analyze your audience. Your writing will be more effective if you can anticipate what your readers know and need to know, what they are interested in, and what their beliefs or attitudes are. As you write for different readers, you will select different kinds of information, organize it in different ways, or write in a more formal or less formal style.

FREEWRITING: WRITING FOR DIFFERENT AUDIENCES

Before you read further, get a pen or pencil and several sheets of paper and do the following exercise.

1. For your eyes only, write about what you did at a recent party. Write for four minutes.

2. On a second sheet of paper, describe for the members of your writing class what you did at this party; you will read it aloud to the class. Stop after four minutes.

3. On a third sheet of paper, write a letter to one of your parents or a relative describing what you did at the party. Stop after four minutes.

AUDIENCE ANALYSIS

If you are writing to communicate to other readers, analyzing your probable audience will help you answer some basic questions.

- What genre should I choose? What genre—or combination of genres— would best enable me to communicate with my audience?

- How much information or evidence is enough? What should I assume my audience already knows? What should I not tell them? What do they believe? Will they readily agree with me, or will they be antagonistic?

- How should I organize my writing? How can I get my readers' attention? Can I just describe my subject and tell a story, or should I analyze everything in a logical order? Should I put my best examples or arguments first or last?

- Should I write informally, with simple sentences and easy vocabulary, or should I write in a more elaborate or specialized style, with technical vocabulary?

Analyze your audience by considering the following questions. As you learn more about your audience, the possibilities for your own role as a writer will become clearer.

1. **Audience profile.** How narrow or broad is your audience? Is it a narrow and defined audience—a single person, such as your Aunt Mary, or a group with clear common interests, such as the zoning board in your city or the readers of *Organic Gardening?* Is it a broad and diverse audience: educated readers who wish to be informed on current events, American voters as a whole, or residents of your state? Do your readers have identifiable roles? Can you determine their age, sex, economic status, ethnic background, or occupational category?

2. **Audience–subject relationship.** Consider what your readers know about your subject. If they know very little about it, you'll need to explain the basics; if they already know quite a bit, you can go straight to more difficult or complex issues. Also estimate their probable attitude toward this subject. Are they likely to be sympathetic or hostile?

3. **Audience–writer relationship.** What is your relationship with your readers? Do you know each other personally? Do you have anything in common? Will your audience be likely to trust what you say, or will they be skeptical about your judgments? Are you the expert on this particular subject and the readers the novices? Or are you the novice and your readers the experts?

4. **Writer's role.** To communicate effectively with your audience, you should also consider your own role or perspective. Of the many roles that you could play (friend, big sister or brother, student of psychology, music fan, employee of a fast-food restaurant, and so on), choose one that will be effective for your purpose and audience. If, for example, you are writing to sixth-graders about nutrition, you could choose the perspective of a concerned older brother or sister. Your writing might be more effective, however, if you assume the role of a person who has worked in fast-food restaurants for three years and knows what goes into hamburgers, french fries, and milkshakes.

Writers may write to real audiences, or they may create audiences. Sometimes the relationship between writer and reader is real (sister writing to brother), so the writer starts with a known audience and writes accordingly. Sometimes, however, writers begin and gradually discover or create an audience in the process of writing. Knowing the audience guides the writing, but the writing may construct an audience as well.

Purpose, Audience, and Genre

In addition to considering your purpose and audience, think also about the possible forms or genres your writing might take. If you are writing to observe or remember something, you may want to write an informal essay, a letter, a memoir, or even an e-mail to reach your audience. If you are writing to inform your readers or explain some idea, you may write an article, essay, letter, report, or pamphlet to best achieve your purpose and address your audience. Argumentative writing—writing to evaluate, persuade, or recommend some position or course of action—takes place in many different genres, from e-mails and letters, to reviews and editorials, to proposals and researched documents. As you select a topic, consider which genre would most effectively accomplish your purpose for your intended audience.

Below are some of the common genres that you will read or write while in college, on the job, or as a member of your community. Each genre has certain organization and style features that readers of this genre expect. Knowing the genre that you are writing or reading helps answer questions about how to write or how to respond to a piece of writing.

GENRE	CONVENTIONS OF ORGANIZATION AND STYLE
Personal essay	Some narrative and descriptive passages Informal; uses first person "I" Applies personal experience to larger social question
Research review	Uses concise, accurate summary May be an annotated bibliography or part of a larger thesis Adheres to MLA, APA, Chicago styles
Argumentative essay	Makes a claim about a controversial topic Responds to alternative or opposing positions Carefully considers audience Supports claims with evidence and examples Uses reasonable tone Has formal paragraphing
Laboratory report	May be informal description of materials, procedures, and results May be formal organization with title, abstract, introduction, method, results, and discussion

Continued

GENRE	CONVENTIONS OF ORGANIZATION AND STYLE
Brochure	Mixes graphics, text, visuals Visually arresting and appealing layout Concise information and language
Letter to the editor	Refers to issue or topic States opinion, point of view, or recommendation Usually concise to fit into editorial page
Posting to an electronic forum	Connects to specific thread in discussion May be informal style Flaming and trolling occur, but are often censured
E-mail and text messaging	Usually short Informal and personal style Often without salutation, caps, or punctuation May use emoticons such as :-), :-(, :-.) (Cindy Crawford), or 8(:-) (Mickey Mouse), or acronyms such as BTW, LOL, FYI, or THX

FREEWRITING: PURPOSE, AUDIENCE, GENRE, AND CONTEXT IN AN IMAGE

Before you read further in this chapter, analyze the rhetorical elements in the photograph by Layne Kennedy that appears at the beginning of this chapter. What is the purpose of this barn painting? Who was the intended audience? How would you describe this genre of art? What was the social and cultural context in which this painting appeared? (Use Yahoo!, Google, or your favorite search engine to discover background information.) Overall, how effective is this painting at achieving its rhetorical purpose for its audience and context? Explain.

The Rhetorical Situation

To review, the rhetorical situation consists of the writer, the occasion, the purpose and audience, the genre and the context. Sometimes several of these are assigned to the writer, but at other times, the writer chooses a purpose, audience, and genre.

The key point to remember is that these terms are all interrelated and interconnected. Your overall purpose often depends on your selected audience. Deciding on a particular audience may mean choosing a particular genre. Thinking about the context and conversation surrounding a particular topic may help you be more persuasive for your selected audience. Writing and revising require reconsidering and revising each of these elements to make them work harmoniously to achieve your rhetorical goal.

The following scenarios illustrate how the writer's purpose, the occasion, the audience, genre, and context work together to define the rhetorical situation. In the following descriptions, identify each of the key parts of the rhetorical situation.

A student majoring in journalism reads accounts by reporters embedded in military units in the Iraq war. After reading several accounts, the student decides that this war was a good test case in the battle between the public's right to receive accurate information and the military's need for security. The advantages of embedded journalists were their on-the-spot reports and film footage; the disadvantages included the journalists' natural bias toward their military unit, their potential violations of privacy and tactical security, and their inability to present a larger picture of the progress of the war. The student decides to write an essay for a conservative online news magazine in which she recommends policy changes for embedded reporters for any future military engagement.

In response to a request by an editor of a college recruiting pamphlet, a student decides to write an essay explaining the advantages of the social and academic life at his university. According to the editor, the account needs to be realistic but should also promote the university. It shouldn't be too academic and stuffy—the college catalog itself contains all the basic information—but it should give high school seniors a flavor of college life. The student decides to write a narrative account of his most interesting experiences during his first week at college.

PURPOSE, AUDIENCE, AND CONTEXT IN TWO ESSAYS

The two short essays that follow appeared as columns in newspapers. Both relate the writers' own experiences. They are similar in genre but have different purposes, they appeal to different readers, and they have different social and cultural contexts. First, read each essay just to understand each writer's point of view. Then reread each essay, thinking particularly about each writer's main purpose, his or her intended audience, and the social and cultural context surrounding each topic.

PROFESSIONAL WRITING

The Struggle to Be an All-American Girl

Elizabeth Wong

It's still there, the Chinese school on Yale Street where my brother and I used to go. Despite the new coat of paint and the high wire fence, the school I knew 10 years ago remains remarkably, stoically the same.

Every day at 5 P.M., instead of playing with our fourth- and fifth-grade friends or sneaking out to the empty lot to hunt ghosts and animal bones, my brother and I had to go to Chinese school. No amount of kicking, screaming, or pleading could dissuade my mother, who was solidly determined to have us learn the language of our heritage.

Forcibly, she walked us the seven long, hilly blocks from our home to school, depositing our defiant tearful faces before the stern principal. My only memory of him is that he swayed on his heels like a palm tree, and he always clasped his impatient twitching hands behind his back. I recognized him as a repressed maniacal child killer, and knew that if we ever saw his hands we'd be in big trouble.

We all sat in little chairs in an empty auditorium. The room smelled like Chinese medicine, and imported faraway mustiness. Like ancient mothballs or dirty closets. I hated that smell. I favored crisp new scents. Like the soft French perfume that my American teacher wore in public school.

Although the emphasis at the school was mainly language—speaking, reading, writing—the lessons always began with an exercise in politeness. With the entrance of the teacher, the best student would tap a bell and everyone would get up, kowtow, and chant, "sing san ho," the phonetic for "How are you, teacher?"

Being ten years old, I had better things to learn than ideographs copied painstakingly in lines that ran right to left from the tip of a *moc but*, a real ink pen that had to be held in an awkward way if blotches were to be avoided. After all, I could do the multiplication tables, name the satellites of Mars, and write reports on "Little Women" and "Black Beauty." Nancy Drew, my favorite book heroine, never spoke Chinese.

The language was a source of embarrassment. More times than not, I had tried to disassociate myself from the nagging loud voice that followed me wherever I wandered in the nearby American supermarket outside Chinatown. The voice belonged to my grandmother, a fragile woman in her seventies who could outshout the best of the street vendors. Her humor was raunchy, her Chinese rhythmless, patternless. It was quick, it was loud, it was unbeautiful. It was not like the quiet, lilting romance of French or the gentle refinement of the American South. Chinese sounded pedestrian. Public.

In Chinatown, the comings and goings of hundreds of Chinese on their daily tasks sounded chaotic and frenzied. I did not want to be thought of as mad, as talking gibberish. When I spoke English, people nodded at me, smiled sweetly, said encouraging words. Even the people in my culture would cluck and say that I'd do well in life. "My, doesn't she move her lips fast," they would say, meaning that I'd be able to keep up with the world outside Chinatown. *8*

My brother was even more fanatical than I about speaking English. He was especially hard on my mother, criticizing her, often cruelly, for her pidgin speech—smatterings of Chinese scattered like chop suey in her conversation. "It's not 'What it is,' Mom," he'd say in exasperation. "It's 'What is it, what is it, what is it!'" Sometimes Mom might leave out an occasional "the" or "a," or perhaps a verb of being. He would stop her in mid-sentence: "Say it again, Mom. Say it right." When he tripped over his own tongue, he'd blame it on her: "See, Mom, it's all your fault. You set a bad example." *9*

After two years of writing with a *moc but* and reciting words with multiples of meanings, I finally was granted a cultural divorce. I was permitted to stop Chinese school. *10*

I thought of myself as multicultural. I preferred tacos to egg rolls; I enjoyed Cinco de Mayo more than Chinese New Year. *11*

At last, I was one of you; I wasn't one of them. *12*

Sadly, I still am. *13*

■ ■ ■

PROFESSIONAL WRITING

I'm O.K., but You're Not

Robert Zoellner

The American novelist John Barth, in his early novel, *The Floating Opera*, remarks that ordinary, day-to-day life often presents us with embarrassingly obvious, totally unsubtle patterns of symbolism and meaning—life in the midst of death, innocence vindicated, youth versus age, etc. *1*

...*continued* I'm O.K., but You're Not, **Robert Zoellner**

The truth of Barth's insight was brought home to me recently while having breakfast in a lawn-bordered restaurant on College Avenue near the Colorado State University campus. I had asked to be seated in the smoking section of the restaurant—I have happily gone through three or four packs a day for the past 40 years.   *2*

As it happened, the hostess seated me—I was by myself—at a little two-person table on the dividing line between the smoking and non-smoking sections. Presently, a well-dressed couple of advanced years, his hair a magisterial white and hers an electric blue, were seated in the non-smoking section five feet away from me.   *3*

It was apparent within a minute that my cigarette smoke was bugging them badly, and soon the husband leaned over and asked me if I would please stop smoking. As a chronic smokestack, I normally comply, out of simple courtesy, with such requests. Even an addict such as myself can quit for as long as 20 minutes.   *4*

But his manner was so self-righteous and peremptory—he reminded me of Lee Iacocca boasting about Chrysler—that the promptings of original sin, always a problem with me, took over. I quietly pointed out that I was in the smoking section—if only by five feet—and that that fact meant that I had met my social obligation to non-smokers. Besides, the idea of morning coffee without a cigarette was simply inconceivable to me—might as well ask me to vote Republican.   *5*

The two of them ate their eggs-over-easy in hurried and sullen silence, while I chain-smoked over my coffee. As well as be hung for a sheep as a lamb, I reasoned. Presently they got up, paid their bill, and stalked out in an ambiance of affronted righteousness and affluent propriety.   *6*

And this is where John Barth comes in. They had parked their car—a diesel Mercedes—where it could be seen from my table. And in the car, waiting impatiently, was a splendidly matched pair of pedigreed poodles, male and female.   *7*

Both dogs were clearly in extremis, and when the back door of the car was opened, they made for the restaurant lawn in considerable haste. Without ado (no pun intended), the male did a doo-doo that would have done credit to an animal twice his size, and finished off with a leisurely, ruminative wee-wee. The bitch of the pair, as might be expected of any well-brought-up female of Republican proclivities, confined herself to a modest wee-wee, fastidious, diffident, and quickly executed.   *8*

Having thus polluted the restaurant lawn, the four of them marshalled   *9*
their collective dignity and drove off in a dense cloud of blue smoke—that
lovely white Mercedes was urgently in need of a valve-and-ring job, its
emission sticker an obvious exercise in creative writing.

As I regretfully watched them go—after all, the four of them had   *10*
made my day—it seemed to me that they were in something of a hurry, and
I uncharitably wondered if the husband was not anxious to get home in order to light the first Fall fire in his moss-rock fireplace, or apply the Fall
ration of chemical fertilizer to his doubtlessly impeccable lawn, thus
adding another half-pound of particulates to the local atmosphere and another 10 pounds of nitrates and other poisons to the regional aquifers. But
that, of course, is pure and unkindly speculation.

In any case, the point of this real-life vignette, as John Barth would in-   *11*
sist, is obvious. The current controversy over public smoking in Fort
Collins is a clear instance of selective virtue at work, coming under the
rubric of, what I do is perfectly OK, but what you do is perfectly awful.

■ ■ ■

QUESTIONS FOR WRITING AND DISCUSSION

1. Choosing only one adjective to describe your main reaction to each essay,
    answer the following question: "When I finished the _____ [Wong,
    Zoellner] essay, I was _____ [intrigued, bored, amused, irritated, curious,
    confused, or _____] because _____. Explain your choice of adjectives in one
    or two sentences.

2. Referring to specific passages, explain the purpose and state the thesis or
    main point of each essay.

3. What personality or role does each writer project? Drawing from evidence in
    the essay, describe what you think both writers would be like if you met them.

4. Both of these essays appeared in newspapers. What kind of reader would find
    each essay interesting? What kind of reader would not enjoy each essay? For
    each essay, find examples of specific sentences, word choices, vocabulary,
    experiences, or references to culture or politics that would appeal to one
    reader but perhaps irritate another.

5. These two essays are similar in genre—they are both informal essays
    narrating personal experiences and explaining what each writer

discovered or learned. There are differences, however, in structure and style. What differences do you notice in the way each essay begins and concludes, in the order of the paragraphs, and in vocabulary or style of the sentences?

6. Each essay has a particular social, cultural, and political context. Describe this context for both essays. Then identify at least three other viewpoints that exist in the cultural, social, or political conversations that surround each of these topics. (For example, what are different points of view about multicultural or bilingual education? What arguments exist both for and against smoking in privately owned business establishments?) How effective is each writer in responding to the ongoing cultural, social, or political context or conversation?

> ❝ I don't see writing as communication of something already discovered, as "truths" already known. Rather, I see writing as a job of experiment. It's like any discovery job; you don't know what's going to happen until you try it. ❞
> —WILLIAM STAFFORD, TEACHER, POET, AND ESSAYIST

Dimensions of the Writing Process

Processes for writing vary from one writer to the next and from one writing situation to the next. Most writers, however, can identify four basic stages, or dimensions, of their writing process: collecting, shaping, drafting, and revising. The writing situation may precede these stages—particularly if you are assigned a subject, purpose, audience, and form. Usually, however, you continue to narrow your subject, clarify your purpose, meet the needs of your audience, and modify your form as you work through the dimensions of your writing process.

| **COLLECTING** | SHAPING | DRAFTING | REVISING | WHOLE PROCESS |

COLLECTING

Mark Twain, author of *The Adventures of Huckleberry Finn*, once observed that if you attempt to carry a cat around the block by its tail, you'll gain a whole lot of information about cats that you'll never forget. You may collect such firsthand information, or you may rely on the data, experience, or expertise of others. In any case, writers constantly collect facts, impressions, opinions, and ideas that are relevant to their subjects, purposes, and audiences. Collecting involves observing, remembering, imagining, thinking, reading, listening, writing, investigating, talking, taking notes, and experimenting. Collecting also involves thinking about the relationships among the bits of information that you have collected.

COLLECTING   **SHAPING**   DRAFTING   REVISING   WHOLE PROCESS

SHAPING

Writers focus and organize the facts, examples, and ideas that they have collected into the recorded, linear form that is written language. When a hurricane hits the Gulf Coast, for example, residents of Texas, Louisiana, Mississippi, Alabama, and Florida are likely to collect an enormous amount of data in just a few hours. Rain, floods, tree limbs snapping in the wind, unboarded windows shattering, sirens blaring—all of these events occur nearly simultaneously. If you try to write about such devastation, you need to narrow your focus (you can't describe everything that happened) and organize your information (you can't describe all of your experiences at the same time).

The genre of the personal essay, weaving description in a chronological order, is just one of the shapes that a writer may choose to develop and organize experience. Such shaping strategies also help writers collect additional information and ideas. Reconstructing a chronological order, for example, may suggest some additional details—perhaps a wet, miserable-looking dog running through the heavy downpour—that you might not otherwise have remembered.

> " The writing process is not linear, moving smoothly in one direction from start to finish. It is messy, recursive, convoluted, and uneven. Writers write, plan, revise, anticipate, and review throughout the writing process. "
>
> —MAXINE HAIRSTON, TEACHER AND AUTHOR OF ARTICLES AND TEXTBOOKS ON WRITING

COLLECTING   SHAPING   **DRAFTING**   REVISING   WHOLE PROCESS

DRAFTING

At some point, writers actually write down a rough version of what will evolve into the finished piece of writing. Drafting processes vary widely from one writer to the next. Some writers prefer to reread their collecting and shaping notes, find a starting point, and launch themselves—figuring out what they want to say as they write it. Other writers start with a plan—a mental strategy, a short list, or an outline—of how they wish to proceed. Whatever approach you use in your draft, write down as much as possible: You want to see whether the information is clear, whether your overall shape expresses and clarifies your purpose, and whether your content and organization meet the needs and expectations of your audience.

> " We must and do write each our own way. "
>
> —EUDORA WELTY, NOVELIST AND ESSAYIST

COLLECTING   SHAPING   DRAFTING   **REVISING**   WHOLE PROCESS

REVISING

When writers revise rough drafts, they literally "resee" their subjects—and then modify drafts to fit new visions. Revision is more than just tinkering with a word here and there; revision leads to larger changes—new examples or details, a different organization, or a new perspective. You accomplish these changes by adding, deleting, substituting, or reordering words, sentences, and paragraphs. Although revision begins the moment you get your first idea, most revisions are based on the reactions—or anticipated reactions—of the audience to your draft. You often play the role of audience yourself by putting the draft aside and rereading it later when you have some distance from your writing. Wherever you feel readers might not get your point, you revise to make it clearer. You may also get feedback from readers in a class workshop, suggesting that you collect more or different information, alter the shape of your draft to improve the flow of ideas, or clarify your terminology. As a result of your rereading and your readers' suggestions, you may change your thesis or write for an entirely different audience.

Editing—in contrast to revising—focuses on the minor changes that you make to improve the accuracy and readability of your language. You usually edit your essay to improve word choice, grammar, usage, or punctuation. You also use a computer spell-check program and proofread to catch typos and other surface errors.

COLLECTING   SHAPING   DRAFTING   REVISING   **WHOLE PROCESS**

THE WHOLE PROCESS

In practice, a writer's process rarely follows the simple, consecutive order that these four stages or dimensions suggest. The writing process is actually recursive: It begins at one point, goes on to another, comes back to the first, jumps to the third, and so forth. A stage may last hours or only a second or two. While writing a letter to a friend, you may collect, shape, revise, and edit in one quick draft; a research paper may require repeated shaping over a two-week period. As writers draft, they may correct a few mistakes or typos, but they may not proofread until many days later. In the middle of reorganizing an essay, writers often reread drafts, go back and ask more questions, and collect more data. Even while editing, writers may throw out several paragraphs, collect some additional information, and draft new sections.

In addition to the recursive nature of the writing process, keep in mind that writing often occurs during every stage, not just during drafting and revising. During collecting, you will be recording information and jotting down ideas. During shaping, you will be writing out trial versions that you may use later when you draft or revise. Throughout the writing process, you use your writing to modify your subject, purpose, audience, and form.

The most important point to keep in mind is that the writing process is unique to each writer and to each writing situation. What works for one writer may be absolutely wrong for you. Some writers compose nearly everything in their heads. Others write only after discussing the subject with friends or drawing diagrams and pictures.

During the writing process, you need to experiment with several collecting, shaping, and drafting strategies to see what works best for you and for a particular piece of writing. As long as your process works, however, it's legitimate—no matter how many times you backtrack and repeat stages. When you are struggling with a piece of writing, remember that numerous revisions are a normal part of the writing process—even for most professionals.

Circling back over what you have already written—to sharpen your thesis, improve the organization, tighten up a paragraph, or add specific details to your examples—is likely to be the most time-consuming, yet worthwhile, part of your writing process. Most professional writers testify to the necessity and value of writing numerous drafts. When you are reworking a piece of writing, scrawling revisions over what you had hoped would be your finished product, remember what Nobel laureate Isaac Bashevis Singer once pointed out: "The wastepaper basket is the writer's best friend."

Writing with a Computer

Even though you have used a computer to help write your essays, you may not have worked in a writing classroom or lab where you have the advantages of a network. Most college writing classes today use many of the advantages of a networked environment, including e-mail, access to a class Web page and class discussion forums, and access to the Internet. In a networked environment, teachers and students send each other e-mail and can e-mail drafts of their work-in-progress. Students no longer need to be in the same room, building, or city in order to be part of their writing community. They can respond electronically to each other's writing in a discussion forum, chat room, blog, or bulletin board. They can collaboratively conduct research, post results using file sharing, and edit each other's drafts online. In the middle of drafting or revising an essay, they can quickly check the Internet or their library's database for other articles or information that they need. Finally, students often publish their essays online or even create their own Web pages using materials they have written for their writing course. In short, networked computers have revolutionized the teaching of writing by allowing discussion and revision to continue even after the class meeting time has finished. Writing in a networked computer environment reinforces the idea that a writing class is a continually supportive, interactive learning community.

WARNING UP: Journal Exercises

The following exercises will help you review and practice the topics covered in this chapter. In addition, you may discover a subject for your own writing. Choose three of the following entries, and write for ten minutes on each.

1. Reread your "authority" list from chapter 1. Choose one of those topics and then explain your purpose, identify a possible audience, and select a genre you would use.

2. From the resources available to you at home or on your computer, find examples of four different genres, such as advertisements, pamphlets, letters, articles, letters to the editor, and so forth. For each sample genre, identify the purpose, audience, and context. Bring these samples to class and be prepared to explain the rhetorical situation for each genre and why each sample is or is not effective.

3. If you have already been given a writing assignment in another course, explain the purpose, the intended audience, and the genre for that assignment. Be prepared to explain in class (or in a discussion forum) how you plan to complete that assignment.

4. During the first week of the term, one of your friends, Mark Lindstrom, is in an accident and is hospitalized. While still under the effects of anesthesia, he scribbles the following note for you to mail to his parents.

   Dear Mom and Dad,

   I arrived here last week. The trip was terrible. Dr. Stevens says that my leg will be better soon. My roommate is very strange. The police say my money is gone forever.

   Please send $1,500 to my new address right away.

   Thanks!

   Your loving son

   Mark

   Because you were at the accident and can fill in the details, Mark asks you to explain everything to his parents. Write a short letter to them. Next, write a paragraph to your best friend that describes what happened to Mark.

5. Explore the availability of computers on your campus. Where is the English department computer lab? What services does it offer? What other computer facilities are available? Write up your report and post it on your class bulletin board or forum.

6. Read Neil Petrie's essay and postscript at the end of this chapter. Then find the best paper you've written during the past year or two and write a "postscript" for it. Describe (a) the rhetorical situation, (b) your purpose, and (c) the process you used to write it.

A Writing Process at Work: Collecting and Shaping

PROFESSIONAL WRITING

Athletes and Education

Neil H. Petrie

In the following essay, which appeared in The Chronicle of Higher Education, *Neil H. Petrie argues that colleges have a hypocritical attitude toward student athletes. Although most universities claim that their athletes—both male and female—are in college to get a good education, in reality the pressures on athletes compromise their academic careers. The problem, Petrie argues, is not the old cliché that jocks are dumb, but the endless hours devoted to practice or spent on road trips, which drain even the good student-athlete's physical and mental energies. Colleges point with pride to a tiny number of athletes who become professionals, but much more frequently the collegiate system encourages athletes to settle for lower grades and incomplete programs. In far too many cases, athletes never graduate. These are the students whom, as Petrie says, "the system uses and then discards after the final buzzer."*

I have spent all my adult life in academe, first as a student and then as a professor. During that time I have seen many variations in the role of intercollegiate athletics in the university, and I've developed sharply split opinions on the subject. On one hand, I despise the system, clinging as it does to the academic body like a parasite. On the other hand, I feel sympathy and admiration for most of the young athletes struggling to balance the task of getting an education with the need to devote most of their energies to the excessive demands of the gym and the field. 1

My earliest experiences with the intrusion of athletics into the classroom came while I was still a freshman at the University of Colorado. While I was in my English professor's office one day, a colleague of hers came by for a chat. Their talk turned to the football coach's efforts to court 2 the favor of the teachers responsible for his gladiators by treating them to dinner and a solicitous discussion of the academic progress of the players. I vividly recall my professor saying, "He can take me out to dinner if he wants, but if he thinks I'll pass his knuckleheads just because of that, he'd better think again."

Later, as a graduate teaching fellow, a lecturer, and then an assistant professor of English, I had ample opportunity to observe a Division I university's athletics program. I soon discovered that the prevailing stereotypes did not always apply. Athletes turned out to be as diverse as any other group of students in their habits, tastes, and abilities, and they showed a wide range of strategies for coping with the stress of their dual roles. *3*

Some of them were poor students. An extreme example was the All-American football player (later a successful pro) who saw college only as a step to a six-figure contract and openly showed his disdain for the educational process. Others did such marginal work in my courses that I got the feeling they were daring me to give them D's or F's. One woman cross-country star, who almost never attended my composition class, used to push nearly illiterate essays under my office door at odd hours. *4*

Yet many athletes were among the brightest students I had. Not so surprising, when you consider that, in addition to physical prowess, success in athletics requires intelligence, competitive drive, and dedication—all qualities that can translate into success in the classroom as well as on the field. The trouble is that the grinding hours of practice and road trips rob student athletes of precious study time and deplete their reserves of mental and physical energy. A few top athletes have earned A's; most are content to settle for B's or C's, even if they are capable of better. *5*

The athletes' educational experience can't help being marred by their numerous absences and divided loyalties. In this respect, they are little different from the students who attempt to go to college while caring for a family or working long hours at an outside job. The athletes, however, get extra help in juggling their responsibilities. Although I have never been bribed or threatened and have never received a dinner invitation from a coach, I am expected to provide extra time and consideration for athletes, far beyond what I give other students. *6*

Take the midterm grade reports, for example. At my university, the athletic department's academic counselor sends progress questionnaires to every teacher of varsity athletes. While the procedure shows admirable concern for the academic performance of athletes, it also amounts to *7*

...continued Athletes and Education, **Neil H. Petrie**

preferential treatment. It requires teachers to take time from other teaching duties to fill out and return the forms for the athletes. (No other students get such progress reports.) If I were a cynic it would occur to me that the athletic department might actually be more concerned with athletes' eligibility than with their academic work.

Special attendance policies for athletes are another example of preferential treatment. Athletes miss a lot of classes. In fact, I think the road trip is one of the main reasons that athletes receive a deficient education. You simply can't learn as much away from the classroom and the library as on the campus. Nevertheless, professors continue to provide make-up tests, alternative assignments, and special tutoring sessions to accommodate athletes. Any other student would have to have been very sick or the victim of a serious accident to get such dispensations. 8

It is sad to see bright young athletes knowingly compromise their potential and settle for much less education than they deserve. It is infuriating, though, to see the ones less gifted academically exploited by a system that they do not comprehend and robbed of any possible chance to grow intellectually and to explore other opportunities. 9

One specific incident illustrates for me the worst aspects of college athletics. It wasn't unusual or extraordinary—just the all-too-ordinary case of an athlete not quite good enough to make a living from athletics and blind to the opportunity afforded by the classroom. 10

I was sitting in my office near the beginning of a term, talking to a parade of new advisees. I glanced up to see my entire doorway filled with the bulk of a large young man, whom I recognized as one of our basketball stars from several seasons ago who had left for the pros and now apparently come back. 11

Over the next hour I got an intensive course on what it's like to be a college athlete. In high school, John had never been interested in much outside of basketball, and, like many other indifferent students, he went on to junior college on an athletic scholarship. After graduating, he came to the university, where he played for two more years, finishing out his eligibility. He was picked in a late round of the N.B.A. draft and left college, but in the end he turned out to be a step too slow for the pros. By that time he had a family to support, and when he realized he could never make a career of basketball, he decided to return to college. 12

We both knew that his previous academic career hadn't been particu- *13*
larly focused, and that because of transferring and taking minimum course
loads during the basketball season, he wouldn't be close to a degree. But I
don't think either one of us was prepared for what actually emerged from
our examination of his transcripts. It was almost as if he had never gone
beyond high school. His junior-college transcript was filled with remedial
and nonacademic courses.

Credit for those had not transferred to the university. Over the next *14*
two years he had taken a hodgepodge of courses, mostly in physical education. He had never received any advice about putting together a coherent program leading to a degree. In short, the academic side of his college
experience had been completely neglected by coaches, advisers, and, of
course, John himself.

By the time we had evaluated his transcripts and worked out a tenta- *15*
tive course of study, John was in shock and I was angry. It was going to take
him at least three years of full-time study to complete a degree. He thanked
me politely for my time, picked up the planning sheets, and left. I was
ashamed to be a part of the university that day. Why hadn't anyone in the
athletic department ever told him what it would take to earn a degree? Or
at least been honest enough to say, "Listen, we can keep you eligible and
give you a chance to play ball, but don't kid yourself into thinking you'll be
getting an education, too."

I saw John several more times during the year. He tried for a while. He *16*
took classes, worked, supported his family, and then he left again. I lost
track of him after that. I can only hope that he found a satisfying job or
completed his education at some other institution. I know people say the
situation has improved in the last few years, but when I read about the
shockingly low percentages of athletes who graduate, I think of John.

Colleges give student athletes preferential treatment. We let them cut *17*
classes. We let them slide through. We protect them from harsh realities.
We applaud them for entertaining us and wink when they compromise
themselves intellectually. We give them special dorms, special meals, special tutors, and a specially reprehensible form of hypocrisy.

I can live with the thought of the athletes who knowingly use the *18*
college-athletics system to get their pro contracts or their devalued degrees. But I have trouble living with the thought of the ones whom the
system uses and then discards after the final buzzer.

■ ■ ■

PROFESSIONAL WRITING

On Writing "Athletes and Education"

Neil H. Petrie

In the following postscript on his writing process, Neil Petrie describes why he wanted to write the paper, how he collected material to support his argument, and how he shaped and focused his ideas as he wrote. His comments illustrate how his purpose—to expose the hypocrisies of collegiate athletics—guided his writing of the essay. In addition, Petrie explains that other key questions affected the shape of his essay: how he should begin, where he should use his best example, and what words he should choose.

This essay has its origin, as all persuasive writing should, in a strongly held opinion. I'm always more comfortable if I care deeply about my subject matter. As a teacher, I hold some powerful convictions about the uneasy marriage of big-time athletics and higher education, and so I wanted to write an essay that would expose what I think are the dangers and hypocrisies of that system. 1

At the beginning of my essay, I wanted to establish some authority to lend credibility to my argument. Rather than gather statistics on drop-out rates of student athletes or collect the opinions of experts, I planned to rely on my own experiences as both a student and teacher. I hoped to convince my readers that my opinions were based on the authority of firsthand knowledge. In this introduction I was also aware of the need to avoid turning off readers who might dismiss me as a "jock hater." I had to project my negative feelings about the athletic system while maintaining my sympathy with the individual student athletes involved in that system. The thesis, then, would emerge gradually as I accumulated the evidence; it would be more implied than explicitly stated. 2

Gathering the material was easy. I selected a series of examples from my personal experiences as a college student and instructor, as well as anecdotes I'd heard from other instructors. Most of these stories were ones that I had shared before, either in private discussions with friends or in classrooms with students. 3

Shaping the material was a little tougher. As I began thinking about my examples and how to order them, I saw that I really wanted to make two main points. The first was that most colleges give preferential treatment to athletes. The second point was that, despite the extra attention, 4 the success of the athlete's academic career is often ignored by all parties involved. Many of my examples, I realized, illustrated the varieties of pressures put upon both athletes and instructors to make sure that the students at least get by in class and remain eligible. These examples seemed to cluster together because they showed the frustrations of teachers and the reactions of athletes trying to juggle sports and academics. This group would make a good introduction to my general exposé of the system. But I had one more example I wanted to use that seemed to go beyond the cynicism of some athletes or the hypocrisy of the educators. This was the case of John, an athlete who illustrated what I thought were the most exploitative aspects of varsity athletics. I originally planned on devoting the bulk of my essay to this story and decided to place it near the end where it would make my second point with maximum emotional effect.

A two-part structure for the essay now emerged. In the first segment 5 following my introductory paragraph, I gave a series of shorter examples, choosing to order them in roughly chronological order (paragraphs 2–4). I then moved from these specific details to a more general discussion of the demands placed upon both students and teachers, such as lengthy practice time, grade reports, road trips, and special attendance policies. This concluded my description of the way the system operates (paragraphs 5–8).

Then it was time to shift gears, to provide a transition to the next part 6 of my essay, to what I thought was my strongest example. I wanted the story of John to show how the system destroyed human potential. To do this, I needed to increase the seriousness of the tone in order to persuade the reader that I was dealing in more than a little bureaucratic boondoggling. I tried to set the tone by my word choice: I moved from words such as "sad," "compromise," and "settle" to words with much stronger emotional connotations such as "infuriating," "exploited," and "robbed," all in a single short transitional paragraph (paragraph 9).

I then introduced my final extended example in equally strong language, identifying it as a worst-case illustration (paragraph 10). I elaborated on John's story, letting the details and my reactions to his situation carry the more intense outrage that I was trying to convey in this second part of the essay (paragraphs 10–16). The first version that I tried was a rambling narrative that had an overly long recounting of John's high school and college careers. So I tightened this section by eliminating such items as his progress through the ranks of professional basketball and his dreams of million-dollar contracts. I also cut down on a discussion of the various courses of study he was considering as options. The result was a sharper

...continued On Writing "Athletes and Education," **Neil H. Petrie**

focus on the central issue of John's dilemma: the lack of adequate degree counseling for athletes.

After my extended example, all that was left was the conclusion. As *8*
I wrote, I was very conscious of using certain devices, such as the repetition of key words and sentence patterns in paragraph seventeen ("We let them . . . We let them . . . We protect them . . . We applaud them . . . We give them . . .") to maintain the heightened emotional tone. I was also conscious of repeating the two-part structure of the essay in the last two paragraphs. I moved from general preferential treatment (paragraph 17) to the concluding and more disturbing idea of devastating exploitation (paragraph 18).

On the whole, I believe that this essay effectively conveys its point *9*
through the force of accumulated detail. My personal experience was the primary source of evidence, and that experience led naturally to the order of the paragraphs and to the argument I wished to make: that while some athletes knowingly use the system, others are used and exploited by it.

■ ■ ■

QUESTIONS FOR WRITING AND DISCUSSION

1. In your journal, describe how your extracurricular activities (athletics, jobs, clubs, or family obligations) have or have not interfered with your education. Recall one specific incident that illustrates how these activities affected your classwork—either positively or negatively.

2. Describe Petrie's audience and purpose for this essay. What sentences reveal his intended audience? What sentences reveal his purpose? What sentences contain his thesis, claim, or main idea? Do you agree with that thesis? Why or why not?

3. Reread Petrie's postscript. Based on his comments and on your reading of the essay, how does Petrie describe or label each of the following sections of his essay:

    paragraphs 1–4
    paragraphs 5–8
    paragraph 9
    paragraphs 10–16
    paragraphs 17–18

4. Who do you think is most to blame for the situation that Petrie describes: The athletes themselves? The colleges for paying their scholarships and then ignoring them when they drop out? The students and alumni who pay to see their teams win?

5. Petrie does not explicitly suggest a solution to the problem that he describes. Assume, however, that he has been asked by the president of his university to propose a solution. Write the letter that you think Petrie would send to the president.

A Writing Process at Work: Drafting and Revising

While drafting and revising, writers frequently make crucial changes in their ideas and language. The first scribbled sentences, written primarily for ourselves, are often totally different from what we later present to other people in final, polished versions. Take, for example, the final version of Abraham Lincoln's Gettysburg Address. It begins with the famous lines "Four score and seven years ago our fathers brought forth on this continent a new nation. . . ." But his first draft might well have begun, "Eighty-seven years ago, several politicians and other powerful men in the American Colonies got together and decided to start a new country. . . ." It is difficult to imagine that language ingrained in our consciousness was once drafted, revised, drafted again, and edited, as the author or authors added, deleted, reordered, and otherwise altered words, sentences, and ideas. In fact, it usually was.

Carl Becker's study of the American Declaration of Independence assembles the early drafts of that famous document and compares them with the final version. Shown below is Thomas Jefferson's first draft, with revisions made by Benjamin Franklin, John Adams, and other members of the Committee of Five that was charged with developing the new document.

Thomas Jefferson's Rough Draft of the Opening Sentences
of the Declaration of Independence

When in the course of human events it becomes necessary for a people to

dissolve the political bands which have connected them with another, and to

~~advance from that subordination in which they have hitherto remained, & to~~

assume among the powers of the earth the ~~equal & independent~~ _{separate and equal} station to which

the laws of nature & of nature's god entitle them, a decent respect to the opinions

of mankind requires that they should declare the causes which impel them to

the separation.
~~the change.~~

We hold these truths, _{self-evident} ~~to be sacred & undeniable~~; that all men are created

equal ~~& independent~~; that _{they are endowed by their creator with} ~~from that equal creation they derive in rights~~ inherent

_{rights; that} & inalienable, among ~~which~~ _{these} are ~~the preservation of~~ life, & liberty, & the pursuit

of happiness. . . .

The Final Draft of the Opening Sentences of the Declaration of Independence, as Approved on July 4, 1776.

When in the Course of human events, it becomes necessary for one people to

dissolve the political bands which have connected them with another, and to

assume among the powers of the earth, the separate and equal station to which

the Laws of Nature and of Nature's God entitle them, a decent respect to the

opinions of mankind requires that they should declare the causes which impel

them to the separation.

We hold these truths to be self-evident, that all men are created equal, that

they are endowed by their Creator with certain inalienable Rights, that among

these are Life, Liberty and the pursuit of Happiness.

QUESTIONS FOR WRITING AND DISCUSSION

1. Describe your reaction to the "rough draft" of the Declaration of Independence. Where did it seem strange or make you feel uncomfortable?

2. Select one change in a sentence that most improved the final version. Explain how the revised wording is more effective.

3. Find one change in a word or phrase that constitutes an alteration in meaning rather than just a choice of "smoother" or more appropriate language. How does this change affect the meaning?

4. Upon rereading this passage from the Declaration of Independence, one reader wrote, "I was really irritated by that 'all men are created equal' remark. The writers were white, free, well-to-do, Anglo-Saxon, mostly Protestant males discussing their own 'inalienable rights.' They sure weren't discussing the 'inalienable rights' of female Americans or of a million slaves or of nonwhite free Americans!" Revise the passage from the Declaration of Independence using this person as your audience.

5. On the Internet, visit the National Archives at http://www.nara.gov to see a photograph of the original Declaration of Independence and learn how the Dunlap Broadside of the Declaration was read aloud to troops. What does this historical context add to what you know about the Declaration of Independence? Do the revisions help make the document more revolutionary or propagandistic? In addition, this site has other treasures from the National Archives including the police blotter listing Abraham Lincoln's assassination, the first report of the *Titanic*'s collision with an iceberg, and Rosa Parks's arrest records. Do you think these documents are as important to our history and culture as the Declaration itself? Explain.

In *American Progress*, John Gast paints his vision of the spirit of westward expansion in the United States during the second half of the nineteenth century. The scene, a popular and widely distributed image of the time, shows settlers moving west, protected by a goddess-like figure, and followed by the expansion of the telegraph and the railroad. Ahead of the settlers, Native Americans and bison flee the onset of progress. Journal entry 7 in this chapter asks you to describe this picture and then compare your notes to a description of the painting written during that time.

Observing

3

In the far corner of a friend's living room is a lighted aquarium. Instead of water, the aquarium has a few inches of white sand, a dish of water, and a small piece of pottery. When you ask about the aquarium, your friend excitedly says, "You mean you haven't met Nino?" In a matter of seconds, you have a small, tannish-brown snake practically in your lap, and your friend is saying, "This is Nino. She—or he—is an African sand boa." You imagined that all boa constrictors were huge snakes that suffocated and then swallowed babies. "Actually," replies your friend, "Nino is very shy. She prefers to burrow in the sand." The snake is fascinating. It is only fifteen inches long, with a strong, compact body and a stub tail. Before it burrows into your coat pocket, you observe it closely so you can describe it to your younger brother, who loves all kinds of snakes.

In the physics laboratory, you're doing an experiment on light refraction. You need to observe how light rays bend as they go through water, so you take notes describing the procedure and the results. During each phase of the experiment, you observe and record the angles of refraction. The data and your notes will help you write up the lab report that is due next Monday.

> " My task . . . is, by the power of the written word, to make you hear, to make you feel—it is, before all, to make you see. "
> —JOSEPH CONRAD, AUTHOR OF *HEART OF DARKNESS* AND OTHER NOVELS

> " Seeing is of course very much a matter of verbalization. Unless I call my attention to what passes before my eyes, I simply won't see it. "
> —ANNIE DILLARD, NATURALIST AND AUTHOR OF *PILGRIM AT TINKER CREEK*

OBSERVING IS ESSENTIAL TO GOOD WRITING. WHETHER YOU ARE WRITING IN A JOURNAL, DOING A LABORATORY REPORT FOR A SCIENCE CLASS, OR WRITING A LETTER TO THE EDITOR OF A NEWSPAPER, KEEN OBSERVATION IS ESSENTIAL. WRITING OR verbalizing what you see helps you discover and learn more about your environment. Sometimes your purpose is limited to yourself: you observe and record to help you understand your world or yourself better. At other times, your purpose extends to a wider audience: You want to share what you have learned with others to help them learn as well. No matter who your audience is or what your subject may be, however, your task is to see and to help your readers see.

Of course, observing involves more than just "seeing." Good writers draw on all their senses: sight, smell, touch, taste, hearing. In addition, however, experienced writers also notice what is *not* there. The smell of food that should be coming from the kitchen but isn't. A friend who usually is present but now is absent. The absolute quiet in the air that precedes an impending storm. Writers should also look for *changes* in their subjects—from light to dark, from rough to smooth, from bitter to sweet, from noise to sudden silence. Good writers learn to use their previous *experiences* and their *imaginations* to draw comparisons and create images. Does a sea urchin look and feel like a pincushion with the pins stuck in the wrong way? Does the room feel as cramped and airless as the inside of a microwave oven? Finally, good writers write from a specific point of view or role: a student describing basic laws of physics or an experienced worker in a mental health clinic describing the clientele.

The key to effective observing is to *show* your reader the person, place, object, or image through *specific detail*. Good description follows the advice of experienced writers: *Show, don't tell*. Showing through vivid detail allows the reader to reach the conclusions that you may be tempted to just tell them. If your reader is going to learn from your observations, you must give the *exact details that you learned from,* not just your conclusions or generalizations. Even in writing, experience is the best teacher, so use specific details to communicate the look, the feel, the weight, the sights and sounds and smells.

Although effective description depends on detailed observation, what we already know about the subject—and what we can learn during our observations—can be crucial. The people, places, objects, or images that we observe are often difficult, complex, or contested. They do not give up their meaning in our first glance. When we look at Stonehenge, what exactly are we seeing? What does the stone circle really mean? If we look at an Impressionist painting, are we seeing pretty colors in shimmering light or just careless, undisciplined brushwork? If we see workers in a field planting or harvesting crops, is it a natural agricultural scene

Photograph of Stonehenge.

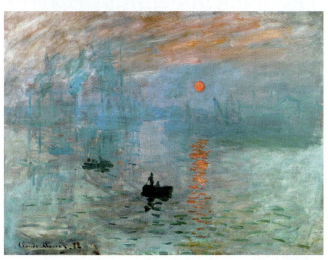

Claude Monet, *Impression: Sunrise*, 1872. This painting gave the Impressionists their name.

Angel Adams, Farm, farm workers, Mount Williamson in background, 1943. Photographs of Japanese-American Internment, Manzanar Relocation Center, California.

> ❝ The real voyage of discovery consists not in seeking new landscapes but in having new eyes. ❞
>
> —MARCEL PROUST,
> AUTHOR OF *REMEMBRANCE OF THINGS PAST*

> ❝ . . . Not that it's raining, but the feel of being rained upon. ❞
>
> —E. L. DOCTOROW,
> AUTHOR OF *RAGTIME* AND OTHER NOVELS

or the exploitation of migrant workers? A key part, then, of effective observation is learning and reading about what we see. An observant eye requires a critical, inquiring mind.

Whether you are a tourist describing the cliff dwellings at Mesa Verde, a student in a chemistry class writing up your laboratory experiment, a social worker observing working and housing conditions of agricultural workers, or a volunteer observing at a community crisis center, your task is to critically observe and then describe your subject—to show your readers, to make them *see*.

TECHNIQUES	PROCESS

Techniques for Writing About Observations

The short passages on the following pages use specific techniques for observing people, places, objects, or images that are described here. In all of the passages, the writer *narrows* or *limits* the scope of the observation and selects specific details that support the *dominant idea* of the passage. The dominant idea reflects the writer's purpose for that particular audience. As you read each passage, notice how the authors use the techniques listed below for making their writing more vivid and effective.

> ❝ When description is just an inventory of sights and sounds, it is not yet an essay. It becomes an essay only when a writer provides an interpretation of the details that catches the reader by surprise. ❞
>
> —JAMES C. RAYMOND,
> AUTHOR OF *WRITING IS AN UNNATURAL ACT*

- **Giving sensory details (sight, sound, smell, touch, taste).** Also include *actual dialogue* and *names of things* where appropriate. Good writers often "zoom in" on crucial details. Use *comparisons* and *images* when appropriate.

- **Describing what is *not* there.** Sometimes keen observation requires stepping back and noticing what is absent, what is not happening, or who is not present.

- **Noting changes in the subject's form or condition.** Even when the subject appears static—a landscape, a flower, a building—good writers look for evidence of changes, past or future: a tree being enveloped by tent worms, a six-inch purple-and-white iris that eight hours earlier was just a green bud, a sandstone exterior of a church being eroded by acid rain.

- **Learning about your subject.** An observant eye requires a critical, inquiring mind. Read about your subject. Ask other people or experts on the subject. Probe to find what is *unusual*, *surprising*, or *contested* about your subject.

- **Writing from a distinct point of view.** Good writers assume distinct roles; in turn, perspective helps clarify what they observe. A lover and a botanist, for example, see entirely different things in the same red rose. *What* is seen depends on *who* is doing the seeing.
- **Focusing on a dominant idea.** Good writers focus on those details and images that clarify the main ideas or discoveries. Discovery often depends on the *contrast* between the reality and the writer's expectations.

These techniques for observing are illustrated in the following two paragraphs by Karen Blixen, who wrote *Out of Africa* under the pen name Isak Dinesen. A Danish woman who moved to Kenya to start a coffee plantation, Blixen knew little about the animals in Kenya Reserve. In this excerpt from her journals, she describes a startling change that occurred when she shot a large iguana. (The annotations in the margin identify all six observing techniques.)

In the Reserve I have sometimes come upon the Iguana, the big lizards, as they were sunning themselves upon a flat stone in a riverbed. They are not pretty in shape, but nothing can be imagined more beautiful than their coloring. They shine like a heap of precious stones or like a pane cut out of an old church window. When, as you approach, they swish away, there is a flash of azure, green and purple over the stones, the color seems to be standing behind them in the air, like a comet's luminous tail.

    Once I shot an Iguana. I thought that I should be able to make some pretty things from his skin. A strange thing happened then, that I have never afterwards forgotten. As I went up to him, where he was lying dead upon his stone, and actually while I was walking the few steps, he faded and grew pale, all color died out of him as in one long sigh, and by the time that I touched him he was grey and dull like a lump of concrete. It was the live impetuous blood pulsating within the animal, which had radiated out all that glow and splendor. Now that the flame was put out, and the soul had flown, the Iguana was as dead as a sandbag.

Role: A newcomer to the Reserve

Comparisons and images

Sensory details

Comparisons and images

Changes in condition

Sensory detail

Learning about the subject

What is not there

Dominant idea: Now colorless and dead

PEOPLE	PLACES	OBJECTS

OBSERVING PEOPLE

Observing people—their dress, facial features, body language, attitudes, behavior, skills, quirks, habits, and conversation—is a pastime that we all share. When writers describe people, however, they zero in on specific details that fit overall patterns or impressions. In an *Esquire* magazine article, for example, Joseph Nocera profiles Steven Jobs, the cocreator of the Apple and Macintosh computers and the ex-chairman of the board of Apple Computer. All of Nocera's details reinforce his dominant idea that Steven Jobs is a temperamental boy genius.

Role: Writer as an outsider looks objectively at Jobs; is probably older

Dominant idea: Youth

Sensory detail: Visual description

Comparison and image

What is not there: Facial hair

What is not there: Tact

Comparison

With personal computers so ubiquitous today, you tend to forget that . . . the Apple II, the machine that began it all, was unleashed upon an unsuspecting world in 1977. You forget, that is, until you sit in a room full of people who have built them and realize how young they are. Jobs himself is only thirty-one. If anything, he looks younger. He is lithe and wiry. He is wearing faded jeans (no belt), a white cotton shirt (perfectly pressed), and a pair of brown suede wing-tipped shoes. There is a bounce to his step that betrays a certain youthful cockiness; the quarterback of your high school football team used to walk that way. His thin, handsome face does not even appear to need a daily shave. And that impression of eternal youth is reinforced by some guileless, almost childlike traits: by the way, for instance, he can't resist showing off his brutal, withering intelligence whenever he's around someone he doesn't think measures up. Or by his almost willful lack of tact. Or by his inability to hide his boredom when he is forced to endure something that doesn't interest him, like a sixth grader who can't wait for class to end.

PEOPLE	PLACES	OBJECTS

OBSERVING PLACES

In the following passage, John Muir describes California and the Yosemite Valley as it looked over 130 years ago. John Muir, of course, was the founder of the Sierra Club, whose first mission was to preserve the vision of Yosemite that Muir paints in the following paragraphs. Notice how Muir uses all of the key techniques for observing as he vividly describes the California Sierra.

Arriving by the Panama steamer, I stopped one day in San Francisco and then inquired for the nearest way out of town. "But where do you want to go?" asked the man to whom I had applied for this important information. "To any place that is wild," I said. This reply startled him. He seemed to fear I might be crazy and therefore the sooner I was out of town the better, so he directed me to the Oakland ferry.

So on the first of April, 1868, I set out afoot for Yosemite. It was the bloom-time of the year over the lowlands and coast ranges; the landscapes of the Santa Clara Valley were fairly drenched with sunshine, all the air was quivering with the songs of the meadow-larks, and the hills were so covered with flowers that they seemed to be painted. Slow indeed was my progress through these glorious gardens, the first of the California flora I had seen. Cattle and cultivation were making few scars as yet, and I wandered enchanted in long wavering curves, knowing by my pocket map that Yosemite Valley lay to the east and that I should surely find it.

Looking eastward from the summit of the Pacheco Pass one shining morning, a landscape was displayed that after all my wanderings still appears as the most beautiful I have ever beheld. At my feet lay the Great Central Valley of California, level and flowery, like a lake of pure sunshine, forty or fifty miles wide, five hundred miles long, one rich furred garden of yellow *Compositae*. And from the eastern boundary of this vast golden flower-bed rose the mighty Sierra, miles in height, and so gloriously colored and so radiant, it seemed not clothed with light, but wholly composed of it, like the wall of some celestial city. Along the top and extending a good way down, was a rich pearl-gray belt of snow; below it a belt of blue and dark purple, marking the extension of the forests; and stretching along the base of the range a broad belt of rose-purple; all these colors, from the blue sky to the yellow valley smoothly blending as they do in a rainbow, making a wall of light ineffably fine. Then it seemed to me that the Sierra should be called, not the Nevada or Snowy Range, but the Range of Light.

In general views no mark of man is visible upon it, nor anything to suggest the wonderful depth and grandeur of its sculpture. None of its magnificent forest-crowned ridges seems to rise much above the general level to publish its wealth. No great valley or river is seen, or group of well-marked features of any kind standing out as distinct pictures. Even the summit peaks, marshaled in glorious array so high in the sky, seem comparatively regular in form. Nevertheless the whole range five hundred miles long is furrowed with canyons 2,000 to 5,000 feet deep, in which once flowed majestic glaciers, and in which now flow and sing the bright rejoicing rivers.

PEOPLE	PLACES	OBJECTS

OBSERVING OBJECTS

In observing an inanimate object such as a cookie, Paul Goldberger—architecture critic for *The New York Times*—brings his special point of view to his description. He totally ignores the cookie's taste, ingredients, and calories, focusing instead on the architectural relationships of function and form. Goldberger's architectural perspective helps focus his observations, creating a dominant idea for each passage.

■ SUGAR WAFER (NABISCO)   There is no attempt to imitate the ancient forms of traditional, individually baked cookies here—this is a modern cookie through and through. Its simple rectangular form, clean and pure, just reeks of mass production and modern technological methods. The two

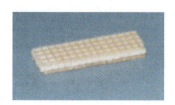

wafers, held together by the sugar-cream filling, appear to float . . . this is a machine-age object.

FIG NEWTON (NABISCO)   This, too, is a sandwich but different in every way from the Sugar Wafer. Here the imagery is more traditional, more sensual even; a rounded form of cookie dough arcs over the fig concoction inside, and the whole is soft and pliable. Like all good pieces of design, it has an appropriate form for its use, since the insides of Fig Newtons can ooze and would not be held in place by a more rigid form. The thing could have had a somewhat different shape, but the rounded tip is a comfortable, familiar image, and it's easy to hold. Not a revolutionary object but an intelligent one.

> **For Godsake, keep your eyes open. Notice what's going on around you.**
> —WILLIAM BURROUGHS, NOVELIST

WARMING UP: Journal Exercises

The following topics will help you practice close, detailed observation and may possibly suggest a subject for your assignment on observing. Read the exercises and then write on the two or three that interest you the most.

1. Go to a public place (library, bar, restaurant, hospital emergency room, gas station, laundromat, park, shopping mall, hotel lobby, police station, beach, skating rink, beauty salon, city dump, tennis court, church, etc.). Sit and observe everything around you. Use your pencil to help you see, both by drawing sketches and by recording sensory details in words. What do you see that you haven't noticed before? Then *narrow* your attention to a single person, *focus* on a restricted place, or *zoom* in on a single object. What do you see that you haven't noticed before?

2. In one of your classes, use your repeated observations of the total learning environment (the room, the seating arrangements, the blackboards, the audiovisual or computer equipment, the teacher, the daily teaching or learning rituals, and the students) to speculate on who has authority, how knowledge is created or communicated, and what the learning goals are for this course.

3. If you are working on a community-service learning project, for your first assignment, go and observe the place, people, and setting for the agency. Start by taking double-entry notes in your journal. On the left-hand side, record visual and sensory details; on the right-hand side, record your reactions and impressions. Use these notes for a description of your agency that will go in your final portfolio for your learning project.

4. Go to a gallery, studio, or museum where you can observe sculpture, paintings, or other works of art. Choose one work of art and draw it. Then describe it as fully as possible. Return to the gallery the next day, reread your first description, observe the work again, and add details that you didn't notice the first time.

5. Visit a local park. Pretend that you are a landscape architect, a photographer, a bird-watcher, an entomologist, an engineer building a road, a jogger, or a mother with two small children. Describe what you see. Now choose another role—you're a social worker, a woman alone in a park at night, a person without a home, a Secret Service agent assigned to protect the President of the United States, a Saint Bernard, or a sixth-grader just out of school for the day. Describe what you see. Then reread both descriptions. Compare them. Briefly explain how and why they are similar or dissimilar.

6. Reprinted below is a painting by Umberto Boccioni titled *Dynamism of a Cylist*. Write a paragraph describing in detail what you see in this painting. After you finish your description, you may wish to learn more about this painting by researching it in your library database or on Yahoo!, Google, or other search engine. After you finish your research, go back and revise your descriptive paragraph.

7. Study the painting by John Gast, *American Progress*, which appears at the beginning of this chapter. Use your observing skills to describe what is happening in this painting and what it appears to mean. After you have written your description and interpretation, compare your notes to the following description, written by George Crofutt, a contemporary of John Gast. How does your description and interpretation compare to Crofutt's version?

> In John Gast's *American Progress* (1872), a diaphanously and precariously clad America floats westward through the air with the "Star of Empire" on her forehead. She has left the cities of the East behind, and the wide Mississippi, and still her course is westward. In her right hand she carries a school book—testimonial of the National enlightenment, while with her left she trails the slender wires of the telegraph that will bind the nation. Fleeing her approach are Indians, buffalo, wild horses, bears, and other game, disappearing into the storm and waves of the Pacific coast. They flee the wondrous vision—the star "is too much for them."
>
> —George Crofutt

PROFESSIONAL WRITING

Take This Fish and Look at It

Samuel H. Scudder

In this essay, Samuel H. Scudder (1837–1911), an American entomologist, narrates his early attempts at scientific observation. Scudder recalls how a famous Swiss naturalist, Louis Agassiz, taught him the skills of observation by having him examine a fish—a haemulon or snapper—closely, carefully, and repeatedly. Agassiz, a professor of natural history at Harvard, taught his students that both factual details and general laws are important. "Facts are stupid things," he said, "until brought into connection with some general law." Scudder, writing about his studies under Agassiz, suggests that repeated observation can help us connect facts or specific details with general laws. The essay shows us an important lesson that Scudder learned: To help us see, describe, and connect, "A pencil is one of the best of eyes."

It was more than fifteen years ago that I entered the laboratory of Profes-   *1*
sor Agassiz, and told him I had enrolled my name in the Scientific School
as a student of natural history. He asked me a few questions about my object in coming, my antecedents generally, the mode in which I afterwards
proposed to use the knowledge I might acquire, and, finally, whether I
wished to study any special branch. To the latter I replied that, while I
wished to be well grounded in all departments of zoology, I purposed to
devote myself specially to insects.

    "When do you wish to begin?" he asked.   *2*

    "Now," I replied.   *3*

    This seemed to please him, and with an energetic "Very well!" he   *4*
reached from a shelf a huge jar of specimens in yellow alcohol. "Take this
fish," he said, "and look at it; we call it a haemulon; by and by I will ask
what you have seen."

    With that he left me, but in a moment returned with explicit instruc-   *5*
tions as to the care of the object entrusted to me.

    "No man is fit to be a naturalist," said he, "who does not know how to   *6*
take care of specimens."

    I was to keep the fish before me in a tin tray, and occasionally moisten   *7*
the surface with alcohol from the jar, always taking care to replace the stop-
per tightly. Those were not the days of ground-glass stoppers and elegantly
shaped exhibition jars; all the old students will recall the huge neckless
glass bottles with their leaky, wax-besmeared corks, half eaten by insects,
and begrimed with cellar dust. Entomology was a cleaner science than
ichthyology, but the example of the Professor, who had unhesitatingly
plunged to the bottom of the jar to produce the fish, was infectious; and
though this alcohol had a "very ancient and fishlike smell," I really dared
not show any aversion within these sacred precincts, and treated the alcohol as though it were pure water. Still I was conscious of a passing feeling
of disappointment, for gazing at a fish did not commend itself to an ardent
entomologist. My friends at home, too, were annoyed when they discovered that no amount of eau-de-Cologne would drown the perfume which
haunted me like a shadow.

    In ten minutes I had seen all that could be seen in that fish, and   *8*
started in search of the Professor—who had, however, left the Museum;
and when I returned, after lingering over some of the odd animals stored
in the upper apartment, my specimen was dry all over. I dashed the fluid
over the fish as if to resuscitate the beast from a fainting fit, and looked

with anxiety for a return of the normal sloppy appearance. This little excitement over, nothing was to be done but to return to a steadfast gaze at my mute companion. Half an hour passed—an hour—another hour; the fish began to look loathsome. I turned it over and around; looked it in the face—ghastly; from behind, beneath, above, sideways, at three-quarter's view—just as ghastly, I was in despair; at an early hour I concluded that lunch was necessary; so, with infinite relief, the fish was carefully replaced in the jar, and for an hour I was free.

On my return, I learned that Professor Agassiz had been at the Museum, but had gone, and would not return for several hours. My fellow-students were too busy to be disturbed by continued conversation. Slowly I drew forth that hideous fish, and with a feeling of desperation again looked at it. I might not use a magnifying-glass; instruments of all kinds were interdicted. My two hands, my two eyes, and the fish: it seemed a most limited field. I pushed my finger down its throat to feel how sharp the teeth were. I began to count the scales in the different rows, until I was convinced that was nonsense. At last a happy thought struck me—I would draw the fish; and now with surprise I began to discover new features in the creature. Just then the Professor returned. 9

"That is right," said he; "a pencil is one of the best of eyes. I am glad to notice, too, that you keep your specimen wet, and your bottle corked." 10

With these encouraging words, he added: "Well, what is it like?" 11

He listened attentively to my brief rehearsal of the structure of parts whose names were still unknown to me: the fringed gill-arches and movable operculum; the pores of the head, fleshy lips and lidless eyes; the lateral line, the spinous fins and forked tail; the compressed and arched body. When I finished, he waited as if expecting more, and then, with an air of disappointment: 12

"You have not looked very carefully; why," he continued more earnestly, "you haven't even seen one of the most conspicuous features of the animal, which is plainly before your eyes as the fish itself; look again, look again!" and he left me to my misery. 13

I was piqued; I was mortified. Still more of that wretched fish! But now I set myself to my task with a will, and discovered one new thing after another, until I saw how just the Professor's criticism had been. The afternoon passed quickly; and when, towards its close, the Professor inquired: 14

"Do you see it yet?" 15

"No," I replied, "I am certain I do not, but I see how little I saw before." *16*

"That is next best," said he, earnestly, "but I won't hear you now; put *17* away your fish and go home; perhaps you will be ready with a better answer in the morning. I will examine you before you look at the fish."

This was disconcerting. Not only must I think of my fish all night, *18* studying, without the object before me, what this unknown but most visible feature might be; but also, without reviewing my discoveries, I must give an exact account of them the next day. I had a bad memory; so I walked home by Charles River in a distracted state, with my two perplexities.

The cordial greeting from the Professor the next morning was reas- *19* suring; here was a man who seemed to be quite as anxious as I that I should see for myself what he saw.

"Do you perhaps mean," I asked, "that the fish has symmetrical sides *20* with paired organs?"

His thoroughly pleased "Of course! Of course!" repaid the wakeful *21* hours of the previous night. After he had discoursed most happily and enthusiastically—as he always did—upon the importance of this point, I ventured to ask what I should do next.

"Oh, look at your fish!" he said, and left me again to my own devices. *22* In a little more than an hour he returned, and heard my new catalogue.

"That is good, that is good!" he repeated; "but that is not all; go on"; *23* and so for three long days he placed that fish before my eyes, forbidding me to look at anything else, or to use any artificial aid. "Look, look, look," was his repeated injunction.

This was the best entomological lesson I ever had—a lesson whose in- *24* fluence has extended to the details of every subsequent study; a legacy the Professor had left to me, as he has left it to so many others, of inestimable value, which we could not buy, with which we cannot part.

A year afterward, some of us were amusing ourselves with chalking *25* outlandish beasts on the Museum blackboard. We drew prancing star-fishes; frogs in mortal combat; hydra-headed worms, stately crawfishes with gaping mouths and staring eyes. The Professor came in shortly after, and was as amused as any at our experiments. He looked at the fishes.

"Haemulons, every one of them," he said; "Mr. _____ drew them." *26*

True; and to this day, if I attempt a fish, I can draw nothing but *27* haemulons.

The fourth day, a second fish of the same group was placed beside the *28* first, and I was bidden to point out the resemblances and differences between the two; another and another followed, until the entire family lay before me, and a whole legion of jars covered the table and surrounding shelves; the odor had become a pleasant perfume; and even now, the sight of an old, six-inch worm-eaten cork brings fragrant memories.

The whole group of haemulons was thus brought in review; and *29* whether engaged upon the dissection of the internal organs, the preparation and examination of the bony framework, or the description of the various parts, Agassiz's training in the method of observing facts and their orderly arrangement was ever accompanied by the urgent exhortation not to be content with them.

"Facts are stupid things," he would say, "until brought into connection *30* with some general law."

At the end of eight months, it was almost with reluctance that I left *31* these friends and turned to insects; but what I had gained by this outside experience has been of greater value than years of later investigation in my favorite groups.

■ ■ ■

vo·cab·u·lar·y

In your journal, write down the meanings of the italicized words in the following phrases.

- my *antecedents* generally **(1)**
- *Entomology* was a cleaner science than *ichthyology* **(7)**
- dared not show any *aversion* **(7)**
- to *resuscitate* the beast **(8)**
- instruments of all kinds were *interdicted* **(9)**
- movable *operculum* **(12)**
- I was *piqued* **(14)**
- with my two *perplexities* **(18)**
- his repeated *injunction* **(23)**
- *hydra-headed* worms **(25)**
- the urgent *exhortation* **(29)**

QUESTIONS FOR WRITING AND DISCUSSION

1. If you have taken any science classes with laboratory sections, describe any observing techniques you used while completing the lab assignments. What were you asked to observe? What were you asked to record? How were these sessions similar to or different from Scudder's experience? Explain.

2. Follow Professor Agassiz's advice about observing: Without looking again at the essay, record in writing what you found to be the most memorable parts of the essay. What parts seemed most vivid? Explain.

3. Apply Scudder's technique of *repeated observation* to his own essay. Read the essay a second time, carefully, looking for techniques for recording observations. Use a pencil to help you read, by underlining or making brief notes. What do you notice on the second reading that you did not see in the first?

4. What is the purpose of this essay? To inform us about fish? To explain how to learn about fish? To persuade us to follow Professor Agassiz's method? To entertain us with college stories? In your estimation, what is the primary purpose?

5. Describe the genre and intended audience for this essay. Review the list of genres on pages 27–28. What features of the essay (such as content, dialogue, paragraphing, narrative voice) help indicate the genre of this piece? Who is the intended audience? Which sentences most clearly address the intended audience?

6. "Facts are stupid things," Agassiz says, "until brought into connection with some general law." Reread paragraph 8. What is the "general law" about scientific observation—or, in this case, the *dominant idea*—created by the specific details describing Scudder's first session with his fish? Explain.

7. On the Internet, access a biography of Louis Agassiz at http://www.ucmp. berkeley.edu/history/agassiz.html. Does this biography explain why Agassiz was one of the scientists who paved the way for Darwin's discoveries but also attacked Darwin's theory of evolution? Should Agassiz's discoveries be discredited because he did not agree with Darwin?

8. Connect Scudder's techniques to those in the other essays in this chapter. Does Farley Mowat use repeated observation to make an important discovery? In your own essay, how can you use Scudder's or Agassiz's advice to make your descriptions more vivid or insightful?

PROFESSIONAL WRITING

Observing Wolves

Farley Mowat

Farley Mowat was born in Ontario in 1921 and received a B.A. from the University of Toronto. He has published over fifty books of fiction and nonfiction, including People of the Deer *(1952),* Never Cry Wolf *(1963), and* Woman in the Mists: The Story of Dian Fossey and the Mountain Gorillas of Africa *(1987).* Never Cry Wolf *(1963), from which "Observing Wolves" was taken, describes how the Canadian government sent Mowat to the Keewatin Barren Lands in the Northwest Territories to prove that the wolves were decimating the caribou herds—and thus should be exterminated. After observing wolves for a few short days, however, Mowat realized that "the centuries-old and universally accepted human concept of wolf character was a palpable lie. . . . I made my decision that, from this hour onward, I would go open-minded into the lupine world and learn to see and know the wolves, not for what they were supposed to be, but for what they actually were." In the first scene, Mowat learns how wolves establish territories; in the second, he discovers something about their diet. Mowat also gives names to each wolf that he observes: Angeline is a female wolf, George is her mate, and Uncle Albert is a male attached to the group.*

I

During the next several weeks I put my decision into effect with the thoroughness for which I have always been noted. I went completely to the wolves. To begin with I set up a den of my own as near to the wolves as I could conveniently get without disturbing the even tenor of their lives too much. After all, I *was* a stranger, and an unwolflike one, so I did not feel I should go too far too fast. 1

Abandoning Mike's cabin (with considerable relief, since as the days warmed up so did the smell) I took a tiny tent and set it up on the shore of the bay immediately opposite to the den esker. I kept my camping gear to the barest minimum—a small primus stove, a stew pot, a teakettle, and a sleeping bag were the essentials. I took no weapons of any kind, although there were times when I regretted this omission, even if only fleetingly. The big telescope was set up in the mouth of the tent in such a way that I could observe the den by day or night without even getting out of my sleeping bag. 2

During the first few days of my sojourn with the wolves I stayed in-   *3*
side the tent except for brief and necessary visits to the out-of-doors which
I always undertook when the wolves were not in sight. The point of this
personal concealment was to allow the animals to get used to the tent and
to accept it as only another bump on a very bumpy piece of terrain. Later,
when the mosquito population reached full flowering, I stayed in the tent
practically all of the time unless there was a strong wind blowing, for the
most bloodthirsty beasts in the Arctic are not wolves, but the insatiable
mosquitoes.

My precautions against disturbing the wolves were superfluous. It   *4*
had required a week for me to get their measure, but they must have
taken mine at our first meeting; and, while there was nothing overtly dis-
dainful in their evident assessment of me, they managed to ignore my
presence, and indeed my very existence, with a thoroughness which was
somehow disconcerting.

Quite by accident I had pitched my tent within ten yards of one of the   *5*
major paths used by the wolves when they were going to, or coming from,
their hunting grounds to the westward; and only a few hours after I had
taken up residence one of the wolves came back from a trip and discovered
me and my tent. He was at the end of a hard night's work and was clearly
tired and anxious to go home to bed. He came over a small rise fifty yards
from me with his head down, his eyes half-closed, and a preoccupied air
about him. Far from being the preternaturally alert and suspicious beast of
fiction, this wolf was so self-engrossed that he came straight on to within
fifteen yards of me, and might have gone right past the tent without seeing it at all, had I not banged my elbow against the teakettle, making a
resounding clank. The wolf's head came up and his eyes opened wide, but
he did not stop or falter in his pace. One brief, sidelong glance was all he
vouchsafed to me as he continued on his way.

It was true that I wanted to be inconspicuous, but I felt uncomfortable   *6*
at being so totally ignored. Nevertheless, during the two weeks which followed, one or more wolves used the track past my tent almost every
night—and never, except on one memorable occasion, did they evince the
slightest interest in me.

By the time this happened I had learned a good deal about my   *7*
wolfish neighbors, and one of the facts which had emerged was that they
were not nomadic roamers, as is almost universally believed, but were settled beasts and the possessors of a large permanent estate with very definite boundaries.

...continued Observing Wolves, **Farley Mowat**

The territory owned by my wolf family comprised more than a hundred square miles, bounded on one side by a river but otherwise not delimited by geographical features. Nevertheless there *were* boundaries, clearly indicated in wolfish fashion.

8

Anyone who has observed a dog doing his neighborhood rounds and leaving his personal mark on each convenient post will have already guessed how the wolves marked out *their* property. Once a week, more or less, the clan made the rounds of the family lands and freshened up the boundary markers—a sort of lupine beating of the bounds. This careful attention to property rights was perhaps made necessary by the presence of two other wolf families whose lands abutted on ours, although I never discovered any evidence of bickering or disagreements between the owners of the various adjoining estates. I suspect, therefore, that it was more of a ritual activity.

9

In any event, once I had become aware of the strong feeling of property rights which existed amongst the wolves, I decided to use this knowledge to make them at least recognize my existence. One evening, after they had gone off for their regular nightly hunt, I staked out a property claim of my own, embracing perhaps three acres, with the tent at the middle, and *including a hundred-yard long section of the wolves' path.*

10

Staking the land turned out to be rather more difficult than I had anticipated. In order to ensure that my claim would not be overlooked, I felt obliged to make a property mark on stones, clumps of moss, and patches of vegetation at intervals of not more than fifteen feet around the circumference of my claim. This took most of the night and required frequent returns to the tent to consume copious quantities of tea; but before dawn brought the hunters home the task was done, and I retired, somewhat exhausted, to observe results.

11

I had not long to wait. At 0814 hours, according to my wolf log, the leading male of the clan appeared over the ridge behind me, padding homeward with his usual air of preoccupation. As usual he did not deign to glance at the tent; but when he reached the point where my property line intersected the trail, he stopped as abruptly as if he had run into an invisible wall. He was only fifty yards from me and with my binoculars I could see his expression very clearly.

12

His attitude of fatigue vanished and was replaced by a look of bewilderment. Cautiously he extended his nose and sniffed at one of my marked bushes. He did not seem to know what to make of it or what to do about

13

it. After a minute of complete indecision he backed away a few yards and sat down. And then, finally, he looked directly at the tent and at me. It was a long, thoughtful, considering sort of look.

Having achieved my object—that of forcing at least one of the wolves *14* to take cognizance of my existence—I now began to wonder if, in my ignorance, I had transgressed some unknown wolf law of major importance and would have to pay for my temerity. I found myself regretting the absence of a weapon as the look I was getting became longer, yet more thoughtful, and still more intent.

I began to grow decidedly fidgety, for I dislike staring matches, and in *15* this particular case I was up against a master, whose yellow glare seemed to become more baleful as I attempted to stare him down.

The situation was becoming intolerable. In an effort to break the im- *16* passe I loudly cleared my throat and turned my back on the wolf (for a tenth of a second) to indicate as clearly as possible that I found his continued scrutiny impolite, if not actually offensive.

He appeared to take the hint. Getting to his feet he had another sniff *17* at my marker, and then he seemed to make up his mind. Briskly, and with an air of decision, he turned his attention away from me and began a systematic tour of the area I had staked out as my own. As he came to each boundary marker he sniffed it once or twice, then carefully placed his mark on the outside of each clump of grass or stone. As I watched I saw where I, in my ignorance, had erred. He made *his* mark with such economy that he was able to complete the entire circuit without having to reload once, or, to change the simile slightly, he did it all on one tank of fuel.

The task completed—and it had taken him no longer than fifteen *18* minutes—he rejoined the path at the point where it left my property and trotted off towards his home—leaving me with a good deal to occupy my thoughts.

II

After some weeks of study I still seemed to be as far as ever from solv- *19* ing the salient problem of how the wolves made a living. This was a vital problem, since solving it in a way satisfactory to my employers was the reason for my expedition.

Caribou are the only large herbivores to be found in any numbers in *20* the arctic Barren Lands. Although once as numerous as the plains buffalo, they had shown a catastrophic decrease during the three or four decades preceding my trip to the Barrens. Evidence obtained by various

Government agencies from hunters, trappers and traders seemed to prove that the plunge of the caribou toward extinction was primarily due to the depredations of the wolf. It therefore must have seemed a safe bet, to the politicians-cum-scientists who had employed me, that a research study of wolf–caribou relationships in the Barrens would uncover incontrovertible proof with which to damn the wolf wherever he might be found, and provide a more than sufficient excuse for the adoption of a general campaign for his extirpation.

21 I did my duty, but although I had searched diligently for evidence which would please my superiors, I had so far found none. Nor did it appear I was likely to.

22 Toward the end of June, the last of the migrating caribou herds had passed Wolf House Bay heading for the high Barrens some two or three hundred miles to the north, where they would spend the summer.

23 Whatever my wolves were going to eat during those long months, and whatever they were going to feed their hungry pups, it would not be caribou, for the caribou were gone. But if not caribou, what *was* it to be?

24 I canvassed all the other possibilities I could think of, but there seemed to be no source of food available which would be adequate to satisfy the appetites of three adult and four young wolves. Apart from myself (and the thought recurred several times) there was hardly an animal left in the country which could be considered suitable prey for a wolf. Arctic hares were present; but they were very scarce and so fleet of foot that a wolf could not hope to catch one unless he was extremely lucky. Ptarmigan and other birds were numerous; but they could fly, and the wolves could not. Lake trout, arctic grayling and whitefish filled the lakes and rivers; but wolves are not otters.

25 About this time I began having trouble with mice. The vast expanses of spongy sphagnum bog provided an ideal milieu for several species of small rodents who could burrow and nest-build to their hearts' content in the ready-made mattress of moss.

26 They did other things too, and they must have done them with great frequency, for as June waned into July the country seemed to become alive with little rodents. The most numerous species were the lemmings, which are famed in literature for their reputedly suicidal instincts, but which, instead, *ought* to be hymned for their unbelievable reproductive capabilities. Red-backed mice and meadow mice began invading Mike's cabin in such numbers that it looked as if *I* would soon be starving unless I could thwart

their appetites for my supplies. *They* did not scorn my bread. They did not scorn my bed, either; and when I awoke one morning to find that a meadow mouse had given birth to eleven naked offspring inside the pillow of my sleeping bag, I began to know how Pharaoh must have felt when he antagonized the God of the Israelites.

I suppose it was only because my own wolf indoctrination had been so [27] complete, and of such a staggeringly inaccurate nature, that it took me so long to account for the healthy state of the wolves in the apparent absence of any game worthy of their reputation and physical abilities. The idea of wolves not only eating, but actually thriving and raising their families on a diet of mice was so at odds with the character of the mythical wolf that it was really too ludicrous to consider. And yet, it was the answer to the problem of how my wolves were keeping the larder full.

Angeline tipped me off. [28]

Late one afternoon, while the male wolves were still resting in prepa- [29] ration for the night's labors, she emerged from the den and nuzzled Uncle Albert until he yawned, stretched and got laboriously to his feet. Then she left the den site at a trot, heading directly for me across a broad expanse of grassy muskeg, and leaving Albert to entertain the pups as best he could.

There was nothing particularly new in this. I had several times seen [30] her conscript Albert (and on rare occasions even George) to do duty as a babysitter while she went down to the bay for a drink or, as I mistakenly thought, simply went for a walk to stretch her legs. Usually her peregrinations took her to the point of the bay farthest from my tent where she was hidden from sight by a low gravel ridge; but this time she came my way in full view and so I swung my telescope to keep an eye on her.

She went directly to the rocky foreshore, waded out until the icy wa- [31] ter was up to her shoulders, and had a long drink. As she was doing so, a small flock of Old Squaw ducks flew around the point of the Bay and pitched only a hundred yards or so away from her. She raised her head and eyed them speculatively for a moment, then waded back to shore, where she proceeded to act as if she had suddenly become demented.

Yipping like a puppy, she began to chase her tail; to roll over and over [32] among the rocks; to lie on her back; to wave all four feet furiously in the air; and in general to behave as if she were clean out of her mind.

I swung the glasses back to where Albert was sitting amidst a gaggle of [33] pups to see if he, too, had observed this mad display, and, if so, what his reaction to it was. He had seen it all right, in fact he was watching Angeline with keen interest but without the slightest indication of alarm.

... *continued* Observing Wolves, **Farley Mowat**

By this time Angeline appeared to be in the throes of a manic 34
paroxysm, leaping wildly into the air and snapping at nothing, the while
uttering shrill squeals. It was an awe-inspiring sight, and I realized that
Albert and I were not the only ones who were watching it with fascination. The ducks seemed hypnotized by curiosity. So interested were they
that they swam in for a closer view of this apparition on the shore.
Closer and closer they came, necks outstretched, and gabbling incredu-
lously among themselves. And the closer they came, the crazier grew
Angeline's behavior.

When the leading duck was not more than fifteen feet from shore, 35
Angeline gave one gigantic leap towards it. There was a vast splash, a
panic-stricken whacking of wings, and then all the ducks were up and
away. Angeline had missed a dinner by no more than inches.

This incident was an eye-opener since it suggested a versatility at 36
food-getting which I would hardly have credited to a human being, let
alone to a mere wolf. However, Angeline soon demonstrated that the
charming of ducks was a mere side line.

Having dried herself with a series of energetic shakes which momen- 37
tarily hid her in a blue mist of water droplets, she padded back across the
grassy swale. But now her movements were quite different from what they
had been when she passed through the swale on the way to the bay.

Angeline was of a rangy build, anyway, but by stretching herself so that 38
she literally seemed to be walking on tiptoe, and by elevating her neck like
a camel, she seemed to gain several inches in height. She began to move
infinitely slowly upwind across the swale, and I had the impression that
both ears were cocked for the faintest sound, while I could see her nose
wrinkling as she sifted the breeze for the most ephemeral scents.

Suddenly she pounced. Flinging herself up on her hind legs like a 39
horse trying to throw its rider, she came down again with driving force,
both forelegs held stiffly out in front of her. Instantly her head dropped;
she snapped once, swallowed, and returned to her peculiar mincing ballet
across the swale. Six times in ten minutes she repeated the straight-armed
pounce, and six times she swallowed—without my having caught a
glimpse of what it was that she had eaten. The seventh time she missed her
aim, spun around, and began snapping frenziedly in a tangle of cotton
grasses. This time when she raised her head I saw, quite unmistakably, the
tail and hind quarters of a mouse quivering in her jaws. One gulp, and it
too was gone.

Although I was much entertained by the spectacle of one of this con- *40*
tinent's most powerful carnivores hunting mice, I did not really take it seriously. I thought Angeline was only having fun; snacking, as it were. But
when she had eaten some twenty-three mice I began to wonder. Mice are
small, but twenty-three of them adds up to a fairsized meal, even for a wolf.

It was only later, by putting two and two together, that I was able to *41*
bring myself to an acceptance of the obvious. The wolves of Wolf House
Bay, and, by inference at least, all the Barren Land wolves who were raising families outside the summer caribou range, were living largely, if not
almost entirely, on mice.

vo·cab·u·lar·y

In your journal, write down the meanings of the italicized words in the following
phrases.

- the den *esker* **(2)**
- *superfluous* **(4)**
- somehow *disconcerting* **(4)**
- *preternaturally* **(5)**
- *evince* the slightest interest **(6)**
- *lupine* **(9)**
- *extirpation* **(20)**
- *her peregrinations* **(30)**

QUESTIONS FOR WRITING AND DISCUSSION

1. Describe what you knew about wolves before you read Mowat's description.
   Which parts of Mowat's description agreed with your preconceptions?
   Which parts gave you new information or a different opinion?

2. *What* is observed depends on *who* is doing the observing. Describe the
   narrator's behavior and personality. How do his preconceptions affect what he
   observes? Should a scientific observer interfere with the lives of the wolves, as
   the narrator does? What does the narrator learn?

3. Some readers complain that Mowat is not scientific. Mowat's genre, a
   personal essay, suggests in fact that he is writing a personal observation, not
   a scientific treatise. For example, compare Mowat's essay with an article

published in *Science,* February 6, 2004, titled "Evolutionary Dynamics of Biological Games," by Martin A. Nowak and Karl Sigmund (full text available at http://www.sciencemag.org. The authors begin their abstract with the following two sentences: "Darwinian dynamics based on mutation and selection form the core of mathematical models for adaptation and coevolution of biological populations. The evolutionary outcome is often not a fitness-maximizing equilibrium but can include oscillations and chaos." Read the opening page or two of this article, and then write a paragraph explaining how Mowat's style and genre is different from the style and genre of this article in *Science.* How does changing a genre affect a writer's purpose?

4. Four keys to effective description are repeated observation, attention to sensory details, noticing changes in the subject or the subject's behavior, and noticing what is not present. Find examples of each of these four strategies in this essay.

5. On the Internet, log on to one of the wolf organization sites such as the International Wolf Center at http://www.wolf.org, the North American Wolf Association at http://www.nawa.org, or Wolfcountry at http://www.wolfcountry.net to check the accuracy of Mowat's essay. For example, the Wolfcountry site explains that wolves are, as Mowat suggests, very opportunistic in their feeding. Although they will prey on deer, moose, bison, elk, and caribou, they also eat beavers, rabbits, rodents, and wild berries. They are also able to catch fish to supplement their diet. Check the information about wolves on these sites: Are Mowat's conclusions about wolf behavior scientifically accurate? Explain.

6. The photograph on the following page shows a gray wolf feeding on a caribou in Denali National Park, Alaska. Assuming that you were arguing that wolves do reduce caribou herd populations and should be controlled, how useful might this image be in supporting your position? Based on this photograph, what logical conclusions could you reach? What conclusions could you *not* logically draw? Explain.

7. Naturalists have reintroduced wolves into Yellowstone National Park. Nearby ranchers, however, are still fearful that wolves will continue to leave the park and kill their livestock. How would Mowat respond to this debate? Imagine that Mowat has logged on to one of the wolf sites and is going to post a response to one of the ranchers. Write the response that Mowat might post.

TECHNIQUES · PROCESS

Observing: The Writing Process

ASSIGNMENT FOR OBSERVING

Do a piece of writing in which you observe a specific person, place, object, or image. Your goal is to show how specific, observed details create dominant ideas about the person, place, object, or image. Your initial purpose is to use your writing to help you observe, discover, and learn about your subject; your final purpose will be to show your reader what you have seen and learned.

While your main purpose is to observe, you also need to think about a possible audience and genre. Are you writing primarily for yourself, to observe and learn? Are you writing for a specific audience? What genre or form would best suit your purpose and audience: a journal entry, a letter to a friend, a personal essay, an editorial, an

Continued

article to be published in a particular magazine, or a posting to an Internet forum?

Important: Repeated observation is essential. Choose a *limited* subject—a person or small group of people, a specific place, a single object or animal, or a recurring event—that *you can reobserve over a period of several days during the writing process.*

CHOOSING   COLLECTING   SHAPING   DRAFTING   REVISING

CHOOSING A SUBJECT

If one of your journal entries suggested an interesting subject, try the collecting and shaping strategies. If none of those exercises caught your interest, consider the following ideas.

- Think about your current classes. Do you have a class with a laboratory—chemistry, physics, biology, engineering, animal science, horticulture, industrial sciences, physical education, social work, drawing, pottery—in which you have to make detailed observations? Use this assignment to help you in one of those classes: Write about what you observe and learn during one of your lab sessions.

- Seek out a new place on campus that is off your usual track. Check the college catalog for ideas about places you haven't yet seen—a theater where actors are rehearsing, a greenhouse, a physical education class in the martial arts, a studio where artists are working, a computer laboratory, or an animal research center. Or visit a class you wouldn't take for credit. Observe, write, and learn about what's there.

- From a magazine that you read, choose an advertisement or an image to describe. Start by observing the composition or arrangement of the figures and the use of color, lines, balance, and contrast in the advertisement or work of art. *Your goals are to describe this image in detail and to analyze the effectiveness of this image in its rhetorical context.* As part of the rhetorical context, consider the artist or sponsor, the occasion, the purpose and intended audience, the genre, and the cultural context of this image.

As you write on your subject, consider a tentative audience and purpose. Who might want to know what you learn from your observations? What do you need to explain? What will readers already know? Jot down tentative ideas about your sub-

"Write about dogs!"

ject, audience, and purpose. Remember, however, that these are not cast in concrete: You may discover some new idea, focus, or angle as you write.

CHOOSING   **COLLECTING**   SHAPING   DRAFTING   REVISING

COLLECTING

Once you have chosen a subject from your journal or elsewhere, begin collecting information. Depending on your purpose, your topic, or even your personal learning preferences, some activities will work better than others. However, you should *practice* all of these activities to determine which is most successful for you and most appropriate to your topic. During these collecting activities, go back and *reobserve your subject.* The second or third time you go back, you may see additional details or more actively understand what you're seeing.

> **❝** We don't take in the world like a camera or a set of recording devices. The mind is an agent, not a passive receiver. . . . The active mind is a composer and everything we respond to, we compose. **❞**
>
> —ANN BERTHOFF,
> AUTHOR AND TEACHER

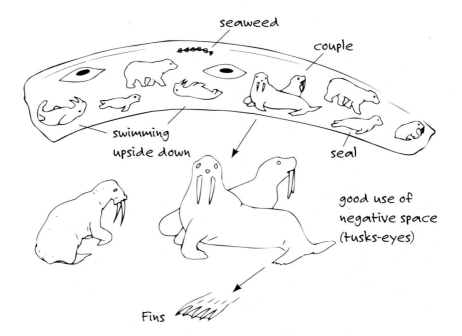

▍ SKETCHING

Begin by *drawing* what you see. The essayist Samuel Scudder says that pen or pencil can be "the best of eyes." Your drawing doesn't have to be great art to suggest other details, questions, or relationships that may be important. Instead of trying to cover a wide range of objects, try to focus on one limited subject and draw it in detail.

Here's an example. Writing student Brad Parks decided to visit an Eskimo art display at a local gallery. As part of his observing notes, he drew these sketches of Eskimo paintings. As he drew, he made notes in the margins of his sketches and zoomed in for more detail on one pair of walruses.

▍ TAKING DOUBLE-ENTRY NOTES

Taking notes in a double-entry format is a simple but effective system for recording observed details. At the top of the page, write the place and time of your observation and your perspective, role, or point of view. Draw a vertical line down the middle of a page in your journal. On the left-hand side, write down description and sensory details. On the right-hand side, record your reactions, thoughts, ideas, and questions.

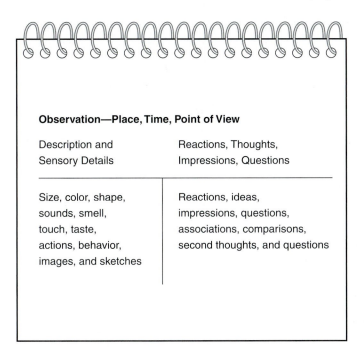

Observation—Place, Time, Point of View

Description and Sensory Details	Reactions, Thoughts, Impressions, Questions
Size, color, shape, sounds, smell, touch, taste, actions, behavior, images, and sketches	Reactions, ideas, impressions, questions, associations, comparisons, second thoughts, and questions

■ **ANSWERING QUESTIONS**   To help you describe the person, place, object, or image, write a short response in your journal to each of the following questions.

- What exactly is it? Can you *define* this person, place, object, or image? If it's an object, are its parts related? Who needs it, uses it, or produces it?
- How much could it change and still be recognizable?
- Compare and contrast it. How is it similar to or different from other comparable people, places, things, or images?
- From what points of view is it usually seen? From what point of view is it rarely seen?

■ **FREEWRITING**   *Freewriting* means exactly what it says. Write about your subject, nonstop, for five to ten minutes. Sometimes you may have to write, "I can't think of anything" or "This is really stupid," but keep on writing. Let your words and ideas suggest other thoughts and ideas. For observing, the purpose of freewriting is to let your imagination work on the subject, usually *after* you have observed and recorded specific details. Freewriting on your subject will also develop more *associations* or *comparisons* for the right-hand side of your double-entry log. It should also help you to identify a dominant idea for your details.

SHAPING

To focus once again on the shaping process, consider your subject, purpose, and audience. Has your purpose changed? Can you narrow your subject to a specific topic? You may know the answers to some questions immediately; others you may not know until after you complete your first draft. Jot down your current responses to the following questions.

> **❝** Your audience is one single reader. I have found that sometimes it helps to pick out one person—a real person you know, or an imagined person—and write to that one. **❞**
> —JOHN STEINBECK, NOVELIST

- **Subject:** What is your general subject?
- **Specific topic:** What aspect of your subject interests you? Try to narrow your field or limit your focus.
- **Purpose:** Why is this topic interesting or important to you or to others? From what point of view will you be writing? What is the *dominant idea* you are trying to convey?
- **Audience:** Who are your readers? What are these readers like, and why might they be interested in this topic? How can you direct your description of your subject to your particular audience?
- **Context:** What is the cultural, political, social, or personal context in which this person, object, or image appears? How does that context affect your subject? How does the context affect you?

With answers to these questions in mind, you should experiment with several of the following genre possibilities and organization strategies. These genres and strategies not only will organize your specific examples but also may suggest related ideas to improve your description.

As you practice these strategies, try to *focus* on your subject. In a profile of a person, for example, focus on key facial features or revealing habits or mannerisms. If you're writing about a place or an event, narrow the subject. Describe, for instance, the street at night, a spider spinning a web in a windowsill, a man in a laundromat banging on a change machine, a bird hovering in midair, a photograph, a fish. Write in depth and detail about a *limited* subject.

With a limited subject, a shaping strategy such as spatial order, chronological order, or comparison/contrast will organize all the specific details for your audience. Shaping strategies give you ways of seeing relationships among the many bits of your description and of presenting them in an organized manner for your reader. Seeing these relationships will also help you discover and communicate the dominant idea to your reader.

▪ **GENRE**   As you begin thinking about organizing or shaping your description, consider what genre would work best for your topic. Should you write an essay? Should you write a letter? Might this be part of your Web page or blog? Would a multigenre or multimedia approach work? Do you want to have text, pictures, graphics, Web links, or added sound? Would text and a paper or digital collage be most effective for your purpose, audience, and occasion?

▪ **SPATIAL ORDER**   Spatial order is a simple way to organize your descriptive details. Choose some sequence—left to right, right to left, bottom to top—and describe your observed details in that sequence. In the following description of his "trashed" dorm room, Dale Furnish, a student who was the victim of a prank, uses spatial order. The italicized words illustrate the spatial order.

> As I walked in the door, I could hardly believe that this scene of destruction used to be my room. *Along the left-hand wall,* nearly hiding my desk and mirror, was a pile of beer cans and bottles, paper cups, and old crumpled newspapers. The small window *on the far wall* was now covered with the mattress of the bed, and the frame of the bunk bed stood on end. The clothes closet, *to the right of the window,* looked as though it were a giant washing machine which had just gone through spin cycle—clothes were plastered all over, and only four hangers remained, dangling uselessly on the pole. *On the right wall,* where the bed had been, was the real surprise. Tied to the heating pipe was a mangy looking sheep. I swear. It was a real sheep. As I looked at it, it turned to face me and loudly and plaintively said, "Baaaa." *Behind me,* in the hall, everyone began laughing. I didn't know whether to laugh or cry.

▪ **CHRONOLOGICAL ORDER**   Chronological order is simply the time sequence of your observation. In the following passage, Gregory Allen, writing from his point of view as a five-foot-six-inch guard on a basketball team, describes sights, sounds, and his feelings during a pickup game. The italicized words emphasize the chronological order.

> The game *begins.* The guy checking me is about 6'1", red hair, freckles, and has no business on the court. He looks slow, so I decide to run him to tire him. I dribble twice, pump fake, and the guy goes for it, thinking that he's going to block this much smaller guy's shot. *Then* I leap, flick my wrist, and the ball glides through the air and flows through the net with a swish as the net turns upside down. I come down and realize that I have been scratched. *Suddenly,* I feel a sharp pain as sweat runs into the small red cut. I wipe the

blood on my shorts and *continue playing* the game. *After* that first play, I begin to hear the common song of the game. There's the squeak of the hightop Nike sneakers, the bouncing ball, the shuffle of feet. *Occasionally,* I hear "I'm open!" "Pass the ball!" "Augghh!" And *then,* "Nice play, man!"

▪ **COMPARISON/CONTRAST**   If what you've observed and written about your subject so far involves seeing similarities or differences, you may be able to use comparison/contrast as a shaping strategy—either for a single paragraph or for a series of paragraphs. The following two paragraphs, for example, are taken from Albert Goldman's biography of Elvis Presley, titled *Elvis.* In these paragraphs, Goldman's dominant idea depends on the striking contrast between what he finds on the front lawn of Graceland, the rock star's mansion in Memphis, and what he notices when he steps through the front door.

> Prominently displayed on the front lawn is an elaborate creche. The stable is a full-scale adobe house strewn with straw. Life-sized are the figures of Joseph and Mary, the kneeling shepherds and Magi, the lambs and ewes, as well as the winged annunciatory angel hovering over the roof beam. Real, too, is the cradle in which the infant Jesus sleeps.
>
> When you step through the ten-foot oak door and enter the house, you stop and stare in amazement. Having just come from the contemplation of the tenderest scene in the Holy Bible, imagine the shock of finding yourself in a *whorehouse!* Yet there is no other way to describe the drawing room of Graceland except to say that it appears to have been lifted from some turn-of-the-century bordello down in the French Quarter of New Orleans. . . . The room is a gaudy melange of red velour and gilded tassels, Louis XV furniture and porcelain bric-a-brac, all informed by the kind of taste that delights in a ceramic temple d'amour housing a miniature Venus de Milo with an electrically simulated waterfall cascading over her naked shoulders.

Examine once again your collecting notes about your subject. If there are striking similarities or differences between the two parts or between various aspects of your subject, perhaps a comparison or contrast structure will organize your details.

▪ **DEFINITION**   Definition is the essence of observation. Defining a person, place, or object requires stating its exact meaning and describing its basic qualities. Literally, a definition sets the boundaries, indicating, for example, how an apple is distinct from an orange or how a canary is different from a sparrow. *Definition,* however, is a catchall term for a variety of strategies. It uses classification and comparison as well as description. It often describes a thing by negation—by saying what it is not. For example, Sidney Harris, a columnist for many years for the *Chicago Daily News,* once defined a "jerk" by referring to several types of people ("boob," "fool," "dope," "bore," "egotist," "nice person," "clever person") and then compared or contrasted these terms to show where "jerk" leaves off and "egotist" begins. In the following excerpt, Harris also defines by negation, saying that a jerk has no grace and is tactless. The result, when combined with a description of qualities he has observed in jerks, is definition.

> Thinking it over, I decided that a jerk is basically a person without insight. He is not necessarily a fool or a dope, because some extremely clever persons can be jerks. In fact, it has little to do with intelligence as we commonly think of it; it is, rather, a kind of subtle but persuasive aroma emanating from the inner part of the personality.
>
> I know a college president who can be described only as a jerk. He is not an unintelligent man, or unlearned, nor even unschooled in the social amenities. Yet he is a jerk *cum laude,* because of a fatal flaw in his nature— he is totally incapable of looking into the mirror of his soul and shuddering at what he sees there.
>
> A jerk, then, is a man (or woman) who is utterly unable to see himself as he appears to others. He has no grace, he is tactless without meaning to be, he is a bore even to his best friends, he is an egotist without charm. All of us are egotists to some extent, but most of us—unlike the jerk—are perfectly and horribly aware of it when we make asses of ourselves. The jerk never knows.

At this stage in the writing process, you have already been defining your subject simply by describing it. But you may want to use a deliberately structured definition, as Harris does, to shape your observations.

■ **SIMILE, METAPHOR, AND ANALOGY**   Simile, metaphor, and analogy create vivid word pictures or *images* by making *comparisons.* These images may take up only a sentence or two, or they may shape several paragraphs.

- A *simile* is a comparison using *like* or *as:* A is like B. "George eats his food like a vacuum cleaner."
- A *metaphor* is a direct or implied comparison suggesting that A is B. "At the dinner table, George is a vacuum cleaner."
- An *analogy* is an extended simile or metaphor that builds a point-by-point comparison into several sentences, a whole paragraph, or even a series of paragraphs. Writers use analogy to explain a difficult concept, idea, or process by comparing it with something more familiar or easier to

understand. If the audience, for example, knows about engines but has never seen a human heart, a writer might use an analogy to explain that a heart is like a simple engine, complete with chambers or cylinders, intake and exhaust valves, and hoses to carry fuel and exhaust.

As an illustration of simile and metaphor, notice how Joseph Conrad, in the following brief passage from *Heart of Darkness*, begins with a simile and then continues to build on his images throughout the paragraph. Rather than creating a rigid structural shape for his details (as classification or comparison/contrast would do), the images combine and flow like the river he is describing.

> Going up that river was like travelling back to the earliest beginnings of the world, when vegetation rioted on the earth and the big trees were kings. An empty stream, a great silence, an impenetrable forest. The air was warm, thick, heavy, sluggish. There was no joy in the brilliance of sunshine. The long stretches of the waterway ran on, deserted, into the gloom of overshadowed distances. On silvery sand-banks hippos and alligators sunned themselves side by side. The broadening waters flowed through a mob of wooded islands; you lost your way on that river as you would in a desert, and butted all day long against shoals, trying to find the channel, till you thought yourself bewitched and cut off forever from everything you had known once—somewhere—far away—in another existence perhaps.

An analogy helps shape the following paragraph by Carl Sagan, author of *The Dragons of Eden* and *Cosmos.* To help us understand a difficult concept, the immense age of the Earth (and, by comparison, the relatively tiny span of human history), Sagan compares the lifetime of the universe to something simple and familiar: the calendar of a single year.

> The most instructive way I know to express this cosmic chronology is to imagine the fifteen-billion year lifetime of the universe . . . compressed into the span of a single year. . . . It is disconcerting to find that in such a cosmic year the Earth does not condense out of interstellar matter until early September; dinosaurs emerge on Christmas Eve; flowers arise on December 28th; and men and women originate at 10:30 P.M. on New Year's Eve. All of recorded history occupies the last ten seconds of December 31; and the time from the waning of the Middle Ages to the present occupies little more than one second.

Consider whether a good analogy would help you shape one or more paragraphs in your essay. Ask yourself, "What is the most difficult concept or idea I'm trying to describe?" Is there an extended point-by-point comparison—an analogy—that would clarify it?

TITLE, INTRODUCTION, AND CONCLUSION Depending on your purpose and audience, you may want a title for what you're writing. At the minimum, titles—like labels—should accurately indicate the contents in the package. In addition, however, good titles capture the reader's interest with some catchy phrasing or imaginative language—something to make the reader want to "buy" the package. Samuel H. Scudder's title is a good label (the essay is about looking at fish) and uses catchy phrasing: "Take This Fish and Look at It." If a title is appropriate for your observation, write out several possibilities in your journal.

The introduction should set up the context for the reader—*who, what, when, where,* and *why*—so that readers can orient themselves. Depending on your audience and purpose, introductions can be very brief, pushing the reader quickly into the scene, or they can take more time, easing readers into the setting. Stephen White, in his essay about Mesa Verde at the end of this chapter, begins mysteriously: "It is difficult for me to say exactly what it was that drew me to this solitary place." White doesn't tell his reader that he's talking about Mesa Verde until the second paragraph.

Conclusions should wrap up the observation, providing a sense of completeness. Conclusions vary, depending upon a writer's purpose and audience, but they tend to be of two types or have two components: a *summary* and a *reference* to the introduction. Mowat uses both components when he concludes his essay. Part II of his essay ends by referring to and then answering the central question of his expedition, that is: How do wolves survive? "The wolves of Wolf House Bay," Mowat tells us, "were living largely, if not almost entirely, on mice."

As you work on shaping strategies and drafting, make notes about possible titles, appropriate introductions, or effective conclusions for your written observations.

CHOOSING	COLLECTING	SHAPING	**DRAFTING**	REVISING

DRAFTING

> **"** The idea is to get the pencil moving quickly. **"**
> —BERNARD MALAMUD, NOVELIST

REREAD JOURNAL ENTRIES AND NOTES FROM COLLECTING AND SHAPING Before you start drafting, review your material so you aren't writing cold. Stop and reread everything you've written on your subject. You're not trying to memorize particular sentences or phrases; you're just getting it all fresh in your mind, seeing what you still like and discarding details that are no longer relevant.

■ **REOBSERVE YOUR SUBJECT** If necessary, go back and observe your subject again. One more session may suggest an important detail or idea that will help you get started writing.

■ **REEXAMINE PURPOSE, AUDIENCE, DOMINANT IDEA, AND SHAPE** After all your writing and rereading, you may have some new ideas about your purpose, audience, or dominant idea. Take a minute to jot these down in your journal. Remember that your specific details should show the main point or dominant idea, whether you state it explicitly or not.

Next, if the shaping strategies suggested an order for your essay, use it to guide your draft. You may, however, have only your specific details or a general notion of the dominant idea you're trying to communicate to your reader. In that case, you may want to begin writing and work out a shape or outline as you write.

■ **CREATE A DRAFT** With the above notes as a guide, you are ready to start drafting. Work on establishing your ritual: Choose a comfortable, familiar place with the writing tools you like. Make sure you'll have no interruptions. Try to write nonstop. If you can't think of a word, substitute a dash. If you can't remember how to spell a word, don't stop to look it up now—keep writing. Write until you reach what feels like the end. If you do get stuck, reread your last few lines or some of your writing process materials. Then go back and pick up the thread. Don't stop to count words or pages. You should shoot for more material than you need because it's usually easier to cut material later, when you're revising, than to add more if you're short.

CHOOSING	COLLECTING	SHAPING	DRAFTING	REVISING

REVISING

■ **GAINING DISTANCE AND OBJECTIVITY** Revising, of course, has been going on since you put your first sentence down on paper. You've changed ideas, thought through your subject again, and observed your person, place, object, or image. After your rough draft is finished, your next step is to revise again to resee the whole thing. But before you do, you need to let it sit at least twenty-four hours, to get away from it for a while, to gain some distance and perspective. Relax. Congratulate yourself.

About the time you try to relax, however, you may get a sudden temptation—even an overwhelming urge—to have someone else read it—immediately! Usually, it's better to resist that urge. Chances are, you want to have someone else read it either because you're bubbling with enthusiasm and you want to share it or because you're certain that it's all garbage and you want to hear the bad news right away. Most read-

❝ All the stuff you see back there on the floor is writing I did last week that I have to rewrite this week. ❞
—ERNEST J. GAINES, AUTHOR OF *THE AUTOBIOGRAPHY OF MISS JANE PITTMAN*

PEER RESPONSE

The instructions below will help you give and receive constructive advice about the rough draft of your observing essay. You may use these guidelines for an in-class workshop, a take-home review, or a computer e-mail response.

Writer: Before you exchange drafts with another reader, write out the following information about your rough draft.

1. What is the dominant impression that you want your description to make? What overall idea or impression do you want your reader to have?
2. What paragraph(s) contains your best and most vivid description? What paragraph(s) still needs some revision?
3. Explain one or two things you would like your reader to comment on as he or she responds to your draft.

Reader: First, without making any marks, read the entire draft from start to finish. As you reread the draft, answer the following questions.

1. What *dominant impression* does the draft create? Does the dominant impression you received agree with the writer's own idea? If not, how might the writer better achieve that overall impression?
2. Look at the writer's responses to question 2. Does the writer, in fact, use vivid description in his or her best paragraph(s)? How might the paragraphs that the writer says need revision be improved? Review the six techniques for descriptive writing at the beginning of this chapter. Where or how might the writer improve the *sensory details, images,* descriptions of what is not there, changes in the subject, or *point of view?* Offer specific suggestions.
3. Reread the assignment for this essay. Explain how this essay should be revised to more clearly meet the assignment. Does the writer understand the *rhetorical situation?* What changes in purpose, audience, genre, or style would help the essay meet the assignment?
4. List the *two most important things* this writer should work on as he or she revises this draft. Explain why these are important.

ers will not find it either as great as you hope *or* as awful as you fear. As a result, their offhand remarks may seem terribly insensitive or condescending. In a day or so, however, you'll be able to see your writing more objectively: Perhaps it's not great yet, but it's not hopeless, either. At that point, you're ready to get some feedback and start your revisions.

█ REREADING AND RESPONDING TO YOUR READERS When you've been away from the draft for a while, you are better able to see the whole piece of writing. Start by rereading your own draft and making marginal notes. Don't be distracted by spelling errors or typos; concentrate on the quality of the details and the flow of the sentences. Focus on the overall effect you're creating, see if your organization still makes sense, and check to make sure that all the details support the dominant idea. Now you're ready to get some peer feedback. Depending on the reactions of your readers, you may need to change the point of view, add a few specific examples or some comparisons or images, fix the organization of a paragraph, reorder some details, delete some sentences, or do several of the above. Be prepared, however, to rewrite several paragraphs to help your readers really see what you are describing.

GUIDELINES FOR REVISION

As you revise your essay, keep the following tips and checklist questions in mind.

- **Reexamine your purpose and audience.** Are you doing what you intended? If your purpose or audience has changed, what other changes do you need to make as you revise?
- **Pay attention to the advice your readers give you, but don't necessarily make all the changes they suggest.** Ask them *why* something should be changed. Ask them specifically *where* something should be changed.
- **Consider your genre.** Does your chosen genre still work for your purpose, audience, and context? Would including pictures, visuals, graphics, poetry, or quotations in a multigenre format be more effective?
- **Consider your point of view.** Would changing to another point of view clarify what you are describing?
- **Consider your vantage point.** Do you have a bird's-eye view, or are you observing from a low angle? Do you zoom in for a close-up of a person or object? Would a different vantage point fit your purpose and audience?
- **Make sure you are using sensory details where appropriate.** Remember, you must *show* your reader the details you observe. If necessary, *reobserve* your subject.
- **Do all your details and examples support your dominant idea?** Reread your draft and omit any irrelevant details.
- **What is *not* present in your subject that might be important to mention?**

- **What changes occur in the form or function of your subject?** Where can you describe those changes more vividly?

- **Make comparisons if they will help you or your reader understand your subject better.** Similes, metaphors, or analogies may describe your subject more vividly.

- **Does what you are observing belong to a class of similar objects?** Would classification organize your writing?

- **Be sure to cue or signal your reader with appropriate transition words.** Transitions will improve the coherence or flow of your writing.
  - **Spatial order:** on the left, on the right, next, above, below, higher, lower, farther, next, beyond
  - **Chronological order.** before, earlier, after, afterward, thereafter, then, from then on, the next day, shortly, by that time, immediately, slowly, while, meanwhile, until, now, soon, within an hour, first, later, finally, at last
  - **Comparison/contrast:** on one hand, on the other hand, also, similarly, in addition, likewise, however, but, yet, still, although, even so, nonetheless, in contrast

- **Revise sentences for clarity, conciseness, emphasis, and variety.**

- **When you have revised your essay, edit your writing for correct spelling and appropriate word choice, punctuation, usage, and grammar.**

> ❝I went for years not finishing anything. Because, of course, when you finish something you can be judged. ❞
> —ERICA JONG,
> AUTHOR OF *FEAR OF FLYING*

POSTSCRIPT ON THE WRITING PROCESS

When you've finished writing this assignment, do one final journal entry. Briefly, answer the following questions.

1. What was the hardest part of this writing assignment for you?

2. Put brackets ([ ]) around the paragraph containing your most vivid sensory details. Explain what makes this paragraph so vivid.

3. What exercise, practice, strategy, or workshop was the "breakthrough" for you? What led you to your discovery or dominant idea?

4. State in one sentence your discovery or the dominant idea of your essay.

5. What did you learn about your writing ritual and process? What did you learn about observing? What did you learn about your rhetorical situation?

STUDENT WRITING

JENNIFER MACKE

Permanent Tracings

Jennifer Macke, a student in Professor Rachel Henne-Wu's class at Owens Community College in Findlay, Ohio, decided to write her observing essay about a tattoo parlor. She visited the Living Color Tattoo Parlor and took notes on the office, the clientele, the conversations, the artwork of the tattoos, and the owner of the establishment. Ms. Macke wrote that her preconceptions about tattoo parlors were that they were "smoke-filled, dimly lit places" where "undesirables gathered." Gradually, her impressions changed as she saw firsthand the high quality and the remarkable artistry of the tattoos. Reprinted below are some of her original notes, questions and answers, an outline, and the final version of her essay.

NOTES ON A VISIT

- A couple with a young school-aged daughter looks at the artwork on the walls for about 15 minutes before saying anything to the owner. They are looking for a design for the wife for her birthday. They appear to be a typical young couple with a limited amount of money. They ask how much a particular design will be and say they will have to save for it. "How much for this ankle bracelet?" he says. "It'll run you between $45 and $60, depending on how thick you want the rose vine," Gasket says.

- Two Latino men enter the waiting room. One peeks his head into the office and says, "I'm here early for my appointment because I'm not sure exactly what I want. Do you have any books or more pictures I can look through?" Gasket gives him six photo albums full of ideas (designs).

- Five young adult black men enter. They begin browsing through the photos on the wall. There are designs with prices below them so you know what it costs without asking. They too look through the photo albums the Latinos left on the floor. One of the black guys announces, "I'll go first 'cause I want to get it over with." One says, "I'm not going to do this. I can't stand the sound of that needle!" Gasket looks at me and says, "It's amazing how many people just think all you have to do is walk through the door like a walk-in barber shop. They don't know I'm booked for at least a week. During the summer, it's three weeks."

- The phone rings and since his daughter, who normally works there, is gone to visit her mother, he tells me to pick it up. The guy on the other end says, "My uncle wants to know if Jeff's cousin works here?" I relay the message to the owner and he replies, "Yes, that's me." Back on the phone, "He says he's the best in the business. Does he have any time today?" Gasket says, "Here we go again." I tell the guy it will be a week. He says, "OK, I'll call back then." I tell Gasket what he said and he comments, "He'll call back next week, and I'll have to tell him it'll be another week. You would not believe the intelligence level of some people."

- The next girl is going to have lips tattooed on her right hip. She is a petite nurse whom you would never guess would even consider such a thing. Her husband put lipstick on and kissed a napkin which she brought to use for the pattern. Gasket took a photocopy of this and made a transfer from it to use as the template. She dropped her shorts to expose where the art would be placed. She lay down on the table which Gasket explained he had gotten in trade for a tattoo. He also said the stirrups were still in the drawer. The girl smiled and talked the whole time he worked. At one point, he asked her, "Does it hurt?" She said, "No." He said, "I can go deeper!" She said, "Are you supposed to?" He said, laughing, "It's just a joke. If I see someone who's comfortable, I'll ask them this." It only took about 30 minutes to complete this one. You would swear someone just kissed her with bright red lipstick. It's amazing how realistic his work looks.

QUESTIONS AND ANSWERS

1. "Why do people get tattoos?"
   "A tattoo is a very personal thing. It's an expression of one's self."

2. "Does it hurt to get a tattoo?"
   "It all depends on the placement and the person. Guys tend to be bigger wimps. I'd rather do women any day. The most painful areas are the ankle and higher up on the belly. I've had the pain described as something annoying but not necessarily painful to such a point that they cannot stand it. I've never had anyone pass out, though."

3. "What kind of person gets a tattoo?"
   "There's not one particular type of person who gets a tattoo. I once had a call from some lawyers from Findlay. They wanted to know if they had five or so people who wanted a tattoo, would I come over? I said, yes, and I tattooed six lawyers at a party."

. . . continued Permanent Tracings, **Jennifer Macke**

4. "What is the process of getting a tattoo?"

   "Depending if it will be freehand or something the people bring in, it starts with drawing the art. It is drawn either on the person or on carbon paper backwards. The carbon design is transferred to the skin with Speed Stick deodorant. The outline is applied first. As the single needle picks up and sews into the skin, excess ink covers the work area."

   As Gasket works, it's hard to see the actual area he's working on because of the excess ink. When asked how he can work with the excess ink obstructing the guidelines, he says he just knows where the line goes. (I wouldn't.) Once the outline is complete he changes to use a 3 or 4 needle set, depending on the coverage necessary. He colorizes the art, which brings it to life. After it's complete, he puts a thick coat of Bacitracin on and covers it with a gauze bandage. The gauze must remain on for one and a half to two hours.

5. "What is the most common place for a tattoo?"

   "Placement runs in cycles, sometimes the upper arm, sometimes the ankle." While we were talking, a man came in with one on the back of his neck.

6. "How expensive are tattoos?"

   The minimum is $30. Depending on how detailed and how big. Gasket has bartered for the tattoos, too.

7. "Do most people get more than one tattoo?"

   "I've seen people go through life with only one or maybe two, but it's said when you get your third, you're hooked. You'll be back for more."

8. "Are there health department requirements?"

   "At the beginning, the requirements (laws) weren't very strict. I knew I wanted to be supersterile, so I put my needles and equipment through a much stricter procedure. Since then, the health department has taken on my policy and requires everyone to process their stuff like me. They drop in to make sure the laws are being followed."

9. "How many times do you use your needles?"

   "They are single-application needles, but they still need to be sterilized. People ask me if they can watch their needles being sterilized so they can make sure. I say fine, but it will be two and a half hours until I can work on you."

OUTLINE

Working Thesis: "Gasket's creative artistic
ability and perfectionist work ethic make his designs
worth sewing into your body for a lifetime."

I. Describe the Tattoo Parlor

    A. Outer area (waiting room)

    B. Inner office

II. Describe the owner

    A. The way he looks

    B. The way he feels about his work

III. Describe the people

    A. People getting a tattoo

    B. People not getting a tattoo

FINAL VERSION
Permanent Tracings

At first glance, the Living Color Tattoo Parlor appears to be just another 1
typical tattoo establishment. You enter through a glass door only to find
a waiting room with the decor reminiscent of the 1970s. The dark pan-
eled walls display numerous types of artwork that range from pencil
sketching to color Polaroid snapshots of newly completed tattoos. The
gold and green davenport looks as if it came from a Saturday morning
garage sale. The inner office is celery green with a dental chair and an obstetrics table that the owner bartered for a tattoo (the stirrups are still in
the drawer). A filing cabinet, desk, and copy machine make you feel as if
you're in a professional office. The sterilizer is in plain sight and is in operation. Bottle after bottle of brightly colored inks are neatly arranged on
a tiered wooden stand. The sound of the oscillating fan that cools the
client interrupts the buzz of the needle sewing the paint into the client's
skin. A freeze-dried turtle is displayed on a table in the office.

    I still wondered, though. Could tattoos actually be a form of art?   2

    As soon as I could, I asked the owner, a man called Gasket, about his   3
occupation. "I was a suit for fifteen years and now I can work as much as I
want. There's always somebody wanting a tattoo or something pierced,"
Gasket said. He's often asked if he'll scratch out the name of a previous

girlfriend, and he always replies that he would never even consider it. "That would be defacement," he said. "When I'm done, the design should look better than when I started." Gasket is not his given name but one he acquired because of his expert repair work on Harley Davidson motorcycles. Gasket is the owner of this establishment, and to look at him, you would never guess he is a college-educated engineer. His long curly, graying hair flows from under his Harley hat, and examples of his handiwork are visible under the rolled up sleeves of his black Harley T-shirt. The harshness of his heavily bearded face is softened by his slate-blue eyes, which mirror his gentle demeanor. If you look past his casual exterior, you will find a code of steel. "At the beginning, the laws weren't very strict. I knew I wanted to be supersterile, so I put my single-use needles and equipment through a much stricter procedure. Since then, the health department has taken on my policy and requires everyone to process their stuff like me," he said.

The appearance of the Living Color Tattoo Parlor may be typical, but two things are distinctly different: the quality and the creativity of the tattoo designs. A young college couple from Toledo was asked why they would drive to Fremont for an appointment. They answered, "Gasket's the best! We wouldn't trust something that's going to be on our body for the rest of our lives to someone other than him." *4*

"I already have two tattoos from you, and I love your work," a middle-aged woman said. Displaying two greeting cards, she asked, "Is it possible to get a combination of these two designs?" *5*

"I can create anything you want," Gasket said. *6*

"I'll have to wait a couple of weeks because I'm not working much and my other bills come first," she said. *7*

"Yes, you have to get your priorities straight. When you're ready, I'm here," he said. *8*

Gasket is performing his tattoo magic on a young college female. He's creating a rose with a heart stem wrapping around her belly button, which is pierced. The girl is nervously seated in the green dental chair, which is tilted back to flatten the skin surface. First, Gasket draws the sketch on her belly. He covers his hands with a thin layer of latex once the exact position and specific details are decided upon. A small device resembling a fountain pen with a brightly colored motor and a single needle moving at 1,000 rpm is used to apply the black outline first. As the needle moves up and down, it picks up a small amount of ink and deposits it just under the surface of the skin. When asked how he can work with the excess ink obstructing the guidelines, he simply said he just knows *9* where the line goes. This is a difficult task because unlike a paint-by-number design, the image not only has to be in his mind but he also has to have the artistic ability to convert the image to the skin. The girl asks a pain-filled question, "How much longer?"

"I can stop and let you take a break at any time," Gasket says. His soft 10 tone and slow-paced voice help soothe the girl. "The higher up on the belly, the more painful," he says. The process of colorizing the tattoo begins once the outline is complete. This is accomplished with a three- or four-needle set, depending on the amount of coverage desired. It takes about forty-five minutes to complete the multicolored masterpiece, which is literally sewn into her skin. Some of Gasket's designs can be compared to Picasso's brilliantly colored, dreamlike images. Upon completion, the girl is directed to a full-length mirror to inspect her permanently altered abs.

"It looks fantastic!" she exclaims. "I was a little vague on how I pic- 11 tured it would look, but it looks even better than I had imagined. I'm thrilled."

Once thought of as green-toned disfigurements that only drunken 12 sailors and lowlife people would don, tattoos are now high fashion. Now it is possible to see skin art on TV stars, sports superstars, and a multitude of individuals you might not suspect. The future of this trendy fashion has its roots firmly planted in today's society. Young people seem to be one of its biggest supporters.

"I'll go first 'cause I want to get it over with," one young black man 13 states to his four companions.

"I'm not going to do this. I can't stand the sound of that needle!" an- 14 other man proclaims.

"It's amazing how many people think all you have to do is just walk 15 through the door like a walk-in barber shop. They don't know I'm booked for at least a week. During the summer, it's three weeks," Gasket claims. He explains this to the young men, who make appointments. They leave, disappointed.

Gasket's tattoo designs can be compared to the famous fashion de- 16 signs by Bob Mackie. Like Mackie's one-of-a-kind designs, they are not mass-produced, but are hand-sewn for a specific individual. As I left, my first impression of the Living Color Tattoo Parlor was changed by the incredibly beautiful skin art and the comments of the satisfied clients. For many, Gasket's artistic ability and perfectionism make his designs worth sewing into your body for a lifetime.

QUESTIONS FOR WRITING AND DISCUSSION

1. Review the techniques for writing observing papers at the beginning of the chapter. Which paragraph(s) in Macke's essay have the best sensory detail, images, comparisons, and other effective bits of description? Which paragraphs might use more descriptive detail?

2. Macke describes the office, the owner, the customers, the process of tattooing, and the prices of a tattoo. Should she also describe several of the tattoos? Should she describe the colors in a typical tattoo? If she did these descriptions, where might she put them in her essay?

3. Reread Macke's notes of her visit, including her questions and answers. What interesting ideas and descriptions in her notes might be included in her final draft? Why might Macke have left these details out? Assume that you are a peer reader for Macke's essay. Fill out the peer response questions printed earlier in this chapter so you can help her with a revision of her essay.

4. List the three things that you like best about Macke's essay. Which of her strategies might work for a revision of your own essay? Make a revision plan for your own essay, based on what you learned from reading "Permanent Tracings."

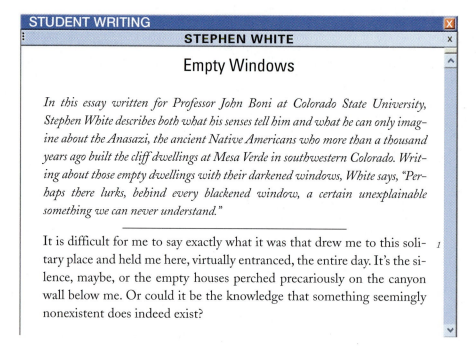

STUDENT WRITING

STEPHEN WHITE

Empty Windows

In this essay written for Professor John Boni at Colorado State University, Stephen White describes both what his senses tell him and what he can only imagine about the Anasazi, the ancient Native Americans who more than a thousand years ago built the cliff dwellings at Mesa Verde in southwestern Colorado. Writing about those empty dwellings with their darkened windows, White says, "Perhaps there lurks, behind every blackened window, a certain unexplainable something we can never understand."

It is difficult for me to say exactly what it was that drew me to this solitary place and held me here, virtually entranced, the entire day. It's the silence, maybe, or the empty houses perched precariously on the canyon wall below me. Or could it be the knowledge that something seemingly nonexistent does indeed exist?

I awoke this morning with a sense of unexplainable anticipation   *2*
gnawing away at the back of my mind, that this chilly, leaden day at Mesa
Verde would bring something new and totally foreign to any of my past
experiences. It was a sensation that began to permeate my entire being as
I sat crouched before my inadequate campfire, chills running up my
spine. Chills which, I am certain, were due not entirely to the dreary gray
of a winter "sunrise."

It had been my plan to travel the so-called Ruins Road early today   *3*
and then complete my visit here, but as I stopped along the road and
stood scanning the opposite wall of the canyon for ruins, I felt as if some
force had seized control of my will. I was compelled to make my way
along the rim.

Starting out upon the rock, I weaved in and out repeatedly as the   *4*
gaping emptiness of the canyon and the weathered standstone of the rim
battled one another for territory. At last arriving here, where a narrow
peninsula of canyon juts far into the stone, I was able to peer back into
the darkness of a cave carved midway in the vertical wall opposite, within
whose smoke-blackened walls huddle, nearly unnoticeable, the rooms of
a small, crumbled ruin.

They are a haunting sight, these broken houses, clustered together   *5*
down in the gloom of the canyon. It presents a complete contrast to the

Cliff Palace at Mesa Verde National Park.

... *continued* Empty Windows, **Stephen White**

tidy, excavated ruins I explored yesterday, lost within a cluster of tourists and guided by a park ranger who expounded constantly upon his wealth of knowledge of excavation techniques and archaeological dating methods. The excavated ruins seemed, in comparison, a noisy, almost modern city, punctuated with the clicking of camera shutters and the bickering of children. Here it is quiet. The silence is broken only by the rush of the wind in the trees and the trickling of a tiny stream of melting snow springing from ledge to ledge as it makes its way down over the rock to the bottom of the canyon. And this small, abandoned village of tiny houses seems almost as the Indians left it, reduced by the passage of nearly a thousand years to piles of rubble through which protrude broken red adobe walls surrounding ghostly jet-black openings, undisturbed by modern man.

Those windows seem to stare back at me as my eyes are drawn to 6 them. They're so horribly empty, yet my gaze is fixed, searching for some sign of the vitality they must surely have known. I yearn for sounds amidst the silence, for images of life as it once was in the bustling and prosperous community of cliff dwellers who lived here so long ago. It must have been a sunny home when the peaceful, agrarian Anasazi, or ancient ones, as the Navajo call them, lived and dreamed their lives here, wanting little more than to continue in their ways and be left alone, only to be driven away in the end by warring people with whom they could not contend.

I long to hear, to see, and to understand, and though I strain all my 7 senses to their limits, my wishes are in vain. I remain alone, confronted only by the void below and the cold stare of those utterly desolate windows. I know only an uneasy sensation that I am not entirely alone, and a quick, chill gust gives birth once again to that restless shiver tracing its path along the length of my spine.

As a gray afternoon fades into a gray evening, I can find neither a 8 true feeling of fear nor one of the quiet serenity one would expect to experience here. It is comforting for me to believe that it was the explorer in me which brought me here, to feel that I was lured to stand above this lonely house by that same drive to find and explore the unknown which motivated the countless others who have come here since seeking knowledge and understanding of the ancient people of the "Green Table." Yet as I begin the journey back to my car and the security of an evening fire, I remain uncomfortably unconvinced.

Perhaps the dreariness of a cloudy day united with my solitude to   9
pave a mental pathway for illusion and mystery. Or perhaps all homes are
never truly empty, having known the multitude of experience which is
human life. Perhaps there lurks, behind every blackened window, a certain unexplainable something we can never understand. I know only that
the Indian has long respected these places and given them wide berth,
leaving their sanctity inviolate.

QUESTIONS FOR WRITING AND DISCUSSION

1. Describe a similar experience you have had with an empty room or a vacant
    house. White says that "perhaps all homes are never truly empty, having
    known the multitude of experience which is human life." Based on your
    experience, do you agree with him?

2. Through his description, what did White help you "see" about the Anasazi
    and their cliff dwellings? What did you learn?

3. Consider once again the basic techniques for observing—using sensory
    detail, comparisons, and images; describing what is not there; noting changes;
    and writing from a clear point of view. Which ones does White use most
    effectively? Cite an example of each technique from his essay.

4. In which paragraphs does White use each of the following shaping strategies:
    spatial order, chronological order, comparisons or contrasts, and simile,
    metaphor, or analogy? Which strategies did you find most effective in
    organizing the experience for you as a reader?

5. White's essay illustrates how the *occasion* for writing can figure prominently
    in a writer's rhetorical situation. What sentences and paragraphs best describe
    the occasion that motivated him to write? Why is occasion so important to
    the success of his essay? Explain.

6. Consider the relationship between the photograph of Cliff Palace at Mesa
    Verde Park and White's essay. Does this image add to the overall effect of the
    essay? Does it detract from the essay by giving the reader an actual picture
    rather than an imagined one? Should the image be retained, replaced with
    another image, or removed altogether? Explain your response.

César Chavez portrait used by special permission of the artist:
Bavi Garcia, 1545 West Dana Street, Mountain View, California 94041,
(650) 961-7305

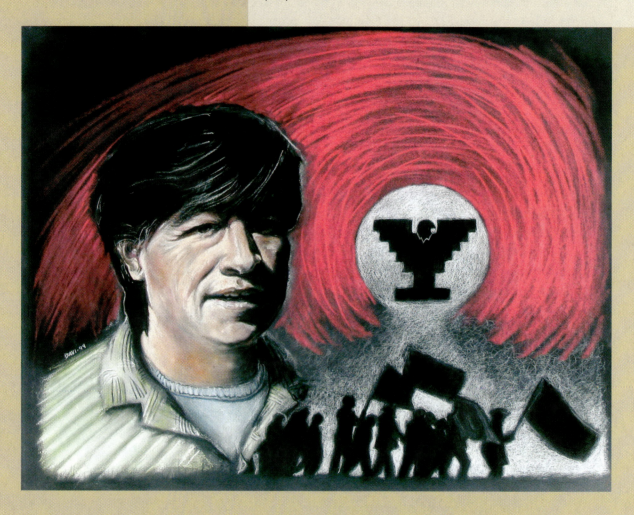

Described by Robert F. Kennedy as "one of the heroic figures of our time," César Chávez
(1927–1993) spent his lifetime improving the conditions of agricultural workers in America. In
1994, President Clinton posthumously awarded Chávez the Presidential Medal of Freedom,
the nation's highest and most prestigious civilian award. In his essay in this chapter, "César
Chávez Saved My Life," Daniel Alejandrez remembers Chávez's influence on his own life.

Remembering

4

You and several coworkers have formed a committee to draft a report for your company's vice president in charge of personnel. You have grievances about workload, pay scale, daily procedures, and the attitudes of supervisors. Your report needs to recommend changes in current policies. The committee decides that each person will contribute part of the report by describing actual incidents that have had negative effects on efficiency and human relations. You decide to describe a day last June when your immediate supervisor expected you to learn a new word-processing system and at the same time meet a 3:00 P.M. deadline for a thirty-seven-page budget analysis.

This morning you accidentally ran into a certain person whom you knew several years ago, and for several hours you've been in a bad mood. You called your best friend, but no one answered the phone. You went to class and then for your usual jog, but you pooped out after only half a mile. You even watched a game show on television in the middle of the afternoon and ate half a bag of potato chips, but you still felt lousy. You yell at the television: "Why do I always react this way when I see that person?" But the television has no reply. So you grab some paper and begin scrawling out every memory you have of your experiences with the person you ran into this morning, hoping to understand your feelings.

> " For me the initial delight is in the surprise of remembering something I didn't know I knew. "
> —ROBERT FROST, POET

> " The fact is that there's no understanding the future without the present, and no understanding where we are now without a glance, at least, to where we have been. "
> —JOYCE MAYNARD, COLUMNIST AND AUTHOR OF *LOOKING BACKWARD: A CHRONICLE OF GROWING UP OLD IN THE SIXTIES*

THE HUMAN BRAIN IS A PACK RAT: NOTHING IS TOO SMALL, OBSCURE, OR MUNDANE FOR THE BRAIN'S COLLECTION. OFTEN THE BRAIN COLLECTS AND DISCARDS INFORMATION WITHOUT REGARD TO OUR WISHES. OUT OF THE COLLECTION MAY ARISE, WITH NO WARNING, the image of windblown whitecaps on a lake you visited more than five years ago, the recipe for Uncle Joe's incomparable chili, or even the right answer to an exam question that you've been staring at for the past fifteen minutes.

Remembering is sometimes easy, sometimes difficult. Often careful concentration yields nothing, while the most trivial occurrence—an old song on a car radio, the acrid smell of diesel exhaust, the face of a stranger—will trigger a flood of recollections. Someone tells a story and you immediately recall incidents, funny or traumatic, from your own life. Some memories, however, are nagging and troublesome, keeping you awake at night, daring you to deal with them. You pick at these memories. Why are they so important? You write about them, usually to probe that mystery of yesterday and today. Sights, sounds, or feelings from the present may draw you to the past, but the past leads, just as surely, back to the present.

Direct observations are important to learning and writing, but so are your memories, experiences, and stories. You may write an autobiographical account of part of your life, or you may recall a brief event, a person, or a place just as an example to illustrate a point. Whatever form your writing from memory takes, however, your initial purpose is to remember experiences so that you can understand yourself and your world. The point is not to write fiction, but to practice drawing on your memories and to write vividly enough about them so that you and others can discover and learn.

The value of remembering lies exactly here: Written memories have the power to teach you and, through the *empathy* of your readers, to inform or convince them as well. At first, you may be self-conscious about sharing your personal memories. But as you reveal these experiences, you realize that your story is worth telling—not because you're such an egotist, but because sharing experiences helps everyone learn.

> ❝ Time passes and the past becomes the present. . . . These presences of the past are there in the center of your life today. You thought . . . they had died, but they have just been waiting their chance. ❞
>
> —CARLOS FUENTES, MEXICAN ESSAYIST AND NOVELIST, AUTHOR OF *THE CRYSTAL FRONTIER*

TECHNIQUES   PROCESS

Techniques for Writing About Memories

Writing vividly about memories includes all the skills of careful observing, but it adds several additional narrative strategies. Listed below are six techniques that writers use to compose effective remembering essays. As you read the essays that follow in this chapter, notice how each writer uses these techniques. Then, when you write your own remembering essay, use these techniques in your own essay. Remember: Not all writing about memories uses all of these techniques, but one or two of them may transform a lifeless or boring account into an effective narrative.

- **Using *detailed observation* of people, places, and events.** Writing vividly about memories requires many of the skills of careful observation. Give actual dialogue where appropriate.

- **Focusing on *occasion* and *cultural context*.** These two aspects of the rhetorical situation are especially important for remembering essays. First, think about the personal *occasion* that motivated you to write. Second, you may want to include details about the cultural context for key events.

- **Creating *specific scenes* set in time and space.** Show your reader the actual events; don't just tell about them. Narrate specific incidents as they actually happened. Avoid monotonously summarizing events or presenting just the conclusions (for instance, "Those experiences really changed my life").

- **Noting *changes, contrasts,* or *conflicts*.** Changes in people or places, contrasts between two different memories or between memories of expectations and realities, and conflicts between people or ideas—any of these may lead to the meaning or importance of a remembered person, place, or event.

- **Making *connections* between past events, people, or places and the present.** The main idea of a narrative often grows out of changes and conflicts or arises from the connections you make between past and present.

- **Discovering and focusing on a *main idea*.** A remembering essay is not a random narrative of the writer's favorite memories. A narrative should have a clear main point, focus on a main idea, or make a discovery. The essay should clearly show why the memories are important.

All of these techniques are important, but you should also keep several other points in mind. Normally, you should write in the *first person*, using *I* or *we* throughout the narrative. Although you will usually write in *past tense*, sometimes you may wish to lend immediacy to the events by retelling them in the *present tense*, as if they are happening now. Finally, you may choose straightforward *chronological order*, or you may begin near the end and use a *flashback* to tell the beginning of the story.

The key to effective remembering, however, is to get beyond *generalities and conclusions* about your experiences ("I had a lot of fun—those days really changed my life"). Your goal is to *recall specific incidents set in time and place* that *show* how and why those days changed your life. The specific incidents should show your *main point* or *dominant idea*.

The following passage by Andrea Lee began as a journal entry during a year she spent in Moscow and Leningrad following her graduation from college. She then combined these firsthand observations with her memories and published them in a collection called *Russian Journal*. She uses first person and, frequently, present tense as she describes her reactions to the sights of Moscow. In these paragraphs, she weaves observations and memories together to show her main idea: The contrast between American and Russian advertising helped her understand both the virtues and the faults of American commercialism. (The annotations in the margin illustrate how Lee uses all five remembering techniques.)

Specific scene

In Mayakovsky Square, not far from the Tchaikovsky Concert Hall, a big computerized electric sign sends various messages flashing out into the night. An outline of a taxi in green dots is accompanied by the words: "Take Taxis—All Streets Are Near." This is replaced by multicolored human figures and a sentence urging Soviet citizens to save in State banks.

Detailed observation

The bright patterns and messages come and go, making this one of the most sophisticated examples of advertising in Moscow. Even on chilly nights when I pass through the square, there is often a little group of Russians standing in front of the sign, watching in fascination for five and ten minutes as the colored dots go through their magical changes. The first few

Connections past and present

times I saw this, I chuckled and recalled an old joke about an American town so boring that people went out on weekends to watch the Esso sign.

Contrast

Advertising, of course, is the glamorous offspring of capitalism and art: Why advertise in a country where there is only one brand, the State brand, of anything, and often not enough even of that? There is nothing here comparable to the glittering overlay of commercialism that Ameri-

Main idea

cans, at least, take for granted as part of our cities; nothing like the myriad small seductions of the marketplace, which have led us to expect to be enticed. The Soviet political propaganda posters that fill up a small

Detailed observation

part of the Moscow landscape with their uniformly cold red color schemes and monumental robot-faced figures are so unappealing that they are dismissable.

Connections past and present

I realize now, looking back, that for at least my first month in Moscow, I was filled with an unconscious and devastating disappointment. Hardly realizing it, as I walked around the city, I was looking for the constant sen-

Contrast and change

sory distractions I was accustomed to in America. Like many others my age, I grew up reading billboards and singing advertising jingles; my idea

Main idea

of beauty was shaped—perniciously, I think—by the models with the painted eyes and pounds of shining hair whose beauty was accessible on every television set and street corner.

PEOPLE	PLACES	EVENTS

REMEMBERING PEOPLE

In the following passage from the introduction to *The Way to Rainy Mountain*, N. Scott Momaday remembers his grandmother. While details of place and event are also recreated, the primary focus is on the character of his grandmother as revealed in several *specific*, recurring actions. Momaday does not give us generalities about his feelings (for instance, "I miss my grandmother a lot, especially now that she's gone."). Instead, he begins with specific memories of scenes that *show* how he felt.

> Now that I can have her only in memory, I see my grandmother in the several postures that were peculiar to her: standing at the wood stove on a winter morning and turning meat in a great iron skillet; sitting at the south window, bent above her beadwork, and afterwards, when her vision failed, looking down for a long time into the fold of her hands; going out upon a cane, very slowly as she did when the weight of age came upon her; praying. I remember her most often at prayer. She made long, rambling prayers out of suffering and hope, having seen many things. I was never sure that I had the right to hear, so exclusive were they of all mere custom and company. The last time I saw her she prayed standing by the side of her bed at night, naked to the waist, the light of a kerosene lamp moving upon her dark skin. Her long, black hair, always drawn and braided in the day, lay upon her shoulders and against her breasts like a shawl. I do not speak Kiowa, and I never understood her prayers, but there was something inherently sad in the sound, some merest hesitation upon the syllables of sorrow. She began in a high and descending pitch, exhausting her breath to silence; then again and again—and always the same intensity of effort, of something that is, and is not, like urgency in the human voice. Transported so in the dancing light among the shadows of her room, she seemed beyond the reach of time. But that was illusion; I think I knew then that I should not see her again.

> "A writer is a reader moved to emulation."
> —SAUL BELLOW,
> AUTHOR OF *HENDERSON THE RAIN KING*

PEOPLE	PLACES	EVENTS

REMEMBERING PLACES

In the following passage from *Farewell to Manzanar*, Jeanne Wakatsuke Houston remembers the place in California where, as Japanese-Americans, her family was imprisoned during World War II. As you read, look for specific details and bits of description that convey her main idea.

> In Spanish, Manzanar means "apple orchard." Great stretches of Owens Valley were once green with orchards and alfalfa fields. It has been a desert

ever since its water started flowing south into Los Angeles, sometime during the twenties. But a few rows of untended pear and apple trees were still growing there when the camp opened, where a shallow water table had kept them alive. In the spring of 1943 we moved to block 28, right up next to one of the old pear orchards. That's where we stayed until the end of the war, and those trees stand in my memory for the turning of our life in camp, from the outrageous to the tolerable.

Papa pruned and cared for the nearest trees. Late that summer we picked the fruit green and stored it in a root cellar he had dug under our new barracks. At night the wind through the leaves would sound like the surf had sounded in Ocean Park, and while drifting off to sleep, I could almost imagine we were still living by the beach.

PEOPLE   PLACES   EVENTS

REMEMBERING EVENTS

In the following essay, called "The Boy's Desire," Richard Rodriguez recalls a particular event from his childhood that comes to mind when he remembers Christmas. In his memory, he sorts through the rooms in his house on Thirty-ninth Street in Sacramento, recalling old toys: a secondhand bike, games with dice and spinning dials, a jigsaw puzzle, and a bride doll. In this passage, Rodriguez describes both the effort to remember and the memory itself—the one memory that still "holds color and size and shape." Was it all right, he wonders, that a boy should have wanted a doll for Christmas?

The fog comes to mind. It never rained on Christmas. It was never sharp blue and windy. When I remember Christmas in Sacramento, it is in gray: The valley fog would lift by late morning, the sun boiled haze for a few hours, then the tule fog would rise again when it was time to go into the house.

The haze through which memory must wander is thickened by that fog. The rooms of the house on 39th Street are still and dark in late afternoon, and I open the closet to search for old toys. One year there was a secondhand bike. I do not remember a color. Perhaps it had no color even then. Another year there were boxes of games that rattled their parts—dice and pegs and spinning dials. Or perhaps the rattle is of a jigsaw puzzle that compressed into an image . . . of what? of Paris? a litter of kittens? I cannot remember. Only one memory holds color and size and shape: brown hair, blue eyes, the sweet smell of styrene.

That Christmas I announced I wanted a bride doll. I must have been seven or eight—wise enough to know not to tell anyone at school, but young enough to whine out my petition from early November.

My father's reaction was unhampered by psychology. A shrug—"Una muñeca?"—a doll, why not? Because I knew it was my mother who would choose all the presents, it was she I badgered. I wanted a bride doll! "Is there something else you want?" she wondered. No! I'd make clear with my voice that nothing else would appease me. "We'll see," she'd say, and she never wrote it down on her list.

By early December, wrapped boxes started piling up in my parents' bedroom closet, above my father's important papers and the family album. When no one else was home, I'd drag a chair over and climb up to see . . . Looking for the one. About a week before Christmas, it was there. I was so certain it was mine that I punched my thumb through the wrapping paper and the cellophane window on the box and felt inside—lace, two tiny, thin legs. I got other presents that year, but it was the doll I kept by me. I remember my mother saying I'd have "to share her" with my younger sister—but Helen was four years old, oblivious. The doll was mine. My arms would hold her. She would sleep on my pillow.

And the sky did not fall. The order of the universe did not tremble. In fact, it was right for a change. My family accommodated itself to my request. My brother and sisters played round me with their own toys. I paraded my doll by the hands across the floor.

> There are two ways to live. One is as though nothing is a miracle, the other is as though everything is.
> —ALBERT EINSTEIN, AUTHOR OF *WHAT I BELIEVE*

> Some very small incident that takes place today may be the most important event that happens to you this year, but you don't know that when it happens. You don't know it until much later.
> —TONI MORRISON, NOBEL PRIZE-WINNING AUTHOR OF *BELOVED* AND *SONG OF SOLOMON*

The other day, when I asked my brother and sisters about the doll, no one remembered. My mother remembers. "Yes," she smiled. "One year there was a doll."

The closet door closes. (The house on 39th Street has been razed for a hospital parking lot.) The fog rises. Distance tempts me to mock the boy and his desire. The fact remains: One Christmas in Sacramento I wanted a bride doll, and I got one.

WARMING UP: Journal Exercises

The following topics will help you practice writing about your memories. Read all of the following exercises, and then write on three that interest you the most. If another idea occurs to you, write a free entry about it.

1. Reread Jeanne Wakatsuke Houston's excerpt from *Farewell to Manzanar* and then re-examine the accompanying image, "Manzanar War Relocation Center." What details of the image's composition stand out? What other elements do you notice? What does the image add to Houston's account? Would a different image be more effective for her excerpt? Why or why not? Explain.

2. Go through old family photographs and find one of yourself, taken at least five years ago. Describe the person in the photograph—what he or she did, thought, said, or hoped. How is that person like or unlike the person you are now?

3. Remember the first job you had. How did you get it, and what did you do? What mistakes did you make? What did you learn? Were there any humorous or serious misunderstandings between you and others?

4. What are your earliest memories? Choose one particular event. How old were you? What was the place? Who were the people around you? What happened? After you write down your earliest memories, call members of your family, if possible, and interview them for their memories of this incident. How does what you actually remember differ from what your family tells you? Revise your first memory to incorporate additional details provided by your family.

5. At some point in the past, you may have faced a conflict between what was expected of you—by parents, friends, family, coach, or employer—and your own personality or abilities. Describe one occasion when these expectations seemed unrealistic or unfair. Was the experience entirely negative or was it, in the long run, positive?

6. At least one point in our lives, we have felt like an outsider. In a selection earlier in this chapter, for instance, Richard Rodriguez recalls feelings of being different, rejected, or outcast. Write about an incident when you felt alienated from your family, peers, or social group. Focus on a key scene or scenes that show what happened, why it was important, and how it affects you now.

7. Read Mike Rose's essay in this chapter and write your own literacy narrative. What are your early memories about learning to read and write? At what points did you struggle or fail? When did you most enjoy reading or writing?

PROFESSIONAL WRITING

Lives on the Boundary

Mike Rose

Mike Rose was born to Italian immigrant parents in 1944, and his family moved to Los Angeles, where he attended Our Lady of Mercy, a private Catholic school. He continued his education at Loyola University, graduating in 1966, and went on to earn his Ph.D. from UCLA in 1981. Rose currently teaches at UCLA and is the author of numerous articles and books, including When a Writer Can't Write: Studies in Writer's Block and Other Composing Problems *(1985),* Lives on the Boundary *(1989), and* Possible Lives: The Promise of Public Education in America *(1995). In the following selection, taken from the second chapter of* Lives on the Boundary, *Rose recalls how he was originally misplaced in a high school vocational track and then was shifted to college prep courses. Rose focuses his memories on his fellow students in the voc. ed. track and on one English teacher, Jack MacFarland, who opened his mind to the world of books and ideas and who helped him get to college and live the "beyond the limiting boundaries" of his South Los Angeles neighborhood.*

My parents used to say that their son would have the best education they   *1*
could afford. Maybe I would be a doctor. There was a public school in our neighborhood and several Catholic schools to the west. They had heard that quality schooling meant private, Catholic schooling, so they somehow got the money together to send me to Our Lady of Mercy, fifteen or so miles southwest of Ninety-first and Vermont.

...continued Lives on the Boundary, **Mike Rose**

It took two buses to get to Our Lady of Mercy. The first started deep   *2*
in South Los Angeles and caught me at midpoint. The second drifted
through neighborhoods with trees, parks, big lawns, and lots of flowers.
The rides were long but were livened up by a group of South L.A. veterans whose parents also thought that Hope had set up shop in the west end
of the county. There was Christy Biggars, who, at sixteen, was dealing and
was, according to rumor, a pimp as well. There were Bill Cobb and Johnny
Gonzales, grease-pencil artists extraordinaire, who left Nembutal-
enhanced swirls of "Cobb" and "Johnny" on the corrugated walls of the bus.
And then there was Tyrrell Wilson. Tyrrell was the coolest kid I knew. He
ran the dozens like a metric half-back, laid down a rap that outrhymed and
outpointed Cobb, whose rap was good but not great—the curse of a moderately soulful kid trapped in white skin. But it was Cobb who would sneak
a radio onto the bus, and thus underwrote his patter with Little Richard,
Fats Domino, Chuck Berry, the Coasters, and Ernie K. Doe's mother-in-
law, an awful woman who was "sent from down below." And so it was that
Christy and Cobb and Johnny G. and Tyrrell and I and assorted others
picked up along the way passed our days in the back of the bus, a funny mix
brought together by geography and parental desire.

Entrance to school brings with it forms and releases and assessments.   *3*
Mercy relied on a series of tests, mostly the Stanford-Binet, for placement,
and somehow the results of my tests got confused with those of another
student named Rose. The other Rose apparently didn't do very well, for I
was placed in the vocational track, a euphemism for the bottom level. Neither I nor my parents realized what this meant. We had no sense that Business Math, Typing, and English-Level D were dead ends. The current
spate of reports on the schools criticizes parents for not involving themselves in the education of their children. But how would someone like
Tommy Rose, with his two years of Italian schooling, know what to ask?
And what sort of pressure could an exhausted waitress apply? The error
went undetected, and I remained in the vocational track for two years.
What a place.

Students will float to the mark you set. I and the others in the voca-   *4*
tional classes were bobbing in pretty shallow water. Vocational education
has aimed at increasing the economic opportunities of students who do not
do well in our schools. Some serious programs succeed in doing that, and
through exceptional teachers—like Mr. Gross in *Horace's Compromise*—
students learn to develop hypotheses and troubleshoot, reason through a

problem, and communicate effectively—the true job skills. The vocational track, however, is most often a place for those who are just not making it, a dumping ground for the disaffected. There were a few teachers who worked hard at education; young Brother Slattery, for example, combined a stern voice with weekly quizzes to try to pass along to us a skeletal outline of world history. But mostly the teachers had no idea of how to engage the imaginations of us kids who were scuttling along at the bottom of the pond.

But I did learn things about people and eventually came into my own socially. I liked the guys in Voc. Ed. Growing up where I did, I understood and admired physical prowess, and there was an abundance of muscle here. There was Dave Snyder, a sprinter and a half-back of true quality. Dave's ability and his quick wit gave him a natural appeal, and he was welcome in any clique, though he always kept a little independent. It was a testament to his independence that he included me among his friends—I eventually went out for track, but I was no jock. Owing to the Latin alphabet and a dearth of Rs and Ss, Snyder sat behind Rose, and we started exchanging one-liners and became friends. *5*

There was Ted Richard, a much-touted Little League pitcher. He was chunky and had a baby face and came to Our Lady of Mercy as a seasoned street fighter. Ted was quick to laugh and he had a loud, jolly laugh, but when he got angry he'd smile a little smile, the kind that simply raises the corner of the mouth a quarter of an inch. For those who knew, it was an eerie signal. Those who didn't found themselves in big trouble, for Ted was very quick. He loved to carry on what we would come to call philosophical discussions: What is courage? Does God exist? He also loved words, enjoyed picking up big ones like *salubrious* and *equivocal* and using them in our conversations—laughing at himself as the word hit a chuckhole rolling off his tongue. Ted didn't do all that well in school—baseball and parties and testing the courage he'd speculated about took up his time. His textbooks were *Argosy* and *Field and Stream*, whatever newspapers he'd find on the bus stop—from the *Daily Worker* to pornography—conversations with uncles or hobos or businessmen he'd meet in a coffee shop, *The Old Man and the Sea*. With hindsight, I can see that Ted was developing into one of those rough-hewn intellectuals whose sources are a mix of the learned and the apocryphal, whose discussions are both assured and sad. *6*

And then there was Ken Harvey. Ken was good-looking in a puffy way and had a full and oily ducktail and was a car enthusiast . . . a hodad. One day in religion class, he said the sentence that turned out to be one of the *7*

... *continued*   Lives on the Boundary,   **Mike Rose**

most memorable of the hundreds of thousands I heard in those Voc. Ed. years. We were talking about the parable of the talents, about achievement, working hard, doing the best you can do, blah-blah-blah, when the teacher called on the restive Ken Harvey for an opinion. Ken thought about it, but just for a second, and said (with studied, minimal affect), "I just wanna be average." That woke me up. Average?! Who wants to be average? Then the athletes chimed in with the clichés that make you want to laryngectomize them, and the exchange became a platitudinous melee. At the time, I thought Ken's assertion was stupid, and I wrote him off. But his sentence has stayed with me all these years, and I think I am finally coming to understand it. . . .

My own deliverance from the Voc. Ed. world began with sophomore biology. Every student, college prep to vocational, had to take biology, and unlike the other courses, the same person taught all sections. When teaching the vocational group, Brother Clint probably slowed down a bit or omitted a little of the fundamental biochemistry, but he used the same book and more or less the same syllabus across the board. If one class got tough, he could get tougher. He was young and powerful and very handsome, and looks and physical strength were high currency. No one gave him any trouble. 8

I was pretty bad at the dissecting table, but the lectures and the textbook were interesting: plastic overlays that, with each turned page, peeled away skin, then veins and muscle, then organs, down to the very bones that Brother Clint, pointer in hand, would tap out on our hanging skeleton. Dave Snyder was in big trouble, for the study of life—versus the living of it—was sticking in his craw. We worked out a code for our multiple-choice exams. He'd poke me in the back: once for the answer under A, twice for B, and so on; and when he'd hit the right one, I'd look up to the ceiling as though I were lost in thought. Poke: cytoplasm. Poke, poke: methane. Poke, poke, poke: William Harvey. Poke, poke, poke, poke: islets of Langerhans. This didn't work out perfectly, but Dave passed the course, and I mastered the dreamy look of a guy on a record jacket. And something else happened. Brother Clint puzzled over this Voc. Ed. kid who was racking up 98s and 99s on his tests. He checked the school's records and discovered the error. He recommended that I begin my junior year in the College Prep program. According to all I've read since, such a shift, as one report puts it, is virtually impossible. Kids at that level rarely cross tracks. The telling thing is how chancy both my placement into and exit from Voc. 9

Ed. was; neither I nor my parents had anything to do with it. I lived in one world during spring semester, and when I came back to school in the fall, I was living in another.

Switching to College Prep was a mixed blessing. I was an erratic stu- *10* dent. I was undisciplined. And I hadn't caught onto the rules of the game: Why work hard in a class that didn't grab my fancy? I was also hopelessly behind in math. Chemistry was hard; toying with my chemistry set years before hadn't prepared me for the chemist's equations. Fortunately, the priest who taught both chemistry and second year algebra was also the school's athletic director. Membership on the track team covered me; I knew I wouldn't get lower than a C. U.S. history was taught pretty well, and I did okay. But civics was taken over by a football coach who had trouble reading the textbook aloud—and reading aloud was the centerpiece of his pedagogy. College Prep at Mercy was certainly an improvement over the vocational program—at least it carried some status—but the social science curriculum was weak, and the mathematics and physical sciences were simply beyond me. . . .

Jack MacFarland couldn't have come into my life at a better time. Mr. *11* MacFarland had a master's degree from Columbia and decided, at twenty-six, to find a little school and teach his heart out. He never took any credentialing courses, couldn't bear to, he said, so he had to find employment in a private system. He ended up at Our Lady of Mercy teaching five sections of senior English. He was a beatnik who was born too late. His teeth were stained, he tucked his sorry tie in between the third and fourth buttons of his shirt, and his pants were chronically wrinkled. At first, we couldn't believe this guy, thought he slept in his car. But within no time, he had us so startled with work that we didn't much worry about where he slept or if he slept at all. We wrote three or four essays a month. We read a book every two to three weeks, starting with the *Iliad* and ending up with Hemingway. He gave us a quiz on the reading every other day. He brought a prep school curriculum to Mercy High.

MacFarland's lectures were crafted, and as he delivered them he would *12* pace the room jiggling a piece of chalk in his cupped hand, using it to scribble on the board the names of all the writers and philosophers and plays and novels he was weaving into his discussion. He asked questions often; raised everything from Zeno's paradox to the repeated last line of Frost's "Stopping by Woods on a Snowy Evening." He slowly and carefully built up our knowledge of Western intellectual history—with facts, with connections, with speculations. We learned about Greek philosophy, about

...*continued* Lives on the Boundary, **Mike Rose**

Dante, the Elizabethan world view, the Age of Reason, existentialism. He analyzed poems with us, had us reading sections from John Ciardi's *How Does a Poem Mean?,* making a potentially difficult book accessible with his own explanations. We gave oral reports on poems Ciardi didn't cover. We imitated the styles of Conrad, Hemingway, and *Time* magazine. We wrote and talked, wrote and talked. The man immersed us in language.

Even MacFarland's barbs were literary. If Jim Fitzsimmons, hung   13 over and irritable, tried to smart-ass him, he'd rejoin with a flourish that would spark the indomitable Skip Madison—who'd lost his front teeth in a hapless tackle—to flick his tongue through the gap and opine, "good chop," drawing out the single "o" in stinging indictment. Jack MacFarland, this tobacco-stained intellectual, brandished linguistic weapons of a kind I hadn't encountered before. Here was this *egghead,* for God's sake, keeping some pretty difficult people in line. And from what I heard, Mike Dweetz and Steve Fusco and all the notorious Voc. Ed. crowd settled down as well when MacFarland took the podium. Though a lot of guys groused in the schoolyard, it just seemed that giving trouble to this particular teacher was a silly thing to do. Tomfoolery, not to mention assault, had no place in the world he was trying to create for us, and instinctively everyone knew that. If nothing else, we all recognized MacFarland's considerable intelligence and respected the hours he put into his work. It came to this: The troublemaker would look foolish rather than daring. Even Jim Fitzsimmons was reading *On the Road* and turning his incipient alcoholism to literary ends.

There were some lives that were already beyond Jack MacFarland's   14 ministrations, but mine was not. I started reading again as I hadn't since elementary school. I would go into our gloomy little bedroom or sit at the dinner table while, on the television, Danny McShane was paralyzing Mr. Moto with the atomic drop, and work slowly back through *Heart of Darkness,* trying to catch the words in Conrad's sentences. I certainly was not MacFarland's best student; most of the other guys in College Prep, even my fellow slackers, had better backgrounds than I did. But I worked very hard, for MacFarland had hooked me. He tapped my old interest in reading and creating stories. He gave me a way to feel special by using my mind. And he provided a role model that wasn't shaped on physical prowess alone, and something inside me that I wasn't quite aware of responded to that. Jack MacFarland established a literacy club, to borrow a phrase of Frank Smith's, and invited me—invited all of us—to join.

In my last semester of high school, I elected a special English course *15*
fashioned by Mr. MacFarland, and it was through this elective that there
arose at Mercy a fledgling literati. Art Mitz, the editor of the school newspaper and a very smart guy, was the kingpin. He was joined by me and
Mark Dever, a quiet boy who wrote beautifully and who would die before
he was forty. MacFarland occasionally invited us to his apartment, and
those visits became the high point of our apprenticeship: We'd clamp on
our training wheels and drive to his salon.

He lived in a cramped and cluttered place near the airport, tucked *16*
away in the kind of building that architectural critic Reyner Banham calls
a *dingbat.* Books were all over: stacked, piled, tossed, and crated, underlined and dog eared, well worn and new. Cigarette ashes crusted with coffee in saucers or spilled over the sides of motel ashtrays. The little bedroom
had, along two of its walls, bricks and boards loaded with notes, magazines,
and oversized books. The kitchen joined the living room, and there was a
stack of German newspapers under the sink. I had never seen anything like
it: a great flophouse of language furnished by City Lights and Café le
Metro. I read every title. I flipped through paperbacks and scanned jackets
and memorized names: Gogol, *Finnegan's Wake,* Djuna Barnes, Jackson
Pollock, *A Coney Island of the Mind,* F. O. Matthiessen's *American Renaissance,* all sorts of Freud, *Troubled Sleep,* Man Ray, the *Education of Henry
Adams,* Richard Wright, *Film as Art,* William Butler Yeats, Marguerite
Duras, *Redburn, a Season in Hell, Kapital.* On the cover of Alain-Fournier's
The Wanderer was an Edward Gorey drawing of a young man on a road
winding into dark trees. By the hotplate sat a strange Kafka novel called
Amerika, in which an adolescent hero crosses the Atlantic to find the Nature Theater of Oklahoma. Art and Mark would be talking about a movie
or the school newspaper, and I would be consuming my English teacher's
library. It was heady stuff. I felt like a Pop Warner athlete on steroids.

Let me be the first to admit that there was a good deal of adolescent *17*
passion in this embrace of the avant-garde: self-absorption, sexually
charged pedantry, an elevation of the odd and abandoned. Still it was a
time during which I absorbed an awful lot of information: long lists of titles, images from expressionist paintings, new wave shibboleths, snippets
of philosophy, and names that read like Steve Fusco's misspellings—
Goethe, Nietzsche, Kierkegaard. Now this is hardly the stuff of deep understanding. But it was an introduction, a phrase book, a Baedeker to a
vocabulary of ideas, and it felt good at the time to know all these words.
With hindsight I realize how layered and important that knowledge was.

...continued Lives on the Boundary, **Mike Rose**

It enabled me to do things in the world. I could browse bohemian *18* bookstores in far-off, mysterious Hollywood; I could go to the Cinema and see events through the lenses of European directors; and, most of all, I could share an evening, talk that talk, with Jack MacFarland, the man I most admired at the time. Knowledge was becoming a bonding agent. Within a year or two, the persona of the disaffected hipster would prove too cynical, too alienated to last. But for a time it was new and exciting: It provided a critical perspective on society, and it allowed me to act as though I were living beyond the limiting boundaries of South Vermont.

■ ■ ■

vo·cab·u·lar·y

In your journal, write the meanings of the italicized words in the following pharses.

- a *euphemism* for the bottom level **(3)**
- picking up big ones like *salubrious* and *equivocal* **(6)**
- a mix of the learned and the *apocryphal* **(6)**
- centerpiece of his *pedagogy* **(10)**
- turning his *incipient* alcoholism to literary ends **(13)**
- beyond Jack MacFarland's *ministrations* **(14)**
- this embrace of the *avant-garde* **(17)**
- new wave *shibboleths* **(17)**
- a *Baedeker* to a vocabulary of ideas **(17)**

QUESTIONS FOR WRITING AND DISCUSSION

1. The title of Mike Rose's book is *Lives on the Boundary*. In this selection, what "boundaries" do the voc. ed. students face? What boundaries does Rose face? Which of these boundaries is Rose able to cross? How are these boundaries similar to or different from the boundaries you faced growing up?

2. Effective remembering essays build on detailed descriptions. Review the *observing* techniques from Chapter 3. Of the techniques discussed there (using sensory details and images, describing what is not present, noting changes, writing from a point of view, and focusing on a dominant idea), which does Rose use most effectively? To support your choice(s), find examples from Rose's essay.

3. Review the remembering techniques listed early in this chapter. Which does Rose use most effectively in his essay? Cite examples to support your choice(s). Which techniques might he add to his essay? Where, for example, might Rose use dialogue to recreate a school scene more vividly?

4. In his essay, Rose creates two voices that represent him as a high school student and as a forty-five-year-old man looking back on his early education. Find examples that illustrate each of these voices. Should Rose interrupt the narration about his high school years with his older reflections? Why or why not?

5. Write your own remembering essay describing a particular teacher from high school or college who impressed you or influenced the direction of your life. Recall scenes from this time in your life that illustrate how this teacher changed your life.

6. Although Rose overcame his misplacement in the voc. ed. track, the consequences of standardized tests can be disastrous. What is your experience with state tests, high stakes tests, exit tests, and SAT tests? Have the results accurately indicated your abilities? Do these tests cause more harm than good? Read the essay by Eric Boese in Chapter 11. Then check out the Fordam Foundation Web site at *http://www.edexcellence.net/topics/standards. html.* Browse through some of the articles. Write your own essay that draws on your experience with educational testing to recommend changes in testing procedures to the administrators of your high school.

PROFESSIONAL WRITING

Beauty: When the Other Dancer Is the Self

Alice Walker

The author of the Pulitzer Prize–winning novel The Color Purple *(1983), Alice Walker has written works of fiction and poetry, including* Love and Trouble: Stories of Black Women *(1973),* Meridian *(1976), and* By the Light of My Father's Smile: A Novel *(1998).* Beauty: When the Other Dancer Is the Self" *originally appeared in* Ms. *magazine and was revised and published in Walker's collection of essays,* In Search of Our Mother's Gardens *(1983). Walker, a former editor of* Ms., *refers in this essay to Gloria Steinem and an interview published in* Ms. *titled* 'Do You Know This Woman? She Knows You—A Profile of Alice Walker." *As you read the essay reprinted here,*

... *continued* Beauty: When the Other Dancer Is the Self, **Alice Walker**

consider Walker's purpose: Why is she telling us—total strangers—about a highly personal and traumatic event that shaped her life?

It is a bright summer day in 1947. My father, a fat, funny man with beautiful eyes and a subversive wit, is trying to decide which of his eight children he will take with him to the county fair. My mother, of course, will not go. She is knocked out from getting us ready: I hold my neck stiff against the pressure of her knuckles as she hastily completes the braiding and then beribboning of my hair. 1

My father is the driver for the rich old white lady up the road. Her name is Miss Mey. She owns all the land for miles around, as well as the house in which we live. All I remember about her is that she once offered to pay my mother thirty-five cents for cleaning her house, raking up piles of her magnolia leaves, and washing her family's clothes, and that my mother—she of no money, eight children, and a chronic earache—refused it. But I do not think of this in 1947. I am two-and-a-half years old. I want to go everywhere my daddy goes. I am excited at the prospect of riding in a car. Someone has told me fairs are fun. That there is room in the car for only three of us doesn't faze me at all. Whirling happily in my starchy frock, showing off my biscuit polished patent leather shoes and lavender socks, tossing my head in a way that makes my ribbons bounce, I stand, hands on hips, before my father. "Take me, Daddy," I say with assurance, "I'm the prettiest!" 2

Later, it does not surprise me to find myself in Miss Mey's shiny black car, sharing the backseat with the other lucky ones. Does not surprise me that I thoroughly enjoy the fair. At home that night I tell all the unlucky ones about the merry-go-round, the man who eats live chickens, and the abundance of Teddy bears, until they say: that's enough, baby Alice. Shut up now, and go to sleep. 3

It is Easter Sunday, 1950. I am dressed in a green, flocked scalloped-hem dress (handmade by my adoring sister Ruth) that has its own smooth satin petticoat and tiny hot-pink roses tucked into each scallop. My shoes, new T-strap patent leather, again highly biscuit polished. I am six years old and have learned one of the longest Easter speeches to be heard in church that day, totally unlike the speech I said when I was two: "Easter lilies/pure and white/blossom in/the morning light." When I rise to give my speech I do so on a great wave of love and pride and expectation. People in the church stop rustling their new crinolines. They seem to hold their breath. 4

I can tell they admire my dress, but it is my spirit, bordering on sassiness (womanishness), they secretly applaud.

"That girl's a little *mess,*" they whisper to each other, pleased.   5

Naturally I say my speech without stammer or pause, unlike those who   6
stutter, stammer, or, worst of all, forget. This is before the word "beautiful" exists in people's vocabulary, but "Oh, isn't she the *cutest* thing!" frequently floats my way. "And got so much sense!" they gratefully add . . . for which thoughtful addition I thank them to this day.

It was great fun being cute. But then, one day, it ended.   7

I am eight years old and a tomboy. I have a cowboy hat, cowboy boots,   8
checkered shirt and pants, all red. My playmates are my brothers, two and four years older than I. Their colors are black and green, the only difference in the way we are dressed. On Saturday nights we all go to the picture show, even my mother: Westerns are her favorite kind of movie. Back home, "on the ranch," we pretend we are Tom Mix, Hopalong Cassidy, Lash LaRue (we've even named one of our dogs Lash LaRue); we chase each other for hours rustling cattle, being outlaws, delivering damsels from distress. Then my parents decide to buy my brothers guns. These are not "real" guns. They shoot "BBs," copper pellets my brothers say will kill birds. Because I am a girl, I do not get a gun. Instantly I am relegated to the position of Indian. Now there appears a great distance between us. They shoot and shoot at everything with their new guns. I try to keep up with my bow and arrows.

One day while I am standing on top of our makeshift "garage"—pieces of tin nailed across some poles—holding my bow and arrow and looking   9
out toward the fields, I feel an incredible blow in my right eye. I look down just in time to see my brother lower his gun.

Both brothers rush to my side. My eye stings, and I cover it with my hand. "If you tell," they say, "we will get a whipping. You don't want that to   10
happen, do you?" I do not. "Here is a piece of wire," says the older brother, picking it up from the roof; "say you stepped on one end of it and the other flew up and hit you." The pain is beginning to start. "Yes," I say. "Yes, I will say that is what happened." If I do not say this is what happened, I know my brothers will find ways to make me wish I had. But now I will say anything that gets me to my mother.

Confronted by our parents we stick to the lie agreed upon. They place me on a bench on the porch and I close my left eye while they examine the   11
right. There is a tree growing from underneath the porch, that climbs past the railing to the roof. It is the last thing my right eye sees. I watch as its trunk, its branches, and then its leaves are blotted out by the rising blood.

. . . continued Beauty: When the Other Dancer Is the Self, **Alice Walker**

I am in shock. First there is intense fever, which my father tries to *12* break using lily leaves bound around my head. Then there are chills: my mother tries to get me to eat soup. Eventually, I do not know how, my parents learn what has happened. A week after the "accident" they take me to see a doctor. "Why did you wait so long to come?" he asks, looking into my eye and shaking his head. "Eyes are sympathetic," he says. "If one is blind, the other will likely become blind too."

This comment of the doctor's terrifies me. But it is really how I look *13* that bothers me most. Where the BB pellet struck there is a glob of whitish scar tissue, a hideous cataract, on my eye. Now when I stare at people—a favorite pastime, up to now—they will stare back. Not at the "cute" little girl, but at her scar. For six years I do not stare at anyone because I do not raise my head.

Years later, in the throes of a mid-life crisis, I ask my mother and sis- *14* ter whether I changed after the "accident." "No," they say, puzzled. "What do you mean?"

What do I mean? *15*

I am eight, and for the first time, doing poorly in school, where I have *16* been something of a whiz since I was four. We have just moved to the place where the "accident" occurred. We do not know any of the people around us because this is a different county. The only time I see the friends I knew is when we go back to our old church. The new school is the former state penitentiary. It is a large stone building, cold and drafty, crammed to overflowing with boisterous, ill-disciplined children. On the third floor there is a huge circular imprint of some partition that has been torn out.

"What used to be here?" I ask a sullen girl next to me on our way past *17* it to lunch.

"The electric chair," says she. *18*

At night I have nightmares about the electric chair, and about all the *19* people reputedly "fried" in it. I am afraid of the school, where all the students seem to be budding criminals.

"What's the matter with your eye?" they ask, critically. *20*

When I don't answer (I cannot decide whether it was an "accident" or *21* not), they shove me, insist on a fight.

My brother, the one who created the story about the wire, comes to *22* my rescue. But then brags so much about "protecting" me, I become sick.

After months of torture at the school, my parents decide to send me *23* back to our old community to my old school. I live with my grandparents and the teacher they board. But there is no room for Phoebe, my cat. By the time my grandparents decide there is room, and I ask for my cat, she cannot be found. Miss Yarborough, the boarding teacher, takes me under her wing, and begins to teach me to play the piano. But soon she marries an African—a "prince," she says—and is whisked away to his continent.

At my old school there is at least one teacher who loves me. She is the 24 teacher who "knew me before I was born" and bought my first baby clothes. It is she who makes my life bearable. It is her presence that finally helps me turn on the one child at the school who continually calls me "one-eyed bitch." One day I simply grab him by his coat and beat him until I am satisfied. It is my teacher who tells me my mother is ill.

My mother is lying in bed in the middle of the day, something I have 25 never seen. She is in too much pain to speak. She has an abscess in her ear. I stand looking down on her, knowing that if she dies, I cannot live. She is being treated with warm oils and hot bricks held against her cheek. Finally a doctor comes. But I must go back to my grandparents' house. The weeks pass, but I am hardly aware of it. All I know is that my mother might die, my father is not so jolly, my brothers still have their guns, and I am the one sent away from home.

"You did not change," they say. 26

Did I imagine the anguish of never looking up? 27

I am twelve. When relatives come to visit I hide in my room. My 28 cousin Brenda, just my age, whose father works in the post office and whose mother is a nurse, comes to find me. "Hello," she says. And then she asks, looking at my recent school picture which I did not want taken, and on which the "glob" as I think of it is clearly visible, "You still can't see out of that eye?"

"No," I say, and flop back on the bed over my book. 29

That night, as I do almost every night, I abuse my eye. I rant and rave 30 at it, in front of the mirror. I plead with it to clear up before morning. I tell it I hate and despise it. I do not pray for sight. I pray for beauty.

"You did not change," they say. 31

I am fourteen and baby-sitting for my brother Bill who lives in 32 Boston. He is my favorite brother and there is a strong bond between us. Understanding my feelings of shame and ugliness, he and his wife take me to a local hospital where the "glob" is removed by a doctor named O. Henry. There is still a small bluish crater where the scar tissue was, but the ugly white stuff is gone. Almost immediately I become a different person from the girl who does not raise her head. Or so I think. Now that I've raised my head, I win the boyfriend of my dreams. Now that I've raised my head, I have plenty of friends. Now that I've raised my head, classwork comes from my lips as faultlessly as Easter speeches did, and I leave high school as valedictorian, most popular student and *queen,* hardly believing my luck. Ironically, the girl who was voted most beautiful in our class (and was) was later shot twice through the chest by a male companion, using a "real" gun, while she was pregnant. But that's another story in itself. Or, is it?

"You did not change," they say. 33

It is now thirty years since the "accident." A beautiful journalist comes 34 to visit and to interview me. She is going to write a cover story for her magazine that focuses on my last book. "Decide how you want to look on the cover," she says. "Glamorous, or whatever."

Never mind "glamorous," it is the "whatever" that I hear. Suddenly all I 35 can think of is whether I will get enough sleep the night before the photography session: if I don't, my eye will be tired and wander, as blind eyes will.

At night in bed with my lover I think up reasons why I should not ap- 36 pear on the cover of a magazine. "My meanest critics will say I've sold out," I say. "My family will now realize I write scandalous books."

"But what's the real reason you don't want to do this?" he asks. 37

"Because in all probability," I say in a rush, "my eye won't be straight." 38

"It will be straight enough," he says. Then, "Besides, I thought you'd 39 made your peace with that."

And I suddenly remember that I have. 40

I remember: 41

I am talking to my brother Jimmy, asking if he remembers anything unusual about the day I was shot. He does not know I consider that day the last time my father, with his sweet home remedy of cool lily leaves, "chose" me, and that I suffered and raged inside because of this. "Well," he says, "all I remember is standing by the side of the highway with Daddy, trying to flag down a car. A white man stopped, but when Daddy said he needed somebody to take his little girl to the doctor, he drove off."

I remember: 42

I am in the desert for the first time. I fall totally in love with it. I am so overwhelmed by its beauty, I confront for the first time, consciously, the meaning of the doctor's words years ago: "Eyes are sympathetic. If one is blind, the other will likely become blind too." I realize I have dashed about the world madly, looking at this, looking at that, storing up images against the fading of the light. But I might have missed seeing the desert! The shock of that possibility—and gratitude for over twenty-five years of sight—sends me literally to my knees. Poem after poem comes—which is perhaps how poets pray.

On Sight

I am so thankful I have seen
The Desert
And the creatures in the desert
And the desert Itself.
The desert has its own moon
Which I have seen
With my own eye
There is no flag on it.
Trees of the desert have arms
All of which are always up
That is because the moon is up
The sun is up
Also the sky
The stars
Clouds
None with flags.
If there were flags, I doubt
the trees would point.
Would you?

But mostly, I remember this: *43*

I am twenty-seven, and my baby daughter is almost three. Since her birth I have worried over her discovery that her mother's eyes are different from other people's. Will she be embarrassed? I wonder. What will she say? Every day she watches a television program called "Big Blue Marble." It begins with a picture of the earth as it appears from the moon. It is bluish, a little battered-looking, but full of light, with whitish clouds swirling around it. Every time I see it I weep with love, as if it is a picture of Grandma's house. One day when I am putting Rebecca down for her nap, she suddenly focuses on my eye. Something inside me cringes, gets ready to try to protect myself. All children are cruel about physical differences, I know from experience, and that they don't always mean to be is another matter. I assume Rebecca will be the same.

...continued Beauty: When the Other Dancer Is the Self, **Alice Walker**

But no-o-o-o. She studies my face intently as we stand, her inside   *44*
and me outside her crib. She even holds my face maternally between her
dimpled little hands. Then, looking every bit as serious and lawyerlike as
her father, she says, as if it may just possibly have slipped my attention:
"Mommy, there's a *world* in your eye." (As in, "Don't be alarmed, or do anything crazy.") And then, gently, but with great interest: "Mommy, where
did you *get* that world in your eye?"

For the most part, the pain left then. (So what if my brothers grew up   *45*
to buy even more powerful pellet guns for their sons and to carry real guns
themselves. So what if a young "Morehouse man" once nearly fell off the
steps of Trevor Arnett Library because he thought my eyes were blue.)
Crying and laughing I ran to the bathroom, while Rebecca mumbled and
sang herself off to sleep. Yes indeed, I realized, looking into the mirror.
There *was* a world in my eye. And I saw that it was possible to love it; that
in fact, for all it had taught me, of shame and anger and inner vision, I *did*
love it. Even to see it drifting out of orbit in boredom, or rolling up out of
fatigue, not to mention floating back at attention in excitement (bearing
witness, a friend has called it), deeply suitable to my personality, and even
characteristic of me.

That night I dream I am dancing to Stevie Wonder's song "Always"   *46*
(the name of the song is really "As," but I hear it as "Always"). As I dance,
whirling and joyous, happier than I've ever been in my life, another bright-
faced dancer joins me. We dance and kiss each other and hold each other
through the night. The other dancer has obviously come through all right,
as I have done. She is beautiful, whole and free. And she is also me.

vo·cab·u·lar·y

In your journal, write the meanings of the italicized words in the following phrases.

- a *subversive* wit **(1)**
- rustling their new *crinolines* **(4)**
- Eyes are *sympathetic* **(12)**
- a hideous *cataract* **(13)**
- *boisterous*, ill-disciplined children **(16)**
- bearing *witness* **(45)**

QUESTIONS FOR WRITING AND DISCUSSION

1. Why does Alice Walker share this story with us? What memories from your own life did her story trigger? Write them down.

2. What does Walker discover or learn about herself? As a reader, what did you learn about your own experiences by reading this essay?

3. Reread the essay, looking for examples of the following techniques for writing about memories: (1) using detailed observations; (2) creating specific scenes; (3) noting changes, contrasts, or conflicts; and (4) seeing relationships between past and present. In your opinion, which of these techniques does she use most effectively?

4. What is Walker's main idea in this autobiographical account? State it in your own words. Where in the essay does she state it most explicitly?

5. How many scenes or episodes does Walker recount? List them according to her age at the time. Explain how each episode relates to her main idea.

6. Walker also uses images of sight and blindness to organize her essay. The story begins with a description of a father who has "beautiful eyes" and ends with her dancing in her dream to a song by Stevie Wonder. Catalog the images of sight and blindness from each scene or episode. Explain how, taken together, these images reinforce Walker's main idea.

7. Walker writes her essay in the present tense, and she uses italics not only to emphasize ideas but to indicate the difference between past thoughts and events and the present. List the places where she uses italics. Explain how the italicized passages reinforce her main point.

8. What is the *occasion* in Walker's life that motivates her to write this narrative? Is it told in the story or does it happen in her life after the story concludes? Explain. Where does Walker include details about the social, historical, or cultural *context* for her story? Locate at least three paragraphs that provide details about context. Explain how these details are important for you as a reader in understanding her narrative.

9. Walker writes a multigenre essay, weaving poetry into her narrative essay. What other multigenre elements—such as photographs, drawings, excerpts from journals, or material from scrapbooks—might also be appropriate in your remembering essay? Might you want to do a "multimedia essay" in which you include not only photographs, images, and childhood artifacts, but also weblog excerpts, streaming video, audio, and Web links?

PROFESSIONAL WRITING

César Chávez Saved My Life

Daniel "Nene" Alejandrez

Labor leader and civil rights worker César Chávez (1927–1993) founded the National Farm Workers Association and used the nonviolent principles of Mahatma Gandhi and Dr. Martin Luther King, Jr. to gain dignity, fair wages, and humane working conditions for farm workers. In addition to his posthumously awarded Presidential Medal of Freedom and his induction into the California Hall of Fame, César Chávez has had his birthday, March 31st, recognized in eight states as an official holiday.

The author of the article, Daniel "Nene" Alejandrez, is the founder of Barrios Unidos and has spent his life fighting poverty, drugs, and gangs in Latino communities. In this essay, written in 2005 for Sojourners *magazine, Alejandrez remembers how the principles and the voice of César Chávez changed his life and inspired him to help others escape the cycle of drugs, violence, and incarceration.*

1   I'm the son of migrant farm workers, born out in a cotton field in Merigold, Mississippi. My family's from Texas. A migrant child goes to five or six different schools in one year, and you try to assimilate to whatever's going on at that time. I grew up not having shoes or only having one pair of pants to wear to school all week. I always remembered my experience in Texas, where Mexicans and blacks couldn't go to certain restaurants. That leaves something in you.

2   I saw how my father would react when Immigration would come up to the fields or the boss man talked to him. I would see my father bow his head. I didn't know why my father wasn't standing up to this man. As a child working in the rows behind him, I said to myself, "I'll never do that." A deep anger was developing in me.

3   But it was also developing in my father; the way that he dealt with it was alcohol. He would become violent when he drank on the weekends. I realized later that the reason he would bow his head to the boss is that he had seven kids to feed. He took that humiliation in order to feed me.

4   I stabbed the first kid when I was 13 years old. I shot another guy when I was 15. I almost killed a guy when I was 17. On and on and on. Then, in the late 1960s, I found myself as a young man in the Vietnam War. I saw more violence, inflicted more violence, and then tried to deal with the violence.

I came back from the war addicted to heroin, as many, many young *5*
men did. I came back to the street war, in the drug culture. Suddenly there
were farm workers—who lost jobs because of the bringing of machines
into the fields—who turned into drug dealers; it's easier money.

But when I was still working in the fields, something happened. I was *6*
17 years old, out in the fields of central California, and suddenly I hear this
voice coming out of the radio, talking about how we must better our conditions and better our lives in the migrant camps. It was like this voice was
talking just to me.

The voice was César Chávez. He said, "You must organize. You must *7*
seek justice. You must ask for better wages."

It's 1967. I'm busting my ass off pitching melons with six guys. Be- *8*
cause we're the youngest, they put us on the hardest job, but we're getting
paid $1.65 an hour. The guys working the harvesting machines are mak-
ing $8 an hour. We said to ourselves, "Something's not right."

Having the words of César Chávez, I organized the young men and *9*
called a strike. After lunch we just stopped working. We didn't go back on
the fields. This was sort of a hard thing because my father was a foreman
to this contractor, so I was going against him. He was concerned that we
were rocking the boat—but I think he was proud of me. We shut down
three of the melon machines, which forced the contractor to come, and
then the landowner came. "What's going on?" he said. We said, "We're on
strike, because we aren't getting our money." After about two hours, they
said, "Okay, we're going to raise it to $1.95."

But it wasn't the $1.95—it was the fact that six young men were be- *10*
ing abused, and that this little short Indian guy, César Chávez, had an influence. I kept his words.

When I wound up in Vietnam, I heard about Martin Luther King and *11*
his stand against the war. Somebody also told me about Mahatma Gandhi.
I didn't know who he was, only that he was a bald-headed dude that had
done this kind of stuff.

In Vietnam I realized that there were people that I had never met be- *12*
fore, that had never done nothing to me, never called me a dirty Mexican
or a greaser or nothing, and all of sudden I had to be an enemy to them.

I started looking at the words of César Chávez in terms of nonvio- *13*
lence. I looked at the violence in the community, in the fields, yet Chávez
was still calling for peace.

It has been an incredible journey since those days. For us this is a spir- *14*
itual movement. In Barrios Unidos, that's the primary thing—our spirit

... *continued* César Chávez Saved My Life, **Daniel "Nene" Alejandrez**

comes first. How do we take care of ourselves? Whatever people believe in, no matter what faith or religion, how do we communicate to the youngsters who are spiritually bankrupt? Many of us were addicted to drugs or alcohol, and we have to find a spiritual connection. Working with gang members, there's a lot of pain, so you have to find ways for healing. As peacemakers, we are wounded peacemakers.

This work has taken us into the prisons. Throughout the years, we've 15 been talking about the high rate of incarceration among our people, and the drug laws. Many people are doing huge amounts of time for nonviolent drug convictions; they did not need to be incarcerated—they need treatment. Currently in this country we deal with treatment by incarcerating people, which leads them to more violence and more negative ways of living.

As community-based organizations, we have had to prove to the cor- 16 rectional institutions that we're not in there to create any revolution. We're there to try to help. I'm asking how I can change the men that have been violent. How do I help change their attitude toward society and toward their own relatives? We see them as our relatives—these are our relatives that are incarcerated. How can we support them?

We go into the prison as a cultural and spiritual group helping men in 17 prison to understand their own culture and those of different cultures. They come from great warrior societies. But the warrior tradition doesn't just mean going to war, but also fighting for peace. The prisoners who help organize the Cinco de Mayo, Juneteenth, and Native powwow ceremonies within the prison system are a true testament of courage to change the madness of violence that has unnecessarily claimed many lives. By providing those ceremonies, we allow them to see who they really are. They weren't born gang members, or drug addicts, or thieves.

My best example of hope in the prisons is when we take the Aztec 18 dancers into the institutions. They do a whole indigenous ceremony. At the end, they invite people to what's called a friendship dance. It's a big figure-eight dance.

The first time that we were in prison in Tracy, California, out on the 19 yard, there were 2,000 men out there. The ceremony was led by Laura Castro, founder of the Xochut Aztec dance group, a very petite woman, very keen to her culture. She says to me, "What do you think, Nane? Do you think that these guys will come out and dance?" I'm looking at those guys—tattoos all over them and swastikas and black dudes that are really big. It's incredible to be in the prison yard. I say to her, "I don't know."

But what ties all those guys together is the drumbeat. Every culture *20* has some ceremonial drum you play. When the drumbeat started in the yard, the men just started coming. They divide themselves by race and then by gang. You got Norteños, Sureños, Hispanos, blacks, whites, Indians, and then "others" (mostly the Asian guys).

When the men were invited into the dance, those guys emptied out *21* the bleachers. They came. They held hands. This tiny woman, Laura, led them through the ceremony of the friendship dance. They went round and round. There were black, white, and brown holding hands, which doesn't happen in prison. And they were laughing. For a few seconds, maybe a minute, there was hope. We saw the smiles of men being children, remembering something about their culture. The COs [correctional officers] came out of the tower wondering what the hell was going on with these men dancing in prison, holding hands. It was an incredible sight. That day, the Creator was present. I knew that God's presence was there. Everyone was given a feeling that something had happened that wasn't our doing.

■ ■ ■

vo·cab·u·lar·y

In your journal, write the meanings of the italicized words in the following phrases.

- try to *assimilate* **(1)**
- took that *humiliation* **(3)**
- the high rate of *incarceration* **(15)**
- a whole *indigenous* ceremony **(18)**

QUESTIONS FOR WRITING AND DISCUSSION

1. The motto for César Chávez and his organization, The National Farm Workers Association, was "Si Se Puede," or "It Can Be Done." Although Alejandrez does not specifically refer to this motto, explain where this theme is most apparent in his essay.

2. One key strategy for writing successful narratives is setting and describing specific scenes. Alejandrez does an excellent job of setting two key scenes— one from his childhood and one from later in life. For each of these scenes, explain how Alejandrez (a) sets up the scene, (b) describes what happens using detailed observations, (c) uses dialogue to make the scene more vivid and dramatic, and (d) makes connections between the past and the present.

3. One key theme or motif in Alejandrez's essay is the idea of a "spiritual connection." Drawing on your description from question 2, explain how the idea of a spiritual connection is important in both of these key scenes. How does this theme connect to the nonviolent movements of Mahatma Gandhi and Martin Luther King, Jr.? How is this theme evoked in the final sentences of Alejandrez's essay? Explain.

4. Using Alejandrez's essay as a guide, write a remembering essay about a person in your life who became a role model or was influential at a key point in your life. Be sure to include key scenes showing how, when, and why this person was influential and then what you were able to accomplish because of that influence.

5. Go to the official Web sites for César Chávez and Barrios Unidos. What parallels are there between the lives of César Chávez and Daniel Alejandrez? How did both organizations use the nonviolent principles of Gandhi and Martin Luther King, Jr.? How are or were the goals of both organizations different? Explain.

TECHNIQUES   PROCESS

Remembering: The Writing Process

ASSIGNMENT FOR REMEMBERING

Write an essay about an important person, place, and/or event in your life. Your purpose is to recall and then use specific examples that *recreate* this memory and *show* why it is so important to you.

Think also about your possible audience and genre. Usually the audience for memories, autobiographical essays, and personal essays is fairly general. Since many people are interested in events from our lives, we may not want to restrict our audience too much. You may want to write just for your family or friends, however, or put your memories in the form of a letter you wish to send to a particular person. Also, you may want to think of a particular magazine that frequently publishes personal essays. Nearly every speciality magazine (sports, nature, outdoors, genealogy, cooking, clothing, style) occasionally publishes personal essays with memories that focus on the subject of the publication. Browsing through magazines may give you an idea for an audience and genre that would work for the event you wish to narrate.

> " Memory is more indelible than ink. "
>
> —ANITA LOOS,
> AUTHOR OF *KISS HOLLYWOOD GOODBYE*

CHOOSING	COLLECTING	SHAPING	DRAFTING	REVISING

CHOOSING A SUBJECT

If one of the journal entry exercises suggested a possible subject, try the collecting and shaping strategies below. If none of those exercises led to an interesting subject, consider the following ideas.

- Interview (in person or over the phone) a parent, a brother or sister, or a close friend. What events or experiences does your interviewee remember that were important to you?

- Get out a map of your town, city, state, or country and spend a few minutes doing an inventory of places you have been. Make a list of trips you have taken, with dates and years. Which of those places is the most memorable for you?

- Dig out a school yearbook and look through the pictures and the inscriptions that your classmates wrote. Whom do you remember most clearly? What events do you recall most vividly?

- Go to the library and look through news magazines or newspapers from five to ten years ago. What were the most important events of those years? What do you remember about them? Where were you and what were you doing when these events occurred? Which events had the largest impact on your life?

- Choose an important moment in your life, but write from the *point of view* of another person—a friend, family member, or stranger who was present. Let this person narrate the events that happened to you.

Note: Avoid choosing overly emotional topics such as the recent death of a close friend or family member. If you are too close to your subject, responding to your reader's revision suggestions may be difficult. Ask yourself if you can emotionally distance yourself from that subject. If you received a C for that essay, would you feel devastated?

CHOOSING	COLLECTING	SHAPING	DRAFTING	REVISING

COLLECTING

Once you have chosen a subject for your essay, try the following collecting strategies.

BRAINSTORMING   Brainstorming is merely jotting down anything and everything that comes to mind that is remotely connected to your subject: words, phrases, images, or complete thoughts. You can brainstorm by yourself or in groups, with everyone contributing ideas and one person recording them.

LOOPING   Looping is a method of controlled freewriting that generates ideas and provides focus and direction. Begin by freewriting about your subject for eight to ten minutes. Then pause, reread what you have written, and *underline* the most interesting or important idea in what you've written so far. Then, using that sentence or idea as your starting point, write for eight to ten minutes more. Repeat this cycle, or "loop," one more time. Each loop should add ideas and details from some new angle or viewpoint, but overall you will be focusing on the most important ideas that you discover.

CLUSTERING   Clustering is merely a visual scheme for brainstorming and free-associating about your topic. It can be especially effective for remembering because it helps you sketch relationships among your topics and subtopics. As you can see from the sample sketch, the sketch that you make of your ideas should help you see relationships between ideas or get a rough idea about an order or shape you may wish to use.

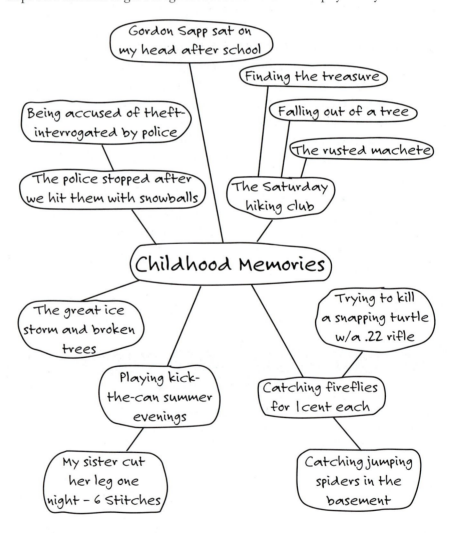

SHAPING

First, reconsider your purpose; perhaps it has become clearer or more definite since you recorded it in your journal entry. In your journal, jot down tentative answers for the following questions. If you don't have an answer, go on to the next question.

- **Subject:** What is your general subject?
- **Specific topic:** What aspect of your subject interests you?
- **Purpose:** Why is this topic interesting or important to you or your readers?
- **Main idea:** What might your main idea be?
- **Audience:** For whom are you writing this? What is your reader like, and why might he or she be interested in this topic?
- **Genre:** What genre might help you communicate your purpose and main idea most effectively to your audience? (See suggestions below.)

As you think about ways to organize and shape your essay, reread your assignment and think about your purpose and possible audience. Consider several possible *genres* or combinations of genres that might work. Then, for particular parts or sections of your essay, review the strategies described below. *Chronological order* will shape a major part of your narrative, but think also about using *comparison/contrast* for highlighting past and present or for contrasting two places, two events, or two key people. In addition, *similes, metaphors,* and *analogies* will make your writing more vivid, and paying attention to your *voice* and *tone* can help your achieve your purpose.

Most important, be sure to *narrow* and *focus* your subject. If you're going to write a three-page essay, don't try to cover everything in your life. Focus on one person, one episode, one turning point, one discovery, or one day, and do that in depth and detail.

GENRE   As you collect ideas, draft sample passages, and discuss your assignment with your peers, think about genre alternatives that might be appropriate for your purpose and audience. You may want to write in a traditional narrative format suitable for informal essays, autobiographical passages, or memoirs. You may want to consider multigenre essays in which you include photographs, graphics, drawings, letters, or material from scrapbooks. You may even want to write a multimedia essay in which you include not only photographs and artifacts but also weblog passages, video, audio, and Weblinks.

CHRONOLOGICAL ORDER   If you are writing about remembered events, you will probably use some form of chronological order. Try making a *chronological* *list of the major scenes or events.* Then go through the list, deciding what you will emphasize by telling about each item in detail and what you will pass over quickly. Normally, you will be using a straightforward chronological order, but you may wish to use a flashback, starting in the middle or near the end and then returning to tell the beginning. In his paragraph about a personal relationship, for example, student writer Gregory Hoffman begins the story at the most dramatic point, returns to tell how the relationship began, and then concludes the story.

> Her words hung in the air like iron ghosts. "I'm pregnant," she said as they walked through the park, the snow crackling beneath their feet. Carol was looking down at the ground when she told him, somewhat ashamed, embarrassed, and defiant all at once. Their relationship had only started in September, but both had felt the uneasiness surrounding them for the past months. She could remember the beginning so well and in such favor, now that the future seemed so uncertain. The all-night conversations by the bay window, the rehearsals at the university theater—where he would make her laugh during her only soliloquy, and most of all the Christmas they had spent together in Vermont. No one else had existed for her during those months. Yet now, she felt duped by her affections—as if she had become an absurd representation of a tragic television character. As they approached the lake, he put his arm around her, "Just do what you think is best, babe. I mean, I think you know how I feel." At that moment, she knew it was over. It was no longer "their" decision. His hand touched her cheek in a benedictorial fashion. The rest would only be form now. Exchanging records and clothes with an aside of brief conversation. She would see him again, in the market or at a movie, and they would remember. But like his affection in September, her memory of him would fade until he was too distant to see.

■ **COMPARISON/CONTRAST**   Although you may be comparing or contrasting people, places, or events from the past, you will probably also be comparing or contrasting the past to the present. You may do that at the beginning, noting how something in the present reminds you of a past person, place, or event. You may do it at the end, as Andrea Lee does in *Russian Journal.* You may do it both at the beginning and at the end, as Richard Rodriguez does in "The Boy's Desire." You may even contrast past and present throughout, as Alice Walker does in "Beauty: When the Other Dancer Is the Self." Comparing or contrasting the past with the present will often clarify your dominant idea.

■ **IMAGE**   Sometimes a single mental picture or recurring image will shape a paragraph or two in an essay. Consider how novelist George Orwell, in his essay "Shooting an Elephant," uses the image of a puppet or dummy to describe his feeling at a moment when he realized that, against his better judgment, he was going to have to shoot a marauding elephant in order to satisfy a crowd of two thousand Burmese who had gathered to watch him. The italicized words emphasize the recurring image.

> Suddenly I realized that I should have to shoot the elephant after all. The people expected it of me and I had got to do it; I could feel their *two thousand wills pressing me forward,* irresistibly. And it was at this moment, as I stood there with the rifle in my hands, that I first grasped the hollowness, the futility of the white man's dominion in the East. Here was I, the white man with his gun, standing in front of the unarmed native crowd— *seemingly the leading actor* of the piece; but in reality I was only an absurd *puppet pushed to and fro* by the will of those yellow faces behind. I perceived in this moment that when the white man turns tyrant it is his own freedom that he destroys. He becomes a sort of *hollow, posing dummy,* the *conventionalized figure* of a sahib. For it is the condition of his rule that he shall spend his life in trying to impress the "natives" and so in every crisis he has got to do what the "natives" expect of him. He *wears a mask,* and his face grows to fit it. I had got to shoot the elephant. I had committed myself to doing it when I sent for the rifle. *A sahib has got to act like a sahib;* he has got to appear resolute, to know his own mind and do definite things.

▪ VOICE AND TONE   When you have a personal conversation with someone, the way you look and sound—your body type, your voice, your facial expressions and gestures—communicates a sense of personality and attitude, which in turn affects how the other person reacts to what you say. In written language, although you don't have those gestures, expressions, or the actual sound of your voice, you can still create the sense that you are talking directly to your listener.

The term *voice* refers to a writer's personality as revealed through language. Writers may use emotional, colloquial, or conversational language to communicate a sense of personality. Or they may use abstract, impersonal language either to conceal their personalities or to create an air of scientific objectivity.

Tone is a writer's attitude toward the subject. The attitude may be positive or negative. It may be serious, humorous, honest, or ironic; it may be skeptical or accepting; it may be happy, frustrated, or angry. Often voice and tone overlap, and together they help us hear a writer talking to us. In the following passage, we hear student writer Kurt Weekly talking to us directly; we hear a clear, honest voice telling the story. His tone is not defensive or guilty: He openly admits he has a "problem."

> Oh no, not another trash day. Every time I see all those trash containers, plastic garbage bags and junk lined up on the sidewalks, it drives me crazy. It all

started when I was sixteen. I had just received my driver's license and the most beautiful Ford pickup. It was Wednesday as I remember and trash day. I don't know what happened. All of a sudden I was racing down the street swerving to the right, smashing into a large green Hefty trash bag filled with grass clippings. The bag exploded, and grass clippings and trash flew everywhere. It was beautiful and I was hooked. There was no stopping me.

At first I would smash one or two cans on the way to school. Then I just couldn't get enough. I would start going out the night before trash day. I would go down the full length of the street and wipe out every garbage container in sight. I was the terror of the neighborhood. This was not a bad habit to be taken lightly. It was an obsession. I was in trouble. There was no way I could kick this on my own. I needed help.

I received that help. One night after an evening of nonstop can smashing, the Arapahoe County Sheriff Department caught up with me. Not just one or a few but the whole department. They were willing to set me on the right path, and if that didn't work, they were going to send me to jail. It was a long, tough road to rehabilitation, but I did it. Not alone. I had the support of my family and the community.

■ **PERSONA**   Related to voice and tone is the *persona*—the "mask" that a writer can put on. Sometimes in telling a story about yourself, you may want to speak in your own "natural" voice. At other times, however, you may change or exaggerate certain characteristics in order to project a character different from your "real" self. Writers, for example, may project themselves as braver and more intelligent than they really are. Or to create a humorous effect, they may create personas who are more foolish or clumsy than they really are. This persona can shape a whole passage. In the following excerpt, James Thurber, a master of autobiographical humor, uses a persona—along with chronological narrative—to shape his account of a frustrating botany class.

> I passed all the other courses that I took at my university, but I could never pass botany. This was because all botany students had to spend several hours a week in a laboratory looking through a microscope at plant cells, and I could never see through a microscope. I never once saw a cell through a microscope. This used to enrage my instructor. He would wander around the laboratory pleased with the progress all the students were making in drawing the involved and, so I am told, interesting structure of flower cells, until he came to me. I would just be standing there. "I can't see anything," I would say. He would begin patiently enough, explaining how anybody can see through a microscope, but he would always end up in a fury claiming that I could too see through a microscope but just pretended that I couldn't. "It takes away from the beauty of flowers anyway,"

I used to tell him. "We are not concerned with beauty in this course," he would say. "We are concerned solely with the mechanics of flowers." "Well," I'd say, "I can't see anything." "Try it just once again," he'd say, and I would put my eye to the microscope and see nothing at all, except now and again a nebulous milky substance—a phenomenon of maladjustment. You were supposed to see a vivid, restless clockwork of sharply defined plant cells. "I see what looks like a lot of milk," I would tell him. This, he claimed, was the result of my not having adjusted the microscope properly, so he would readjust it for me, or rather, for himself. And I would look again and see milk. I finally took a deferred pass, as they called it, and waited a year and tried again. (You had to pass one of the biological sciences or you couldn't graduate.) The professor had come back from vacation brown as a berry, bright-eyed, and eager to explain cell-structure again to his classes. "Well," he said to me, cheerily, when we met in the first laboratory hour of the semester, "we're going to see cells this time, aren't we?" "Yes, sir," I said. Students to the right of me and to the left of me and in front of me were seeing cells; what's more, they were quietly drawing pictures of them in their notebooks. Of course, I didn't see anything.

"We'll try it," the professor said to me, grimly, "with every adjustment of the microscope known to man. As God is my witness, I'll arrange this glass so that you see cells through it or I'll give up teaching. In twenty-two years of botany, I—" He cut off abruptly for he was beginning to quiver all over, like Lionel Barrymore, and he genuinely wished to hold onto his temper; his scenes with me had taken a great deal out of him.

So we tried it with every adjustment of the microscope known to man. With only one of them did I see anything but blackness or the familiar lacteal opacity, and that time I saw, to my pleasure and amazement, a variegated constellation of flecks, specks, and dots. These I hastily drew. The instructor, noting my activity, came back from an adjoining desk, a smile on his lips and his eyebrows high in hope. He looked at my cell drawing. "What's that?" he demanded, with a hint of a squeal in his voice. "That's what I saw," I said. "You didn't, you didn't, you didn't!" he screamed, losing control of his temper instantly, and he bent over and squinted into the microscope. His head snapped up. "That's your eye!" he shouted. "You've fixed the lens so that it reflects! You've drawn your eye!"

▪ **DIALOGUE**   Dialogue, which helps to *recreate* people and events rather than just tell about them, can become a dominant form and thereby shape your writing. Recreating an actual conversation, you could possibly write a whole scene using nothing but dialogue. More often, however, writers use dialogue occasionally for dramatic effect. In the account of his battle with the microscope, for instance, Thurber uses dialogue in the last two paragraphs to dramatize his conclusion:

> "We'll try it," the professor said to me, grimly, "with every adjustment of the microscope known to man. As God is my witness, I'll arrange this glass so that you see cells through it or I'll give up teaching. In twenty-two years of teaching botany, I—"... "What's that?" he demanded.... "That's what I saw," I said. "You didn't, you didn't, you didn't!" he screamed.... "You've fixed the lens so that it reflects! You've drawn your eye!"

▍**TITLE, INTRODUCTION, AND CONCLUSION** In your journal, sketch out several possible titles you might use. You may want a title that is merely an accurate label, such as *Russian Journal* or "The Boy's Desire," but you may prefer something less direct that gets your reader's attention. For example, for his essay about his hat that appears at the end of this chapter, student writer Todd Petry uses the title "The Wind Catcher." As a reader, what do you think about Alice Walker's title, "Beauty: When the Other Dancer Is the Self"?

Introductions or beginning paragraphs take several shapes. Some writers plunge the reader immediately into the action—as Gregory Hoffman does—and then later fill in the scene and context. Others are more like Kurt Weekly, announcing the subject—trash cans—and then taking the reader from the present to the past and the beginning of the story: "It all started when I was sixteen...." At some point, however, readers do need to know the context—the *who, what, when,* and *where* of your account.

Conclusions are also of several types. In some, writers will return to the present and discuss what they have learned, as Andrea Lee does in *Russian Journal.* Some, like Alice Walker, end with an image or even a dream. Some writers conclude with dramatic moments, or an emotional scene, as student writer Juli Bovard does in the essay "The Red Chevy" that appears at the end of this chapter. But many writers will try to tie the conclusion back to the beginning, as Richard Rodriguez does at the end of "The Boy's Desire": "The closet door closes ... the fog rises." In your journal, experiment with several possibilities until you find one that works for your subject.

> *I start at the beginning, go on to the end, then stop.*
> —GABRIEL GARCÍA MÁRQUEZ, AUTHOR OF *ONE HUNDRED YEARS OF SOLITUDE*

> *I always know the ending; that's where I start.*
> —TONI MORRISON, NOBEL PRIZE-WINNING NOVELIST

CHOOSING COLLECTING SHAPING **DRAFTING** REVISING

DRAFTING

When you have experimented with the above shaping strategies, reconsider your purpose, audience, and main idea. Have they changed? In your journal, reexamine the notes you made before trying the shaping activities. If necessary, revise your statements about purpose, audience, or main idea based on what you have actually written.

Working from your journal material and from your collecting and shaping activities, draft your essay. It is important *not* to splice different parts together or just recopy and connect segments, for they may not fit or flow together. Instead, reread what you have written, and then start with a clean sheet of paper. If you're working on a computer file, you can start with your list of events or one of your best shaping strategies and expand that file as you draft. Concentrate on what you want to say and write as quickly as possible.

To avoid interruptions, choose a quiet place to work. Follow your own writing rituals. Try to write nonstop. If you cannot think of the right word, put a line or a dash, but keep on writing. When necessary, go back and reread what you have previously written.

CHOOSING	COLLECTING	SHAPING	DRAFTING	REVISING

REVISING

Revising begins, of course, when you get your first idea and start collecting and shaping. It continues as you redraft certain sections of your essay and rework your organization. In many classes, you will give and receive advice from the other writers in your class. Use the guidelines below to give constructive advice about a remembering essay draft.

> " The difference between the right word and the nearly right word is the same as that between lightning and the lightning bug. "
> —MARK TWAIN, AUTHOR OF *THE ADVENTURES OF HUCKLEBERRY FINN*

GUIDELINES FOR REVISION

- **Reexamine your purpose and audience.** Are you doing what you intended?

- **Reconsider the genre you selected.** Is it working for your purpose and audience? Can you add multigenre elements to make your narrative more effective?

- **Revise to make the main idea of your account clearer.** You don't need a "moral" to the story or a bald statement saying, "This is why this person was important." Your reader, however, should know clearly why you wanted to write about the memory that you chose.

- **Revise to clarify the important relationships in your story.** Consider relationships between past and present, between you and the people in your story, between one place and another place, between one event and another event.

- **Close and detailed observation is crucial.** *Show,* don't just tell. Can you use any of the collecting and shaping strategies for observing discussed in Chapter 3?

PEER RESPONSE

The instructions below will help you give and receive constructive advice about the rough draft of your remembering essay. You may use these guidelines for an in-class workshop, a take-home review, or a computer e-mail response.

Writer: Before you exchange drafts with another reader, write out the following information about your own rough draft.

1. State the main idea that you hope your essay conveys.
2. Describe the best *one* or *two* key scenes that your narrative creates.
3. Explain one or two problems that you are having with this draft that you want your reader to focus on.

Reader: Without making any comments, read the *entire* draft from start to finish. As you *reread* the draft, answer the following questions.

1. Locate one or two of the *key scenes* in the narrative. Are they clearly set at an identified time and place? Does the writer use vivid description of the place or the people? Does the writer use dialogue? Does the writer include his or her reflections? Which of these areas need the most attention during the writer's revision? Explain.
2. Write out a *time line* for the key events in the narrative. What happened first, second, third, and so forth? Are there places in the narrative where the time line could be clearer? Explain.
3. When you finished reading the draft, *what characters or incidents were you still curious about?* Where did you want more information? What characters or incidents did you want to know more about?
4. What *overall idea* does the narrative convey to you? How does your notion of the main idea compare to the writer's answer to question 1? Explain how the writer might revise the essay to make the main idea clearer.
5. Answer the *writer's questions* in question 3.

After you have some feedback from other readers, you need to distance yourself and objectively reread what you have written. Review the advice you received from your peer readers. Remember, you will get both good and bad advice, so *you* must decide what you think is important or not important. If you are uncertain about advice you received from one of your peers, ask for a third or fourth opinion. In addition, most writing centers will have tutors available who can help you sort through the advice you have received on your draft and figure out a revision plan. Especially for this remembering essay, make sure your memories are recreated on paper. Don't be satisfied with suggesting incidents that merely trigger your own memories: You must *show* people and events vividly for your reader.

- **Revise to show crucial changes, contrasts, or conflicts more clearly.** Walker's essay, for instance, illustrates how *conflict and change* are central to an effective remembering essay. See if this strategy will work in your essay.

- **Have you used a straight chronological order?** If it works, keep it. If not, would another order be better? Should you begin in the middle and do a flashback? Do you want to move back and forth from present to past or stay in the past until the end?

If you are using a chronological order, cue your reader by occasionally using transitional words to signal changes: *then, when, first, next, last, before, after, while, as, sooner, later, initially, finally, yesterday, today.*

- **Be clear about point of view.** Are you looking back on the past from a viewpoint in the present? Are you using the point of view of yourself as a child or at some earlier point in your life? Are you using the point of view of another person or object in your story?

- **What are the key images in your account?** Should you add or delete an image to show the experience more vividly?

- **What voice are you using?** Does it support your purpose? If you are using a persona, is it appropriate for your audience and purpose?

- **Revise sentences to improve clarity, conciseness, emphasis, and variety.**

- **Check your dialogue for proper punctuation and indentation.** See the essay by Alice Walker in this chapter for a model.

- **When you are relatively satisfied with your draft, edit for correct spelling, appropriate word choice, punctuation, and grammar.**

POSTSCRIPT ON THE WRITING PROCESS

After you finish writing, revising, and editing your essay, you will want to breathe a sigh of relief and turn it in. But before you do, think about the problems that you solved as you wrote this essay. *Remember:* Your major goal for this course is to learn to write and revise more effectively. To do that, you need to discover and adapt your writing processes so you can anticipate and solve the problems you face as a writer. Take a few minutes to answer the following questions. Be sure to hand in this postscript with your essay.

1. Review your writing process. Which collecting, shaping, and revising strategies helped you remember and describe incidents most quickly and clearly? What problems were you unable to solve?

Continued

2. Reread your essay. With a small asterisk [*], identify in the margin of your essay sentences where you used sensory details, dialogue, or images to show or recreate the experience for your reader.

3. If you received feedback from your peers, identify one piece of advice that you followed and one bit of advice that you ignored. Explain your decisions.

4. Rereading your essay, what do you like best about it? What parts of your essay need work? What would you change if you had another day to work on this assignment?

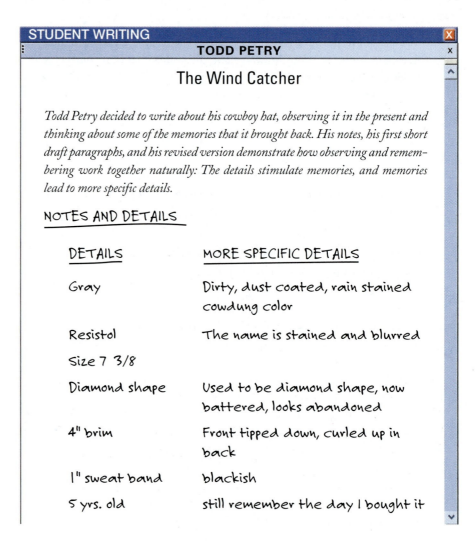

STUDENT WRITING

TODD PETRY

The Wind Catcher

Todd Petry decided to write about his cowboy hat, observing it in the present and thinking about some of the memories that it brought back. His notes, his first short draft paragraphs, and his revised version demonstrate how observing and remembering work together naturally: The details stimulate memories, and memories lead to more specific details.

NOTES AND DETAILS

DETAILS	MORE SPECIFIC DETAILS
Gray	Dirty, dust coated, rain stained cowdung color
Resistol	The name is stained and blurred
Size 7 3/8	
Diamond shape	Used to be diamond shape, now battered, looks abandoned
4" brim	Front tipped down, curled up in back
1" sweat band	blackish
5 yrs. old	still remember the day I bought it

4x beaver

What it is not:	it is unlike a hat fresh out of the box
What it compares to:	point of crown like the north star like a pancake with wilted edges battered like General Custer's hat
What I remember:	the day I bought the hat a day at Pray Mesa

FIRST DRAFT
The Wind Catcher

The other day while I was relaxing in my favorite chair and listening to Ian Tyson, I happened to notice my work cowboy hat hanging on the wall. Now I look at that old hat no less than a dozen times a day without too much thought, but on that particular day, my eyes remained fixed on it and my mind went to remembering.

I still remember I had $100 cash in my pocket the day I went hat shopping. The local tack, feed, and western wear CO-OP was my first and only stop. Finding a hat to meet my general specifications was no big deal. I wanted a gray Resistol, size 7 3/8, with a 4-inch brim and diamond-shaped crown. From there on, though, my wants became very particular. I took 30 minutes to find the one that had the right fit, and five times that long to come to terms with the hat shaper. Boy, but I was one proud young fellow the next day when I went to school sporting my new piece of head gear. I've had that wind catcher five years through rough times, but in a way, it really looks better now, without any shape, dirty, and covered with dust and cowdung.

REVISED VERSION
The Wind Catcher

The other day, while I was relaxing in my favorite chair and listening to Ian Tyson, I happened to notice my work cowboy hat hanging on the wall. Now, I look at that old hat no less than a dozen times a day without too much thought, but on that particular day, my eyes remained fixed on it and my mind went to remembering.

...*continued* The Wind Catcher, **Todd Petry**

I was fifteen years old and had $100 cash in my pocket the day I went   *2*
hat shopping five years ago. The local tack, feed, and western wear
CO-OP was my first and only stop. Finding a hat to meet my general
specifications was no big deal. I wanted a gray 4X Resistol, size 7 3/8, with
a four-inch brim and diamond-shaped crown. I wanted no flashy feathers or gaudy hatbands, which in my mind were only for pilgrims. From
there on, though, my wants became very particular. I took thirty minutes
to find the one that had the right fit, and five times that long to come to
terms with the hat shaper. Boy, but I was one proud young fellow the next
day when I went to school sporting my new piece of head gear.

About that time, Ian Tyson startled me out of my state of reminis-   *3*
cence by singing "Rose in the Rockies," with that voice of his sounding
like ten cow elk cooing to their young in the springtime. As I sat there
listening to the music and looking at that old hat, I had to chuckle to myself because that wind catcher had sure seen better days. I mean it looked
rode hard and put up wet. The gray, which was once as sharp and crisp as
a mountain lake, was now faded and dull where the sun had beat down.
Where the crown and brim met, the paleness was suddenly transformed
into a gritty black which ran the entire circumference of the hat. This
black was unlike any paint or color commercially available, being made
up of head sweat, dirt, alfalfa dust, and powdered cow manure. Water
blemishes from too much rain and snow mottled the brim, adding to the
colors' turbidity. Inside the crown and wherever the slope was less than
ninety degrees, dust had collected to hide the natural color even more.

After a while, my attention lost interest in the various colors and be-   *4*
gan to work its way over the hat's shape, which I was once so critical of.
General Custer's hat itself could not have looked worse. All signs of uniformity and definite shape had disappeared. The diamond-shaped crown,
which was once round and smooth, now bowed out on the sides and had
edges as blunt as an orange crate. The point, which once looked like the
North Star indicating the direction, now was twisted off balance from excessive right hand use. Remembering last spring, how I threw that hat in
the face of an irate mother cow during calving, I had to chuckle again.
Throwing that hat kept my horse and me out of trouble but made the
"off-balance look" rather permanent. As I looked at the brim, I was reminded of a three-day-old pancake with all its edges wilted. The back of
that brim curled upward like a snake ready to strike, and the front had become so narrow and dipped, it looked like something a dentist would use
on your teeth.

For probably half an hour, I sat looking at the wear and tear on that   *5*
ancient hat. Awhile back, I remember, I decided to try to make my old
hat socially presentable by having it cleaned and blocked, removing those
curls and dips and other signs of use. However, when a hat shop refused
to even attempt the task, I figured I'd just leave well enough alone. As I
scanned my eyes over the hat, I noticed several other alterations from its
original form, such as the absent hat band, which was torn off in the
brush on Pray Mesa, and the black thread that drew together the edges
of a hole in the crown. However, try as I might, I could not for the life of
me see where any character had been lost in the brush, or any flair had
been covered with cowdung.

QUESTIONS FOR WRITING AND DISCUSSION

1. Close observation often leads to specific memories. In the opening paragraph
   of his revised version, Todd Petry says that "on that particular day, my eyes
   remained fixed on it and my mind went to remembering." He then recalls
   the time when he was fifteen years old and bought his hat. Identify two
   other places where observation leads Petry to remember specific scenes from
   the past.

2. Petry chose "The Wind Catcher" as the title for his essay. Reread the essay
   and then brainstorm a list of five other titles that might be appropriate for
   this short essay. Which title do you like best?

3. Where does Petry most clearly express the main idea of his essay? Write out
   the main idea in your own words.

STUDENT WRITING

JULI BOVARD

The Red Chevy

*In the following essay, Juli Bovard recalls several of the most traumatic days of her
life. She remembers not just the day she was raped by an unknown assailant, but
the days she had to spend in the police station, the day she confronted her attacker
in the courtroom, and the days she spent regaining control of her life. In the end,
Bovard helps us understand how she overcame being a rape victim and reclaimed
her life.*

... *continued* The Red Chevy, **Juli Bovard**

From the moment the man in the Chevy stopped to offer me a ride on that *1* blistering September afternoon, I knew I was in trouble. Before I could say, "No, but thanks anyway," the man in the passenger side of the car jumped at me, twisted my arm and held a shiny piece of steel to my side. I was pushed into the car and driven 30 miles over the county line. During the ride, I did everything every article or specialist on abduction had advised against: I cried, I babbled, and I lost control. In the end it was all futile. Two hours later—after they dumped me off near my home—I was another statistic. I had been raped, and was now a victim of the brutal, demeaning, sad violent crime of sexual assault. I was officially one of the 1,871 rapes that occur each day in the United States ("Sexual Assault Statistics").

Rape not only has physical repercussions, but has an enormous psy- *2* chological and emotional impact as well. During my "event" as I like to call it, I remembered an initial feeling of shock and numbness, and soon found myself babbling incoherently. I begged my attackers to let me go. I tried to talk my way out of the car. I even tried to beg or bargain my way out. However, the driver was very much in control of the situation, and my weak efforts failed. Eventually my babbling gave way to cold reason, and I became convinced that not only would I be raped, but that I would also die. My life did not pass before me—as is said to happen to dying people. In fact, I did not think of the past at all, but only the future and all the things I had not yet done. I had never ridden a horse other than the ponies at the fair. I had not learned to play golf—though I had intended to—or learned to snow ski down a mountain with my son. There were too many people I had not told how I really felt, too many people to whom I wanted to say good-bye. I seriously doubted I would ever be given another chance.

I did not die. In fact, other than a few bruises and scratches from the *3* field grass (where I was forced to lie during my rape), and several cuts on my neck and cheek—left by the brass knuckle style knife, I was remarkably, physically unhurt. The greatest trauma was to my mind. The psychological and emotional wounds in the ensuing months were far worse than the actual sexual assault.

Within a week of my report, the man who raped me was arrested and *4* held without bail (he had previously been convicted of attempted rape), his accomplice was not accused since he agreed to turn state's evidence— which means he made a deal to cover himself and agreed to testify against my assailant. What followed these events, I remember, was a long investigation that involved many tedious hours in the police station, and numbing revisits to the scene of the crime. Through it all I was alone, and I halfheartedly tried to comfort myself for enduring the stress so well. By late October, the month of the preliminary hearing, I had gone back to work, and was back in control of my life—or so I thought. The actual hearing proved me wrong.

Though I do not remember much about the actual courtroom or its proceedings, I will always remember the warmth of the day and the overwhelming odor of my perpetrator's cologne (to this day I become nauseous if I smell the cologne Obsession). Seeing my assailant again had an effect on me that I was not prepared for. I felt the same fear that I had experienced the day of my rape, and for the second time in my life I felt terror so deep it paralyzed me. The pressure from the entire incident finally overwhelmed me, and when I returned home that afternoon I climbed into bed and did not leave it for three days. I spent seventy-two hours staring at the ceiling and vomiting. When I finally emerged from my emotional coma, I could not eat or sleep. Everything seemed unreal and unclear to me. It was weeks before I could focus on everyday tasks, even something as simple as showering.

By the middle of November, I had lost close to fifteen pounds. I had constant diarrhea, my menstrual cycle had stopped, and I was constantly bombarded by anxiety attacks. I could no longer get up each day and go to work and act like nothing had happened. Leaving the house left me with cold sweats, and sleeping through the night became impossible. I became paranoid and despondent. I knew I would have to seek professional help.

Fortunately, through counseling I learned that my reactions were very common, and are shared by most rape victims. Through research, I found that all the feelings I was having were very normal. My fear that the rapist would return was natural, and my inability to face unfamiliar situations or people was a classic symptom. I also learned that the guilt that plagued me, which made me think that somehow I had provoked the rape or "wore" the wrong clothes to entice the rapist, was simply untrue. I was feeling a great amount of shame and embarrassment—a stigma I learned society often places on rape victims. My anger, which was the most natural response, was also the most helpful. When you are angry, you tend to want to fight back. My way of fighting back was to get on with living. Still I asked, "Why me?" I had followed all the rules set by society. I did not walk the streets at night, hang out in bars, or talk to strangers. I was an actively employed member of society. So why me? I found it wasn't just me or something I did. It could have been any woman

...*continued* The Red Chevy, **Juli Bovard**

walking the streets that day, and it went far beyond what I wore or how I walked, something noted author Susan Brownmiller eloquently affirms in her statement that, "any female may become a victim of rape. Factors such as youth, advanced age, physical homeliness and virginal lifestyle do not provide a fool-proof deterrent to render a women impervious to sexual assault" (Brownmiller 348).

Through my experience and in talking with other victims I have learned that rape has no typical "face." Certainly the man who raped me looked normal (He was not obscene, ugly, or disfigured). He could have been my neighbor, my grocer, or even my boyfriend. Rape victims and its perpetrators are colorless and ageless. There is no stereotypical rapist *or* victim. We can be doctors, lawyers, mothers, or fathers. We are tall, short, fat, and skinny. And, as in most victims' cases, simply in the wrong place at the wrong time. 8

After the question of "why me?" I asked, "WHY, at all?" Why *does* a man rape a woman? Initially I thought it was obvious—for sex. But I was wrong. The motivations of rape include anger, aggression, dominance, hostility, and power, but generally are not usually associated with just the actual act of sex. Quite simply it is violence. Men who rape do so because they are violent and psychotic. There is no other reason, and no valid excuse. 9

In the end, before I was to testify, the man who attacked me changed his plea to guilty. I walked out of the district attorney's office and never asked how many years the rapist would serve in prison. It did not matter. He would be behind bars, but more importantly, I would be free to begin living again. Now, instead of dreading the month of September, I celebrate it. I celebrate the month, in which, instead of just existing, I started living. I was a victim of rape, but through years of counseling and support *I am not a victim any longer.* 10

Works Cited

Brownmiller, Susan. *Against Our Will.* New York: Simon and Schuster, 1975.

"Sexual Assault Statistics." Sexual Assault Site. *Abuse Counseling and Treatment.* 22 Oct. 2000 http://actabuse.com/SAstatistics.html.

vo·cab·u·lar·y

In your journal, write down the meanings of the italicized words in the following phrases.

- babbling *incoherently* **(2)**
- the greatest *trauma* **(3)**
- a *stigma* **(7)**
- render a woman *impervious* **(7)**
- they are violent and *psychotic* **(9)**

QUESTIONS FOR WRITING AND DISCUSSION

1. Psychological research has shown that people remember traumatic events more vividly and with more detail than other events. Has that been true in your experience? Recall two experiences—one happy, one traumatic—and consider whether your experiences support or do not support the research.

2. Remembering essays should have a purpose—that is, they should focus on having a specific effect on their audience. Why is Juli Bovard writing about this experience? What effect does she want to have on her readers? Is she just giving information or does she want to convince us about something? Explain.

3. Review the techniques for writing a remembering essay listed at the beginning of this chapter. Which of these techniques does Bovard use? Where does she use them? Which are, in your opinion, most effective? Why?

4. In addition to remembering specific scenes, Bovard uses some research and explains the causes and effects of the event. Should she have research and cite sources in a narrative essay? Do her explanations and her research help achieve her purpose or do they detract from the story? Support your response by citing specific sentences from her essay.

5. Bovard chose the title "The Red Chevy" for her essay. Brainstorm five other titles she might use for her essay. Compare your ideas with those of your classmates. Did you come up with titles that might be more effective for the purpose of her essay? Explain.

Diego Rivera
The Flower Carrier (formerly *The Flower Vendor*) (1934)
© Estate of Diego Rivera, Courtesy Banco de México

Often called the greatest modern Mexican painter, Diego Rivera is most famous for his mural paintings showing the lives of working people. The journal exercise on page 166 provides ideas for writing and research about Diego Rivera and his paintings.

Reading

5

After discussing in class how to write letters to the editor, you decide to respond to Margaret Atwood's "Letter to America." Atwood, the award-winning Canadian author of *Surfacing* and *The Handmaid's Tale*, addresses America personally, arguing that what was great about America in previous centuries—its great writers like Twain and Dickinson, its great films, and its history and Constitution—is now being lost through its deteriorating economy and foreign policy. In your response, you acknowledge areas where you agree with Atwood, but then argue that not everything in America's past was as rosy as Atwood portrays. Moreover, even current events show flaws but also continued signs of greatness. America, you conclude, "is still that city upon a hill."

As an assignment in class, you are reading and critiquing an article by Deborah Tannen on how men and women respond differently during class conversations. As you read the article, you have trouble locating the main focus of the article, and then you are disturbed by some unsupported assertions that she makes about typical behavior of men and women. Do men really like to argue and dominate class discussions? Do women always benefit from smaller, more intimate group discussions? You reread the article and make notes in the margin. After discussing your reactions with other readers, you decide to argue that readers should expect clearer organization and fewer unsupported assertions about the gender-based differences between men and women.

> **If we think of it, all that a University, or final highest School can do for us, is still but what the first School began doing—teach us to read.**
> —THOMAS CARLYLE, AUTHOR OF *ON HEROES AND HERO WORSHIP*

> **Reading is not a passive process by which we soak up words and information from the page, but an active process by which we predict, sample, and confirm or correct our hypotheses about the written text.**
> —CONSTANCE WEAVER, AUTHOR OF *READING PROCESS AND PRACTICE*

A T FIRST GLANCE, A CHAPTER ON READING IN A TEXTBOOK ON WRITING MAY CATCH YOU BY SURPRISE. THIS CHAPTER, HOWEVER, IS NOT ABOUT LEARNING YOUR ABC'S OR ABOUT READING *THE CAT IN THE HAT*. IT IS ABOUT LEARNING TO READ TEXTS ACTIVELY AND critically. It is about learning how to summarize and respond to what you read. It is about using reading—along with observing and remembering—as a source for your writing.

At the beginning of this chapter, we need to define two key terms: *texts* and *reading*. Normally, when you think about a text, you may think of a textbook. A text, however, can be any graphic matter—a textbook, an essay, a poem, a newspaper editorial, a photograph, or an advertisement. Some people expand the definition of texts to include any thing or phenomenon in the world. In this widest sense, the layout of a restaurant, the behavior of children on a playground, or clouds in the sky could be "texts" that can be read.

Similarly, the term *reading* has both narrow and broad senses. In a narrow sense, reading is simply understanding words on a page. But reading has a variety of wider meanings as well. Reading can mean analyzing, as when an architect "reads" blueprints and knows how to construct a roof. Reading can also mean interpreting, as when a sailor "reads" the sky and knows that the day will bring winds and rough weather. Reading can also mean examining texts or cultural artifacts and perceiving messages of racism, gender bias, or cultural exploitation. All of these "readings" require close, critical reading of the text and an ability to engage, analyze, probe, respond to, and interpret the text.

In this chapter, you will practice active, critical reading and responding to academic and cultural texts. (In Chapter 6, you will focus specifically on analyzing and responding to images, photographs, advertisements, and other visual texts.) Implied in active, critical reading are both writing about the texts and discussing the texts with other readers. Writing requires reading with your pen in your hand to annotate the texts you read with comments, questions, and observations. You can also write double-entry logs that will help you become an active, critical reader. You may consider reading a solitary activity, but texts appear in social contexts and should be read in social contexts. Active reading, therefore, also involves sharing ideas in small groups, engaging in a class conversation, posting e-mail responses, or writing for an online discussion forum.

This chapter provides guidelines for critical reading, tips for summarizing ideas accurately, and techniques for responding to academic essays, editorials, and other texts you will encounter in college, on the job, and in your community.

Techniques for Writing About Reading

- **Using active and responsive reading, writing, and discussing strategies.** Preview the author's background and the writing context. Prewrite about your own experiences with the subject. Read initially for information and enjoyment. As you reread, make annotations, write questions, or do a double-entry log. Discuss the text with other readers.

- **Summarizing the main ideas or features of the text.** A summary should *accurately* and *objectively* represent the key ideas. Summaries cite the author and title, accurately represent the main ideas, quote directly key phrases or sentences, and describe main features of the text.

- **Responding to or critiquing the ideas in the text.** A response should focus on your ideas and reactions. Types of responses include *analysis* of the rhetorical situation, argument, organization, or evidence in the text; *agreement* or *disagreement* with the author/text; or *interpretation* of the text.

- **Supporting the response with evidence.** As supporting evidence for the response, writers should analyze key features of the text, cite evidence from other relevant texts, and/or use examples from personal experience.

- **Combining summary and response into a coherent essay.** Usually, the summary appears first, followed by the reader's response, but be sure to *integrate* the two parts. Focus early on a main idea for your response. Use transitions between the summary and the response.

> ❝ Reading involves a fair measure of push and shove. You make your mark on a book and it makes its mark on you. Reading is not simply a matter of hanging back and waiting for a piece, or its author, to tell you what the writing has to say. ❞
>
> —DAVID BARTHOLOMAE AND ANTHONY PETROSKY, AUTHORS OF *WAYS OF READING*

As you work on these techniques, don't simply read the text, listen to a class discussion, and write out your critique. Instead, annotate the text by circling key ideas and writing your questions and responses in the margin. Continue reading and discussing your ideas after you have written out a draft. Use the interactive powers of reading, writing, and discussing to help you throughout your writing process.

CRITICAL READING STRATEGIES

Critical reading does not mean that you always criticize something or find fault. *Critical reading simply means questioning what you read.* You may end up liking or praising certain features of a text, but you begin by asking questions, by resisting the text, and by demanding that the text be clear, logical, reliable, thoughtful, and honest.

You begin your critical reading by asking questions about every element in the rhetorical situation. Who is the *author,* and what is his or her background or potential bias? What was the *occasion,* and who was the intended *audience?* Is the writer's *purpose* achieved for that occasion and audience? Did the writer understand and fairly represent other writers' positions on this topic? Did the writer understand the *genre* and use it to achieve the purpose? How did the *cultural context* affect the author and the text? How did the context affect you as a reader?

You continue your critical reading by asking about the writer's claim or argument, the representation of the background information, the organization, the logical use of evidence, and the effectiveness of the style, tone, and word choice. You may find these elements effective or ineffective, but you start your critical reading by reading and then rereading, by probing key passages, by looking for gaps or ideas not included, by discussing the text with other readers, by assessing your position as a reader, and by continually making notes and asking questions.

▪ **DOUBLE-ENTRY LOG**   One of the most effective strategies to promote critical reading is a double-entry log. Draw a line down the middle of a page in your

Author and Title:_____

Summary	**Response**
Main ideas, key features	Your reactions, comments, and questions

notebook. On the left-hand side, keep a running summary of the main ideas and features that you notice in the text. On the right-hand side, write your questions and reactions.

■ **CRITICAL REREADING GUIDE**   If your double-entry log did not yield some good ideas, try the ideas and suggestions in this rereading guide. First, read the essay in its entirety. Then, let the following set of questions guide your rereading. The questions on the left-hand side will help you summarize and analyze the text; the questions on the right-hand side will start your critical reading and help focus your response.

DESCRIPTION

I. Purpose
   • Describe the author's overall *purpose* (to inform, explain, explore, evaluate, argue, negotiate, or other purpose).
   • How does the author/text want to affect or change the reader?

II. Audience/Reader
   • Who is the *intended* audience?
   • What *assumptions* does the author make about the reader's knowledge or beliefs?
   • From what *point of view* or *context* is the author writing?

III. Occasion, Genre, Context
   • What was the *occasion* for this text?
   • What *genre* is this text?
   • What is the *cultural* or *historical context* for this text?

CRITICAL RESPONSE

   • Is the overall purpose clear or muddled?
   • Was the actual purpose different from the stated purpose?
   • How did the text actually affect you?

   • Are you part of the intended audience?
   • Does the author misjudge the reader's knowledge or beliefs?
   • Examine your own personal or cultural bias or point of view. How does that hinder you from being a critical reader of this text?

   • What ideas or conversation was taking place on this topic?
   • Does the author's chosen genre help achieve the purpose for the audience?
   • What passages show the cultural forces at work on the author and the text?

DESCRIPTION

IV. Thesis and Main Ideas
- What key *question* or *problem* does the author/text address?
- What is the author's *thesis?*
- What *main ideas* support the thesis?
- What are the key passages or key moments in the text?

V. Organization and Evidence
- Where does the author *preview* the essay's organization?
- How does the author *signal* new sections of the essay?
- What kinds of *evidence* does the author use (personal experience, descriptions, statistics, interviews, other authorities, analytical reasoning, or other)?

VI. Language and Style
- What is the author's *tone* (casual, humorous, ironic, angry, preachy, academic, or other)?
- Are *sentences* and *vocabulary* easy, average, or difficult?
- What key *words* or *images* recur throughout the text?

CRITICAL RESPONSE

- Where is the thesis stated?
- Are the main ideas related to the thesis?
- Where do you agree or disagree?
- Does the essay have contradictions or errors in logic?
- What ideas or arguments does the essay omit or ignore?
- What experience or prior knowledge do you have about the topic?
- What are the implications or consequences of the essay's ideas?

- At what point could you accurately predict the organization of the essay?
- At what points were you confused about the organization?
- What evidence was most or least effective?
- Where did the author rely on assertions rather than on evidence?
- Which of your own personal experiences did you recall as you read the essay?

- Did the tone support or distract from the author's purpose or meaning?
- Did the sentences and vocabulary support or distract from the purpose or meaning?
- Did recurring words or images relate to or support the purpose or meaning?

Remember that not all these questions will be relevant to any given essay or text, but one or two of these questions may suggest a direction or give a *focus* to your overall response. When one of these questions suggests a focus for your response to the essay, *go back to the text, to other texts, and to your experience* to gather *evidence* and *examples* to support your response.

GUIDELINES FOR CLASS DISCUSSION

Class discussions are an important part of the reading, writing, and discussing process. Often, however, class discussions are not productive because not everyone knows the purpose of the discussion or how to discuss openly and fairly. Following is a suggested list of goals for class discussion. Read them carefully. Make notes about any suggestions, revisions, or additions for your class. Your class will then review these goals and agree to adopt, modify, or revise them for your own class discussions for the remainder of the semester.

Discussion Goals

1. To understand and accurately represent the views of the author(s) of an essay. The first discussion goal should be to summarize the author's views fairly.
2. To understand how the views and arguments of individual authors relate to each other. Comparing and contrasting different authors' views help clarify each author's argument.
3. To encourage all members of the class to articulate their understanding of each essay and their response to the ideas in each essay. Class discussions should promote multiple responses rather than focus on a single "right" interpretation or response.
4. To hear class members' responses in an open forum. All points of view must be recognized. *Discussions in class should focus on ideas and arguments, not on individual class members.* Class members may attack ideas but not people.
5. To relate class discussions to the assigned reading/writing task. What effective writing strategies are illustrated in the essay the class is discussing? How can class members use any of these strategies in writing their own essays?

TECHNIQUES   SUMMARIZING/RESPONDING   PROCESSES

Summarizing and Responding to an Essay

Following is an essay by Barbara Ehrenreich, "Teach Diversity—with a Smile." First, write for five minutes on the suggested Prereading Journal Entry that precedes the essay. The purpose of the journal entry is to allow you to collect your thoughts about the subject *before* you read Ehrenreich's essay. You will be a much more responsive reader if you reflect on your experiences and articulate your opinions *before* you are influenced by the author and her text. If possible, discuss your experiences and opinions with your classmates after you write your entry but before you read the essay. Next, read the introductory note about Barbara Ehrenreich to understand her background and the context for the essay. Finally, practice active reading techniques as you read. Read first for information and enjoyment. Then, reread with a pen in your hand. Either write your comments and questions directly in the text or do a double-entry log, summarizing the main ideas on one side of a piece of paper and writing your questions and reactions on the other.

PREREADING JOURNAL ENTRY

Describe the ethnic groups of people who live in your neighborhood or who attended your previous school. List all the groups you can recall. Then choose one of the following terms and briefly explain what it means: *diversity, multiculturalism,* or *political correctness.* Finally, describe one personal experience that taught you something about diversity or political correctness. What was the experience and how did you react?

PROFESSIONAL WRITING

Teach Diversity—with a Smile

Barbara Ehrenreich

Barbara Ehrenreich was born in Butte, Montana, in 1941 and received a B.A. degree from Reed College and a Ph.D. from Rockefeller University. She has been a health policy adviser and a professor of health sciences, but since 1974, she has spent most of her time writing books and articles about socialist and feminist issues. She has received a Ford Foundation Award and a Guggenheim Fellowship for her writings, which include The Worst Years of Our Lives: Irreverent Notes from a Decade of Greed *(1990),* The Snarling Citizen: Essays *(1995), and* Nickel and Dimed: On (Not) Getting by in America *(2001). Her articles and essays have appeared in* Esquire, Mother Jones, Ms., New Republic, The New York Times Magazine, *and* Time. *The following essay on cultural diversity appeared in* Time *magazine.*

Something had to replace the threat of communism, and at last a workable   *1*
substitute is at hand. "Multiculturalism," as the new menace is known, has
been denounced in the media recently as the new McCarthyism, the new
fundamentalism, even the new totalitarianism—take your choice. According to its critics, who include a flock of tenured conservative scholars, multiculturalism aims to toss out what it sees as the Eurocentric bias in
education and replace Plato with Ntozake Shange and traditional math
with the Yoruba number system. And that's just the beginning. The
Jacobins of the multiculturalist movement, who are described derisively as
P.C., or politically correct, are said to have launched a campus reign of terror against those who slip and innocently say "freshman" instead of "fresh-
person," "Indian" instead of "Native American" or, may the Goddess
forgive them, "disabled" instead of "differently abled."

So you can see what is at stake here: freedom of speech, freedom of   *2*
thought, Western civilization and a great many professorial egos. But before we get carried away by the mounting backlash against multiculturalism, we ought to reflect for a moment on the system that the P.C. people
aim to replace. I know all about it; in fact it's just about all I *do* know, since
I—along with so many educated white people of my generation—was a
victim of monoculturalism.

American history, as it was taught to us, began with Columbus's "dis-   *3*
covery" of an apparently unnamed, unpeopled America, and moved on to
the Pilgrims serving pumpkin pie to a handful of grateful red-skinned
folks. College expanded our horizons with courses called Humanities or
sometimes Civ, which introduced us to a line of thought that started with
Homer, worked its way through Rabelais and reached a poignant climax in
the pensées of Matthew Arnold. Graduate students wrote dissertations on
what long-dead men had thought of Chaucer's verse or Shakespeare's dra-
mas; foreign languages meant French or German. If there had been high
technology in ancient China, kingdoms in black Africa or women anywhere, at any time, doing anything worth noticing, we did not know it, nor
did anyone think to tell us.

Our families and neighborhoods reinforced the dogma of monocul-   *4*
turalism. In our heads, most of us '50s teenagers carried around a social
map that was about as useful as the chart that guided Columbus to the "Indies." There were "Negroes," "whites" and "Orientals," the latter meaning
Chinese and "Japs." Of religions, only three were known—Protestant,
Catholic and Jewish—and not much was known about the last two types.
The only remaining human categories were husbands and wives, and that

...continued Teach Diversity—with a Smile, **Barbara Ehrenreich**

was all the diversity the monocultural world could handle. Gays, lesbians, Buddhists, Muslims, Malaysians, Mormons, etc. were simply off the map.

So I applaud—with one hand, anyway—the multiculturalist goal of 5 preparing us all for a wider world. The other hand is tapping its fingers impatiently, because the critics are right about one thing: when advocates of multiculturalism adopt the haughty stance of political correctness, they quickly descend to silliness or worse. It's obnoxious, for example, to rely on university administrations to enforce P.C. standards of verbal inoffensiveness. Racist, sexist and homophobic thoughts cannot, alas, be abolished by fiat but only by the time-honored methods of persuasion, education and exposure to the other guy's—or, excuse me, woman's—point of view.

And it's silly to mistake verbal purification for genuine social reform. 6 Even after all women are "Ms." and all people are "he or she," women will still earn only 65¢ for every dollar earned by men. Minorities by any other name, such as "people of color," will still bear a hugely disproportionate burden of poverty and discrimination. Disabilities are not just "different abilities" when there are not enough ramps for wheelchairs, signers for the deaf or special classes for the "specially" endowed. With all due respect for the new politesse, actions still speak louder than fashionable phrases.

But the worst thing about the P.C. people is that they are such poor 7 advocates for the multicultural cause. No one was ever won over to a broader, more inclusive view of life by being bullied or relentlessly "corrected." Tell a 19-year-old white male that he can't say "girl" when he means "teen-age woman," and he will most likely snicker. This may be the reason why, despite the conservative alarms, P.C.-ness remains a relatively tiny trend. Most campuses have more serious and ancient problems: faculties still top-heavy with white males of the monocultural persuasion; fraternities that harass minorities and women; date rape; alcohol abuse; and tuition that excludes all but the upper fringe of the middle class.

So both sides would be well advised to lighten up. The conservatives 8 ought to realize that criticisms of the great books approach to learning do not amount to totalitarianism. And the advocates of multiculturalism need to regain the sense of humor that enabled their predecessors in the struggle to coin the term P.C. years ago—not in arrogance but in self-mockery.

Beyond that, both sides should realize that the beneficiaries of 9 multiculturalism are not only the "oppressed peoples" on the standard

P.C. list (minorities, gays, etc.). The "unenlightened"—the victims of monoculturalism—are oppressed too, or at least deprived. Our educations, whether at Yale or at State U, were narrow and parochial and left us ill-equipped to navigate a society that truly is multicultural and is becoming more so every day. The culture that we studied was, in fact, *one* culture and, from a world perspective, all too limited and ingrown. Diversity is challenging, but those of us who have seen the alternative know it is also richer, livelier and ultimately more fun.

■ ■ ■

SUMMARIZING   EXAMPLE SUMMARY   RESPONDING   EXAMPLE RESPONSE

SUMMARIZING

The purpose of a summary is to give a reader a condensed and objective account of the main ideas and features of a text. Usually, a summary has between one and three paragraphs or one hundred to three hundred words, depending on the length and complexity of the original essay and the intended audience and purpose. Typically, a summary will do the following:

- **Cite the author and title of the text.** In some cases, the place of publication or the context for the essay may also be included.

- **Indicate the main ideas of the text.** Accurately representing the main ideas (while omitting the less important details) is the major goal of a summary.

- **Use direct quotation of key words, phrases, or sentences.** *Quote* the text directly for a few key ideas; *paraphrase* the other important ideas (that is, express the ideas in your own words).

- **Include author tags.** ("According to Ehrenreich" or "as Ehrenreich explains") to remind the reader that you are summarizing the author and the text, not giving your own ideas. *Note:* Instead of repeating "Ehrenreich says," choose verbs that more accurately represent the purpose or tone of the original passage: "Ehrenreich argues," "Ehrenreich explains," "Ehrenreich warns," "Ehrenreich asks," "Ehrenreich advises."

- **Avoid summarizing specific examples or data** unless they help illustrate the thesis or main idea of the text.

- **Report the main ideas as objectively as possible.** Represent the author and text as accurately and faithfully as possible. Do not include your reactions; save them for your response.

> " Inferences about the writer's intentions appear to be an essential building block—one that readers actively use to construct a meaningful text. "
>
> —LINDA FLOWER,
> AUTHOR OF "THE CONSTRUCTION OF PURPOSE"

SUMMARIZING **EXAMPLE SUMMARY** RESPONDING EXAMPLE RESPONSE

SUMMARY OF "TEACH DIVERSITY— WITH A SMILE"

Following is a summary of Ehrenreich's essay. Do *not* read this summary, however, until you have tried to write your own. After you have made notes and written a draft for your own summary, you will more clearly understand the key features of a summary. *Note:* There are many ways to write a good summary. If your summary conveys the main ideas and has the features described previously, it may be just as good as the following example. (Key features of a summary are annotated in the margin.)

Title and author

Main idea

Paraphrase

Context for essay

Author tag

Direct quotations

Main idea

Paraphrase

Author tag

Main idea

Paraphrase

In "Teach Diversity—with a Smile," journalist Barbara Ehrenreich explains the current conflict between people who would like to replace our Eurocentric bias in education with a multicultural approach and those critics and conservative scholars who are leading the backlash against multiculturalism and "political correctness." Writing for [readers of *Time* magazine] Ehrenreich uses her own experience growing up in the 1950s to explain that her narrow education left her a "victim of monoculturalism," ill-equipped to cope with America's growing cultural diversity. Ehrenreich applauds multiculturalism's goal of preparing people for a culturally diverse world, but she is impatient at the "haughty stance" of the P.C. people because they mistake "verbal purification for genuine social reform" and they arrogantly bully people and "correct" their language. Since actions speak louder than words, Ehrenreich argues, the multiculturalists should focus more on genuine social reform—paying equal salaries to men and women, creating access for people with disabilities, and reducing date rape and alcohol abuse. The solution to the problem, according to Ehrenreich, is for both sides to "lighten up." The conservatives should recognize that criticizing the great books of Western civilization is not totalitarian, and the multiculturalists should be less arrogant and regain their sense of humor.

SUMMARIZING EXAMPLE SUMMARY **RESPONDING** EXAMPLE RESPONSE

RESPONDING

A response requires your reaction and interpretation. Your own perspective—your experiences, beliefs, and attitudes—will guide your particular response. Your response, as the Viuti cartoon illustrates, may be totally different from another reader's

VIUTI
Buenos Aires
ARGENTINA

Cartoonists & Writers Syndicate

VIUTI

Cartoonists & Writers Syndicate

response, but that does not necessarily make yours better or worse. Good responses say what you think, but then they *show why* you think so. They show the relationships between your opinions and the text, between the text and your experience, and between this text and other texts.

Depending on its purpose and intended audience, a response to a text can take several directions. Responses may focus on one or more of the following strategies. Consider your purpose and audience or check your assignment to see which type(s) you should emphasize.

> Reading the world always precedes reading the word, and reading the word implies continually reading the world.
>
> —PAULO FREIRE
> AUTHOR OF *LITERACY: READING THE WORD AND THE WORLD*

TYPES OF RESPONSES

- **Analyzing the effectiveness of the text.** In this case, the response analyzes key features such as the clarity of the main idea, the rhetorical situation, the organization of the argument, the logical reasoning of an argument, the quality of the supporting evidence, and/or the effectiveness of the author's style, tone, and voice.

- **Agreeing and/or disagreeing with the ideas in the text.** Often responders react to the ideas or the argument of the essay. In this case, the responders show why they agree and/or disagree with what the author/text says.
- **Interpreting and reflecting on the text.** The responder explains key passages or examines the underlying assumptions or the implications of the ideas. Often, the responder reflects on how his or her own experiences, attitudes, and observations relate to the text.

Analyzing, agreeing/disagreeing, and interpreting are all slightly different directions that a response may take. But regardless of the direction, responses must be supported by evidence, examples, facts, and details. A responder cannot simply offer an opinion or agree or disagree. Good responses draw on several kinds of supporting evidence.

KINDS OF EVIDENCE

- **Personal experience.** Responders may use *examples* from their personal experiences to show why they interpreted the text as they did, why they agreed or disagreed, or why they reacted to the ideas as they did.
- **Evidence from the text.** Responders should cite *specific phrases or sentences* from the text to support their explanation of a section, their analysis of the effectiveness of a passage, or their agreement or disagreement with a key point.
- **Evidence from other texts.** If appropriate, responders may bring in ideas and information from other relevant essays, articles, books, or graphic material.

Not all responses use all three kinds of supporting evidence, but all responses *must* have sufficient examples to support the responder's ideas, reactions, and opinions. Responders should not merely state their opinions. They must give evidence to *show* how and why they read the text as they did.

One final—and crucial—point about responses: A response should make a coherent, overall main point. It should not be just a laundry list of reactions, likes, and dislikes. Sometimes the main point is that the text is not convincing because it lacks evidence. Sometimes the overall point is that the text makes an original statement even though it is difficult to read. Perhaps the basic point is that the author/text stimulates the reader to reflect on his or her experience. Every response should focus on a coherent main idea.

RESPONSE TO "TEACH DIVERSITY— WITH A SMILE"

Following is one possible response to Ehrenreich's essay. Before you read this response, however, write out your own reactions. You need to decide what you think before other responses influence your reading. There are, of course, many different but legitimate responses to any given essay. As you read this response, note the marginal annotations indicating the different types of responses and the different kinds of evidence this writer uses.

What I like best about Barbara Ehrenreich's article is her effective use of personal experience to clarify the issues on both sides of the multiculturalism debate. However, her conclusion, that we should "lighten up" and accept diversity because it's "more fun," weakens her argument by ignoring the social inequalities at the heart of the debate. The issue in this debate, I believe, is not just enjoying diversity, which is easy to do, but changing cultural conditions, which is much more difficult.

Analyzing effectiveness of text

Responder's main point

Ehrenreich effectively uses her own experiences—and her common sense—to let us see both the virtues and the excesses of multiculturalism. When she explains that her monocultural education gave her a social map that was "about as useful as the chart that guided Columbus to the 'Indies,'" she helps us understand how vital multicultural studies are in a society that is more like a glass mosaic than a melting pot. Interestingly, even her vocabulary reveals—perhaps unconsciously—her Western bias: *Jacobins, pensées, fiat,* and *politesse* are all words that reveal her Eurocentric education. When Ehrenreich shifts to discussing the P.C. movement, her commonsense approach to the silliness of excessive social correctness ("the other guy's—or, excuse me, woman's—point of view") makes us as readers more willing to accept her compromise position.

Evidence from text

Evidence from text

My own experience with multiculturalism certainly parallels Ehrenreich's impatience with the "haughty stance" of the P.C. people. Of course, we should avoid racist and sexist terms and use our increased sensitivity to language to reduce discrimination. But my own backlash began several years ago when a friend said I shouldn't use the word *girl.* I said, "You mean, not ever? Not even for a ten-year-old female child?" She replied that the word had been so abused by people referring to a "woman" as a "girl" that the word *girl* now carried too many sexist connotations. Although I understood my friend's point, it seems that *girl* should still be a perfectly good word for a female child under the age of twelve. Which reminds me of a book I saw recently, *The Official Politically Correct Dictionary.* It is loaded with examples of political correctness out of control: Don't say *bald,*

Reflecting on the text

Personal experience

Evidence from other texts

say *hair disadvantaged.* Don't use the word *pet,* say *nonhuman companion.* Don't call someone *old,* say that they are *chronologically gifted.*

Analyzing effectiveness of text

Ehrenreich does recommend keeping a sense of humor about the P.C. movement, but the conclusion to her essay weakens her argument. Instead of focusing on her earlier point that "it's silly to mistake verbal purification for genuine social reform," she advises both sides to lighten up and have fun with the diversity around us. Instead, I wanted her to conclude by reinforcing her point that "actions still speak louder than fashionable phrases." Changing the realities of illiteracy, poverty, alcohol abuse, and sexual harassment should be the focus of the multiculturalists. Of course, changing language is crucial to changing the world, but the language revolution has already happened—or at least begun. Ehrenreich's article would be more effective, I believe, if she concluded her essay with a call for both sides to help change cultural conditions rather than with a reference to the silly debate about what to call a teenage woman.

Responder's main point

▮ WARMING UP: Journal Exercises

The following topics will help you practice your reading and responding.

1. Study the painting by Diego Rivera, *The Flower Carrier,* at the beginning of this chapter. Then use your search engine or library databases to find out information about the work of Diego Rivera. What are major themes in his art? What is his attitude toward workers and how is that reflected in this portrait? How does Rivera's style and message compare to a similar image by Dorothea Lange in Chapter 6?

2. If you have a community-service learning project in your class, go to your agency or organization and collect texts, images, and brochures that advertise the organization or explain its mission. Choose one or two documents and write a summary and response addressed both to your classmates and to the organization itself. Consider the rhetorical context of these documents (author, purpose, audience, occasion, genre, and cultural context) as you explain why they are or are not effective or appropriate and/or how you interpret the assumptions and implications contained in these texts or images. Your goal is to provide constructive suggestions about ways to revise or improve these texts.

3. Study the print by Maurits Escher reproduced here. How many different ways of perceiving this picture can you see? Describe each perspective. How is "reading" this picture similar to reading a printed text? How is it different?

Day and Night by M. C. Escher. © 1997 Cordon Art-Baarn-Holland.
All rights reserved.

4. Because previewing material is an important part of active reading, most recent psychology and social science textbooks use previewing or prereading strategies at the beginning of each new chapter. Find one chapter in a textbook that uses these previewing techniques. How does the author preview the material? Does the preview help you understand the material in the chapter?

5. Reading the following paragraph illustrates how our prior experience can combine with our predictions to make meaning. The following passage describes a common procedure in our lives. Read the passage. Can you identify the procedure?

> The procedure is actually quite simple. First, you arrange things into different groups. Of course, one pile may be sufficient depending on how much there is to do. If you have to go somewhere else because of lack of facilities, that is the next step; otherwise you are pretty well set. It is important not to overdo things. That is, it is better to do too few things at once than too many. In the short run this may not seem important, but complications can easily arise. A mistake can be expensive as well. At first, the whole procedure will seem complicated. Soon, however, it will become just another facet of life. It is difficult to foresee any end to the necessity for this task in the immediate future, but then one can never tell. After the procedure is completed, one arranges the materials into different groups again. Then they can be put into their appropriate places. Eventually, they will be used once

more, and the whole cycle will then have to be repeated. However, that is part of life.

As you read, record your guesses. What words helped to orient you? Where did you make wrong guesses? Discuss your reactions in class.

6. Reprinted below is a letter written by Margaret Atwood, which appeared in *The Nation*. The editors of *The Nation* had asked several foreign writers and political commentators to "share their reflections" about the debate concerning America's foreign policy. An award-winning Canadian novelist, Margaret Atwood has written many volumes of poetry and short fiction as well as over a dozen novels, including *Surfacing* (1973), *The Handmaid's Tale* (1986), and *Oryx and Crake* (2003). Read her "Letter to America," and then write your own summary and response to her ideas.

LETTER TO AMERICA
Margaret Atwood

Dear America:

This is a difficult letter to write, because I'm no longer sure who you are. Some of you may be having the same trouble.

I thought I knew you: We'd become well acquainted over the past fifty-five years. You were the Mickey Mouse and Donald Duck comic books I read in the late 1940s. You were the radio shows—*Jack Benny, Our Miss Brooks*. You were the music I sang and danced to: the Andrews Sisters, Ella Fitzgerald, the Platters, Elvis. You were a ton of fun.

You wrote some of my favorite books. You created Huckleberry Finn, and Hawkeye, and Beth and Jo in *Little Women,* courageous in their different ways. Later, you were my beloved Thoreau, father of environmentalism, witness to individual conscience; and Walt Whitman, singer of the great Republic; and Emily Dickinson, keeper of the private soul. You were Hammett and Chandler, heroic walkers of mean streets; even later, you were the amazing trio, Hemingway, Fitzgerald and Faulkner, who traced the dark labyrinths of your hidden heart. You were Sinclair Lewis and Arthur Miller, who, with their own American idealism, went after the sham in you, because they thought you could do better.

You were Marlon Brando in *On the Waterfront,* you were Humphrey
Bogart in *Key Largo,* you were Lillian Gish in *Night of the Hunter.*
You stood up for freedom, honesty and justice; you protected the
innocent. I believed most of that. I think you did, too. It seemed
true at the time.

You put God on the money, though, even then. You had a way of
thinking that the things of Caesar were the same as the things of
God: That gave you self-confidence. You have always wanted to be a
city upon a hill, a light to all nations, and for a while you were. Give
me your tired, your poor, you sang, and for a while you meant it.

We've always been close, you and us. History, that old entangler, has
twisted us together since the early seventeenth century. Some of us
used to be you; some of us want to be you; some of you used to be
us. You are not only our neighbors: In many cases—mine, for
instance—you are also our blood relations, our colleagues and our
personal friends. But although we've had a ringside seat, we've never
understood you completely, up here north of the 49th parallel. We're
like Romanized Gauls—look like Romans, dress like Romans, but
aren't Romans—peering over the wall at the real Romans. What are
they doing? Why? What are they doing now? Why is the haruspex
eyeballing the sheep's liver? Why is the soothsayer wholesaling the
Bewares?

Perhaps that's been my difficulty in writing you this letter. I'm not
sure I know what's really going on. Anyway, you have a huge posse
of experienced entrail-sifters who do nothing but analyze your every
vein and lobe. What can I tell you about yourself that you don't
already know?

This might be the reason for my hesitation: embarrassment,
brought on by a becoming modesty. But it is more likely to be
embarrassment of another sort. When my grandmother—from a
New England background—was confronted with an unsavory topic,
she would change the subject and gaze out the window. And that is
my own inclination: Keep your mouth shut, mind your own
business.

But I'll take the plunge, because your business is no longer merely
your business. To paraphrase Marley's Ghost, who figured it out too

late, mankind is your business. And vice versa: When the Jolly Green Giant goes on the rampage, many lesser plants and animals get trampled underfoot. As for us, you're our biggest trading partner: We know perfectly well that if you go down the plug-hole, we're going with you. We have every reason to wish you well.

I won't go into the reasons why I think your recent Iraqi adventures have been—taking the long view—an ill-advised tactical error. By the time you read this, Baghdad may or may not be a pancake, and many more sheep entrails will have been examined. Let's talk, then, not about what you're doing to other people but about what you're doing to yourselves.

You're gutting the Constitution. Already your home can be entered without your knowledge or permission, you can be snatched away and incarcerated without cause, your mail can be spied on, your private records searched. Why isn't this a recipe for widespread business theft, political intimidation and fraud? I know you've been told that all this is for your own safety and protection, but think about it for a minute. Anyway, when did you get so scared? You didn't used to be easily frightened.

You're running up a record level of debt. Keep spending at this rate and pretty soon you won't be able to afford any big military adventures. Either that or you'll go the way of the USSR: lots of tanks, but no air conditioning. That will make folks very cross. They'll be even crosser when they can't take a shower because your shortsighted bulldozing of environmental protections has dirtied most of the water and dried up the rest. Then things will get hot and dirty indeed.

You're torching the American economy. How soon before the answer to that will be not to produce anything yourselves but to grab stuff other people produce, at gunboat-diplomacy prices? Is the world going to consist of a few mega-rich King Midases, with the rest being serfs, both inside and outside your country? Will the biggest business sector in the United States be the prison system? Let's hope not.

If you proceed much further down the slippery slope, people around the world will stop admiring the good things about you. They'll decide that your city upon the hill is a slum and your democracy is a sham, and therefore you have no business trying to impose your sullied vision on them. They'll think you've abandoned the rule of law. They'll think you've fouled your own nest.

The British used to have a myth about King Arthur. He wasn't dead, but sleeping in a cave, it was said: and in the country's hour of greatest peril, he would return. You too have great spirits of the past you may call upon: men and women of courage, of conscience, of prescience. Summon them now, to stand with you, to inspire you, to defend the best in you. You need them.

PROFESSIONAL WRITING

Vows

Christopher Caldwell

A senior editor at The Weekly Standard, *Christopher Caldwell is a prolific journalist and a regular contributor to dozens of newspapers and magazines, including the* Financial Times, *the* New York Times, *the* Wall Street Journal, Commentary, *the* National Review, *and the* Washington Post. *When he is not writing about cultural and political relationships between Europe and the United States, he reviews popular and controversial books. In this book review, Caldwall summarizes and responds to the arguments in Jonathan Rauch's recent book,* Gay Marriage: Why It Is Good for Gays, Good for Straights, and Good for America *(2004). As you read his review, consider your own views about same-sex marriage but also evaluate Caldwell's response. Does Caldwell's summary represent Rauch's arguments clearly? Does his response include analysis of Rauch's argument, points where he agrees or disagrees with Rauch, and/or interpretations or examination of the implications of Rauch's ideas?*

The average American views same-sex marriage as a bad idea whose time   1
has come. Solid majorities—generally around two-thirds—oppose it. But now that Vermont has introduced "civil unions" for gays, Belgium and the Netherlands have legalized gay marriages and courts have mandated them in both Ontario and Massachusetts, stopping gay marriage appears to require measures (like an amendment to the Constitution) more reactionary than Americans will countenance. What opponents of single-sex marriage

...continued Vows, **Christopher Caldwell**

have failed miserably to do is enunciate a rationale for blocking it that the country can rally behind.

There's a reason for that, according to the veteran Washington journalist Jonathan Rauch. Most arguments against gay marriage, he writes in a closely argued new polemic, are "overblown, at best, often just fanciful, and sometimes hypocritical." Worse, they ignore the possibility that gays, once admitted to marriage, would have a stake in defending its traditions.

Some people may support same-sex marriage only as a roundabout means to recognition for gays. Not Rauch. Gay himself, he seeks it because he wants to get married, and thinks everyone should. His idea of marriage is old-school, even sentimental. ("I mean two souls bonded in each other's eyes and together clasped to their community's bosom.") Of those gays who fear that marriage will force them to trade in a libertine lifestyle for a bourgeois heterosexual one, Rauch says, "I believe that they are largely right, and that gay integration into the mainstream would be, on balance, a good thing."

Marriage has a "special power" to bind people into communities and into other families, Rauch thinks. Its two primary purposes are setting young adults into a web of commitments and providing caregivers to the old and infirm. Since homosexuals can and do carry out the responsibilities of marriage, they deserve to accede to its rights. A marriage regime that excludes homosexuals "no longer accords with liberal justice or the meaning of marriage as it is practiced today." Neither, Rauch writes, do Vermont-style civil unions (which he calls "marriage-lite") and corporate partnership plans (which he thinks should be abolished the moment gay marriage is passed). These not only keep gays stranded on a different plane of citizenship but also threaten to undermine marriage for straights. Should a legal challenge make them universally available, they will compete with the marriages they're meant to defend.

So while traditionalists complain that marriage is embattled, and while gay activists complain that marriage is unfair, Rauch insists that marriage is embattled because it's unfair. When gays can marry, they will appear in a new light—as allies, not interlopers; relations between gays and straights will improve, because what makes homosexuals appear most "grotesque and threatening" is not their sexual orientation but the outlawry against convention to which the unavailability of marriage consigns them. For Rauch, the best way to defend marriage is by letting gays in, not keeping them out.

But even if gays deserve the right to marry, can they be given their due   6
without altering marriage? Over the course of several chapters, Rauch
holds up to close examination some key arguments used to defend the marital status quo. There is, for instance, what he calls the "Anything Goes" argument, which holds that if gay marriage is allowed, then polygamists and
incestuous pairs will demand marriage under the same logic. Rauch's reply
is that incestuous marriage "is an option no one needs and no one even
seems to want," and that Americans will easily recognize that polygamy
does considerably more damage to a liberal-democratic order than his own
preferred policy of "one person, one spouse" possibly could. To the "Men
Behaving Badly" argument—that what "settles" men is not the institution
of marriage but the need to negotiate a modus vivendi with women—he
narrows the discussion to adultery and finds the jury still out. Even if gay
men are more likely to cheat on their partners than heterosexuals, Rauch
points out, there would be a clear net gain to society in having them disciplined into discretion by a marital vow.

Rauch's points do not close any arguments. Strands of two large   7
American religions, Islam and Mormonism, will surely demand polygamy
once gay marriage passes; and the question of whether women help settle
men might look different if Rauch used the lens of, say, substance abuse or
violence. But his discussion is enough to reassure anyone not already dug
in against gay marriage. Even more important, it puts on display his arguing style, an appealing combination of prosecutorial logic and gentlemanly
forbearance. Rauch strains to find merit even in the positions of intemper-
ate talk-show hosts. He neither twists words nor tweaks statistics. He takes
pains not to leave angles unexamined.

And yet he commits an important error of emphasis, which is not fa-   8
tal to his case for gay marriage but damages his case that gay marriage can
be traditional marriage. It concerns the importance of childbearing. "I
hope I won't be accused of saying that children are a trivial reason for marriage," he says early in the book. "They just cannot be the only reason." It
is true that marriage has historically served many purposes. But alongside
that of providing a nonanarchic context for producing children, they all
look like moons against Jupiter. Rauch hates this argument. He finds it "in-
coherent, incorrect and antimarriage." He is happy to speak of the welfare
of children, but skirts the production of children, dismissing it as a "sex-
centered view."

Rauch is not being prudish, only unreasonable. "If the possibility   9
of procreation is what gives meaning to marriage," he writes, "then a

postmenopausal woman who applies for a marriage license should be turned away at the courthouse door. What's more, she should be hooted at and condemned for breaking the crucial link between marriage and procreation." Not necessarily. The state's reluctance to engage in purposeless Maoist persecution of the infertile does not mean the state has no interest in fertility. (And, in fact, traditional marriage has been consistently heartless towards infertile heterosexuals, particularly women.)

Rauch believes the argument-from-procreation is made in bigoted bad faith. "Well, there is one thing no homosexual couple can do, and that is to procreate," he writes. "So gay-marriage opponents come back time and again, at the outset and then as a last resort, to the claim that marriage is inseparable from procreation." That word "So" contains an accusation. And it is not a slip, for Rauch writes elsewhere, "With the rise of the gay-marriage debate, another view has come to the fore: marriage is about children." Rauch has this exactly backward. Far from being a recent pretext, the idea that marriage is about producing children is an ancient understanding, and a steadily weakening one.   10

Those who make this argument today are guilty only of failing to re-examine ideas that have passed down from earlier understandings of marriage. That is why they claim to be defending "tradition." Traditional society never had any reason to marry gays, even in periods of relative tolerance, because it never had any need for homosexual sex. Nor does it today. What has happened to render gay marriage suddenly more logical is society's waning need for married people's sex. Sex, childbearing and childrearing—which marriage once bound as tightly as an atomic nucleus—have been disaggregated. This has happened partly through law (on divorce and adoption), partly through technology (contraception, abortion and artificial insemination), partly through convention (cohabitation) and partly through knowledge (on the innateness of homosexuality, for instance).   11

Rauch may have too high an opinion of the sort of marital club that would have gays as members. It seems unlikely that marriage could simultaneously be flexible enough to admit homosexuals and rigid enough to offer them the same protection and rights (and discipline) it offered heterosexuals in the old days. But it seems even less likely that, as Rauch hopes, the gay-marriage movement will be able to shore up an institution that has for decades been undermined legally, socially, medically, theolog-   12 ically, philosophically, psychologically and politically. Gays will soon accede to marriage, but only because marriage is losing its old set of purposes and is becoming, irrevocably, something else.

■ ■ ■

vo·cab·u·lar·y

In your journal, write the meaning of the italicized words in the following phrases.

- new *polemic* **(2)**
- a *libertine* lifestyle **(3)**
- deserve to *accede* to its rights **(4)**
- as allies, not *interlopers* **(5)**
- *incestuous* marriage **(6)**
- negotiate a *modus vivendi* with women **(6)**
- disciplined into *discretion* **(6)**
- providing a *nonanarchic* context **(8)**
- made in *bigoted* bad faith **(10)**
- have been *disaggregated* **(11)**
- on the *innateness* of homosexuality **(11)**

QUESTIONS FOR WRITING AND DISCUSSION

1. Analyze yourself as a reader and responder to arguments about same-sex marriage. First, consider your own background and beliefs. What are your parents' religious, political, and cultural beliefs on this issue, and how do your beliefs differ? What experiences have shaped your beliefs on this issue? Second, would you describe yourself as a person in favor of same-sex marriage, a person in favor of a compromise position such as civil unions, a person in favor of having individual states decide the issue rather than favoring a constitutional amendment, or a person who is, as Caldwell says, "already dug in against gay marriage?"

2. Based on your answer to question 1, how has your reading of this article and your previous reading and conversation on this topic altered your beliefs? What passages in this article provided new ideas, arguments, or issues that you had not previously considered? How did they affect your position?

3. Review the strategies for summary given earlier in the chapter. Which of those strategies (cite author and title, accurately represent main ideas, use direct quotation for key ideas, include author tags, and report ideas objectively) does Caldwell model? Find at least one example from his review illustrating each of those techniques.

4. After reviewing the chapter's discussion of types of responses and kinds of evidence, comment on Caldwell's response to Rauch's argument. Find two examples where Caldwell analyzes the effectiveness of Rauch's argument. Find two passages where Caldwell either agrees or disagrees with Rauch. Find at least one passage where Caldwell offers an interpretation or reflects on the implications of Rauch's argument. Based on your analysis, how effective is Caldwell's response to Rauch? Explain.

5. The cultural context and the ongoing conversation surrounding a topic are important parts of the rhetorical situation surrounding any controversial topic. Use your library's online full-text databases (such as EBSCO or Lexis Nexis) to find at least three other reviews of Jonathan Rauch's book. What other ideas or arguments from Rauch's book do those reviewers cite that Caldwell omits? Examine the responses of the reviewers. How are their responses similar to or different from Caldwell's? Illustrate those similarities or differences by citing at least two examples from each of the other reviews. Are the responses more conservative or more liberal than Caldwell's? How do those responses reflect the policies of the magazines or newspapers in which they appear?

PROFESSIONAL WRITING

Responses to the Intergovernmental Panel on Climate Change

The importance of critical reading, interpretation, and responding is dramatically illustrated today in our ongoing debate and conversation about global warming and climate change. Although most people are familiar with popular representations of climate change (such as Al Gore's An Inconvenient Truth*), discussions of climate change actually begin with scientific research reports—the so-called "primary texts." These texts focus on data collection and hypothesis testing. The next step is the collection and synthesis of hundreds of scientific docu-*

ments into a single document that describes overall trends. The reports of the Intergovernmental Panel on Climate Change (IPCC) represent this next step of synthesis, with added interpretations and conclusions. Articles and editorials that comment on scientific articles and the IPCC reports are "secondary texts," and are more interpretive, more opinionated, and often more important for guiding public opinion and setting public policy.

The following selection of texts moves from a summary and response to the fourth IPCC Report written by the editor of Environmental Science & Technology *magazine to several editorials and articles that appeared in magazines and newspapers. As you read each of these short articles, ask the following questions: How much of each article is devoted to summarizing and how much to response? Does the summary give sufficient and detailed information about the IPCC report? Does the response focus on the data and conclusions from the IPCC report? Does it consider related political, cultural, or environmental issues? Does the response reflect a known bias of the author or of the magazine or journal? What is that bias? What key questions and issues emerge from the ongoing conversation about climate change?*

The IPCC Fourth Assessment

Jerald L. Schnoor, Editor
Environmental Science & Technology

Will history show that February 2, 2007, marked the beginning of the end   1
of the fossil-fuel age? That's when the scientific basis of the Intergovernmental Panel on Climate Change's (IPCC's) Fourth Assessment Report (AR4) was unveiled in Paris. It also may be the day when we first took seriously the threat of human-induced global warming, the gravest environmental problem of our time.

Climate Change 2007: The Physical Science Basis AR4 from Working   2
Group 1 is a consensus report written by 150 authors from 100 countries and vetted by 600 reviewers. It states, with 90% certainty, that human activities, especially the burning of fossil fuels, have *caused* global warming during the past 50 years. Predicting a warming for the 21st century of 2.0–4.5 °C, it narrows the range of 1.4–5.8 °C from the Third Assessment

Report. The tone of the assessment has become more strident (and certain) with each report:

". . . the observed increase could be largely due to this natural variability; alternatively this variability and other human factors could have offset a still larger human-induced greenhouse warming."—IPCC First Assessment Report, 1990

"The balance of evidence suggests a discernible human influence on global climate."—IPCC Second Assessment Report, 1995

"There is new and stronger evidence that most of the warming over the last 50 years is attributable to human activities."—IPCC Third Assessment Report, 2001

Despite the fact that these reports are *consensus* documents, the reality   3
is still lost on many Americans. The Bush Administration has done an amazingly effective job of creating confusion where little existed. And the press has contributed to the fiasco by "fair and balanced" reporting, that is, by always finding an opposing quotation despite the lack of support for its research content or the questionable credentials of the interviewee.

AR4 tracks 20 climate models from groups all over the world. Unan-   4
imous agreement exists among model results that the 21st century will be significantly warmer. Modelers disagree only on exactly how much warmer it will be. Understanding climate sensitivity to increasing CO_2 is still crucial, and the uncertainties are narrowing.

Like a vigilant lawyer, the report lays out multiple lines of evidence as   5
to how we know that humans are causing global warming: satellite corroboration of land surface warming, parallel ocean warming and commensurate sea-level rise, stratospheric cooling, increasing nighttime minimum temperatures, and melting ice shelves and glaciers.

Why is AR4 so important? For the first time, it seeks to define "dan-   6
gerous climate interference". Earth's vulnerabilities include the potential disintegration of Greenland and Antarctic ice sheets, increased storm severity, rapidly rising sea levels, and shutdown of the thermohaline circulation in the North Atlantic. Most researchers estimate that those effects initiate at 2 °C of total warming. Because we have already experienced 0.6 °C of warming and we likely have already loaded an additional ~1.0 °C of warming into the sluggish climate system, we don't have much leeway before anthropogenic interference becomes dangerous. That is why nations must begin to reduce emissions within the next decade or so.

Drastic measures are needed—an −80% cut in emissions to stabilize   *7*
the atmospheric concentration of CO_2 at 550 ppmv by 2100 (a doubling
from preindustrial times). The Kyoto Protocol was designed to achieve a
reduction of a few percent, and it will fall short of that target. Eighty percent is a formidable goal, a much greater challenge than sending a man to
the moon or rebuilding Europe and Japan after World War II. It is *the* environmental challenge defining our century and future generations.

Actually, I'm optimistic that (finally) we are beginning to accept and   *8*
respond to the challenge. Bob Dylan sang that you don't need a weather-
man to know which way the wind blows and, for the first time, you can feel
the winds shifting. Companies in the EU, North America, Japan, and even
China are announcing their own emission reduction programs; states are
passing legislation to serve as incubators for greenhouse-gas mitigation;
and people understand that emitting CO_2 has consequences and that
there's a price to pay. The much-debated Stern report from the U.K., *The
Economics of Climate Change*, states that price: 5–20% of gross world product (GWP) if we fail to act, compared with 1% of GWP if we respond now.
I believe even the laggard U.S. will enact a cap-and-trade program within
the next year.

In case you missed the nuance, the release of the IPCC report coin-   *9*
cided with Groundhog Day in the U.S., the day when that awkward furry
animal wakes from hibernation to predict what the weather will be in the
future. Let's hope the U.S. can make the right choice.

Planet Gore

Editor
National Review

The U.N.'s Intergovernmental Panel on Climate Change (IPCC) has re-   *1*
leased a summary of its latest report. The release has had the intended effect: generating fresh gloom and doom about global warming. The *New
York Times* described the report as "a grim and powerful assessment of the
future of the planet." Meteorologists who dissent from the "consensus" on
warming are already being ostracized. And the chairman of the IPCC,
Rajendra Pachauri, has said, quite forthrightly, "I hope this report will
shock people."

The shock, however, is that the latest summary contains very little that *2* was not in the IPCC's last report, in 2001. What is new, moreover, is a retreat from earlier, gloomier claims. Notwithstanding the authors' bold assertion of 90 percent confidence that human activity causes warming, it appears from the short summary of the full report that there has been only slight progress over the past five years in refining our climate models and resolving key uncertainties.

The 2001 report identified twelve factors in climate "forcings" (i.e., *3* factors such as greenhouse-gas emissions, clouds, and solar radiation that "force" temperatures higher or lower). These twelve factors went into the computer models to generate predictions about future warming, but the IPCC said in 2001 that the level of scientific understanding for seven of the twelve factors was "very low." Most of the seven are significant "negative forcings" that cool the planet, and may be underestimated in climate models. The new report has consolidated the twelve factors into just nine; yet the IPCC still says our level of understanding is "low" or "medium-low" for six of the nine.

Gone from the latest summary is the infamous "hockey stick" of the *4* 2001 report. This was a graphic purporting to show that the planet is warmer today than at any time in the last thousand years, a demonstration that required erasing the inconvenient medieval warm period. The new IPCC report has also reduced its estimate of the human influence on warming by one-third (though this change was not flagged for the media, so few news accounts took notice of it). That reduction is one reason the IPCC narrowed the range of predicted future warming, and lowered the new midpoint—i.e., the most likely temperature increase—by half a degree, from 3.5 degrees Celsius in 2001 to 3 degrees in this report. The new assessment also cuts in half the range of predicted sea-level rise over the next century. Now the maximum prediction is about 17 inches, as compared with the 20 to 30 feet Al Gore dramatizes in his horror film. (Which truths are inconvenient now?) There are murmurs from the green warriors that the new report is a disappointment, and no wonder.

Keep in mind that this summary covers only one of the three IPCC *5* working groups that will report their findings later this year. Good news for insomniacs: The three complete reports, covering science, impacts, and mitigation, will run to nearly 5,000 pages. The IPCC's release of only one summary in advance of the complete reports is a clear attempt to spin the media.

Climate change is real—the world is warming modestly, and this fact *6* should be taken seriously. But the continuing panic of Gore & Co. in the face of growing evidence that previous predictions were exaggerated and politicized should bolster the position of those who advocate sensible climate policy. Such policy would emphasize development of new energy technologies, and eschew the starvation diet of the Kyoto Protocol.

On the Climate Change Beat, Doubt Gives Way to Certainty

William K. Stevens
The New York Times

In the decade when I was the lead reporter on climate change for this *1* newspaper, nearly every blizzard or cold wave that hit the Northeast would bring the same conversation at work.

Somebody in the newsroom would eye me and say something like, "So *2* much for global warming." This would often, but not always, be accompanied by teasing or malicious expressions, and depending on my mood the person would get either a joking or snappish or explanatory response. Such an exchange might still happen, but now it seems quaint. It would be out of date in light of a potentially historic sea change that appears to have taken place in the state and the status of the global warming issue since I retired from *The New York Times* in 2000.

Back then I wrote that one day, if mainstream scientists were right *3* about what was going on with the earth's climate, it would become so obvious that human activity was responsible for a continuing rise in average global temperature that no other explanation would be plausible.

That day may have arrived. *4*

Similarly, it was said in the 1990s that while the available evidence of *5* a serious human impact on the earth's climate might be preponderant enough to meet the legal test for liability in a civil suit, it fell short of the more stringent "beyond a reasonable doubt" test of guilt in a criminal case.

Now it seems that the steadily strengthening body of evidence about *6* the human connection with global warming is at least approaching the higher standard and may already have satisfied it.

The second element of the sea change, if such it is, consists of a *7* demonstrably heightened awareness and concern among Americans about

... *continued* On the Climate Change Beat, Doubt Gives Way to Certainty, **William K. Stevens**

global warming. The awakening has been energized largely by dramatic reports on the melting Arctic and by fear—generated by the spectacular horror of Hurricane Katrina—that a warmer ocean is making hurricanes more intense.

I've been avidly watching from the sideline as the strengthening evidence of climate change has accumulated, not least the discovery that the Greenland ice cap is melting faster than had been thought. The implications of that are enormous, though the speed with which the melting may catastrophically raise sea levels is uncertain—as are many aspects of what a still hazily discerned climatic future may hold. *8*

Last week, in its first major report since 2001, the world's most authoritative group of climate scientists issued its strongest statement yet on the relationship between global warming and human activity. The Intergovernmental Panel on Climate Change said the likelihood was 90 percent to 99 percent that emissions of heat-trapping greenhouse gases like carbon dioxide, spewed from tailpipes and smokestacks, were the dominant cause of the observed warming of the last 50 years. In the panel's parlance, this level of certainty is labeled "very likely." *9*

Only rarely does scientific odds-making provide a more definite answer than that, at least in this branch of science, and it describes the endpoint, so far, of a progression: *10*

In 1990, in its first report, the panel found evidence of global warming but said its cause could be natural as easily as human.

In a landmark 1995 report, the panel altered its judgment, saying that "the balance of evidence suggests a discernible human influence on global climate."

In 2001, it placed the probability that human activity caused most of the warming of the previous half century at 66 percent to 90 percent—a "likely" rating.

And now it has supplied an even higher, more compelling seal of numerical certainty, which is also one measure of global warming's risk to humanity.

To say that reasonable doubt is vanishing does not mean there is no doubt at all. Many gaps remain in knowledge about the climate system. Scientists do make mistakes, and in any case science continually evolves and changes. That is why the panel's findings, synthesized from a vast body of scientific studies, are generally couched in terms of probabilities and sometimes substantial margins of error. So in the recesses of the mind, *11* there remains a little worm of caution that says all may not be as it seems, or that the situation may somehow miraculously turn around—or, for that matter, that it may turn out worse than projected.

In several respects, the panel's conclusions have gotten progressively *12* stronger in one direction over almost two decades, even as many of its hundreds of key members have left the group and new ones have joined. Many if not most of the major objections of contrarians have evaporated as science works its will, although the contrarians still make themselves heard.

The panel said last week that the fact of global warming itself could *13* now be considered "unequivocal," and certified that 11 of the last 12 years were among the 12 warmest on record worldwide. (The fact of the warming is one thing contrarians no longer deny.)

But perhaps the most striking aspect of the 2007 report is the sheer *14* number and variety of directly observed ways in which global warming is already having a "likely" or "very likely" impact on the earth.

In temperate zones, the frequency of cold days, cold nights and frosts *15* had diminished, while the frequency of hot days, hot nights and heat waves has increased. Droughts in some parts of the world have become longer and more intense. Precipitation has decreased over the subtropics and most of the tropics, but increased elsewhere in the Northern and Southern Hemispheres.

There have been widespread increases in the frequency of "heavy pre- *16* cipitation events," even in areas where overall precipitation has gone down. What this means is that in many places, it rains and snows less often but harder—well-documented characteristics of a warming atmosphere. Remember this in the future, when the news media report heavy, sometimes catastrophic one-day rainfalls—four, six, eight inches—as has often happened in the United States in recent years. Each one is a data point in a trend toward more extreme downpours and the floods that result.

All of these trends are rated 90 percent to 99 percent likely to continue. *17*

The list goes on. *18*

And for the first time, in the wake of Hurricane Katrina, the panel re- *19* ported evidence of a trend toward more intense hurricanes since 1970, and said it was likely that this trend, too, would continue.

Some of the panel's main conclusions have remained fairly stable over *20* the years. One is that if greenhouse gas emissions continue unabated, they will most likely warm the earth by about 3 to 7 degrees Fahrenheit by the end of this century, with a wider range of about 2 to 12 degrees possible.

The warming over the Northern Hemisphere is projected to be higher than the global average, as is the case for the modest one-degree warming observed in the last century.

The projected warming is about the same as what the panel estimates would be produced by a doubling of atmospheric concentrations of greenhouse gases, compared with the immediate preindustrial age. It would also be almost as much warming as has occurred since the depths of the last ice age, 20,000 years ago. *21*

Some experts believe that no matter what humans do to try to rein in greenhouse gas emissions, a doubling is all but inevitable by 2100. In this view, the urgent task ahead is to keep them from rising even higher. *22*

If the concentrations were to triple, and even if they just double, there is no telling at this point what the world will really be like as a result, except to speculate that on balance, most of its inhabitants probably won't like it much. If James E. Hansen, one of the bolder climate scientists of the last two decades, is right, they will be living on a different planet. *23*

It has been pointed out many times including by me, that we are engaged in a titanic global experiment. The further it proceeds, the clearer the picture should become. At age 71, I'm unlikely to be around when it resolves to everyone's satisfaction—or dissatisfaction. Many of you may be, and a lot of your descendants undoubtedly will be. *24*

Good luck to you and to them. *25*

Global Warming and Hot Air

Robert J. Samuelson
The Washington Post

You could be excused for thinking that we'll soon do something serious about global warming. Last Friday, the Intergovernmental Panel on Climate Change (IPCC)—an international group of scientists—concluded that, to a 90 percent probability, human activity is warming the Earth. Earlier, Democratic congressional leaders made global warming legislation a top priority; and 10 big U.S. companies (including General Electric and DuPont) endorsed federal regulation. Strong action seems at hand. *1*

Don't be fooled. The dirty secret about global warming is this: We have no solution. About 80 percent of the world's energy comes form fos- *2* sil fuels (coal, oil, natural gas), the main sources of man-made greenhouse gases. Energy use sustains economic growth, which—in all modern societies—buttresses political and social stability. Until we can replace fossil fuels or find practical ways to capture their emissions, governments will not sanction the deep energy cuts that would truly affect global warming.

Considering this reality, you should treat the pious exhortations to "do *3* something" with skepticism, disbelief or contempt. These pronouncements are (take your pick) naive, self-interested, misinformed, stupid or dishonest. Politicians mainly want to be seen as reducing global warming. Companies want to polish their images and exploit markets created by new environmental regulations. As for editorialists and pundits, there's no explanation except superficiality or herd behavior.

Anyone who honestly examines global energy trends must reach these *4* harsh conclusions. In 2004, world emissions of carbon dioxide (CO_2, the main greenhouse gas) totaled 26 billion metric tons. Under plausible economic and population assumptions, CO_2 emissions will grow to 40 billion tons by 2030, projects the International Energy Agency. About three-quarters of the increase is forecast to come from developing countries, two-fifths from China alone. The IEA expects China to pass the United States as the largest source of carbon dioxide by 2009.

Poor countries won't sacrifice economic growth—lowering poverty, *5* fostering political stability—to placate the rich world's global warming fears. Why should they? On a per-person basis, their carbon dioxide emissions are only about one-fifth the level of rich countries. In Africa, less than 40 percent of the population even has electricity.

Nor will existing technologies, aggressively deployed, rescue us. The *6* IEA studied an "alternative scenario" that simulated the effect of 1,400 policies to reduce fossil fuel use. Fuel economy for new U.S. vehicles was assumed to increase 30 percent by 2030; the global share of energy from "renewables" (solar, wind, hydropower, biomass) would quadruple, to 8 percent. The result: by 2030, annual carbon dioxide emissions would rise 31 percent instead of 55 percent. The concentration levels of emissions in the atmosphere (which presumably cause warming) would rise.

Since 1850, global temperatures have increased almost 1 degree *7* Celsius. Sea level has risen about seven inches, though the connection is unclear. So far, global warming has been a change, not a calamity. The IPCC projects wide ranges for the next century: temperature increases from 1.1 degrees Celsius to 6.4 degrees; sea level rises from seven inches to almost two feet. People might easily adapt; or there might be costly disruptions (say, frequent flooding of coastal cities resulting from melting polar ice caps).

...continued Global Warming and Hot Air, **Robert J. Samuelson**

I do not say we should do nothing, but we should not delude ourselves. 8
In the United States, the favored remedy is "cap and trade." It's environmental grandstanding—politicians pretending they're doing something.

Companies would receive or buy quotas ("caps") to emit carbon diox- 9
ide. To exceed the limits, they'd acquire some other company's unused
quotas ("trade"). How simple. Just order companies to cut emissions. Businesses absorb all the costs.

But in practice, no plausible "cap and trade" program would signifi- 10
cantly curb global warming. To do that, quotas would have to be set so low
as to shut down the economy. Or the cost of scarce quotas would skyrocket
and be passed along to consumers through much higher energy prices.
Neither outcome seems likely. Quotas would be lax. The program would
be a regulatory burden with little benefit. It would also be a bonanza for
lobbyists, lawyers and consultants, as industries and localities besieged
Washington for exceptions and special treatment. Hello, influence-
peddling and sleaze.

What we really need is a more urgent program of research and devel- 11
opment, focusing on nuclear power, electric batteries, alternative fuels and
the capture of carbon dioxide. Naturally, there's no guarantee that socially
acceptable and cost-competitive technologies will result. But without
them, global warming is more or less on automatic pilot. Only new technologies would enable countries—rich and poor—to reconcile the immediate imperative of economic growth with the potential hazards of climate
change.

Meanwhile, we could temper our energy appetite. I've argued before 12
for a high oil tax to prod Americans to buy more fuel-efficient vehicles.
The main aim would be to limit insecure oil imports, but it would also
check CO2 emissions. Similarly, we might be better off shifting some of
the tax burden from wages and profits to a broader tax on energy or carbon. That would favor more fuel-efficient light bulbs, appliances and industrial processes.

It's a debate we ought to have—but probably won't. Any realistic re- 13
sponse would be costly, uncertain and no doubt unpopular. That's one truth
too inconvenient for almost anyone to admit.

vo·cab·u·lar·y

In your journal, write the meanings of the italicized words in the following phrases.

"The IPCC Fourth Assessment"

- *vetted* by 600 reviewers **(2)**
- has become more *strident* **(2)**
- due to this natural *variability* **(2)**
- contributed to the *fiasco* **(3)**
- satellite *corroboration* of land and surface warming **(5)**
- shutdown of the *thermohaline* circulation **(6)**
- *anthropogenic* interference **(6)**
- greenhouse-gas *mitigation* **(8)**

"Planet Gore"

- who *dissent* from the "consensus" **(1)**
- already being *ostracized* **(1)**
- has *consolidated* the twelve factors **(3)**
- the *infamous* "hockey stick" **(4)**
- *purporting* to show **(4)**
- clear attempt to *spin* the media **(5)**
- *eschew* the starvation diet **(6)**

"On the Climate Change Beat"

- may *catastrophically* raise sea levels **(8)**
- *synthesized* from a vast body of scientific studies **(11)**
- generally *couched* in terms of probabilities **(11)**
- major objections of *contrarians* **(12)**
- be considered *"unequivocal"* **(13)**
- if greenhouse gas emissions continue *unabated* **(20)**

"Global Warming and Hot Air"

- the *pious exhortations* **(3)**
- as for editorialists and *pundits* **(3)**
- *placate* the rich world's global warming fears **(5)**
- has been a change, not a *calamity* **(7)**
- we should not *delude* ourselves **(8)**
- the immediate *imperative* of economic growth **(11)**

QUESTIONS FOR WRITING AND DISCUSSION

1. In a group in class or on your online forum, choose one of the above articles and analyze it for the summary skills presented earlier in this chapter. Where does the author cite the original IPCC study? Where does the author give the main ideas of the IPCC report? Does the author use paraphrase and direct quotations from the report? Does the writer use author tags for the report or for other commentators? If the writer uses specific data or examples, do these details support the main ideas of the report? Does the writer accurately and objectively represent the ideas in the report?

2. Analyze each of the articles in this section for its balance of summary and response. In each article, how many paragraphs are devoted to summary of the IPCC report? How many paragraphs focus on response or contain statements of opinion? Do some paragraphs contain both summary and response? Explain.

3. In Jerald L. Schnoor's editorial in *Environmental Science & Technology*, he says, in paragraph 3, that the press has contributed to the confusion about global warming by "always finding an opposing quotation" despite the lack of credible evidence for an opposing view. Review all of the articles in this section. Which authors take a one-sided view? Which articles discuss alternative or opposing viewpoints? Are those opposing views credible? Are there always two sides to every argument, or are there multiple "sides"? Analyze each article or editorial for its presentation of alternate or opposing views.

4. Climate change debates focus primarily on three issues: the degree to which the planet is warming and will continue to warm; the consequences of this warming; and what should be done to slow or prevent this warming. Analyze each of the articles above for its focus on these three issues. Which articles focus primarily on the first two issues? Which articles focus on the third issue? Is the focus of the debate about climate changing? Explain.

5. Using your library's databases or reliable Internet sites such as that sponsored by the Environmental Protection Agency, research the latest information about climate change, its probable effects, and ideas to reduce carbon emissions. How has the conversation or the focus of the debate changed since the last IPCC report? Write your own summary and response to one or more articles or editorials that you discover.

Reading and Writing Processes

ASSIGNMENT FOR READING/WRITING

Write an essay that summarizes and then responds to one or more essays, articles, or advertisements. As you review your particular assignment, make sure you understand what text or texts you should respond to, how long your summary and response should be, and what type(s) of responses you should focus on.

Your purpose for this assignment is to represent the text(s) accurately and faithfully in your summary and to explain and support your response. Taken together, your summary and response should be a coherent essay, with a main idea and connections between summary and response. Assume that your audience is other members of the class, including the instructor, with whom you are sharing your reading.

Your instructor's assignment should indicate your audience and appropriate genres. You need to know your intended audience in order to decide and what kinds of evidence will make your analysis and response convincing and how detailed your summary should be. If your audience is not familiar with your text, for example, you'll need a more detailed summary. Typically, responses take the form of an essay, but a letter to the editor may be appropriate.

CHOOSING   COLLECTING   SHAPING   OUTLINING   DRAFTING   REVISING

CHOOSING A SUBJECT

Suggested processes, activities, and strategies for reading and writing will be illustrated in response to the following essay by Dudley Erskine Devlin.

PROFESSIONAL WRITING

Teaching Tolerance in America

Dudley Erskine Devlin

Dudley Erskine Devlin was born in Syracuse, New York, and attended the University of Kansas. Originally trained as a scientist, he currently teaches English at Colorado State University and writes columns and editorials on contemporary problems. The targets for his editorials are often the large and complicated issues of the day, such as education, violence, health care, and the media. "My first goal as a writer," Devlin said in a recent interview, "is to provoke response. If just one reader is angry enough to write me a letter of response, then my time is not wasted." As you read Devlin's essay, note places where you agree or disagree with his ideas. How would you respond to Devlin's argument?

In the past few years, American high schools have struggled with a variety   1
of forces that have threatened to tear them apart: reduced funding, increased class sizes, fewer music and art classes, violence in schools, and racial and class divisions among students. Although educational reform in America tends to focus on curriculum issues, class sizes, and security issues, one lesson seems increasingly hard to teach—helping students appreciate and welcome differences in culture, racial heritage, and personal identity. Despite the emphasis on increasing respect and tolerance in schools, teenagers still bring the social and racial divisions found in society at large back into the halls of high schools across America. Social cliques based on race, gender, athletic prowess, income, social class, dress, and even body piercings still define the culture at most schools.

America, we fervently believe, is still the land of opportunity, the land   2
where we can be judged on our merits and achievements, not on stereotypes or preconceptions or prejudices. Yet the social clique is based on the notion that one group imagines it is superior to another and thus can ridicule, taunt, or even bully another group. And nowhere does the social clique have more devastating and long-lasting effects than in our high schools.

High school cliques, which reproduce the class divisions found in so-   3
ciety, originate from three distinct sources: racial differences, gender differences, and social differences. Racial problems in high schools need no explanation. Every high school in America has racial problems that have led to continuing conflicts. A reporter visiting one typical suburban high

school found that each ethnic group—Hispanics, whites, blacks, Asians—had a place where they gathered between classes and after school. Although individual members in an ethnic group gain security from being in the group, they make outsiders—people who do not belong to their racial group—feel insecure and often threatened. As one student put it, "The problem is that some people think they are better than others. So they make disparaging remarks about one another, creating tension and conflict in the school."

The ongoing gender problems in America's high schools are mentioned—if at all—on the back pages of newspapers, as if the sexist treatment of girls is a normal and inconsequential behavior. Nan Stein, author of *Classrooms and Courtrooms: Facing Sexual Harassment in K-12 Schools,* recounts numerous incidents where school administrations overlook student-on-student sexual harassment. In a recent interview with *Harvard Educational Letter,* Stein recalled a case in which "15 boys harassed this one girl verbally, mooing like cows whenever they saw her and talking about the size of her breasts. They did this outside of school, in school, on the way to school. Other kids heard it and saw it. Teachers and custodians told the administrator, who kept saying, 'It's not a big deal.'" When the case involves males of status, the chances are even more likely that school administrators will look the other way. Ignoring the flagrant behavior of the popular students happens at every school in America—despite a recent Supreme Court ruling that now holds schools liable in such cases of sexual harassment.

Finally, the differences in social classes among the various cliques—most notably between the jocks and the geeks, between the powerful and the weak—is a continuing source of conflict. As one student put it, "If you're not a jock in this school . . . you're not part of it." The outsiders, geeks, and gays are ridiculed by everyone and harassed, bullied, and picked on by the jocks and by other members of the elite social class. Bullying is sometimes connected to cliques and gangs, and it affects both boys and girls. Allan Beane, author of *The Bully-Free Classroom,* writes that he has "heard from so many adults who are still very angry and hurt from when they were mistreated in school." Frequently school bullies are boys—and the ridicule and intimidation they inflict has played a role, Beane says, in "almost all of the school shootings that have outraged the nation in the past two years." Hara Marano, an editor for *Psychology Today,* points out that girls, too, engage in physical aggression even though they are "more apt to be masters of indirect bullying, spreading lies and rumors and destroying reputations." The result is that about one in seven schoolchildren is either a bully or a victim of bullying.

How do we solve these problems? First we need to eliminate those liberal solutions that simply aren't working—thus releasing funds for more effective deterrents. Many schools, for example, have introduced diversity issues into English and social studies classes, and some schools even have sensitivity training classes that seek to "instill respect for others and training students how to speak up when they hear insulting or intimidating comments." However, most students react negatively to such classes. In a recent report, one student said that he really didn't like having notions of tolerance and acceptance drilled into him: "It's like shoving something down our throats." Besides, we want students to be able to express their feelings—if more students were like John Rocker of the Atlanta Braves, then we would have more of these problems out in the open.   6

There are, however, some real and sensible solutions that could solve the intolerance problem in our high schools. For years, parents and educators have recommended that schools adopt uniforms, so that every student wears the same clothing to school. Already, many schools ban specific colors or types of hats, shirts, or jewelry. We need uniforms not just to eliminate gangs, but to reduce the visual cues that enable one group to maintain social power. And we need to enforce those dress rules with a zero tolerance policy. Second, schools need to make single-sex classes a standard practice. Not only do boys and girls learn better in single-sex environments, but the segregated classes will reduce the differences and thus reduce conflicts. Finally, schools need to improve security—both to protect students from the outside and to protect students from each other. Schools need more video cameras, drug sniffing dogs, and spot checks of cars and lockers. Governor Jesse Ventura had an excellent idea when he suggested that every school needs to have teachers with paramilitary and anti-riot training. Last but not least, students need to wear picture ID tags hung on ribbons around their necks—so videotapes can easily identify any troublemakers.   7

The class system that is created and perpetuated by student cliques is the most important problem in our high schools today. In any high school on any day, we see the strong picking on the weak, the bullies intimidating the outcasts, and the jocks and the social elite dominating everyone else. Only when we apply our zero tolerance policy to the dress code, the gender makeup of our classes, and the security of our schools will students learn how to treat all people and social classes with acceptance and tolerance.   8

| CHOOSING | **COLLECTING** | SHAPING | OUTLINING | DRAFTING | REVISING |

COLLECTING

Once a text or texts have been selected or assigned for your summary and response, try the following reading, writing, and discussing activities.

PREREADING JOURNAL ENTRY

In your journal, write what you already know about the subject of the essay. The following questions will help you to recall your prior experiences and think about your own opinions before you read the essay. The purpose of this entry is to think about your own experiences and opinions *before* you are influenced by the arguments of the essay.

- What classes or programs at your high school were designed to improve tolerance of social differences among students? Did they increase or decrease tolerance for social, sexual, or racial difference among students at your school?

- Were cliques a big problem at your school? Did your high school have bullies who picked on other students? Were the jocks or the upper-class students given preferential treatment?

- What measures to increase security, reduce potential violence, and increase tolerance has your high school taken in the last few years? Were these changes necessary? Did they improve the quality of your education? Did they make you feel more secure at school?

▌**TEXT ANNOTATION**   Most experts on reading and writing agree that you will learn more and remember more if you actually write out your comments, questions, and reactions in the margins of the text you are reading. Writing your responses helps you begin a conversation with the text. Reproduced below are one reader's marginal responses to paragraph 7 of Devlin's essay.

Second, schools need to make single-sex classes a (standard practice.) Not only do

Why not have them optional for some subjects?

boys and girls learn better in single-sex environments, but the segregated classes

will reduce the differences and thus reduce conflicts. Finally, schools need to

In the real world men and women work together, so why not start now?

improve security—both to protect students from the outside and to protect

A few cameras will pro-
vide security, but spot
checks invade our
privacy.

What? Schools are not
wrestling arenas and we
don't have riots.

Students should not be
treated like jail inmates!

students from each other. Schools need more video cameras, drug sniffing dogs, and spot checks of cars and lockers. Governor Jesse Ventura had an excellent idea when he suggested that every school needs to have teachers with paramilitary and anti-riot training. Last but not least, students need to wear picture ID tags hung on ribbons around their necks—so videotapes can easily identify any trouble-makers.

■ **READING LOG**   A reading log, like text annotation, encourages you to inter-act with the author/text and write your comments and questions as you read. While text annotation helps you identify specific places in the text for commentary, a read-ing log encourages you to write out longer, more thoughtful responses. In a reading log, you can keep a record of your thoughts *while you read and reread* the text. Often, reading-log entries help you focus on a key idea to develop later in your response.

Below is one reader's response to Devlin's ideas about single-sex classes and bullying.

> I attended a private elementary school and junior high where a school uni-form was required and some of the classes were single-sex. Personally, I can say that the uniform did not make a bit of difference where bullying was an issue. Kids still made fun of other kids no matter what they were wear-ing. The real reason that kids make fun of others is because of social dif-ferences and because they themselves do not want to be picked on, so they deflect the attention onto others.
>
> It is true that bullying is carried on with people throughout life, which is why there should be no tolerance at all for teasing. For example, I was talking with a very good friend of mine who told me that he is still haunted by memories of when children would call him a "fag" on the playground. This has affected him for a long time, and he is still fearful of admitting his homosexuality because he feels as if he is letting the bullies win and proving that they were right.

CHOOSING   COLLECTING   **SHAPING**   OUTLINING   DRAFTING   REVISING

SHAPING

Summaries and responses have several possible shapes, depending on the writer's purpose and intended audience. Keep in mind, however, that in a summary/

Avoiding Plagiarism

Plagiarism is knowingly and deliberately using the language, ideas, or visual materials from another person or text without acknowledging that person or source. Use the following guidelines to avoid plagiarism.

- Do not use language, ideas, or graphics from any essay, text, or visual image that you find online, in the library, or from commercial sources without acknowledging the source.
- Do not use language, ideas, or visual images from any other student's essay without acknowledging the source.

Students who deliberately plagiarize typically fail the course and face disciplinary action by the university.

Sometimes, however, students plagiarize out of carelessness or inadequately citing words, specific languages, ideas, or visual images. You can avoid this *inadvertent* plagiarism by learning how to quote accurately from your sources, how to paraphrase using your own words, and how to cite your sources accurately. In this chapter, you will learn how to quote accurately, to paraphrase without plagiarizing, and to use author tags to indicate your sources. In addition, Chapter 7, "Investigating," and Chapter 13, "Writing a Research Paper," have examples illustrating how to do in-text citation and how to do a Works Cited page.

The best way to avoid inadvertent plagiarism is to ask your instructor how to document a source you are using. Your instructor will help you with conventions of direct quotation, paraphrasing, and in-text reference or citation.

---

response essay or critique, *the summary and the response should be unified by the writer's overall response.* The summary and the response may be organized or drafted separately, but they are still parts of one essay, focused on the writer's most important or overall response.

CHOOSING   COLLECTING   **SHAPING**   OUTLINING   DRAFTING   REVISING

SUMMARY SHAPING

Summaries should convey the main ideas, the essential argument, or the key features of a text. The purpose should be to represent the author's/text's ideas as accurately and as faithfully as possible. Summaries rely on description, paraphrase, and direct quotation. Below are definitions and examples for each of these terms.

DESCRIPTION   The summary should *describe* the main features of an essay, including the author and title, the context or place of publication of the essay (if appropriate), the essay's thesis or main argument, and any key text features, such as sections, chapters, or important graphic material.

In the article "Teaching Tolerance in America," Dudley Erskine Devlin reports some disturbing issues concerning America's high schools. Devlin states that intimidation, through dress, social cliques, gender, and race, is causing tension and danger in high schools today. According to Devlin, sexual harassment is allowed and condoned, and that in some cases jocks bully geeks and racial and social groups intimidate one another. As a solution, Devlin suggests that schools enforce strict, zero-tolerance dress codes, segregate the sexes in classes, increase security through surveillance cameras and drug-sniffing dogs, and require students to wear photo IDs.

■ PARAPHRASE   A paraphrase restates a passage or text in different words. The purpose of a paraphrase is to recast the author's/text's words in your own language. A good paraphrase retains the original meaning without plagiarizing from the original text.

ORIGINAL: High school cliques, which reproduce the class divisions found in society, originate from three distinct sources: racial differences, gender differences, and social differences.

PARAPHRASE: Peer groups in high school mirror society's class distinctions, which stem from differences in race, gender, and social status.

PLAGIARISM: Peer groups in high school *reproduce the class divisions found in society* and come *from three distinct sources: race, gender, and social differences.* [This is plagiarism because the writer uses exact phrases (see italics) from the original without using quotation marks.]

■ DIRECT QUOTATION   Often, summaries directly quote a few key phrases or sentences from the source. *Remember: Any words or phrases within the quotation marks must be accurate, word-for-word transcriptions of the original.* Guidelines for direct quotation and examples are as follows. Use direct quotations sparingly to convey the key points in the essay:

> Devlin focuses on what he believes is the school system's largest problem today, the issue of "helping students appreciate and welcome differences in culture, racial heritage, and personal identity."

Use direct quotations when the author's phrasing is more memorable, more concise, or more accurate than your paraphrase might be:

> Devlin claims that teenagers "still bring the social and racial divisions found in society at large back into the halls of high schools across America."

Use direct quotations for key words or phrases that indicate the author's attitude, tone, or stance:

> According to Devlin, we should "eliminate those liberal solutions that simply aren't working" in order to fund his solutions.

Don't quote long sentences. Condense the original sentence to the most important phrases. Use just a short phrase from a sentence or use an ellipsis (three spaced points . . .) to indicate words that you have omitted.

ORIGINAL: Although educational reform in America tends to focus on curriculum issues, class sizes, and security issues, one lesson seems increasingly hard to teach—helping students appreciate and welcome differences in culture, racial heritage, and personal identity.

CONDENSED QUOTATION: Educational reform, according to Devlin, should focus less on curriculum issues and class sizes and more on helping students "appreciate . . . differences in culture, racial heritage, and personal identity."

CHOOSING   COLLECTING   **SHAPING**   OUTLINING   DRAFTING   REVISING
SAMPLE SUMMARIES

Following are summaries of Devlin's essay written by two different readers. Notice that while both convey the main ideas of the essay by using description, paraphrase, and direct quotation, they are not identical. Check each summary to see how well it meets these guidelines:

- Cite the author and title of the text.
- Indicate the main ideas of the text.
- Use direct quotation of key words, phrases, or sentences.
- Include author tags.
- Do not summarize most examples or data.
- Be as accurate, fair, and objective as possible.

Summary 1

Dudley Erskine Devlin's essay "Teaching Tolerance in America" addresses several hot topics concerning the American public school system. Devlin focuses on what he believes is the school system's largest problem today, the issue of "helping students appreciate and welcome differences in culture, racial heritage, and personal identity." According to Devlin, the root of the problem lies within the social clique, particularly the social cliques found inside the halls of your local high school. According to Devlin, these cliques originate from three different sources: social, racial, and gender differences. Devlin suggests that we solve the problems these cliques create by eliminating "those liberal solutions that simply aren't working—thus releasing funds for more effective deterrents." Devlin's solutions to eradicate the intolerance are to impose dress codes or uniforms, to create single-sex classrooms, and to markedly increase security at every high school.

Summary 2

The idea of social reform in education has been a pressing issue given the increase in youth violence in high schools across America. In Dudley Erskine Devlin's article "Teaching Tolerance in America," he outlines some of the problems in schools caused by members of cliques and bullies who feed on the "racial differences, gender differences, and social differences" found in society at large. Devlin's argument then moves on to attack the "liberal solutions" (such as introducing diversity issues in classes) and proposes to replace them with "more effective deterrents" such as instituting single-sex classes, school uniforms, picture IDs, and heightened security measures. This zero-tolerance policy, Devlin believes, will teach students how to accept diversity and "appreciate and welcome differences in culture, racial heritage, and personal identity."

CHOOSING   COLLECTING   **SHAPING**   OUTLINING   DRAFTING   REVISING
RESPONSE SHAPING

Strategies for organizing a response depend on the purpose of the response. Typically, responses include one or more of the following three purposes:

- Analyzing the effectiveness of the text.
- Agreeing and/or disagreeing with the ideas in the text.
- Interpreting and reflecting on the text.

As the following explanations illustrate, each of these types of responses requires supporting evidence from the text, from other texts, and/or from the writer's own experience.

ANALYZING   Analysis requires dividing a whole into its parts in order to better understand the whole. In order to analyze a text for its effectiveness, start by examining key parts or features of the text, such as the purpose, the intended audience, the thesis and main ideas, the organization and evidence, and the language and style. Notice how the following paragraph analyzes Devlin's illogical argument.

> Devlin's essay has some clear problems with the logic of his argument. The title of his essay is "Teaching Tolerance in America," but his solutions contradict his stated purpose. Devlin's proposal to tighten security in our high schools is not going to teach tolerance in high schools across America. As a teenager in a post-Columbine era, I can tell you that ID card checks, patrolling security officers, and hall monitors do not create an atmosphere conducive to teaching tolerance. Students who are treated like prisoners in a maximum security ward do not feel increased warm wishes to faculty and administrators nor are they more likely to tolerate differences in their classmates. Being watched like a hawk by a hall monitor does nothing to make a person more socially outgoing or more tolerant of difference. These security measures will increase fear during the school hours and not encourage tolerance once students leave the school grounds. In short, Devlin's solutions do not, in fact, solve the problems with tolerance created by racial, gender, or social differences.

▌ AGREEING/DISAGREEING

Often, a response to a text focuses on agreeing and/or disagreeing with its major ideas. Responses may agree completely, disagree completely, or agree with some points but disagree with others. Responses that agree with some ideas but disagree with others are often more effective because they show that the responder sees both strengths and weaknesses in an argument. In the following paragraphs, notice how the responder agrees and disagrees and then supports each judgment with evidence.

> About Devlin's recommendation that schools can "reduce conflicts" and teach tolerance by creating single-sex classrooms, I have mixed feelings. From my own personal experience, I agree that single-sex classes can have benefits. Perhaps I am biased, but attending an all-girls high school was very beneficial for me and many of my classmates. Although I have always been a very outgoing individual, I watched many of my friends grow from timid, shy freshmen to independent, strong women. Furthermore, I was never sexually harassed by a classmate, nor did I hear of any of the kinds of harassment Devlin mentions. On the other hand, however, I must disagree with Devlin that single-sex classes are a long-term solution. In the real world, women and men constantly interact, so they need to learn how to positively interact as girls and boys in school. Students need to be comfortable and learn to work with the opposite sex in preparation for college and the workplace. Although my high school gave me academic confidence, it did not really prepare me for the diverse world I met once I went to

college. Single-sex classrooms may just postpone learning about tolerance and difference rather than actually teaching it.

▪ **INTERPRETING AND REFLECTING**   Many responses contain interpretations of passages that might be read from different points of view or reflections on the assumptions or implications of an idea. An interpretation says, "Here is what the text says, but let me explain what it means, what assumptions the argument carries, or what the implications might be." Here is a paragraph from an interpretive response to Devlin's essay.

If we stop a moment and reflect on the purpose of schools, we realize that schools should be a place where learning and growth can take place. All of Devlin's solutions, however, are designed to increase security and control rather than actually teach tolerance. Perhaps Devlin has modeled his "final solution" on prisons, where students as inmates would have no rights, no privacy, no room to express either tolerance or hatred. Rather than place students in a maximum security prison, we should return to the more liberal approach of teaching tolerance and understanding—the very solution that Devlin initially rejects. While the simple method of teaching about cultural, social, and ethnic differences does not guarantee a conflict-free school environment, it does ensure that students have the opportunity to embrace rather than just accept differences. The forced tolerance that Devlin recommends through dress codes and maximum security measures ultimately discourages students from using their schools to actively examine and freely embrace the differences among their peers.

CHOOSING   COLLECTING   SHAPING   **OUTLINING**   DRAFTING   REVISING
OUTLINES FOR SUMMARY/ RESPONSE ESSAYS

Three common outlines for summary/response essays follow. Select or modify one of these outlines to fit your audience, purpose, and kind of response. Typically, a summary/response takes the following form

 I. Introduction to text(s)

 II. Summary of text(s)

 III. Response(s)

   A. Point 1

   B. Point 2

   C. Point 3, etc.

 IV. Conclusion

A second kind of outline focuses initially on key ideas or issues and then examines the text or texts for their contribution to these key ideas. This outline begins with the issues, then summarizes the text(s), and then moves to the reader's responses

I. Introduction to key issues

II. Summary of relevant text(s)

III. Response(s)
    A. Point 1
    B. Point 2
    C. Point 3, etc.

IV. Conclusion

A third outline integrates the summary and the response. It begins by introducing the issue and/or the text, gives a brief overall idea of the text, but then summarizes and responds point by point.

I. Introduction to issues and/or text(s)

II. Summary of text's Point 1/response to Point 1

III. Summary of text's Point 2/response to Point 2

IV. Summary of text's Point 3/response to Point 3, etc.

V. Conclusion

CHOOSING   COLLECTING   SHAPING   OUTLINING   **DRAFTING**   REVISING

DRAFTING

If you have been reading actively, you have been writing throughout the reading/writing/discussing process. At some point, however, you will gather your best ideas, have a rough direction or outline in mind, and begin writing a draft. Some writers like to have their examples and evidence ready when they begin drafting. Many writers have outlines in their heads or on paper. Perhaps you like to put your rough outline on the computer and then just expand each section as you write. Finally, most writers like to skim the text and *reread their notes* immediately before they start their drafts, just to make sure everything is fresh in their minds.

Once you start drafting, keep interruptions to a minimum. Because focus and concentration are important to good writing, try to keep writing as long as possible. If you come to a spot where you need an example that you don't have at your fingertips, just put in parentheses—(put the example about cosmetics and animal abuse here)—and keep on writing. Concentrate on making all your separate responses add up to a focused, overall response.

REVISING

Revision means, literally, *reseeing*. Revising requires rereading the text and rewriting your summary and response. While revision begins as you read and reread the text, it continues until—and sometimes after—you turn in a paper or send it to its intended audience.

A major step in your revision is receiving responses from peer readers and deciding on a revision plan, based on the feedback. Use the following guidelines as you read your peers' papers and respond to their advice.

GUIDELINES FOR REVISION

- **Review the purpose and audience for your assignment.** Is your draft addressed to the appropriate audience? Does it fulfill its intended purpose?

- **Reconsider the genre you selected.** Is the genre you selected (essay, letter, letter to the editor) still working for your audience and purpose? Are there multigenre elements you could add to make your summary and response more effective?

- **Continue to use your active reading/writing/discussing activities as you revise your draft.** If you are uncertain about parts of your summary or response, reread the text, check your notes, or discuss your draft with a classmate.

- **Reread your summary for key features.** Make sure your summary indicates author and title, cites main ideas, uses an occasional direct quotation, and includes author tags. Check your summary for accuracy and objectivity.

- **Check paraphrases and direct quotations.** If you are paraphrasing (without quotation marks), you should put the author's ideas into your own language. If you are quoting directly, make sure the words within the quotation marks are accurate, word-for-word transcriptions.

- **Review the purpose of your response.** Are you analyzing, agreeing/disagreeing, interpreting, or some combination of all three? Do your types of responses fit the assignment or address your intended audience and satisfy your purpose?

- **Amplify your supporting evidence.** Summary/response drafts often need additional, relevant evidence. Be sure you use sufficient personal experience, evidence from the text, or examples from other texts to support your response.

PEER RESPONSE

The instructions below will help you give and receive constructive advice about the rough draft of your summary/response essay. You may use these guidelines for an in-class workshop, a take-home review, or a computer e-mail response.

Writer: Before you exchange drafts with another reader, write out the following information about your own rough draft.

1. On your draft, *label* the parts that are summary and the parts that are your own response.
2. *Underline* the sentence(s) that signal to the reader that you are shifting from objective summary to personal response.
3. Indicate your purpose, intended audience, and any special genre features such as graphs or images.
4. Explain *one or two problems* that you are having with this draft that you want your reader to comment on.

Reader: Without making any comments, read the *entire* draft from start to finish. As you *reread* the draft, answer the following questions.

1. Review the guidelines for writing summaries. Has the writer remained *objective* in his or her summary? Does the summary *omit* any key ideas? Does the writer use *author tags* frequently and accurately? Can you clearly understand the main ideas of the article? Is the summary written in language appropriate for the intended audience? Do any added images or graphic material support the writer's purpose?
2. Review the guidelines for writing responses. What type(s) of response is the writer using? In the margin, label the types. What kinds of evidence does the writer use in support of his or her response? In the margin, label the kinds of supporting evidence. Is this response addressed appropriately to the audience?
3. In your own words, state the main idea or the focus that organizes the writer's response.
4. Write out your own reactions to the writer's response. Where do you disagree with the writer's analysis or interpretation? Explain.
5. Answer the writer's questions in number 4, above.

- **Focus on a clear, overall response.** Your responses should all add up to a focused, overall reaction. Delete or revise any passages that do not maintain your focus.
- **Revise sentences to improve clarity, conciseness, emphasis, and variety.** (See Handbook.)
- **Edit your final version.** Use the spell check on your computer. Have a friend help proofread. Check the Handbook for suspected problems in usage, grammar, and punctuation.

POSTSCRIPT ON THE WRITING PROCESS

1. As you finish your essay, what questions do you still have about how to summarize? What questions do you have about writing a good response?

2. Which paragraphs in your response contain your most effective supporting evidence? What kinds of evidence (analysis of the text, evidence from other texts, or personal experience) did you use?

3. What sentences in your response contain your overall reaction to the text?

4. If you had one more day to work on your essay, what would you change? Why?

5. Review the guidelines for critical reading at the beginning of this chapter. Which of those strategies was most successful for you? What did you learn about active, critical reading that you applied to the writing of your response? Cite one passage that illustrates what you learned about critical reading.

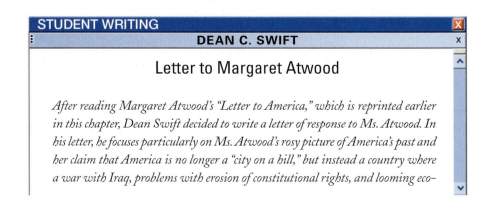

STUDENT WRITING

DEAN C. SWIFT

Letter to Margaret Atwood

After reading Margaret Atwood's "Letter to America," which is reprinted earlier in this chapter, Dean Swift decided to write a letter of response to Ms. Atwood. In his letter, he focuses particularly on Ms. Atwood's rosy picture of America's past and her claim that America is no longer a "city on a hill," but instead a country where a war with Iraq, problems with erosion of constitutional rights, and looming eco-

*nomic problems have threatened America's standing in the world. In his letter of
response, Swift argues that the America in the past faced significant problems with
civil rights, with assassinations of our great leaders, and with a severe economic
depression. Before you read Swift's response, however, be sure to read Atwood's letter and form your own opinion.*

1763 Fox Wood Ct.
Rockford, IL 61106
March 11, 2004

Ms. Margaret Atwood
C/o Editors, *The Nation*
33 Irving Place
New York, New York 10003

Dear Ms. Atwood:

I am writing in response to your "Letter to America." Although I do
not agree totally with everything you say in the letter, I do agree that
you can get a much better sense of your country through the eyes of
another. There are many things we do not see or realize as Americans
until we look at America from the outside. We get tunnel vision. Yet
when reading your letter and hearing your description of the America you "once knew," I believe you also have tunnel vision. Throughout the letter you seem to compare the negative things about America
today to all the positive things of the past. You fail to mention any
negative aspects of America during those days. Maybe you should
take a look at someone else's view on America today versus America
in the past.

You started your letter by relating the America you once knew to its
popular culture. For one thing, I don't really think that is an appropriate subject on which to judge a country. There are more important aspects to our history than what the hit movies and songs were. But on
that subject, of course it has changed—that was fifty years ago! You
can't expect all the music and books to be the same; we are a completely different generation. Now we have our Dave Mathews Band
and our Jennifer Lopez—we go to the movies to see *Lord of the Rings*.
What is wrong with that? You've drawn us a picture that the America you once knew was flawless. Why don't you try to tell that to the
African Americans living in this country back at that time? Would

...*continued* Letter to Margaret Atwood, **Dean C. Swift**

they really believe that America was so much better back then? I'll guarantee that if you were to ask Rosa Parks today whether America has changed for the better or worse, she would go on for hours on how great this country has become. African Americans have been used as slaves, abused, discriminated against, and even tortured to death for hundreds of years until the later 1950s and '60s. Violent race riots and disturbing demonstrations took place during the Civil Rights Movement. Didn't it bother you that women didn't have equal rights until 1964? How was that such a perfect country when people were being discriminated against and in some cases beaten, simply because of their race or gender?

Our economy now and the debt we have gotten ourselves into is frustrating to everyone, but what about the economy in the past? Were there no problems with it in the 1930s during the Great Depression? I understand that you feel there are many corrupt things in our country today, but it is no more corrupt than it was in the past. Our country has been going to war as far back as our history dates. What about all the assassinations that took place back then? Your generation lost some great people. Throughout America's history, these tragedies have taken place: the assassination of President Lincoln and President Kennedy, Martin Luther King, Jr., Senator Robert Kennedy—yet these disturbing events don't seem to have left an impression on you.

On the subject of gutting the constitution, it's hard to draw a clear line as to where I stand on that issue. On the one hand, according to our amendments, it is wrong for the government to be able to do such things as tap phone lines, enter a home without a warrant, and incarcerate suspects without cause. These are our rights as Americans. But is this invasion of our privacy really wrong? Why should this bother us unless we are on the guilty side or under suspicion of a crime? I know I don't have anything to hide myself. Although everyone in the U.S. should be entitled to certain privacy rights, isn't it in our best interest—for safety purposes—to go sacrifice some rights in order to gain better knowledge and leads on subjects such as terrorism, gang violence, drug deals, and other serious matters? From my point of view, I believe that the Patriot Act is good for our country, and for our own safety. If you have nothing to hide, then why worry—if you are guilty or have information on something serious, then it should be in our best interest to apprehend the suspects or information by any means possible.

You say that our "city upon a hill" is slipping to the slums, but I say you are far from the truth. Though we have fallen in some ways, we have also risen in many. Look at all the technological and medical advances we have made. Our efforts to improve equal rights among all people have clearly improved since your time. We are still a great country. To be sure, there are flaws along the way, but that doesn't change for any country, at any time in history. I felt you were a little narrow minded in your judgment about how America has changed since the time period you grew up in. From generation to generation, people will always have different views on other time periods. I think you should try to open your mind and see that there were many flaws in your time also, and that although there are still many today, we have changed many things for the better. America is still that city upon a hill.

Sincerely,

Dean C. Swift

QUESTIONS FOR WRITING AND DISCUSSION

1. Reread Margaret Atwood's "Letter to America" reprinted earlier in this chapter. Write your own summary of her main ideas. Then reread Dean Swift's essay. Which of her points or arguments does he mention and respond to? Which ones does he ignore? Would he have a more effective letter if he responded to all of her points? Why or why not?

2. Dean Swift chose to use the genre of a letter to respond to Atwood's own letter. How are the stylistic conventions of a letter different from the conventions of an academic essay? How would Swift's response be different if he were writing a letter to the editor of *The Nation?* Does Swift use the more informal conventions of a letter to make his point in a more effective or per sonal way? Explain.

3. Responses typically analyze the logic and presentation of the argument, agree or disagree with the main ideas, and/or offer an interpretation or an

examination of assumptions and implications behind an argument. Which of these does Swift do most effectively? Where could he add more supporting analysis, evidence, or interpretation? Should he use more of his own personal experience? Explain, referring to specific paragraphs in his essay.

STUDENT WRITING   ✕

JENNIFER KOESTER AND SONJA H. BROWE

Two Responses to Deborah Tannen

The two essays reprinted here were written in response to an essay by Deborah Tannen, "How Male and Female Students Use Language Differently," which appears in Chapter 8. Jennifer Koester and Sonja H. Browe have opposite responses to Tannen's essay. Jennifer Koester, a political science major at Colorado State University, argues that Tannen's essay is effective because she uses sufficient evidence and organizes her essay clearly. On the other hand, Sonja Browe, an English education major at the University of Wyoming, writes an essay that is critical of Deborah Tannen's focus and supporting evidence. Be sure to read Tannen's essay and decide for yourself before you read the following essays.

A Response to Deborah Tannen's Essay

JENNIFER KOESTER

Deborah Tannen's "How Male and Female Students Use Language Differ- 1 ently" addresses how male and female conversational styles influence classroom discussions. Tannen asserts that women speak less than men in class because often the structure of discussion is more "congenial" to men's style of conversing.

Tannen looks at three differences between the sexes that shape class- 2 room interaction: classroom setting, debate format, and contrasting attitudes toward classroom discussion. First, Tannen says that during childhood, men "are expected to seize center stage: by exhibiting their skill, displaying their knowledge, and challenging and resisting challenge." Thus, as adults, men are more comfortable than women when speaking in front of a large group of strangers. On the other hand, women are more comfortable in small groups.

Second, men are more comfortable with the debate format. Tannen 3 asserts that many classrooms use the format of putting forth ideas followed by "argument and challenge." This too coincides with men's conversational experiences. However, Tannen asserts that women tend to "resist discussion they perceive as hostile."

Third, men feel it is their duty to think of things to say and to voice *4* them. On the other hand, women often regulate their participation and hold back to avoid dominating discussion.

Tannen concludes that educators can no longer use just one format *5* to facilitate classroom discussion. Tannen sees small groups as necessary for any "non-seminar" class along with discussion of differing styles of participation as solutions to the participation gap between the sexes.

Three things work together to make Deborah Tannen's essay "How *6* Male and Female Students Use Language Differently" effective: the qualifications of her argument, the evidence used, and the parallel format of comparison/contrast.

First, Tannen's efforts to qualify her argument prevent her from com- *7* mitting logical errors. In the first paragraphs of her essay, she states, "This is not to say that all men talk in class, nor that no women do. It is simply that a greater percentage of discussion time is taken by men's voices." By acknowledging exceptions to her claim, Tannen avoids the mistake of oversimplification. She also strengthens her argument because this qualification tells the reader that she is aware of the complexity of this issue.

Later, Tannen uses another qualification. She says, "No one's conver- *8* sational style is absolute; everyone's style changes in response to the context and others' styles." Not only does this qualification avoid a logical fallacy, but it also strengthens Tannen's argument that classroom discussion must have several formats. By acknowledging that patterns of participation can change with the setting, Tannen avoids oversimplifying the issue and adds to her argument for classroom variety.

Second, Tannen's evidence places a convincing argument before her *9* reader. In the beginning of her essay, Tannen states that a greater percentage of discussion time in class is taken by men and that those women who attend single-sex schools tend to do better later in life. These two pieces of evidence present the reader with Tannen's jumping-off point. These statistics are what Tannen wants to change.

In addition, Tannen effectively uses anecdotal evidence. She presents *10* the reader with stories from her colleagues and her own research. These stories are taken from the classroom, a place which her audience, as educators, are familiar with. Her anecdotal evidence is persuasive because it appeals to the common sense and personal experiences of the audience. While some might question the lack of hard statistics throughout the

...continued A Response to Deborah Tannen's Essay, **Jennifer Koester**

essay, the anecdotal evidence serves Tannen best because it reminds her audience of educators of their own experiences. When she reminds the audience of their experiences, she is able to make them see her logic.

Third, the parallel format of comparison/contrast between the gen- *11* ders highlights for the reader Tannen's main points. Each time Tannen mentions the reactions of one gender, she follows with the reaction of the other gender. For example, Tannen states, "So one reason men speak in class more than women is that many of them find the 'public' classroom setting more conducive to speaking, whereas most women are more comfortable speaking in private to a small group of people they know well." Here, Tannen places the tendencies of men and of women together, thus preventing the reader from having to constantly refer back to another section of the essay.

In an earlier example, Tannen discusses men's comfort with the de- *12* bate format in class discussion. The majority of that paragraph relates why men feel comfortable with that format. After explaining this idea, Tannen then tells the reader how women feel about the debate structure. Because how men and women feel about the debate format is placed within a paragraph, the readers easily see the difference between the genders. Tannen's use of the parallel format in the above examples and the rest of the essay provides a clear explanation of the differences in men's and women's interactions in the classroom.

Tannen writes her essay effectively. She makes the essay convincing by *13* qualifying her claims about gender participation. This strengthens her argument that just as the classroom is diverse, so should the format be diverse. Her supporting evidence is convincing because it comes from Tannen's own experience, reminds the audience of its own experiences, and appeals to the audience's common sense. Finally, her parallel format for discussing the differences between men and women enhances the reader's understanding. Overall, Tannen's essay is effective because she qualifies her argument, uses convincing evidence, and makes clear how men and women use language differently through a parallel comparison/contrast format.

Is Deborah Tannen Convincing?

SONJA H. BROWE

In her article entitled "How Male and Female Students Use Language Dif- *1* ferently," Deborah Tannen explores the issue of gender as it affects the way we use language to communicate. Specifically, she discusses how differences in the way males and females are socialized to use language affect their classroom interactions. She explains that as females are growing up, they learn to use language to talk to friends, and to tell secrets. She states that for females, it is the "telling of secrets, the fact and the way they talk to each other, that makes them best friends." Boys, on the other hand, are "expected to use language to seize center stage: by exhibiting their skill, displaying their knowledge, and challenging and resisting challenge."

According to Tannen, these differences make classroom language use more conducive to the way males were taught to use language. Tannen suggests that speaking in front of groups and the debatelike formats used in many classrooms are more easily handled by male students. 2

Finally, Tannen describes an experiment she conducted in her own classroom which allowed students to evaluate their own conversation transcripts. From this experience, she deduced that small-group interaction is essential in the classroom because it gives students who don't participate in whole-class settings the opportunity for conversation and interaction. 3

Though Tannen's research is a worthwhile consideration and provides information which could be of great interest to educators, this particular article lacks credibility and is unfocused. The points she is trying to make get lost in a world of unsupported assertions, and she strays from her main focus, leaving the reader hanging and confused. 4

Tannen does take some time at the beginning of her article to establish her authority on linguistic analysis, but we may still hold her accountable for supporting her assertions with evidence. However, Tannen makes sweeping declarations throughout the essay, expecting the reader to simply accept them as fact. For example, when discussing the practice of the teacher playing devil's advocate and debating with the students, she states that "many, if not most women would shrink from such a challenge, experiencing it as public humiliation." Following such an assertion, we expect to see some evidence. Whom did Tannen talk to? What did they say? What percentage of women felt this way? This sort of evidence is completely lacking, so that what Tannen states as fact appears more like conjecture. 5

Tannen makes another such unsupported pronouncement when she discusses the debatelike formats used in many classrooms. She explains that this type of classroom interaction is in opposition to the way that females, in contrast to males, approach learning. She states that "it is not that females don't fight, but that they don't fight for fun. They don't ritualize opposition." Again, where is Tannen's evidence to support such a claim? 6

. . . *continued* Is Deborah Tannen Convincing?, **Sonja H. Browe**

When Tannen does bother to support her assertions, her evidence is *7* trite and unconvincing. For example, she reviews Walter Ong's work on the pursuit of knowledge, in which he suggested that "ritual opposition . . . is fundamental to the way males approach almost any activity." Tannen supports this claim of Ong's in parentheses, saying, "Consider, for example, the little boy who shows he likes a little girl by pulling her braids and shoving her." This statement may serve as an example but is not enough to convince the reader that ritual opposition is fundamental to the way males approach "almost any activity."

Other evidence which Tannen uses to support her declarations *8* comes in the form of conversations she has had with colleagues on these issues. Again, though these may provide examples, they do not represent a broad enough database to support her claims.

Finally, Tannen takes three pages of her article to describe in detail *9* an experiment she conducted in her classroom. Though the information she collected from this experiment was interesting, it strayed from the main point of the essay. Originally, Tannen's article was directed specifically at gender differences in communication. In this classroom activity, she looked at language-use differences in general, including cultural differences. She states that some people may be more comfortable in classes where you are expected to raise your hand to speak, while others prefer to be able to talk freely. She makes no mention of gender in regard to this issue.

Finally, at the close of her essay, where we can expect to get the thrust *10* of her argument or at least some sort of summary statement which ties into her main thesis, Tannen states that her experience in her classroom convinced her that "small-group interaction should be a part of any classroom" and that "having students become observers of their own interaction is a crucial part of their education." Again, these are interesting points, but they stray quite a bit from the original intention of the article.

In this article, Tannen discusses important issues of which those of *11* us who will be interacting with students in the classroom should be aware. However, her article loses a great deal of its impact because she does not stay focused on her original thesis and fails to support her ideas with convincing evidence.

QUESTIONS FOR WRITING AND DISCUSSION

1. Do your own double-entry log for Tannen's essay (see Chapter 8). On the left-hand side of a piece of paper, record Tannen's main points. On the right-hand side, write your own questions and reactions. Compare your notes to Koester's and Browe's responses. Whose response most closely matches your own? Where or how does your response differ from each?

2. Review the critical reading strategies at the beginning of this chapter (see page 155). Identify specific places in both Koester's and Browe's essays where they analyze elements of the rhetorical situation—such as purpose, audience, or context. Where do they analyze the effectiveness of the organization, use of evidence, or the style? Based on your analyses of both essays, which writer does a better job of critically reading Tannen's essay? Explain your choice.

3. Responses to texts may analyze the effectiveness of the text, agree or disagree with the ideas in the text, and/or interpret or reflect on the text. What kinds of responses do Koester and Browe give? Would a different kind of response work better for either writer? Why or why not?

4. Koester focuses on three writing strategies that Tannen uses to make her essay more effective. What are they? What weaknesses of Tannen's essay does Koester ignore or downplay?

5. Browe's response focuses on two criticisms of Tannen's essay. What are they? In which paragraphs does Browe develop each criticism? What strengths of Tannen's essay does Browe ignore or downplay?

6. Neither Browe nor Koester uses personal experience as supporting evidence. Think of one experience that you have had in a specific class illustrating the conversational preferences of men and women. Write out that specific example. Could either Browe or Koester use such a specific example? Where might each writer use it in her response?

7. Reread the essays by Tannen, Koester, and Browe. Review your reactions with your classmates. Then write your own summary and response. In your response, mention both the strengths and the weaknesses of Tannen's article. Then indicate whether or not you found Tannen's essay, in general, thought-provoking or convincing.

The plate above is taken from a fourteenth-century illuminated manuscript
by Guillaume de Machaut, Le Remède de Fortune. The plate is titled *The
Lover Sings as his Lady Dances*. In this narrative, de Machaut recounts how
he hid in a park from his lady love, too embarrassed to sing a ballad he had
composed for her. In this picture, however, de Machaut returns to the castle
where he finds his lady dancing a "carole" in the company of her friends.
The lady, second from the right in the larger group, encourages de
Machaut, standing to her left, to sing his song. See Journal Exercise
page 239, which invites you to analyze the composition of the painting.

Analyzing and Designing Visuals

6

For one of your composition class projects, you work with the managers of a local adult fitness center in writing a brochure that they can use to promote their fitness, healthy diet, and weight loss programs. First you research information about healthy approaches to weight loss programs. Then you prepare a draft with information organized into key topics from your research and, working with the adult center, decide how to best select, organize, and present this information for their adult clients. As you revise, you focus on giving good, concise advice for adults, presented in an easy-to-read, visually appealing document. Your final product is a four-color brochure with your information, advice, photographs, and graphs that the center will print and distribute.

The editor of your college newspaper asks you to write an article calling attention to upcoming events celebrating Cesar Chavez Day on March 31. You interview organizers of the day's activities to gather basic information. After researching Cesar Chavez's life, however, you decide to write your article primarily to let readers know about his life and accomplishments. You plan to have a calendar of the day's events accompany your biographical information. Your final article features your profile, two pictures of Cesar Chavez, and a sidebar of the campus and community activities.

> " Graphic design creates visual logic and seeks an optimal balance between visual sensation and graphic information. Without the visual impact of shape, color, and contrast, pages are graphically boring and will not motivate the viewer. "
> —PATRICK LYNCH AND SARAH HORTON,
> *WEB STYLE GUIDE*

> " Now we make our networks, and our networks make us. "
> —WILLIAM MITCHELL,
> *CITY OF BITS*

COMMUNICATION IN THE 21ST CENTURY IS, INCREASINGLY, MULTI-MEDIA COMMUNICATION. WRITTEN TEXTS ARE INTERWOVEN WITH PICTURES, NEWS PHOTOGRAPHS, GRAPHIC DESIGNS, WORKS OF ART, CHARTS, AND DIAGRAMS. IN ADDITION, WEB SITES AND ELEC-tronic communication contain sound and video, with music, podcasts, and video clips often only a mouse click away. High-tech cell phones now offer true mul-timedia communication, with e-mail, text messaging, photographs, news up-dates, video and text files, and music.

Although much is new in our contemporary digital world, much is still the same. The illuminated medieval manuscript that opens this chapter is a multimedia text, with a picture of a young man meeting (and dancing with) a lady of the court, with Latin script explaining the context, and with music accompanying the story represented in the scene. This manuscript is very high tech—for its day and ours. Illuminators of medieval manuscripts were multimedia artists who had mastered the process of adding gold leaf to the page, thus making the manuscript more attractive, more influential, and more effective in conveying its message.

Even though our digital-age technology is new, our means for analyzing and designing visuals remains very traditional. In every case, we analyze and design by asking basic rhetorical questions. What is the purpose of this image or bit of media? Who is the intended audience? In what social, political, or cultural context does this visual appear? Who is the author or group of authors? What appeals to logic, emo-tion, or character do these hybrid or multimedia texts make?

This chapter begins by providing the rhetorical questions you need to analyze visuals and hybrid texts. After you understand how to analyze visuals, you can prac-tice composing and designing hybrid texts of your own. This chapter focuses prima-rily on visuals as one key element of a multimedia text, but the rhetorical principles will help you analyze other kinds of media as well. The diagram on the following page will help you analyze visuals, their contexts, and their meanings.

The chapter begins with you as the reader, viewer, or member of the audi-ence. You will examine the visual and its relationship to any accompanying text. Then you will consider how the visual and the text interact with the cultural, po-litical, or social context in which the image appears. The context is both immedi-ate (the magazine, newspaper, essay, Web site, or blog in which the image appears) and more general (the cultural context of the image, the written or spoken con-versation that is occurring about this image). Finally, throughout the process of analyzing, you will estimate the rhetorical effect: What is the purpose and audi-ence for this image and its text? What appeals to logic and reason, to emotion and

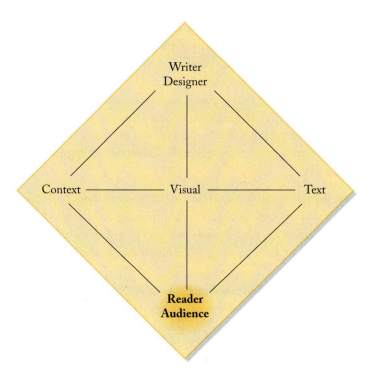

feelings, to reliability and character is the writer making? How effective are those appeals?

After you practice analyzing the rhetorical effect of visuals, you will be better prepared to switch roles from reader or audience to writer or designer of visuals for your own documents. In the second half of this chapter, you will practice several possible visual or design choices. You will analyze which visuals help support your purpose for your specific audience, and how effectively the visuals add to your audience appeals.

ANALYZING   DESIGNING   PROCESSES
Techniques for Analyzing Visuals

As you analyze images and visuals—as well as any accompanying text or surrounding context—always consider the rhetorical situation, the purpose of the visual, and the intended audience for the visual or hybrid text. The techniques explained here help you **analyze**—that is, look at each part of the visual separately—but the ultimate goal is to **synthesize**, to put the pieces together in an explanation that shows how the parts work together (or do not work together) to achieve a rhetorical purpose for an intended audience. Your conclusion about the visual's significance or meaning becomes your **claim**. These techniques shouldn't necessarily be followed in lock-step order. If you begin by analyzing the genre of a visual, for example, you may more quickly see how the text and the visual work together. Similarly, returning to analyze the visual *after* you know more about the context can be very important.

- **Analyzing the visual itself.** Describe the layout, balance, color, key figures, symbols, and cultural references. What message or messages are being conveyed? Based on your analysis, what is the purpose and who is the audience? What claim can you make about the significance or meaning of the visual?

- **Analyzing the visual in combination with any text.** Do the text and the visual work together? How does the text add to (or distract from) the visual? What do the words help you notice in the visual? What do the words keep you from noticing? Do the words and text work together to achieve the same purpose for the intended audience?

- **Analyzing the visual and the text in context.** In what magazine, essay, or newspaper, or on what Web site does the visual appear? What does this context tell you about purpose and audience? In what larger cultural, political, or social context does the visual appear? Are these images and their meanings supported or critiqued by their context? Are there conversations (articles, essays, blogs) surrounding these visuals and their context? How does this analysis help you arrive at your thesis or claim?

- **Analyzing the genre of the visual.** Visuals that share common features belong to a genre—a type or kind. Visual genres include advertisements, photographs, art, graphics, posters, brochures, and charts. Compare the visual or hybrid text you are analyzing to other similar ones: What features do they share? How is your example different? How do those similarities/ differences affect the overall meaning and purpose of the visual or its effect on the audience?

- **Analyzing the rhetorical appeals of a visual.** Focus on the purpose and the overall effect on the audience: What appeals to reason and logic, to emotion, or to character and credibility does the visual make? Does the writer or designer use multiple appeals (to reason and to emotion, for example)? How effective are these appeals in achieving the writer's purpose for the intended audience? How does your analysis of these appeals affect your thesis or claim?

VISUALS	WITH TEXT	IN CONTEXT	GENRE	RHETORICAL APPEALS

ANALYZING VISUALS

When we analyze stand-alone visuals and images, we need to pay particular attention to the details of composition, focus, narrative, and genre. We rely primarily on this analysis to reach conclusions about the purpose, intended audience, and effectiveness of the visual. These conclusions will become your claim or thesis for your analysis. Use the following sets of questions to guide your analysis. Depending on the particular image, of course, some questions will be more important than others.

COMPOSITION

- Who or what is pictured in the main figure?
- How are key images arranged or organized on the page?
- What is the relationship between the main figure and the background?
- What is excluded from the main figure or background?
- When and where was the image or photograph made?
- What use of color, contrasts of light and shade, or repeated figures are present?
- How do these composition details come together to create a purpose or message for the intended audience/viewer?

FOCAL POINT

- What point or image first draws your attention?
- Is this focal point centered or offset?
- Do background figures or diagonal lines draw your attention to or away from the focal point?
- How does the focus (or lack of focus) contribute to the purpose or message of the image?

NARRATIVE

- What story or narrative does the image or visual suggest?
- Do certain objects or figures act as symbols or metaphors?
- How do these story elements support (or not support) the purpose or message for the intended audience?

THEMES

- Who has the power in this visual? Who does not? Who is included or excluded?
- What sexist, racist, or body image stereotypes exist? Are these stereotypes promoted and reproduced or are they resisted or challenged? Explain.
- What is this image trying to sell? Does the image make a commodity out of social or cultural values, including holidays (Christmas or Independence Day), ideals (patriotism, charity, or religion), or personal values (integrity or status)?

Now practice applying these questions to two photographs taken by Dorothea Lange. One of America's most famous documentary photographers of migrant workers and sharecroppers, Lange took the following images during the Great Depression of the 1930s, near Berkeley, California.

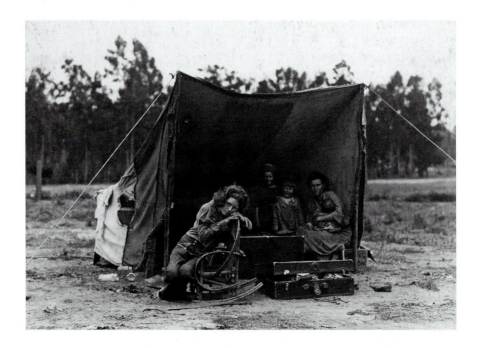

In the first picture, the composition focuses on several main figures—the two women and the three children. The makeshift tarp helps to frame these figures, and the diagonal lines from the chair and the woman on the left bring the viewer's focus to the children standing in the center and then to the mother holding her child on the right. The half-opened suitcase of clothes appears in the foreground. The background helps establish the rural, agricultural setting.

In contrast, the second picture has much a much stronger **composition**. The main figure is the woman, with her two children, looking away from the camera. The background—the tent—does not distract from this central, pyramid-like image. The children's faces are also turned away from the camera, leaving the **focal point** on the mother. The picture is in black and white, which helps focus the viewer's attention on the figures of the mother and the children. Even the angle of the mother's arm, and her chin in her hand, lead the eye to the woman's face. Her expression is determined, but without much hope. All of these compositional features support the purpose and message of the photograph: A migrant mother is caring for her family, as best as she can, in the most primitive of environments.

As viewers, we can construct our own **narrative** based on the information in the picture. This woman is caring for her children in a migrant worker environment. She has no apparent support. This shelter appears to be where she is living, both during the day and at night. She may have other family members working in the area, but we can only guess at their whereabouts.

Our own conjectural narrative is, in fact, not very different from the description that Dorothea Lange herself gives of the day when she took these photographs:

"I saw and approached the hungry and desperate mother, as if drawn by a magnet. I do not remember how I explained my presence or my camera to her, but I do remember she asked me no questions. I made five exposures, working closer and closer from the same direction. I did not ask her name or her history. She told me her age, that she was thirty-two. She said that they had been living on frozen vegetables from the surrounding fields, and birds that the children killed. She had just sold the tires from her car to buy food. There she sat in that lean-to tent with her children huddled around her, and seemed to know that my pictures might help her, and so she helped me. There was a sort of equality about it." (*Popular Photography*, Feb., 1960)

We can put all these analytical pieces together to better understand the purpose and meaning of this photograph. For its **theme**, the photograph brings something hidden (the human story of poverty and exploitation) out into the open and gives it dignity. Lange's purpose was to call attention to the predicament of migrant workers in order to gather support for governmental reform. Her purpose was thus persuasive: she hoped to change public awareness as a first step to improving governmental assistance programs.

VISUALS   **WITH TEXT**   IN CONTEXT   GENRE   RHETORICAL APPEALS
ANALYZING VISUALS WITH TEXT

> There can be no words without images.
> —ARISTOTLE,
> AUTHOR OF *RHETORIC*

Analyzing visuals with accompanying words or text requires considering how the composition of the image and the written text function together. Text serves to call attention to and support the message of the visual. Often, words serve as a focusing device, calling our attention to key features, guiding us to "read" the visual in a certain way. (Of course, a text that encourages us to see one meaning in the visual may keep us from seeing other possible meanings or messages in that visual.) Ideally, image and text should not just duplicate each other; they should each contribute something unique so that the combined effect is more powerful, appealing, or persuasive than either the text or the image taken separately.

> My eyes make pictures when they are shut.
> —SAMUEL TAYLOR COLERIDGE,
> AUTHOR OF "THE RIME OF THE ANCIENT MARINER"

In the following recruiting poster for the American Red Cross, the text is spare, simple, and direct: "Join." Notice how the composition of the picture supports this appeal. The foreground figure contrasts clearly with the less distinct background, a representation of a flood-ravaged town. And the figures in the background—a run-down house and a Red Cross nurse who is caring for children—seem to hover in the middle distance, perhaps connected, perhaps not, to the flooded town. The nurse in the foreground extends her hand to the viewer, inviting her or him to join. Thematically, women rather than men are featured in the foreground and back-

ground in this stereotypical service role. The patriotic red, white, and blue colors of the nurse's blouse and cape are repeated as a motif in the red of the cross, the blue of the word *join*, and the white of the immediate foreground. The focus on the foreground figure, the color, the center focal point, and the balance of the background figures on the right and left function with the text and the implied narrative (Join the Red Cross and serve your country!) to achieve this visual's persuasive purpose.

In the next image with accompanying text, photographer Jim Goldberg effectively illustrates how visual and text should combine to create a more powerful message than either word or image alone. The photograph, taken in San Francisco in 1982, shows the lady of the house, Mrs. Stone, standing in her modern kitchen with her servant, Vickie Figueroa, standing in the background. The diagonal lines of the white counter and window to the right send us first to the figure of Mrs. Stone, and then to Ms. Figueroa in the background. This foreground/background juxtaposition sets up a power relationship, confirmed by Mrs. Stone's hands grasping (and owning) the counter while Ms. Figueroa's hands are tucked behind her. The contrast between the pointed and poignant writing and the rather conventional kitchen

My dream Was to became a shool teacher.
Mrs Stone is rich.
I have talents but not opportunity.
I ~~am~~ am used to standing behind
Mrs Stone.
I have been a servant for 40 years.
Vickie Figueroa.

Jim Goldberg, USA, San Francisco, 1982

scene gives the visual a special, combined power. The language in Ms. Figueroa's note supports the power relationship of the image: "I am used to standing behind Mrs. Stone." Finally, Goldberg's choice to present the text in what is apparently Ms. Figueroa's own handwriting, complete with crossed out letters, uneven lines, and signature, gives her lost dream of becoming a school teacher remarkable power. If Goldberg had simply put her note in typeface, much of the authenticity and power of the visual would be lost.

VISUALS   WITH TEXT   **IN CONTEXT**   GENRE   RHETORICAL APPEALS

ANALYZING VISUALS IN CONTEXT

Often, the key to analyzing a visual lies in understanding and explaining the context of the image. The context is the publication or medium in which the image

appeared, but taken more widely, the context is the surrounding political, social, and cultural context of the times. The image of Michael J. Fox on the right does not, in itself, appear to be unusual. But this still photograph actually represents a frame in a video in which Fox is speaking in support of a political candidate who supports stem cell research. On the video, Fox shows visible tremors, a symptom of his battle with Parkinson's disease. As a result of the controversy created by Rush Limbaugh's criticism of the video—followed by Limbaugh's apology—this image has become a focal point in a larger cultural and political battle over governmental support for stem cell research.

In the following short commentary in *Newsweek*, one of hundreds of articles and editorials appearing in the media at the time, Jonathan Alter explains how the video image impacted the political debate on stem cell research.

Progress or Not

Oct. 25, 2006—"The ad was in extremely poor taste," said a spokesman for Michael Steele, Republican candidate for the Senate in Maryland, referring to a TV spot made for his opponent, Rep. Ben Cardin.

That will be the line of Republicans under assault from what could become one of the most powerful political advertisements ever made. The new ad features an ailing Michael J. Fox talking about politicians who oppose embryonic stem-cell research. This is not just another celebrity ad, like those cut by the late Christopher Reeve. It's a celebrity shot to the solar plexus of the GOP. Whatever happens in the campaign, the ad is already a classic and will be mentioned in the same breath as LBJ's famous 1964 "Daisy" ad and other unforgettable political moments on television.

Rush Limbaugh helped cement the ad's place in history with his astonishingly insensitive remark that Fox "was either off his medication or was acting." Limbaugh quickly apologized but the damage to his own reputation was already done.

Fox, star of megahit TV shows and movies like "Family Ties" and *Back to the Future,* was for years one of the most popular actors in the United States. He still works, but is clearly debilitated by Parkinson's. Throughout the ad, he sways back and forth, showing signs of advanced disease.

In the version cut for Democrat Claire McCaskill, who is running against Sen. Jim Talent in Missouri, the actor, wearing a blue blazer and open-collared shirt, says, "Senator Talent even wanted to criminalize the science that gives us a chance for hope." This is in apparent reference to Talent's early support for Sen. Sam Brownback's view that embryonic stem-cell research should be illegal. Then comes the clincher: "They say all politics is local, but it's not always the case. What you do in Missouri matters to millions of Americans—Americans like me."

> " In any hypertext, the
> text originates in an
> interaction that neither
> the author nor the
> reader can completely
> predict or control. "
> —JAY DAVID BOULTER,
> "LITERATURE IN THE
> ELECTRONIC WRITING SPACE"

Sometimes, the accompanying text for a visual carries a message that in the larger social context creates controversy and anger. Consider the following two photographs showing people wading through the floodwaters in New Orleans following hurricane Katrina in 2005. The first, taken by Associated Press photographer Dave Martin, has a caption stating that the young man, an African American, was "looting a grocery store." The second, taken by photographer Chris Graythen for Getty Images, has a caption stating that two white residents are wading through the floodwaters after "finding bread and soda from a local grocery store." Several Internet sites and bloggers picked up these photographs and highlighted the key words with a red box in order to illustrate racial bias in media coverage of Hurricane Katrina.

A young man walks through chest deep flood water after looting a grocery store in New Orleans on Tuesday, Aug. 30, 2005. Flood waters continue to rise in New Orleans after Hurricane Katrina did extensive damage. Associated Press

Two residents wade through chest-deep water after finding bread and soda from a local grocery store after Hurricane Katrina came through the area in New Orleans, Louisiana. (AFP/Getty Images/Chris Graythen) AFP/Getty Images Tue Aug 30, 3:47 AM ET

The controversy created by these images was reported one week later by Tania Ralli in a *New York Times* article titled "Who's a Looter?" Read her account of the circumstances surrounding this media event. When you finish reading her article, you may want to Google the photographers, Dave Martin and Chris Graythen, to read more about their accounts of the events and the story surrounding their photographs. This controversy shows the dramatic power of images, but it also emphasizes the power of our reading or interpretation of these images. A picture may be worth a thousand words, but sometimes a single word is more powerful than a dramatic picture.

Who's a Looter?

Two news photographs ricocheted through the Internet last week and set off a debate about race and the news media in the aftermath of Hurricane Katrina.

The first photo, taken by Dave Martin, an Associated Press photographer in New Orleans, shows a young black man wading through water that has risen to his chest. He is clutching a case of soda and pulling a floating bag. The caption provided by The A.P. says he has just been "looting a grocery store."

The second photo, also from New Orleans, was taken by Chris Graythen for Getty Images and distributed by Agence France-Presse. It shows a white couple up to their chests in the same murky water. The woman is holding some bags of food. This caption says they are shown "after finding bread and soda from a local grocery store."

Both photos turned up Tuesday on Yahoo News, which posts automatic feeds of articles and photos from wire services. Soon after, a user of the photo-sharing site Flickr juxtaposed the images and captions on a single page, which attracted links from many blogs. The left-leaning blog Daily Kos linked to the page with the comment, "It's not looting if you're white."

The contrast of the two photo captions, which to many indicated a double standard at work, generated widespread anger toward the news media that quickly spread beyond the Web.

On Friday night, the rapper Kanye West ignored the teleprompter during NBC's live broadcast of "A Concert for Hurricane Relief," using the opportunity to lambast President Bush and criticize the press. "I hate the way they portray us in the media," he said. "You see a black family, it says they're looting. You see a white family, it says they're looking for food."

Many bloggers were quick to point out that the photos came from two different agencies, and so could not reflect the prejudice of a single media outlet. A writer on the blog BoingBoing wrote: "Perhaps there's more factual substantiation behind each copywriter's choice of words than we know. But to some, the difference in tone suggests racial bias, implicit or otherwise."

According to the agencies, each photographer captioned his own photograph. Jack Stokes, a spokesman for The A.P., said that photographers are told to describe what they have seen when they write a caption.

Mr. Stokes said The A.P. had guidelines in place before Hurricane Katrina struck to distinguish between "looting" and "carrying." If a photographer sees a person enter a business and emerge with goods, it is described as looting. Otherwise The A.P. calls it carrying.

Mr. Stokes said that Mr. Martin had seen the man in his photograph wade into a grocery store and come out with the sodas and bag, so by A.P.'s definition, the man had looted.

The photographer for Getty Images, Mr. Graythen, said in an e-mail message that he had also stuck to what he had seen to write his caption, and had actually given the wording a great deal of thought. Mr. Graythen described seeing the couple near a corner store from an elevated expressway. The door to the shop was open, and things had floated out to the street. He was not able to talk to the couple, "so I had to draw my own conclusions," he said.

In the extreme conditions of New Orleans, Mr. Graythen said, taking necessities like food and water to survive could not be considered stealing. He said that had he seen people coming out of stores with computers and DVD players, he would have considered that looting.

"If you're taking something that runs solely from a wall outlet that requires power from the electric company—when we are not going to have power for weeks, even months—that's inexcusable," he said.

Since the photo was published last Tuesday Mr. Graythen has received more than 500 e-mail messages, most of them supportive, he said.

Within three hours of the photo's publication online, editors at Agence France-Presse rewrote Mr. Graythen's caption. But the original caption remained online as part of a Yahoo News slide show. Under pressure to keep up with the news, and lacking the time for a discussion about word choice, Olivier Calas, the agency's director of multimedia, asked Yahoo! to remove the photo last Thursday.

Now, in its place, when readers seek the picture of the couple, a statement from Neil Budde, the general manager of Yahoo! News, appears in its place. The statement emphasizes that Yahoo! News did not write the photo captions and that it did not edit the captions, so that the photos can be made available as quickly as possible.

Mr. Calas said Agence France-Presse was bombarded with e-mail messages complaining about the caption. He said the caption was unclear and should have been reworded earlier. "This was a consequence of a series of negligences, not ill intent," he said.

For Mr. Graythen, whose parents and grandparents lost their homes in the disaster, the fate of the survivors was the most important thing. In his e-mail message he wrote: "Now is no time to pass judgment on those trying to stay alive. Now is no time to argue semantics about finding versus looting. Now is no time to argue if this is a white versus black issue."

ANALYZING THE GENRE OF THE VISUAL

Visuals, like other texts, are of certain kinds or types that we call *genres*. Common visual genres are advertisements, works of art, photographs, charts, and other kinds of graphics. We can learn more about the purpose, audience, and context by understanding how a visual that we are analyzing is similar to (and different from) other visuals belonging to its genre. The World War II posters on this page, for example, illustrate a visual genre from the 1940s. The purpose of these posters was to recruit men and women to the war effort. The posters featured here were intended to appeal to women to help with war-related tasks or even to join the Women's Army Corps.

Rosie the Riveter

The first poster is possibly the most famous example of this genre: Rosie the Riveter. The focus is on Rosie's strong right arm, with her sleeves rolled up, ready for work. The strong diagonal of her arm points back to Rosie's face and to the text at the top of the poster. The purpose of this poster was to encourage women to participate in the war effort, both by direct exhortation ("We Can Do It!") and by offering an image of an attractive, capable, and courageous woman. The Rosie the Riveter poster helped revolutionize gender images during the war.

The second poster, "She's a WOW," presents a similarly strong image designed to recruit women for ordnance work. Like Rosie, she is capable, attractive, and ready for work, with her hair wrapped in a red and white bandana. Although she is in the foreground against the background image of the soldier, the text keeps her in a supportive role: "The Girl He Left Behind Is Still Behind Him." She is not looking out at the viewer, as Rosie is, but back at the soldier. Still, her color image, accented in red and white, is larger than the soldier's background picture.

A third poster from this genre shows a uniformed, professional figure against the background of the U.S. flag. "Join the WAC Now!" relies on a dominant foreground image of a professional woman in uniform against the patriotic red, white, and blue colors. The flag's diagonal helps connect the messages at the bottom ("Join the WAC Now!" and "Thousands of Army Jobs Need Filling!") with the more emotional appeal at the top: "Are you a girl with a Star-Spangled heart?"

The genre of visuals used to recruit women for a war effort has evolved so that now, during the war in Iraq, the official army recruiting

"She's a WOW"

"Join the WAC Now!"

site posts photos of women serving in the army with an accompanying caption, explaining the service that women perform. This image shows the children who will be helped by this new women's center, and it shows the other women soldiers who have contributed to this effort. However, the person cutting the tape is a man, and he screens the woman in the aqua dress who, presumably, is a key figure for the new women's center.

The war poster genre continues in contemporary satiric posters questioning our Homeland Security laws. The poster on the following page suggests that patriotism requires being silent and refraining from speaking out against these laws, against the war in Iraq, or against other government policies. It uses a popular and patriotic image to imply that the Homeland Security Office is trying to silence freedom of speech. We understand this message partly from the words and partly from the genre of the patriotic wartime poster.

Col. Debra Lewis

Patriotism Means Silence

VISUALS   WITH TEXT   IN CONTEXT   GENRE   RHETORICAL APPEALS

RHETORICAL APPEALS
TO THE AUDIENCE

All of the features of visuals analyzed earlier—the composition of the visual, the ac-companying text, the context, and the genre—contribute to the overall rhetorical purpose and the effect on its audience or viewer. Visuals, like written texts, also make specific rhetorical appeals to reason and logic (logos), to emotion (pathos), and to character and credibility (ethos).

APPEAL TO REASON Usually charts, graphs, and diagrams contain appeals to reason, logic, facts, and other kinds of data. The following visual diagram, which accompanied a newspaper story about alternative sources of energy, illustrates the appeal to reason (logos). Using a sequence of logical steps, it explains in text and in image how wind could be used to generate hydrogen to power electric grids as well as automobiles. Its purpose is apparently to inform or explain, but because the information for the graphic is provided by an energy company, its more subtle purpose is to improve public relations by persuading customers that Xcel Energy is doing its part in the search for alternative energies.

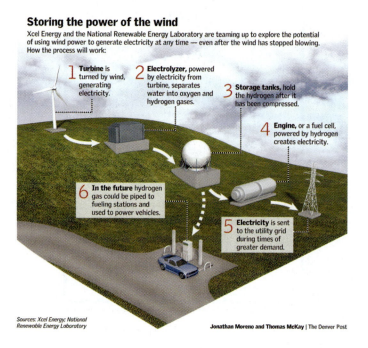

Storing the power of the wind

Xcel Energy and the National Renewable Energy Laboratory are teaming up to explore the potential of using wind power to generate electricity at any time — even after the wind has stopped blowing. How the process will work:

1 **Turbine** is turned by wind, generating electricity.

2 **Electrolyzer,** powered by electricity from turbine, separates water into oxygen and hydrogen gases.

3 **Storage tanks,** hold the hydrogen after it has been compressed.

4 **Engine,** or a fuel cell, powered by hydrogen creates electricity.

6 **In the future** hydrogen gas could be piped to fueling stations and used to power vehicles.

5 **Electricity** is sent to the utility grid during times of greater demand.

Sources: Xcel Energy; National Renewable Energy Laboratory

Jonathan Moreno and Thomas McKay | The Denver Post

▪ **APPEAL TO EMOTION**   Typically, advertisements use strong appeals to emotion (pathos), simply because emotions are so effective in persuading viewers to buy a product. Emotional appeals include positive feelings (beauty, sex, status, image, and sometimes even humor) as well as negative emotions (fear, anxiety, insecurity, and pity). These appeals come from the composition of the image, the text, the context, and even the genre of the visual. Magazines are a good source for advertisements relying primarily on emotional appeals.

▪ **APPEAL TO CHARACTER AND CREDIBILITY**   Often visuals use a strong appeal to character and credibility (ethos) to convince, move, or persuade viewers. This appeal is not to the character of any person pictured in the visual, but to the character and credibility of the designer or creator of the image. If viewers sense that the visual conveys a sense of integrity and authenticity, that the maker of the image is sincere and is not relying on cheap emotional appeals, or that the visual communicates a sense of humanity and goodwill, the appeal to character is successful. Look again at Dorothea Lange's images of a migrant mother. These pictures have an emotional appeal, to be sure, but they are composed with an integrity and credibility that give them a strong character appeal, too. Lange's pictures give the mother and her children dignity at the same time that they call attention to her plight.

COMBINED APPEALS   Often visuals and their texts will combine appeals to logic, emotion, and character. Consider the following spoof-ad posted on Adbusters of the popular ads for Absolut, a brand of vodka. Emotional appeals emerge from the blood-colored reds and dramatic blacks, the long shadows and spilt liquids, the white chalk outline of the body (the bottle), the police officer taking notes, and the red taillights of the car. The bold caption, "Absolute End," (notice how the spelling has been changed from *Absolut* to *Absolute*) and the statistics cited below the picture appeal to logic, connecting the 100,000 alcohol ads teenagers see with the fact that 50% of automobile fatalities are linked to alcohol. This visual also generates an ethos or character appeal because the creator of the ad is apparently someone we can trust, someone of good character whose goal is to prevent the needless and tragic fatalities associated with drinking and driving.

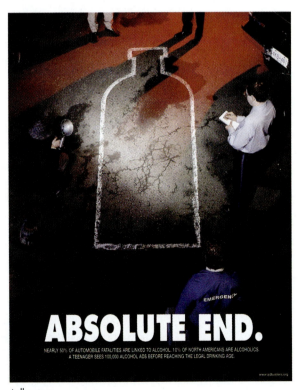

As you practice analysis of a variety of visuals, remember three important points. First, not all types of analysis will be important for a particular visual or hybrid text. Focus on the kinds of analysis that work best for your project. Second, techniques for analysis should be repeated or combined until you discover the key features of the visual. Start with the visual, work through accompanying text, consider the context and the genre, and analyze the rhetorical appeals, but come back to the visual after you know more about the context and have thought about appeals. Third, remember that the

Adbusters

ultimate goal of your analysis will be **synthesis**. You examine the parts and pieces of a multimedia text in order to support your synthesis of these parts into a meaningful whole. Your explanation of the meaning and significance of the visual or the rhetorical purpose and effectiveness of the visual in its context becomes your thesis or **claim**.

When you practiced analyzing visuals, you were the reader or audience in the diagram shown here, judging the visual with its accompanying text, in its context, and considering how the creator of the image worked to achieve a particular purpose for the intended audience.

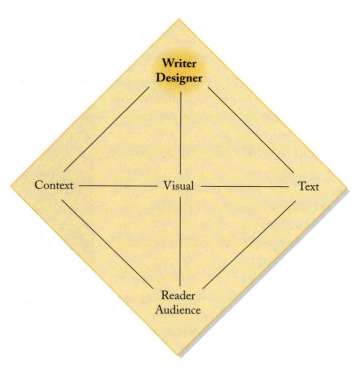

Now you need to switch roles. After you have practiced analyzing a variety of visuals for their overall rhetorical effect, you are better prepared to add or design visuals for your own essay, article, pamphlet, or Web site. As the primary designer or creator, you will likely be using visuals and diagrams, but you should also consider the layout of your text as a visual element: typeface, size of font, margins, color, and use of white space all have visual appeal for your readers. As you design your document, keep the following techniques in mind.

TECHNIQUES FOR DESIGNING VISUALS

Visuals, illustrations, graphics, photographs, and document design are all elements of your writing that have a rhetorical effect. Use the following techniques as you consider visuals and text layout possibilities for your essay, article, brochure, or other document.

- **Designing for your audience and purpose.** Use your analytical skills to work backward from your intended audience and purpose. Your purpose and audience should guide your selection of appropriate genre, most effective visuals, and clear document design.

- **Choosing and understanding your genre.** Collect and study several examples of your genre, whether it is an article, brochure, poster, or Web site. Does your genre use many visuals and only a few words? Does it use mostly text with few visuals or diagrams? Take notes on the layout typically used. Choose the best features and creatively modify them for your own purposes.

- **Selecting or designing visuals for your document.** Choose or design visual elements with strong compositional features: key figures, strong diagonals, appropriate color, and balance. Make your diagrams, graphs, and charts clear and easy to understand. Choose the most striking illustrations, and use them sparingly. Avoid clutter.

- **Designing your written text to support your purpose.** Choose typeface, font, and margins with an eye to your purpose and audience. Balance chunks of text with visuals on a page. Use bold type and white space to create emphasis. Make your visuals or illustrations compatible with your text.

The following layout strategies, featuring the article about Michael J. Fox, show several design features you can create with your own computer. If you are not familiar with how to use columns, text box features, sidebars, color shading, or pulled quotations, check with your instructor or computer lab assistant. The "Help" feature on your computer will also guide you through the steps to create these layout features.

> **“** Effective visual presentation . . . [requires] minimizing the possibility of competition between picture and text and ensuring that the pictures used are relevant to the material presented. **”**
> —JENNIFER WILEY, "COGNITIVE AND EDUCATIONAL IMPLICATIONS OF VISUAL RICH MEDIA"

Creating Columns and Adding Images in Text Boxes

PROGRESS OR NOT

Oct. 25, 2006—"The ad was in extremely poor taste," said a spokesman for Michael Steele, Republican candidate for the Senate in Maryland, referring to a TV spot made for his opponent, Rep. Ben Cardin.

That will be the line of Republicans under assault from what could become one of the most powerful political advertisements ever made. The new ad features an ailing Michael J. Fox talking about politicians who oppose embryonic stem-cell research. This is not just another celebrity ad, like those cut by the late Christopher Reeve. It's a celebrity shot to the solar plexus of the GOP. Whatever happens in the campaign, the ad is already a classic and will be mentioned in the same breath as LBJ's famous 1964 "Daisy" ad and other unforgettable political moments on television.

Rush Limbaugh helped cement the ad's place in history with his astonishingly insensitive remark that Fox "was either off his medication or was acting." Limbaugh quickly apologized but the damage to his own reputation was already done.

Fox, star of megahit TV shows and movies like "Family Ties" and *Back to the Future,* was for years one of the most popular actors in the United States. He still works, but is clearly debilitated by Parkinson's. Throughout the ad, he sways back and forth, showing signs of advanced disease.

Adding Boxes, Drop Caps, Color, and Quotations in the Margins

PROGRESS OR NOT

Oct. 25, 2006—"The ad was in extremely poor taste," said a spokesman for Michael Steele, Republican candidate for the Senate in Maryland, referring to a TV spot made for his opponent, Rep. Ben Cardin.

That will be the line of Republicans under assault from what could become one of the most powerful political advertisements ever made. The new ad features an ailing Michael J. Fox talking about politicians who

> **Whatever happens in the campaign, the ad is already a classic....**

oppose embryonic stem-cell research. This is not just another celebrity ad, like those cut by the late Christopher Reeve. It's a celebrity shot to the solar plexus of the GOP. Whatever happens in the campaign, the ad is already a classic and will be mentioned in the same breath as LBJ's famous 1964 "Daisy" ad and other unforgettable political moments on television.

Rush Limbaugh helped cement the ad's place in history with his astonishingly insensitive remark that Fox "was either off his medication or was acting." Limbaugh quickly apologized but the damage to his own reputation was already done.

Fox, star of megahit TV shows and movies like "Family Ties" and *Back to the Future,* was for years one of the most popular actors in the United States. He still works, but is clearly debilitated by Parkinson's. Throughout the ad, he sways back and forth, showing signs of advanced disease.

"He is exaggerating the effects of the disease," Limbaugh told listeners. "He's moving all around and shaking and it's purely an act. . . . This is really shameless of Michael J. Fox. He was either off his medication or he's acting."

Source: *The Washington Post*, October 25, 2006

Adding Sidebars, Tables, Charts, and Graphs

PROGRESS OR NOT

Oct. 25, 2006—"The ad was in extremely poor taste," said a spokesman for Michael Steele, Republican candidate for the Senate in Maryland, referring to a TV spot made for his opponent, Rep. Ben Cardin.

The struggle for funds to support Parkinson's disease is illustrated by the following chart. Most of the funds for medical research go to research for the nation's greatest killers: heart disease, cancer, stroke, and lung disease. AIDS and diabetes kill far more people than Parkinson's, which causes death less than a fraction of one percent of the time. People are far more likely to die from anorexia, salmonella, or measles than from Parkinson's.

Causes of Death

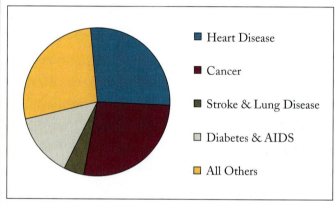

- Heart Disease
- Cancer
- Stroke & Lung Disease
- Diabetes & AIDS
- All Others

Source: *Time*, Dec. 4, 2006, p. 68.

That will be the line of Republicans under assault from what could become one of the most powerful political advertisements ever made. The new ad features an ailing Michael J. Fox talking about politicians who oppose embryonic stem-cell research. This is not just another celebrity ad, like those cut by the late Christopher Reeve. It's a celebrity shot to the solar plexus of the GOP. Whatever happens in the campaign, the ad is already a classic and will be mentioned in the same breath as LBJ's famous 1964 "Daisy" ad and other unforgettable political moments on television.

Rush Limbaugh helped cement the ad's place in history with his astonishingly insensitive remark that Fox "was either off his medication or was acting." Limbaugh quickly apologized but the damage to his own reputation was already done.

▍ WARMING UP: Journal Exercises

The following exercises will help you practice analyzing visuals and hybrid texts. Respond to these exercises individually, in groups, or on your class Web site.

1. Analyze the chapter opening art, *The Lover Sings as his Lady Dances.* Look at composition, focal point(s), use of color, and perspective in the painting. Why are the details of dress realistic while the sky is a stylistic red? What kind of perspective is used to draw the castle and the well? What is the social purpose of this image?

2. Analyze the spoof-ad below that appears on Adbuster's Web site. First, examine the visual for composition, focus, narrative, theme, and rhetorical appeals. After you have written your analysis, search the Internet and your library databases for a short, full-text news article, report, editorial, or op-ed column that discusses the dietary or health problems associated with fast foods. Download a full-text version of this article into a word file, and then download and insert this image in an appropriate place in that article. Write a paragraph explaining why this McDonald's spoof-ad is (or perhaps is not) appropriate to the purpose and audience of that article.

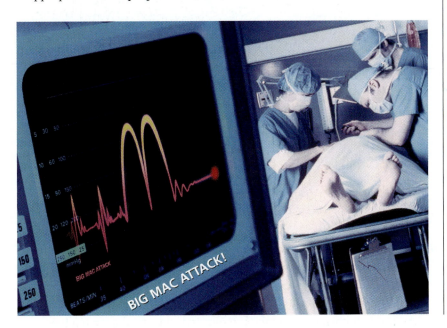

3. In a visual that contains text or a caption, the image and the words should complement each other, working toward a single meaning. *The New Yorker* regularly sponsors a cartoon caption contest. Drawings are initially published without captions, and readers are invited to contribute their best lines during the next two weeks. Study the following cartoon. By yourself or in a group, suggest possible captions. Once you have a caption or two, explain why your entry complements the drawing. (Below the cartoon are the three finalist suggestions, printed upside down. Don't read them until you've made your own suggestions.)

"Well, then, it's unanimous." Anne Whiteside, San Francisco, Calif. (The winning caption.)
"So that settles it. This year, instead of cooking the books, we'll bake them in a light, flaky pastry." Michael Hirson, Washington, D.C.
"Who else found Gary's report a little too angry, white, and male?" Grant Ruple, Morristown, N.J.

4. Study the two famous photographs presented on the next page. Choose one and write your own analysis of that image. First, analyze the image. Then write a narrative of what you imagine happened before, during, and after the moment recorded in this image. Finally, *research* these two photographs and their photographers on the Internet and add a final paragraph explaining how the information you discovered confirms or revises your analysis and your narrative.

Gordon Parks, *American Gothic*

5. Find three advertisements in magazines that advertise the same product (or same kind of product, such as cars, jeans, or perfume) in different magazines directed at different audiences. For example, you might find similar ads in *Time*, *Wired*, and *Seventeen*. Analyze each ad for its compositional features, and then describe how the ad changes in its composition, focus, narrative, theme, or appeals based on different target audiences. Which of these ads is most effective for its target audience? Why?

6. Choose an essay that you have already written for this course or for a previous writing course. Revise and format it on your computer for a more public audience, choosing the genre of a short newspaper article, brochure, flyer, or poster. Practice using the layout features (sidebars, inserted visuals, double columns, pulled quotations, drop caps, tables, and color) appropriate for that genre. As a postscript for your revision, explain why you made the choices you did during your revision.

7. Analyze the following cartoon, which appeared in *The New Yorker*. What are the main compositional features? Is this cartoon humorous, serious, or

both? If you were looking for a visual to use in an article about possible cell phone legislation, would this image be effective? Research your library's databases for recent newspaper articles or editorials about cell phone use and abuse. Find a short article or editorial, copy it into your computer word file, and insert this image at an appropriate place. Then write a paragraph explaining why this image complements the message of the article. On Google Images, find another image about cell phone use that would be effective for your article or editorial. Which of the two images (the cartoon shown here or the visual you found) would be more effective? Explain.

"I was distracted for a moment. Go on."

8. Imagine that you are a news magazine editor who is responsible for choosing visuals to accompany articles about global warming. Your magazine is going to print a report about the United Nations Inter-governmental Panel on Climate Change (IPCC). (See sample articles in Chapter 5.) Consider the images reprinted here. Which images contain appeals to emotion? Which appeal to logic? Which to ethos? Which of these images would you prefer for this context? Find another image on Google Images that might be even more effective. Explain your choice(s).

Global Warming Projections

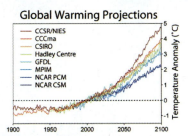

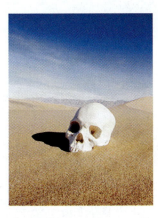

9. The editor of your local or college newspaper has asked you to write an article calling attention to Cesar Chavez Day on March 31. Your purpose is to describe the highlights of Chavez's career and accomplishments. Write a short (300–400-word) report that describes upcoming activities on Cesar Chavez Day and that briefly outlines his career and accomplishments. You have room for one image to accompany your short article. Examine the images on the next page. Analyze each image for its effectiveness in supporting the purpose of your article. Explain which one you would choose and why.

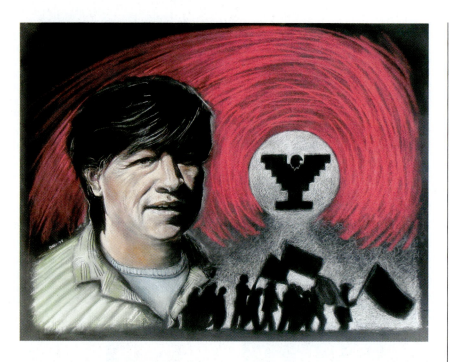

PROFESSIONAL WRITING

Miss Clairol's "Does She . . . Or Doesn't She?": How to Advertise a Dangerous Product

James B. Twitchell

A longtime professor of English at the University of Florida, James B. Twitchell has written a dozen books on a variety of academic and cultural topics. His recent books on advertising and popular culture include Carnival Culture: The Trashing of Taste in America *(1992),* Adcult USA: The Triumph of Advertising in American Culture *(1996), and* Living It Up: Our Love Affair with Luxury *(2002). In "Miss Clairol's 'Does She . . . Or Doesn't She?'" taken from* Twenty Ads That Shook the World *(2000), Twitchell examines the Miss Clairol advertising campaign, which was designed by Shirley Polykoff. Twitchell explains how Polykoff's ads, which ran for nearly twenty years, revolutionized the hair-coloring industry. Part of the success of the ad was in the catchy title, Twitchell notes, but equally important were the children in the ads and the follow-up phrase, "Hair color so natural, only her hairdresser knows for sure." (Before you read Twitchell's essay, however, look at several of Polykoff's Clairol ads by searching for Shirley Polykoff on Google.)*

...continued Miss Clairol's "Does She ... Or Doesn't She?", **James B. Twitchell**

Two types of product are difficult to advertise: the very common and the very radical. Common products, called "parity products," need contrived distinctions to set them apart. You announce them as "New and Improved, Bigger and Better." But singular products need the illusion of acceptability. They have to appear as if they were *not* new and big, but old and small.

So, in the 1950s, new objects like television sets were designed to look like furniture so that they would look "at home" in your living room. Meanwhile, accepted objects like automobiles were growing massive tail fins to make them seem bigger and better, new and improved.

Although hair coloring is now very common (about half of all American women between the ages of thirteen and seventy color their hair, and about one in eight American males between thirteen and seventy does the same), such was certainly not the case generations ago. The only women who regularly dyed their hair were actresses like Jean Harlow, and "fast women," most especially prostitutes. The only man who dyed his hair was Gorgeous George, the professional wrestler. He was also the only man to use perfume.

In the twentieth century, prostitutes have had a central role in developing cosmetics. For them, sexiness is an occupational necessity, and hence anything that makes them look young, flushed, and fertile is quickly assimilated. Creating a full-lipped, big-eyed, and rosy-cheeked image is the basis of the lipstick, eye shadow, mascara, and rouge industries. While fashion may come *down* from the couturiers, face paint comes *up* from the street. Yesterday's painted woman is today's fashion plate.

In the 1950s, just as Betty Friedan was sitting down to write *The Feminine Mystique*, there were three things a lady should not do. She should not smoke in public, she should not wear long pants (unless under an overcoat), and she should not color her hair. Better she should pull out each gray strand by its root than risk association with those who bleached or, worse, dyed their hair.

This was the cultural context into which Lawrence M. Gelb, a chemical broker and enthusiastic entrepreneur, presented his product to Foote, Cone & Belding. Gelb had purchased the rights to a French hair-coloring process called Clairol. The process was unique in that unlike other available hair-coloring products, which coated the hair, Clairol actually penetrated the hair shaft, producing softer, more natural tones. Moreover, it contained a foamy shampoo base and mild oils that cleaned and conditioned the hair.

When the product was first introduced during World War II, the application process took five different steps and lasted a few hours. The users were urban and wealthy. In 1950, after seven years of research and development, Gelb once again took the beauty industry by storm. He introduced the new Miss Clairol Hair Color Bath, a single-step hair-coloring process. *7*

This product, unlike any haircolor previously available, lightened, darkened, or changed a woman's natural haircolor by coloring and shampooing hair in one simple step that took only twenty minutes. Color results were more natural than anything you could find at the corner beauty parlor. It was hard to believe. Miss Clairol was so technologically advanced that demonstrations had to be done onstage at the International Beauty Show, using buckets of water, to prove to the industry that it was not a hoax. This breakthrough was almost too revolutionary to sell. *8*

In fact, within six months of Miss Clairol's introduction, the number of women who visited the salon for permanent hair-coloring services increased by more than 500 percent! The women still didn't think they could do it themselves. And *Good Housekeeping* magazine rejected hair-color advertising because they too didn't believe the product would work. The magazine waited for three years before finally reversing its decision, accepting the ads, and awarding Miss Clairol's new product the "Good Housekeeping Seal of Approval." *9*

FC&B passed the "Yes you *can* do it at home" assignment to Shirley Polykoff, a zesty and genial first-generation American in her late twenties. She was, as she herself was the first to admit, a little unsophisticated, but her colleagues thought she understood how women would respond to abrupt change. Polykoff understood emotion, all right, and she also knew that you could be outrageous if you did it in the right context. You can be very naughty if you are first perceived as being nice! Or, in her words, "Think it out square, say it with flair." And it is just this reconciliation of opposites that informs her most famous ad. *10*

She knew this almost from the start. On July 9, 1955, Polykoff wrote to the head art director that she had three campaigns for Miss Clairol Hair Color Bath. The first shows the same model in each ad, but with slightly different hair color. The second exhorts "Tear up those baby pictures! You're a redhead now," and plays on the American desire to refashion the self by rewriting history. These two ideas were, as she says, "knock-downs" en route to what she really wanted. In her autobiography, appropriately titled *Does She . . . Or Doesn't She?: And How She Did It*, Polykoff explains the third execution, the one that will work: *11*

. . . continued Miss Clairol's "Does She . . . Or Doesn't She?", **James B. Twitchell**

#3. Now here's the one I really want. If I can get it sold to the client. Listen to this: "*Does she . . . or doesn't she?*" (No, I'm not kidding. Didn't you ever hear of the arresting question?) Followed by: "*Only her mother knows for sure!*" or "*So natural, only her mother knows for sure!*"

I may not do the mother part, though as far as I'm concerned mother is the ultimate authority. However, if Clairol goes retail, they may have a problem of offending beauty salons, where they are presently doing all of their business. So I may change the word "mother" to "hairdresser." This could be awfully good business—turning the hairdresser into a color expert. Besides, it reinforces the claim of naturalness, and not so incidentally, glamorizes the salon.

The psychology is obvious. I know from myself. If anyone admires my hair, I'd rather die than admit I dye. And since I feel so strongly that the average woman is me, this great stress on naturalness is important [Polykoff 1975, 28–29].

While her headline is naughty, the picture is nice and natural. Exactly *12* what "Does She . . . or Doesn't She" do? To men the answer was clearly sexual, but to women it certainly was not. The male editors of *Life* magazine balked about running this headline until they did a survey and found out women were not filling in the ellipsis the way they were.

Women, as Polykoff knew, were finding different meaning because *13* they were actually looking at the model and her child. For them the picture was not presexual but postsexual, not inviting male attention but expressing satisfaction with the result. Miss Clairol is a mother, not a love interest.

If that is so, then the product must be misnamed: it should be *Mrs.* *14* Clairol. Remember, this was the mid-1950s, when illegitimacy was a powerful taboo. Out-of-wedlock children were still called bastards, not love children. This ad was far more dangerous than anything Benetton or Calvin Klein has ever imagined.

The naughty/nice conundrum was further intensified *and* diffused by *15* some of the ads featuring a wedding ring on the model's left hand. Although FC&B experimented with models purporting to be secretaries, schoolteachers, and the like, the motif of mother and child was always constant.

So what was the answer to what she does or doesn't do? To women, *16* what she did had to do with visiting the hairdresser. Of course, men couldn't understand. This was the world before unisex hair care. Men still went to barber shops. This was the same pre-feminist generation in which the solitary headline "Modess . . . because" worked magic selling female sanitary products. The ellipsis masked a knowing implication that excluded men. That was part of its attraction. Women know, men don't. This you-just-don't-get-it motif was to become a central marketing strategy as the women's movement was aided *and* exploited by Madison Avenue nichemeisters.

Polykoff had to be ambiguous for another reason. As she notes in her *17* memoir, Clairol did not want to be obvious about what they were doing to their primary customer—the beauty shop. Remember that the initial product entailed five different steps performed by the hairdresser, and lasted hours. Many women were still using hairdressers for something they could now do by themselves. It did not take a detective to see that the company was trying to run around the beauty shop and sell to the end-user. So the ad again has it both ways. The hairdresser is invoked as the expert—only he knows *for sure*—but the process of coloring your hair can be done without his expensive assistance.

The copy block on the left of the finished ad reasserts this intimacy, *18* only now it is not the hairdresser speaking, but another woman who has used the product. The emphasis is always on *returning* to young and radiant hair, hair you used to have, hair, in fact, that glistens exactly like your current companion's—your child's hair.

The copy block on the right is all business and was never changed *19* during the campaign. The process of coloring is always referred to as "automatic color tinting." *Automatic* was to the fifties what *plastic* became to the sixties, and what *networking* is today. Just as your food was kept automatically fresh in the refrigerator, your car had an automatic transmission, your house had an automatic thermostat, your dishes and clothes were automatically cleaned and dried, so, too, your hair had automatic tinting.

However, what is really automatic about hair coloring is that once you *20* start, you won't stop. Hair grows, roots show, buy more product . . . automatically. The genius of Gillette was not just that they sold the "safety razor" (they could give the razor away), but that they also sold the concept of being *clean-shaven*. Clean-shaven means that you use their blade every day, so, of course, you always need more blades. Clairol made "roots showing" into what Gillette had made "five o'clock shadow."

As was to become typical in hair-coloring ads, the age of the model was *21* a good ten years younger than the typical product user. The model is in her early thirties (witness the age of the child), too young to have gray hair.

...continued Miss Clairol's "Does She ... Or Doesn't She?", **James B. Twitchell**

This aspirational motif was picked up later for other Clairol products: 22 "If I've only one life . . . let me live it as a blonde!" "Every woman should be a redhead . . . at least once in her life!" "What would your husband say if suddenly you looked 10 years younger?" "Is it true blondes have more fun?" "What does he look at second?" And, of course, "The closer he gets the better you look!"

But these slogans for different brand extensions only work because 23 Miss Clairol had done her job. She made hair coloring possible, she made hair coloring acceptable, she made at-home hair coloring—dare I say it— empowering. She made the unique into the commonplace. By the 1980s, the hairdresser problem had been long forgotten and the follow-up lines read, "Hair color so natural, they'll never know for sure."

The Clairol theme propelled sales 413 percent higher in six years and 24 influenced nearly 50 percent of all adult women to tint their tresses. Ironically, Miss Clairol, bought out by Bristol-Myers in 1959, also politely opened the door to her competitors, L'Oreal and Revlon.

Thanks to Clairol, hair coloring has become a very attractive business 25 indeed. The key ingredients are just a few pennies' worth of peroxide, ammonia, and pigment. In a pretty package at the drugstore it sells for four to ten dollars per application. To put it mildly, the cost-revenue spread is what is really enticing. Gross profits of 70 percent are standard. As is common in the beauty industry, advertising and promotion cost far more than the product.

If you want to see how well this Clairol campaign did, just look at how 26 L'Oreal sells its version of hair dye. In L'Oreal's pitch, a rapturous beauty proudly proclaims that her coloring costs more, but that "I'm worth it." In a generation, hair coloring has gone from a surreptitious whisper (Does she . . .?) to a heroic trumpet (You better believe I do!). The user may be dangerous, the product certainly isn't. L'Oreal now dominates the world-wide market.

But by taking control of how the new woman presented herself, Miss 27 Clairol did indeed make it possible to come a long way, baby. In a current ad for Miss Clairol's descendant Nice 'n' Easy, the pixieish Julia Louis Dreyfus, from *Seinfeld*, shows us how the unique and dangerous has become common and tame. In her Elaine persona, she interrupts a wedding, telling the bride, "Even if your marriage doesn't last, your haircolor will." The guests are not shocked; they nod understandingly.

vo·cab·u·lar·y

In your journal, write down the meanings of the following words.

- is quickly *assimilated* **(4)**
- from the *couturiers* **(4)**
- enthusiastic *entrepreneur* **(6)**
- *reconciliation* of opposites **(10)**
- filling in the *ellipsis* **(12)**
- models *purporting* to be secretaries **(15)**
- the *motif* of mother and child **(15)**
- had to be *ambiguous* **(17)**

QUESTIONS FOR WRITING AND DISCUSSION

1. Recall the first time you colored your hair—or cut or styled it in a particular way. What was your attitude toward making a change? Did you change because of influences from peers, family, friends, advertisements, or other social pressure? What was the effect of the change on your attitude, personality, or relationships with others?

2. A key part of any successful advertising campaign is understanding the rhetorical situation: the product, the purpose and audience, the occasion, the selected text and images, and the cultural context. First consider the cultural context. Twitchell subtitles his essay, "How to Advertise a Dangerous Product." According to Twitchell, what was culturally "dangerous" about a hair-coloring product at that time? What specifically were the dangers? How did Shirley Polykoff's Miss Clairol ads diffuse each of those dangers?

3. Understanding and successfully appealing to the audience is a second key to any successful text or advertisement. Who was the audience or audiences for the Clairol advertisements? Cite particular paragraphs where Twitchell explains how the Clairol advertisements anticipated and successfully managed the problem of audience.

4. Key word choices (diction) played an important role in the success of the Clairol advertisements. Find three examples from the essay that show how Polykoff used—or didn't use—a key word in order to make the advertisement more successful.

5. In paragraph 15, Twitchell briefly mentions the "motif of mother and child" that appears in every Miss Clairol advertisement. Using the Internet or your

library's databases, research cultural images of mother and child. Start by examining traditional Christian imagery. Consider Dorothea Lange's famous photograph of a migrant mother. How does the mother-child imagery work in these pictures to make them more effective? Then, working in a small group in your class, develop Twitchell's idea about the motif of mother and child. Why is this image culturally so important? Why was it rhetorically so important in the Miss Clairol advertisements?

ANALYZING   DESIGNING   PROCESSES

Processes for Analyzing and Designing Visuals

ASSIGNMENT FOR ANALYZING AND DESIGNING VISUALS

Write an essay, letter, forum response, commentary, or blog entry in which you analyze the effectiveness of a visual by itself or with accompanying text and social context. For example, you might choose or be assigned an advertising campaign, political document with photographs, prize-winning or historical photograph, fine art, Internet visual, or other scientific, cultural, or social text that uses images and visuals as a key part of the document. Your assignment is to analyze the relationship of the image to its context and intended audience, to compare similar images to determine which is rhetorically more effective, to research how the image is related to its social or historical context, and/or to design accompanying images for an assignment you have already written or are currently writing.

Your purpose for this assignment is to analyze the visual for its composition, focus, narrative, themes, and rhetorical appeals in order to show how—and how effectively—it works with any accompanying text, in its social context, for the intended purpose and audience. You will analyze all the specific components in order to combine or synthesize them into an explanation of *what* the overall meaning or significance of the visual is and/or *how* and *why* the visuals are or are not effective for that context. Be sure to focus your explanation on your purpose for your intended audience.

CHOOSING   COLLECTING   SHAPING   DRAFTING   REVISING

CHOOSING A SUBJECT

Unless you have a particular assignment, choose a contemporary image that you find incorporated in your reading for your other classes, reading and research that you do for your job, news items, Internet sites, billboards, or any other place where visuals appear in a clear rhetorical context. (If you choose to analyze a Web site, read the essay "Evaluating a Web Site," reprinted on pages 414–417.) Video clips from the Internet can work if they are short and if you are submitting your document online or in a digital environment. You may wish to choose a visual and compare it to other examples from that genre. You may wish to consider several similar images used for different gender, racial, or cultural contexts. Your assignment may even be to analyze a variety of possible visuals you could choose for an essay you are writing and to show why the ones you select are best suited to your purpose, audience, and genre. *Remember that when you download images from the Internet, you must give credit to the photographer, artist, or designer of the visual.*

CHOOSING   **COLLECTING**   SHAPING   DRAFTING   REVISING

COLLECTING

Many images are available on the Internet through Google or Yahoo! searches, or on popular image sites such as Corbis. Once you locate several appropriate visuals, begin by analyzing and taking notes on them, looking for key parts of the composition, focus, narrative, themes, and rhetorical appeals. However, you should also collect and analyze any accompanying texts or evidence that illustrates the social or historical context. Collecting visuals belonging to the same genre (historical photographs, advertising campaigns, political photographs, or Internet images) will also provide evidence helpful for your analysis. Researching the background, context, origin, or maker/designer of the image can be important, as is finding other commentaries and analyses of your particular type or genre of visuals. Use your *critical reading skills* to understand key points in these commentaries. Be sure to use your *observing* skills to help your analysis. Try closing your eyes and drawing the visual for yourself—what details did you remember and reproduce and what details did you forget? If you have any particular *memories* of this image or of the first time you saw this visual, you may want to add those to your account.

SHAPING

How you organize your analysis depends on the assignment, purpose, audience, and genre for your analysis. Three effective strategies for organizing are explained and illustrated here.

■ ANALYSIS FOCUSED ON THE VISUAL

Often the specific details of the visual are the primary focus of the analysis. This is often the case with detailed or complex images whose meaning or significance may not be immediately obvious. The analysis focuses on composition, arrangement, focus, foreground and background images, images in the center and on the margin, symbols, cultural references, and key features of the genre. Only after analyzing these details will the commentary explain how these details are related to the cultural or historical context and thus contribute to the overall meaning.

The following analysis, by Charles Rosen and Henri Zerner, appeared in the *New York Review of Books*, and is of a painting by Norman Rockwell that appeared on the cover of *The Saturday Evening Post* in 1960. The authors devote over half of their essay to an analysis of the picture before they interpret the significance of Rockwell's self-portrait. Before you read Rosen's and Zerner's analysis, however, study the painting presented here. What are the important details in the picture? What is the overall meaning or significance, based on your analysis?

Printed by permission of the Norman Rockwell Family Agency, © 1960 the Norman Rockwell Family Entities.

Triple Self-Portrait

Triple Self-Portrait of 1960 is clever and witty. It is not simply a portrait of the artist by himself but represents the process of painting a self-portrait, and in the bargain Rockwell takes the opportunity to comment on his brand of "realism" and his relation to the history of art. A sheet of preparatory drawings in different poses is tacked onto the left of the canvas. The artist represents himself from the back; the canvas he works on already has a fully worked-out black-and-white drawing of his face with the pipe in his mouth, based on the central drawing of the sketch sheet. The artist gazes at his own reflection in a mirror propped up on a chair. The reflection we see in the mirror is similar to, but not identical with, the portrait sketched on the canvas. The artist wears glasses, and the glare of the lenses completely obliterates his gaze, while the portrait he works on is without glasses and a little younger-looking, certainly less tense than the reflection. Rockwell seems to confess that the reality of his depicted world, compelling as it may be, is in fact a make-believe.

Tacked on the upper right corner of the canvas is a series of reproductions of historical self-portraits: Dürer, Rembrandt, Van Gogh, and Picasso—grand company to measure oneself against, although the humorous tone of the image preserves it from megalomania. But there is a problem: "If Rockwell nodded humbly in Picasso's direction," as Robert Rosenblum suggests, how humbly was it? It is "most surprising," Rosenblum observes, that Rockwell chose "a particularly difficult Picasso that mixes in idealized self-portrait in profile with an id-like female monster attacking from within" rather than something easily recognizable. This was a cover for *The Saturday Evening Post*. The strength of Rockwell is that he knew his public, and knew that such subtleties would be entirely lost on its readers, that most of them would not recognize the Picasso as a self-portrait at all but would consider it as pretentious humbug compared to Rockwell's honest picture and those of the illustrious predecessors he claims. Nor does he seem to have been particularly anxious to change their minds, whatever he himself may have thought.

Claim: The portrait is a clever and witty comment on his own art.

Layout and composition of portrait

Description of details

More description of details

Interpreting the meaning and significance of the painting

■ **ANALYSIS FOCUSED ON THE SOCIAL CONTEXT**   Often the visual or image is not detailed or complex, but the social, political, or historical context is complex, involved, or highly controversial. The following analysis, "Out of the Picture on the Abortion Ban," by Ellen Goodman, appeared in the *Boston Globe*. In this case, the photograph is not particularly complex or difficult, but it reveals much about the political and social context. The photograph is described at the beginning and then referred to at the end, providing a framework for Goodman's comment about the abortion debate.

Out of the Picture on the Abortion Ban

Early reference to another frequently appearing photograph

Short description and analysis of the photograph

Analysis: What is missing from the photograph

Analysis: How the photograph connects to abortion

Maybe this picture isn't worth a thousand words. That honor probably belongs to the flight deck portrait of the president under the sign, "Mission Accomplished." Maybe the presidential photo op now flying around the Internet and soon to be available on your local T-shirt is only worth 750 words.

The picture shows the president surrounded by an all-male chorus line of legislators as he signs the first ban on an abortion procedure. It's a single-sex class photo of men making laws governing something they will never have: a womb.

This was not just a strategic misstep, a rare Karl Rove lapse. It perfectly reflected the truth of the so-called partial-birth abortion law. What's wrong with this picture? The legislators had indeed erased women. They used the law as if it were Photoshop software, to crop out real women with real problems.

Indeed, just days after the shutter snapped, three separate courts ordered a temporary halt to the ban on these very grounds: It doesn't have any exemption for the health of a woman.

This is what brings me back, kicking and screaming, to the subject of abortion. I don't want to write about this. Like most Americans, I want the abortion debate to end. I want abortion to be safe and rare. That's safe and rare. And early.

Over the years, I've rejoiced at sonograms and picked names for what we call a baby when it's wanted and a fetus when it isn't. I'm aware that medicine has put the moment of viability on a collision course with the

moment of legal abortion. And I am also aware that not every pregnancy goes well, that sometimes families face terrible, traumatic choices.

Social and political contexts

Sixty-eight percent of Americans have been convinced by a public relations coup that this new law bans only a fringe and outrageous procedure. But the refusal to include an exception for the health of a pregnant woman takes this from the fringe to the heart of the debate. It's a deliberate, willful first strike at some of the most vulnerable women, those who need medical help the most.

The moment the anti-abortion leaders invented the term "partial-birth abortion," they made women invisible. The cartoon figures shown at congressional debates were, literally, drawings of a headless womb holding a perfect Gerber baby of some six or more months.

As Priscilla Smith, legal director of the Center for Reproductive Rights, said, "they turned the argument from the right of a woman to have an abortion to the reasons women have abortions." And then they declared those reasons to be frivolous.

Social and political contexts

The headless womb belonged to a generic woman who, as one opponent said, would get an abortion to fit into a prom dress. She would carry a pregnancy for months and then casually flip a coin between birth and an abortion "inches from life."

Time and again, abortion-rights supporters said they too would vote for the ban if opponents recognized that some pregnancies go terribly awry for the fetus or the woman and that some doctors found this procedure safest. But anti-abortion forces simply declared—against the evidence of the AMA or the American College of Obstetrics and Gynecology—that it was never medically necessary.

Reference to the abortion ban being signed in the photograph

Some years ago, when President Clinton vetoed a similar bill, he was surrounded by women. These women had been through pregnancies that came with words like hydrocephalus and polyhydramnia, and came with risks like hysterectomies. But the men around Bush see a health exception as a giant loophole. They believe a woman would leap through this loophole to get to the prom.

Reminder that another president had not signed a similar bill

Behind this is simply a mistrust of women as moral decision-makers. A mistrust so profound that their health is now in the hands of the courts. Not long ago, the Supreme Court ruled by exactly one vote that a law similar to this one violated the Constitution.

This should be a wake-up call to young women, because it's their health at risk, their role as moral decision-makers disparaged.

The most reliable supporters of abortion rights today are women over 50. It is, ironically, post-menopausal women who still lead the struggle to keep abortion legal for younger women. Everyone will tell you that the younger generation simply doesn't remember a time when abortion was illegal. They can't believe that it will ever be illegal again. How many believe they could be among those who need it?

Final reference to the omission of women in the photograph and in the making of laws directly affecting women

Days before signing this ban, the president tried to reassure voters that it wasn't the time to "totally ban abortions." But young women should put this picture up on their desktops. The folks in that photo op don't trust you. They don't even see you.

▎**ANALYSIS FOCUSED ON THE STORY** In this organizational pattern, the visual or photograph receives some analysis and commentary, but most of the analysis is of the history of the photograph and the life story of the key figures in the photograph. A narrative or story can often be very effective as a means of understanding the significance or true meaning behind a picture. The following example, "Coming Home," by Carolyn Kleiner Butler, was published in *Smithsonian* in 2003. Her article appeared at a time when many families in the United States had loved ones serving in Iraq or Afghanistan. Butler chooses to analyze a famous Vietnam era photograph by Sal Veder, which he titled *Burst of Joy* and which won a Pulitzer Prize in 1974. Usually an analysis of an image focuses on what the image reveals and what it represents. In this case, however, Butler emphasizes how the reality behind the photograph contrasts sharply with the reality in the photograph. In other words, Butler contrasts the happy story of what the image reveals with the reality that it conceals.

A hero's welcome: Lorrie, Robert Jr., Cindy, Loretta and Roger Stirm greet Lt. Col. Robert Stirm after his six years as a prisoner of war.

Coming Home

*To a war-weary nation, a U.S. POW's return from captivity
in Vietnam in 1973 looked like the happiest of reunions*

SITTING IN THE BACK SEAT of a station wagon on the tarmac at Travis Air Force Base, in California, clad in her favorite fuchsia miniskirt, 15-year-old Lorrie Stirm felt that she was in a dream. It was March 17, 1973, and it had been six long years since she had last seen her father, Lt. Col. Robert L. Stirm, an Air Force fighter pilot who was shot down over Hanoi in 1967 and had been missing or imprisoned ever since. She simply couldn't believe they were about to be reunited. The teenager waited while her father stood in front of a jubilant crowd and made a brief speech on behalf of himself and other POW's who had arrived from Vietnam as part of "Operation Homecoming."

The minutes crept by like hours, she recalls, and then, all at once, the car door opened. "I just wanted to get to Dad as fast as I could," Lorrie says. She tore down the runway toward him with open arms, her spirits—and feet—flying. Her mother, Loretta, and three younger siblings—Robert Jr., Roger and Cindy—were only steps behind. "We didn't know if he would ever come home," Lorrie says. "That moment was all our prayers answered, all our wishes come true."

Associated Press photographer Slava "Sal" Veder, who'd been standing in a crowded bullpen with dozens of other journalists, noticed the sprinting family and started taking pictures. "You could feel the energy and the raw emotion in the air," says Veder, then 46, who had spent much of the Vietnam era covering antiwar demonstrations in San Francisco and Berkeley. The day was overcast, meaning no shadows and near-perfect light. He rushed to a makeshift darkroom in a ladies' bathroom on the base (United Press International had commandeered the men's). In less than half an hour, Veder and his AP colleague Walt Zeboski had developed six remarkable images of that singular moment. Veder's pick, which he instantly titled *Burst of Joy*, was sent out over the news-service wires, published in newspapers around the nation and went on to win a Pulitzer Prize in 1974.

It remains the quintessential homecoming photograph of the time. Stirm, 39, who had endured gunshot wounds, torture, illness, starvation and despair in North Vietnamese prison camps, including the infamous Hanoi Hilton, is pictured in a crisp new uniform. Because his back is to the camera, as Veder points out, the officer seems anonymous, an everyman who represented not only the hundreds of POW's released that spring but all the troops in Vietnam who would return home to the mothers, fathers, wives, daughters and sons they'd left behind. "It's a hero's welcome for guys who weren't always seen or treated as heroes," says Donald Goldstein, a retired Air Force lieutenant colonel and a coauthor of *The Vietnam War: The*

The story just before the photograph was taken

Lorrie's memories of her feelings when her dad returned

Shift to the photographer's story

The photographer's recollection of the emotions of that day

The story from the soldier's or father's point of view

Stories and The Photographs, of the Stirm family reunion picture. "After years of fighting a war we couldn't win, a war that tore us apart, it was finally over, and the country could start healing."

Events behind the moment of this photograph

But there was more to the story than was captured on film. Three days before Stirm landed at Travis, a chaplain had handed him a Dear John letter from his wife. "I can't help but feel ambivalent about it," Stirm says today of the photograph. "I was very pleased to see my children—I loved them all and still do, and I know they had a difficult time—but there was a lot to deal with." Lorrie says, "So much had happened—there was so much that my dad missed out on—and it took a while to let him back into our lives and accept his authority." Her parents were divorced within a year of his return. Her mother remarried in 1974 and lives in Texas with her husband. Robert retired from the Air Force as a colonel in 1977 and worked as a corporate pilot and businessman. He married and was divorced again. Now 72 and retired, he lives in Foster City, California.

How the lives of all the family members have changed

As for the rest of the family, Robert Jr. is a dentist in Walnut Creek, California; he and his wife have four children, the oldest of whom is a marine. Roger, a major in the Air Force, lives outside Seattle. Cindy Pierson, a waitress, resides in Walnut Creek with her husband and has a daughter in college. And Lorrie Stirm Kitching, now 47, is an executive administrator and mother of two sons. She lives in Mountain View, California, with her husband. All four of Robert Stirm Sr.'s children have a copy of *Burst of Joy* hanging in a place of honor on their walls. But he says he can't bring himself to display the picture.

Three decades after the Stirm reunion, the scene, having appeared in countless books, anthologies and exhibitions, remains part of the nation's collective consciousness, often serving as an uplifting postscript to Vietnam. That the moment was considerably more fraught than we first assumed makes it all the more poignant and reminds us that not all war casualties occur on the battlefield.

Concluding comments leading up to Butler's thesis: Pictures do not always tell the complete story, and not all casualties occur on the battlefield.

"We have this very nice picture of a very happy moment," Lorrie says, "but every time I look at it, I remember the families that weren't reunited, and the ones that aren't being reunited today—many, many families—and I think, I'm one of the lucky ones."

DRAFTING

Before you begin drafting, collect all your notes, your visuals, and your research. Based on your materials, determine what you want the *focus* of your analysis to be—the visual itself, its relationship to any accompanying text or context, its relation to other images in its genre, or the rhetorical appeals that the visual makes. Depending on the assignment, your visuals, and your own purpose, narrow the strategies to the few that are most helpful in understanding the rhetoric of the visual.

If you are designing your own document, write out your accompanying text in a draft, and then experiment with the overall placement of text, images, and graphs. Cut out and arrange/rearrange the chunks of your text and visuals on a blank page until you find a combination of text, image, and use of white space that has the best effect for your purpose and audience.

Finally, obtain feedback or peer response to help you as you move from drafting to revising.

PEER RESPONSE

The instructions that follow will help you give and receive constructive advice about the rough draft of your visual analysis or design document. Use these guidelines for an in-class workshop, a take-home review, or an electronic class forum response.

Writer: Before you exchange drafts, write out your responses to the following questions.

1. **Purpose** Briefly describe the purpose and intended audience of your essay or document. What is the main point you are trying to communicate?

2. **Revision Plans** Point out one part of your essay that is successful at achieving your purpose. Describe the parts of your essay that do not seem to be working or are not yet completed.

3. **Questions** Write out one or two specific questions that you still have about your visual analysis or your design. Where exactly would you like help on this project?

Reader: First, read the entire draft or document from start to finish without making any comments. Then as you reread the draft, answer the following questions.

Continued

1. **Techniques for analyzing visuals** Where in the draft do you see the writer using the techniques for analyzing visuals discussed in this chapter? Which techniques should be more developed to help achieve the writer's purpose? Explain.
2. **Context** Where do you see the writer analyzing or using the social, political, or cultural context of the visuals? What other aspects of context might the writer consider?
3. **Responses to visuals** Write out your response to these visuals. What key elements of these visuals do you see that the writer does not comment on? Where would you disagree with the writer's analysis? Explain.
4. **Response to design** Analyze the writer's document design. Is it too busy, cluttered, or crowded? Does the document need more text and fewer visuals? Does it need to cut text and increase white space? What might the audience for this document say about its attractiveness, simplicity of message, or overall effectiveness?
5. **Response to the assignment** The visual analysis or document design needs to respond to the assignment. Where does this draft respond to the assignment? Where doesn't it respond to the assignment? Explain.
6. **Answer the writer's questions** Briefly respond to the writer's questions listed above.

CHOOSING   COLLECTING   SHAPING   DRAFTING   **REVISING**

REVISING

As you revise your visual analysis or visual design project, consider your peer-response feedback. Some of it will be helpful, but some may not help you achieve your purpose. You must decide which changes to make.

GUIDELINES FOR REVISION

- **Review the purpose and audience for your assignment.** Does your draft analyze the key parts of the visual? If you are designing a document, give a draft to someone who is your intended audience or who might understand the needs of your intended audience. What suggestions does that person have?
- **Reexamine the visual.** What else do you notice about its composition, focus, narrative, or themes?

- **Reconsider relationships between the image and its text and context.** Much of the meaning and impact of the visual depends on the accompanying text and on the social, political, and cultural context. Look again at these possible relationships.

- **Reconsider the genre of your visual or your document.** If you are analyzing a visual, have you collected other examples of visuals in that genre? How are these examples similar to or different from your visual? If you are designing a document, have you checked other documents belonging to this genre? How does yours compare to them? How could you use their ideas to improve your document?

- **Check your visual or your document for its rhetorical appeals.** Make sure your draft comments on or makes use of appropriate rhetorical appeals to logic, to character, and to emotion. Are these appeals effective for the purpose and audience of the visual or the document?

- **Organize your analysis.** Check your draft to make sure the parts of your analysis add up to or contribute to your overall thesis or claim.

- **Revise and edit sentences to improve clarity, conciseness, and emphasis.** Check your handbook for suspected problems with usage, grammar, and punctuation. Be sure to spell check your final version.

POSTSCRIPT ON THE WRITING PROCESS

1. Describe the process you used to analyze your visual in its context or to design your own document. What did you do first? How did your research help? What advice did you get from your peers? What major change(s) did you make for your final version?

2. Write out the sentence or sentences that contain your thesis or main claim of your visual analysis. If you are designing a document, explain where you put the focus and how you related both your text and your images to that focus or main idea.

3. Explain the two or three most important things you learned about visual analysis or document design as you wrote your analysis or worked through your project.

4. What parts of your analysis or document still need revision? If you had one more day to work on the project, what changes would you make? Explain.

KARYN M. LEWIS

Some Don't Like Their Blues at All

Karyn Lewis decided to write an analysis of an advertisement for Fila jeans that she found in a magazine. She chose this particular advertisement because it created an image for the product that was based on stereotyped portrayals of gender roles. Instead of using its power to break down gender stereotypes, Fila deliberately used common stereotypes (men are strong and hard; women are weak and soft) to help sell their clothing. Lewis's analysis explains how Fila's images perpetuate the myth that men are "creatures of iron," while women are soft and "silly bits of fluff," leaving viewers of the advertisement without positive gender role models.

1　He strides toward us in navy and white, his body muscled and heavy-set, one arm holding his casually flung jeans jacket over his shoulder. A man in his prime, with just the right combination of macho and sartorial flair.

2　He is also black.

3　She is curled and giggling upon a chair, her hair loose and flowing around her shoulders, leaning forward innocently—the very picture of a blossoming, navy flower.

4　She is white.

5　They are each pictured on a magazine page of their own, situated opposite each other in a complementary two-page spread. They are stationed in front of a muted photograph which serves as a background for each one. They both merit their own captions: bold indigo letters presiding over them in the outer corners of each page.

6　His says: SOME LIKE THEIR BLUES HARD.

7　Hers says: SOME LIKE THEIR BLUES SOFT.

8　His background depicts a thrusting struggle between a quarterback and a leaping defender, a scene of arrested violence and high tension.

9　Her background is a lounging, bikini-clad goddess, who looks at the camera with intriguing, calm passion. She raises her hand to rest behind her head in a languid gesture as she tries to incite passion within the viewer.

10　At the bottom of the page blazes the proud emblem of the company that came up with this ad: FILA JEANS.

11　This advertisement blatantly uses stereotypes of men and women to sell its product. It caters to our need to fit into the roles that society has deemed right for the individual sexes ever since patriarchal rule rose up and replaced the primitive worship of a mother goddess and the reverence for women. These stereotypes handed down to us throughout the centuries spell out to us that men are violence and power incarnate, and that the manly attitude has no room for weakness or softness of nature. And we find our role model of women in the compliant and eager female who obeys her man in all things, who must not say no to a male, and who is not very bright—someone who flutters her eyelashes, giggles a lot, and uses tears to get her way.

This ad tells us, by offering the image of a hard, masculine male, who *12* is deified in violence, that he is the role model men should aspire to, and that for women, their ideal is weak but sexual, innocent and at the same time old enough to have sex. In viewing this ad, we see our aspirations clothed in Fila jeans, and to be like them, we must buy the clothes pictured here. This ad also suggests that a man can become hard and powerful (or at least look it) dressed in these jeans; a woman can become sexually intense and desirable dressed in Fila's clothing.

The words of the captions tantalize with their sexual innuendo. The *13* phrase "Some like their blues hard" hints at male sexual prowess. Most men and women in this country are obsessed with males' need to prove their virility, and Fila plays on this obsession. Females too have their own stereotype of what constitutes their sexuality. "Some like their blues soft" exemplifies this ideal: A woman should be soft and yielding. Her soft, sensuous body parts, which so excite her partners, have been transformed into her personal qualities. By using the term *soft*, Fila immediately links the girl with her sexuality and sexual organs.

We are shown by the models' postures that men and women are (ac- *14* cording to Fila) fundamentally different and total antonyms of one another. He is standing and walking with purpose; she sits, laughing trivially at the camera. Even the background hints at separation of the sexes.

The football players on the man's page are arranged in a diagonal line *15* which starts at the upper left-hand corner and runs to the opposite corner, which is the center of the ad. On her page, the enchanting nymph in the bathing suit runs on a diagonal; beginning where his ends, and traveling up to the upper right-hand corner of her page. These two photos in effect create a *V*, which both links the two models and suggests movement away from one another. Another good example of their autonomy

...*continued* Some Don't Like Their Blues at All, **Karyn M. Lewis**

from one another is their skin color. He is a black man, she's white. Black is the opposite color of white on an artist's color wheel and palette and symbolizes dynamically opposed forces: good and evil, night and day, man and woman. This ad hits us with the idea that men and women are not parallel in nature to one another but are fundamentally different in all things. It alienates the sexes from each other. Opposites may attract, but there is no room for understanding a nature completely alien to your own.

So in viewing this ad, and reading its captions, the consumer is left 16 with the view that a woman must be "soft" and sensual, a male's sexual dream, and must somehow still retain her innocence after having sex. She must be weak, the opposite of the violence which contrasts with her on the opposite page. The men looking at this ad read the message that they are supposed to be well-dressed and powerful and possess a strength that borders on violence. As we are told by the caption, men should be "hard." Furthermore, men and women are opposite creatures, as different as two sides of a coin.

This ad is supposed to cause us to want to meet these requirements, 17 but it fills me with a deep-rooted disgust that we perpetuate the myth that men are unyielding creatures of iron and women are silly bits of fluff. The ad generates no good role models to aspire to, where men and women are equal beings, and both can show compassion and still be strong. Fila may like their blues hard and soft, but I don't like their blues at all.

QUESTIONS FOR WRITING AND DISCUSSION

1. Fila did not grant permission to reproduce their advertisement for this text. However, Lewis does an excellent job of describing the layout, balance, color, key figures, diagonals, and background. In the margin of this essay, indicate those sentences where Lewis describes the advertisement, enabling us to clearly visualize it.

2. Parts of Lewis's essay describe and analyze the text that accompanies the advertisement, but she spends most of her time discussing the social, cultural, and gendered contexts of the advertisement. In the margin of the essay,

indicate places where she analyzes the accompanying *text* and where she analyzes the *context* of the advertisement. Where in her analysis do you see her showing how text and context relate to each other? Explain.

3. Examine how Lewis *organizes* her analysis of the Fila advertisement. How does her organization reflect her thesis that the two figures, hers and his, are opposites? In other words, where and how does she use sentences and paragraphs to show that these two figures are "fundamentally different and total antonyms of each other"?

4. The genre of the Fila promotion is the clothing or fashion advertisement. Find at least three other advertisements for clothing or fashion. Use Lewis's strategy and analyze how the images, text, and context function together. How are the overall messages in these advertisements similar to or different from the messages that Lewis finds? Explain.

STUDENT WRITING   [X]

LAWRENCE FLETCHER   x

Weight Loss 101 for the Adult Fitness Program

For his class assignment, Lawrence Fletcher was asked to work with a community organization to produce a brochure, flyer, or pamphlet. Fletcher's site partner was the Adult Fitness Center, which needed a four-page informative pamphlet to help increase its members' understanding of weight-loss strategies that use good nutrition and dieting practices. After researching effective dieting strategies, Fletcher wrote a sixteen-page document for the adult members, which he then revised and cut down to the length required by the center. To make his pamphlet more attractive, Fletcher used bulleted lists, photographs, and charts to illustrate key strategies and highlight important information.

Are you working hard in the gym and still not shedding the pounds? Is   *1*
your face dripping in sweat and you're out of breath from the cardio, but you still have unwanted weight? Are your muscles sore from weightlifting, but your arms are just not as toned as you think they should be? If you have answered YES to even one of these questions, you can do one more thing to fight the fat and enjoy that fit and youthful body you have always wanted. The key to obtaining your weight loss goal is through choosing a healthy diet!

Two main ways adults become overweight are through eating too much food and not being active enough (kind of a no brainer, right?). We all know the reasons why we get big, but fighting the problem is not so easy.

With good nutritional habits combined with the right fitness levels, you should have no trouble in dropping extra pounds to feel healthy and good about yourselves. Take the challenge of fighting the fat and become the new you! It will be fun and easy!

FAD DIETS—KICK EM' OUT!

In our fast paced world, we are very concerned with the quick and easy solution to weight loss. People discuss the low-fat, low-carb, and miracle diets that swarm our everyday lives. These diets are not the key to long-term weight loss.

The low-carbohydrate diet popularized through the Atkins and South Beach programs poses many health risks to a person. Low intake of fruits and vegetables from the diet limits the vitamins, minerals, phytochemicals, and especially fiber you can get through the course of a day leaving yourself nutrient deficient. Meals rich in saturated fats from the diet produce long-term negative health effects such as heart disease according to Dr. Chris Melby, a professor of Advanced Nutrition at CSU. The low-carb diet is not an eating regimen you could possibly meet the rest of your life. Forget the low-carb craze!

Low-fat diets are not the best solution to shed pounds. Low-fat foods associated with diets can be extremely high in sugar content and will actually make a person overeat and gain weight. Low-fat cookies and ice cream are not your friends. Forget the fads! Let's focus on a safe and easy approach to weight loss that will last a lifetime.

CALORIE BALANCE = A HEALTHY WEIGHT

The American Dietetic Association claims calorie balance is the one easy and correct way to your weight loss solution. Dieters must simply manage their calories to ensure weight loss success. Making sure you eat fewer calories than what you use in a day will guarantee that you finally lose that extra baggage you carry around today.

One pound of body fat is equal to 3,500 calories. So to lose 1 pound of fat in a week, a person must cut out 3,500 calories from their diet in that week. Dropping 1 pound may sound like a lot of work, but it's not if you follow a few simple rules.

TO CUT OUT THE CALORIES, YOU MUST:

- Know your nutritional requirements

- Eat the right foods

- Understand food labels

- Control the portions you eat

- Diet while dining out

FABULOUS FOODS

The key to a good diet is the food you are "allowed to eat." But let's not think of it as the food we're allowed to eat but rather the food we choose to eat to get that flat stomach. *9*

Here are a few tips in choosing the right foods for you: *10*

- Eat more fruits and vegetables. Your mother has always told you this, and she was right. Eating fruits and vegetables replaces those "bad" foods high in sugar and fat which plague your body into obesity.

- Eat a variety of fruits! Eatright.org, supervised by the American Dietetic Association, suggests eating 2 cups of fruit each day whether frozen, fresh, canned, or dried.

- Eat your fruit, don't just drink them. Eat whole fruits rather than drinking fruit juices. Juices contain many sugar calories. Whole fruits will maintain your feeling of fullness longer.

- Vary your vegetables! Choose a wide variety of veggies including orange and dark green varieties like carrots, sweet potatoes, broccoli, and dark leafy greens to fill your appetite.

- Eat the lean meat! Meats such as fish and poultry are the champions.

- Stay away from the red meat! Red meat is loaded with saturated fat which is hard for the body to shed. If you prefer red meat, the US department of Agriculture claims the leanest beef cuts include round steaks and roasts as well as top loin and top sirloin.

- Choose turkey, ham, or roast beef for your sandwiches. These are the lean deli meats. Salami, bologna, and bacon should be eaten minimally because they contain much more fat and calories than other luncheon meats.

...continued Weight Loss 101 for the Adult Fitness Program, **Lawrence Fletcher**

- Eat whole grains in your diet, while tossing the refined carbohydrates (sugars and white floured grains) into the garbage.

- Drink fewer alcoholic beverages. Alcohol is a temptation which leads to big bellies and thighs. Many adults get home from work and want to enjoy a glass of beer or wine to relax. Another way to relax is to enjoy a nice cup of green tea full of anti-oxidants which fight cancer as well as being low in calories.

- Drink six to eight glasses of water each day. Drinking water helps one feel a sense of fullness which limits your need or urge to eat. Good hydration will also lead to increased energy. Energy is motivation to burn more calories in the gym!

- Choose dairy products which are low in fat or fat free. Many cheeses, creams, and milk products are loaded with fat. Fat-free cottage cheese or yogurt are smart choices for any dieter's dairy needs.

- Eat foods with more monounsaturated fats than polyunsaturated fat and saturated fat. Olive oil, avocados, natural peanut butter, and cold water fish contain good fats that are highly monounsaturated.

- Choose foods prepared by baking, grilling, and broiling more often than frying. Fried foods are high in fat and calories that contribute to becoming overweight. Forget the hot wings; try something else! Grilled chicken also pleases the taste buds.

- Eat Breakfast! Breakfast jumpstarts your metabolism and helps you curb hunger throughout your day so you will be less prone to overeating.

Your Metabolism Will
Burn More Calories!

By following some of these simple guidelines, weight loss will be within your reach!

READING THE LABELS AND COUNTING THE CALORIES

Keep your calories in check. Counting the calories you consume is *11* not a hard task and will aid in your weight loss. The key to your success in limiting calories will be to understand the food label placed on every food package in your cabinet and refrigerator.

Understanding the Label   *12*

- Check the food's fat and calorie content listed on the label. Choose foods that are lower in fats, especially saturated and trans fats, and low in calories. Foods with a smaller fat content will help you cut calories from your normal diet and lose some pounds with ease.

- Servings per container can be deceiving. One container may be more than 1 serving. Don't eat the whole box! Eat the appropriate serving size for your weight loss goal.

- Let the percent daily values (DVs) guide you to your weight loss goals. Use DVs to assist you in deciding how a particular food should fit into your diet.

...continued Weight Loss 101 for the Adult Fitness Program, **Lawrence Fletcher**

- The FDA claims that DVs on labels today for the energy-producing nutrients such as protein, fat, and carbohydrates are based on the number of calories a person eats per day. The reference amount is 2000 calories, so do not be fooled. If you require more than 2000 calories per day, your DVs will be larger than what the label reads. If you require less than 2000 calories a day to maintain your weight, your DVs will be less than what the label says.

PORTION CONTROL: BE THE LEADER!

Portion control is a major part to winning your battle in weight loss. Overeating is a common problem among Americans because of increased portion sizes. Super-sized foods and bigger bags of chips are leading to bigger waistlines in this fast-food nation. 13

You can still enjoy your favorite foods by keeping them in moderation. Read the labels to determine if 3 cookies are really OK for your snack. ONE cookie may be more reasonable. 14

To lose weight, the Department of Health and Human Services lists many suggestions to control portion sizes. 15

- Serve food on individual plates! Placing food on individual plates helps reduce the opportunity to overeat by keeping excess food out of reach.

- Keep the serving dishes off the table and out of sight so you will not be tempted to dig in a second or third time.

- Take control when eating out! Split large entrees with a friend so you do not overeat and keep some money in your pocket and fat off your stomach.

- Ask your server for a "to-go" box as your food comes out so that you can split the meal in half and limit your intake at one meal. Now you will have food for tomorrow's lunch as well.

- Ask about child size portions that may be available to you.

- Order an appetizer as your entrée.

- Control portions by creating a diet-friendly environment! One suggestion is to replace a candy or cookie jar with a fruit basket, so you'll steal a piece of nutritious food between meals.

For a quick reference of your portion sizes, here are some easy reminders 16 provided by the American Dietetic Association:

Food	Serving Size	About the size of ...
Meat, Poultry, Fish	2 to 3 ounces	Deck of cards or palm of your hand
Pasta, Rice	1/2 cup	Small computer mouse or the size of your fist
Cooked Vegetables	1/2 cup	Small computer mouse
Fruit	1/2 cup	Small computer mouse or a medium apple, pear, or orange
Cheese	1 1/2 ounces hard cheese	C battery or your thumb

American Dietetic Association—eatright.org

CALCULATE THE CALORIES—JOT THEM DOWN

To keep yourself in check while cutting calories, try making a diary of the 17 food you eat and the beverages you consume throughout the course of a week. Record the calories at each meal and your total calories for a day. Jotting down all of your calories will assist in exposing hidden calories you did not realize you were taking in.

...continued Weight Loss 101 for the Adult Fitness Program, **Lawrence Fletcher**

EATING OUT, DON'T LET IT RUIN YOUR GOAL!

Eating out on a regular basis can ruin your plan for weight loss as well as [18] diminish your healthy lifestyle. The Heart and Stroke Foundation has filled out the Fast Food Report Card and has reported failing grades for your fast-food choices!

Fast foods tend to be high in fat, calories, and sodium content. Eat- [19] ing excess fat, especially saturated and trans fats, at your favorite fast-food establishment can increase your blood cholesterol levels, which puts you at a higher risk for heart disease, stroke, diabetes, and cancer. These excess calories from that burger and fries will also lead to weight gain, which is your enemy today!

If you are like many Americans who find it hard to make time to [20] cook nutritious meals at home or rely on the inexpensive option of fast-food meals, here's some advice to think about before you swallow that juicy burger:

- Stay away from the fried foods. French fries, fried fish, and fried chicken, like the world famous McNuggets, are villains to a healthy lifestyle. Instead of fried foods, choose grilled varieties of foods from your favorite fast-food stop.

- Grilled options such as chicken and fish are cooked without added fat, therefore will lack the fat and calorie content their fried counterparts have.

- Get rid of the fattening condiments. Condiments such as mayonnaise, ranch, and bleu cheese dressings are loaded with fat calories. Stay away from these unhealthy condiments and choose items such as ketchup, barbeque sauce, salsa, and hot sauce in moderation to add to your sandwich.

- Stay clear of the big sodas! Soda is composed mostly of high fructose corn syrup, also known as sugar, which can destroy your diet. A large 32-ounce soda may contain as much as 310 calories. Drink diet beverages instead.

- Drink tea without added sugar or water at a fast food joint. Tea and water are low in calories.

BEYOND FAST FOOD

As adults, it is fun to go out with friends, family, and coworkers for the oc- *21* casional meal full of hearty foods and good drinks. Your diet should not restrict the good times to be had! When you are out for a night on the town, make good decisions about what you eat so that you can stay true to your diet and weight loss goals.

The Heart and Stroke Foundation offers great suggestions for *22* healthy choices.

- *At the coffee shop* eat healthier options, such as a low-fat whole-grain muffin or bagel with a small amount of light cream cheese, coffee or tea.

- *At the deli or sandwich counter* good options include: whole-grain bread or bun; lean meats like ham, chicken, turkey, and roast beef; green salad, fruit salad, or bean salad; unsweetened juices or low-fat milk.

- *At the pizza place* choose smart options like: vegetarian or Hawaiian pizza, whole-wheat or grain crust, and lower-fat toppings such as ham, chicken, mushrooms, peppers, tomatoes, zucchini, artichokes, and low-fat cheese. Red-pepper is fine to give your pizza a little spice, but put the parmesan cheese back on the table. Your pizza already has plenty of cheese. Extra cheese equals extra fat and calories.

- *At the Asian café* healthy options include: steamed dumplings and buns; grilled/steamed/or stir-fried veggies; spring rolls, sushi, and cucumber salad; steamed rice (not fried!), noodles in soup, and light soy sauce with no MSG (monosodium glutamate).

- *At your best burger stand* cut some calories with these choices: plain or child-size burgers (stay away from the double and triple patties if you want to lose extra pounds), light menu items, chili, and veggie burgers. Choose buffalo burgers over beef because buffalo is naturally a leaner meat.

- *At your Italian bistro* excellent choices include broiled, baked, grilled, or poached fish, grilled chicken, or veal. Pasta with vegetables in a red sauce will include the least amount of fat and calories. Stay clear of the lasagna and pastas drenched in creamy sauces. White sauce = excessive fat + calories!

Enjoy your favorite restaurants by choosing healthy options on your *23* quick and easy path to weight loss success. Many restaurants will include a "healthy options" section on their menu.

. . . continued Weight Loss 101 for the Adult Fitness Program, **Lawrence Fletcher**

DEVELOP ENERGY FOR LIFE WITH GOOD NUTRITION! GET OFF THE COUCH AND GET ACTIVE!

GET ON YOUR PATH TO SUCCESSFUL WEIGHT LOSS

It's now time to apply the 24 knowledge in this brochure to successfully shed those unwanted pounds! Get back into your favorite pair of jeans, tone those arms, and feel better about yourself today. Nutritional discipline combined with an effective workout routine (supplied to you by the wonderful people at the Adult Fitness Program) will lead you to your goal of a shaped and toned body and higher energy levels to take on the day.

Good luck meeting your 25 **weight loss goals!**

Further Information for Dieters:

In addition to this brochure, additional information to assist in your weight loss success can be found at many government supported Web sites which include:

www.mypyramid.gov
www.eatright.org
www.nutrition.gov
www.smallstep.gov

QUESTIONS FOR WRITING AND DISCUSSION

1. The first principle of designing documents with accompanying visuals is to consider purpose and audience. What is the purpose of Fletcher's brochure? Where do you find him stating or restating that purpose? Where do you find him adapting his text and his visuals to his adult audience? Find examples of both specific sentences and visuals that address his audience. Are there places where he could revise his language or his visuals to appeal more effectively to his audience? Explain.

2. To be effective, visuals must be relevant to the accompanying text. Ideally, however, they should not only be relevant, but they should also add attractiveness and impact that the text does not have by itself. Choose three of Fletcher's visuals and analyze their relevance, attractiveness, and impact. Which are his strongest and which are his weakest visuals? What substitutions might you suggest?

3. Assume that you are one of the managers of the Adult Fitness Center, and that you are going to revise and then actually print this brochure. What typeface and fonts would you use? Where would you want more white space? What colors might you use? Would you want to use Fletcher's text in a full-page brochure, or in a folding brochure? Would you add a sidebar indicating diet or exercise classes at your center? Write out your complete design plan for the finished brochure.

4. At your place of work, talk to your managers about a poster, flyer, instructional leaflet, or brochure that they could use. The project might be addressed to current customers, future customers, or even to employees. The resulting document should use both text and visuals, should be attractively designed, and should be addressed to and clearly appeal to its audience. Write your first draft of that document.

Jan Vermeer Van Delft, (1632–1675)
The Astronomer (1668)
Oil on canvas, 31.5 x 45.5 cm
Musée du Louvre, Département des Peintures, Paris, France
Photograph © Erich Lessing, Art Resource, NY

At the time of this painting, scientific discoveries in mathematics, navigation, and astronomy in Europe were laying the groundwork for modern science. The globe at which the astronomer gazes was modeled on one made by Jococus Hondius in 1600. Vermeer himself is credited with using a *camera obscura,* a precursor of the modern camera, to help generate the optical effects of his paintings. As a possible topic for investigation, the journal entry on page 295 invites you to compare this painting with recent images from the NASA Web site.

Investigating

7

While watching joggers running in the park one day, you notice their straining muscles, their labored breathing, and the grimaces etched on their faces. Why, you wonder, do people go through the pain of running? Does it have a physical or a psychological benefit? Or can it even become an addiction for those people who *have* to run every day? You decide to investigate this question in runners' magazines and professional journals and then interview a few serious runners to determine their motives and the effects that running has on them, both physically and psychologically. The results of your report, you hope, will prove interesting to those who run as well as to those who merely watch others run.

Your boss at the local self-service gas station wants to expand the station's range of convenience items. Currently, you sell only snacks such as soda pop, candy, and ice cream. Your boss asks you to find out what is sold at other convenience stores. Next, she wants you to design a survey for your customers, asking which items they would like to have the station carry. After tabulating questionnaires from thirty-five customers, you write a short report for the boss outlining what the competition stocks, how you designed your questionnaire, and what the responses from your customers indicate.

NVESTIGATING BEGINS WITH QUESTIONS. WHAT CAUSES THE GREENHOUSE EFFECT? WHEN WILL THE WORLD BEGIN TO RUN OUT OF OIL? HOW DOES ILLITERACY AFFECT A PERSON'S LIFE? HOW WAS THE WORLD WIDE WEB CREATED? HOW DOES RAPE AFFECT THE LIVES OF WOMEN IN AMERICA? How do colleges recruit applicants? What can you find out about a famous person's personality, background, and achievements? At what age do children first acquire simple mathematical abilities? Why are sunsets yellow, then orange, red, and finally purple?

Investigating also carries an assumption that probing for answers to such questions—by observing and remembering, researching sources, interviewing key people, or conducting surveys—will uncover truths not generally known or accepted. As you dig for information, you learn *who, what, where,* and *when.* You may even learn *how* and *why.*

The purpose of investigating is to uncover or discover facts, opinions, information, and reactions and then to report that information to other people who want to know. Although no writing is ever free from cultural or personal bias, a report strives to be as neutral and objective as possible. It may summarize other people's judgments, but it does not consciously editorialize. It may represent opposing viewpoints or arguments, but it does not argue for one side or the other. A report attempts to be a window on the world, allowing readers to see the information for themselves.

TECHNIQUES   PROCESS

Techniques for Investigative Writing

> **"** Curiosity is my natural state and has led me headlong into every worthwhile experience . . . I have ever had. **"**
> —ALICE WALKER,
> AUTHOR OF
> *THE COLOR PURPLE*

Investigative writing begins with asking questions and finding informed sources: published material, knowledgeable people, or both. In most cases, collecting information in an investigation requires the ability to use a library and then to summarize, paraphrase, and quote key ideas accurately from other people's writing. In addition, personal interviews are often helpful or necessary. For an investigation, you might talk to an expert or an authority, an eyewitness or participant in an event, or even the subject of a personality profile. Finally, you may wish to survey the general public to determine opinions, trends, or reactions. Once you have collected your information, you must then present your findings in a written form suitable for your audience, with clear references in the text to your sources of information.

Investigative writing uses the following techniques.

- **Beginning with an interesting title and a catchy lead sentence or paragraph.** The first few sentences arouse your readers' *interest* and focus their attention on the subject.

- **Giving background information by answering relevant who, what, when, where, and why questions.** Answering the *reporter's "Wh" questions* ensures that readers have sufficient information to understand your report.

- **Stating the main idea, question, or focus of the investigation.** The purpose of a report is to convey information as *clearly* as possible. Readers shouldn't have to guess the main idea.

- **Summarizing or quote information from written or oral sources; cite sources in the text.** Quote *accurately* any statistics, data, or sentences from your sources. Cite authors and titles.

- **Following appropriate genre conventions.** A news report, a profile, an interview, and an investigative report require different form and style conventions. Learn the key features of the particular genre with which you are working.

- **Writing in a readable and interesting style appropriate to the intended audience.** Clear, direct, and readable language is essential in a report. Use graphs and charts as appropriate.

The following reports illustrate several types of investigative writing: the *summary* of a single book or article, the *investigation* of a controversial issue (using multiple sources), and the *profile* of a person. These types may overlap (the investigation of a controversial issue may contain a personality profile, for instance), and all three types may use summaries of written material, questionnaires, and interviews. While some investigative reports are brief, intended to be only short news items, others are full-length features.

The intended audience for each report is often determined by the publication in which the report appears: *Psychology Today* assumes that its readers are interested in personality and behavior; *Discover* magazine is for readers interested in popular science; readers of *Ms.* magazine expect coverage of contemporary issues concerning women.

SUMMARY   REPORT   INVESTIGATION   PROFILE   INTERVIEW
SUMMARY OF A BOOK OR ARTICLE

The following report from *Psychology Today,* by journalist Jeff Meer, summarizes information taken from an article by Charlene L. Muehlenhard and Melaney A. Linton that appeared in the *Journal of Counseling Psychology.* Although the *Psychology Today* report summarizes only that one article, it demonstrates several key features of an investigative report.

PROFESSIONAL WRITING

Date Rape: Familiar Strangers

Attention-getting title

Lead-in paragraph

Focus of investigation or report

Who, what, where questions answered

Summary of results

Summary of results

Summary of results

Quotation

By now, everyone knows the scenario. Boy meets girl, they go to a party, get drunk, return to his apartment, and he forces her to have sex. *1*

Most people assume that date rape occurs on a first or second date between relative strangers. But new research supports a different conclusion: The individuals involved generally know each other fairly well. *2*

Psychologist Charlene L. Muehlenhard and undergraduate Melaney A. Linton asked more than 600 college men and women about their most recent dates, as well as their worst experience with "sexual aggression"— any time a woman was forced to participate in acts, ranging from kissing to intercourse, against her will. More than three quarters of the women and more than half of the men admitted to having an experience with sexual aggression on a date, either in high school or in college. And nearly 15 percent of the women and 7 percent of the men said they had intercourse against the woman's will. *3*

The researchers found that when a man initiated the date, drove to and from and paid for the date, sexual aggression was more likely. They also found that if both people got drunk (at a party, for example) and "parked," or found themselves in the man's dorm room or apartment, the date was more likely to end with the woman being forced to perform against her wishes. Men and women who thought of themselves as having traditional values and those who were more accepting of violence were also more likely to have been involved in date rape. *4*

But contrary to what one might expect, date rape and sexual aggression were much more likely to happen between partners who knew each other. On average, students said they had known the partner almost a year before the incident. "If women were more aware of this, they might be less surprised and more prepared to deal with sexual aggression by someone they know well," Muehlenhard says. *5*

She points out that communication is often a big problem on dates during which there is sexual aggression. Both men and women reported that the man had felt "led on" during such dates. Men said that women *6* desired more sexual contact on these dates than had others on previous dates. Women said that they had desired less sexual contact than usual.

Muehlenhard believes that a direct approach, such as a woman saying "I don't want to do anything more than kiss," might clear up confusion better than simply saying "No."

Summary

Quotation

7

■ ■ ■

SUMMARY   **REPORT**   INVESTIGATION   PROFILE   INTERVIEW

A BRIEF REPORT WITH GRAPHICS

The following passage illustrates the genre of the brief report with graphics that was popularized by *USA Today*. Abigail Sullivan Moore's report, which appeared in the Education Life section of the *New York Times*, illustrates how a simple graphic can enhance the impact of a report.

PROFESSIONAL WRITING

Gimme an A (I Insist!)

Abigail Sullivan Moore

Grade inflation seems to be reaching record levels at the nation's high schools, according to a new survey of incoming freshmen at more than 400 colleges and universities. Almost half reported an A average in high school, up from 18 percent in 1968. "Something is amiss," says Linda J. Sax, who directed the survey of 276,000 students for the Higher Education Research Institute at the University of California at Los Angeles. At the same time, she says, "students are studying, but not as often as they were."

Based on conversations with educators, Dr. Sax believes that parents and pupils are pushing teachers for higher grades amid the intense competition for desirable colleges. Also, she says: "What I'm hearing is that teachers feel a pressure to not shatter students' self-esteem. Teachers are caught up in this web of pressure."

A study by the College Board released in January confirms the findings: high school seniors' grades have climbed but SAT scores remain nearly unchanged. Wayne J. Camara, the board's vice president for research

...*continued* Gimme an A (I Insist!), **Abigail Sullivan Moore**

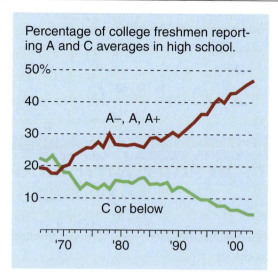

Percentage of college freshmen reporting A and C averages in high school.

and development, says the trend started to accelerate in the early 90's, when "more and more middle-income families had much more awareness of college, and at the same time there was more discretionary income" to pay for the expensive, hard-to-get-into institutions. He predicts a correction is due. "Everyone can't get A's," he says.

■ ■ ■

SUMMARY   REPORT   **INVESTIGATION**   PROFILE   INTERVIEW

INVESTIGATION USING MULTIPLE SOURCES

Most investigative reports draw on multiple sources: books, articles, research reports, and interviews. Some interviews are conducted in person, but interviews on the phone or via e-mail are common. The following article, "That Parent-Child Conversation Is Becoming Instant, and Online," by John Schwartz, appeared in the *New York Times* on January 3, 2004. As you read this report, first notice its genre features: short paragraphs, catchy quotations, and focus on contemporary features of instant messaging rather than an in depth, academic analysis. After you read the article, go back and reread, looking for all the sources Schwartz uses and cites. Schwartz cites over a dozen different sources—can you identify all of them and guess how he gathered his information?

PROFESSIONAL WRITING

That Parent-Child Conversation Is Becoming Instant, and Online

John Schwartz

Nina Gordon types out an instant message and sends it. The data travels   *1*
some 500 miles, from the computer in her living room in Queens to America Online's servers in Northern Virginia, and then to her son Schuyler's computer, which just happens to be in the next room—about 20 feet away from where she is sitting.

　you hungry for dinner?

After a little online banter over dining options, her son, a 17-year-old   *2*
with a wicked sense of humor and no shortage of attitude, sends his request:

　an insty pizza and a beer
　　don't push your luck, comes the reply.

Instant messaging, long a part of teenagers' lives, is working its way   *3*
into the broader fabric of the American family. The technology "has really grown up in the last 18 months," said Michael Gartenberg, vice president and research director at Jupiter Research. "It's certainly not just for kids anymore."

Almost three-quarters of all teenagers with online access use instant   *4*
messaging and about half of all adults have tried the services, surveys show. Adults, who generally began using the services from AOL, Microsoft and Yahoo! to stay in touch with co-workers during the day, Mr. Gartenberg said, are saying "this stuff I'm using for work is actually useful in my personal life as well."

Use among adults has grown to include friends and far-flung family   *5*
members, particularly children away at college. AOL, which provides the most popular service, reports that more than one billion instant messages each day flow through its networks.

And now, as families own more than one computer, the machines   *6*
spread beyond the den, and home networks relying on wireless connections become increasingly popular, instant messaging is taking root within the home itself.

Although it might seem lazy or silly to send electronic messages instead   *7*
of getting out of a chair and walking into the next room, some psychologists

say that the role of the technology within families can be remarkably positive. In many cases, they say, the messages are helping to break down the interpersonal barriers that often prevent open communication.

"Conversation between parents and teenagers could be highly emotional and not necessarily productive," said Elisheva F. Gross, a psychology researcher at the Children's Digital Media Center at the University of California at Los Angeles. When young people are online, however, "it's their turf," she said. "It may be a way for parents to communicate in a language and in a space that their children are more comfortable with." *8*

Teenagers already use online communications to take on difficult topics with one another, said Katelyn McKenna, a research assistant professor in psychology at New York University. Preliminary results from a study she conducted last year, she said, suggest that "they are able to talk with one another about issues that bother them more readily online than when they are talking face to face." *9*

Lissa Parsonnet said that her daughter, Dorrie, is sometimes more open to talking with her and her husband online about difficult subjects, like conflicts with friends, than in person. *10*

"She talks to us as if we're people, not parents," she said. *11*

Ms. Parsonnet, a psychotherapist, said that the online back channel strips away some of the parts of face-to-face communication that complicate matters: "They don't see your face turning red," she said. "They don't see you turning cross—all the things that will shut them up immediately." *12*

Both instant messages and e-mail messages can help smooth things over after a fight, said Nora Gross, a 17-year-old in Manhattan who said that electronic communications had helped strengthen her relationship with her father. "I can remember a few times when we've had little blowups and sent apology letters over e-mail," she said. "We're both writers, so I guess it's easier for us to put our feelings into words through text." *13*

While even quicker than e-mail, instant messages also have the advantage of not actually being instant, Ms. Parsonnet said, because the medium at least gives the user time to compose his or her thoughts and comments before hitting the button. *14*

"You know all the times you wish you'd counted to 10 before you said something?" she said with a laugh. With instant messages, she said, "you have a built-in counting-to-10." *15*

For users, instant-messaging software typically displays, in a small box on the computer screen, a "buddy list" of friends who are online at any *16* given moment. Most instant messaging conversations are one-to-one, but it is also possible to include several people in a group discussion—and to carry on multiple sessions with several people at once.

Ms. Parsonnet said that the instant messaging habit began naturally *17* with Dorrie. One night, she wanted to ask Dorrie a question, but "I didn't want to go chasing her around the house." She didn't have to wander around the family's Short Hills, N.J., home, though, because "I could hear her instant message thing bleeping."

She signed on, saw that Dorrie was indeed online, and sent a note. "It *18* was so easy," she recalled.

That ease of use is essential for adopting any new technology, said *19* Michael Osterman, an industry analyst who studies the instant messaging market. The concept should even seem familiar to the many baby boomers who grew up in post-World War II suburban houses with built-in home intercom systems. But families rarely used the clunky devices to talk from room to room, he noted.

Instant messaging puts a much simpler, more effective intercom sys- *20* tem at every set of fingertips. "It's an old idea that's been made practical," he said. "Instead of yelling downstairs, 'Hey, is there any fried chicken left?' You can I.M. downstairs.' "

Using instant messages to reach out to adolescents fits into the broad *21* structure of experimentation and adaptation that family therapists gener- ally recommend, said A. Rae Simpson, program director for parenting ed- ucation and research at the M.I.T. Center for Work, Family & Personal Life in Cambridge, Mass.

"People who are having difficulty communicating with each other *22* write to each other," Ms. Simpson said, similar to the way that many par- ents and adolescents find they can talk more freely in the car than at home because they are not looking directly at each other. "It takes the intensity out of the eye-to-eye contact."

The uses of instant messages in the home can be banal, playful or pro- *23* found. Lily Mandlin, 15, who lives with her mother and two siblings in a four-bedroom apartment on Manhattan's Upper West Side, said that an instant message is sometimes the best way to get her older brother to turn down his stereo.

"A little ping on the computer actually gets to him a lot quicker than *24* screaming, 'Turn the music down!' " she said.

Mr. Gartenberg, the industry analyst, said, "there has been more *25* than one time when I have been checking something late at night and

...continued That Parent-Child Conversation, **John Schwartz**

discovered one of the kids was logged on. And I said, 'What are you doing? Go to bed!' "

Sometimes the messages are more, well, adult. Ms. Gordon, the 26 Queens mother, said that when she and her husband first got laptop computers with wireless cards, they would even send messages to each other as they worked at home, sitting across from each other in bed.

What messages would they send back and forth when they were sit- 27 ting so close?

"Use your imagination," she said. "Sparks flying across the wireless 28 network, so to speak!"

Kathy Grace, a Web site designer in Austin, said that she is more likely 29 to send instant messages to her husband, Dennis, than to her daughter Ariel, because "we're on different systems." Ariel is on AOL; Ms. Grace and her husband favor Microsoft Messenger, which he uses at work.

Husband and wife will pop a message back and forth while she is 30 working on the laptop at the dining room table and he is using the bedroom PC, even though the house is small, Ms. Grace said. "We keep the bedroom doors closed, and it's easier than shouting," she said.

For all the advantages many families and experts see in instant mes- 31 saging, some adolescents say that they simply do not want their parents on their buddy list.

"People can be easily misunderstood online," one teenager, who asked 32 that her name not be used, wrote in an I.M. interview. "I am not as reserved when I talk to people online than in real life, so really, it would just exacerbate whatever problem was there."

Back at the Gordon home, the chatter is often just for the fun of word- 33 play—and that, too, can strengthen the bond between generations.

It is another night, another dinner. Takeout seafood. 34

want another clam? Nina Gordon asks her son, eating in the next room.

    i havent started the crab yet, he replies. A pun-fest ensues.
    don't be crabby, she writes.
    don't be coy, he replies.
    never, she counters. oy, not coy.

While instant messages and e-mail may helpfully supplement face-to- 35 face discussion, experts warn that it should not be relied on as the principal means of communication.

**"Dear Andy: How have you been?
Your mother and I are fine. We miss you.
Please sign off your computer and come
downstairs for something to eat. Love, Dad."**

"The question is whether you can use it constructively, to bring it back *36*
to the face-to-face," said Sherry Turkle, director of the Initiative on Technology and Self at the Massachusetts Institute of Technology. If the conversation is strictly virtual, she said, "it's not so different from saying, 'I have a wonderful epistolary relationship with my husband, who I can't stand.'"

· ■ ■

| SUMMARY | REPORT | INVESTIGATION | **PROFILE** | INTERVIEW |

PROFILE OF A PERSON

The following passage is a profile of a person—a biographical sketch intended to give a sense of the person's appearance, behavior, character, and accomplishments. The paragraphs are part of a profile, "Rick Steves's Not-So-Lonely Planet," by Sara Corbett, that appeared in the *New York Times Magazine*. The passage gives the first five paragraphs of the profile.

The guy is just another tourist. Or that's how it appears, anyway, to Cristina, the prim Portuguese woman holding down the front desk at the Residencia Roma, a spartan three-star hotel on a quiet side street in Lisbon. No two tourists are the same, of course, but there is something familiar, even iconic, in this man's eager-beaver smile, his unstylish windbreaker and leather walking shoes, his broken-spined guidebook to Spain and Portugal. Like most Americans, he doesn't pretend to speak anything but English. He inquires about rates—60 euros for a double—then asks to see a room. Cristina shrugs, hands the man a key and waves him toward a set of stairs leading up into the hotel's interior, unaware that she has just set a dervish loose in her establishment.

Safely beyond her gaze, Rick Steves accelerates up the stairs and rockets down a dim hallway, quickly shedding all pretense of leisure. This is what he calls a "blitz," a 10-minute undercover rampage during which he will poke mattresses and inspect toilet seats, prowling the hotel like an unleashed hound. Earlier in the day, as we ate breakfast together, Steves had spelled out his plan for seeing Lisbon. "We'll just blitz the Bairro Alto and the castle, then the restaurants," he said, spooning yogurt into his mouth at double the pace most of us think of as normal. "And after that, we'll blitz the museums." With this, he peered under the breakfast table at my feet, adding, "I hope those shoes are comfortable."

Dashing through the Residencia Roma qualifies as an unscheduled side blitz, but its small sign caught Steves's eye as he passed by on the street, and he couldn't resist taking a look. This is often how it goes with Steves, who has written 27 eponymous guidebooks to Europe, stars in a public-television travelogue series called "Rick Steves's Europe" and also runs Europe Through the Back Door, a $20-million-a-year tour business he started in his hometown of Edmonds, Wash. At the age of 49, he is a methodical, even obsessive, planner, but he remains a sucker for a worthy diversion. In many respects, this is the root of Steves's character: a fastidious mind coupled with an explorer's sense of whimsy. After 30 years of professional travel, he has built a fortune from veering off course, discovering and expertly promoting what he calls the "backdoors" to Europe—the alleyway pension, the forgotten Alpine village, the poorly lighted restaurant with the souvlaki to die for.

On camera and off, Steves comes across as a perambulating, mildly mischievous Mister Rogers, relentlessly chipper and almost painfully square, delivering feel-good messages about travel with an earnestness that could be mistaken for naïveté. "This is fun!" he bubbles when he is having fun. "Wouldya look at that?" he exclaims, happening upon a pretty view or a pigeon-covered plaza.

This enthusiasm has found a fertile audience, even in an era when many Americans have grown more afraid of traveling abroad. Last year, as the United Nations chafed at the U.S. decision to invade Iraq, as American tourists reportedly received extra-snarly treatment in France and orange alerts crawled across the bottom of the CNN screen, Rick Steves still managed to sell more than 600,000 guidebooks and sign up some 5,000 people for his company's bus tours. For the last three years, Steves's guide to Italy has outsold those from Frommer's, Fodor's and Lonely Planet; several of his foreign phrase books—which include translations like "If you don't slow this taxi down, I will throw up"—have become more popular than Berlitz.

SUMMARY   REPORT   INVESTIGATION   PROFILE   **INTERVIEW**

EXTENDED INTERVIEW

Extended interviews with newsmakers, writers, and celebrities are a common genre in newspapers and magazines. The following is an interview with demographer Harold Hodgkinson, author of many books and articles, including "Educational Demographics: What Teachers Should Know," which appeared in *Educational Leadership* in 2001. Interviewing Hodgkinson is Karen Arenson, an education reporter for *The New York Times*. Arenson has written articles on education fund raising, honors programs, award-winning teachers, and illegal immigrants at CUNY. In the following interview, which appeared in *The New York Times* in August, 2001, Arenson asks Hodgkinson to explain how population trends are affecting America's colleges and universities. Hodgkinson reports that poor children are still underrepresented in colleges while the number of older, nontraditional students has continued to increase. As you read this interview, consider how Arenson directs the interview to provide information to her audience, which consists of teachers and administrators as well as immigrant and nontraditional students.

READING STATISTICAL TEA LEAVES

Harold Hodgkinson likes to say that "demography is destiny." As a demographer focused on education, he has looked at how births, ethnic backgrounds, family income and other factors shape education. He is convinced that careful scrutiny of such data can lead to better education policy. A former dean at Simmons and Bard colleges, Dr. Hodgkinson led the National Institute of Education under President Gerald R. Ford. Since 1987, he has directed the Center for Demographic Policy at the Institute for Educational Leadership in Washington.

What is the most important demographic trend affecting higher education?

The No. 1 demographic change is probably the increase in ethnic diversity in America. If you look 20 years out, 63 percent of the new population growth in the United States will be Hispanic and Asian. And virtually all of the diversity in America is concentrated in 10 states. Hispanics are now the largest minority group in the United States, and 34 percent of them live in California, 19 percent in Texas, 10 percent in New York and 7 percent in Florida. All of the other states are under 5 percent. Of the Asian population in America, nearly half live in three metropolitan areas, San Francisco, Los Angeles and New York. And 75 percent of the black population is in the Southeast and the Mississippi Delta.

What does that mean for colleges?

There is a move afoot to have every college be a mirror of the national population distribution. Given that 80 percent of kids going to college do so in their own state, looking like the country as a whole becomes a challenge in a state where minorities are 10 percent of the population. It also raises the issue of whether you should have the same proportion of minority faculty. The recruitment of minority faculty becomes a real crisis, because graduate schools are not turning out that many minority Ph.D.'s. One area where there will be a real problem is in developing new teachers. There has been a fairly pervasive decline in the number of blacks and Hispanics majoring in education—a decline of about 30 percent.

You say you like demographics because population trends are predictable. Have there been any surprises in the last 20 years?

There was only one surprise: the percentage of children living below the poverty line.

The strong economy pushed it down somewhat in recent years, but for decades the number was about 20 percent of American children. Any lessons there for colleges and universities?

For the lowest 20 percent, the amount of household income required to send children to college has increased, while their income has not increased at all. Tuition as a proportion of income has risen. But as we look at programs to help the poor, we have to remember that they are not all minorities. We tend to associate poverty mostly with minorities. But the largest number of poor children are white. Of the 14 million poor children in 1999, 8.9 million were white, 4 million were black and 3.9 million were Hispanic. But the children in poverty represented 16 percent of all white children, 37 percent of all black children and 36 percent of Hispanic children.

What are some of the other demographic trends?

People are moving much more frequently. About 43 million Americans move every year. That means people are changing jobs, and employers need to know who they are and what they can do. So they need a piece of paper—a college diploma or a certificate stating their skills. That is putting pressure on universities and colleges for those pieces of paper to mean the same thing. But there is almost no way you can guarantee that they do. It will only be a matter of time before states require tests to show what students have learned in college. But that would be terrible.

Did anyone predict there would be so many adult students?

Nobody in 1980 assumed that the number of adults going to college would be so high today. Of the 15 million students in college, almost half of them are adults with kids and jobs. The Joe College stereotype—the 18-to-22-year-old full-time student in residence on a campus—accounts for only 20 percent of the 15 million students.

Has the increase in older students run its course, or do you think it will continue?

I think it will continue. A lot of people are beginning to come back to higher education for a capstone experience in their 40's, 50's and 60's. Not for a better job, but for a vindication of their life. I was speaking at a commencement a few months ago and an older man walked across the stage to receive his doctoral degree. Someone shouted out, "Way to go, grandpa." I just love it. There is no reason to think that higher education was designed solely for the post-pubescent adolescent.

What does that mean for colleges faced with serving such students?

Older students have different needs. A whole lot of 30- and 40-year-olds have been out of education a long time. They may have a lot of innate smarts, but they don't remember the quadratic equation. So a lot of remedial education is to get 40-year-olds to remember how to write a good theme, and that is fine.

Many of the immigrants who come to the United States count on higher education to help them make it. How well does it work for them?

American higher education performs a unique function. No other country takes such a diverse group of people and turns them into the middle class. In the 1900's, it worked for Italians, Germans, French and English-speaking immigrants. Now it is working for Koreans and the Hmong. It is even working for the black population that is already here. Twenty percent of black households now have a higher income than the average for white households. That's never been true before. The mobility machine is clicking along like it should. We're very cynical, especially about our education system. But we need some appreciation for the kind of miracle we accomplish that doesn't happen in other countries—it's all due to our system of education.

So is college really available to all?

The percentage of college students who are minorities is virtually the same in every state as the percentage of high school students who are minorities. In California, for example, 54 percent of high school graduates are minorities, while 53 percent of college students are minorities. In Minnesota, 10 percent of high school graduates are minorities, while 9 percent of college students are minorities.

If you had a billion dollars to invest in education, how would you spend it?

I would spend most of it on the years before college, not on colleges. Money spent on Head Start and Trio and other precollege programs saves lots of money later on. To remediate someone at age 20 when their last 14 years were misused is really a chore. It can be done. But it is not efficient. College is really the icing on the cake.

WARMING UP: Journal Exercises

The following exercises will help you practice investigative writing. Read all of the following exercises and then, in your journal, write about the three that interest you most. One of these exercises may suggest an idea for your investigative essay.

1. Write an "authority" list of topics about which you have some information or experience. Consider your hobbies, academic interests, job skills, community experiences, or other experience with art, music, sports, travel, films, and so forth. Jot down a few sentences about three or four possible topics. Then go to the Internet and use your favorite search engine to continue investigating these topics. When you are finished browsing, write out the key questions you could answer about each of these topics.

2. Page through the notebooks and texts from another course you are currently taking. What subjects mentioned in class or referred to in the text might you investigate? Make a list of topics for investigation that would help you in that course. During that class, jot down any other suggestions that occur to you. While the topics should not be assignments for essays already assigned in that course, they could relate to relevant background reading.

3. Next semester, you will be taking a course in your major field, but you aren't sure which professor you should pick. To investigate the differences among the teachers, interview several students who have taken this course from different professors. Prepare questions that encourage factual responses: How many papers or tests does the teacher require? What is the grade distribution? What textbook is required? What is the reading or homework load? What are typical lecture topics? Is the teacher available outside class?

4. As a member of the student governing board, your job is to solicit student opinions about some aspect of campus life that needs improving. Choose a subject such as dorms, classes, the library, parking, student clubs, the film or fine art series, or recreational opportunities. Then choose a question to focus your investigation and write a one-page questionnaire that you might distribute to students. (See the section on writing questionnaires in this chapter.)

5. Watch an investigative news show such as *60 Minutes* or *Nightline,* taking notes on the interviewer's techniques. Is there a sequence to the questions— say, from gentle and polite to critical or controversial? What information does the interviewer have *before* the interview? Can you tell which questions are planned or scripted and which are spontaneous? After taking notes on a show, explain what you think are the three most important tips for successful interviewing.

6. Interview a classmate for a 200- to 250-word "personality profile." Your object is to profile this person and one of his or her major interests. First, in your daybook, prepare questions you need to ask for biographical information. Then, in an eight- to ten-minute interview, ask questions about the person and about several topics from that person's "authority" list. After the interview, take two or three minutes to review your notes. At home, write up the results of your interview, which will appear in your local or campus newspaper.

7. In early 2004, NASA landed two rovers, *Opportunity* and *Spirit,* on the surface of Mars. On the following page is an image from the NASA Web site. Observe the details of this image. Consider the rhetorical context: authoring agency, purpose, occasion, audience, composition, and cultural context. Then compare this image with the painting by Vermeer van Delft, *The Astronomer,* which appears at the beginning of this chapter. Using the Internet and your library's online databases, investigate the scientific, artistic, and/or cultural backgrounds of both of these images. What did scientists know about astronomy and our solar system when Vermeer painted his picture in 1668? What do we know—or not know—today? Use your research to start your own investigative article about some aspect of astronomy and space exploration then and now.

8. Read the following article by Elizabeth Larson, "Surfin' the Louvre." Use her model to write your own investigative essay comparing online learning to a traditional textbook-based course. Choose a course you are taking or

Image available at: *http://www.dfrc.nasa.gov/Newsroom/X-Press/images/072503/EC03016606.jpg*

have recently taken, and then find and report on key Web sites that enable you to learn about your subject without going to a single class, reading a textbook, or taking an exam.

PROFESSIONAL WRITING

Surfin' the Louvre

Elizabeth Larsen

I first studied art history the old-fashioned way: scribbling notes in a dark auditorium as a parade of yellowing slides whizzed past in an overwhelming progression from ancient Greece to Andy Warhol. Four years and tens of thousands of dollars later, I had traveled from the ruins of Tikal in Guatemala to a tiny Giotto-decorated chapel in Padua to Rodin's Paris atelier without ever leaving my college's urban campus.

Today it's possible to get a similar education—minus the sometimes inspired (and sometimes not-so-inspired) comments of a professor—on the Internet. In the past few years, virtually every museum of note has established a presence on the World Wide Web. While some sites still stick to the basics (cost of admission, hours, information about the permanent collection and current exhibits), more and more institutions are following the lead of the Fine Arts Museums of San Francisco (www.thinker.org/index.shtml) which is using the Web to promote its new commitment to "behave more like a resource and less like a repository." Currently the site houses over 65,000 images—from Mary Cassatt's *Woman Bathing* to more than 3,000 examples of Japanese ukiyo-e printmaking—with plans to double that number as the museum digitizes its entire collection.

That's a heck of a lot more reproductions than you'll find in that chiropractically unfriendly art history text, H. W. Janson's *History of Art*. Inspired by the sheer volume of images available on FAMSF's "Imagebase," I decided to try my hand at digitally designing my own art education.

My self-directed syllabus started in Spain at the new Guggenheim Museum in Bilbao (www.bm30.es/guggenheim), the recently opened critic's darling designed by maverick California architect Frank Gehry. As befits a museum where the architecture is as much a piece of art history as the works it houses, much of the site is devoted to Gehry's oddly gorgeous design, which looks like a cross between a medieval fortress and a bouquet of flowers sculpted in titanium. But there's a lot of other great stuff as well, including reproductions of the museum's most famous acquisitions—like Richard Serra's *Snake,* an appropriately jarring-yet-graceful panel of curving steel set smack dab in the middle of a gallery.

Eager to see more, I moved on to the Museums page of the World Wide Web Virtual Library (www.comlab.ox.ac.uk/archive/other/museums.html). A clearinghouse of links to museums, the site is most helpful for those who want to search according to the countries the museums are in. I started in Italy, which I soon discovered doesn't include that country-within-a-country, the Vatican (www.christusrex.org/www1citta/O-Citta.html). At the Uffizi Gallery in Florence (www.italink.com/eng/egui/hogui.html), I checked out a number of Renaissance heavy hitters, including Botticelli's The Birth of Venus and Paolo Ucello's Battle of San

...*continued* Surfin' the Louvre, **Elizabeth Larsen**

Romano. To get more of a feeling for Florentine art as it exists on the streets and in the churches of Florence, I used the Florence Art Guide to take me all over the city, from the Ponte Vecchio to the Piazzale Michelangelo.

My next stop was Paris, where my first visit was to—where else?—the Louvre (www.mistral.culture.fr/Louvre/Louvrea.html), where I lingered over a Watteau and a Poussin before getting absorbed in the history of the building. From there it was an easy trek to the countryside and the Giverny home page (www.giverny.org/index.html) to check out the gardens that inspired Monet.

From Giverny I hopped over to Greece and the Hellenic Ministry of Culture's Guide to Athens (www.culture.gr/maps/sterea/attiki/athens. html) where I gazed out over the Acropolis. Then I spent the rest of the afternoon in Japan at the Kyoto National Museum (www.kyohaku.go.jp/), where I studied up on the intricacies of Chinese and Japanese lacquerware.

I know I'm starting to sound pretty starry-eyed about my cyber-education, so I'll temper my enthusiasm with a few caveats. From the vantage point of my office chair, I obviously wasn't able to glean insights from the people standing next to me as I contemplated de Kooning's *Woman I*. But I don't require that every symphony I listen to be live, and I'm equally comfortable with the trade-offs inherent in a digital visual experience. Especially since I won't need to worry about those threatening form letters from the bursar's office.

■ ■ ■

PROFESSIONAL WRITING

Plotting a Net Gain

Connie Koenenn

In this profile of sociologist and computer guru Sherry Turkle, Los Angeles Times staff writer Connie Koenenn gives her readers information on Turkle's book, Life on the Screen: Identity in the Age of the Internet, *as well as perspectives on Turkle's private life. In writing this profile, notice how Koenenn interweaves material from interviews with Turkle, quotations and information from Turkle's book, information from a radio interview, and personal observations about Turkle's lifestyle.*

Microsoft Chairman Bill Gates looks at the Internet and sees a transforma-   *1*
tion in the way we get information. MIT sociologist Sherry Turkle looks at
the Internet and sees a transformation in the way we view ourselves.

Despite all the hype and babble about the information super-highway,   *2*
Turkle says, most people actually have underestimated the coming knowledge revolution. When we log onto a bulletin board, chat room, forum or
other cyberspace sites, she says, we are entering a world of possibility.
There, we can change our name, our appearance, even our sex, and test ourselves in that different persona. "We can easily move through multiple
identities," Turkle says, "and we can embrace—or be trapped by—cyberspace as a way of life."

This is the theme of her new book, *Life on the Screen: Identity in the Age*   *3*
of the Internet (Simon & Schuster). It's based on her studies, which started
20 years ago when she noticed the way MIT students used computer language ("Let's debug this relationship") in everyday life.

And although Turkle has been tracking the emerging computer culture   *4*
for two decades, the exploding popularity of the Internet world has turned
a new spotlight on her. *Newsweek* magazine listed her among "50 for the
Future" for 1995 and *Time* dubbed her the "Margaret Mead of Silicone."

"Sherry Turkle is an important thinker and very perspicacious—she   *5*
was way ahead of the curve," says Constance Hale, associate managing editor of *Wired* magazine, which is excerpting Turkle's book in its January issue. "Her book is groundbreaking. Her theory—that the computer isn't a
tool but that it is giving you access to parts of yourself that you didn't have
before—is revolutionary."

Like Gates, Turkle says we are on the brink of a revolution, now that   *6*
computers inhabit life at every turn. But while Gates's new book, *The Road*
Ahead (Viking), focuses on the outward shapes of the computers and software (such as a wallet PC), Turkle is more concerned with the loosening of
the boundaries between people and their computers. "If you want to call
this an 'information revolution,' you can," she said on a recent visit to Los
Angeles. "I think it is more than that."

Turkle, 47, who was wearing a trim black pantsuit and carrying an   *7*
immense leather handbag, had just been a guest on Michael Jackson's
CABC-AM (790) talk show. The discussion had turned to such new phenomena as "cyber-infidelity." Turkle had mentioned a wife who decided her husband's online affair was better than his looking around for real-life women.

That brought up the question of what constitutes infidelity in a world   *8*
where nothing is physical. "I think when you can connect via the computer,
you can adopt a persona somewhat different than the one you ordinarily

have," she told the radio audience. "People feel that the anonymity and distance allow them to experience different aspects of themselves."

Later, she elaborates. In person, Turkle is an engaging conversationalist, jumping from thought to thought with energy and humor. "People can experience other aspects of themselves online," she says. "I have seen it happen!"   9

She has seen how people, talking online in a low-risk setting, have slowly developed social skills or been able to discuss physical problems, such as weight or disabilities, that they previously repressed. She has watched men and women gradually move from virtual online worlds into real relationships ("Rush Limbaugh met his wife on CompuServe," she says).   10

Turkle put six years into writing *Life on the Screen.* Despite its catchy title and rich use of case studies, the heavily footnoted book, interweaving psychological and social analysis with an overview of intelligent machine development, is not light reading. "The meaning of the computer presence in people's lives is very different from what most expected in the late 1970s," Turkle writes. "One way to describe what has happened is to say we are moving from a modernist culture of calculation toward a postmodernist culture of simulation." In short, computers have moved from machines that do things for us (our tax returns or spreadsheets) to machines that do things to us, such as provide experiences that will affect our social and emotional life.   11

Describing e-mail as a "return to conversation over the backyard fence," Turkle notes that in the Massachusetts Institute of Technology Media Lab, where she works, she can log on any morning and scroll through the staff messages. "Someone has died, someone has a baby, someone has won an award—it's like a small-town newspaper."   12

Now, her interest is turning to families. She recently interviewed a woman whose son, just off to college, was studying for his first physics test. The woman had gotten America Online so they could keep in touch, and when she sent her first e-mail message, he replied, "Mom, you did it right!" She had insomnia and got up about 5 A.M. and, on an impulse, sent him another message. When he answered immediately, she realized he was very nervous about the test and had been studying all night. So she sent him a reassuring message that his parents will love him however he does on tests. "Here was a socially acceptable way to talk. She would never have called him at 5 in the morning, but this allows him to be in control, which is what kids that age need to be," Turkle says.   13

Computers were not on the agenda when Turkle graduated in 1976 *14* from Harvard with a double doctorate in sociology and personality psychology. She had spent a year in France analyzing how Freudian thought had been rejected and then accepted by the French; her first book, *Psychoanalytic Politics: Jacques Lacan & Freud's French Revolution,* has been reissued (Guilford Press, 1992).

"I thought I would have a career studying how complicated ideas come *15* into everyday life. I didn't anticipate the next set of ideas I would look at would be from computer science," Turkle says.

She was hired because MIT wanted somebody who studied the cul- *16* tural diffusion of scientific ideas. As technophobe Turkle began listening to the computer-savvy students, she realized they were using computer ideas (instead of "Freudian slip," they would say "information-processing error") to describe their lives. "It was like a 'Eureka!' experience to me," she says.

Beginning in her own backyard, Turkle organized pizza parties for *17* students playing MUDS (Multi-User Domains), the intricate online games in which participants can alter their real-life identities to improvise elaborate melodramas. She interviewed them at length about their experiences in the fantasies that grew out of the Dungeons and Dragons fantasy games of the early 1970s. She also studied children who were being introduced to computer toys. More recently, she began monitoring Internet chat and bulletin boards.

"I just kept studying people and machines," says Turkle, who has *18* steadily written articles for academic journals about the computer culture—about women and computers, physicists and computers, children and computers. Ten years ago she wrote *The Second Self: Computers and the Human Spirit* (Simon & Schuster).

Turkle estimates that she has interviewed more than 1,000 people. *19* Mitchel Resnick, a colleague at the MIT Media Lab, admires Turkle's ability to get people to open up in interviews. "She can make people feel comfortable sharing their deepest feelings," he says. "I think often they have been transformed by these [online] experiences and most people don't understand that world."

Although Turkle may meet her subjects online, she insists on inter- *20* viewing them in person, usually in her MIT office. She doesn't even have a computer there—it's reserved for seeing RL (real life) students and colleagues, she explains.

She is, however, surrounded by computers at home. Turkle is married *21* to consultant Ralph Willard, and they have a daughter, 4. Her routine in

...continued Plotting a Net Gain, **Connie Koenenn**

their Boston home is to wake up at 6 A.M. and devote two hours to e-mail, sitting at her Macintosh with a Powerbook nearby to receive faxes. "I have a little computer for my daughter and a palmtop I travel with. I don't watch TV and I write very few letters anymore—I spend a fair amount of time Internet-surfing."

And although she signs on daily to a huge amount of e-mail, she says 22 it is worth it. She recently heard from an old high school friend who had seen an article about her in a Boston paper. He had thought about contacting her previously, but with e-mail it was too easy to pass up, he said. She was delighted. "To me, making possible that kind of connection with your past, with people all over the world, is so precious. I am willing to bite the bullet and sort through all the e-mail."

And although she acknowledges a darker side of cyberspace (people 23 can get stuck in the selves they have created on the screen, or hurt by an online relationship that turns out to be fraudulent, she says), Turkle has great hopes for the emerging computer culture.

"Here's the good news," she says briskly. "Being online can help you 24 develop parts of yourself that have been underdeveloped and it can help your personal growth. Here's the bad news: Some people find themselves just acting out the same problems they have in real life in virtual life. If they've been hostile, they become the 'flamers' on the Internet, using the anonymity to act out their hangups."

She doesn't like the question, "Is cyberspace good or bad?" The point 25 is, it is, she says. "It's going to demand ongoing conversations about the new definition of work, of marriage, of sexuality, of child care, of every aspect of our lives."

She thus welcomes the fuss over pornography on the Internet as a sig- 26 nal that we are living in a very different time. "It's setting the stage for that longer-term reflection. It's important to keep in mind that we are not going to sort this out in the next two months or two years."

■ ■ ■

vo·cab·u·lar·y

In your journal, write the meanings of the italicized terms or words in the following phrases.

- *Margaret Mead* of Silicone **(4)**
- very *perspicacious* **(5)**

- *postmodernist* culture **(11)**
- cultural *diffusion* of scientific ideas **(16)**
- *technophobe* Turkle **(16)**
- *Freudian slip* **(16)**

QUESTIONS FOR WRITING AND DISCUSSION

1. Investigative essays focus on answering at least one key question. The question for Connie Koenenn's article might be "Who is Sherry Turkle and what does she think about the Internet?" Reread the article, focusing on Koenenn's answer to the second part of that question. Find at least three specific passages that reveal what Turkle finds important about the Internet.

2. Typically, profiles have certain identifying features, such as physical description, personal quotations, and informal observations as well as comments about professional achievements, articles or books written, awards received, and plans for the future. Reread Koenenn's profile "Plotting a Net Gain," and list all the features that you find. When you finish your list, write a paragraph that describes the profile as a genre.

3. Reread Koenenn's article, looking for evidence of the sources she used in writing this essay. Next to major paragraphs, indicate the probable source of the quotations, facts, or information. Does Koenenn rely most on quotations and information from a personal interview, on information from Turkle's books, on outside biographical information, on additional third-party interviews, on transcripts of a radio interview, or on other sources? Write a list of the kinds of sources Koenenn probably used.

4. Write your own investigative profile about a person from your school, an employee at your place of work, or a member of your family. Schedule an interview to find out about this person. Use your own observations. Interview other people about their acquaintance with this person. Read anything this person may have written. Assume that your profile will appear in a local or campus newspaper.

5. Sherry Turkle continues to be interviewed about her views on how computers and the Internet are changing and—especially—how they are changing us. Use your library databases to find recent full-text articles on Sherry Turkle. In one interview published in *Fortune* magazine, Turkle had the following comments: "The Internet is a place of experimentation on your identity—in positive as well as negative ways." "The more complicated computer networks get, the more people use them as models for their own minds." "It's going to

create a crisis about the simulated and the real. The notion of what it is to live in a culture of simulation . . . is going to become more and more [important]." What new information can you find about how computers are changing our identity, our culture, and our sense of what is real and what is only simulated?

PROFESSIONAL WRITING

The Homeless and Their Children

Jonathan Kozol

In his most famous book, Illiterate America (1985), *Jonathan Kozol says that because more than one-third of America's adults are at least partially illiterate, we should organize a massive government and volunteer army to liberate people imprisoned by illiteracy. More recently, Kozol has written about children in underclass America in* Amazing Grace: The Lives of Children and the Conscience of a Nation (1996) *and* Ordinary Resurrections (2000). *In "The Homeless and Their Children,"* taken from Rachel and Her Children (1988), *Kozol investigates individual cases of poverty in a New York City welfare hotel. Although welfare laws have changed and the Martinique Hotel has since been renovated, Kozol's investigative report accurately chronicles the effects of illiteracy on the lives of the poor. Kozol uses his own observations and interview transcripts to demonstrate vividly the connection between illiteracy and poverty. However, instead of arguing indignantly for literacy programs to save the lives of the poor and illiterate, Kozol simply reports the case of a single illiterate woman trying to raise her four children. The woman he calls Laura cannot decipher labels on products at the grocery store, cannot read notices from the welfare office, and cannot understand letters from the hospital warning of her children's lead poisoning.*

The Martinique Hotel, at Sixth Avenue and Thirty-second Street, is one *1* of the largest hotels for homeless people in New York City. When I visited it, in December of 1985, nearly four hundred homeless families, including some twelve hundred children, were lodged in the hotel, by arrangement with the city's Human Resources Administration. One of the residents I spoke to at some length was an energetic, intelligent woman I'll call Kim. During one of our conversations, she mentioned a woman on the seventh floor who had seemingly begun to find her situation intolerable.

Kim described this woman as "a broken stick," and offered to arrange for us to meet.

The woman—I will call her Laura, but her name, certain other names, and certain details have been changed—is so fragile that I find it hard to start a conversation when we are introduced, a few nights later. Before I begin, she asks if I will read her a letter from the hospital. The oldest of her four children, a seven-year-old boy named Matthew, has been sick for several weeks. He was tested for lead poisoning in November, and the letter she hands me, from Roosevelt Hospital, says that the child has a dangerous lead level. She is told to bring him back for treatment. She received the letter some weeks ago. It has been buried in a pile of other documents that she cannot read.

Although Laura cannot read, she knows enough about the dangers of lead to grasp the darker implications of this information. The crumbling plaster in the Martinique Hotel is covered with sweet-tasting paint, and children eat or chew chips of the paint as it flakes off the walls. Some of the paint contains lead. Children with lead poisoning may suffer loss of coordination or undergo convulsions. The consequences of lead poisoning may be temporary or long lasting. They may appear at once or not for several years. This final point is what instills so much uneasiness; even months of observation cannot calm a parent's fear.

Lead poisoning, then, is Laura's first concern, but she has other problems. The bathroom plumbing has overflowed and left a pool of sewage on the floor. A radiator valve is broken, and every now and then releases a spray of scalding steam at the eye level of a child. A crib provided by the hotel appears to be unstable. A screw that holds two of its sides together is missing. When I test the crib with my hand, it starts to sway. There are four beds in the room, and they are dangerous, too. They have metal frames with unprotected corners, and the mattresses do not fit the frames; at one corner or another, metal is exposed. If a child has the energy or the playfulness to jump or turn a somersault or wrestle with a friend, and if he falls and strikes his head against the metal corner, the consequences can be serious. The week before, a child on the fourteenth floor fell in just this way, cut his forehead, and required stitches. Most of these matters have been brought to the attention of the hotel management; in Laura's case, complaints have brought no visible results.

All of this would be enough to make life difficult for an illiterate young woman in New York, but Laura has one other urgent matter on her hands. It appears that she has failed to answer a request for information from her welfare office, and, for reasons that she doesn't understand, she did not receive her benefits this week. The timing is bad; it's a weekend. The city operates a crisis center in the Martinique, where residents can go for food and other help, but today the crisis center is not open, so there's nobody around to tide her over with emergency supplies. Laura's children have been eating cheese and bread and peanut butter for two days. "Those on welfare," the Community Service Society of New York said in a report published in 1984, may be suddenly removed from welfare rolls "for reasons unrelated to their actual need," or even to eligibility standards. Welfare workers in New York City call this practice "churning." Laura and her children are being churned.

The room is lighted by fluorescent tubes in a ceiling fixture. They cast   6
a stark light on four walls of greenish paint smeared over with sludge draining from someone's plumbing on the floor above. In the room are two boys with dark and hollowed eyes and an infant girl. A third boy is outside and joins us later. The children have the washed-out look of the children Walker Evans photographed for "Let Us Now Praise Famous Men." Besides the four beds and the crib, the room contains two chairs, a refrigerator, and a television set, which doesn't work. A metal hanger serves as an antenna, but there is no picture on the screen. Instead, there is a storm of falling flakes and unclear lines. I wonder why Laura keeps it on. There are no table lamps to soften the fluorescent glare, no books, no decorations. Laura tells me that her father is of Panamanian birth but that she went to school in New York City. Spanish is her first language. I don't speak Spanish well. We talk in English.

"I cannot read," Laura says. "I buy the New York *Post* to read the pic-   7
tures. In the grocery, I know what to buy because I see the pictures."

What of no-name products—generic brands, whose labels have no   8
pictures but which could save her a great deal of money?

"If there are no pictures, I don't buy it," she says. "I want to buy pan-   9
cakes, I ask the lady, 'Where's the pancakes?' So they tell me."

She points to the boys and says, "He's two. He's five. Matthew's seven.   10
My daughter is four months. She has this rash." She shows me ugly skin eruptions on the baby's neck and jaw. "The carpets, they was filthy from the stuff, the leaks that come down on the wall. All my kids have rashes, but the worst she has it. There was pus all over. Somewhere here I have a letter from the nurse." She shuffles around but cannot find the letter. "She got something underneath the skin. Something that bites. The only way you can get rid of it is with a cream."

She finds the letter. The little girl has scabies.   *11*

Laura continues, "I have been living here two years. Before I came   *12*
here, I was in a house we had to leave. There was rats. Big ones, they crawl
on us. The rats, they come at night. They come into our house, run over my
son's legs. The windows were broken. It was winter. Snow, it used to come
inside. My mother lived with us before. Now she's staying at my grandma's
house. My grandma's dying in the bed. She's sixty-five. My mother comes
here once a week to do the groceries. Tomorrow she comes. Then she goes
back to help my grandma."

"I know my name, and I can write my name, my children's names. To   *13*
read, I cannot do it. Medicines, I don't know the instructions. I was living
here when I was pregnant with Corinne. No, I didn't see no doctor. I was
hungry. What I ate was rice and beans, potato chips and soda. Up to now
this week we don't have food. People ask me, 'Can you help? Do you got
this? Do you got that?' I don't like to tell them no. If I have something, I
give it. This week, I don't got. I can read baby books—like that, a little bit.
If I could read, I would read newspapers. I would like to know what's going on. Matthew, he tells me I am stupid. 'You can't read.' You know, because he wants to read. He don't understand what something is. I tell him,
'I don't know it. I don't understand.' People laugh. You feel embarrassed.
On the street. Or in the store." She weeps. "There's nothing here."

Laura sweeps one hand in a wide arc, but I can't tell whether she   *14*
means the gesture to take in the room or something more. Then she makes
her meaning clear: "Everything I had, they put it on the sidewalk when I
was evicted. I don't know if that's the law. Things like that—what is the
law, what isn't? I can't read it, so I didn't understand. I lost everything I had.
I sign papers. Somebody could come and take my children. They could
come. 'Sign this. Sign that.' I don't know what it says. Adoption papers—
I don't know. This here paper that I got I couldn't understand."

She hands me another letter. This one is from the management of the   *15*
hotel: "This notice is to inform you that your rent is due today. I would appreciate your cooperation in seeing to it that you go to your center today."
Another form that she hands me asks her to fill out the names and the ages
of her children.

"Papers, documents—people give it to me. I don't know it: I don't un-   *16*
derstand." She pauses, and then says, "I'm a Catholic. Yes—I go two weeks
ago to church. This lady say they have these little books that learn me how
to spell. You see the letters. Put them together. I would like to read. I go to
St. Francis' Church. Go inside and kneel—I pray. I don't talk to the priest.
I done so many things—you know, bad things. I buy a bottle of wine. A

...continued The Homeless and Their Children, **Jonathan Kozol**

bottle of beer. That costs a dollar. I don't want to say to God. I get a hundred and seventy-three dollars restaurant allowance. With that money I buy clothes. Food stamps, I get two hundred dollars. That's for groceries. Subway tokens I take out ten dollars. Washing machine, I do downstairs. Twenty-five dollars to dry and wash. Five dollars to buy soap. Thirty dollars twice a month."

Another woman at the Martinique calculates her laundry costs at my 17 request, and they come out to nearly the same figure. These may be the standard rates for a midtown site. The difficulty of getting out and traveling to find lower prices, whether for laundromats or for groceries, cannot be overstated. Families at the Martinique are trapped in a commercial district.

I ask Laura who stays with the children when she does her chores. 18

"My mother keeps the children when I do the wash," she replies. "If 19 she can't, I ask somebody on the floor. 'Give me three dollars. I watch your kids.' For free? Nothing. Everything for money. Everybody's poor."

Extending a hand, she says, "This is the radiator. Something's wrong." 20 She shows me where the steam sprays out. I test it with my hand. "Sometimes it stops. The children get too close. Then it starts—like that! Leak is coming from upstairs down." I see the dark muck on the wall. "The window is broke. Lights broke." She points to the fluorescent tubes. They flicker on and off. "I ask them, 'Please, why don't you give me ordinary lights?' They don't do nothing. So it been two weeks. I go downstairs. They say they coming up. They never come. So I complain again. Mr. Tuccelli— Salvatore Tuccelli, the manager of the Martinique—said to come here to his office. Desks and decorations and a lot of pictures. It's above the lobby. So the manager was there. Mr. Tuccelli sat back in his chair. He had a gun. He had it here under his waist. You know, under his belt. I said, 'Don't show it to me if you isn't going to use it.' I can't tell what kind of gun it was. He had it in his waist. 'You are showing me the gun so I will be afraid.' If he was only going to show it, I would not be scared. If he's going to use it, I get scared."

"So he says, 'You people bring us trouble.' I said, 'Why you give my 21 son lead poison and you didn't care? My child is lead-poisoned.' He said, 'I don't want to hear of this again.' What I answer him is this: 'Listen. People like you live in nice apartments. You got a home. You got TV. You got a family. You got children in a school that learn them. They don't got lead poison.' "

"I don't know the reason for the guards. They let the junkies into the 22 hotel. When my mother comes, I have to sign. If it's a family living good, they make it hard. If it's the drug dealers, they come in. Why they let the junkies in but keep away your mother? The guards, you see them taking women in the corner. You go down twelve-thirty in the night, they're in the corner with the girls. This is true. I seen it."

She continues, "How I know about the lead is this: Matthew sits there 23 and he reaches his fingers in the plaster and he put it in his mouth. So I ask him, 'Was you eating it?' He says, 'Don't hit me. Yes, I was.' So then I took him to the clinic and they took the blood. I don't know if something happen to him later on. I don't know if it affects him. When he's older . . .'"

I ask Laura why she goes to church. 24

"I figure: Go to church. Pray God. Ask Him to help. I go on my knees. 25 I ask Him from my heart. 'Jesus Christ, come help me, please. Why do you leave me here?' When I'm lying down at night, I ask, 'Why people got to live like this?' On the street, the people stare at you when you go out of the hotel. People look. They think, I wonder how they live in there. Sometimes I walk out this door. Garbage all over in the stairs. When it's hot, a lot of bugs around the trash. Sometimes there are fires in the trash. I got no fire escape. You have to get out through the hall. I got no sprinkler. Smoke detector doesn't work. When I cook and food is burning, it don't ring. If I smoke, it starts to ring. I look up. I say, 'Why you don't work? When I need you, you don't work. I'm gonna knock you down.' I did!" She laughs.

There is a sprinkler system in the corridor. In 1987, the hotel manage- 26 ment informed residents that the fire-alarm system was "inoperable."

I ask Laura if the older children are enrolled in school. Nodding at 27 Michael, her middle son, she says, "This one doesn't go to school. He's five. I need to call tomorrow. Get a quarter. Then you get some papers. Then you got to sign those papers. Then he can start school."

"For this room I pay fifteen hundred dollars for two weeks. I don't pay. 28 The welfare pays. I got to go and get it." The room, although it is undivided, was originally a two-room suite and is being rented at the two-room rate. "They send me this. I'm suppose to sign. I don't know what it is. Lots of things you suppose to sign. I sign it but I don't know what it is."

While we are talking, Matthew comes in and sits beside his mother. 29 He lowers his eyes when I shake his hand.

Laura goes on, "Looking for a house, I got to do it." She explains that 30 she's required to give evidence that she is searching for a place to live. "I can't read, so I can't use the paper. I get dressed. I put my makeup on. If I go like this, they look afraid. They say, 'They going to destroy the house!' You got to dress the children and look nice. Owners don't want homeless. Don't want welfare. Don't want kids. What I think? If they pay one thousand and five hundred dollars every two weeks, why not pay five hundred dollars for a good apartment?"

She hands me another paper. "Can you tell me what is this?"   *31*

It's a second letter from the hospital, telling her to bring her son for   *32* treatment.

She says, "Every day, my son this week, last week was vomiting. Every   *33* time he eat his food, he throw it right back out. I got to take him to the clinic."

"Christmas, they don't got. For my daughter I ask a Cabbage Patch.   *34* For my boys I ask for toys. I got them stockings." She shows me four cotton stockings tacked to the wall with nothing in them. "They say, 'Mommy, there's no toys.' I say not to worry. 'You are going to get something.' But they don't. They don't get nothing. I could not afford. No, this isn't my TV. Somebody lended it to me. Christmas tree I can't afford. Christmas I don't spend it happy. I am thinking of the kids. What we do on Christmas is we spend it laying on the bed. If I go outside, I feel a little better. When I'm here, I see those walls, the bed, and I feel sad. If I had my own apartment, maybe there would be another room. Somewhere to walk. Walk back and forth."

I ask her, "How do you relax?"   *35*

"If I want to rest, relax, I turn out the light and lie down on the bed,"   *36* she says. "When I met his father, I was seventeen." She says she knew him before she was homeless, when she lived in Brooklyn with her mother. He was working at a pizza parlor near her mother's home. "One night, he bought me liquor. I had never tasted. So he took me to this hallway. Then my mother say that what I did is wrong. So I say that I already did it. So you have to live with what you did. I had the baby. No. I did not want to have abortion. The baby's father I still see. When he has a job, he brings me food. In the summer, he worked in a flower store. He would bring me flowers. Now he don't have any job. So he don't bring me flowers."

She sweeps her hand in a broad arc and says again, "Nothing here. I   *37* feel embarrassed for the room. Flowers, things like that, you don't got. Pretty things you don't got. Nothing like that. No."

In the window is a spindly geranium plant. It has no flowers, but some   *38* of the leaves are green. Before I go, we stand beside the window. Blowing snow hits the panes and blurs the dirt.

"Some of the rooms high up, they got a view," Laura says. "You see the   *39* Empire State."

I've noticed this—seen the building from a window. It towers high *40* above the Martinique.

"I talk to this plant. I tell him, 'Grow! Give me one flower!' He don't *41* do it." Then, in an afterthought, "No pets. No. You don't got. Animals. They don't allow."

It occurs to me that this is one of the few places I have been except a *42* hospital or a reform school where there are hundreds of children and virtually no pets. A few people keep cats illegally.

"I wish I had a dog," Laura says. "Brown dog. Something to hug." *43*

■ ■ ■

vo·cab·u·lar·y

In your journal, write the meanings of the italicized words in the following phrases.

- the darker *implications* (3)
- call this practice "*churning*" (5)
- ugly skin *eruptions* (10)
- girl has *scabies* (11)

QUESTIONS FOR WRITING AND DISCUSSION

1. Describe your intellectual and emotional reaction to Kozol's article. What information about the lives of the poor and illiterate did you already know? What information surprised you? How did Kozol's essay make you feel about this problem?

2. The purpose of an investigative report is to give information without editorializing or arguing for or against a solution. In which paragraphs does Kozol remain most objective and unemotional? Which passages reveal Kozol's sympathy for Laura's situation? Does he avoid editorializing?

3. Reread the essay, marking those places where Laura's illiteracy causes her problems. Based on your notes, explain how her illiteracy (rather than her poverty) causes or magnifies her problems.

4. Describe the investigative techniques that Kozol probably used to write his essay. In addition to his interviews with Laura, what were his other probable sources of information?

5. According to the information provided by Kozol, what support does the welfare system provide Laura and her children? How does the welfare system encourage

Laura to improve her life? List three changes that you believe the welfare system should make to solve Laura's problems and make her more self-sufficient.

6. On your next trip to the grocery store, see which products would appeal to an illiterate person. List the items (and their prices) that you might buy based on the pictures on the labels. Write a paragraph describing your findings. Is Kozol correct in assuming that Laura pays too much for her groceries?

7. Jonathan Kozol's latest investigative book, *Ordinary Resurrections* (2000), is a postscript to his earlier works such as *Savage Inequalities: Children in America's Schools* (1992) and *Amazing Grace: The Lives of Children and the Conscience of a Nation* (1995). Use the Internet to access full-text reviews of *Ordinary Resurrections*. On Amazon.com, you will find interesting but mostly positive comments—Amazon is, after all, in the business of selling books. A review in *Newsweek* by Ellis Cose is also positive, but check out Sol Stern's review, "America's Most Influential—and Wrongest—School Reformer," available in full text from Lexis-Nexis. Stern claims, for example, that "Kozol's mistaken but hugely influential diagnosis leads education advocates to keep proposing still more of the wrong cure [giving resources to these schools], while the real causes of school failure—the monopoly public education system, the teachers' unions, and the ed schools—go on wreaking their damage unimpeded, and inner-city schools keep on failing." Read all of Stern's review. Do you agree or disagree with Stern's analysis? Explain.

TECHNIQUES   PROCESS

Investigating: The Writing Process

ASSIGNMENT FOR INVESTIGATING

Choose a subject to investigate: one aspect of a current social or political policy, a scientific discovery or principle, a historical event, a profile of a controversial public figure, or perhaps just an ordinary event, person, process, or place that you find interesting. Your initial purpose should be to discover or learn about your subject. Then, with a specific audience in mind, report your findings. A report presents the information that you find; it should not argue for or against any idea or plan. With the final copy of your investigative report, turn in photocopies of any sources you have summarized or cited, notes from your interview(s), and/or copies of questionnaires that you used.

Selecting your audience and genre is especially important for your investigative piece. If an audience is not specified in your assignment, check out newspapers, magazines, and Web sites for appropriate audiences and genres. You may want to do an investigative essay, but perhaps a pamphlet, Web site, or letter would be more effective. Limiting your audience and selecting a possible newspaper, journal, magazine, forum, or Web site will help you focus your information. Where possible, think globally but focus locally—what global topic has local implications that you can investigate, and what local publication might be interested in your essay?

CHOOSING COLLECTING RESEARCH SHAPING DRAFTING REVISING

CHOOSING A SUBJECT

If one of your journal topics does not suggest a subject for your investigation, consider the following ideas. If you have a subject, go on to the collecting and shaping strategies.

- Choose some idea, principle, process, or theory discussed in a class that you are currently taking. In biology, you might focus on the Krebs cycle; in art, investigate the Dutch school of painters; or in education, investigate community literacy programs. In physics, research low-temperature conductivity or hydrogen fuels, or in astronomy, investigate competing theories about the formation of the universe. Begin by interviewing a professor, graduate students, or classmates about how to research the history, development, or personalities behind this idea. With information from the interview, continue your investigation in the library and online. As you read, focus your question to one narrow or specific area.

- Investigate and report on a campus or community service organization. Choose any academic, minority, cultural, or community organization. Visit the office. Interview an official. Read the organization's literature. Talk to students or community members who have used the service. Check the library for background information. Find people who are dissatisfied with or critical of the organization. Select an audience who might use this service or who might be interested in volunteering for the organization, and report the relevant *who, what, when, where, why,* and/or *how* information.

- At your workplace, investigate how something does or does not work, research how the business (or your part of the business) is organized, do a profile of a coworker, or survey your customers to find out what they like best or least about your store or company.

- For practice, investigate one of the following questions on the Internet and/or in the library (be prepared to explain your answers to your class members): How can you minimize jet lag? Can aspirin prevent heart attacks? How expensive is television advertising? What is a wind tunnel used for? Why is the Antarctic ice shelf melting? How do endorphins work? What is a melanoma? What causes seasonal affective disorder? How does a "Zamboni" work? What effects does Megan's law have? Do Americans spend more money on cosmetics than on education? What are the newest ways to repair torn ACLs (anterior cruciate ligaments) in your knee? What is computer morphing, and how does it work?

- Investigate an academic major, a career, or a job in which you are interested. List some of the *who, what, when, where,* and *why* questions you want to answer. Who is interested in this major? What background or courses are required? What is the pay scale or opportunities for advancement? What appeals to you about this major or job? What are the disadvantages of this major or career? Research your major or career on the Internet and in the library. Plan to interview an adviser, a friend who majors in the field, or a person who works at that job. Be prepared to report your findings to your classmates.

CHOOSING **COLLECTING** RESEARCH SHAPING DRAFTING REVISING

COLLECTING

The collecting strategies discussed in Chapters 3, 4, and 5 (brainstorming, clustering, looping, mapping, sketching, reading, summarizing, taking double-entry notes) may be useful as you collect ideas. Other strategies particularly useful for investigating are suggested here. Try each of the following collecting strategies for your subject.

ASKING QUESTIONS Asking the *right questions* is crucial to investigative writing. Sets of questions (often called *heuristics*) will help you narrow and focus your subject and tailor your approach to the expectations or needs of your audience. You don't know what information you need to collect until you know what questions your investigation needs to answer.

1. The "reporter's" or the familiar "Wh" questions are one basic heuristic: Who? What? When? Where? Why? Asking these questions of a topic ensures that

> " Had I known the answer to any of these questions, I would never have needed to write. "
> —JOAN DIDION, ESSAYIST AND NOVELIST

COMMUNITY SERVICE LEARNING

If you have a service-learning project connected with your writing course, below is some background information that will help you understand your project.

Definition Community-service learning is simply a mutually beneficial partnership with a community agency.

Goals Teachers, students, and the partnering agency work together to set mutual goals promoting both civic action and academic learning. The agency receives your assistance with projects involving planning, writing, and communicating. You receive valuable experience related to your writing class goals: working and writing collaboratively, assessing and addressing agency needs, and getting practice with real-world writing situations, tasks, and genres.

Requirements Most service-learning projects require both a certain number of hours of service and a portfolio of pieces of writing *about* the agency, *for* the agency, and *with* the agency. A major requirement of service-learning projects is a reflective account about your participation, about the agency and its mission, and about what you have learned.

Writing Situations and Genres Depending on the goals and mission of the agency, you may write any combination of the following genres or kinds of writing: journal writing, online discussion forums, observation of the agency, profile of the agency, research, needs assessment, audience analysis, interviews, pamphlets, Web site design, public service announcements, feature articles, and impact assessment.

Benefits The agency benefits from your help with its ongoing projects (but remember that it also gives its time to help you learn). You benefit from getting to write in real-world situations—not just for your teacher and classmates. You also gain civic and crosscultural awareness, experience in working and writing collaboratively, increased problem-solving skills, contacts for possible job or career choices, and personal satisfaction for helping with a worthy civic cause.

---

you're not leaving out any crucial information. If, for example, you are investigating recreational opportunities in your city or on campus, you might ask the following questions to focus your investigation (remember to ask the negative version of each question, too).

- *Whom* is the recreation for?
- *Who* runs the programs?
- *Who* is excluded from the programs?
- *Who* pays for the programs?
- *What* is the program?
- *What* sports are included in the program?

- *What* sports are not included?
- *What* is the budget for these programs?
- *When* are these opportunities available or not available?
- *Where* do the activities take place?
- *Where* are they restricted?
- *Why* are these programs offered?
- *Why* are certain activities not offered?
- *Why* have activities been changed?

These questions might lead you to focus your investigation on the scheduling, on why soccer has been excluded, or on why participants are charged a fee for one class or program but not for another.

2. The classical "topics" provide a second set of questions for an investigation.

Definition:	What is it?
Comparison:	What is it like or unlike?
Relationship:	What caused it? What are its consequences?
Testimony:	What has been said or written about it?

These questions can be used in conjunction with the reporter's questions to focus an investigation. Applied to the topic on recreational opportunities, the questions might be as follows.

Definition:	What activities exist?
	How can the activities be described, classified, or analyzed?
Comparison:	What are similarities to or differences from other programs?
Relationship:	What caused these programs to be offered?
	What causes people to use or avoid these activities?
	What are the consequences of these programs?
Testimony:	What do students think about these activities?
	What do administrators think?
	What have other schools done?
	What does research show?
	What proverbs or common sayings apply here?

These two sets of questions will *expand* your information, helping you collect facts, data, examples, and ideas—probably more than you can use in a short essay. Once you have all of this information, you can then *narrow* your topic.

THE FAR SIDE®   BY GARY LARSON

USING WRITTEN AND ELECTRONIC SOURCES

- **When printed copies are not available directly from your computer access, make photocopies of relevant articles.** The small amount of money you spend on copies will enable you to reread articles if necessary, quote or paraphrase from them accurately, and cite them accurately as references. (The money you spend is also excellent antifrustration insurance, in case you return to the library stacks and discover that someone else has checked out your magazine or book.) On your photocopies, be sure to write *source information:* magazine or book title, author, publisher, date and place of publication, volume, and page numbers. For this investigative report, remember that you must turn in photocopies of any pages of articles or books you use.

- **Make notes and summaries from your photocopied sources.** As you collect information from photocopied sources, jot down key facts, ideas, and direct quotations. For every note you take, record the author, title, publishing information, and page numbers. You may *paraphrase* another writer's ideas, examples, sentences, or short passages by writing them in

Research Tips

As you work on your investigating essay, use the following research strategies.

Library Orientation Every library is different, so be sure to take your library's tour and find out how the online catalog searches and databases work. Knowing which databases to use and how to effectively use their search strategies makes your research quicker and more effective.

Internet Searches Use Internet search engines such as Google, Yahoo!, or Altavista primarily for introductory or background information. Remember that the sites you find online may not be as reliable as information you find through your library's academic databases.

Evaluate Your Sources For all your Internet and library database sources, be sure to carefully evaluate the reliability, accuracy, and bias of your sources. Is the author of the text or Web site an authority on the subject? What is the author's connection to the subject, point of view, or bias? Has the text been published by a reputable magazine, or is it a self-published Web site?

Talk to Your Reference Librarian An informal interview with a reference librarian may be the most important ten minutes you spend doing research. Start by telling the librarian about your assignment—the topic and issue you're investigating—and then ask which databases, sources, or reference guides might be most helpful. Remember, there are no stupid questions in a library. Everyone has to learn how electronic databases work.

Include Field Research Field research, including personal observations, interviews, and questionnaires, can be effective in almost every research project. An interview with a campus or community expert on your topic may be a great place to start. A questionnaire for other students or potential readers may give you a better sense of what your audience knows or does not know about your topic and what points of view they have on the issue.

your own words. Use *direct quotation* when words or phrases in a source are more striking than your paraphrase might be. You may edit a direct quotation by (1) deleting any irrelevant or unnecessary words or phrases by using ellipsis points (three spaced periods) to indicate the deleted words and by (2) inserting your own words in square brackets [ ] if you need to clarify a quoted passage. Otherwise, the words within the quotation marks must accurately reproduce the original: No altered spellings, changed words, or rephrasings are allowed.

- **Avoid plagiarism.** Use quotation marks whenever you quote more than a word or two from your source. Paraphrase in your own words rather than stringing together phrases and sentences written by someone else. Give credit for ideas, facts, and language by citing your sources. In informal investigative writing, you may simply mention the author and title of written sources, citing page numbers of direct quotations in parentheses. (All formal research papers and some investigative essays cite sources in full in a "Works Cited" section at the end. See Chapter 13, "Writing a Research Paper," for more details.)

SUMMARIZING   As explained in Chapter 5, a *summary* is a concise explanation of the main and supporting ideas in a passage, report, essay, book, or speech. It is usually written in the present tense. It identifies the author and title of the source; it may refer to the context or the actual place where the study took place; it contains the passage's main ideas; and it may quote directly a few forceful or concise sentences or phrases. It will not usually cite the author's examples. A *paraphrase* usually expresses all the information in the passage—including examples—in your own words. Summary, paraphrase, and direct quotation often occur together as you use sources. (See Chapter 5 for more details.)

CITING SOURCES IN YOUR TEXT   As you collect information, you should note authors, titles of books or magazines, dates of publication, publishers, and page numbers to give proper credit to your sources. For some journalistic writing, you may need to cite only the author, the title of your source, or both:

> According to Constance Hale, associate managing editor of *Wired* magazine, "Sherry Turkle . . . was way ahead of the curve" **(2)**.

> *Newsweek* magazine listed Sherry Turkle among their "50 for the Future" **(2)**.

For a more formal, academic context, the MLA (Modern Language Association) requires that the author and page numbers be given, in parentheses, at the end of the sentence—for example, "(Turkle 24–25)":

> A key point in *Life on the Screen: Identity in the Age of the Internet* is that we can "embrace—or be trapped by—cyberspace as a way of life" (Turkle 25).

If you refer to the author in the sentence that contains the citation, indicate just the page numbers in parentheses.

> In her book *Life on the Screen: Identity in the Age of the Internet*, Turkle argues that we can "embrace—or be trapped by—cyberspace as a way of life" (25).

For additional information on formal, in-text citation, consult Chapter 13, "Writing a Research Paper."

DOING FIELD RESEARCH

Field research is essential for many kinds of investigative reports. Typically, field research—as opposed to library research—involves first-hand observations, interviews, and questionnaires. For observing strategies, see Chapter 3, "Observing." Using interviews and writing questionnaires are discussed below.

■ INTERVIEWING   After you have done some initial research, interviews are a logical next step. Remember that the more you know about the subject (and the person you're interviewing), the more productive the interview will be. In planning an interview, keep the following steps in mind.

1. Make an *appointment* with the person you wish to interview. Although you may feel hesitant or shy about calling or e-mailing someone for an interview, remember that most people are flattered that someone else is interested in them and wants to hear their opinions or learn about their areas of expertise.

2. Make a *list of questions,* in an appropriate *sequence,* that you can ask during the interview. The interview itself will generate additional topics, but your list will jog your memory if the interview gets off track. Begin with relatively objective or factual questions and work your way, gradually, to more subjective questions or controversial issues. Try to phrase your questions so that they require more than a yes or no answer.

3. Begin the interview by *introducing yourself* and describing your investigation. Keep your biases or opinions out of the questions. Be sure to *listen* carefully and ask follow-up questions: "What information do you have on that? What do the statistical studies suggest? In your opinion, do these data show any trends? What memorable experiences have you had relating to this topic?" Like a dog with a good bone, a reporter doesn't drop a topic until the meat's all gone.

4. During the interview, *take notes* and, if appropriate, use a tape recorder to ensure accuracy. Don't hesitate to ask your interviewee to repeat or clarify a statement. Remember: People want you to get the facts right and quote them accurately. Especially if you're doing a personality profile, describe notable features of your interviewee: hair color, facial features, stature, dress, gestures, and nervous habits, as well as details about the room or surroundings. Finally,

don't forget to ask your interviewee for additional leads or sources. At the conclusion of the interview, *express your thanks* and ask if you can check with him or her later, perhaps by e-mail, for additional details or facts.

5. Immediately after the interview, *go over your notes*. If you recorded the interview, listen to the tape and transcribe important responses. List other questions you may still have.

■ **WRITING QUESTIONNAIRES**   Questionnaires are useful when you need to know the attitudes, preferences, or opinions of a large group of people. If you are surveying customers in your business, you may discover that 39 percent of those surveyed would prefer that your business stay open an additional hour, from 5 P.M. to 6 P.M. If you are surveying students to determine their knowledge of geography, you might discover that only 8 percent can correctly locate Beirut on a map of the Middle East. The accuracy and usefulness of a survey depend on the kinds of questions you ask, on the number of people you survey, and on the sample of people you select to respond to your questionnaire.

Open questions are easy to ask, but the answers can be difficult to interpret. For example, if you want to survey customers at a department store where you work, you might ask questions requiring a short written response:

* What is your opinion of the service provided by clerks at Macy's?
* What would make your shopping experience at Macy's more enjoyable?

While these questions may give you interesting—and often reliable—responses, the results may be difficult to tabulate. Open questions are often valuable in initial surveys because they can help you to determine specific areas or topics for further investigation.

Closed questions are more typical than open questions in surveys. They limit responses so that you can focus on a particular topic and accurately tabulate the responses. Following are several types of closed questions.

* *Yes/no questions:* Have you shopped at Macy's in the last three months?
  _____ Yes
  _____ No
* *Multiple choice:* How far did you travel to come to Macy's?
  _____ 0–5 miles
  _____ 5–10 miles
  _____ 10–15 miles
  _____ Over 15 miles

- How would you characterize the salespeople at Macy's?
  - _____ Exceptionally helpful
  - _____ Helpful
  - _____ Indifferent
  - _____ Occasionally rude
  - _____ Usually rude
- *Checklists:* Which departments at Macy's do you usually visit?
  - _____ Women's Wear
  - _____ Sporting Goods
  - _____ Children's Wear
  - _____ Lingerie
  - _____ Men's Wear
  - _____ Household Goods
- *Ranking lists:* Rank the times you prefer to shop (1 indicates most convenient time, 2 indicates slightly less convenient, and so on).
  - _____ 9 A.M.–11 A.M.
  - _____ 11 A.M.–1 P.M.
  - _____ 1 P.M.–4 P.M.
  - _____ 4 P.M.–8 P.M.

As you design, administer, and use your questionnaire, keep the following tips in mind.

- Limit and focus your questions so that respondents can fill out the questionnaire quickly.
- Avoid loaded or biased questions. For example, don't ask, "How do you like the high-quality merchandise in Macy's sports department?"
- At the top of your questionnaire, write one or two sentences describing your study and thanking participants.
- Pretest your questionnaire by giving it to a few people. Based on their oral and written responses, focus and clarify your questions.
- Use a large sample group. Thirty responses will give you more accurate information about consumer attitudes than will three responses.
- Make your sample as *random* or as evenly representative as possible. Don't survey customers on only one floor, in only one department, or at only one time of day.
- Be sure to include a copy of your questionnaire with your article or essay.

Note: If you intend to do a formal study using questionnaires, check your library for additional sources to help you design and administer statistically reliable surveys.

CHOOSING   COLLECTING   RESEARCH   **SHAPING**   DRAFTING   REVISING

SHAPING

As you begin shaping your material, reconsider your purpose and audience. Limit your subject to create a *narrowed* and *focused* topic. Don't try to cover everything; focus on *the most interesting questions and information*. Take the time to write out a statement of your topic, key questions, purpose, and audience. Then try the following strategies.

■ INVERTED PYRAMID   A common form for reports, especially in journalism, is the *inverted pyramid*. The writer begins with a succinct but arresting title, opens the story with a sentence or short paragraph that answers the reporter's "Wh" questions, and then fills in the background information and details in order of importance, from the *most important* to the *least important*.

Writers use the inverted pyramid when concrete information and the convenience of the reader are most important. The advantage of the inverted pyramid is that a hurried reader can quickly gather the most important information and determine whether the rest of the story is worth reading. The disadvantage is that some details or information may be scattered or presented out of clear sequence. In investigative writing, therefore, writers often supplement the inverted pyramid with other forms of development: chronological order, definition, classification, or comparison/contrast.

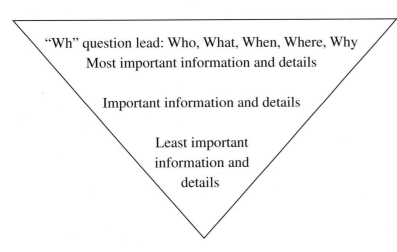

"Wh" question lead: Who, What, When, Where, Why
Most important information and details

Important information and details

Least important
information and
details

> ❝ But for whom have I tried so steadfastly to communicate? Who have I worried over in this writing? Who is my audience? ❞
> —CHERRIE MORAGA,
> SOCIAL CRITIC AND POET

■ CHRONOLOGICAL ORDER   Often, writers present their information in the order in which they discovered it, enabling the reader to follow the research as if it were a narrative or a story. In this format, the writer presents the steps of the investigation, from the earliest incidents, to the discoveries along the way, to the final pieces of information.

Elizabeth Larsen, for example, uses chronological order to make a story out of her report on Web sites in art history. The following sentences—most of them appearing at the beginning of paragraphs—illustrate how she uses time signals ("first," "today," "started," "my next stop," and "then") to create an interesting story about surfing the Web.

I first studied art history the old-fashioned way: scribbling notes in a dark auditorium . . .

Inspired by the sheer volume of images available . . . I decided to try my hand at digitally designing my own art education.

My self-directed syllabus started in Spain . . .

Eager to see more, I moved on to the Museums page of the World Wide Web Virtual Library.

I started in Italy, which I soon discovered doesn't include . . . the Vatican.

My next stop was Paris, where my first visit was to . . . the Louvre.

From Giverny I hopped over to Greece . . .

As these sentences illustrate, chronological order can transform a potentially boring list of Web sites into an interesting narrative journey through the information.

■ DEFINITION   Definitions are central to investigating and reporting, whether they shape only a sentence or two or several paragraphs. In her article on Sherry Turkle, Connie Koenenn uses an informal definition of MUDS in order to shape one paragraph. Her definition helps us understand how the Internet can alter our real-life identity:

> Beginning in her own backyard, Turkle organized pizza parties for students playing MUDS (Multi-User-Domains), the intricate online games in which participants can alter their real-life identities to improvise elaborate melodramas.

■ COMPARISON AND CONTRAST   Comparison and contrast are as essential to investigating and reporting as they are to observing and remembering. In "Surfin' the Louvre," Elizabeth Larsen organizes her essay around a comparison between her traditional campus art course and her online education. Jonathan Kozol, in "The Homeless and Their Children," concludes his investigative report about Laura and her children with a comparison to other places where children have no pets: "It occurs to me that this is one of the few places I have been except a hospital or a reform school where there are hundreds of children and virtually no pets."

■ **ADDITIONAL SHAPING STRATEGIES**   Other shaping strategies, discussed in previous chapters, may be useful for your investigation, too. *Classifying people, places,* or *things* may help organize your investigation. *Simile, metaphor,* or *analogy* may develop and shape parts of your article. Even in investigative reporting, writers may create an identifiable *persona* or adopt a humorous tone. In the example report given earlier in this chapter, Jeff Meer assumes a reporter's objective persona and uses a serious, straightforward tone. In contrast, Elizabeth Larsen, in "Surfin' the Louvre," establishes a friendly and humorous tone: "That's a heck of a lot more reproductions than you'll find in that chiropractically unfriendly art history text, H. W. Janson's *History of Art.*" Larsen demonstrates that even journalistic writing can have a sense of fun.

■ **TITLE, INTRODUCTION, AND CONCLUSION**   Especially in an investigative report, a catchy title is important to help get your readers' interest and attention. Jot down several ideas for titles now and add to that list *after* you've drafted your essay.

In your introductory paragraph(s), answering the "Wh" questions will help focus your investigation. Or you may wish to use a short *narrative,* as Larsen does in "Surfin' the Louvre." Other types of lead-ins, such as a short *description,* a *question,* a *statement of a problem,* a *startling fact* or *statistic,* or an arresting *quotation,* may get the reader's interest and focus on the main idea you wish to investigate. (See Chapter 7 for additional examples of lead-ins.)

The conclusion should resolve the question or questions posed in the investigation, summarize the most important information (useful primarily for long or complicated reports), and give the reader a sense of completion, often by picking up an idea, fact, quotation, narrative, or bit of description used in the introduction.

Some writers like to have a title and know how they're going to start a piece of writing before they begin drafting. However, if you can't think of the perfect title or introduction, begin drafting and continue working on the title, the introduction, and the conclusion after the first draft.

CHOOSING COLLECTING RESEARCH SHAPING **DRAFTING** REVISING
DRAFTING

Before you begin a first draft, reconsider your purpose in writing and further focus your questions, sense of audience, and shaping strategies.

The actual drafting of an investigative essay requires that you have all your facts, statistics, quotations, summaries, notes from interviews, or results of surveys ready to use. Organize your notes, decide on an overall shaping strategy, or write a sketch outline. In investigative writing, a primary danger is postponing writing too long in

PEER RESPONSE

The instructions that follow will help you give and receive constructive advice about the rough draft of your investigating essay. You may use these guidelines for an in-class workshop, a take-home review, or a computer e-mail response.

Writer: Before you exchange drafts with another reader, write out the following on your essay draft or in an e-mail message.

1. **Purpose** Briefly describe your purpose and intended audience. For your audience, write out the title of a newspaper or magazine that might print your investigative report.
2. **Revision plans** Obviously, your draft is just a draft. What still needs work as you continue revising? Explain. (You don't want your reader to critique problems you are already intending to fix.)
3. **Questions** Write out one or two questions that you still have about your draft. What questions would you like your reader to answer?

Reader: First, read the entire draft from start to finish. As you reread the draft, answer the following questions.

1. **Purpose** Remember that the purpose of this essay is to accurately and objectively report information, not argue or editorialize. Does this writer go beyond reporting to editorializing or arguing? If so, point out specific sentences that need revision.
2. **Evidence** List the kinds of evidence the writer uses. What additional kinds of sources might the writer use: An additional interview? A source on the Web? Personal observation? Other print sources? A survey? Make a specific suggestion about additional, appropriate sources.
3. **Key investigative question** When you read the essay, the key question should become apparent. Write it out. If there are places in the essay that don't relate to that key question, should they be omitted? Explain. Are there other aspects of the key question that the writer should address? Explain.
4. **Reader's response** An investigative essay should satisfy your curiosity about the topic. What did you want to learn about the topic that the essay did not answer? Write out any questions that you would like the writer to answer as he or she revises the essay.
5. **Answer the writer's questions in number 3.**

the mistaken belief that if you read just one more article or interview just one more person, you'll get the information you need. At some point, usually *before* you feel ready, you must begin writing. (Professional writers rarely feel they know enough about their subject, but deadlines require them to begin.) Your main problem, you'll quickly discover, will be having too much to say rather than not enough. If you have too much, go back to your focusing questions and see whether you can narrow your topic further.

> **❝** All good writing is swimming under water and holding your breath. **❞**
>
> —F. SCOTT FITZGERALD, AUTHOR OF *THE GREAT GATSBY*

| CHOOSING | COLLECTING | RESEARCH | SHAPING | DRAFTING | **REVISING** |

REVISING

After you have drafted your essay, you may wish to get some feedback from your peers about your work in progress. The peer response guidelines below will help you to review your goals for this investigative assignment and to construct a revision plan. When you read other students' drafts or ideas, be as constructively critical as possible. Think carefully about the assignment. Be honest about your own reactions as a reader. What would make the draft better?

GUIDELINES FOR REVISION

As you add, delete, substitute, or rearrange materials, keep the following tips in mind.

- **Reexamine your purpose and audience.** Are you doing what you intended? You should be *reporting* your findings; you should *not* be arguing for or against any idea.

- **Is the genre of your report responsive to audience needs and expectations?** Use samples of other writing for your audience (from newspapers, magazines, or journals) as models. Would visuals be appropriate or effective in your essay?

- **Can you add any of your own observations or experiences to the investigation?** Remember that your own perceptions and experiences as a reporter are also relevant data.

- **Review the reporter's "Wh" questions.** Are you providing your readers with relevant information *early* in the report and also catching their interest with a key statistic, fact, quotation, example, question, description, or short narrative?

- **Recheck your summaries, paraphrases, or direct quotations.** Are they accurate, and have you cited these sources in your text?

- **Use signals, cues, and transitions to indicate your shaping strategies.**
  Chronological order: before, then, afterward, next, soon, later, finally, at last
  Comparison/contrast: likewise, similarly, however, yet, even so, in contrast
  Analysis: first, next, third, fourth, finally

- **Revise sentences for directness, clarity, and conciseness.** Avoid unnecessary passive voice.

- **Edit your report for appropriate word choice, usage, and grammar.** Check your writing for problems in spelling and punctuation.

> **"** We are all apprentices at a craft where no one ever becomes a master. **"**
> —ERNEST HEMINGWAY, NOVELIST

POSTSCRIPT ON THE WRITING PROCESS

While the process of writing an investigative essay is still fresh in your mind, answer the following questions in your journal.

1. What sources of information (articles, books, interviews, surveys) were most helpful in your investigation? Explain.

2. Most researchers discover that the more they learn, the more they still need to know about their subjects. If you had more time to work on this essay, which sources would you investigate further?

3. What was the most difficult problem you had to solve during your collecting, shaping, drafting, and revising? What helped you most as you tried to solve this problem (further reading, additional writing, advice from peers)? Explain.

4. What was the single most important thing you learned about investigating as you wrote this paper?

5. What do you like best about the final version of your investigative report?

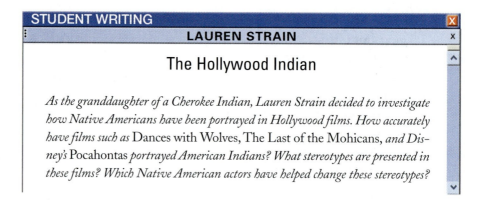

STUDENT WRITING

LAUREN STRAIN

The Hollywood Indian

As the granddaughter of a Cherokee Indian, Lauren Strain decided to investigate how Native Americans have been portrayed in Hollywood films. How accurately have films such as Dances with Wolves, The Last of the Mohicans, *and Disney's* Pocahontas *portrayed American Indians? What stereotypes are presented in these films? Which Native American actors have helped change these stereotypes?*

In order to answer these questions, Strain watched old films, interviewed her grandfather, and researched several popular films about American Indians.

INVESTIGATING PAPER PROPOSAL

Being a quarter Indian, I have grown up with only a few Indian images in my life. Those images come from my grandfather, a Cherokee, and from the Indians in movies and on television. I have always been curious about Hollywood's portrayal of Indians. My grandfather, being adopted, did not grow up with any traditional Indian beliefs or values, so I heard of none. So I wonder if my perceptions about Indian culture and value systems are correct. I would like to look into that more for my paper.

Using sources from movies, TV, photos and articles, I would like to go into the Native American resource center and speak to a full-blood Indian who has experienced some of the traditional ways and values. Using my grandfather as a resource will also be an option. I would like to ask him how he felt seeing the images of Indians on television, and if he thought that they truly reflected how he saw himself as an Indian.

I would start out my paper with the perception of Tonto in *The Lone Ranger*. Using Sherman Alexie's story, *The Lone Ranger and Tonto Fistfight in Heaven* as one view of Tonto, I would continue with written accounts of the actor who played Tonto in the TV show. Next, I would look at Hollywood's perceptions of Indians on reservations. I could use *Smoke Signals* and other movies for those images. I will also look for movie reviews in journals in the library's database for any articles on Indians in Hollywood. I will finish my paper with the perception of the traditional "soak" Indian in Hollywood—I mean when Indians had just been taken over by the white man. For this I will use old westerns and the written and visual accounts of the movies *Dances with Wolves* and *The Last of the Mohicans*.

I am looking forward to this assignment, although it will be challenging to collect all of the information. It will, however, give me the chance to talk with other Indians and perhaps I will be able to grow as a person as well as a Cherokee Indian. I will also have a reason to ask my grandfather all of the questions that I have had for him ever since I was a child. I would like to direct this paper to all white and red people to help them see that although many of us believe almost everything we see on television and in movies, some of that information might be false. It will be a journey to find out what is true and what is false about some of the first people to inhabit America.

...*continued* The Hollywood Indian, **Lauren Strain**

OUTLINE: THE HOLLYWOOD INDIAN

I. Introduce Topic

    A. How are Indians portrayed in Hollywood?

    B. Grandfather Cherokee and how I grew up with the TV and movie Indians as my models.

    C. Introduce movies like *Dances with Wolves* and *The Last of the Mohicans.*

II. Movie portrayal of Native Americans

    A. The accurate portrayal and inaccurate portrayal of *Dances with Wolves.*

    B. *The Last of the Mohicans*—are they really gone?

    C. *Pocahontas*—an inaccurate portrayal of true women?

    D. Jack Strain's account of Indians on the reservation in the movie theaters.

    E. Tonto.

III. Indian actors and their movies

    A. *Outlaw Josey Wales* (Chief Dan George)

    B. *Maverick* (Graham Green)

    C. *Last of the Mohicans* (Russell Means)

IV. Movies and ideals of Native Americans throughout history

    A. The early movie portrayal of Native Americans

    B. President Ulysses S. Grant's quote and ideal

    C. John Ford's *Stagecoach* interprets Indians as enemies

V. Conclusions

    A. My own beliefs of how Native Americans are portrayed in Hollywood

    B. Interview with a Native American student at CSU and what his or her views are about Native Americans in movies

THE HOLLYWOOD INDIAN

I am the granddaughter of an adopted Cherokee who grew up knowing only the ways of the white man. Not knowing much about the traditional American Indian, my only perceptions of them were through movies and Hollywood. Now that I am older, I stop and ask myself: What is the perception of Indians in Hollywood movies? Some of the most popular movies portraying Indians came out in my younger years (late 1980's early 1990's). I remember sneaking in to watch *Dances with Wolves* with my parents in the movie theater, which is a source of my perceptions of Indians. I even watched *Last of the Mohicans* in my freshman history class. Not only do I wonder how accurate movies like these are, I am very curious about the actors who play the Indians. During this research I want to answer certain questions. Are recent movies historically correct and do they eliminate stereotypes that people have given to Native Americans? What Native American actors have helped to portray their people accurately? And lastly, how has history helped to portray Native Americans better?

Three films that, despite historical inaccuracies, helped to popular- 2 ize the life and culture of Native Americans were *Dances with Wolves, Last of the Mohicans,* and *Pocahontas. Dances with Wolves* has been the most critically acclaimed movie that portrays the "correct" Indian. When asking my grandfather about whether or not he thought this movie was a correct portrayal, he said, "Yes, except for one thing." He told me that at the end of the movie, you see a winter camp deep in the mountains. The Indians would never keep their camp that deep in the mountains during the winter; they would move on to a warmer place. This was a detail that I had never known about. In Armando J. Prats' essay about the comparison between the two cinematic versions of *Dances with Wolves,* he states that there was a normal film version shown in the theaters and the one released in a TV miniseries that added scenes. He brings up a very valid point: even though, in this movie, the Indians are portrayed in a valid way, the story's main character is a white man. This title is even the white man's given Indian name (6). Watching the movie myself, I noticed that the portrayal of the Sioux Indians was very human and realistic to tradition. The film showed strong bonds between family and tribesmen. I too—as well as many others I know—also have strong bonds with family and friends. The Indian characters even had a sense of humor, which also helped me connect to them easier.

The movie *Last of the Mohicans* is also a very realistic film but it has 3 some historical misrepresentations. It takes place during the French and Indian War in 1757. This movie was shown to me in my freshman history class to illustrate brutalities of the war itself. Those details of the movie were portrayed very clearly. In one scene, an Indian from the Mohawk tribe eats the heart of a British general. I am not quite sure whether or not this type of brutality actually happened but I do know that scalpings were regular occurrences during the French and Indian War. Just like humans today, people kill people in savage ways. And although there are many accurate historical details about the war itself, like the Mohegan tribe helping out the settlers in Canada, there are misrepresentations about the details concerning the Mohegan tribe.

One plot point that is incorrect is that the Mohegan tribe is extinct, 4 as the movie suggests. Melissa Sayet, in her essay "The Lasting of the Mohegans," tells us "[I am] a Mohegan Indian, alive and well in 1993" (55). The Mohegan tribe still exists, although it is very small, in Uncasville, Connecticut. The small tribe has a church, museum and an all-Indian run institution that has existed for sixty-two years to help show their history. Sayet tells us that the media is responsible for putting the thought into people's heads that the tribe has been dead for a long time. The myth was actually created by Lydia Howard Sigourney. Sayet writes, "It seems that it was far easier for Lydia to romanticize dead Mohegans than to deal with the realities of alcoholism and poverty among living ones" (56). A well-known poet that knew of the Mohegan tribe, Sigourney wrote of their extinction anyway.

An additional inaccuracy in *The Last of the Mohicans,* although it may 5 be small, is that the spelling of the tribe's name is different in the movie compared to the spelling that the tribe uses (Mohican vs. Mohegan). According to Sayet, this was because of the miscommunication between the tribe and Europeans during first contact. The Mohegan tribe did not have an alphabet to help convey the correct spelling (56). Another reason for the misspelling is the fact that there are two tribes with the same name spelled differently. One tribe comes from Connecticut and the other from the Hudson Valley in New York. The author of *The Last of the Mohicans* just accidentally switched the names unknowingly, according to the First Nations Web Site (*First Nations*).

When I watched the movie, I saw the romantic reasons for saying 6 that the tribe was extinct at the end. The Mohegan men were very stoic, smart, athletic and heroic. I have never met a Mohegan Indian, so I am not sure how they carry themselves. I do know that not all the Indians were known heroes. It was hard not to fall in love with these characters, though. The movie was designed to pull at your heart. In the end, when the character Changachook, the father of Uncas and the second-to-last Mohegan, tells us he is the only remaining Mohegan, it is very convincing and sad. This is how Hollywood wants us to feel. If movies did not leave people with any type of feeling, whether humor, sadness or happiness, then there would be no reason to watch.

In contrast to the more accurate portrayals of Native Americans in   *7*
Dances with Wolves and *Last of the Mohicans,* a third popular Native
American film, *Pocahontas,* is very inaccurate historically speaking.
Disney's version of *Pocahontas* focuses on a very historic American Indian. This movie is very factually inaccurate, however. The Indians
were portrayed as very peaceful and loving in this film. Pocahontas is
an Indian princess who falls in love with the handsome John Smith, an
English soldier looking for land in the New World. She ends up saving his life, and he asks her to come with him back to England to be
his wife. She declines his offer, saying she could never leave her family and her land.

The true story of Pocahontas is different in many ways. The age of   *8*
the character in the Disney movie seems to be in her early twenties. The
real Pocahontas was sixteen years old. She did save the life of John Smith,
but she fell in love with his friend, John Rolfe. She also ended up leaving
America and going to England to marry him. Shortly upon her arrival,
she died of smallpox. Although the film is historically inaccurate, telling
children the real story of Pocahontas would not have been a wise decision
on the part of Disney. They like to show a happy story that promotes values. A sixteen-year-old girl marrying an older man is not a common
thing these days. Plus, the main character never dies in Disney movies. I
can see why Disney changed the story. They did, however, keep the happy
and peaceful image of the Indians, thus promoting them; but they didn't
tell the story in a historically correct manner.

The second question that I had was who were/are the Native Amer-   *9*
ican actors who have helped Hollywood portray a historically unstereo-
typical Indian? Three of the most recognized Indian actors in Hollywood
who have portrayed historically accurate Indian characters are Graham
Green, Russell Means, and Chief Dan George.

Graham Green is best known for his portrayal of Kicking Bird in   *10*
Dances with Wolves. He received an Academy Award Nomination for best
supporting actor for that role. Green is also a well-known draftsman, steel
worker, civil technologist, and sound engineer. He graduated from a Native American theater school, where his comedy skills shined (*Graham
Green*).

We see Green's comic acting shine through in the movie *Maverick.*   *11*
In this movie, his character, Joseph, is earning money for his tribe by running around in war paint and having his tribe beat their drums for a European who wants to experience the "real west." When we see him
encounter the European, he begins to speak the man's native language.

When the European tells Joseph to speak as they do in the movies, Joseph says "How, white man," a stereotypical greeting. Joseph tells his friend Maverick how stupid he feels acting as if he is foolish and savage when in fact we see he is a very intellectual person (*Maverick*). I believe that Graham Green chose this role because he was able to show people how inaccurate and stupid the stereotypical Indian can be, when in reality Indians can be intellectual, caring people.

Russell Means is known more for his work outside Hollywood, but 12 he is still praised for the roles he has taken in movies. He has been involved in civil rights for Native Americans since the 1960s. He has also done work with the United Nations for over twelve years. His most recent spot in the public eye was not in a movie, but rather in the demonstration against Columbus Day celebrations. Means got involved in acting in 1991. His most recognizable role was in *Last of the Mohicans*, where he plays the eldest Mohegan, a wise and brave man. His character was the leader of the family of Mohegans in this movie and he never strayed and helped to keep the spirit of the tribe alive when it was "lost" with the passing of his son.

Chief Dan George (1899–1981) also helped to show film viewers 13 that American Indians were intelligent and civilized and not the typical savages. George was the chief of the Salish Band in the Burrard Inlet, in British Columbia, Canada. He was a very gifted actor and the author of many books, such as *My Heart Soars* and *My Spirit Soars*. George was also nominated for an Academy Award for his role in *Little Big Man*. He was also in the TV miniseries "Centennial" (*Chief Dan George*).

In the movie *The Outlaw Josey Wales*, Chief Dan George's character, 14 Lone Watie, explains to Josey Wales how he was part of the tribe the white man called "the civilized tribe," or the Cherokee. His character is wearing a top hat and a suit when we first see him in the film. He tells Wales that he dressed up as Abe Lincoln to impress Lincoln when he met him. Later we see Watie burning his clothes, wearing less casual traveling garments. He tells Wales how he forgot things and lost his way when he became "civilized" (*The Outlaw Josie Wales*). The clothes Chief Dan George wore in that movie were very symbolic in the story that he told. Although these were the words of a fictional character, I believe that they helped reflect the struggle of a Native American to be accepted as "civilized." Because of Hollywood, these struggles and lifestyles were able to get out to movie watchers.

The final question I was curious about was when and if historical *15* events helped to change the portrayal of Native Americans in Hollywood. The change from the savage enemy Indian came with World War II because the Nazis became the enemy rather than Native Americans. Angela Aleiss writes, "Previous images of menacing warriors who blocked Westward expansion gradually began to fade into one in which Indians stood as allies—rather than enemies—alongside America's frontier heroes" (25). Most movies changed stereotypes, but there were still some that had inaccurate portrayals like *Geronimo* (1939) and *They Died With Their Boots On* (1941).

In addition to the change brought on by World War II, Aleiss tells *16* us that there were three other contributions. The first one was to keep the relations between America, the United Kingdom, and Canada on good terms. Puritanical leaders wanted a good portrayal of Americans with other races. The second contribution, Alesiss says, is "the pro-interventionist politics of Hollywood studios [that] helped to create a mindset that would reshape the Indians image at least two years before America's entry into the war" (26). Hollywood executives were trying to rid the movie industry of fascist ideals. The final element was that the image of the ally Indian was not a fad, but rather a gateway for other Western movie themes.

My grandfather grew up next to a reservation before World War II, *17* so I asked him in my interview how Native Americans reacted to the westerns depicting them as the enemy. He told me that most of them went to the movies for the cartoons before the movie itself. "They did not show any emotional reaction to it," he said. I found it interesting that they would even go to the movies at all. When telling my grandfather this, he told me that, "It was a way for the Indians to break into the western culture." That helped me to understand their reasons for going.

When conducting my survey of students in my class, three out of ten *18* thought that movies still portray Indians in a stereotypically savage manner. Two of them thought that Hollywood was doing a good job in the portrayal of the "correct" Native American. One person wrote, "Hollywood is more worried about offending anybody who is not white. Because people today are very sensitive, everyone, including Hollywood, watches what they say and do."

Throughout my research, I have found that Native Americans are *19* portrayed in a very positive light. The negative stereotypical Indian has slowly faded with images of "the true west." Although there are still few

...continued The Hollywood Indian, **Lauren Strain**

exceptions, one aspect that I see in movies with Native Americans is historical details being left out. For example, the Mohegan tribe still existing and the movie *Last of the Mohicans* portraying their extinction. Also, the Indians in the last scene of *Dances with Wolves,* who use an incorrect stopping ground during the winter. I believe that Hollywood is concerned about offending Native Americans, but historical context comes into play in what they write and put in movies. Hollywood has a duty to add accurate historical context to the films; movies are taken very seriously in today's culture. Children learn from what they see in movies and on TV. But should Hollywood risk a good story just for entertainment value? I believe that the film industry can mix fact and fiction while still pulling off a good story. They should learn the correct history of America and all its people.

Works Cited

Aleiss, Angela. "Prelude to World War II: Racial Unity and the Hollywood Indian." *Journal of American Culture* 18 (Summer 1995): 25–34.

"Chief Dan George." *Indigenous Peoples' Literature.* 14 Dec. 1998. 7 May 2001 <http://www.indians.org/welker/dangeorg.htm>.

First Nations. Ed. Jordan S. Dill. 2000. 23 Apr. 2001 <http://www.dickshovel.com/www.html>.

Graham Green. Home page. 16 Jan. 2000. 6 May 2001 <http://www.geocities.com/Hollywood/guild/9621/grahamgreen.html>.

The Last of the Mohicans. Dir. Michael Mann. Perf. Russell Means and Daniel Day-Lewis. Twentieth Century Fox, 1992.

Maverick. Dir. Richard Donner. Perf. Graham Green and Mel Gibson. Warner Brothers, 1994.

The Outlaw Josey Wales. Dir. Clint Eastwood. Perf. Clint Eastwood and Chief Dan George. Warner Brothers, 1976.

Prats, Armando J. "The Image of the Other and the Other 'Dances with Wolves': The Refigured Indian and the Textual Supplement." *Journal of Film and Video* 50.1 (Spring 1998): 3–19.

Sayet, Melissa F. "The Lasting of the Mohegan." *Essence* 23.11 (March 1993): 55–57.

Strain, Jack. Phone interview. 11 April 2001.

Strain, Lauren. Personal survey. 3 May 2001.

vo·cab·u·lar·y

In your journal, write down the meanings of the italicized words in the following sentences.

- some historical *misrepresentations* **(3)**
- the *romantic* reasons **(6)**
- *pro-interventionist* politics of Hollywood studios **(16)**
- rid the movie industry of *fascist* ideals **(16)**

QUESTIONS FOR WRITING AND DISCUSSION

1. Make a list of films you have seen that have Native American characters. Choose two of those films—one older, one more recent. Which characters in both films seemed most realistic and which most stereotypical? Describe the changes you notice between these two films' representations of Native American culture, language, politics, or heritage.

2. At the end of her essay, Strain says that Hollywood can "mix fact and fiction" while still creating a good story. Would you agree with that statement, or do you think historical accuracy should come first and entertainment values second? Choose a film about Native Americans—or any ethnic group—and explain what that film loses or gains by placing entertainment values over historical and cultural accuracy (or, conversely, by giving historical/cultural accuracy much more importance than entertainment values).

3. Strain conducts both a short survey and an interview which she reports on at the end of her paper. Assume you are in a peer-response group, giving her feedback on her essay. Would you advise her to integrate the information in paragraphs 17 and 18 earlier in her essay rather than tacking them on at the end? Where might that information fit? (How do you plan to integrate any interview or survey information in your own essay?)

4. Read the essay by Margaret Lazarus in Chapter 9, titled "All's Not Well in Land of 'The Lion King.' " Rent *Pocahontas* from a video store and watch it. Are there racist or sexist scenes or images in Disney's version of *Pocahontas?* Does the film ultimately promote Native American cultural values or mainstream white American values? Explain.

BRIDGID STONE   ✕

My Friend Michelle, an Alcoholic

Bridgid Stone, a student at Southeast Missouri State University, decided to write her investigative essay on alcoholism. In the library, she was able to find quite a lot of information and statistics about alcohol. In her friend, Michelle, she had a living example of the consequences of alcohol abuse. The question, however, was how to combine the two. As you read her essay, notice how she interweaves description and dialogue with facts and statistics.

1   Five million teenagers are problem drinkers, according to *Group* magazine's article "Sex, Drugs, and Alcohol." One of these five million teenagers is my friend, Michelle.

2   "I can't wait to go out tonight and get drunk," Michelle announces as she walks into my dorm room. I just sigh and shake my head. Michelle has been drunk every night since Wednesday. In the last three days, she has been to more fraternity parties than classes.

3   We leave a few hours later for a Sig Tau party. Even though I have been attending these parties for weeks now, the amount of alcohol present still amazes me. Almost everyone is walking around with a twelve-pack of beer. Others are carrying fifths of vodka or Jack Daniels whiskey. As cited in *Fraternities and Sororities on Contemporary College Campuses*, 73 percent of fraternity advisers believe that alcohol is a problem in fraternities. I wish the other 27 percent could be here now. Fraternities are synonymous with drinking.

4   Michelle and I both have innocent-looking squeeze bottles, but inside are very stiff screwdrivers. They probably have more vodka than orange juice. Michelle finishes her drink before I am halfway through mine. So she finishes off mine, too, before disappearing into the throng of people at the party. The next time I see her, she is holding a beer in each hand. Her speech is slurred, and she can barely stand up on her own.

5   We head back to the dorm when Michelle starts vomiting. Once we are in her room, I help her undress and put her to bed.

6   "Bridgid, I am so sorry," Michelle cries, "I promise never to drink again."

7   "Okay, just get some sleep," I tell her as I leave.

8   It's Thursday night and Michelle is ready to party again.

"I haven't been to my Friday 8:00 class in a month. Do you think I 9 should just stay up all night after the party and go to class drunk? Or should I just not go to class and sleep in?" Michelle asks.

"Don't go out and get drunk. Stay home tonight and get up and go 10 to your classes tomorrow," I advise.

"I am just going to sleep in," Michelle informs me as she leaves for 11 the party.

Like Michelle, an estimated 4.6 million adolescents experience neg- 12 ative consequences of alcohol abuse, such as poor school performance. This was reported in a survey conducted by NIAAA for a United States Congressional report.

Early Friday morning, I get a phone call from the on-duty resident 13 adviser. Michelle has passed out in the lobby of the Towers Complex. She couldn't remember her phone number or even what floor she lived on, but I had written my phone number on Michelle's hand, so she could call me if she got into any trouble. The R.A. had seen my number and decided to call, since Michelle was too drunk to dial the four digits.

"Could you please escort your friend up to your room?" the R.A. 14 asks. She doesn't sound very happy.

"Sure, I will be down in a few minutes," I promise. It takes me and 15 another girl from our floor to get Michelle onto the elevator. She keeps lying down or passing out. Thirty minutes later, we get Michelle into bed. She is mumbling incoherently, and she reeks of alcohol. Needless to say, Michelle doesn't make it to her 8:00 A.M. class, again.

Saturday afternoon, I confront Michelle about the Thursday night 16 incident. This is rather hard to do, since she doesn't remember any of it.

"I just drink to loosen up. I'm much more fun if I've been drinking," 17 Michelle tells me.

"You are not much fun when you are puking or passing out," I reply. 18 A desire to loosen up is one of the main reasons that teenagers drink, reports *Group* magazine. Other reasons include a need to escape and to rebel.

"I have to release steam every once in a while," she argues. "School is 19 really stressing me out."

"Michelle, you don't even go to class," I tell her. 20

"Everyone else drinks!" she says. "Why are you picking on me?" She 21 stomps out of my room.

Michelle was partially correct, though, when she stated, "Everyone 22 else drinks." As reported in *Alcohol and Youth,* more than 80 percent of all college students surveyed had been drinking in the previous month. But this doesn't mean that what Michelle is doing is any less serious. In all probability, Michelle is an alcoholic.

A test that is often used to determine if someone has a drinking 23 problem can be found in *Getting Them Sober,* by Toby Rice Andrews. There are twenty questions on the test. A "yes" answer to two of the questions indicates a possible drinking problem. Questions include: "Do you miss time from school or work due to drinking?" "Do you drink to escape from worries or troubles?" "Do you drink because you are shy?" "Have you ever had a memory loss due to drinking?" Michelle would probably have answered "yes" to all of the above questions.

I moved out of the dorm at the beginning of the second semester, so 24 I haven't seen much of Michelle. The last time I saw her was about three weeks ago. She had gotten arrested while in New Orleans for spring break. Apparently, Michelle had been out drinking and eventually had been arrested for public drunkenness.

"It wasn't that bad," she told me. "I don't even remember being in the 25 jail cell. I was pretty trashed."

Works Cited

Andrews, Toby Rice. *Getting Them Sober.* South Plainfield, N.J.: Bridge Publishing, 1980.

Barnes, Grace. *Alcohol and Youth.* Westport, Conn.: Greenwood Press, 1982.

Pruett, Harold, and Vivian Brown. *Crisis Intervention and Prevention.* San Francisco: Jossey-Bass Inc., 1987.

"Sex, Drugs, and Alcohol." *Group.* February 1992: 17–20.

Van Pelt, Rich. *Intensive Care.* Grand Rapids, Mich.: Zondervan Publishing House, 1988.

Winston, Roger, William Nettles III, and John Opper, Jr. *Fraternities and Sororities on Contemporary College Campuses.* San Francisco: Jossey-Bass Inc., 1987.

QUESTIONS FOR WRITING AND DISCUSSION

1. Investigative reports should provide information without editorializing or arguing for or against one perspective or another. Even though Stone is writing about her friend, Michelle, does she sympathize with Michelle or make excuses for her? Does she censure Michelle for her behavior? How effectively does Stone maintain a reporter's distance as she describes Michelle's behavior and presents statistics and other background information? Explain, referring to specific passages in the essay.

2. Who is Stone's audience for her essay? Where would you recommend that Stone send her essay for possible publication? List two possible publication sources (magazines or newspapers), and explain your choices.

3. If Stone were revising her essay, what advice would you give her about balancing statistics and personal experience? Should she have more statistics? Should she have more narrative? Refer to specific paragraphs and examples in your response.

4. Stone's use of the present tense adds dramatic impact to her essay. Reread her essay, noticing where she uses the present tense and where she shifts to the past tense. Where was the use of the present tense most effective? Did her tense shifting confuse you at any point? Where?

5. Compare Stone's essay with Kozol's essay earlier in this chapter. What reporting strategies does Stone adapt from Kozol? How are their reporting strategies different? Explain your response by referring to specific passages from each author.

Marie Louise Elisabeth Vigée-Lebrun (1755–1842)
Marie Antoinette and her Children (1787) Oil on canvas, 9' 1/4" × 7' 5/8"
Musée National du Château de Versailles et des Trianons,
© Photo RMN-Gerard Blot

A prolific painter of portraits before and after the French Revolution, Elisabeth Vigée-Lebrun specialized in paintings of the rich and famous of her time. Shortly after completing this portrait, Vigée-Lebrun escaped from France and lived in exile for over a decade. The journal question on page 354 asks you to compare her work with a photograph by Dorthea Lange made in California in 1936 of a migrant mother and her children.

Explaining

You have decided to quit your present job, so you write a note to your boss giving thirty days' notice. During your last few weeks at work, your boss asks you to write a three-page job description to help orient the person who will replace you. The job description should include a list of your current duties as well as advice to your replacement on how to execute them most efficiently. To write the description, you record your daily activities, look back through your calendar, comb through your records, and brainstorm a list of everything you do. As you write up the description, you include specific examples and illustrations of your typical responsibilities.

As a gymnast and dancer, you gradually become obsessed with losing weight. You start skipping meals, purging the little food you do eat, and lying about your eating habits to your parents. Before long, you weigh less than seventy pounds, and your physician diagnoses your condition: anorexia nervosa. With advice from your physician and counseling from a psychologist, you gradually begin to control your disorder. To explain to others what anorexia is, how it is caused, and what its effects are, you write an essay in which you explain your ordeal, alerting other readers to the potential dangers of uncontrolled dieting.

> " Become aware of the two-sided nature of your mental make-up: one thinks in terms of the connectedness of things, the other thinks in terms of parts and sequences. "
> —GABRIELE LUSSER RICO, AUTHOR OF *WRITING THE NATURAL WAY*

> " What [a writer] knows is almost always a matter of the relationships he establishes, between example and generalization, between one part of a narrative and the next, between the idea and the counter idea that the writer sees is also relevant. "
> —ROGER SALE, AUTHOR OF *ON WRITING*

E XPLAINING AND DEMONSTRATING RELATIONSHIPS IS A FREQUENT PURPOSE FOR WRITING. EXPLAINING GOES BEYOND INVESTIGATING THE FACTS AND REPORTING INFORMATION; IT ANALYZES THE COMPONENT PARTS OF A SUBJECT AND THEN SHOWS HOW THE PARTS FIT in relation to one another. Its goal is to clarify for a particular group of readers *what* something is, *how* it happened or should happen, and/or *why* it happens.

Explaining begins with assessing the rhetorical situation: the writer, the occasion, the intended purpose and audience, the genre, and the cultural context. As you begin thinking about a subject, topic, or issue to explain, keep in mind your own interests, the expectations of your audience, the possible genre you might choose to help achieve your purpose (essay, article, pamphlet, multigenre essay, Web site), and finally the cultural or social context in which you are writing or in which your writing might be read.

Explaining any idea, concept, process, or effect requires analysis. Analysis starts with dividing a thing or phenomenon into its various parts. Then, once you explain the various parts, you put them back together (synthesis) to explain their relationship or how they work together.

Explaining how to learn to play the piano, for example, begins with an analysis of the parts of the learning process: playing scales, learning chords, getting instruction from a teacher, sight reading, and performing in recitals. Explaining why two automobiles collided at an intersection begins with an analysis of the contributing factors: the nature of the intersection, the number of cars involved, the condition of the drivers, and the condition of each vehicle. Then you bring the parts together and show their *relationships:* you show how practicing scales on the piano fits into the process of learning to play the piano; you demonstrate why one small factor—such as a faulty turn signal—combined with other factors to cause an automobile accident.

The emphasis you give to the *analysis* of the object or phenomenon and the time you spend explaining *relationships* of the parts depends on your purpose, subject, and audience. If you want to explain how a flower reproduces, for example, you may begin by identifying the important parts, such as the pistil and stamen, that most readers need to know about before they can understand the reproductive process. However, if you are explaining the process to a botany major who already knows the parts of a flower, you might spend more time discussing the key operations in pollination or the reasons why some flowers cross-pollinate and others do not. In any effective explanation, analyzing parts and showing relationships must work together for that particular group of readers.

Because its purpose is to teach the reader, *expository writing,* or writing to explain, should be as clear as possible. Explanations, however, are more than organized pieces of information. Expository writing contains information that is focused by your point of view, by your experience, and by your reasoning powers. Thus, your explanation of a thing or phenomenon makes a point or has a thesis: This is the *right* way to define *happiness*. This is how one *should* bake lasagne or do a calculus problem. These are the *most important* reasons why the senator from New York was elected. To make your explanation clear, you show what you mean by using specific support: facts, data, examples, illustrations, statistics, comparisons, analogies, and images. Your thesis is a *general* assertion about the relationships of the *specific* parts. The support helps your reader identify the parts and see the relationships. Expository writing teaches the reader by alternating between generalizations and specific examples.

TECHNIQUES   PROCESSES

Techniques for Explaining

> **“** The main thing I try to do is write as clearly as I can. **”**
>
> —E. B. WHITE,
> JOURNALIST AND COAUTHOR OF
> *ELEMENTS OF STYLE*

Explaining requires first that you assess your rhetorical situation. Your purpose must work for a particular audience, genre, and context. You may revise some of these aspects of the rhetorical situation as you draw on your own observations and memories about your topic. As you research your topic, conduct an interview, or do a survey, keep thinking about issues of audience, genre, and context. Below are techniques for writing clear explanations.

- **Considering (and reconsidering) your purpose, audience, genre, and social context.** As you change your audience or your genre, for example, you must change how you explain something as well as how much and what kind of evidence and support you use.

- **Getting the reader's attention and stating the thesis.** Devise an accurate but interesting *title*. Use an attention-getting *lead-in*. State the *thesis* clearly.

- **Defining key terms and describing *what* something is.** Analyze and *define* by describing, comparing, classifying, and giving examples.

- **Identifying the steps in a process and showing *how* each step relates to the overall process.** Describe how something should be done or how something typically happens.

- **Describing causes and effects and showing *why* certain causes lead to specific effects.** Analyze how several causes lead to a single effect, or show how a single cause leads to multiple effects.

- **Supporting explanations with specific evidence.** Use descriptions, examples, comparisons, analogies, images, facts, data, or statistics to *show* what, how, or why.

In *Spirit of the Valley: Androgyny and Chinese Thought,* psychologist Sukie Colgrave illustrates many of these techniques as she explains an important concept from psychology: the phenomenon of *projection.* Colgrave explains how we "project" attributes missing in our own personality onto another person—especially someone we love:

> A one-sided development of either the masculine or feminine principles has [an] unfortunate consequence for our psychological and intellectual health: it encourages the phenomenon termed "projection." This is the process by which we project onto other people, things, or ideologies, those aspects of ourselves which we have not, for whatever reason, acknowledged or developed. The most familiar example of this is the obsession which usually accompanies being "in love." A person whose feminine side is unrealised will often "fall in love" with the feminine which she or he "sees" in another person, and similarly with the masculine. The experience of being "in love" is one of powerful dependency. As long as the projection appears to fit its object nothing awakens the person to the reality of the projection. But sooner or later the lover usually becomes aware of certain discrepancies between her or his desires and the person chosen to satisfy them. Resentment, disappointment, anger and rejection rapidly follow, and often the relationship disintegrates. . . . But if we can explore our own psyches we may discover what it is we were demanding from our lover and start to develop it in ourselves. The moment this happens we begin to see other people a little more clearly. We are freed from some of our needs to make others what we want them to be, and can begin to love them more for what they are.

Explaining what: Definition example

Explaining why: Effects of projection

Explaining how: The process of freeing ourselves from dependency

EXPLAINING WHAT	EXPLAINING HOW	EXPLAINING WHY

EXPLAINING *WHAT*

Explaining *what* something is or means requires showing the relationship between it and the *class* of beings, objects, or concepts to which it belongs. *Formal definition,* which is often essential in explaining, has three parts: the thing or term to be defined, the class, and the distinguishing characteristics of the thing or term. The thing being defined can be concrete, such as a turkey, or abstract, such as democracy.

THING OR TERM	CLASS	DISTINGUISHING CHARACTERISTICS
A turkey is a	bird	that has brownish plumage and a bare, wattled head and neck; it is widely domesticated for food.
Democracy is	government	by the people, exercised directly or through elected representatives.

Frequently, writers use *extended definitions* when they need to give more than a mere formal definition. An extended definition may explain the word's etymology or historical roots, describe sensory characteristics of something (how it looks, feels, sounds, tastes, smells), identify its parts, indicate how something is used, explain what it is not, provide an example of it, and/or note similarities or differences between this term and other words or things.

The following extended definition of democracy, written for an audience of college students to appear in a textbook, begins with the etymology of the word and then explains—using analysis, comparison, example, and description—what democracy is and what it is not:

> Since democracy is government of the people, by the people, and for the people, a democratic form of government is not fixed or static. Democracy is dynamic; it adapts to the wishes and needs of the people. The term *democracy* derives from the Greek word *demos,* meaning "the common people," and *-kratia,* meaning "strength or power" used to govern or rule. Democracy is based on the notion that a majority of people creates laws and then everyone agrees to abide by those laws in the interest of the common good. In a democracy, people are not ruled by a king, a dictator, or a small group of powerful individuals. Instead, people elect officials who use the power temporarily granted to them to govern the society. For example, the people may agree that their government should raise money for defense, so the officials levy taxes to support an army. If enough people decide, however, that taxes for defense are too high, then they request that their elected officials change the laws or they elect new officials. The essence of democracy lies in its responsiveness: Democracy is a form of government in which laws and lawmakers change as the will of the majority changes.

Formal definition

Description: What democracy is

Etymology: Analysis of the word's roots

Comparison: What democracy is not

Example

Formal definition

Figurative expressions—vivid word pictures using similes, metaphors, or analogies—can also explain what something is. During World War II, for example, the Writer's War Board asked E. B. White (author of *Charlotte's Web* and many *New Yorker* magazine essays, as well as other works) to provide an explanation of democracy. Instead of giving a formal definition or etymology, White responded with a series of imaginative comparisons showing the *relationship* between various parts of American culture and the concept of democracy.

> Surely the Board knows what democracy is. It is the line that forms on the right. It is the don't in Don't Shove. It is the hole in the stuffed shirt through which the sawdust slowly trickles; it is the dent in the high hat. Democracy is the recurrent suspicion that more than half of the people are right more than half of the time. It is the feeling of privacy in the voting

booths, the feeling of communion in the libraries, the feeling of vitality everywhere. Democracy is the score at the beginning of the ninth. It is an idea which hasn't been disproved yet, a song the words of which have not gone bad. It's the mustard on the hot dog and the cream in the rationed coffee. Democracy is a request from a War Board, in the middle of a morning in the middle of a war, wanting to know what democracy is.

Often, we think that explanations of technical subjects must be academic and complex, but sometimes writers about technical subjects use images and metaphors to get their point across. In the following definition of Web robots—so-called "bots," Andrew Leonard, writing for a contemporary audience in *Wired* magazine, enlivens his explanation by personifying these software programs.

Web robots—spiders, wanderers, and worms. Cancelbots, Lazarus, and Automoose. Chatterbots, soft bots, userbots, taskbots, knowbots, and mailbots. . . . In current online parlance, the word "bot" pops up everywhere, flung around carelessly to describe just about any kind of computer program—a logon script, a spellchecker—that performs a task on a network. Strictly speaking, all bots are "autonomous"—able to react to their environments and make decisions without prompting from their creators; while the master or mistress is brewing coffee, the bot is off retrieving Web documents, exploring a MUD, or combatting Usenet spam. . . . Even more important than function is behavior—bona fide bots are programs with personality. Real bots talk, make jokes, have feelings—even if those feelings are nothing more than cleverly conceived algorithms.

EXPLAINING WHAT EXPLAINING HOW EXPLAINING WHY
EXPLAINING *HOW*

Explaining *how* something should be done or how something happens is usually called *process analysis*. One kind of process analysis is the "how-to" explanation: how to cook a turkey, how to tune an engine, how to get a job. Such recipes or directions are *prescriptive:* You typically explain how something *should* be done. In a second kind of process analysis, you explain how something happens or is typically done—without being directive or prescriptive. In a *descriptive* process analysis, you explain how some natural or social process typically happens: how cells split during mitosis, how hailstones form in a cloud, how students react to the pressure of examinations, or how political candidates create their public images. In both prescriptive and descriptive explanations, however, you are analyzing a *process*—dividing the sequence into its parts or steps—and then showing how the parts contribute to the whole process.

Cookbooks, automobile-repair manuals, instructions for assembling toys or appliances, and self-improvement books are all examples of *prescriptive* process analysis. Writers of recipes, for example, begin with analyses of the ingredients and the steps in preparing the food. Then they carefully explain how the steps are related, how to avoid problems, and how to serve mouth-watering concoctions. Farley Mowat, naturalist and author of *Never Cry Wolf,* gives his readers the following detailed—and humorous—recipe for creamed mouse. Mowat became interested in this recipe when he decided to test the nutritional content of the wolf's diet. "In the event that any of my readers may be interested in personally exploiting this hitherto overlooked source of excellent animal protein," Mowat writes, "I give the recipe in full."

Souris à la Crème

INGREDIENTS:

One dozen fat mice	Salt and pepper	One cup white flour
Cloves	One piece sowbelly	Ethyl alcohol

Skin and gut the mice, but do not remove the heads; wash, then place in a pot with enough alcohol to cover the carcasses. Allow to marinate for about two hours. Cut sowbelly into small cubes and fry slowly until most of the fat has been rendered. Now remove the carcasses from the alcohol and roll them in a mixture of salt, pepper and flour; then place in frying pan and sauté for about five minutes (being careful not to allow the pan to get too hot, or the delicate meat will dry out and become tough and stringy). Now add a cup of alcohol and six or eight cloves. Cover the pan and allow to simmer slowly for fifteen minutes. The cream sauce can be made according to any standard recipe. When the sauce is ready, drench the carcasses with it, cover and allow to rest in a warm place for ten minutes before serving.

Explaining *how* something happens or is typically done involves a *descriptive* process analysis. It requires showing the chronological relationship between one idea, event, or phenomenon and the next—and it depends on close observation. In *The Lives of a Cell,* biologist and physician Lewis Thomas explains that ants are like humans: while they are individuals, they can also act together to create a social organism. Although exactly how ants communicate remains a mystery, Thomas explains how they combine to form a thinking, working organism.

[Ants] seem to live two kinds of lives: they are individuals, going about the day's business without much evidence of thought for tomorrow, and they are at the same time component parts, cellular elements, in the huge, writhing, ruminating organism of the Hill, the nest, the hive. . . .

A solitary ant, afield, cannot be considered to have much of anything on his mind; indeed, with only a few neurons strung together by fibers, he can't be imagined to have a mind at all, much less a thought. He is more like a ganglion on legs. Four ants together, or ten, encircling a dead moth on a path, begin to look more like an idea. They fumble and shove, gradually moving the food toward the Hill, but as though by blind chance. It is only when you watch the dense mass of thousands of ants, crowded together around the Hill, blackening the ground, that you begin to see the whole beast, and now you observe it thinking, planning, calculating. It is an intelligence, a kind of live computer, with crawling bits for its wits.

At a stage in the construction, twigs of a certain size are needed, and all the members forage obsessively for twigs of just this size. Later, when outer walls are to be finished, thatched, the size must change, and as though given new orders by telephone, all the workers shift the search to the new twigs. If you disturb the arrangement of a part of the Hill, hundreds of ants will set it vibrating, shifting, until it is put right again. Distant sources of food are somehow sensed, and long lines, like tentacles, reach out over the ground, up over walls, behind boulders, to fetch it in.

EXPLAINING WHAT	EXPLAINING HOW	EXPLAINING WHY

EXPLAINING *WHY*

"Why?" may be the question most commonly asked by human beings. We are fascinated by the reasons for everything that we experience in life. We ask questions about natural phenomena: Why is the sky blue? Why does a teakettle whistle? Why do some materials act as superconductors? We also find human attitudes and behavior intriguing: Why is chocolate so popular? Why do some people hit small leather balls with big sticks and then run around a field stomping on little white pillows? Why are America's family farms economically depressed? Why did the United States go to war in Iraq? Why is the Internet so popular?

Explaining *why* something occurs can be the most fascinating—and difficult—kind of expository writing. Answering the question "why" usually requires analyzing *cause-and-effect relationships*. The causes, however, may be too complex or intangible to identify precisely. We are on comparatively secure ground when we ask *why* about physical phenomena that can be weighed, measured, and replicated under laboratory conditions. Under those conditions, we can determine cause and effect with precision.

Fire, for example, has three *necessary* and *sufficient* causes: combustible material, oxygen, and ignition temperature. Without each of these causes, fire will not occur (each cause is "necessary"); taken together, these three causes are enough to cause fire (all three together are "sufficient"). In this case, the cause-and-effect relationship can be illustrated by an equation:

Cause 1	+	**Cause 2**	+	**Cause 3**	=	**Effect**
(combustible material)		(oxygen)		(ignition temperature)		(fire)

Analyzing both necessary and sufficient causes is essential to explaining an effect. You may say, for example, that wind shear (an abrupt downdraft in a storm) "caused" an airplane crash. In fact, wind shear may have *contributed* (been necessary) to the crash but was not by itself the total (sufficient) cause of the crash: an airplane with enough power may be able to overcome wind shear forces in certain circumstances. An explanation of the crash is not complete until you analyze the full range of necessary *and* sufficient causes, which may include wind shear, lack of power, mechanical failure, and even pilot error.

Sometimes, explanations for physical phenomena are beyond our analytical powers. Astrophysicists, for example, have good theoretical reasons for believing that black holes cause gigantic gravitational whirlpools in outer space, but they have difficulty explaining why black holes exist—or whether they exist at all.

In the realm of human cause and effect, determining causes and effects can be as tricky as explaining why black holes exist. Why, for example, do some children learn math easily while others fail? What effect does failing at math have on a child? What are necessary and sufficient causes for divorce? What are the effects of divorce on parents and children? Although you may not be able to explain all the causes or effects of something, you should not be satisfied until you have considered a wide range of possible causes and effects. Even then, you need to qualify or modify your statements, using such words as *might, usually, often, seldom, many,* or *most,* and then giving as much support and evidence as you can.

In the following paragraphs, Jonathan Kozol, a critic of America's educational system and author of *Illiterate America*, explains the multiple effects of a single cause: illiteracy. Kozol supports his explanation by citing specific ways that illiteracy affects the lives of people:

Illiterates cannot read the menu in a restaurant.

They cannot read the cost of items on the menu in the window of the restaurant before they enter.

Illiterates cannot read the letters that their children bring home from their teachers. They cannot study school department circulars that tell them of the courses that their children must be taking if they hope to pass the SAT exams. They cannot help with homework. They cannot write a letter to the teacher. They are afraid to visit in the classroom. They do not want to humiliate their child or themselves. . . .

Many illiterates cannot read the admonition on a pack of cigarettes. Neither the Surgeon General's warning nor its reproduction on the package can alert them to the risks. Although most people learn by word of mouth that smoking is related to a number of grave physical disorders, they do not get the chance to read the detailed stories which can document this danger with the vividness that turns concern into determination to resist. They can see the handsome cowboy or the slim Virginia lady lighting up a filter cigarette; they cannot heed the words that tell them that this product is (not "may be") dangerous to their health. Sixty million men and women are condemned to be the unalerted, high-risk candidates for cancer. . . .

Illiterates cannot travel freely. When they attempt to do so, they encounter risks that few of us can dream of. They cannot read traffic signs and, while they often learn to recognize and to decipher symbols, they cannot manage street names which they haven't seen before. The same is true for bus and subway stops. While ingenuity can sometimes help a man or woman to discern directions from familiar landmarks, buildings, cemeteries, churches, and the like, most illiterates are virtually immobilized. They seldom wander past the streets and neighborhoods they know. Geographical paralysis becomes a bitter metaphor for their entire existence. They are immobilized in almost every sense we can imagine. They can't move up. They can't move out. They cannot see beyond.

▮ WARMING UP: Journal Exercises

The following exercises will help you practice writing explanations. Read all of the following exercises and then write on the three that interest you most. If another idea occurs to you, write about it.

1. Write a one-paragraph explanation of an idea, term, or concept that you have discussed in a class that you are currently taking. From biology, for example, you might define *photosynthesis* or *gene splicing*. From psychology, you might define *psychosis* or *projection*. From computer studies, you might define *cyberspace* or *morphing*. First, identify someone who might need to know about this subject. Then give a definition and an illustration. Finally, describe how the term was discovered or invented, what its effects or applications are, and/or how it works.

2. Imitating E. B. White's short "definition" of democracy, use imaginative comparisons to write a short definition—serious or humorous—of one of the following words: *freedom, adolescence, mathematics, politicians, parents, misery, higher education, luck,* or a word of your own choice.

once defined courage as "grace under
on, explain how you or someone you know
in a difficult situation.

ouis Armstrong replied, "Man, if you gotta ask
now quite a bit about jazz, explain what
se a familiar subject to which the same remark
'explained" about that subject, and what cannot?

cquired (for example, playing a musical
chine, playing a sport, drawing, counseling others,
, dieting) and explain to a novice how he or she
ad what you've written. Then write another version
hat parts can you leave out? What must you add?

andard definitions to explain a key term, but
esist conventional definition in order to make a
eleventh-grader in West Philadelphia, was faced
r to check her racial identity. Like many Americans
she decided not to check one box. In the following
om National Public Radio's *All Things Considered,*
w she decided to (re)define herself. As you read her
you might need to resist a conventional definition in
ay.

Multiracialness

Caucasian, African-American, Latin American, Asian-American.
Check one. I look black, so I'll pick that one. But, no, wait, if I pick
that, I'll be denying the other sides of my family. So I'll pick white.
But I'm not white or black, I'm both, and part Native American, too.
It's confusing when you have to pick which race to identify with, especially when you have family who, on one side, ask, "Why do you
talk like a white girl?" when, in the eyes of the other side of your family, your behind is black.

I never met my dad's mom, my grandmother, Maybelle Dawson
Boyd Steptoe, and my father never knew his father. But my aunts or
uncles or cousins all think of me as black or white. I mean, I'm not the
lightest-skinned person, but my cousins down South swear I'm white.
It bothers them, and that bothers me, how people could care so much
about your skin color.

My mother's mother, Sylvia Gabriel, lives in Connecticut, near
where my aunt, uncle and cousins on that side of the family live. Now,

they're white, and where my grandma lives, there are very few black people or people of color. And when we visit, people look at us a lot, staring like, "What is that woman doing with those people?" It shocks the heck out of them when my brother and I call her Grandma.

My mother's side is Italian. I really didn't get any Italian culture except for the food. My father was raised much differently from my mother. My father is superstitious; he believes that a child should know his or her place and not speak unless spoken to. My father is very much into both his African-American and Native American heritage.

Multiracialness is a very tricky subject for my father. He'll tell people that I'm Native, African-American and Caucasian American, but at the same time he'll say things like, "Listen to jazz, listen to your cultural music." He says, "LaMer, look in the mirror. You're black. Ask any white person: they'll say you're black." He doesn't get it. I really would rather be colorless than to pick a race. I like other music, not just black music.

The term African-American bugs me. I'm not African. I'm American as a hot dog. We should have friends who are yellow, red, blue, black, purple, gay, religious, bisexual, trilingual, whatever, so you don't have a stereotypical view. I've met mean people and nice people of all different backgrounds. At my school, I grew up with all these kids, and I didn't look at them as white or Jewish or heterosexual; I looked at them as, "Oh, she's funny, he's sweet."

I know what box I'm going to choose. I pick D for none of the above, because my race is human.

7. Use your explaining skills to analyze visual images. For example, the work of art that opens this chapter is Elisabeth Vigée-Lebrun's 1788 portrait of Marie Antoinette and her children. Use your browser to search for information about Marie Antoinette, her role in the French Revolution, and the career of Vigée-Lebrun. Then study the photograph on the following page by Dorothea Large of a migrant woman and her children, taken in California in 1936. Do some Internet research on Dorothea Lange and her series of photographs of migrant workers in California. Write an essay comparing and contrasting the artists (Elisabeth Vigée-Lebrun and Dorothea Lange), the composition of these two images, and/or the social/cultural conditions surrounding each image. Assume that your audience is a group of your peers in your composition class.

Lange, Dorothea, photographer, "Migrant Agricultural Worker's Family." February 1936. America from the Great Depression to World War II: Black-and-White Photographs from the FSA-OWI, 1935–1945, Library of Congress.

PROFESSIONAL WRITING

How to Take Control of Your Credit Cards

Suze Orman

The author of several best selling books, including The Nine Steps to Financial Freedom *(1997),* The Money Book for the Young, Fabulous & Broke *(2005), and* Women and Money: Owning the Power to Control Your Destiny *(2007), Suze Orman was born in 1951 in Chicago, earned a degree in social work from the University of Illinois, and started her career not as a financial expert but as a waitress in Berkeley, California. After working at a restaurant for seven years, she talked her way into a job as a financial advisor with Merrill Lynch. She then started her own business and published her first book* You've Earned It, Don't Lose It. *Six of her most recent books have been* New York Times *bestsellers. Now that she is young(ish), fabulous, and very wealthy,*

Suze Orman has her own CNBC TV show, and she appears on Oprah, *the* Today Show, The View, *and* Larry King. *She is also the winner of 2 Emmy Awards for her PBS special and has been the recipient of the most GRACIE Awards in the history of the AWRT (American Women in Radio and Television). "How to Take Control of Your Credit Cards" appeared originally as one of her regular columns for Money Matters on Yahoo! Finance.*

I'm all for taking credit where credit is due, but when it comes to credit   *1*
cards, way too many of you are overdoing it. For Americans who don't
pay their entire credit card bill each month, the average balance is close
to $4,000. And when we zoom in on higher-income folks—those with
annual incomes between $75,000 and $100,000—the average balance
clocks in at nearly $8,000. If you're paying, say, 18 percent interest on an
$8,000 balance, and you make only the 2 percent minimum payment
due each month, you are going to end up paying more than $22,000 in
interest over the course of the 54 years it will take to get the balance
down to zero.

That's absolute insanity.   *2*

And absolutely unnecessary.   *3*

If you have the desire to take control of your credit card mess, you can.   *4*
It's just a matter of choice. I am not saying it will be easy, but there are
plenty of strategies that can put you on a path out of credit card hell. And
as I explain later, even those of you who can't seem to turn the corner and
become credit responsible on your own, can get plenty of help from qualified credit counseling services.

How to Be a Credit Card Shark

If you overspend just because you like to buy buy buy on credit, then you   *5*
are what I call Broke by Choice. You are willfully making your own
mess. I am not going to lecture you about how damaging this is; I'm
hoping the fact that you're reading this article means you are ready to
make a change.

But I also realize that some of you are Broke by Circumstance. I actu-   *6*
ally tell young adults in the dues-paying stage of their careers to lean on
their credit cards if they don't yet make enough to always keep up with
their bills. But the key is that if you rely on your credit cards to make ends
meet, you must limit the plastic spending to true necessities, not indulgences. Buying groceries is a necessity. Buying dinner for you and your pals
at a swank restaurant is an indulgence you can't afford if it will become part
of your unpaid credit card balance.

But whether you are broke by choice or by circumstance, the strategy *7* for getting out of credit card debt is the same: to outmaneuver the card companies with a strategy that assures you pay the lowest possible interest rate, for the shortest possible time, while avoiding all of the many snares and traps the card companies lay out for you.

Here's how to be a Credit Card Shark. *8*

Take an Interest in Your Rate

The average interest rate charged on credit cards is 15 percent, with plenty *9* of folks paying 18 percent, 20 percent, or even more. If you carry a balance on any credit cards, your primary focus should be to get that rate down as low as possible.

Now then. If you have a FICO score of at least 720, and you make at *10* least the minimum payment due each month, on time, you should be able to negotiate with your current credit card issuer to lower your rate. Call 'em up and let them know you plan to transfer your entire balance to another card with a lower rate—more on this in a sec—if they don't get your rate down.

If your card issuer doesn't step up to the plate and give you a better *11* deal, then do indeed start shopping around for a new card with a sweet intro offer. For those of you with strong FICO scores, a zero-rate deal ought to be possible. You can search for top card deals at the Yahoo! Finance Credit Card Center.

Don't forget, though, that the key with balance transfer offers is to find *12* out what your rate will be when the intro period expires in six months to a year. If your zero rate will skyrocket to 20 percent, that's a crappy deal, unless you are absolutely 100 percent sure you will get the balance paid off before the rate changes. (And if you got yourself into card hell in the first place, I wouldn't be betting on you having the ability to wipe out your problem in just six months. . . .)

Once you are approved for the new low- or zero-rate card, move as *13* much of your high-rate balances onto this new card. But don't—I repeat, do NOT—use the new card for new purchases. Hidden in the fine print on these deals are provisions stating, first, that any new purchases you make on the card will come with a high interest rate, and second, that you'll be paying that high interest on the entirety of your new purchase charges until you pay off every last cent of the balance transfer amount. This, to put it mildly, could really screw up your zero-rate deal. So please, use the new card only to park your old high-rate debt, and not to shop with.

Another careless mistake you can make is to cancel your old cards. *14* Don't do that either. Those cards hold some valuable "history" that's used to compute your FICO credit score. If you cancel the cards, you cancel your history, and your FICO score can take a hit. If you are worried about the temptation of using the cards, just get out your scissors and give them a good trim. That way you can't use 'em, but your history stays on your record.

Coddle Your New Card

When you do a balance transfer, you need to protect your low rate as if it 15 were an endangered species—because if the credit card issuer has anything to say about it, it will be. Look, you don't really think the card company is excited about charging you no interest, do you? How the heck do they make money off of that? They only offer up the great deal to lure you over to their card. Then they start working overtime trying to get you to screw up so they have an excuse to change your zero interest rate, often to as much as 20 percent or more.

And the big screw-up they are hoping you don't know about is buried 16 down in the fine print of your card agreement: make one late payment and you can kiss your zero deal good-bye. Even worse is that card companies are now scouring all your credit cards—remember, they can check your credit reports—to see if you have been late on any card, not just their card. So even if you always pay the zero-rate card on time, if you are late on any other card, your zero deal can be in jeopardy.

That's why I want you to make sure every credit card bill is paid ahead 17 of schedule. Don't mail it in on the day it is due; that's late. Mail it in at least five days early. Better yet, convert your card to online bill pay so you can zap your payments over in time every month. And remember, it's only the minimum monthly payment that needs to be paid. That's not asking a lot.

Dealing with High-Rate Debt

Okay, I realize not everyone is going to qualify for these low-rate balance 18 transfer deals, so let's run through how to take control of your cards if you are stuck with higher rates.

I want you to line up all your cards in descending order of their inter- 19 est rates. Notice I said the card with the highest interest rate comes first. Not the one with the biggest balance.

Your strategy is to make the minimum monthly payment on every 20 card, on time, every month. But your card with the highest interest rate gets some special treatment. I want you to pay more than the minimum amount due on this card. The more you can pay, the better; but everyone should put in, at the minimum, an extra $20 each month. Push yourself hard to make that extra payment as large as possible. It can save you thousands of dollars in interest charges over time.

Keep this up every month until your card with the highest rate is paid *21* off. Then turn your attention to the card with the next highest rate. In addition to the usual monthly minimum payment due on that second card, I want you to add in the entire amount you were previously paying on the first card (the one that's now paid off). So let's say you were paying a total of $200 a month on your original highest-rate card, and making a $75 monthly minimum on the second card. Well, now you are going to fork over $275 a month to the second card. And, of course, you'll continue to make the minimum monthly payment due on any other cards. Once your second card is paid off, move on to the third. If your monthly payment on that second card was $275, then that's what you should add to the minimum payment due on your third card. Get the idea? Rinse and repeat as often as needed, until you have all your debt paid off. For some of you this may take a year, for others it may take many years. That's okay. Just get yourself moving in the right direction and you'll be amazed how gratifying it is to find yourself taking control of your money rather than letting it control you.

And be sure to keep an eye on your FICO credit score. As you pay *22* down your card balances—and build a record of paying on time—your score is indeed going to rise. Eventually your score may be high enough to finally qualify for a low-rate balance transfer offer.

Is Credit Counseling Right for You?

There is plenty of help available if you can't seem to get a solid grip on deal- *23* ing with your credit card debt. But not all the help is good. Given that so many Americans are drowning in card debt, it's really no surprise that some enterprising—and underhanded—folks have figured out a way to make money off of this epidemic by charging high fees for counseling and advice.

So you need to make sure you choose an honest and fair credit coun- *24* seling service. Start by getting references from the National Foundation for Credit Counseling.

Next, make an appointment to talk with a counselor face-to-face. A *25* good counselor will question you thoroughly and in detail about your financial situation before proposing anything. If you are simply told right off

...continued How to Take Control of Your Credit Cards, **Suze Orman**

the bat that you need a Debt Management Plan (see below), you should run out the door PDQ. That firm is not interested in truly helping you. They just want to hit you up with a bunch of fees.

A good counselor is also going to require that you attend education   26 classes. This is not punishment! On the contrary, it's the best help you can get. Quite often, you can make the changes necessary to take control of your credit card spending just by learning a few good habits.

vo·cab·u·lar·y

In your journal, write the meaning of the italicized words in the following phrases.

- true necessities, not *indulgences* **(6)**
- to *outmaneuver* the card companies **(7)**
- you have a *FICO* score **(10)**
- deal can be in *jeopardy* **(16)**
- make money off this *epidemic* **(23)**

QUESTIONS FOR WRITING AND DISCUSSION

1. Writers of effective explaining essays focus their thesis for a specific audience. Describe the audience Orman addresses in her essay. Which sentences help you identify this audience? Which sentences in Orman's essay most clearly express her thesis?

2. Explaining essays typically use definition of terms, explanation of processes, and analyses of causes and effects. Identify at least one example of each of the following strategies in Orman's essay: definition, process analysis, and causal analysis. In each case, decide if the information Orman gives is clear to you. Where do you need additional information or clarification?

3. Two strategies that Orman uses to connect with her readers is addressing them in the second person, "you," and using informal language such as "you and your pals," "call 'em up," "more on this in a sec," and "sweet intro offer." Find other examples of informal language in her essay. Does this language work for her audience? Does it make the essay more lively and readable for you? Is this language appropriate in an essay about finances? Explain.

4. Appeals to the audience often involve more than simply using informal language. Effective appeals connect to the readers' sense of identity and their

personal and social values. Read the following introduction to Chapter I in Orman's latest book, *Women and Money: Owning the Power to Control Your Destiny.* Cite specific sentences from the following paragraph to explain how Orman identifies with her readers while at the same time suggesting that they need to make changes in their lives.

> I never thought I'd write a book about money just for women. I never thought it was necessary. So then why am I doing just that in my eighth book? And why now? Let me explain. All my previous books were written with the belief that gender is not a factor on any level in mastering the nuts and bolts of smart financial management. Women can invest, save, and handle debt just as well and skillfully as any man. I still believe that— why would anyone think differently? So imagine my surprise when I learned that some of the people closest to me in my life were in the dark about their own finances. Clueless. Or, in some cases, willfully resisting doing what they knew needed to be done.

5. Find one of the offers for credit cards that you, a friend, or a family member has recently received. Study the fine print. Then, in your own words, explain what the fine print means in language that another member of your class can understand. Is Orman right about the "many snares and traps" that the card companies set for their customers?

6. Write a profile of Suze Orman that recounts key events in her life and explains why she has been so successful as a writer, motivator, and financial advisor. Check your online library databases as well as online reviews and Web sites. Write your profile so that it could appear in a local newspaper, on a Web site, or as a promotion for one of Suze Orman's latest books.

PROFESSIONAL WRITING

How Male and Female Students Use Language Differently

Deborah Tannen

Everyone knows that men and women communicate differently, but Deborah Tannen, a linguist at Georgetown University, has spent her career studying how and why their conversational styles are different. Tannen's books include Conversational Style: Analyzing Talk Among Friends *(1984), her best-selling* You Just Don't Understand: Women and Men in Conversation *(1990), and* I Only Say This Because I Love You *(2001). In the following article from* The Chronicle of Higher Education, *Tannen applies her knowledge of*

... *continued* How Male and Female Students Use Language Differently, **Deborah Tannen**

conversational styles to the classroom. How do men and women communicate differently in the classroom? What teaching styles best promote open communication and learning for both sexes? As you read her essay, think about your own classes. Do the men in your classes talk more than the women? Do men like to argue in large groups, while women prefer conversations in small groups? How clearly—and convincingly—does Tannen explain discussion preferences and their effects in the classroom?

When I researched and wrote my latest book, *You Just Don't Understand: Women and Men in Conversation,* the furthest thing from my mind was reevaluating my teaching strategies. But that has been one of the direct benefits of having written the book.   1

The primary focus of my linguistic research always has been the language of everyday conversation. One facet of this is conversational style: how different regional, ethnic, and class backgrounds, as well as age and gender, result in different ways of using language to communicate. *You Just Don't Understand* is about the conversational styles of women and men. As I gained more insight into typically male and female ways of using language, I began to suspect some of the causes of the troubling facts that women who go to single-sex schools do better in later life, and that when young women sit next to young men in classrooms, the males talk more. This is not to say that all men talk in class, nor that no women do. It is simply that a greater percentage of discussion time is taken by men's voices.   2

The research of sociologists and anthropologists such as Janet Lever, Marjorie Harness Goodwin, and Donna Eder has shown that girls and boys learn to use language differently in their sex-separate peer groups. Typically, a girl has a best friend with whom she sits and talks, frequently telling secrets. It's the telling of secrets, the fact and the way that they talk to each other, that makes them best friends. For boys, activities are central: their best friends are the ones they do things with. Boys also tend to play in larger groups that are hierarchical. High-status boys give orders and push low-status boys around. So boys are expected to use language to seize center stage: by exhibiting their skill, displaying their knowledge, and challenging and resisting challenges.   3

These patterns have stunning implications for classroom interaction. Most faculty members assume that participating in class discussion is a necessary part of successful performance. Yet speaking in a classroom is more congenial to boys' language experience than to girls', since it entails   4 putting oneself forward in front of a large group of people, many of whom are strangers and at least one of whom is sure to judge speakers' knowledge and intelligence by their verbal display.

Another aspect of many classrooms that makes them more hospitable to most men than to most women is the use of debate-like formats as a learning tool. Our educational system, as Walter Ong argues persuasively in his book *Fighting for Life* (Cornell University Press, 1981), is fundamentally male in that the pursuit of knowledge is believed to be achieved by ritual opposition: public display followed by argument and challenge. Father Ong demonstrates that ritual opposition—what he calls "adversativeness" or "agonism"—is fundamental to the way most males approach almost any activity. (Consider, for example, the little boy who shows he likes a little girl by pulling her braids and shoving her.) But ritual opposition is antithetical to the way most females learn and like to interact. It is not that females don't fight, but that they don't fight for fun. They don't *ritualize* opposition.

Anthropologists working in widely disparate parts of the world have found contrasting verbal rituals for women and men. Women in completely unrelated cultures (for example, Greece and Bali) engage in ritual laments: spontaneously produced rhyming couplets that express their pain, for example, over the loss of loved ones. Men do not take part in laments. They have their own, very different verbal ritual: a contest, a war of words in which they vie with each other to devise clever insults.

When discussing these phenomena with a colleague, I commented that I see these two styles in American conversation: many women bond by talking about troubles, and many men bond by exchanging playful insults and put-downs, and other sorts of verbal sparring. He exclaimed: "I never thought of this, but that's the way I teach: I have students read an article, and then I invite them to tear it apart. After we've torn it to shreds, we talk about how to build a better model."

This contrasts sharply with the way I teach: I open the discussion of readings by asking, "What did you find useful in this? What can we use in our own theory building and our own methods?" I note what I see as weaknesses in the author's approach, but I also point out that the writer's discipline and purposes might be different from ours. Finally, I offer personal anecdotes illustrating the phenomena under discussion and praise students' anecdotes as well as their critical acumen.

These different teaching styles must make our classrooms wildly different places and hospitable to different students. Male students are more likely to be comfortable attacking the readings and might find the inclusion of personal anecdotes irrelevant and "soft." Women are more likely to resist discussion they perceive as hostile, and, indeed, it is women in my classes who are most likely to offer personal anecdotes.

A colleague who read my book commented that he had always taken 10 for granted that the best way to deal with students' comments is to challenge them; this, he felt it was self-evident, sharpens their minds and helps them develop debating skills. But he had noticed that women were relatively silent in his classes, so he decided to try beginning discussion with relatively open-ended questions and letting comments go unchallenged. He found, to his amazement and satisfaction, that more women began to speak up.

Though some of the women in his class clearly liked this better, per- 11 haps some of the men liked it less. One young man in my class wrote in a questionnaire about a history professor who gave students questions to think about and called on people to answer them: "He would then play devil's advocate . . . *i.e.,* he debated us. . . . That class *really* sharpened me intellectually. . . . We as students do need to know how to defend ourselves." This young man valued the experience of being attacked and challenged publicly. Many, if not most, women would shrink from such "challenge," experiencing it as public humiliation.

A professor at Hamilton College told me of a young man who was up- 12 set because he felt his class presentation had been a failure. The professor was puzzled because he had observed that class members had listened attentively and agreed with the student's observations. It turned out that it was this very agreement that the student interpreted as failure: since no one had engaged his ideas by arguing with him, he felt they had found them unworthy of attention.

So one reason men speak in class more than women is that many of 13 them find the "public" classroom setting more conducive to speaking, whereas most women are more comfortable speaking in private to a small group of people they know well. A second reason is that men are more likely to be comfortable with the debate-like form that discussion may take. Yet another reason is the different attitudes toward speaking in class that typify women and men.

Students who speak frequently in class, many of whom are men, as- 14 sume that it is their job to think of contributions and try to get the floor to express them. But many women monitor their participation not only to get the floor but to avoid getting it. Women students in my class tell me that if they have spoken up once or twice, they hold back for the rest of the class because they don't want to dominate. If they have spoken a lot one week, they will remain silent the next. These different ethics of participation are, of course, unstated, so those who speak freely assume that those who remain silent have nothing to say, and those who are reining themselves in assume that the big talkers are selfish and hoggish.

When I looked around my classes, I could see these differing ethics 15 and habits at work. For example, my graduate class in analyzing conversation had twenty students, eleven women and nine men. Of the men, four were foreign students: two Japanese, one Chinese, and one Syrian. With the exception of the three Asian men, all the men spoke in class at least occasionally. The biggest talker in the class was a woman, but there were also five women who never spoke at all, only one of whom was Japanese. I decided to try something different.

I broke the class into small groups to discuss the issues raised in the 16 readings and to analyze their own conversational transcripts. I devised three ways of dividing the students into groups: one by the degree program they were in, one by gender, and one by conversational style, as closely as I could guess it. This meant that when the class was grouped according to conversational style, I put Asian students together, fast talkers together, and quiet students together. The class split into groups six times during the semester, so they met in each grouping twice. I told students to regard the groups as examples of interactional data and to note the different ways they participated in the different groups. Toward the end of the term, I gave them a questionnaire asking about their class and group participation.

I could see plainly from my observation of the groups at work that 17 women who never opened their mouths in class were talking away in the small groups. In fact, the Japanese woman commented that she found it particularly hard to contribute to the all-woman group she was in because "I was overwhelmed by how talkative the female students were in the female-only group." This is particularly revealing because it highlights that the same person who can be "oppressed" into silence in one context can become the talkative "oppressor" in another. No one's conversational style is absolute; everyone's style changes in response to the context and others' styles.

Some of the students (seven) said they preferred the same-gender 18 groups; others preferred the same-style groups. In answer to the question "Would you have liked to speak in class more than you did?" six of the seven who said yes were women; the one man was Japanese. Most startlingly, this response did not come only from quiet women; it came from women who had indicated they had spoken in class never, rarely, sometimes, and often. Of the eleven students who said the amount they had spoken was fine, seven were men. Of the four women who checked "fine," two added qualifications indicating it wasn't completely fine: One wrote in "maybe more," and one wrote, "I have an urge to participate but often feel I should have something more interesting/relevant/wonderful/intelligent to say!!"

I counted my experiment a success. Everyone in the class found the 19 small groups interesting, and no one indicated he or she would have preferred that the class not break into groups. Perhaps most instructive, however, was the fact that the experience of breaking into groups, and of talking about participation in class, raised everyone's awareness about classroom participation. After we had talked about it, some of the quietest women in the class made a few voluntary contributions, though sometimes I had to ensure their participation by interrupting the students who were exuberantly speaking out.

Americans are often proud that they discount the significance of cul- 20 tural differences: "We are all individuals," many people boast. Ignoring such issues as gender and ethnicity becomes a source of pride: "I treat everyone the same." But treating people the same is not equal treatment if they are not the same.

The classroom is a different environment for those who feel comfort- 21 able putting themselves forward in a group than it is for those who find the prospect of doing so chastening, or even terrifying. When a professor asks, "Are there any questions?" students who can formulate statements the fastest have the greatest opportunity to respond. Those who need significant time to do so have not really been given a chance at all, since by the time they are ready to speak, someone else has the floor.

In a class where some students speak out without raising hands, those 22 who feel they must raise their hands and wait to be recognized do not have equal opportunity to speak. Telling them to feel free to jump in will not make them feel free; one's sense of timing, of one's rights and obligations in a classroom, are automatic, learned over years of interaction. They may be changed over time, with motivation and effort, but they cannot be changed on the spot. And everyone assumes his or her own way is best. When I asked my students how the class could be changed to make it easier for them to speak more, the most talkative woman said she would prefer it if no one had to raise hands, and a foreign student said he wished people would raise their hands and wait to be recognized.

My experience in this class has convinced me that small-group inter- 23
action should be part of any class that is not a small seminar. I also am convinced that having the students become observers of their own interaction
is a crucial part of their education. Talking about ways of talking in class
makes students aware that their ways of talking affect other students, that
the motivations they impute to others may not truly reflect others' motives,
and that the behaviors they assume to be self-evidently right are not universal norms.

The goal of complete equal opportunity in class may not be attainable, 24
but realizing that one monolithic classroom-participation structure is not
equal opportunity is itself a powerful motivation to find more-diverse
methods to serve diverse students—and every classroom is diverse.

◼ ◼ ◼

vo·cab·u·lar·y

In your journal, write the meanings of the italicized words in the following phrases.

- ritual opposition is *antithetical* **(5)**
- personal *anecdotes* **(8)**
- *conducive* to speaking **(13)**
- *ethics* of participation **(14)**
- *monolithic* classroom-participation structure **(24)**

QUESTIONS FOR WRITING AND DISCUSSION

1. Reread Tannen's essay, noting places where your experiences as a student
   match or do not match her observations. In what contexts were your
   experiences similar to or different from Tannen's? Explain what might
   account for the different observations.

2. In her essay, Tannen states and then continues to restate her thesis. Reread
   her essay, underlining all the sentences that seem to state or rephrase her
   main idea. Do her restatements of the main idea make her essay clearer?
   Explain.

3. Explaining essays may explain *what* (describe and define), explain *how*
   (process analysis), and/or explain *why* (causal analysis). Find one example of
   each of these strategies in Tannen's essay. Which of these three is the
   dominant shaping strategy? Support your answer with references to specific
   sentences or paragraphs.

4. Effective explaining essays must have supporting evidence—specific examples, facts, quotations, testimony from experts, statistics, and so on. Choose four consecutive paragraphs from Tannen's essay and list the kinds of supporting evidence she uses. Based on your inventory, rate her supporting evidence as weak, average, or strong. Explain your choice.

5. Does the style of Tannen's essay support her thesis that men and women have different ways of communicating? Does Tannen, in fact, use a "woman's style" of writing that is similar to women's conversational style? Examine Tannen's tone (her attitude toward her subject and audience), her voice (the projection of her personality in her language), and her supporting evidence (her use of facts and statistics or anecdotal, contextual evidence). Cite specific passages to support your analysis.

6. In another class where students discuss frequently, sit in the back row where you can observe the participation of men and women. First, record the number of men and the number of women in the class. Then, during one class period, record the following: (a) when the teacher calls on a student, record whether the student is male or female; (b) when a student talks without raising his or her hand, record whether the student is male or female; and (c) when students speak in class, record how long they talk and whether they are male or female. Once you have collected and analyzed your data, explain whether they seem to support or refute Tannen's claims.

7. On the Internet, visit Deborah Tannen's home page at http://www.georgetown.edu/faculty/tannend. Click on the link "Interviews with Deborah Tannen." How do her responses during these interviews shed light on the conversational styles of men and women? What points does she make that might apply to how men and women communicate and learn differently in the classroom?

TECHNIQUES   PROCESSES

Explaining: The Writing Process

ASSIGNMENT FOR EXPLAINING
After assessing your rhetorical situation, *explain* what something means or is, *how* it should be done or *how* it occurs, and/or *why* something

occurs. Your purpose is to explain something as clearly as possible for your audience by analyzing, showing relationships, and demonstrating with examples, facts, illustrations, data, or other information.

With a topic in mind, think about your audience and a possible genre. As in your investigating paper, the amount and kind of detail you need depend on how much your readers are likely to know about your topic. What do they already know? What have you discovered in your research that will help explain the topic for them? Is an essay the most appropriate genre, or would an article, editorial, Internet posting, pamphlet, or letter be more effective?

CHOOSING COLLECTING SHAPING DRAFTING REVISING

CHOOSING A SUBJECT

If one of your journal entries suggested a possible subject, go on to the collecting and shaping strategies. If you still need an interesting subject, consider the following suggestions.

> You can write about anything, and if you write well enough, even the reader with no intrinsic interest in the subject will become involved.
> —TRACY KIDDER, NOVELIST

- Reread your authority list or the most interesting journal entries from previous chapters. Do they contain ideas that you might define or explain, processes suitable for how-to explanations, or causes or effects that you could analyze and explain for a certain audience?

- Reread your notes from another class in which you have an upcoming examination. Select some topic, idea, principle, process, famous person, or event from the text or your notes. Investigate other texts, popular magazines, or journals for information on that topic. If appropriate, interview someone or conduct a survey. Explain this principle or process to a member of your writing class.

- If you are doing a community-service-learning project, consider a writing project explaining the agency's mission to the public or to a potential donor. You might also write an article for a local or campus newspaper explaining some aspect of their service or a recent contribution the agency has made to the community.

- Consider writing an artistic, cultural, historical, or social explanation of a particular visual image or a set of visual images. One excellent Web site for famous photographs is the Pulitzer site at http://www.gallerym.com/pulitzerphotos.htm. Decide on a particular audience, genre, and context appropriate for the photograph.

• Choose a current controversy to explain. Instead of arguing for one side or the other, however, explain the different points of view in this controversy. Who are the leading figures or groups representing each of several different positions? Choose a particular audience, genre, and context, and explain what each of these people or groups have to gain or lose and how their personal investments in the topic determine their position.

CHOOSING   **COLLECTING**   SHAPING   DRAFTING   REVISING

COLLECTING

▌**QUESTIONS**   Once you have a tentative subject and audience in mind, consider which of the following will be your primary focus (all three may be relevant).

• *What* something means or is
• *How* something occurs or is done (or should be done)
• *Why* something occurs or what its effects are

To explain *what* something is, jot down answers to each of the following questions. The more you can write on each question, the more details you'll have for your topic.

• What are its class and distinguishing characteristics?
• What is its etymology?
• How can you describe it?
• What examples can you give?
• What are its parts or its functions?
• What is it similar to? What is it *not*?
• What figurative comparisons apply?
• How can it be classified?
• Which of the above is most useful to your audience?

To explain *how* something occurs or is done, answer the following questions.

• What are the component parts or steps in the whole process?
• What is the exact sequence of steps or events?
• Are several of the steps or events related?
• If steps or events were omitted, would the outcome change?
• Which steps or events are most crucial?
• Which steps or events does your audience most need to know?

To explain *why* something occurs or what its effects are, consider the following issues.

- Which are the necessary or sufficient causes?
- Which causes are remote in time, and which are immediate?
- What is the order or sequence of the causes? Do the causes occur simultaneously?
- What are the effects? Do they occur in a sequence or simultaneously?
- Do the causes and effects occur in a "chain reaction"?
- Is there an action or situation that would have prevented the effect?
- Are there comparable things or events that have similar causes or effects?
- Which causes or effects need special clarification for your audience?

■ **BRANCHING**   Often, *branching* can help you visually analyze your subject. Start with your topic and then subdivide each idea into its component parts. The resulting analysis will not only help generate ideas but may also suggest ways to shape an essay.

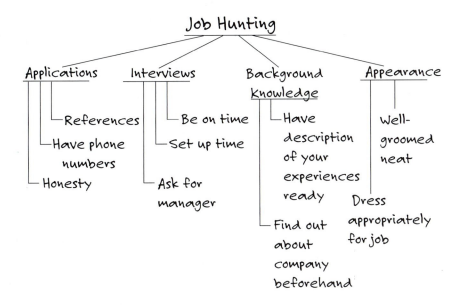

Branching can also take the form of a tree, with a main trunk for the subject and separate branches for each subtopic. For an essay on effective job hunting, information might be diagrammed this way.

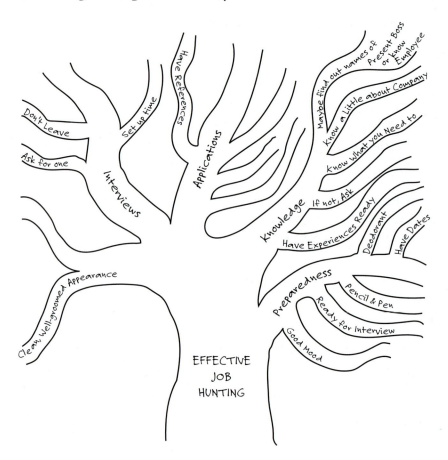

■ **OBSERVING**   If you can observe your subject, try drawing it, describing it, or taking careful notes. Which senses can you use to describe it—sight, sound, touch, smell, taste? If it is a scientific experiment that you can reproduce or a social situation you can reconstruct, go through it again and observe carefully. As you observe it, put yourself in your readers' shoes: what do you need to explain it to them?

■ **REMEMBERING**   Your own experience and memory are essential for explaining. *Freewriting, looping,* and *clustering* may all generate detailed information, good examples, and interesting perspectives that will make your explanation clearer and move vivid. (See Chapter 4 for an explanation of looping and clustering.)

Research Tips

Review your topic for research possibilities. Four research strategies are direct *observation*, use of *memories* and personal experience, *field research* (including interviews and surveys), and *library/Internet research*. (See Chapter 7 for interview and survey techniques. See Chapter 13 on using and documenting sources.) Tips to remember: Make *photocopies* of all the sources that you plan to cite in your essay. When you make copies, be sure to *write all relevant information* on the photocopies, such as author, date, publisher, place of publication, journal title, and volume numbers. When you cite sources in the text, be sure to *introduce* your sources. Make sure your direct quotations are *accurate* word-for-word transcriptions.

█ READING   When you find written texts about your subject, be sure to use your active reading strategies. You may need only a few sources if you reread them carefully. Write out a short summary for each source. Respond to each source by analyzing its effectiveness, agreeing or disagreeing with its ideas, or interpreting the text. The quality of your understanding is more important than the sheer number of sources you cite.

█ INVESTIGATING   Use sources available in the library, textbooks containing relevant information, or interviews with teachers, participants, or experts. Interview your classmates about their own subjects for this assignment: someone else's subject may trigger an idea that you can write about or may suggest a fresh approach to the subject that you have already chosen.

> ❝ Readers may be strangers who have no immediate reason to care about your writing. They want order, clarity, and stimulation. ❞
>
> —ELIZABETH COWAN NEELD,
> TEACHER AND AUTHOR

CHOOSING	COLLECTING	**SHAPING**	DRAFTING	REVISING

SHAPING

As you collect information and generate ideas from your collecting activities, be sure to *narrow* and *focus* your subject into a topic suitable for a short essay. You will not be able to cover everything you've read, thought, or experienced about your subject. Choose the most interesting ideas—for you and for your audience—and shape, order, and clarify those ideas.

█ AUDIENCE AND GENRE   As you consider ways to organize and shape your explaining essay, think about a possible audience and genre. An essay directed at a general audience composed of peers like your classmates is just one possibility. A letter to the editor, a pamphlet for a community agency, a job analysis for your employer, an article for a local or school newspaper, a posting or response to a listserve, or an essay for students in your major are other possibilities. Once you have a tentative audience and genre, you'll have a better idea about how to organize your explanation. Reread your assignment for specific suggestions and guidelines about audience and genre.

DEFINITION AND CLASSIFICATION   An essay explaining *what* something means or is can be shaped by using a variety of definition strategies or by classifying the subject.

Definition itself is not a single organizing strategy; it supports a variety of strategies that may be useful in shaping your essay: description, analysis of parts or function, comparison/contrast, development by examples, or figures of speech such as simile, metaphor, and analogy.

Classification, on the other hand, is a single strategy that can organize a paragraph or even a whole essay quickly. Observers of human behavior, for example, love to use classification. Grocery shoppers might be classified by types: racers (the ones who seem to have just won forty-five seconds of free shopping and run down the aisles filling their carts as fast as possible), talkers (the ones whose phone must be out of order because they stand in the aisles gossiping forever), penny-pinchers (who always have their calculators out and read the unit price labels for everything), party shoppers (who camp out in the junk food aisles, filling their carts with potato chips, dip, candy, peanuts, and drink mixers), and dawdlers (who leave their carts crosswise in the aisles while they read twenty-nine different soup can labels). You can write a sentence or two about each type or devote a whole paragraph to explaining a single type.

EXAMPLE   Development by example can effectively illustrate what something is or means, but it can also help explain how or why something happens. Usually, an example describes a specific incident, located at a certain place and occurring at a particular time, that *shows* or *demonstrates* the main idea. In the following paragraph from *Mediaspeak,* Donna Woolfolk Cross explains what effects soap operas can have on addicted viewers. This paragraph is developed by several examples—some described in detail, others referred to briefly.

> Dedicated watchers of soap operas often confuse fact with fiction. . . . Stars of soap operas tell hair-raising stories of their encounters with fans suffering from this affliction. Susan Lucci, who plays the promiscuous Erica Kane on "All My Children," tells of a time she was riding in a parade: "We

were in a crowd of about 250,000 traveling in an antique open car moving ver-r-ry slowly. At that time in the series I was involved with a character named Nick. Some man broke through, came right up to the car and said to me, 'Why don't you give me a little bit of what you've been giving Nick?' " The man hung onto the car, menacingly, until she was rescued by the police. Another time, when she was in church, the reverent silence was broken by a woman's astonished remark, "Oh, my god, Erica prays!" Margaret Mason, who plays the villainous Lisa Anderson in "Days of Our Lives," was accosted by a woman who poured a carton of milk all over her in the supermarket. And once a woman actually tried to force her car off the Ventura Freeway.

■ VOICE AND TONE

Writers also use voice and tone to shape and control whole passages, often in combination with other shaping strategies. In the following paragraph, Toni Bambara, author of *The Salt Eaters* and numerous short stories, explains *what* being a writer is all about. This paragraph is shaped both by a single extended example and by Bambara's voice talking directly to the reader.

> When I replay the tapes on file in my head, tapes of speeches I've given at writing conferences over the years, I invariably hear myself saying—"A writer, like any other cultural worker, like any other member of the community, ought to try to put her/his skills in the service of the community." Some years ago when I returned south, my picture in the paper prompted several neighbors to come visit. "You a writer? What all you write?" Before I could begin the catalogue, one old gent interrupted with—"Ya know Miz Mary down the block? She need a writer to help her send off a letter to her grandson overseas." So I began a career as the neighborhood scribe—letters to relatives, snarling letters to the traffic chief about the promised stop sign, nasty letters to the utilities, angry letters to the principal about that confederate flag hanging in front of the school, contracts to transfer a truck from seller to buyer, etc. While my efforts have been graciously appreciated in the form of sweet potato dumplings, herb teas, hair braiding, and the like, there is still much room for improvement—"For a writer, honey, you've got a mighty bad hand. Didn't they teach penmanship at that college?" Another example, I guess, of words setting things in motion. What goes around, comes around, as the elders say.

■ CHRONOLOGICAL ORDER AND PROCESS ANALYSIS

Writers use chronological order in expository writing to help explain how to do something or how something is typically done. In her essay "Anorexia Nervosa," student writer

TIPS FOR INTEGRATING IMAGES

For your explaining essay, you may wish to integrate images (photographs, images, graphics, or charts), and you may wish to work with your document design. To integrate images with your text, first consider your rhetorical situation.

- **What is your purpose?** Does the visual contribute to your thesis or main idea, or is it just a distraction?
- **Who is your audience?** Is the image appropriate for your target audience? Would it make your document more appealing or attractive? Would it offend them? Would it amuse them? Would it make your point in a way that words could not?
- **What is your intended genre?** Look at other examples of your genre. Find several examples of the kind of essay, pamphlet, Web page, article, advertisement, brochure, laboratory report, letter, or flyer. How do they use images or graphics?
- **What is the social/cultural context of your text?** Consider whether the subject, topic, or issue you are discussing could or should be illustrated with an image or a certain document design.

Use search engines and library sources to find a variety of images relevant to your topic. Start with an image search on Google or Yahoo!, but don't forget that your library has a wealth of online image databases. If you're looking for paintings or fine art, check Web sites for museums around the world. Having several potential images enables you to choose the one most effective for your rhetorical situation.

Finally, don't forget about your document design. Start with your purpose, audience, and genre. Consider how the genre you have selected uses the following document features.

- **Columns** Would a text with two columns work for your purpose?
- **Margins and white space** Avoid overcrowding words, images, and graphics on a page. Use margins and white space to emphasize key parts of your text.
- **Fonts** Use a font appropriate to your purpose, genre, and audience. Times New Roman and Palatino Linotype are widely accepted, but do you need **Franklin Gothic Demi** for particular parts of your text? For special situations, perhaps consider a script face such as Felt Tip or a bolder face such as TRADE GOTHIC. If appropriate for your purpose, genre, and audience, play around with the available fonts on your computer.
- **Sidebars** If appropriate for your text, use a sidebar for text emphasis or to add related information.

Is the image appropriate for your target audience?
Does the image contribute to your thesis?

Nancie Brosseau uses transitional words to signal the various stages of anorexia. In the following sentences, taken from the third paragraph of her essay, the *italicized* words mark the chronological stages of her anorexia.

> Several serious health problems bombarded me, and it's a wonder I'm still alive. . . . *As my weight plummeted,* my circulation grew *increasingly worse.* . . . My hair *started* to fall out, and my whole body took on a very skeletal appearance. . . . I would force myself to vomit *as soon as possible* if I was forced to eat. The enamel on my teeth *started to be eaten away* by the acid in the vomit, and my lips cracked and bled regularly. I *stopped* menstruating completely because I was not producing enough estrogen. . . . *One time,* while executing a chain of back handsprings, I broke all five fingers on one hand and three on the other because my bones had become so brittle. . . . I chose to see a psychologist, and she helped me sort out the emotional aspects of anorexia, *which in turn* solved the physical problems.

▌ CAUSAL ANALYSIS   In order to explain *why* something happens or what the effects of something are, writers often use one of the following three patterns of cause and effect to shape their material:

Cause 1 + Cause 2 + Cause 3 . . . + Cause n → Effect

In the case of fire, for example, we know that three causes lead to a single effect. These causes do not occur in any special sequence; they must all be present at the same time. For historical events, however, we usually list causes in chronological order.

Sometimes one cause has several effects. In that case, we reverse the pattern:

Cause → Effect 1 + Effect 2 + Effect 3 . . . + Effect n

For example, an explanation of the collapse of the economy following the stock market crash of 1929 might follow this pattern. The crash (itself a symptom of other causes) led to a depreciated economy, widespread unemployment, bankruptcy for thousands of businesses, foreclosures on farms, and so forth. An essay on the effects of the crash might devote one or two paragraphs to each effect.

In the third pattern, causes and effects form a pattern of chain reactions. One cause leads to an effect that then becomes the cause of another effect, and so on:

Cause 1 → Effect 1 (Cause 2) → Effect 2 (Cause 3) → Effect 3

We could analyze events in the Middle East during and after the Iraq War as a series of actions and reactions in which each effect becomes the cause of the next effect in the chain of car bombings, air raids, terrorist hijackings, and kidnappings.

An essay on the chain reaction of events in the Middle East might have a paragraph or two on each of the links in this chain.

■ **INTRODUCTIONS AND LEAD-INS** Often, the first sentences of the introductory paragraph of an essay are the hardest to write. You want to get your reader's attention and focus on the main idea of your essay, but you don't want to begin, boringly, with your thesis statement. Below are several kinds of opening sentences designed to grab your reader's interest. Consider your topic—see if one of these strategies will work for you.

A Personal Example

I knew my dieting had gotten out of hand, but when I could actually see the movement of my heart beating beneath my clothes, I knew I was in trouble.

—"Anorexia Nervosa," Nancie Brosseau

A Description of a Person or Place

He strides toward us in navy and white, his body muscled and heavy-set, one arm holding his casually flung jeans jacket over his shoulder. A man in his prime, with just the right combination of macho and sartorial flair.

—"Some Don't Like Their Blues at All," Karyn M. Lewis

It's still there, the Chinese school on Yale Street where my brother and I used to go. Despite the new coat of paint and the high wire fence, the school I knew ten years ago remains remarkably, stoically the same.

—"The Struggle to Be an All-American Girl," Elizabeth Wong

An Example from a Case Study

Susan Smith has everything going for her. A self-described workaholic, she runs a Cambridge, Massachusetts, real estate consulting company with her husband Charles and still finds time to cuddle and nurture their two young kids, David, 7, and Stacey, 6. What few people know is that Susan, 44, needs a little chemical help to be a supermom: She has been taking the antidepressant Prozac for five years.

—"The Personality Pill," Anastasia Toufexis

A Startling Statement, Fact, or Statistic

Embalming is indeed a most extraordinary procedure, and one must wonder at the docility of Americans who each year pay hundreds of millions of dollars for its perpetuation, blissfully ignorant of what it is all about, what is done, how it is done.

—"To Dispel Fears of Live Burial," Jessica Mitford

A Statement from a Book

The American novelist John Barth, in his early novel *The Floating Opera,* remarks that ordinary, day-to-day life often presents us with embarrassingly obvious, totally unsubtle patterns of symbolism and meaning—life in the midst of death, innocence vindicated, youth versus age, etc.

—"I'm O.K., but You're Not," Robert Zoellner

A Striking Question or Questions

Do non-human animals have rights? Should we humans feel morally bound to exercise consideration for the lives and well-being of individual members of other animal species? If so, how much consideration, and by what logic?

—"Animal Rights and Beyond," David Quammen

A Common Error or Mistaken Judgment

There was a time when, in my search for essences, I concluded that the canyonland country has no heart. I was wrong. The canyonlands did have a heart, a living heart, and that heart was Glen Canyon and the golden, flowing Colorado River.

—"The Damnation of a Canyon," Edward Abbey

Combined Strategies

Last December a man named Robert Lee Willie, who had been convicted of raping and murdering an 18-year-old woman, was executed in the Louisiana state prison. In a statement issued several minutes before his death, Mr. Willie said: "Killing people is wrong. . . . It makes no difference whether it's citizens, countries, or governments. Killing is wrong."

—"Death and Justice," Edward Koch

■ **LEAD-IN, THESIS, AND ESSAY MAP**   The introduction to an explaining essay—whether one paragraph or several—usually contains the following features.

- **Lead-in:** Some example, description, startling statement, statistic, short narrative, allusion, or quotation to get the reader's interest *and* focus on the topic the writer will explain.
- **Thesis:** Statement of the main idea; a "promise" to the reader that the essay fulfills.
- **Essay map:** A sentence, or part of a sentence, that *lists* (in the order in which the essay discusses them) the main subtopics for the essay.

In her essay on anorexia nervosa at the end of this chapter, Nancie Brosseau's introductory paragraph has all three features.

Lead-in: Startling statement

Description

Statistics

Thesis

Essay map

I knew my dieting had gotten out of hand, but when I could actually see the movement of my heart beating beneath my clothes, I knew I was in trouble. At first, the family doctor reassured my parents that my rapid weight loss was a "temporary phase among teenage girls." However, when I, at fourteen years old and five feet tall, weighed in at sixty-three pounds, my doctor changed his diagnosis from "temporary phase" to "anorexia nervosa." Anorexia nervosa is the process of self-starvation that affects over 100,000 young girls each year. Almost 6,000 of these girls die every year. Anorexia nervosa is a self-mutilating disease that affects its victim both physically and emotionally.

The essay map is contained in the phrase "both physically and emotionally": The first half of the essay discusses the physical effects of anorexia nervosa; the second half explains the emotional effects. Like a road map, the essay map helps the reader anticipate what topics the writer will explain.

■ **PARAGRAPH TRANSITIONS AND HOOKS**   Transition words and paragraph hooks are audience cues that help the reader shift from one paragraph to the next. These connections between paragraphs help the reader see the relationships of the various parts. Transition words—*first, second, next, another, last, finally,* and so forth—signal your reader that a new idea or a new part of the idea is coming up. In addition to transition words, writers often tie paragraphs together by using a key word or idea from a previous paragraph in the first sentence of the following paragraph to "hook" the paragraphs together. The following paragraphs from James Twitchell's "Miss Clairol's 'Does She . . . Or Doesn't She?' " illustrate how transition words and paragraph hooks work together to create smooth connections between paragraphs. (The complete essay appears in Chapter 6.)

As was to become typical in hair-coloring ads, the age of the model was a good ten years younger than the typical product user. The model is in her early thirties (witness the age of the child), too young to have gray hair.

This (inspirational motif) was picked up later for other Clairol products: "If I've only one life . . . let me live it as a blonde!" "Every woman should be a redhead . . . at least once in her life!" "What would your husband say if suddenly you looked 10 years younger?" "Is it true blondes have more fun?" "What does he look at second?" And, of course, "The closer he gets, the better you look!"

Hook: "aspirational motif"

But (these slogans) for different brand extensions only work because Miss Clairol had done her job. She made hair coloring possible, she made hair coloring acceptable, she made at-home hair coloring—dare I say it—empowering. She made the unique into the commonplace. By the 1980s, the hairdresser problem had been long forgotten and the follow-up lines read, "Hair color so natural, they'll never know for sure."

Transition: "But"

Hook: "these slogans"

■ **BODY PARAGRAPHS**   Body paragraphs in expository writing are the main paragraphs in an essay, excluding any introductory, concluding, or transition paragraphs. They often contain the following features.

- **Topic sentence:** To promote clarity and precision, writers often use topic sentences to announce the main ideas of paragraphs. The main idea should be clearly related to the writer's thesis. A topic sentence usually occurs early in the paragraph (first or second sentence) or at the end of the paragraph.

- **Unity:** To avoid confusing readers, writers focus on a single idea for each paragraph. Writing unified paragraphs helps writers—and their readers—concentrate on one point at a time.

- **Coherence:** To make their writing flow smoothly from one sentence to the next, writers supplement their shaping strategies with coherence devices: repeated key words, pronouns referring to key nouns, and transition words.

The following body paragraphs from James Twitchell's "Miss Clairol's 'Does She . . . Or Doesn't She?'" illustrates these features. The second sentence in the first paragraph is the *topic sentence* for the first paragraph—and the second paragraph as well. That topic sentence focuses our attention on the process of "automatic color tinting." These two paragraphs have *unity* because they keep the focus on the "automatic" process of hair tinting. The two paragraphs also achieve *coherence* through the use of transitions and repeated key words and ideas.

Topic sentence

Coherence & repeated key words

Transitions

The copy block on the right is all business and was never changed during the campaign. *The process of coloring is always referred to as "automatic color tinting."* Automatic was to the fifties what *plastic* became to the sixties, and what *networking* is today. Just as your food was kept automatically fresh in the refrigerator, your car had an automatic transmission, your house had an automatic thermostat, your dishes and clothes were automatically cleaned and dried, so, too, your hair had automatic tinting.

However, what is really automatic about hair coloring is that once you start, you won't stop. Hair grows, roots show, buy more product . . . automatically. The genius of Gillette was not just that they sold the "safety razor" (they could give the razor away), *but that they also sold* the concept of being *clean-shaven.* Clean-shaven means that you use their blade every day, so, of course, you always need more blades. Clairol made "roots showing" into what Gillette had made "five o'clock shadow."

CHOOSING	COLLECTING	SHAPING	DRAFTING	REVISING

DRAFTING

Before you begin drafting, reconsider your purpose and audience. What you explain depends on what your audience needs to know or what would demonstrate or show your point most effectively.

As you work from an outline or from an organizing strategy, remember that all three questions—*what, how,* and *why*—are interrelated. If you are writing about causes, for example, an explanation of *what* the topic is and *how* the causes function may also be necessary to explain your subject clearly. As you write, balance your sense of plan and organization with a willingness to pursue ideas that you discover as you write. While you need to have a plan, you should be ready to change course if you discover a more interesting idea or angle.

CHOOSING	COLLECTING	SHAPING	DRAFTING	REVISING

REVISING

As you revise your explaining essay, concentrate on making yourself perfectly clear, on illustrating with examples where your reader might be confused, and on signaling the relationship of the parts of your essay to your reader.

GUIDELINES FOR REVISION

- **Review your purpose, audience, and genre.** Is your purpose clear to your target audience? Should you modify your chosen genre to appeal to your audience?

- **Review possibilities for visuals or graphics.** What additions or changes to images might be appropriate for your purpose, genre, or audience?

- **Compare your thesis sentence with what you say in your conclusion.** You may have a clearer statement of your thesis near the end of your paper. Revise your original thesis sentence to make it clearer, more focused, or more in line with what your essay actually says.

- **Explaining means *showing* and *demonstrating* relationships.** Be sure to follow general statements with *specific examples, details, facts, statistics, memories, dialogues,* or other *illustrations.*

- **In a formal definition, be sure to include the class of objects or concepts to which the term belongs.** Avoid ungrammatical writing, such as "Photosynthesis is *when* plants absorb oxygen" or "The lymphatic system is *where* the body removes bacteria and transports fatty cells."

- **Avoid introducing definitions with "Webster says. . . ."** Instead, read definitions from several dictionaries and give the best or most appropriate definition.

- **Remember that you can modify the dictionary definition of a term or concept to fit your particular context.** For example, to you, *heroism* may mean having the courage to *say* what you believe, not just to endanger your life through selfless actions.

- **Don't mix categories when you are classifying objects or ideas.** If you are classifying houses *by floor design* (ranch, bilevel, split-level, two-story), don't bring in other categories, such as passive-solar, which could be incorporated into any of those designs.

- **In explaining *how* something occurs or should be done, be sure to indicate to your audience which steps are *most important.***

- **In cause-and-effect explanations, avoid post hoc fallacies.** This term comes from the Latin phrase *post hoc, ergo propter hoc:* "After this, therefore because of this." For example, just because Event B occurred after Event A, it does not follow, necessarily, that A caused B. If, for example, statistics

> **❝** I wish he would explain his explanation. **❞**
> —LORD BYRON,
> POET

PEER RESPONSE

The instructions that follow will help you give and receive constructive advice about the rough draft of your explaining essay. You may use these guidelines for an in-class workshop, a take-home review, or a computer e-mail response.

Writer: Before you exchange drafts with another reader, write out the following on your essay draft.

1. **Purpose** Briefly describe your purpose, genre, and intended audience.
2. **Revision plans** What do you still intend to work on as you revise your draft?
3. **Questions** Write out one or two questions that you still have about your draft. What questions would you like your reader to answer?

Reader: First, read the entire draft from start to finish. As you reread the draft, answer the following questions.

1. **Clarity** What passages were clearest? Where were you most confused? Refer to specific sentences or passages to support your response. How and where could the writer make the draft clearer?
2. **Evidence** Where does the writer have good supporting evidence (specific examples, facts, visuals, statistics, interview results, or citations from sources)? Where does the writer need additional evidence? Refer to specific sentences or passages to support your response.
3. **Organization** Summarize or briefly outline the main ideas of the essay. Where was the organization most clear? Where were you confused? Refer to specific passages as you suggest ways to improve the draft.
4. **Purpose** Underline sentences that express the purpose or contain the thesis of the essay. Does your understanding of the essay's purpose match the writer's statement about purpose? Explain. How might the writer clarify the thesis for the intended audience?
5. **Reader's response** Overall, describe what you liked best about the draft. Then identify one major area that the writer should focus on during the revision. Does your suggestion match the writer's revision plans? Explain. Answer the writer's own question or questions about the draft.

show that traffic fatalities in your state actually declined after the speed limit on interstate highways was increased, you should not conclude that higher speeds actually caused the reduction in fatalities. Other causes—increased radar patrols, stiffer drunk-driving penalties, or more rigorous vehicle-maintenance laws—may have been responsible for the reduction.

- **As you revise to sharpen your meaning or make your organization clearer, use appropriate transitional words and phrases to signal the** *relationships among the various parts of your subject.*
  —*To signal relation in time:* before, meanwhile, later, soon, at last, earlier, thereafter, afterward, by that time, from then on, first, next, now, presently, shortly, immediately, finally
  —*To signal similarity:* likewise, similarly, once again, once more
  —*To signal difference:* but, yet, however, although, whereas, though, even so, nonetheless, still, on the other hand, on the contrary
  —*To signal consequences:* as a result, consequently, therefore, hence, for this reason

---

POSTSCRIPT ON THE WRITING PROCESS

Before you hand in your essay, reflect on your writing and learning process. In your journal, spend a few minutes answering the following questions.

1. Describe the purpose and intended audience for your essay.

2. What was the best workshop advice that you received? What did you revise in your draft because of that advice? What piece of advice did you ignore? Why?

3. What caused you the most difficulty with this essay? How did you solve the problem—or attempt to solve it? With what parts are you still least satisfied?

4. What are the best parts of your paper? Refer to specific paragraphs—what do you like most about them?

5. If you added visual images or special document-design features to your essay, explain how they supported your purpose or rhetorical goals.

6. What was the most important thing you learned about writing or your writing process as you wrote this paper?

STUDENT WRITING   ✕

CHRISTINE BISHOP   x

English Only

Christine Bishop decided to write on "English Only" as one of her semester portfolio topics. She had become interested in the topic in a previous year when she went to a speech tournament that debated the English-only issue. She wrote the following essay as the first step in her semester portfolio project. Following this explaining essay, she wrote a persuasive essay, arguing against English-only legislation. For this initial essay, however, she focused on reading key articles about English only, exploring the issues in each article, and explaining key arguments on both sides. Her goal was not to argue for one side or the other, but to explore the issues and explain the arguments on both sides of the English-only debate. As you read her essay, see if she explains the major arguments for both sides in a clear and balanced manner.

PREWRITING FOR TOPIC PROPOSAL

The English-only issue is a very controversial issue. Some say America should adopt an official language policy. Others think that this is a very racist idea. I have been reviewing reports of a recent vote on making Puerto Rico a state. Part of the legislation centered on making the people of Puerto Rico (which is predominantly Spanish-speaking) adopt English as their official language. Supporters of this bill claim that it is necessary that the Puerto Ricans learn English to become Americanized. Other people feel this will take away their language rights. Some people speculate that the English-only movement is a xenophobic reaction to the 1960 immigration amendments. These amendments made it illegal to restrict citizenship to America based on race. With this new amendment, there has been an influx in immigrants from diverse places. This influx of people could lead to xenophobia (fear of strangers or foreigners). I feel this speculation may be true. In 1912, when New Mexico became a state, it was allowed to keep Spanish as its official language provided that English was also an official language. Why such a radical change in policy when Puerto Rico applies to be a state? Is America afraid that it will lose its identity to non-English-speaking people? America started out as a conglomerate of immigrants who did not all speak the same language. What now?

I would like to explore this topic more. The two main positions on English-only legislation are as follows:

1. English needs to be the official language of the United States because we need one unifying language. Without English-only laws, immigrants will not learn English and will not contribute to society.

2. It is unfair to expect current citizens in the United States to learn English. Making English official will make people not learn other languages.

I know some about this subject, but I haven't done much research on my own. The questions I have are whether I could tie this into racism and whether I will be able to get enough information in the library and on the Internet.

FIRST DRAFT

The issue has been raised that the United States needs to make English the official language of the nation. Currently, the Senate is reviewing a proposal to require Puerto Rico to adopt English as its official language before considering it for statehood. While everyone agrees that it is important for all Americans to speak English, there is disagreement as to whether the government should adopt an official language policy. Those who support an official language policy (such as Richard Rodriguez) believe that without a policy, immigrants to America will not learn English. Those who do not support this policy believe that there is enough pressure on immigrants, and that they have enough desire to learn English quickly on their own. Some who oppose an official English policy believe that this policy will alienate immigrants and that Americans who support this policy are having a xenophobic reaction to recent immigrants from more diverse cultures initiated by 1960s immigration laws. I would like to explain exactly what these opposing positions are, using essays written by Richard Rodriguez, Samuel Hayakawa, James Crawford, and James Fallows.

As a champion of English-only legislation, Richard Rodriguez believes that without the government to push them into learning English, immigrants will not learn the language. In "Aria: A Memoir of a Bilingual Childhood," Mr. Rodriguez states, "What I did not believe was that I could speak a single public language. . . . It would have pleased me to hear my teachers address me in Spanish. . . . But I would have delayed—for how long postponed?—having to learn the language of public society [English]." Although Rodriguez was born in the United States, being the son of migrant workers, he had not been exposed to English until he had entered school. Without the church (he attended a Catholic school) to force him to learn English, he believes he would never have learned to speak English. Like all people on both sides of the issue, Rodriguez believes that it is necessary to speak English to succeed in the United States. Because Rodriguez was not motivated to speak English as a child, he feels that it is imperative for the government to push immigrants to learn English by making English the official language of the United States. People opposing English being the official language believe immigrants desire to learn English.

Both James Fallows, in "Viva Bilingualism," and James Crawford, author of *Hold Your Tongue: Bilingualism and the Politics of English Only,* oppose English-only legislation. Fallows, an English-speaking American who lived in Japan, feels that his experiences are contradictory to these beliefs. While living in Japan—a country that "makes many more accommodations to the English language than America does to Spanish"—Fallows found that most English-speaking people learned Japanese in order to participate in society. In America, Fallows thinks the incentives for immigrants to learn English are greater. The only way to get any kind of white-collar job or to attend college, according to Fallows, is through learning English. English is how communities in America are built.

Other English-only supporters, like former Senator Samuel Hayakawa, feel that a common language in the United States would better unite Americans. Hayakawa uses the example of Chinese- and Japanese-Americans, who didn't get along during World War II. Now they have begun to form Asian-American groups. Hayakawa believes this is the result of having learned English. Hayakawa states, "A common tongue encourages trust while reducing racial hostility and bigotry." Hayakawa believes that unless the United States implements an English-only policy, we will head the way of Quebec or India—"a chaotic mess which has led to countless problems in the government's efforts to manage the nation's business." According to Hayakawa, this problem is already apparent. He blames the 50 percent dropout rate among Hispanic students on the current bilingual policy.

People who do not support English-only, like James Crawford, do not believe that the differences in language will cause chaos. They further believe that an official English policy will separate Americans. In his book, James Crawford quotes Raul Yazquirre, President of the National Council of La Raza, as saying: "U.S. English is to Hispanics as the Ku Klux Klan is to blacks." Crawford says that this is the consensus among Latino leaders. Crawford goes on to say that Latino leaders believe English only "is a Xenophobic, intolerant act."

Because I believe that Rodriguez's experience might be unique and that there are many other people's experiences pointing the other way—including my own—I think Hayakawa's argument may be shaky. Possibly, Crawford and Fallows, because of their experience, may be correct. Crawford has spent ten years researching the issue, which gives his argument credibility. I think that although it is quite debatable, the new push for English as an official language may be due to a backlash against the recent influx of more diverse groups into the United States. But determining exactly how government laws might affect the motivation of immigrants to learn English is difficult. We seem to have different personal testimonies: Hayakawa and Rodriguez think an English-only policy will encourage immigrants to learn English; Fallows and Crawford think immigrants already have enough incentives to learn English.

FINAL DRAFT
English Only

English-only laws have been in the news again, with a recent debate in the   *1*
Senate over a requirement that Puerto Rico adopt English as its official language before being allowed to become a state (Gugliotta 1). In the United States, English-only laws currently exist in twenty-three states—having passed recently in Alaska and Missouri—but they suffered a setback in Arizona, where the United States Supreme Court upheld a decision that struck down an Arizona law that passed originally in 1988 (Denniston 1). Basically, English-only laws such as Arizona's state that "this state and all political subdivisions of this state shall act in English and no other language" (Denniston 2). While everyone agrees that it is important for all Americans to speak English, there is disagreement as to whether state governments should adopt an official language policy.

The debate over "English only" continues as groups such as U.S.   *2*
English try to promote language laws in every state. Those who support

...*continued* English Only, **Christine Bishop**

an official language policy believe that without a policy, immigrants will not learn English. Those who oppose an official English policy believe that English-only laws alienate immigrants and that Americans who support these laws are having a xenophobic reaction to the flood of recent immigrants from more diverse cultures. In order to explain what this debate is about and what the major issues are on both sides, I will look primarily at four authors who have written about English-only laws. Two writers who support English only are the late Senator Samuel Hayakawa and Richard Rodriguez, author of *Hunger of Memory*. Two authors who oppose English only are James Fallows, Washington editor of *Atlantic* magazine, and James Crawford, author of *Hold Your Tongue: Bilingualism and the Politics of English Only*.

Those who support an English-only policy feel that it will encourage immigrants and non-English-speaking Americans to speak English. In his essay, "Bilingualism in America: English Should Be the *Only* Language," Hayakawa uses the example of Chinese- and Japanese-Americans, who didn't get along during World War II. Now they have begun to form Asian-American groups (252). Hayakawa believes this is the result of having learned English. Hayakawa states, "A common tongue encourages trust while reducing racial hostility and bigotry" (252). Hayakawa, one of the original founders of U.S. English, believes that unless the United States implements an English-only policy, we will head the way of Quebec or India: India's "ten official languages" have created a situation that is "a chaotic mess which has led to countless problems in the government's efforts to manage the nation's business" (253). According to Hayakawa, the problem in the United States is already apparent. He blames the 50 percent dropout rate among Hispanic students on the current bilingual policy (254). Writers such as Hayakawa forecast a Tower of Babel. They believe that unless we adopt an English-only policy, immigrants will not learn English and U.S. citizens will not be able to communicate with each other. Of course, Hayakawa's analogy with Quebec and India may be difficult to support, because immigrants to the United States have always learned English, whereas in Quebec and India, people have always spoken different languages.

As a champion of English-only legislation, Richard Rodriguez, like the late Senator Hayakawa, believes that without the government to push immigrants into learning English, they will not learn English. In "Aria:

A Memoir of a Bilingual Childhood," Rodriguez states, "What I needed to learn in school was that I had the right, and the obligation, to speak the public language. . . . It would have pleased me to hear my teachers address me in Spanish. . . . But I would have delayed—postponed for how long?—having to learn the language of public society" (270). Although Rodriguez was born in the United States, the son of migrant workers, he was not exposed to English until he entered school. Without his Catholic schoolteachers' forcing him to learn English, Rodriguez believes that he would never have learned to speak the public language (271). Like people on both sides of the English-only issue, Rodriguez believes that to succeed in the United States, it is necessary to be proficient in English. Because Rodriguez was not motivated to speak English as a child, he feels that it is imperative for the government to push immigrants to learn English by making English the official language of the United States.

In addition, the website for U.S. English agrees with Hayakawa and 5 Rodriguez that without English-only legislation, immigrants will "fail to learn English and separate into linguistic enclaves. This division of the United States into separate language groups contributes to racial and ethnic conflicts" (U.S. English 1). This is, of course, a controversial position because many other people believe that immigrants have plenty of incentive to learn English on their own, and those people have history to cite as evidence.

On the other side of the English-only debate, James Fallows, a Wash- 6 ington editor of *Atlantic* magazine and author of "Viva Bilingualism," believes that there are enough incentives for immigrants to learn English without adding pressure to the situation. Fallows, an English-speaking American who lived in Japan, feels that his experiences show that English-only laws are unnecessary. When living in Japan, a country that "makes many more accommodations to the English language than America does to Spanish," Fallows found that he, as well as most English-speaking people, needed to learn Japanese to participate in society (262). In America, Fallows thinks the incentives for immigrants to learn English are greater. The only way to get a white-collar job or to attend college, according to Fallows, is to learn English. As Fallows puts it, in America, you can't take the SATs in Spanish or even watch *David Letterman* (262).

Writers such as James Fallows who do not support an English-only 7 policy do not believe that the differences in language will cause chaos. However, some believe that an official English-only policy will actually separate Americans. James Crawford, author of *Hold Your Tongue: Bilingualism and the Politics of English Only*, argues that English-only laws are racist and xenophobic. Crawford quotes Raul Yazguierre, President of the National Council of La Raza, as saying, "U.S. English is to Hispanics as the Ku Klux Klan is to blacks" (1). Crawford says that this is the consensus among Latino leaders. Crawford goes on to say that Latino leaders believe English only is a xenophobic, intolerant act (1). When Spanish leaders are saying that English only is similar to something extreme like the KKK, something has to be wrong. That Latino leaders link English only to the KKK, coupled with the fact that immigrants have always learned English on their own, seems to be compelling evidence that many people think English-only laws are unnecessary and possibly destructive.

If there is any middle ground in this debate, I find it difficult to 8 explain. Often, arguments on both sides seem to come down to personal experiences. Rodriguez thinks his experiences show that there should be the pressure of English-only laws; Fallows's experiences in Japan persuade him that there are already sufficient pressures to encourage immigrants to learn English. Hayakawa does point to real problems in countries such as Canada and India, but his statistics may be shaky. Hayakawa quotes Hispanics as having a 50 percent dropout rate, saying that this could be due to the lack of English proficiency, and then later states that 90 percent of the Hispanics in the United States are fluent in English (254,255). These two statements are contradictory and weaken Hayakawa's position. Crawford and Fallows, because of their experience, do have legitimate points. Crawford spent ten years of research on the issue, which adds to his credibility. In addition, Fallows has personal experience similar to my own. When I was living in a foreign country, I felt continual pressure to learn the language spoken in my host country, and because I did not have my family around, I couldn't hide from the new language and culture.

It is difficult to determine the long-term effects of English-only legislation. I haven't found any evidence that the laws in twenty-three states 9 have increased the number of immigrants who speak English, but I have found evidence that the debate about these laws can be heated and divisive. Although this issue is certainly debatable, I believe that the new push for English as an official language may be due to a backlash against the recent influx of more diverse groups into the United States. If state governments continue to support that backlash, it may further alienate our new citizens. On the other hand, many immigrants don't learn English very quickly, and they survive in linguistic enclaves, separated by language barriers from mainstream American culture. Possibly the economic pressures of earning a living will have a far greater effect on encouraging immigrants to learn English than any official English laws. If the momentum for English-only laws persists in state legislatures, we will continue to see arguments from both sides used in the debate.

Works Cited

Crawford, James. *Hold Your Tongue: Bilingualism and the Politics of English Only.* Reading, MA: Addison Wesley, 1992. 24 Sept. 1998. http://ourworld. compuserve.com/homepages/JWCRAWFORD/home.html.

Denniston, Lyle. "English-Only Measure Dealt Blow." *Baltimore Sun.* 12 Jan. 1998. 11 Jan. 1999. http://www.sunspot.net/cgibin/editorial.

Fallows, James. "Viva Bilingualism." *Exploring Language.* Ed. Gary Goshgarian. 8th ed. New York: Addison Wesley Longman, 1998. 259–63.

Gugliotta, Guy. "House Passes Puerto Rico Bill." *Washington Post Online.* 5 March 1998. 24 Sept. 1998. http://ourworld.compuserve.com/homepages/ JWCRAWFORD/WPOST4.html.

Hayakawa, S. I. "Bilingualism in America: English Should Be the *Only* Language." *Exploring Language.* Ed. Gary Goshgarian. 8th ed. New York: Addison Wesley Longman, 1998. 251–56.

Rodriguez, Richard. "Aria: A Memoir of a Bilingual Childhood." *Exploring Language.* Ed. Gary Goshgarian. 8th ed. New York: Addison Wesley Longman, 1998. 266–75.

U.S. English Page. 13 Jan. 1999. http://www.us-english.org/why.htm.

QUESTIONS FOR WRITING AND DISCUSSION

1. Compare Bishop's first and revised drafts. What information and explanations did she add in the revised version? How did she reorganize her essay for the revised version? Explain.

2. Bishop's purpose in this first essay for her portfolio was to explore the arguments on each side of the English-only debate and then explain these arguments to her reader. She did *not* want to argue for or against English only until the final essay in her portfolio. What paragraphs does she devote to

the advocates of the English-only movement? What paragraphs explain the arguments of those who oppose English only. Does she balance the arguments without taking sides herself? Explain.

3. Explaining essays should define key terms, concepts, or ideas. What terms or ideas does Bishop explain or define? Are there other terms or ideas that she needed to define? Explain.

4. Assume that Bishop wants your advice about how to revise her essay into an argumentative essay, arguing against English-only legislation. Consult the Guidelines for Revision in this chapter. What audience or publication might she choose? In terms of revising the genre, should she write an editorial in a newspaper or a longer essay that might be published in a magazine? Are there additional cultural viewpoints she might consider to make her argument effective for her audience? Would more background information or definitions be helpful? Write out your recommendations.

STUDENT WRITING   X

NANCIE BROSSEAU   x

Anorexia Nervosa

In her essay on anorexia nervosa, Nancie Brosseau writes from her own experience, explaining what anorexia nervosa is and what its effects are. Her essay succeeds not only because it is organized clearly, but also because it is so vivid and memorable. Relying on specific details, her explanation shows the effects of anorexia on her life.

I knew my dieting had gotten out of hand, but when I could actually see   1
the movement of my heart beating beneath my clothes, I knew I was in trouble. At first, the family doctor reassured my parents that my rapid weight loss was a "temporary phase among teenage girls." However, when I, at fourteen years old and five feet tall, weighed in at sixty-three pounds, my doctor changed his diagnosis from "temporary phase" to "anorexia nervosa." Anorexia nervosa is the process of self-starvation that affects over 100,000 young girls each year. Almost 6,000 of these girls die every year. Anorexia nervosa is a self-mutilating disease that affects its victim both physically and emotionally.

    As both a gymnast and a dancer, I was constantly surrounded by   2
lithe, muscular people, all of them extremely conscious about their

weight. Although I wasn't overweight to begin with, I thought that if I lost five to ten pounds I would look, feel, dance, and tumble better. I figured the quickest way to accomplish this was by drastically limiting my intake of food. By doing this, I lost ten pounds in one week and gained the approval of my peers. Soon, I could no longer control myself, and ten pounds turned into twenty, twenty into forty, and so on, until I finally ended up weighing fifty-eight pounds.

Several serious health problems bombarded me, and it's a wonder   *3* I'm still alive. Because my body was receiving no nourishment at all, my muscles and essential organs, including my heart, liver, kidneys, and intestines, started to compensate by slowly disintegrating. My body was feeding on itself! As my weight plummeted, my circulation grew increasingly worse. My hands, feet, lips, and ears took on a bluish-purple tint, and I was constantly freezing cold. My hair started to fall out and my whole body took on a very skeletal appearance. My eyes appeared to have sunken into my face, and my forehead, cheekbones, and chin protruded sharply. My wrists were the largest part of my entire arm, as were my knees the widest part of my legs. My pants rubbed my hips raw because I had to wear my belts at their tightest notch to keep them up. I would force myself to vomit as soon as possible if I was forced to eat. The enamel on my teeth started to be eaten away by the acid in the vomit, and my lips cracked and bled regularly. I stopped menstruating completely because I was not producing enough estrogen. Instead of improving my skills as a dancer and a gymnast, I drastically reduced them because I was so weak. One time, while executing a chain of back handsprings, I broke all five fingers on one hand and three on the other because my bones had become so brittle. My doctor realized the serious danger I was in and told me I either had to see a psychologist or be put in the hospital. I chose to see a psychologist, and she helped me sort out the emotional aspects of anorexia, which in turn solved the physical problems.

The emotional problems associated with anorexia nervosa are   *4* equally disastrous to the victim's health. Self-deception, lying, and depression are three examples of the emotions and actions an anorexic often experiences. During my entire bout with anorexia, I deceived myself into thinking I had complete control over my body. Hunger pains became a pleasant feeling, and sore muscles from overexercising just proved to me that I still needed to lose more weight. When my psychologist showed me pictures of girls that were of normal weight for my age group,

…continued   Anorexia Nervosa, **Nancie Brosseau**

they honestly looked obese to me. I truly believed that even the smallest amount of food would make me extremely fat.

Another problem, lying, occurred most often when my parents tried to force me to eat. Because I was at the gym until around eight o'clock every night, I told my mother not to save me dinner. I would come home and make a sandwich and feed it to my dog. I lied to my parents every day about eating lunch at school. For example, I would bring a sack lunch and sell it to someone and use the money to buy diet pills. I always told my parents that I ate my own lunch. I lied to my doctor when he asked if I was taking an appetite suppressant. I had to cover one lie with another to keep from being found out, although it was obvious that I was not eating by looking at me.

Still another emotion I felt, as a result of my anorexia, was severe depression. It seemed that, no matter how hard I tried, I kept growing fatter. Of course, I was getting thinner all the time, but I couldn't see that. One time, I licked a postage stamp to put on a letter and immediately remembered that there was 1/4 of a calorie in the glue on the stamp. I punished myself by doing 100 extra situps every night for one week. I pinched my skin until it bruised as I lay awake at night because I was so ashamed of the way I thought I looked. I doomed myself to a life of obesity. I would often slip into a mood my psychologist described as a "blue funk." That is, I would become so depressed, I seriously considered committing suicide. The emotional instabilities associated with anorexia nervosa can be fatal.

Through psychological and physical treatment, I was able to overcome anorexia nervosa. I still have a few complications today due to anorexia, such as dysmenorrhea (severe menstrual cramps) and the tendency to fast. However, these problems are minute compared to the problems I would have had if I hadn't received immediate help. Separately, the physical and emotional problems that anorexia nervosa creates can greatly harm its victim. However, when the two are teamed together, the results are deadly.

QUESTIONS FOR WRITING AND DISCUSSION

1. Without looking back at this essay, jot down the specific examples that you found most memorable. How would you describe these examples: tedious and commonplace, eye-opening, shocking, upsetting, persuasive? Explain.

2. Identify the thesis statement and essay map. Referring to paragraph numbers, show how the essay map sets up the organization of the essay.

3. Reread the opening sentences of each body paragraph. Identify one opening sentence that creates a smooth transition from the previous paragraph. Identify one opening sentence in which the transition could be smoother. Revise this sentence to improve the transition with a paragraph hook.

4. In this essay, Brosseau defines anorexia nervosa, explains its physical and emotional effects (and hints at its causes), and analyzes the process of the disorder, from its inception to its cure. Identify passages that illustrate each of these strategies: definition, cause-and-effect analysis, and process analysis.

5. A recent study by Judith Rabek-Wagener and her colleagues has shown that the "mass marketing of body images through print media and television and advertising" has helped cause nearly 65 percent of young women and 35 percent of young men to "experience significant dissatisfaction with their body size, shape, condition, or appearance." For the complete article, see "The Effect of Media Analysis on . . . Body Image Among College Students" in the *Journal of American College Health*, August 1, 1998. Read the research on the connection between the media and eating disorders and then write your own essay explaining the causes of eating disorders or the effects that the media have on college students' self-images.

Diego Rivera (1886–1957)
Portrait of Ramón Gómez de la Serna
Oil on canvas
Private Collection, Christie's Images

Spanish writer Ramón Gómez de la Serna (1888–1963), the subject of this painting by Diego Rivera, was a prolific and creative novelist, biographer, and critic. The journal exercise on page 413 invites you to compare the style of this painting with Rivera's style in *The Flower Carrier* on page 150.

Evaluating

9

During your fall semester library-orientation tour, you discover a small office tucked away in the corner of the library building: the interlibrary loan office. Because you occasionally need to see articles and books that your library does not have, you decide to investigate the interlibrary loan service and evaluate the helpfulness of the staff as well as the convenience, speed, and cost of obtaining materials. As part of your evaluation, you interview the office coordinator as well as several teachers and students who have used the service. Their responses—combined with your own observations—indicate that although an interlibrary loan can sometimes take a couple of weeks, the loan office gets high marks for its service. The staff is always helpful and patient, the service is easily accessible through electronic mail, and the cost of books and articles is surprisingly low.

In a letter to your parents, you explain that you are considering transferring to a different school for the following year. You have some misgivings about your decision to change, but after listing your criteria and ranking them in order from most to least important, you are convinced that you're making the right choice. In the letter, you explain your decision, based on your criteria, and ask that your parents continue to support your education.

> ❝ When we evaluate, we have in mind . . . an ideal of what a good thing—pianist, painting, or professor—should be and do, and we apply that ideal to the individual instance before us. ❞
> —JEANNE FAHNESTOCK AND MARIE SECOR, AUTHORS OF *A RHETORIC OF ARGUMENT*

> ❝ Purpose and craftsmanship—ends and means—these are the keys to your judgment. ❞
> —MARYA MANNES, JOURNALIST AND SOCIAL COMMENTATOR

Hardly a day passes that we do not express our likes or dislikes. We constantly pass judgment on people, places, objects, events, ideas, and policies. "Sue is a wonderful person." "The food in this cafeteria is horrible." "That movie we saw Saturday night ought to get an Oscar nomination for best picture." "Going to war with Iraq was the wrong response to international terrorism." "The Atkins diet is nothing more than a passing fad." In addition to our own reactions, we are constantly exposed to the opinions of our friends, family members, teachers, and business associates. The media also barrage us with claims about products, famous personalities, and candidates for political office.

A claim or opinion, however, is not an *evaluation.* Your reaction to a person, a sports event, a meal, a movie, or a public policy becomes an evaluation *only* when you support your value judgment with clear standards and specific evidence. Your goal in evaluating something is not only to express your viewpoint, but also to *persuade* others to accept your judgment. You convince your readers by indicating the standards for your judgment and then supporting it with evidence: "The food in this cafeteria is horrible [your claim]. I know that not all cafeteria food tastes great, but it should at least be sanitary [one standard of judgment]. Yesterday, I had to dig a piece of green mold out of the meat loaf, and just as I stuck my fork into the green salad, a large black roach ran out [evidence]."

Most people interested in a subject agree that certain standards are important, for example, that a cafeteria be clean and pest-free. The standards that you share with your audience are the *criteria* for your evaluation. You convince your readers that something is good or bad, ugly or beautiful, tasty or nauseating by analyzing your subject in terms of your criteria. For each separate criterion, you support your judgment with specific *evidence:* descriptions, statistics, testimony, or examples from your personal experience. If your readers agree that your standards or criteria are appropriate, and if you supply detailed evidence, your readers should be convinced. They will take your evaluation seriously—and think twice about eating at that roach-infested cafeteria.

TECHNIQUES   **PROCESS**

Techniques for Writing Evaluations

The most common genre for evaluations is the review. Most frequently, we read reviews of films, books, restaurants, commercial products, public performances, and works of art. Reviews vary widely depending on the topic, the place of publication, and the social context. Some reviews seem to be little more than thinly disguised promotions, while other reviews are thorough, complex, and highly critical. For any substantive evaluation, the review must set standards of judgment, rely on fair criteria, balance positive and negative evaluations, and provide sufficient evidence to persuade its readers. Use the following techniques as you write your evaluation.

> *It is as hard to find a neutral critic as it is a neutral country in a time of war.*
> —KATHERINE ANNE PORTER,
> NOVELIST AND SHORT STORY WRITER

- **Assessing the rhetorical situation.** What is the social occasion and context for your review? Find examples of the genre you propose to write—where are these reviews typically published? Who is the audience, and what do they already believe or know about the topic?

- **Stating an *overall claim* about your subject.** This statement serves as the *thesis* for your evaluation.

- **Describing the person, place, object, text, event, service, or performance being evaluated.** Readers need basic information—*who, what, when,* and *where*—to form a clear judgment.

- **Clarifying the *criteria* for your evaluation.** A criterion is a standard of judgment that most people interested in your subject agree is important. A criterion serves as a yardstick against which you measure your subject.

- **Stating a *judgment* for each criterion.** The overall claim is based on your judgment of each separate criterion. Include both positive *and* negative judgments.

- **Supporting each judgment with *evidence*.** Support can include detailed description, facts, examples, testimony, or statistics.

- **Balancing your evaluation with both positive and negative judgments about your subject.** Evaluations that are all positive are merely advertisements; evaluations that are entirely negative may seem too harsh or mean-spirited.

In the following evaluation of a Chinese restaurant in Washington, D.C., journalist and critic Phyllis C. Richman illustrates the main features of an evaluation

Hunan Dynasty

215 Pennsylvania Ave. SE. 546–6161

Open daily 11 A.M. to 3 P.M. for lunch, 3 P.M. to 10 P.M. for dinner, until 11 P.M. on Friday and Saturday.

Reservations suggested for large parties.

Prices for lunch: appetizers $2 to $4.50, entrees $4.75 to $6.50. For dinner: appetizers $1 to $13.95 (combination platter), entrees $6.75 to $18.

Complete dinner with wine or beer, tax, and tip about $20 a person.

Information and description

Description

Chinese restaurants in America were once places one went just to eat. Now one goes to dine. There are now waiters in black tie, cloths on the tables and space between those tables, art on the walls and decoratively carved vegetables on the plate—elegance has become routine in Chinese restaurants. What's more, in Chinese restaurants the ingredients are fresh (have you ever found frozen broccoli in a Chinese kitchen?), and the cooking almost never sinks below decent. . . . And it is usually moderately priced. In other words, if you're among unfamiliar restaurants and looking for good value, Chinese restaurants now are routinely better than ever.

Overall claim

The Hunan Dynasty is an example of what makes Chinese restaurants such reliable choices. A great restaurant? It is not. A good value? Definitely. A restaurant to fit nearly any diner's need? Probably.

Criterion #1: Nice setting

Judgment: Attractive

Evidence

First, it is attractive. There are no silk tassels, blaring red lacquer or Formica tables; instead there are white tablecloths and subtle glass etchings. It is a dining room—or dining rooms, for the vastness has been carved into smaller spaces—of gracefulness and lavish space.

Criterion #2: Good service

Judgment: Often expert

Evidence

Second, service is a strong priority. The waiters look and act polished, and serve with flourishes from the carving of a Peking duck to the portioning of dishes among the diners. I have found some glitches—a forgotten appetizer, a recommendation of two dishes that turned out nearly identical—but most often the service has been expert. . . .

Criterion #3: Good main dishes

Judgment: Good but not memorable

Evidence

As for the main dishes, don't take the "hot and spicy" asterisks too seriously, for this kitchen is not out to offer you a test of fire. The peppers are there, but not in great number. And, like the appetizers, the main dishes are generally good but not often memorable. Fried dishes—and an inordinate number of them seem to be fried—are crunchy and not greasy. Vegetables are bright and crisp. Eggplant with hot garlic sauce is properly unctuous; Peking duck is as fat-free and crackly-skinned as you could hope (though pancakes were rubbery). And seafoods—shrimp, scallops, lobster—are tenderly cooked, though they are not the most full-flavored examples of those ingredients.

Criterion #3 cont.

Judgment: Sometimes bad

Evidence

I have found only one dismal main dish in a fairly broad sampling: lemon chicken had no redeeming feature in its doughy, greasy, overcooked and underseasoned presentation. Otherwise, not much goes wrong. Crispy shrimp with walnuts might be preferable stir-fried rather than batter-fried, but the tomato-red sauce and crunchy walnuts made a good dish. Orange beef could use more seasoning but the coating was nicely crusty and the meat tender. . . .

Overall claim restated

So with the opening of the Hunan Dynasty, Washington did not add a stellar Chinese restaurant to its repertoire, but that is not necessarily what the city needed anyway. Hunan Dynasty is a top-flight neighborhood restaurant—with good food, caring service and very fair prices—that is attractive enough to set a mood for celebration and easygoing enough for an uncomplicated dinner with the family after work.

| PRODUCTS/SERVICES | ART | PERFORMANCES |

EVALUATING COMMERCIAL PRODUCTS OR SERVICES

Writers frequently evaluate commercial products or services. Consumer magazines test and rate every imaginable product or service—from cars and dishwashers to peanut butter and brokerage houses. Guidebooks evaluate tourist spots, restaurants, colleges, and hunting lodges. Specialty magazines, such as *Modern Photography, Road and Track, Skiing,* and *Wired,* often rate products and services of interest to their readers. To qualify as evaluation—and not just advertising—the authors and the publishers must maintain an independent status, uninfluenced by the manufacturers of the products or services they are judging.

Consider, first, the following "evaluation" of a wine, found on a bottle of Cabernet Sauvignon:

> This Cabernet Sauvignon is a dry, robust, and complex wine whose hearty character is balanced by an unusual softness.

This "evaluative" language is so vague and esoteric that it may mean very little to the average consumer who just wants some wine with dinner. *Dry:* How can a liquid be dry? *Robust:* Does this refer to physique? *Soft:* Wine is not a pillow, though it might put you to sleep. *Complex:* Are they describing a wine or conducting a psychological analysis? While an independent evaluator may legitimately use these terms for knowledgeable wine drinkers, this particular description suggests that the wine is absolutely everything the buyer would like it to be—dry yet robust, hearty but at the same time soft. Apparently, the writer's purpose here is not to evaluate a product but to flatter readers who imagine themselves connoisseurs of wine.

Now consider the following evaluation of the gas/electric hybrid car, the Toyota Prius. In the following excerpt from *Consumer Reports,* the editors compare the Prius with the Honda Civic Hybrid in terms of fuel economy, clean emissions, size, and engine technology. In this report, notice also document design and graphics features, including the ratings graph and a sidebar on "The Hybrid Report Card."

The Hybrid Grows Up

Achieving 44 mpg overall in our tests and with near-zero emissions, according to the California Air Resources Board, the redesigned Toyota Prius hybrid car scored well enough in our testing to be named our Top Pick in the Green Car category in the April Auto issue. Its gas mileage is the highest we've recorded in a five-passenger vehicle.

The Prius also outscored the 4 midsized family sedans here and finished sixth out of the 15 similarly priced sedans we've tested (see the Ratings on the next page).

If fuel economy and clean emissions are a priority, the Prius's attributes in these areas combined with its roomy interior, five-passenger seating, and hatchback versatility make it a good alternative to many conventional small or midsized sedans.

However, if you want an excellent all-around family sedan regardless of fuel economy, there are several models, such as the four-cylinder versions of the Honda Accord, Toyota Camry, Mazda6, and Nissan Altima, that are similarly priced and have scored better overall in our tests. The overall fuel economy of those four vehicles ranged from 22 to 24 mpg.

A hybrid vehicle couples an electric motor with a gasoline engine to boost fuel economy and provide cleaner emissions. The Prius uses a 76-hp, 1.5-liter gas engine and a 67-hp electric motor. In contrast to dedicated electric vehicles, hybrids do not need to be plugged in for recharging; the batteries recharge as the car is being driven.

This version of the Prius uses Toyota's second-generation hybrid technology. The car is a significant improvement over the first version, with more interior space, quicker acceleration, better gas mileage, and cleaner emis-

close**up**   THE HYBRID REPORT CARD

Hybrid technology is still new, so some long-term questions remain unanswered. Here are some of the considerations regarding hybrid vehicles.

Price. Hybrids typically cost more than similarly sized and equipped conventional cars. The new Prius, however, has reduced the difference.

Reliability. Reliability for the previous Prius and the Honda Civic Hybrid have been excellent, according to our subscribers survey.

Fuel savings. Fuel costs should be about half what they are for comparable cars. At $1.50 per gallon, cars in this class burn about $1,000 worth of fuel in 15,000 miles. At that rate, the Prius would save about $500 per year.

Depreciation. The previous Prius is holding its value fairly well. After three years it loses about 42 percent of its initial value, compared with about 45 percent of the average car.

Battery pack. Hybrids haven't been around long enough for us to collect data on battery-pack reliability, but the Prius's battery pack is guaranteed for 8 years/100,000 miles (10 years/150,000 in states with California emission rules). Toyota estimates that the replacement cost for the battery pack would be about $3,000 to $3,500 if it's not covered by the warranty. But the company expects the price to drop significantly in coming years.

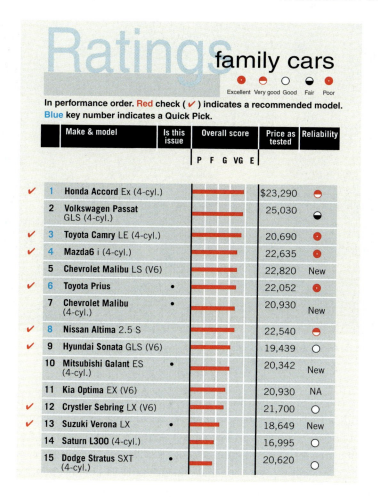

sions, all for about the same price. With optional side and head-protection air bags, our Prius stickered at $22,052. In contrast to the Honda Civic Hybrid sedan, which got 36 mpg overall and uses a smaller electric motor to provide a power boost for the gas engine, the Prius can operate on electric or gasoline power or both, depending on the driving conditions. Overall the scores for the Prius and Civic Hybrid are very close.

PRODUCTS/SERVICES	ART	PERFORMANCES

EVALUATING WORKS OF ART

Evaluations of commercial products and services tend to emphasize usefulness, practicality, convenience, and cost. Evaluations of works of art, on the other hand,

Francisco de Goya, *Los fusilamientos del 3 de Mayo, 1808* (1814). Oil on canvas, 8'6" × 11'4". © Museo Nacional Del Prado Madrid.

focus on form, color, texture, design, balance, image, or theme. Even the phrase "appreciating a work of art" suggests that we are making a value judgment, though usually not one based on money. Through evaluation, writers teach us to appreciate all kinds of art: paintings, sculpture, photographs, buildings, antique cars or furniture, novels, short stories, essays, poems, and tapestries. A Dior fashion, a quilt, a silverware pattern, even an old pair of jeans might be evaluated primarily on aesthetic rather than practical grounds.

In the following selection, art critic Mark Stevens evaluates Francisco Goya's painting *The Third of May*, which is reprinted here. This painting depicts the execution of Spanish hostages by Napoleon's forces, in retaliation for an attack by a mob on the previous day. As Stevens explains, Goya does not portray the doomed hostages as heroic martyrs; instead, he tries to show the horrors of war and death. In doing that, Stevens believes, Goya "told the truth: what happened on the third of May was a butchering."

> The iconography, the color and light, the composition—all contribute to the power of this picture. Its most impressive aspect, in my view, is that Goya . . . transformed the conventions of hope into those of despair. This makes the horror all the greater, for we can see what we have lost, in

(Detail) Francisco de Goya, *Los fusilamientos del 3 de Mayo, 1808* (1814). Oil on canvas, 8'6" × 11'4". © Museo Nacional Del Prado Madrid.

addition to what we have. In the background, for example, the spire of the church is a dark, dim reminder, certainly not a cause for hope. The cruelty of the execution, which takes place in a melodramatic light, reminds us of acts of martyrdom—but without the traditional promise of heavenly reward.

Of course, the outstretched arms of the central figure also recall the Crucifixion, and the man's hands bear stigmata. However, the traditional religious gesture of acceptance—the outstretched arms of Christ—has here been turned into an expression of outrage, terror and meaninglessness. What is the victim saying? There is nothing he can say, for his situation is one in which neither faith nor reason matter. His outflung arms are mirrored by those of the corpse in the foreground: such is the promise of resurrection. The corpse itself is perhaps the most truthful ever painted, for it exhibits the unbearable banality, the crumpled emptiness of death.

The men around the central victim display a variety of other reactions to their fate, none noble. One looks heavenward, but his expression is groveling. The praying man cannot raise his eyes. A third hides his face, as do the victims who await execution. Goya's use of light enhances their horror. The light contains no spiritual overtone, but rather emanates from a common lantern; an intense glow is cast on the small, grisly scene, but it cannot pierce the dark reaches. This light—glaring, without delicacy, lurid, almost artificial—seems peculiarly modern. . . .

In addition to his brilliant use of light and shade, which isolates the central figure, Goya used several other formal devices to make his point. He employed sweeping diagonal lines to scissor the picture into sharp, claustrophobic spaces. He foreshortened the corpse, so that the body seems to draw toward the viewer. (It almost looks as though the dead man is bidding the viewer welcome.) Otherwise, Goya has positioned the figures so that the viewer, curiously, is placed on the side of the executioners. You and I, observing, are implicated in mankind's folly.

PRODUCTS/SERVICES	ART	PERFORMANCES

EVALUATING PERFORMANCES

Evaluating live, recorded, or filmed performances of people in sports, dance, drama, debate, public meetings or lectures, and music may involve practical criteria, such as the prices of tickets to sports events or rock concerts. However, there are also aesthetic criteria that apply to people and their performances. In film evaluations, for example, the usual criteria are good acting and directing, an entertaining or believable story or plot, memorable characters, dramatic special effects, and so forth.

In the following evaluation of *The Lord of the Rings: The Return of the King,* Richard Alleva, writing in *Commonweal* magazine shortly before *The Lord of the Rings* received eleven Academy Awards, compares the trilogy of books to the film version and then evaluates features of the film's narrative, acting, imagery, gender issues, humor, and themes. Typical of the genre of film review, Alleva balances description of the film with evaluation of the film's strengths and weaknesses.

PROFESSIONAL WRITING

Peter Jackson's Sorcery

Richard Alleva

Peter Jackson's three-part film of *The Lord of the Rings* (LOTR) may or   *1* may not please votaries of J.R.R. Tolkien's prose epic, but it is a godsend to anyone like me. I love the book's "northness," its landscape of towering forests and monster-housing caves, and the creatures that inhabit that landscape; my problem is with the prose that conveys this world. Though

Tolkien could write well—witness the charming prose of *The Hobbit* and the incisiveness of his scholarly essays—LOTR the novel contains too many sentences like this one: "The onslaught of Mordor broke like a wave on the beleaguered hills, voices roaring like a tide amid the wreck and crash of arms." The author certainly can't be accused of mixing his metaphors but this is too much of a wet thing. LOTR is lengthy, and a lengthy book needs fresher language than Tolkien could provide.

In the film adaptation, of course, the prose is gone, and Middle-earth floods into movie theaters by way of gorgeous photography and the latest digital tricks. For some, the movie will seem a desecration precisely because it is so visually forceful. You thought you knew what the wizard Gandalf looked like as he took shape within your mind as you read? Well, gaze on Sir Ian McKellen for just five seconds and kiss your inner-eye wizard goodbye. This movie isn't merely an adaptation; it's a coup d'etat. It overthrows our reading responses with a giant's sneer and brushes aside our psychological collaboration with the author. So, caveat lector.

Rather than write a formal movie review, I'm just going to walk around the film trilogy (*The Fellowship of the Ring, The Two Towers,* and *The Return of the King*) and point out interesting features, just as I would walk around a hydroelectric dam or a new skyscraper. Do these comparisons imply something inhuman, or at least grandiose about this movie? Perhaps, but like Gandalf, let us not be petty in the face of a monster.

Narrative: Tolkien's book wasn't just a literary endeavor but a huge verbal Lego project that he assembled in his study with the quiet fanaticism of a child putting together a toy monster or a train station. He gorged the reader on Middle-earth genealogy, flora and fauna, weather, culture, hobbit music, dwarf etiquette, elf ethics, giant cookery, etc., etc., and the whole project spilled over into Tolkien's *Silmarillion,* a prequel set in the same universe as LOTR. Fiction or mythic anthropology? Narrative propulsion was the goal for the moviemakers, not mythic saturation. I'm not surprised that Miranda Otto (who plays the human princess Eowyn) remarked, "I don't like to think of *Rings* as a fantasy, and, actually, Pete [Jackson] wanted to shoot it like a historical [piece]." Indeed, the whole thing comes across very much like one of those medieval adventure stories you saw in your youth—*Prince Valiant, The Black Shield of Falworth*—only much, much bigger and much, much better.

Nonreaders of LOTR may occasionally be puzzled, however. As in the book (albeit one of its appendixes), Aragorn marries the elf princess Arwen, but does the human princess Eowyn get a consolation prize? During my first viewing of *Return of the King,* I blinked and missed the split-second shot of Eowyn and Prince Faramir standing together like a loving couple. I caught it the second time around, yes, but surely this is compression taken too far. And what is the meaning of the crystal ball-like object that the hobbit Pippin finds and that Gandalf treats with trepidation? I found the brief verbal explanation incomprehensible, but readers will know that several of these orbs are used by the arch-fiend Sauron both to spy and to impose false predictions upon gullible creatures such as the steward of the human kingdom of Gondor (the royal line of heirs has been broken—hence the need for the king to return), who comes across on screen as an unmotivated psychopath rather than a man deceived. This is a compression that distorts. Nevertheless, the scriptwriters, Jackson, Fran Walsh, and Philippa Boyens, must be praised for generally keeping a lengthy movie both richly textured and sleek.

Acting: With dozens of roles so well cast and acted, one hardly knows whom to single out. For that very reason let me bypass the usual accolade-gatherers (McKellen, Sean Astin, Elijah Wood) and draw attention to players who might be overlooked. Because she is so beautiful, Liv Tyler has always been scanted as an actress. But in *The Two Towers,* Arwen's scene with her father (who is trying to dissuade her from loving a mortal) is made truly poignant by Tyler's acting, and she achieves this while speaking a language that doesn't really exist (though Elvish sounds like Welsh). Not for nothing do acting teachers make their students study subtext so that the phone book may be recited as if it were Shakespeare. 6

King Theoden of Rohan is such a sere figure that Bernard Hill's underplaying may be overshadowed by the more flamboyant performances, but if you watch him closely you'll find a fascinating portrayal of a man temperamentally drawn to despair yet determined to fight the good fight. 7

There really is an actor at the core of Gollum and he's called Andy Serkis. Peter Jackson's special-effects house, Weta Digital, took Serkis's performance, caught by motion-capture cameras, and overlaid the computer-generated monster we see on Serkis's movements. And whatever sound engineering did to the actor's voice, there is a human 8 note somewhere in there. Gollum comes across as a Dostoyevsky character who's been given a makeover by the Brothers Grimm, and Serkis surely deserves some credit for that kernel of complexity.

Imagery: Yes, the computer-generated work is impressive, occasion- 9
ally overwhelming. Still, some of the most memorable shots are simply good camera setups of actors delivering the emotional goods, just as in nonfantasy movies: Merry the hobbit riding to war while seated in front of Eowyn, his face alight with the discovery of a new way of being in the world; Aragorn (now the returned king), exhausted before the final battle, suddenly smiling at his troops and quietly uttering the mildest of war cries: "For Frodo."

But there are too many camera arcs over rolling plains as the Fel- 10
lowship theme swells up on the soundtrack. And if I ever have to look at another troupe of horsemen clattering through castle gates, I may throw myself over the nearest battlement.

Feminism: It's not that the film invented the warrior princesses, 11
Eowyn and Arwen. They're in the book too, but Tolkien always seemed a little theoretical in his presentation of women. Here the actresses playing them make them specific, mercurial, and commanding. When Eowyn confronts the Lord of the Nazgûl, he who cannot be killed by any man, with the fact that "I am no man," and then thrusts her sword in his face, I could feel battalions of women cheering her on. I cheered too.

Humor: We can feel a fatherly smile pervading the books, but the 12
movie grins. The body-count rivalry between good guys Gimli the dwarf and Legolas the elf is typical of boys' adventure tales but it leads up to, "That still counts as only one!" which, in context (Legolas has miraculously taken down a gigantic mammoth-like beast carrying scads of enemies), is one of the funniest movie lines of the decade. There is also dry wit, as when (in *Towers*) Aragorn impulsively embraces an elf general for coming to the rescue, and the fastidious warrior registers fleeting repugnance at being hugged by a—ugh!—human.

Themes (spoilers follow): The literary LOTR contains many themes 13
but I venture that the leading one is the necessity to cling stubbornly and absolutely to virtue (no matter how modest) in the face of absolute evil. (This is what makes Tolkien basically conservative. Liberals don't believe in absolute evil.) The movie's climax is the same as the book's:

...continued Peter Jackson's Sorcery, **Richard Alleva**

Frodo's failure to throw the ring into the fires of Mount Doom shows that he lacks absolute devotion to virtue, but this very human failure is rescued by Gollum's greedy intervention. Ironically, good comes out of evil; fate is stronger than character.

However, because the movie's script and Sean Astin's wonderfully *14* unfissured performance spotlight Sam's absolute devotion to Frodo, the preclimactic scene in which Sam carries Frodo up Mount Doom conveys an emotional charge that the morally messy climax doesn't. So Sam emerges as the true hero of the film trilogy, and the most important virtue, it seems, is the capacity for friendship, not the more general devotion to abstract virtue.

Though the creator of Middle-earth feared and hated many aspects of *15* technology, the technology of the movies has treated Tolkien with respect. Peter Jackson, master of technomagic and generalissimo of a thousand technicians and actors, has made of Tolkien's deliberately archaic epic a fresh, bracing revel.

■ ■ ■

WARMING UP: Journal Exercises

The following exercises will help you practice writing evaluations. Read all of the following exercises and then write on the three that interest you most. If another idea occurs to you, write about it

1. Choose the best of the courses that you are currently taking. To persuade a friend to take it, evaluate the course, the teacher, or both. What criteria and evidence would you select to persuade your friend?

2. Evaluate an object related to one of your hobbies or special interests—stereo or video equipment, water or snow skis, a cooking appliance or utensil, diving or hiking equipment, photography or art equipment, ranching or farming apparatus, fishing rods or reels, some part of a car, or computers. Write an evaluation of that object following the format used by *Consumer Reports.*

3. Evaluate a TV show that you find particularly irritating, boring, or insipid, but that you find yourself watching occasionally anyway. Watch the show,

taking notes about scenes, characters, dialogue, and plot. Write a critique of the show for other students in this class.

4. To gather some information for yourself about a possible job or career, interview a person in your prospective field about his or her job or profession. Focus your questions on the person's opinions and judgments about this career. What criteria does this person use to judge it? What other jobs serve as a good basis for comparison? What details from this person's daily routine support his or her judgments?

5. At your place of work, evaluate one of your products or services. Write down the criteria and evidence that your business might use to determine whether it is a "good" product or service. Then list the criteria and evidence that your customers or patrons probably use. Are these two sets of criteria and evidence identical? Explain.

6. Choose a piece of modern art (painting, drawing, poster, sculpture, ceramics, and so forth). Describe and evaluate it for an audience that is indifferent or possibly even hostile to contemporary art. Explain why your readers should appreciate this particular art object.

7. Reexamine the painting of Ramón Gómez de la Serna by Diego Rivera that appears at the beginning of this chapter. Describe the people, objects, use of color, and perspective in this painting. Then compare this painting with the painting of *The Flower Carrier*, also by Diego Rivera, on page 150. Compare these two paintings in order to evaluate which is the better, more interesting, or more effective painting. Consider their styles (realism versus cubism), dynamic use of color, effective arrangement and perspective, interesting subject matter, effective theme, and so forth. Do some research on the Web about Diego Rivera's paintings. Use your evaluation and research to explain, in two or three paragraphs, which is the most interesting or effective painting.

8. Read the following short essay, "Evaluating a Web Site," by Robin Williams and John Tollett. Using the guidelines and criteria that they develop in their essay, evaluate a Web site that you choose or a site that you are designing. Which areas are especially effective? Which are least effective? How might the site be improved? Explain how you would evaluate the site overall. (For additional ideas about putting the authors' guidelines into practice, check out their own Web site at www.peachpit.com.)

PROFESSIONAL WRITING

Evaluating a Web Site

Robin Williams and John Tollett

The World Wide Web is relatively new in this old world of ours and has become an important and integral communication tool around the world. Standards have been developed and users expect certain features to exist. Every time you land on a Web page you automatically evaluate how well the site works, how the page design impacts you, what makes the site usable, and what sorts of things hinder the communication. Your gut reactions determine whether or not you'll return to that site.

When John and I design a new site or visit a site we haven't been to before (many times a day, of course), we consciously evaluate a large number of features. Whether designing the site or visiting it, our evaluation criteria is pretty much the same. These are the sorts of things we look at:

Style: Does the theme or graphic style fit the goals of the site and appeal to the target audience? This is an extremely important consideration. Imagine if the Gumps.com site looked like the Disney site—would that suit the market for Gumps customers?

Animation and Flash and lots of large images can be perfectly appropriate on a site designed for a tech-savvy target audience, an audience you assume has a fast computer and the latest software. If the target audience is seniors who have inherited older machines from their kids, the site should probably have fewer flashy gizmos that require up-to-the-minute hardware and software.

Organization: Web sites can contain huge amounts of information. Organization is the critical element that makes the information accessible, and this can make or break a site. Organizing information on a large Web site requires serious thought and planning and testing and more thought and planning and testing. The Apple and Adobe Web sites are incredible examples of clear organization—each site has thousands of pages, but you can find what you need in seconds.

Recently I needed to buy a new carafe for my coffee pot. I went to the Web site our local store recommended, and in THREE SECONDS I found exactly the carafe I needed. The site wasn't beautiful, but I didn't need beautiful—I needed a carafe. This site (that sold hundreds of coffee-related products) was so well organized that I could scan and find the first topic I needed in about one second; I clicked the button and saw the second level of information; I clicked the button, and there was exactly the carafe I needed. Amazing.

Presentation: Web pages don't have to be masterpieces of art, but they do need to be pleasant and easy to look at. A very simple, well-organized page is more pleasing than an over-designed, busy page that is badly organized. When Google.com first appeared, long before we recognized what a superior search engine it used, we loved it because it was simple. All of the other existing search pages were horrendously busy and cluttered and obnoxious; Google was white and clean with almost nothing on the page except the field in which to type my search. It was so comforting that since I found that site, I have never used another search page.

These are some of the features we see on poorly presented sites. These are easily fixable:

Too much bold text, especially when it is in color on a colored background.

Busy, distracting backgrounds.

Long lines of text that stretch out across the page.

Text in lots of all caps or italic.

Underlined text that is not a link.

Meaningless graphics.

Giant link buttons.

Borders turned on in tables.

Anything that blinks.

Anything that makes me scroll sideways (unless it is a specific and conscious design element).

Too many focal points on the page.

Clutter.

Logical and consistent: We don't like sites that are a puzzle we're expected to solve. We don't have time to figure out that if we click on a bubble as it floats up the page, we'll find the photographer's portfolio—I'll spend the time finding another photographer instead. We might find that kind of site interesting—for about twelve seconds.

Every page must be as intuitive and logical as possible and consistent with other pages in the site. You never know where visitors are going to drop into a site; they might find an obscure page through a search tool and

...*continued* Evaluating a Web Site, **Robin Williams and John Tollett**

pop into the archives. This means that no matter where visitors enter your site, they should know instantly whose site it is, have a rough idea of what the site is about, and know how to get to the home page.

The entire site should feel familiar so the visitor feels comfortable and confident wherever they are in it. Don't invent a variety of ways to navigate from page to page. Don't use underlines on the links on most pages, then eliminate them from other pages. Don't arbitrarily change the color scheme or layout.

Forgiving: Site visitors often make mistakes—they go to the wrong page or click a wrong button. If a site design is forgiving, a mistake is not a big problem. Every page should have familiar navigation to make it easy to return to any section of the site.

We hate orphan pages, which are those that dead end without links to return to previous pages or to the home page. Visitors often bookmark pages and return by choosing that bookmark; if they go to a bookmarked orphan page, they may not be able to find the rest of the site.

No chain-yanks: A chain-yank sets you up with expectations, then abruptly disappoints you. For example, you click a link next to a graphic that says "Click here for a larger image." You click, expecting a larger image and perhaps some additional information, but you get a page with the same image on a bare page, or perhaps the image is a quarter-inch larger. This makes you feel stupid. Or worse, it makes you think the Web site is stupid. If there is a link to another page, it must be worth the trip.

I read an online article about Steve Wozniak, co-creator of the Macintosh computer. The article included a paragraph on how Woz felt about his father, and the word "father" was an underlined link. Now, where would you expect that link to go? Probably to a page about Wozniak's father, right? No—the link was to Fathers.com, a nice site but totally irrelevant to the article. Chain-yank.

Link visibility: The underline below text is a visual clue that indicates a link. I agree that it's an ugly look. Designers sometimes remove the underline and use colored text to indicate the links. The problem with removing the underline is that if the designer uses more than one color on the Web page, it's difficult to tell which text is a link and which is just in color. I'm forced to run the mouse over any text in any color on the page to see whether or not it's a link. The only pages I've seen where this was done well were pages where no other text colors were used (see the Adobe.com site for a great example).

It's better to make text links obvious and easy with an underline than to have a fancier page that's harder to use. Whether or not you choose to use the underline, be consistent so the visitor doesn't get confused.

Communication, not decoration: Visuals should enhance the content or repeat a design theme, making pages seem familiar, friendly, consistent, and useful. When photos or illustrations merely decorate a page, they have little effect other than slowing the download time. Now, we're not discouraging visual elements—it's just that every element should have a purpose. Nothing should be on the page arbitrarily.

Dazzle me sparingly: There are many dazzling techniques, such as Flash animation, that advanced Web designers can add to a site. Flash is great stuff. Love it, love it, love it. It can be entertaining, dramatic, and compelling. It can also be annoying, especially when it's so dazzling you can't figure out how to get to another page. Most of us have grown tired of circles and squares that get bigger, then smaller, then fade out. The sites that use Flash effectively, use it sparingly. Visit the Adobe Flash Web pages and notice that even the creators of Flash use it in small bits. If I have to wait for a Flash animation to load before I can even see the first link, I'm gone.

Pop-up windows: Pop-up windows can be wonderful when used appropriately. They are great for giving visitors extra bits of information without making them go to an entirely different page. (Pop-up ads are hateful and annoying!)

Help: Large sites can be cumbersome even with good design. Any good, large site will have a site map, a site outline with links to all pages, or a search feature that a visitor can use to locate information.

This is just a brief overview of the sorts of things that one can evaluate on any Web site in just a few minutes. It's a good exercise to spend an hour or so with a complex Web site and really see what makes it work or not work. Try to accomplish a task, such as find a particular item, buy a product, search for information, contact someone, print a page, dig down deep in the structure and see if you can get out easily. Is the design consistent so you always know when you are in the site? Can you easily find what you need through the navigation bar? Is the search feature useful or annoying? Can you scan the page and know what the major topics of the site are? Is it so cluttered that it's difficult to find what you need? Once you spend the time to really evaluate a large site, you will feel more confident in appraising and using any Web site.

The following two articles present other alternatives for writing reviews. In the first example, Margaret Lazarus writes a cultural critique of Walt Disney's *The Lion King*. Instead of the typical review that evaluates the plot, acting, and cinematography, Lazarus focuses on the cultural stereotyping contained in a film targeted at children. Read her review and decide if you find her evaluation persuasive. In the second short review, David Sedaris, author of the best-selling *Me Talk Pretty One Day*, uses humor to evaluate one of the "precious little bistros" that have sprung up in New York. Sedaris provides an excellent model of how to use a personal narrative and humor to create a memorable review.

PROFESSIONAL WRITING

All's Not Well in Land of "The Lion King"

Margaret Lazarus

It's official: Walt Disney's *The Lion King* is breaking box-office records. Unfortunately, it's not breaking any stereotypes.

My sons, along with millions of other kids around the world, joyously awaited *The Lion King*. I was intrigued because this time Disney appeared to be skipping the old folk-tales with their traditional and primal undercurrents.

I hoped Disney had grown weary of reinforcing women's subordinate status by screening fables about a beauty who tames an angry male beast or a mermaid who gives up her glorious voice and splits her body to be with a prince.

So off we went to the movies, figuring we would enjoy an original, well-animated story about animals on the African plain. Even before the title sequence, however, I started to shudder.

Picture this (and I apologize for spilling the plot): The golden-maned—that is, good—lion is presenting his first born male child to his subjects. All the animals in the kingdom, known as Pride Lands, are paying tribute to the infant son that will someday be their king. These royal subjects are basically lion food—zebras, monkeys, birds, etc.—and they all live together in supposed harmony in the "circle of life."

Outside the kingdom, in a dark, gloomy, and impoverished elephant graveyard, are the hyenas. They live dismally jammed together among bones and litter. The hyenas are dark—mostly black—and they are nasty, menacing the little lion prince when he wanders into their territory.

One of their voices is done by Whoopie Goldberg, in a clearly inner-city dialect. If this is not the ghetto, I don't know what is.

All is not perfect inside Pride Lands, however. The king's evil brother Scar has no lionesses or cubs. Scar has a black mane, and speaks in an effeminate, limp-pawed, British style done by Jeremy Irons—seemingly a gay caricature.

Scar conspires with the hyenas to kill the king and send the prince into exile. In exchange for their support, Scar allows the hyenas to live in Pride Lands. But property values soon crash: The hyenas overpopulate, kill all the game, and litter the once-green land with bones.

Already Disney has gays and blacks ruining the "natural order," and the stereotypes keep rolling. The lionesses never question whether they should be serving Scar and the hyenas—they just worry a lot. They are mistreated, but instead of fighting back these powerful hunters passively await salvation. (Even my 7-year-old wondered why the young, strong lioness didn't get rid of Scar.)

The circle of life is broken; disaster awaits everyone. But then the first-born male returns to reclaim power. The royal heir kills the gay usurper, and sends the hyenas back to the dark, gloomy, bone-filled ghetto. Order is restored and the message is clear: Only those born to privilege can bring about change.

This is not a story about animals—we know animals don't behave like this. This is a metaphor for society that originated in the minds of Disney's creators. These bigoted images and attitudes will lodge deeply in children's consciousness.

I'm not sure I always understand the law of the Hollywood jungle, but my boys definitely don't. Scared and frightened by *The Lion King*, they were also riveted, and deeply affected. But entranced by the "Disney magic," they and millions of other children were given hidden messages that can only do them—and us—harm.

PROFESSIONAL WRITING

Today's Special

David Sedaris

It is his birthday, and Hugh and I are seated in a New York restaurant, awaiting the arrival of our fifteen-word entrées. He looks very nice, dressed in the suit and sweater that have always belonged to him. As for me, I own

. . . *continued* Today's Special, **David Sedaris**

only my shoes, pants, shirt, and tie. My jacket belongs to the restaurant and was offered as a loan by the maître d', who apparently thought I would feel more comfortable dressed to lead a high-school marching band.

I'm worrying the thick gold braids decorating my sleeves when the waiter presents us with what he calls "a little something to amuse the palette." Roughly the size and color of a Band-Aid, the amusement floats on a shallow, muddy puddle of sauce and is topped with a sprig of greenery.

"And this would be . . . what, exactly?" Hugh asks.

"This," the waiter announces, "is our raw Atlantic sword-fish served in a dark chocolate gravy and garnished with fresh mint."

"Not again," I say. "Can't you guys come up with something a little less conventional?"

"Love your jacket," the waiter whispers.

As a rule, I'm no great fan of eating out in New York restaurants. It's hard to love a place that's outlawed smoking but finds it perfectly acceptable to serve raw fish in a bath of chocolate. There are no normal restaurants left, at least in our neighborhood. The diners have all been taken over by precious little bistros boasting a menu of indigenous American cuisine. They call these meals "traditional," yet they're rarely the American dishes I remember. The patty melt has been pushed aside in favor of the herb-encrusted medallions of baby artichoke hearts, which never leave me thinking, Oh, right, those! I wonder if they're as good as the ones my mom used to make.

Part of the problem is that we live in the wrong part of town. SoHo is not a macaroni salad kind of place. This is where the world's brightest young talents come to braise carmelized racks of corn-fed songbirds or offer up their famous knuckle of flash-seared crappie served with a collar of chided ginger and cornered by a tribe of kiln-roasted Chilean toadstools, teased with a warm spray of clarified musk oil. Even when they promise something simple, they've got to tart it up—the meatloaf has been poached in sea water, or there are figs in the tuna salad. If cooking is an art, I think we're in our Dada phase.

I've never thought of myself as a particularly finicky eater, but it's hard to be a good sport when each dish seems to include no fewer than a dozen ingredients, one of which I'm bound to dislike. I'd order the skirt steak with a medley of suffocated peaches, but I'm put off by the aspirin sauce. The sea scallops look good until I'm told they're served in a broth of malt liquor and mummified litchi nuts. What I really want is a cigarette, and I'm always searching the menu in the hope that some courageous young chef has finally recognized tobacco as a vegetable. Bake it, steam it, grill it, or stuff it into littleneck clams, I just need something familiar that I can hold on to.

When the waiter brings our entrées, I have no idea which plate might be mine. In yesterday's restaurants it was possible both to visualize and to recognize your meal. There were always subtle differences, but for the most part, a lamb chop tended to maintain its basic shape. That is to say that it looked choplike. It had a handle made of bone and a teardrop of meat hugged by a thin rind of fat. Apparently, though, that was too predictable. Order the modern lamb chop, and it's likely to look no different than your companion's order of shackled pompano. The current food is always arranged into a senseless, vertical tower. No longer content to recline, it now reaches for the sky, much like the high-rise buildings lining our city streets. It's as if the plates were valuable parcels of land and the chef had purchased one small lot and unlimited air rights. Hugh's saffron linguini resembles a miniature turban, topped with architectural spires of shrimp. It stands there in the center while the rest of the vast, empty plate looks as though it's been leased out as a possible parking lot. I had ordered the steak, which, bowing to the same minimalist fashion, is served without the bone, the thin slices of beef stacked to resemble a funeral pyre. The potatoes I'd been expecting have apparently either been clarified to an essence or were used to stoke the grill.

"Maybe," Hugh says, "they're inside your tower of meat."

This is what we have been reduced to. Hugh blows the yucca pollen off his blackened shrimp while I push back the sleeves of my borrowed sport coat and search the meat tower for my promised potatoes.

"There they are, right there." Hugh uses his fork to point out what could easily be mistaken for five cavity-riddled molars. The dark spots must be my vegetable.

Because I am both a glutton and a masochist, my standard complaint, "That was so bad," is always followed by "And there was so little of it!"

Our plates are cleared, and we are presented with dessert menus. I learn that spiced ham is no longer considered just a luncheon meat and that even back issues of *Smithsonian* can be turned into sorbets.

"I just couldn't," I say to the waiter when he recommends the white chocolate and wild loganberry couscous.

"If we're counting calories, I could have the chef serve it without the crème fraîche."

"No," I say. "Really, I just couldn't."

...continued Today's Special, **David Sedaris**

We ask for the check, explaining that we have a movie to catch. It's only a ten-minute walk to the theater, but I'm antsy because I'd like to get something to eat before the show. They'll have loads of food at the concession stand, but I don't believe in mixing meat with my movies. Luckily there's a hot dog cart not too far out of our way.

Friends always say, "How can you eat those? I read in the paper that they're made from hog's lips."

"And . . . ?"

"And hearts and eyelids."

That, to my mind, is only three ingredients and constitutes a refreshing change of pace. I order mine with nothing but mustard, and am thrilled to watch the vendor present my hot dog in a horizontal position. So simple and timeless that I can recognize it, immediately, as food.

■ ■ ■

PROFESSIONAL WRITING

Watching the Eyewitless News

Elayne Rapping

Culture critic Elayne Rapping is a professor of communications at Adelphi University and is the author of several books, including The Looking Glass World of Nonfiction TV *(1987),* Mediations: Forays into the Culture and Gender Wars *(1994), and* The Culture of Recovery: Making Sense of the Self-Help Movement in Women's Lives *(1996). She has also published dozens of articles about a variety of social, cultural, and media-related issues. "Watching the Eyewitless News," which originally appeared as a column in* The Progressive, *evaluates the local "Eyewitness" news programs featured daily in regional television markets.*

Jimmy Cagney, the ultimate street-smart wise guy, used to snap, "Whadya hear? Whadya know?" in the days of black-and-white movies and READ ALL ABOUT IT! headlines. But that was then and this is now. Today, when gangsta rap has replaced gangster movies, and television has replaced newsprint as the primary source of information (for two-thirds of us, the *only* source), Cagney's famous question is not only antiquated, it is beside the point. What we hear when we consume "the news" has only the most marginal relationship to what we *know* about anything.

I'm not referring here to CNN or the "evening news" on the national broadcast networks. I'm referring here to what passes for news in the homes and minds of the vast majority of Americans today: The Eyewitless, Happy Talk local newscasts that run in many cities for as much as an hour and a half to two hours a day, on as many as seven or eight different channels.   2

The rise of local news, the infotainment monster that ate the news industry, is a long and painful story about a key battle-front in the endless media war between capitalism and democracy, between the drive for profits and the constitutional responsibility of those licensed to use the airwaves to serve the public interest. We know who's winning, of course. The game was rigged from the start. . . .   3

Local news as we know it was invented in 1970, the brainchild of a marketing research whiz hired by the industry to raise ratings by finding out what audiences "wanted to see." The Jeffersonian notion that public media should cover what citizens "need to know" was not a big consideration. Nor was it a concern to respect the audience's intelligence or diversity.   4

The researchers offered a limited, embarrassingly vapid list of choices of formats and subjects, while ignoring the possibility that different groups might want different kinds of information and analysis. More annoying still, they ignored the possibility that individual viewers, of all kinds, might want and need different things at different times for different reasons. Nope, said the marketing whizzes, this master model of "The News" will buy us the most overall-ratings bang per buck. Wrap it up and send it out.   5

And it worked. Their invention has conquered the TV world. The set, the news lineups, the anchors, the weather maps, the sports features—all developed for a New York City market—quickly became a universal formula, sent out to every network affiliate and independent station in America, complete with fill-in-the-blanks guidelines for adaptation to any community, no matter how large or small, urban or rural. Local news today is the single most profitable form of nonfiction television programming in the country and, for most stations, the only thing they actually produce. Everything else comes from the networks. As time went by, this tendency toward cookie-cutter formulas, exported far and wide from a central media source, reached ever more depressing depths. The trend has led to ever more nationally produced, generic features exported to local stations to be passed off as "local."   6

So today we have a phenomenon euphemistically called "local news," although it is anything but, filled with images of a pseudo-community called "America," which is actually closer to Disney World in its representation of American life. But why should that surprise us, in a national landscape now filled, from coast to coast, with identical, mass-produced shopping malls that pass for town marketplaces, and hotels and airports that pass for village inns? In postmodern America, after all, this kind of brand-name synthetic familiarity appears to be the only thing that holds us—a nation of endlessly uprooted and mobile strangers—together.

When you turn on the news, whether at home or in an airport or Holiday Inn in some totally strange locale, you see a predictable, comforting spectacle. The town or city in question, whether Manhattan or Moose Hill, Montana, is presided over by a group of attractive, charming, well-dressed performers—whose agents, salaries, and movements up and down the ladder of media success, gauged by the size of the "market" they infiltrate, are chronicled each week in *Variety*. They seem to care endlessly for each other and us. "Tsk, tsk," they cluck at news of yet another gang rampage or Congressional scandal. "Ooh," they sigh, at news of earthquakes and plane crashes, far and near.

If it bleeds, it leads is the motto of the commercial news industry and local news. Its endless series of fires, shootouts, collapsing buildings, and babies beaten or abandoned or bitten by wild dogs is the state-of-the-art showcase for the industry. As Don Henley once put it, in a scathing song about the local news phenomenon, "It's interesting when people die." And it's especially interesting when they die in bizarre or inhuman situations, when their loved ones are on camera to moan and wail, when a lot of them die at once. And since so much of our news is indeed personally terrifying and depressing, we need to have it delivered as cleverly and carefully as possible. And so we have the always smiling, always sympathetic, always confidently upbeat news teams to sugarcoat the bad news.

Not that local news ignores the politically important stories. Well, not entirely anyway. When wars are declared or covered, when elections are won or lost, when federal budgets and plant closings do away with jobs and services or threaten to put more and more of us in jail, for less and less cause, the local news teams are there to calm our jagged nerves and reassure us that we needn't worry.

This reassurance is sometimes subtle. National news items typically take up less than two minutes of a half-hour segment. And what's said and seen in that brief interlude is hardly enlightening. On the contrary, the hole for "hard news" is generally filled with sound bites and head shots, packaged and processed by the networks, from news conferences with the handful of movers and shakers considered "newsworthy"—the President and his key henchmen and adversaries, mostly.

But even local issues of serious import are given short shrift on these *12* newscasts. Hard news affecting local communities takes up only a minute or two more airtime than national events. And local teams are obsessed with "man-on-the-street" spot interviews. Neighbors on local TV are forever gasping and wailing the most clichéd of reflex responses to actual local horrors, whether personal or social.

"It's so horrible," they say over and over again, like wind-up dolls with *13* a limited repertoire of three-word phrases, when asked about a local disaster. And when the crisis affects them directly—a school budget cut or neighborhood hospital closing, for example—their on-air responses are equally vapid. "I don't know what we're going to do without any teachers or books," they say with puzzled, frenzied expressions as they try desperately to articulate some coherent reply to a complex issue they've just heard about.

"Glad you brought that up, Jim. The latest research on polls has turned up some interesting variables. It turns out, for example, that people will tell you any old thing that pops into their heads."

I am not suggesting that the news should not feature community residents' views and experiences. Of course it should. But the local news teams' way of presenting such community responses is deliberately demeaning and fatuous. No one could say much worth saying in such a format. And if someone managed to come up with something serious and intelligent, rest assured it would be cut in favor of a more sensational, emotional response. 14

But real news, even about cats in trees or babies in wells, is hardly what takes up the most airtime. "Don't bother too much about that stuff," say the guys and gals in the anchor chairs. Here's Goofy Gil with the weather, or Snappy Sam with the sports—the two features which, on every local newscast, are given the longest time slots and the most elaborate and expensive props. The number and ornateness of the weather maps on local news, and the endlessly amazing developments in special-effects technology to observe climate changes and movements of impending "fronts" is truly mind-boggling. 15

Who needs this stuff? But we're forgetting that this is not the question to ask. "Who wants it?" is the criterion for news producers, and it is, understandably, the weather and sports that most people, most of the time, are likely to sit still for. If local news is meant to be a facsimile of a sunny Disneyesque community of happy, cozy campers, in which the bothersome bad guys and events of the day are quickly dealt with so that community harmony may once more reign, at least for the moment—and that *is* the intended fantasy—then what better, safer, kind of information than weather reports. Historically, after all, the weather is the standard small-talk item for people wishing to be pleasant and make contact without getting into anything controversial or heavy. It is the only kind of news we can all share in—no matter what our race, class, gender, or political differences—as members of a common community. 16

The researchers are not entirely wrong, after all, about what people in this kind of society want. They do want comfort, reassurance, and a community where they belong and feel safe. And why shouldn't they? They find precious little of those things in the streets and buildings they traverse and inhabit in their daily lives. In my urban neighborhood, parents warn children never to make eye contact with anyone on the street or subway; never to speak to anyone, even in case of tragedy or emergency; never to look at or listen to the pathetic souls who regularly beg for money or ramble incoherently in the hope that someone, anyone, will take pity and respond. 17

Remember when California was God's country, the Promised Land of   *18*
Milk and Honey, to which people migrated for clean air, good jobs, and
single-dwelling homes? Try to find these things in overpopulated, polluted, socially vexed and violent LA today. . . . But if we can't all dream of
moving to sunny California anymore, there's always TV, where something
resembling that innocent dream still exists. Eyewitness News and its various clones allow us to believe, just for a moment, that there really is a Santa
Claus, a Mary Poppins, a Good Samaritan giving away fortunes to the
needy, a spirit of Christmas Past to convert the most cold-hearted of corporate Scrooges. Indeed, this kind of "good news" is another staple of the
genre. Charities, celebrations, instances of extraordinary good luck or good
works by or for local residents are ever-present on local newscasts. Every
day, in the midst of even the most dreadful and depressing news, there are
legions of friends and neighbors to mourn and console each other, offering
aid, bringing soup and casseroles to the victims of natural and manmade
disasters, stringing lights and hanging balloons for festive neighborhood
gatherings.

The news teams themselves often play this role for us. They march at   *19*
the head of holiday parades and shake hands and kiss babies at openings
of malls and industrial parks. They are the neighbors—often thought of
as friends by the loneliest among us—we wish we had in real life, there to
do the right thing on every occasion. That is their primary function. They
are not trained in journalism. They often cannot pronounce the local
names and foreign words they read from teleprompters. But they sure can
smile. . . .

Sociologist Joshua Gamson has suggested, in an insightful essay, that   *20*
there is a lesson to be learned from the enormous popularity of tabloid
television—a category in which I would certainly include local news. The
lesson is not that people are stupid, venal, "addicted," or otherwise blame-
worthy for their fascinated interest in junk TV. On the contrary, it is those
responsible for the quality of our public life who are more deserving of such
terms of contempt and opprobrium. For it is, says Gamson, "Only when
people perceive public life as inconsequential, as not their own, [that] they
readily accept the invitation to turn news into play." And people most certainly do perceive public life as inconsequential and worse these days,
whether outside their doors or in Washington or on Wall Street.

Only I don't think it is primarily the desire to "play" that drives peo-   *21*
ple in droves to local newscasts, or even the trashier tabloid shows like *Hard
Copy*. What people are getting from local newscasts—and here the re-

. . . continued Watching the Eyewitless News, **Elayne Rapping**

searchers were right on the money, literally—is indeed what they want, in the most profound and sad sense of that phrase. They are getting what they always sought in fantasy and fiction, from *The Wizard of Oz* to *As the World Turns*. They are getting, for a brief moment, a utopian fantasy of a better, kinder, more decent and meaningful world than the one that entraps them.

It is not only that public life is inconsequential, after all. It is, far more   22 tragically, that public and private life today are increasingly unjust, inhumane, painful, even hopeless, materially and spiritually, for many of us. And there is no relief in sight except, ironically, on the local newscasts that are a respite from reality. Only, unlike the utopian villages of soap opera and fairy tale, these "imagined communities" are supposed to be, pretend to be, real and true. And for that reason they are more troubling than the trashiest or silliest of pop-culture fictions.

◼ ◼ ◼

vo·cab·u·lar·y

In your journal, write the meaning of the italicized words in the following phrases.

- is not only *antiquated* **(1)**
- *euphemistically* called "local news" **(7)**
- are given short *shrift* **(12)**
- a limited *repertoire* **(13)**
- equally *vapid* **(13)**
- demeaning and *fatuous* **(14)**
- be a *facsimile* **(16)**
- a *utopian* fantasy **(21)**

QUESTIONS FOR WRITING AND DISCUSSION

1. When you finish reading Elayne Rapping's essay, write your personal responses. Did you agree or disagree with her analysis? Did you find her essay humorous or were you angry at her pronouncements? Were her judgments believable? Did her judgments fit with your own experiences watching your local news programs? Explain your reactions as fully as possible.

2. Reread Rapping's essay, identifying the criteria behind her judgments. In this case, criteria are statements describing what an ideal news program should be; for example, "Good news programs should provide what the people need, not necessarily what they want." Find and list as many of these criteria as you can. Then make a three-column log for this essay, indicating the judgment that Rapping makes about each criterion and the supporting evidence that she provides.

3. Referring to the three-column log from question 2 above, assess Rapping's use of supporting evidence—specific examples from local news shows illustrating her point. Which of Rapping's judgments have supporting evidence? Which are merely unsupported assertions? Based on your analysis, do you think Rapping has written an effective evaluative essay? Explain.

4. Examine the cartoon by Charles Saxon included in this essay. Is this cartoon an effective visual for Rapping's essay? What makes it effective and appropriate? Why might it not be effective? Would another visual be more effective? Explain. (*Note:* This cartoon did not appear in the original version of Rapping's essay.)

5. Observe a local news program. If possible, videotape the program. As you replay your videotape, list each segment of the news: local events, national news, weather, sports, business news, international news, medical and health issues, and so forth. Note any transitional sections (segues) that contain small talk among the anchors. Next to each segment, record the length of time. Next, indicate your opinion about quality or depth of coverage. Finally, record any evidence about the newscasters' personalities, on-camera style, or journalistic ability. Based on your observations and evidence, write an essay responding to Elayne Rapping. How accurately do her observations apply to the case you have observed? What other general conclusions about Rapping's article or about local news programs might you make?

6. Using Rapping's method of cultural analysis, observe and then analyze/evaluate a particular social, cultural, or media-related event. You might choose hall or club meetings at your university, lecture or lab classes, sports events, class registration rituals, TV sitcoms, Internet home pages—the list is bounded only by your imagination. (Be sure to focus on only one particular kind of cultural event or media program.) Your purpose is both to evaluate these cultural "events" and to explain why the cultural event itself is or is not constructed to avoid limited, stereotypical visions of reality or of people.

7. A study by the Kaiser Family Foundation and the Center for Media and Public Affairs found that "the five most common topics in local TV news coverage are crime (20 percent of news items), weather (11 percent), accidents and disasters (9 percent), human interest stories (7 percent), and health stories (7 percent), with all other topics ranking below the top five." "Local TV news wouldn't cover crime as much as it does if the public didn't reward such coverage with high ratings," according to Drew Altman, President of the Kaiser Family Foundation. "But," he continues, "does anyone seriously believe that crime is twice as important as any other issue that the public needs to learn about from local television news?" On the Internet, access Academic Search Premier and search for recent articles on "network news" and "local news." How do the findings described above or in the articles you locate compare with Rapping's argument? Write your own analysis of local or network TV news using the sources you find.

❝ I love criticism so long as it's unqualified praise. **❞**
—NOEL COWARD,
PLAYWRIGHT, SONGWRITER, NOVELIST, DIRECTOR, AND PERFORMER

TECHNIQUES   PROCESS

Evaluating: The Writing Process

ASSIGNMENT FOR EVALUATING

With a specific audience in mind, evaluate a product or service, a work of art, or a performance. Choose a subject that is *reobservable*—that you can revisit or review as you write your essay. Select criteria appropriate for your subject and audience. Collect evidence to support or determine a judgment for each criterion.

The review is the most common genre for evaluating pieces, but "reviews" cover a wide range of documents. Some film reviews are academic and critical while others merely indicate the major plot line without much evaluation. Similarly, some reviews of performances or products are short, informal, and intended mainly as information and entertainment for the reader. After you choose your topic, then be sure to consider the requirements or expectations of your audience. Are they expecting merely to be informed or entertained, or do they want the thorough and critical evaluation described in this chapter?

CHOOSING A SUBJECT

If you have already settled on a possible subject, try the following collecting and shaping strategies. If you have not found a subject, consider these ideas

- Evaluating requires some expertise about a particular person, performance, place, object, or service. You generate expertise not only through experience but also through writing, reading, and rewriting. Review your authority list from Chapter 7. Which of those subjects could you evaluate? Reread your journal entries on observing and investigating. Did you observe or investigate some person, place, or thing that you could write about again, this time for the purpose of evaluating it?

- Comparing and contrasting lead naturally to evaluation. For example, compare two places you've lived, two friends, or two jobs. Compare two newspapers for their coverage of international news, local features, sports, or business. Compare two famous people from the same profession. Compare your expectations about a person, place, or event with the reality. The purpose of your comparison is to determine, for a specific audience, which is "better," based on the criteria you select and the evidence you find.

- Evaluating a possible career choice can help you choose courses, think about possible summer jobs, and prepare for job interviews. Begin by describing several jobs that fit your particular career goals. Then go to several of the following Web sites and gather information.

  http://www.monster.com　　　　http://www.bestjobsusa.com
  http://www.careers.com　　　　money.cnn.com/services/careerbuilder
  http://careers.yahoo.com　　　　http://www.getthatgig.com

  Choose the career criteria that are most important for you, such as job satisfaction, location, benefits, salary, education requirements, and so forth. Decide which criteria are most important for **you**. Is job satisfaction more important than pay or location? Choose your criteria and rank them in order of importance. Then write an evaluation of one or two jobs that you find described on the Internet or in your local newspaper.

- Community service-learning projects often require an assessment at the end of the period of service. These reflective evaluations start with the goals of the agency, the goals of your class project, and your goals as a learner as the major criteria. Then you gather evidence to see how well the actual experiences and projects met these overall project goals. Sometimes participants use short evaluation questionnaires to get feedback at the midpoint and then again at the end of the project. If you are participating in a community service-learning project, check with your teacher or coordinator about how to write this assessment.

CHOOSING **COLLECTING** SHAPING DRAFTING REVISING APPENDIX

COLLECTING

Once you have a tentative subject and audience in mind, ask the following questions to focus your collecting activities

- Can you *narrow*, *restrict*, or *define* your subject to focus your paper?
- What *criteria* will you use to evaluate your subject?
- What *evidence* might you gather? As you collect evidence, focus on three questions:

    What *comparisons* can you make between your subject and similar subjects?
    What are the *uses* or *consequences* of this subject?
    What *experiments* or *authorities* might you cite for support?

- What initial *judgments* are you going to make?

OBSERVING   Observation and description of your subject are crucial to a clear evaluation. In most cases, your audience will need to know *what* your subject is before they can understand your evaluation.

- Examine a place or object repeatedly, looking at it from different points of view. Take notes. Describe it. Draw it, if appropriate. Analyze its component parts. List its uses. To which senses does it appeal—sight, sound, touch, smell, taste? If you are comparing your subject to other similar subjects, observe them carefully. Remember: The second or third time you observe your subject, you will see even more key details.

- If you are evaluating a person, collect information about this person's life, interests, abilities, accomplishments, and plans for the future. If you are able to observe the person directly, describe his or her physical features, write down what he or she says, and describe the person's environment.

- If you are evaluating a performance or an event, a tape recording or videotape can be extremely useful. If possible, choose a concert, film, or play on tape so that you can stop and review it if and when necessary. If a tape recording or videotape is not available, attend the performance or event twice.

Making notes in a *three-column log* is an excellent collecting strategy for evaluations. Using the following example from Phyllis Richman's evaluation of the Hunan Dynasty restaurant, list the criteria, evidence, and judgments for your subject.

Subject: Hunan Dynasty Restaurant

Criteria	Evidence	Judgment
Attractive setting	No blaring red-lacquer tables	Graceful
	White tablecloths	
	Subtle glass etchings	
Good service	Waiters serve with flourishes	Often expert
	Some glitches, such as forgotten appetizer	

▪ **REMEMBERING**   You are already an authority on many subjects, and your personal experiences may help you evaluate your subject. Try *freewriting, looping, branching,* or *clustering* your subject to help you remember relevant events, impressions, and information. In evaluating appliances for consumer magazines, for example, reporters often use products over a period of months, recording data, impressions, and experiences. Those experiences and memories are then used to support criteria and judgments. Evaluating a film often requires remembering similar films that you have liked or disliked. An evaluation of a great athlete may include your memories of previous performances. A vivid narrative of those memories can help convince an audience that a performance is good or bad.

▪ **READING**   Some of the ideas and evidence for your evaluation may come from reading descriptions of your subject, other evaluations of your subject, or the testimony of experts. Be sure you read these texts critically: Who is the intended audience for the text? What evidence does the text give? What is the author's bias? What are other points of view? Read your potential sources critically.

▪ **INVESTIGATING**   All evaluations involve some degree of formal or informal investigation as you probe the characteristics of your subject and seek evidence to support your judgments.

Use the Library or the Internet   Check the library and Internet resources for information on your subject, for ideas about how to design and conduct an evaluation of that subject, for possible criteria, for data in evaluations already performed, and for a sense of different possible audiences. In its evaluation of chocolate chip cookies, for example, *Consumer Reports* suggests criteria and outlines procedures. The magazine rated some two dozen popular store-bought brands, as well as four "boutique" or freshly baked varieties, on "strength of chocolate flavor and aroma, cookie and chip texture, and freedom from sensory defects." When the magazine's evaluators faced a problem sampling the fresh cookies in the lab, they decided to move the lab: "We ended up loading a station wagon with scoresheet, pencils, clipboards, water containers, cups, napkins . . . and setting off on a tasting safari to shopping malls."

Gather Field Data   You may want to supplement your personal evaluation with a sample of other people's opinions by using *questionnaires* or *interviews*. (See Chapter 7.) If you are rating a film, for example, you might give people leaving the theater a very brief *questionnaire,* asking for their responses on key criteria relating to the movie that they just saw. If you are rating a class, you might want to *interview* several students in the class to support your claim that the class was either effective or ineffective. The interviews might also give you some specific examples: descriptions of experiences that you can then use as evidence to support your own judgments.

CHOOSING COLLECTING **SHAPING** DRAFTING REVISING APPENDIX
SHAPING

While the shaping strategies that you have used in previous essays may be helpful, the strategies that follow are particularly appropriate for shaping evaluations.

▍AUDIENCE AND GENRE   As you consider ways to organize and shape your explaining essay, think about your probable audience and genre. Reviews vary greatly in length, critical depth, complexity, and reader appeal. Think about your own purpose and goal; find several magazines, newspapers, or Web sites that publish the kind of review you would like to write, and use the best ones as genre models—not as blueprints—to guide your own writing.

▍ANALYSIS BY CRITERIA   Often, evaluations are organized by criteria. You decide which criteria are appropriate for the subject and audience, and then you use those criteria to outline the essay. Your first few paragraphs of introduction establish your thesis or overall claim and then give background information: what the subject is, why you are evaluating it, what the competition is, and how you gathered your data. Then you order the criteria according to some plan: chronological order, spatial order, order of importance, or another logical sequence. Phyllis Richman's evaluation of the Hunan Dynasty restaurant follows the criteria pattern:

- **Introductory paragraphs:** *information* about the restaurant (location, hours, prices), general *description* of Chinese restaurants today, and *overall claim:* The Hunan Dynasty is reliable, a good value, and versatile.

- **Criterion #1/judgment:** Good restaurants should have an attractive setting and atmosphere/Hunan Dynasty is attractive.
- **Criterion #2/judgment:** Good restaurants should give strong priority to service/Hunan Dynasty has, despite an occasional glitch, expert service.
- **Criterion #3/judgment:** Restaurants that serve moderately priced food should have quality main dishes/Main dishes at Hunan Dynasty are generally good but not often memorable. (*Note:* The most important criterion—the quality of the main dishes—is saved for last.)
- **Concluding paragraphs:** Hunan Dynasty is a top-flight neighborhood restaurant.

■ **COMPARISON AND CONTRAST**   Many evaluations compare two subjects in order to demonstrate why one is preferable to another. Books, films, restaurants, courses, music, writers, scientists, historical events, sports—all can be evaluated by means of comparison and contrast. In evaluating two Asian restaurants, for example, student writer Chris Cameron uses a comparison-and-contrast structure to shape her essay. In the following body paragraph from her essay, Cameron compares two restaurants, the Unicorn and the Yakitori, on the basis of her first criterion—an atmosphere that seems authentically Asian.

> Of the two restaurants, we preferred the authentic atmosphere of the Unicorn to the cultural confusion at the Yakitori. On first impression, the Yakitori looked like a converted truck stop, sparsely decorated with a few bamboo slats and Japanese print fabric hanging in slices as Bruce Springsteen wailed loudly in the ears of the customers. The feeling at the Unicorn was quite the opposite as we entered a room that seemed transported from Chinatown. The whole room had a red tint from the light shining through the flowered curtains, and the place looked truly authentic, from the Chinese patterned rug on the wall to the elaborate dragon on the ceiling. Soft oriental music played as the customers sipped tea from small porcelain cups and ate fortune cookies.

Cameron used the following *alternating* comparison-and-contrast shape for her whole essay.

- Introductory paragraph(s)
- **Thesis:** Although several friends recommended the Yakitori, we preferred the Unicorn for its more authentic atmosphere, courteous service, and well-prepared food.
- **Authentic atmosphere:** Yakitori versus Unicorn
- **Courteous service:** Yakitori versus Unicorn

- **Well-prepared food:** Yakitori versus Unicorn
- Concluding paragraph(s)

On the other hand, Cameron might have used a *block* comparison-and-contrast structure. In this organizational pattern, the outline would be as follows.

- Introductory paragraph(s)
- **Thesis:** Although several friends recommended the Yakitori, we preferred the Unicorn for its more authentic atmosphere, courteous service, and well-prepared food.
- **The Yakitori:** atmosphere, service, and food
- **The Unicorn:** atmosphere, service, and food as compared to the Yakitori's
- Concluding paragraph(s)

▌ **CHRONOLOGICAL ORDER**   Writers often use chronological order, especially in reviewing a book or a film, to shape parts of their evaluations. Film reviewers rely on chronological order to sketch the main outlines of the plot as they comment on the quality of the acting, directing, or cinematography. At the end of this chapter, for example, Kent Y'Blood's review of the film *The Big Chill* uses chronological order to organize the middle paragraphs of his essay.

▌ **CAUSAL ANALYSIS**   Analyzing the *causes or effects* of a place, object, event, or policy can shape an entire evaluation. Evaluations of works of art or performances, for example, often measure the *effect* on the viewers or audience. Mark Stevens, for example, claims that Goya's painting has several definite effects on the viewer; those specific effects become the evidence that supports the claim.

- **Criterion #1/judgment:** The iconography, or use of symbols, contributes to the powerful effect of this picture on the viewer.
  EVIDENCE: The church as a symbol of hopefulness contrasts with the cruelty of the execution. The spire on the church emphasizes for the viewer how powerless the Church is to save the victims.
- **Criterion #2/judgment:** The use of light contributes to the powerful effect of the picture on the viewer.
  EVIDENCE: The light casts an intense glow on the scene, and its glaring, lurid, and artificial qualities create the same effect on the viewer that modern art sometimes does.

- **Criterion #3/judgment:** The composition or use of formal devices contributes to the powerful effect of the picture on the viewer.
  EVIDENCE: The diagonal lines scissor the picture into spaces that give the viewer a claustrophobic feeling. The corpse is foreshortened, so that it looks as though the dead man is bidding the viewer welcome.

▌ **TITLE, INTRODUCTION, AND CONCLUSION** Titles of evaluative writing tend to be short and succinct, stating what product, service, work of art, or performance you are evaluating ("The Big Chill" or "Watching the Eyewitless News") or suggesting a key question or conclusion in the evaluation ("Borrowers Can Be Choosy").

Introductory paragraphs provide background information and description and usually give an overall claim or thesis. In some cases, however, the overall claim comes last, in a concluding "Recommendations" section or in a final summary paragraph. If the overall claim appears in the opening paragraphs, the concluding paragraph may simply review the strengths or weaknesses or may just advise the reader: This *is* or *is not* worth seeing, reading, watching, doing, or buying.

> ❝ I have to stop being afraid of being wrong; I can't wait until everything is perfect before the work comes out. I don't have that kind of time. ❞
> —SHERLEY ANNE WILLIAMS, NOVELIST AND CRITIC

Research Tips ⬚ GO

Before you draft your evaluating essay, stop for a moment and *evaluate your sources* of information and opinion. If you are citing ideas or information from library articles—or especially from the Internet—be skeptical. How reliable is your source? What do you know about your source's reliability or editorial slant? Does the author have a particular bias? Be sure to *qualify* any biased or absolute statements you use from your sources. (See Chapter 13 for additional ideas on evaluating written sources.)

If you cite observations or field sources (interviews, surveys), evaluate the information you collected. Does it reflect only one point of view? How is it biased? Are your responses in surveys limited in number or point of view? Remember: You may use sources that reflect a limited perspective, but *be sure to alert your readers to those limitations.* For example, you might say, "Obviously, these reactions represent only four viewers who saw this film, but . . ." or "Of course, the administrator wanted to defend this student program when he said. . . ."

PEER RESPONSE

The instructions that follow will help you give and receive constructive advice about the rough draft of your evaluating essay. You may use these guidelines for an in-class workshop, a take-home review, or an e-mail computer response.

Writer: Before you exchange drafts, write out the following information about your essay draft.

1. **Purpose, audience, and genre.** Briefly, describe your overall purpose, your genre, and your intended audience. Do you plan to incorporate visuals? If so, where?
2. **Revision plans.** What do you know you still need to work on as you revise your draft?
3. **Questions.** Write one or two questions about your draft that you would like your reader to answer.

Reader: Before you answer the following questions, read the entire draft from start to finish. As you *reread* the draft, do the following.

1. Underline the sentence(s) that state the writer's *overall claim* about the subject.
2. In the margin, put large brackets [ ] around paragraphs that *describe* what the writer is evaluating.
3. On a separate piece of paper or at the end of the writer's essay, make a *three-column log* indicating the writer's criteria, evidence, and judgments. (Does the log include both positive and negative judgments?)
4. Identify with an asterisk (*) any passages in which the writer needs more *evidence* to support the judgments.
5. Write out one *criterion* that is missing or that is not appropriate for the given subject.
6. Assess how well the writer explains the purpose and addresses the intended audience. Do you agree with the writer about his or her revision plans? Finally, answer the writer's questions.

Writer: As you read your peer reviewer's notes and comments, do the following.

1. Consider your peer reviewer's comments and notes. Has your reviewer correctly identified your overall claim? Do you need to add more description of your subject? Does the reviewer's three-column log look like yours? Do you need to revise your criteria or add additional evidence? Do you balance positive and negative judgments?
2. Based on your review, draw up a *revision plan.* Write out the three most important things you need to do as you revise your essay.

CHOOSING COLLECTING SHAPING **DRAFTING** REVISING APPENDIX

DRAFTING

With your criteria in front of you, your data or evidence at hand, and a general plan or sketch outline in mind, begin writing your draft. As you write, focus on your audience. If your evaluation needs to be short, you may have to use only those criteria that will appeal most effectively to your audience. As you write, check occasionally to be sure that you are including your key criteria. While some parts of the essay may seem forced or awkward as you write, other parts will grow and expand as you get your thoughts on paper. As in other papers, don't stop to check spelling or worry about an occasional awkward sentence. If you stop and can't get going, reread what you have written, look over your notes or sketch outline, and pick up the thread again.

> **❝** I have rewritten—often several times—word I have ever published. My pencils outlast their erasers. **❞**
> —VLADIMIR NABOKOV, NOVELIST

CHOOSING COLLECTING SHAPING DRAFTING **REVISING** APPENDIX

REVISING

Remember that revision is not just changing a word here and there or correcting occasional spelling errors. Make your evaluation more effective for your reader by including more specific evidence, changing the order of your paragraphs to make them clearer, cutting out an unimportant point, or adding a point that one of your readers suggests.

GUIDELINES FOR REVISION

* **Review your purpose, audience, and genre.** Is your purpose clear to your target audience? Should you modify your chosen genre to appeal to your audience?

* **Review possibilities for visuals or graphics.** What additions or changes to images might be appropriate for your purpose, genre, or audience?

* **Criteria are *standards of value*.** They contain categories and judgments, as in "good fuel economy," "good reliability," or "powerful use of light and shade in a painting." Some categories, such as "price," have clearly implied judgments ("low price"), but make sure that your criteria refer implicitly or explicitly to a standard of value.

* **Examine your criteria from your audience's point of view.** Which criteria are most important in evaluating your subject? Will your readers agree that the criteria you select are indeed the most important ones? Will changing the order in which you present your criteria make your evaluation more convincing?

- **Include both positive and negative evaluations of your subject.** If all of your judgments are positive, your evaluation will sound like an advertisement. If all of your judgments are negative, your readers may think you are too critical.

- **Be sure to include supporting evidence for each criterion.** Without any data or support, your evaluation will be just an opinion that will not persuade your reader.

- **Avoid overgeneralizing in your claims.** If you are evaluating only three software programs, you cannot say that Lotus 1-2-3 is the best business program around. You can say only that it is the best among the group or the best in the particular class that you measured.

- **Unless your goal is humor or irony, compare subjects that belong in the same class.** Comparing a Ford Focus to a BMW is absurd because they are not similar cars in terms of cost, design, or purpose.

- **If you need additional evidence to persuade your readers, review the questions at the beginning of the "Collecting" section of this chapter.** Have you addressed all the key questions listed there?

- **If you are citing other people's data or quoting sources, check to make sure your summaries and data are accurate.**

- *Signal* **the major divisions in your evaluation to your reader using clear transitions, key words, and paragraph hooks.** At the beginning of new paragraphs or sections in your essay, let your reader know where you are going.

- **Revise sentences for directness and clarity.**

- **Edit your evaluation for correct spelling, appropriate word choice, punctuation, usage, and grammar.**

POSTSCRIPT ON THE WRITING PROCESS

When you finish writing your essay, answer the following questions.

1. Who is the intended audience for your evaluation? Write out one sentence from your essay in which you appeal to or address this audience.

2. Describe the main problem that you had writing this essay, such as finding a topic, collecting evidence, or writing or revising the draft.

3. What parts or paragraphs of your essay do you like best? Indicate the words, phrases, or sentences that make it effective. What do you like about them?

4. Explain what helped you most with your revision: advice from your peers, conference with the teacher, advice from a writing center tutor, rereading your draft several times, or some other source.

5. Write out one question that you still have about the assignment or about your writing and revising process.

STUDENT WRITING ☒

LINDA MEININGER ✕

Borrowers Can Be Choosy

Linda Meininger wrote her evaluation essay on the Interlibrary Loan Office at her campus library. Her purpose was to advise her readers—other students—about the usefulness of the interlibrary loan service. In order to gather information for her essay, she visited the office, learned how to access an interlibrary loan with her computer, interviewed the coordinator of the office, and surveyed nine people who had used the library service. Overall, she discovered that the interlibrary loan office provided a surprisingly convenient, helpful, and inexpensive service. Included here are the following writing-process materials: a draft of her interview and survey questions, a three-column log, her first rough draft, questions for a conference with her instructor, and her final draft.

DRAFT OF INTERVIEW AND SURVEY QUESTIONS

Interview Questions for Interlibrary Loan Office (ILL) Coordinator

1. Have you surveyed your clients to get their impressions about the service? Results? Favorable—why? Unfavorable—why? Valid or not—why?

2. How do you and your employees rate your service?

3. Do you offer any special services for your clients?

4. Have you received any recognition for your work in the ILL?

5. What institutions lend documents to our library?

6. How convenient do you make it for clients to use your services?

... *continued*   Borrowers Can Be Choosy, **Linda Meininger**

Survey Questions

1. Were you satisfied with the interlibrary loan service you received? Why? Why not?
2. How often do you use the service?
3. How much lead time did you allow for your request?
4. What was your area of research?
5. What type of materials did you request? Periodicals? Books? Documents? Theses?
6. What was the cost of using the service?

DRAFT OF THREE-COLUMN LOG

CLAIM: The Interlibrary Loan Office runs a well-organized and efficient operation.

AUDIENCE: Students.

PURPOSE: To evaluate the service and encourage students to use it.

CRITERIA	EVIDENCE	JUDGMENT
1. Timely delivery of materials	Survey results	Mixed
2. Helpful service	Personal experience	Positive
3. Convenience for users	Survey	Positive
4. Scope of libraries available	Interview and brochure	Positive
5. Reasonable cost	Survey and interview	Positive

FIRST ROUGH DRAFT

Are you someone who has searched endlessly through the library's computer database or the card catalog only to have that elusive title never appear? Go directly to Room 210, Morgan Library, and collect an Interlibrary Loan request card, or if that's too far to walk, place your order via e-mail from your PC.

How useful can this service be to you? Stay tuned and I'll show you everything you need to know about Morgan Library Interlibrary Loan (ILL). In evaluating this service, available to all who are affiliated with CSU as a student or employee, I will be looking at the following criteria: convenience and ease of use; timely arrival of materials requested; cooperation and assistance from the ILL staff; and reasonable fees for use of loaned materials.

Jane Smith of the ILL department informed me that request cards can be found in many locations in the library. These color-coded cards are used to request documents, periodicals, theses, or books. The color of the card corresponds to the type of material. Requests may be left at any of the reference desks, or you may drop off your request in person in Room 210 of the library, Monday through Friday. *3*

Students and employees with a PC and a modem may request materials from their office or home. According to Jane Smith, electronic access was developed in-house by the ILL department. A new service has also been established, called the Library Retrieval and Delivery Service (LRDS). This is available to disabled students on campus. Requests may be made by the computer or manually. *4*

Jane Smith of the ILL office informed me that normal turnaround for requests is 24 hours. That translates to one day from the time the requests leave the ILL office for another lending institution. Unless . . . it's spring semester. Then, look out! Deadlines for theses and research are closing in and everyone is in need of the materials yesterday. Then the turnaround time is a week. Most likely materials will not arrive until the end of the school year. Requests in spring semester jump to 300–400 per day compared to a norm of approximately 200 daily. *5*

I would say that being able to fill 300 requests for material is efficient by my standards. Jane was delighted to inform me that Morgan Library was chosen most efficient in the state by other ILLs in Colorado. I think that could be comparable to a Good Housekeeping Seal of Approval or a five-star rating by AAA. *6*

When I visited the ILL office I discovered a staff willing to answer my questions and with a sense of humor. They made me feel comfortable and at ease. One of the brochures I picked up was a pamphlet with their job descriptions: Queen of the World, Resident Geek, ILL's Mouthpiece, Double Agent, ILL's Movie Star and answer to Greta Garbo, and Leading (Lending) Lady. The pamphlet shows me that these people like what they do and can laugh at themselves and their idiosyncrasies. I believe this impression is relayed to their patrons. *7*

CONFERENCE QUESTIONS

1. Are the criteria I have sufficient? Should I have chosen more of the criteria from my log? Or other criteria from my list?
2. My development needs improvement. I need more evidence to substantiate my criteria. What if I didn't secure the surveys necessary (ten) to be fairly objective?

3. Should I introduce my criteria in a subtle manner or just come right out and state them?

4. After class today, I felt that I needed to state judgments for each of my criteria, although they could change after the survey results.

5. Does it sound like I'm writing to a student audience?

REVISED VERSION
Borrowers Can Be Choosy

Are you someone who has searched endlessly through the library's com-   *1*
puter listing, the card catalog, or even the stacks, only to have that elusive
title never appear? Don't give up. Go directly to Room 210, Morgan
Library, and collect an Interlibrary Loan request card. If that's too far to
walk, just place your order via e-mail with your PC, a modem, and some
communications software.

This service can be useful to you during your four-year educational   *2*
experience at Colorado State University. So stay tuned, and I'll review
four characteristics of Morgan Library Interlibrary Loan (ILL). In evaluating this service, which is available to all CSU students, faculty, or staff,
I will be looking at the following criteria: convenience and ease of use,
timely arrival of materials requested, reasonable fees for materials, and
cooperation and assistance from the ILL staff. To gain evidence about the
performance of this department, I interviewed the staff, observed their
operation, and conducted a survey of CSU students, faculty, and employees (see Appendix for results of survey). Out of nine survey respondents,
the level of usage varied from four one-time users to two weekly users.

The convenience and ease of using the interlibrary loan service was   *3*
definitely a high point. Jane Smith of the ILL department informed me
that request cards have been placed in many locations in the library for
convenient access. These color-coded cards are used to request documents, periodicals, theses, or books. The color of the card corresponds to
the type of material requested. Cards may be left at any of the reference
desks, or you may drop off your request in person in Room 210 of the
library, just off to your left at the top of the stairs, Monday through
Friday, 8:00 A.M.–5:00 P.M.

The addition of computer access to interlibrary loans also adds to the   *4*
ease of requesting materials. At the present time, students, faculty, and
employees with a PC and a modem may request materials from their

office or home. According to Ms. Smith, electronic access was developed in-house by the ILL department, making their service available 24 hours per day. Julie Wessling, coordinator of the Interlibrary Loan department, said, "About one third of our users request their specific information via our electronic service."

The ILL has also established another convenient new service, called Library Retrieval and Delivery Service (LRDS). This is available to disabled students on campus and other off-campus users. Requests may be made by computer or by using the request cards. Delivery or notice of nonavailability of materials will be made within 48 hours to three sites on campus: Braiden Hall, the RDS Office in 116 Student Services Building, and the ILL office. There is also dial-up access to the library's computer listings. This service is especially valuable to off-campus users or students with mobility problems. The ILL staff retrieves requests, most of which—according to Ms. Wessling—are in the CSU stacks, and then delivers them to one of the collection sites for pickup by the patron.

Overall, I found the request forms and located the ILL office without any problem, and according to nine out of the nine people surveyed, the ILL service was "easy to use and locate." Judy Lira, a Rocky Mountain High School media specialist, faxes her requests and feels that the technology is a service to the staff and students at her school. Bonnie Mueller, a Morgan Library cataloguing employee, uses LAN to order materials, and she states, "It's wonderful!" While I was in the ILL office, a student was filling out request cards. I tried to enlist her aid for my survey, but she declined, saying that this was her first time using the Interlibrary Loan service. However, she did have one comment for me: "They [the ILL office] need to make us [students] more aware of this." It appears that the convenient access to the ILL system makes it an asset to CSU students and to the local schools.

I wished to experiment personally with the ILL to evaluate the timely arrival of requests, but Ms. Smith explained to me that it would be impossible to receive anything within the time frame I was allotted to finish this essay. Therefore, I will be relying on the experiences and testimony of others.

The normal processing turnaround time for requests, Ms. Smith informed me, is 24 hours. That means that it takes one day from the time the request is made by the borrower to the time it leaves the ILL office for another lending institution. Unless . . . it's spring semester. Then look out! Deadlines for theses and research papers are closing in, and students and faculty need their materials yesterday. Ms. Smith related the story of a student who recently came in on a Wednesday and wanted the item by Monday. She had to tell him, "Sorry, it's not possible, especially now." She said at this time of the year—spring semester—the processing time is approximately one week, and that's just until the request leaves the CSU ILL office. Most likely, materials will not arrive until April or the end of the school year. Normal arrival time seems to vary between ten days and two weeks, according to survey results. Requests at spring semester jump to 300–400 per day, and these requests include not only the CSU customers, but the borrowers from other institutions who are requesting materials from Morgan Library, reported Ms. Wessling.

The normal processing time can be speeded up, however, in some   9
cases. Ms. Wessling explained that "the use of e-mail allows us to locate and help process customers' requests faster. This allows the student or professor to receive the information more quickly. The only thing holding the process back is the time it takes to get the specific request in the mail." Also, articles from periodicals or a document can be sent electronically or by fax. When materials are needed in a hurry, a RUSH may be affixed to the card and a last usable date recorded. This will bring the request to the attention of the office, and they will give it priority to try to locate a copy at a nearby library for pickup by the client. Of the nine people I surveyed, six reported that their materials arrived within 24 hours to two weeks, but one person reported that it took eight weeks and didn't arrive in time to be of use. He allowed two weeks of lead time, but he ordered the material in April. Another person stated that she had to wait over six weeks for materials to arrive. Her materials were "very difficult to locate." My accounting professor, Dr. Middlemist, usually allows a two-week lead time when ordering and said that the "time taken to arrive depended on where the materials were coming from." Dr. Middlemist stated that she uses the service 10–12 times per year, maybe more, depending on what her needs are.

By my standards, being able to fill 300 requests for materials is effi-   10
cient. In addition, Ms. Smith was delighted to inform me that Morgan Library was chosen most efficient by other ILLs in Colorado and will be "looked over" by a team from the state so that their efficient and innovative ideas may be used in other libraries. I think that could be comparable to a Good Housekeeping Seal of Approval or a four-star rating by AAA.

While the timely arrival of materials was a problem, especially in the *11* spring semester, the cost of materials received was very reasonable. For most requests, there is no charge for the service. I found that only on the journal request card was there a line item for maximum cost. This is in the event that there could be photocopying charges. Eight of my nine respondents said they received their materials (books, theses, and journals) free of charge, and the other paid a reasonable fee for Xeroxing one time. It is through the lending and borrowing reciprocal agreement between libraries that the ILL service can be offered at no cost or low cost to the user.

Perhaps the strongest feature of the ILL service was the willingness *12* of the staff to help patrons, answer questions, and keep their sense of humor. They made me feel comfortable and at ease. One of the brochures I picked up was a pamphlet with their job descriptions: Queen of the World, Resident Geek, ILL's Mouthpiece, Double Agent, ILL's Movie Star and Answer to Greta Garbo, and Leading (Lending) Lady. This pamphlet shows that these people like what they do and can laugh at themselves and their idiosyncrasies. Something else Ms. Smith said really sticks in my mind. She said, "I think we're the only department in the whole library where everyone really likes what they do." I believe this impression is relayed to the patrons. My survey results concurred with this, as seven respondents felt that the staff was friendly and helpful. One dissenting student felt that the office could have presented the information she needed over the phone, saving her a trip to the library. The other person felt there wasn't any follow-up on a trace request to see if a book had been lost. Morgan Library has lost this patron to another library. Some of the positive comments received were as follows: "The ILL personnel went out of their way to help me." "What I needed was extremely obscure, and they got most of it." "They found a German book in Berlin, and they Xeroxed it and sent the whole thing FREE!"

As a result of my investigation and evaluation of the ILL office, I *13* hope I have occasion to use their service in the future. I know from my conversations with the staff and other users of ILL that the service and staff are reliable and willing to assist at any time (during office hours, of course). The cost is well within the reach of all patrons, and we have two methods of booking our requests: manually on cards and electronically by computer. So the next time you need an item that the CSU library doesn't own, remember that you do have another resource available at your fingertips: Morgan Library's Interlibrary Loan.

...*continued* Borrowers Can Be Choosy, **Linda Meininger**

Works Cited

Interlibrary Loan. Fort Collins: Colorado State University, 1992.

It's Here! Fort Collins: Colorado State University, 1992.

Libraries Retrieval and Delivery Service. Fort Collins: Colorado State University, 1992.

Morgan Library Interlibrary Loan Survey. Personal Survey. 2 March 1992.

Self-Guided Tour of Morgan Library. Fort Collins: Colorado State University, 1992.

Smith, Jane. Personal Interview. 27 Feb. and 2 March 1992.

Wessling, Julie. Personal Interview. 2 March 1992.

APPENDIX

MORGAN LIBRARY INTERLIBRARY LOAN SURVEY

The following survey was completed by nine students and faculty members. Responses follow each question.

1. What was the subject area of the materials requested?

   Accounting—1   Ben Jonson—17th C writer & critic—1
   Agriculture—1   Cognitive development—1
   Ancient Roman Art—1   Popular fiction—1
   Anthropology—1   Travelogues—1800s—1
   Archaeology—1   Various subjects—1

2. What type of material did you request?

   Book—7   Journal—6
   Thesis—1   Documents—0

3. How much lead time did you allow the Interlibrary Loan office to secure your materials?

   No deadline—5
   24 hours—1
   1 week—1
   2 weeks—2

4. At what time of the year did you request materials?

   Fall semester   Specify month   3 in Oct, Nov, and Dec
   Spring semester   Specify month   1—Jan, 4—Feb & Mar,
                                        2—April, 1—May

5. Did your materials arrive in a timely manner? How much time did it take?

24 hours—1	Very quickly—1
1 week—1	Not more than 1½–2 months—1
8 weeks—1	Over 3 weeks—1
Typically timely—1	10 days—1

6. Were you satisfied with the service you received? Why? Why not?
No, not friendly, no follow-up if lost—1
Yes, friendly and helpful—1
Yes—2
Yes, very satisfied—1
Very, needed extremely obscure stuff & got most of it—1
Extremely satisfied, wonderful to have access to otherwise unreachable materials—1
No problem with service or individuals, satisfied—1
Friendly—1

7. How often do you use the service?

1 time—3	Weekly—1
2 times/year—1	One semester a lot of times—1
10–12 times/year—1	
Goes to Boulder-CU library—1	
2–3 times/week avg., usually turns in requests in batches—1	

8. Was there a charge for your requested materials? If so, did you feel the charge was reasonable or not? How much was it?
No charge—8
Xeroxing charge, reasonable—1

9. Was the staff of the Interlibrary Loan office helpful? Friendly? Did it give out-of-the-ordinary service?
Not friendly, not helpful, no out-of-ordinary service—1
Could have presented info over phone, save trip to library—1
Staff went out of their way to help—1
Worked hard on obscure stuff—1
Always do their best—1

Very friendly—3	Friendly & helpful—3
Regular service—1	Fax requests—1

...continued Borrowers Can Be Choosy, **Linda Meininger**

10. Did you feel that the service was convenient to use (e.g., easy to order materials and pick them up, forms to be filled out, the open hours of the office)?

Easy to use—2   Very—2   Yes—2

Used LAN—1

Yes, feels guilty about amt. of paper involved in all of the requests—1

Fax technology availability real service to students & staff—1

11. From which institution did you receive your materials?

Northwestern—1

Dartmouth—1

Berlin—1

Denver Public Library—1

Oklahoma State University—1

CU-Boulder—1

Don't know—2

QUESTIONS FOR WRITING AND DISCUSSION

1. Evaluate Meininger's final draft, using the peer response guidelines in this chapter. What are the strengths and weaknesses of her essay? Now read Meininger's first rough draft. Which areas did she improve most in her revision?

2. Based on her final draft, make a revised version of Meininger's three-column log. Write out each criterion, the main supporting evidence for that criterion, and the judgment. Indicate the paragraphs (by number) that Meininger devotes to each of her criteria.

3. In her postscript, Meininger wrote, "I revised my criteria and rearranged them in a different order after we talked in class. I didn't want to have my weakest criteria last." Compare her criteria (see her three-column log) with her revised draft. Explain how her additions, deletions, and reordering improved her criteria—and her essay.

4. Reread the questionnaire in Meininger's Appendix. How might she improve that questionnaire? What questions might she add or delete? How might she rephrase the questions?

5. Brainstorm a list of other campus services or organizations that you could evaluate. Choose one of those services or organizations and write a three-column log, indicating the subject, the audience, the criteria, and the possible kinds of evidence that you might collect for your essay.

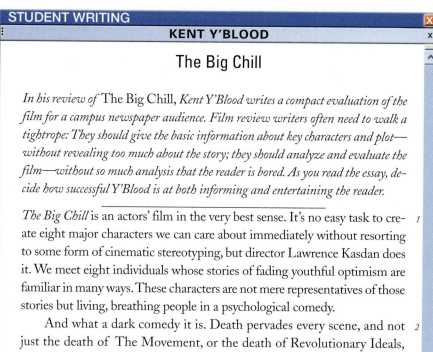

STUDENT WRITING

KENT Y'BLOOD

The Big Chill

In his review of The Big Chill, *Kent Y'Blood writes a compact evaluation of the film for a campus newspaper audience. Film review writers often need to walk a tightrope: They should give the basic information about key characters and plot—without revealing too much about the story; they should analyze and evaluate the film—without so much analysis that the reader is bored. As you read the essay, decide how successful Y'Blood is at both informing and entertaining the reader.*

The Big Chill is an actors' film in the very best sense. It's no easy task to create eight major characters we can care about immediately without resorting to some form of cinematic stereotyping, but director Lawrence Kasdan does it. We meet eight individuals whose stories of fading youthful optimism are familiar in many ways. These characters are not mere representatives of those stories but living, breathing people in a psychological comedy.   1

And what a dark comedy it is. Death pervades every scene, and not just the death of The Movement, or the death of Revolutionary Ideals, or the death of The Spirit of a Generation. Those generalizations have little place here. *The Big Chill* is about a real, particular death: that of Alex Marshall, permanent dropout, college friend of Sam, Sarah, Michael, Nick, Harold, Meg, and Karen. He committed suicide in Harold and Sarah's house, where he was staying with his young girlfriend, Chloe. The old friends, who haven't seen much of each other in years, regroup for his funeral and all decide to spend a weekend at Harold and Sarah's house in Georgia to try to sort out their confusion over Alex's act.   2

At the beginning of the film, Kasdan packs plenty of character information into a relatively short space so that we get to know the people   3

...*continued* The Big Chill, **Kent Y'Blood**

well. As they make their various ways to the funeral, spread out across the country as they are, we begin to learn about them. Sam (Tom Berenger) lines up four miniature vodka bottles on his airplane tray and charms the stewardess out of just one more. Nick (William Hurt) empties out a collection of pills on the seat of his Porsche, downs a couple, and the car roars out ahead of the camera. We get glimpses of the other characters intercut with shots of a man dressing in a pinstripe suit and white shirt, all to the tune of Marvin Gaye's "I Heard It Through the Grapevine." Kasdan ends this scene with a shocker. As a sewn-up wrist is slipped beneath a white cuff, we realize it was Alex's corpse we saw being dressed. This combination of expository information with emotionally powerful action is superb movie making, and Kasdan does not let down after the promise of this opening sequence.

At the funeral itself, we learn more about the principals. Michael (Jeff 4 Goldblum) obviously wants more than comfort from Chloe (Meg Tilly). Harold (Kevin Kline) intones a eulogy and breaks down as he remembers, "There was something about Alex that was too good for this world." His wife, Sarah (Glenn Close), weeps but holds together admirably. Throughout the film, all the characters are true to our first impressions of them but are not mechanically programmed to act predictably. They can still surprise us, and they all do. Later, when the characters get assigned their bedrooms, we get a glimpse of their luggage. Knowing who brings the economy-size bottle of Maalox, who the TV script and a volume of Kafka, and who has many pairs of designer men's underwear just adds that much more to our sense of who each of these people is. It is a weekend of talk, but the talk is supplemented by what we've observed about these people, so the dialogue doesn't have to carry all the weight in the film.

When they do talk, the chat is brilliant. Their sentiment is constantly 5 undercut by jokes that don't weaken their emotions, just complicate them. When Beth rises to play Alex's favorite song on the organ at the funeral (Rolling Stones' "You Can't Always Get What You Want"), it is simultaneously funny and heartbreaking. The friends collectively try to work out how they failed Alex, how they failed their younger selves by becoming successful and rich, and how the people they were became the people they are.

The Big Chill is beautifully edited and masterfully acted and has a 6 script that has more depth than anything I've seen in a long time. The film directly confronts such tough themes as the endurance of friendship, the question of suicide, isolation, meaninglessness—and all to the '60s music of the Temptations, Smokey Robinson, and the Rascals. That's what I call a good movie.

QUESTIONS FOR WRITING AND DISCUSSION

1. Profile yourself as a typical reader of this review: Give your age, note whether you frequently go to movies, describe the kinds of films you enjoy, describe your attitude toward music or events from the sixties, and indicate whether or not you have seen *The Big Chill*. With these notes, come to class prepared to discuss whether or not Y'Blood's review succeeded. Did it make you want to see the movie? If you've seen the film already, was his evaluation convincing? Was it entertaining?

2. Y'Blood's writing-process materials are not reproduced here, but how do you suppose that he collected all the information and supporting evidence for his review? Describe a plausible sequence for his collecting activities.

3. In his review, Y'Blood emphasizes Lawrence Kasdan's skills in directing this film. However, if he had chosen to focus on one particular actor's performance (for example, William Hurt's performance as Nick) or on the relationship of the songs to the story, how would that have changed the review? For practice, rewrite the opening paragraph of this review, focusing either on one principal actor or on the sixties songs.

4. Kent Y'Blood's review, while clearly written, does not discuss any of the film's weaknesses. Does his review sound too positive or too much like an advertisement or blurb for the film? How do you think Y'Blood should have handled this problem? Should he have found some weaknesses in the film to make his evaluation more credible? Explain.

5. Y'Blood's review was written for a campus newspaper. His assignment (the occasion for the review) was to review classic films that college students might want to watch. Where might Y'Blood appeal to this audience more directly? Should he make references to other classic films that college students watch on video or DVD? What other revisions might make his essay more effective for his purpose, the occasion, and his audience? Explain.

Jan Vermeer van Delft
The Lacemaker (1670)
Oil on canvas transferred to panel
Musée du Louvre, Paris

Vermeer's painting of a young woman engaged in the delicate craft of lacemaking appears to celebrate the virtue of skill and work. Notice the nearly photographic reproduction of the details of lacemaking in this painting. A journal entry on page 463 asks you to compare Vermeer's image with a contemporary photograph of a young boy in Cholomo, Honduras, stitching softballs to be sold in the United States.

Problem Solving

10

I n your writing class, you read a conversation between two minority women about racial tensions in African-American and Asian-American communities. The problems, you realize, are continuing and widespread. Publicized instances include a boycott by blacks of Korean shops in New York City and the looting of Korean stores during the Los Angeles riots. As a member of the American-Korean community, you decide to propose your solutions to promote education and understanding. You write up your analysis of the problems and offer solutions for members of your community.

Trying to take notes in your Psych I lecture class—along with 250 other students—you realize that you are completely lost and confused. So you raise your hand to ask a question, but the professor keeps on talking, throwing out more new terms and examples. You look at your neighbor, who just shrugs and keeps on writing. After class, when you think about how hard you've worked to pay your tuition, you realize that you deserve better classes for your money. The problem, you decide, is in the large lecture format—there are just too many students for the teacher to answer questions and explain difficult concepts. So you decide to write a letter to the head of the psychology department (with a copy to the dean of arts and sciences) outlining your problems with this class and proposing that Psychology I be taught in classes no larger than fifty.

> " This country has more problems than it should tolerate and more solutions than it uses. "
> —RALPH NADER,
> CONSUMER RIGHTS ADVOCATE AND PRESIDENTIAL CANDIDATE

> " Whenever life doesn't seem to give an answer, we create one. "
> —LORRAINE HANSBERRY
> AUTHOR OF *A RAISIN IN THE SUN*

W
E DON'T HAVE TO LOOK DILIGENTLY TO LOCATE PROBLEMS IN OUR LIVES. THEY HAVE A HABIT OF SEEKING US OUT. IT SEEMS THAT IF SOMETHING CAN GO WRONG, IT WILL. COUNTRIES ARE FIGHTING EACH OTHER, THE ENVIRONMENT is polluted, prejudice is still rampant, television shows are too violent, sports are corrupted by drugs and money, education is too impersonal, and people drive so recklessly that you take your life in your hands every time you go across town. Everywhere we look, someone else creates problems for us—from minor bureaucratic hassles to serious or life-threatening situations. (On rare occasions, of course, we're part of the problem ourselves.)

Once we identify a potential problem, we must critically question and investigate the issue. Just because we think something is a problem does not mean that other people in other social, political, or cultural contexts will agree that it is a problem. For example, let's critically analyze what appears to be a straightforward issue: grade inflation. First, notice the language used to describe the issue. In this case, the word *inflation* suggests a negative bias; we are predisposed to think that any "inflation" is a bad thing. Next, we need to know who is involved in this issue and who has the most to gain or lose by its existence. What different positions are students, teachers, parents, school administrators, admissions officers at colleges, and companies who hire applicants likely to take on this issue? Some of these groups may see grade inflation as a serious problem, while others may not agree that it is a problem or that it even exists. Finally, we must gather the "facts" about grade inflation and the various definitions commonly used to describe it. There are statistics both proving and disproving that grade inflation exists and a variety of definitions for grade inflation.

Once you can identify something that is actually a problem for a specific group of people, the difficult part is to propose a solution and then persuade others that your solution will in fact solve the problem—without creating new problems and without costing too much. Because your proposal may ask readers to take some action, vote in a certain way, or actually work to implement your proposal, you must make sure that your readers vividly perceive the problem and agree that your plan outlines the most logical and feasible solution.

Techniques for Problem Solving

Problem solving requires all your skills as a writer. You need to observe carefully to see if a problem exists. You may need to remember experiences that illustrate the seriousness of the problem. You need to read and investigate which solutions have worked or have not worked. You often have to explain what the problem is and why or how your proposal would remedy the situation. You may need to evaluate both the problem and alternative solutions. To help you identify the problem and convince your readers of the soundness of your proposal, keep the following techniques in mind.

> *You see things; and you say, "Why?" But I dream things that never were; and I say, "Why not?"*
> —GEORGE BERNARD SHAW, DRAMATIST

- **Critically analyzing the political, social, and cultural** *context*. When, where, and why do some people perceive this issue as a problem? What groups of people are affected, and what do they have to gain or lose? Who would be most affected by a particular solution?

- **Identifying and understanding your** *audience*. If you want something done, fixed, changed, improved, subsidized, banned, reorganized, or made legal or illegal, make sure that you are writing to the appropriate audience.

- **Demonstrating that a** *problem exists*. Some problems are so obvious that your readers will readily acknowledge them: high crime rates, conflicts in Africa and the Middle East, air pollution in industrialized nations, and drug and alcohol abuse. Often, however, you must first convince your audience that a problem exists: Are food preservatives really a serious problem, or would eliminating them cause even more problems?

- **Proposing a** *solution* **that will solve the problem.** After convincing your readers that a serious problem exists, you must then propose a remedy, plan, or course of action that will eliminate or reduce the problem.

- **Persuading your readers that your** *proposal will work*, that it is *feasible,* or that it is better than the *alternative solutions*. You convince your readers by supporting your proposal with *reasons* and *evidence*.

As you start your problem-solving paper, concentrate on ways to *narrow and focus* your topic. When you think about possible topics, follow the advice of environmentalists: "Think Globally, Act Locally." Rather than talk about education or drugs or crime or pollution on a national scale, find out how your community or campus is dealing with a problem. A local focus will help narrow your topic—and provide possibilities for using firsthand observations, personal experience, and interviews.

DEMONSTRATING THAT A PROBLEM EXISTS

A proposal begins with a description of a problem. Demonstrating that the problem exists (and is serious) will make your readers more receptive to your plan for a solution. The following selection from Frank Trippett's *Time* magazine essay "A Red Light for Scofflaws" identifies a problem and provides sufficient examples to demonstrate that scofflawry is pervasive and serious enough to warrant attention. Even if we haven't been personally attacked while driving the Houston or Miami or Los Angeles freeways, Trippett convinces us that *scofflawry*—deliberately disobeying ("scoffing at") laws—is serious. His vivid description makes us aware of the problem.

Demonstrating that a problem exists

Law and order is the longest-running and probably the best-loved political issue in U.S. history. Yet it is painfully apparent that millions of Americans who would never think of themselves as lawbreakers, let alone criminals, are taking increasing liberties with the legal codes that are designed to protect and nourish their society. Indeed, there are moments today—amid outlaw litter, tax cheating, illicit noise, and motorized anarchy—when it seems as though the scofflaw represents the wave of the future. Harvard sociologist David Riesman suspects that a majority of Americans have blithely taken to committing supposedly minor derelictions as a matter of course. Already, Riesman says, the ethic of U.S. society is in danger of becoming this: "You're a fool if you obey the rules."

Evidence: Authority

Evidence: Examples

The dangers of scofflawry vary wildly. The person who illegally spits on the sidewalk remains disgusting, but clearly poses less risk to others than the company that illegally buries hazardous chemical waste in an unauthorized location. The fare beater on the subway presents less threat to life than the landlord who ignores fire safety statutes. The most immediately and measurably dangerous scofflawry, however, also happens to be the most visible. The culprit is the American driver, whose lawless activities today add up to a colossal public nuisance. The hazards range from routine double parking that jams city streets to the drunk driving that kills some 25,000 people and injures at least 650,000 others yearly.

Evidence: Statistics

The most flagrant scofflaw of them all is the red-light runner. The flouting of stop signals has got so bad in Boston that residents tell an anecdote about a cabby who insists that red lights are "just for decoration." The power of the stoplight to control traffic seems to be waning everywhere. In Los Angeles, red-light running has become perhaps the city's most common traffic violation. In New York City, going through an intersection is like Russian roulette. Admits Police Commissioner Robert J.

McGuire: "Today it's a 50–50 toss-up as to whether people will stop for a red light." Meanwhile, his own police largely ignore the lawbreaking.

Evidence: Authority

    The prospect of the collapse of public manners is not merely a matter of etiquette. Society's first concern will remain major crime, but a foretaste of the seriousness of incivility is suggested by what has been happening in Houston. Drivers on Houston freeways have been showing an increasing tendency to replace the rules of the road with violent outbreaks. Items from the Houston police department's new statistical category—freeway traffic violence: (1) Driver flashes high-beam lights at car that cut in front of him, whose occupants then hurl a beer can at his windshield, kick out his tail lights, slug him eight stitches worth. (2) Dump-truck driver annoyed by delay batters trunk of stalled car ahead and its driver with steel bolt. (3) Hurrying driver of 18-wheel truck deliberately rear-ends car whose driver was trying to stay within 55 m.p.h. limit.

Evidence: Examples

DEMONSTRATING	PROPOSING

PROPOSING A SOLUTION AND CONVINCING YOUR READERS

Once you have vividly described the problem, you are ready to propose a solution and persuade your readers. In the following selection from his book *Fist Stick Knife Gun,* Geoffrey Canada proposes ways to create a safer world for our children. Geoffrey Canada is president and CEO of Harlem's Rheedlen Center for Children and Families, an organization that serves at-risk inner-city children. As you read Canada's proposal, notice how he narrows the problem to saving the lives of inner-city children. When he makes a recommendation, he talks about the advantages of his solution, but he talks about *feasibility problems* and real drawbacks. At several points, he gives *reasons* why we must change and supports his reasons with *evidence* from statistics and from his own personal experience.

    If I could get the mayors, the governors, and the president to look into the eyes of the 5-year-olds of this nation, dressed in old raggedy clothes, whose jacket zippers are broken but whose dreams are still alive, they would know what I know—that children need people to fight for them. To stand with them on the most dangerous streets, in the dirtiest hallways, in their darkest hours. We as a country have been too willing to take from our weakest when times get hard. People who allow this to happen must be educated, must be challenged, must be turned around.

Personal experience

    If we are to save our children we must become people they will look up to. We must stand up and be visible heroes. I want people to understand the crisis and I want people to act: Either we address the murder and mayhem

Proposal

in our country or we simply won't be able to continue to have the kind of democratic society that we as Americans cherish. Violence is not just a problem of the inner cities or of the minorities in this country. This is a national crisis and the nation must mobilize differently if we are to solve it.

Part of what we must do is change the way we think about violence. Trying to catch and punish people after they have committed a violent act won't deter violence in the least. In life on the street, it's better to go to jail than be killed, better to act quickly and decisively even if you risk being caught.

Specific recommendations

There are, however, things that governments could and should do right away to begin to end the violence on our streets. They include the following:

Specific details

Create a peace officer corps. Peace officers would not be police; they would not carry guns and would not be charged with making arrests. Instead they would be local men and women hired to work with children in their own neighborhoods. They would try to settle "beefs" and mediate disputes. They would not be the eyes and ears of the regular police force. Their job would be to try to get these young people jobs, to get them back into school, and, most importantly, to be at the emergency rooms and funerals where young people come together to grieve and plot revenge, in order to keep them from killing one another.

Recommendation

Reduce the demand for drugs. Any real effort at diverting the next generation of kids from selling drugs must include plans to find employment for these children when they become teenagers. While that will require a significant expenditure of public funds, the savings from reduced hospitalization and reduced incarceration will more than offset the costs of employment. . . .

Recommendation

Reduce the amount of violence on television and in the movies. Violence in the media is ever more graphic, and the justification for acting violently is deeply implanted in young people's minds. The movie industry promotes the message that power is determined not merely by carrying a gun, but by carrying a big gun that is an automatic and has a big clip containing many bullets.

Reason + evidence

What about rap music, and especially "gangsta rap"? It is my opinion that people have concentrated too much attention on this one source of media violence. Many rap songs are positive, and some are neither positive nor negative—just kids telling their stories. But there are some rap singers who have decided that their niche in the music industry will be the most violent and vile. I would love to see the record industry show some restraint in limiting these rappers' access to fame and fortune.

Reduce and regulate the possession of handguns. I believe all handgun sales should be banned in this country. Recognizing, however, that other Americans may not be ready to accept a ban on handguns, I believe there are still some things we must do.

Recommendation

Licensing. Every person who wants to buy a handgun should have to pass both a written test and a field test. The cost for these new procedures should be paid by those who make, sell, and buy handguns. . . .

Recommendation

Gun buy-backs. The federal government, which recently passed a $32 billion crime bill, needs to invest billions of dollars over the next ten years buying guns back from citizens. We now have more than 200 million guns in circulation in our country. A properly cared-for gun can last for decades. There is no way we can deal with handgun violence until we reduce the number of guns currently in circulation. We know that young people won't give up their guns readily, but we have to keep in mind that this is a long-term problem. We have to begin to plan now to get the guns currently in the hands of children out of circulation permanently.

Recommendation

Statistics

The truth of the matter is that reducing the escalating violence will be complicated and costly. If we were fighting an outside enemy that was killing our children at a rate of more than 5,000 a year, we would spare no expense. What happens when the enemy is us? What happens when those Americans' children are mostly black and brown? Do we still have the will to invest the time and resources in saving their lives? The answer must be yes, because the impact and fear of violence has over-run the boundaries of our ghettos and has both its hands firmly around the neck of our whole country. And while you may not yet have been visited by the spectre of death and fear of this new national cancer, just give it time. Sooner or later, unless we act, you will. We all will.

Response to feasibility problems

Evidence

Statistics

Call to action

▌ WARMING UP: Journal Exercises

The following exercises will help you practice problem solving. Read all of the following exercises and then write on one or two that interest you most. If another idea occurs to you, write about it.

1. Wishful-thinking department: Assume that you are a member of the student government, and your organization has $10,000 to spend on a campus improvement project. Think of some campus problem that needs solving. Describe why it is a problem. Then outline your plan for a solution, indicating how you would spend the money to help solve the problem.

> ❝ A good solution solves more than one problem, and it does not make new problems. I am talking about health as opposed to almost any cure, coherence of pattern as opposed to almost any solution produced piecemeal or in isolation. ❞
>
> —WENDELL BERRY,
> AUTHOR OF *THE GIFT OF THE GOOD LAND*

> ❝ God, give us grace to accept with serenity the things that cannot be changed, courage to change the things which should be changed, and the wisdom to distinguish the one from the other. ❞
>
> —REINHOLD NIEBUHR,
> AUTHOR AND THEOLOGIAN

2. Reread Frank Trippett's analysis of the scofflaw problem. Write a letter to the city council recommending a solution to one of the problems that Trippett identifies—a solution that the city council has the power to implement.

3. Eldridge Cleaver once said, "You're either part of the solution or part of the problem." Examine one of your activities or pastimes—sports, shopping, cruising, eating, drinking, or even studying. How does what you do possibly create a problem from someone else's point of view? Explain.

4. "Let the buyer beware" is a time-honored maxim for all consumers. Unless you are vigilant, you can easily be ripped off. Write a letter to the Better Business Bureau explaining some consumer problem or rip-off that you've recently experienced and suggest a solution that will prevent others from being exploited.

5. The following visual, with an accompanying paragraph, appears on the United Nations Children's Fund (UNICEF) Web site at http://www.unicef.

A small boy sleeps at the table where he was making softballs in the village of Cholomo, Honduras.

Some people say that boycotts—that is, refusing to buy goods made by children—will help put an end to child labour. But boycotts can also hurt working children and their families, as the children lose their jobs, and then their families have even less money to live on. If employers provided parents with jobs at a living wage, fewer children would be forced to go to work. (UNICEF/89-0052/Vauclair) org. Analyze the effectiveness of the image and text in demonstrating the problem of child labor. What details in the picture support the argument that child labor is a problem we must solve?

6. Changing the rules of some sports might make them more enjoyable, less violent, or fairer: moving the three-point line farther out, introducing the 30-second clock in NCAA basketball, using TV instant replays in professional and college football and basketball, imposing stiffer fines for brawls in hockey games, requiring boxers to wear padded helmets, giving equal pay and media coverage to women's sports. Choose a sport you enjoy as a participant or observer, identify and explain the problem you want to solve, and justify your solution in a letter to the editors of *Sports Illustrated.*

7. After studying the text and image in question 5, reexamine the Vermeer painting, *The Lacemaker,* which appears at the beginning of this chapter. Art critic Mark Harden says the following about this painting: "Contemporary Dutch painting portrayed industriousness as an allegory of domestic virtue. While the inclusion of the prayer book pays fealty to this theme, it is a secondary concern to the depiction of the handicraft of lacemaking, and in the highest sense, the creative act itself." Compare and contrast the Vermeer painting with the UNICEF photograph in terms of the details of composition, the work being done, the social class and age of the central figures, and the cultural/social context of the two images. Why does one image seem to suggest a social problem while the other appears to depict a social virtue?

8. Read the following short essay on grade inflation, which appeared in the *New York Times Magazine* in May 2004. Michael Bérubé, the Paterno Family professor of literature at Pennsylvania State University, proposes a solution to grade inflation based on scoring systems used in figure skating and gymnastics. Using the guidelines for problem solving given at the beginning of this chapter, write a journal entry evaluating the effectiveness of Bérubé's analysis of the problem and his proposal for his audience of *New York Times* readers.

How to End Grade Inflation: A Modest Proposal
Michael Bérubé

Last month, Princeton University announced it would combat grade inflation by proposing that A-minuses, A's and A-pluses be awarded to no more than the top 35 percent of students in any course. For those of us in higher education, the news has come as a shock, almost as if Princeton had declared that spring in central New Jersey would begin promptly on March 21, with pleasant temperatures in the 60s and 70s through the end of the semester. For until now, grade inflation was like the weather: it got worse every year, or at least everyone said so, and yet hardly anybody did anything about it.

There is nothing inherently wrong with grade inflation. Imagine a system of scoring on a scale from 1 to 6 in which everyone gets a 5 and above, or a scale of 1 to 10 in which the lowest posted score is around 8.5. Such are the worlds of figure skating and gymnastics. If colleges employed similar scoring systems, the class valedictorian would come in with a 4.0, followed closely by hundreds of students above 3.95, trailed by the class clown at 3.4.

Critics would argue that we must be perilously close to such a system right now. Several years ago, Harvard awarded "honors" to 90 percent of its graduates. For its part, Princeton has disclosed that A's have been given 47 percent of the time in recent years, up from 31 percent in the mid-1970s. Perhaps grade inflation is most severe at the most elite colleges, where everyone is so far above average that the rules of the Caucus Race in "Alice in Wonderland" apply: everybody has won, and all must have prizes. At the school where I teach, Penn State, grade inflation over the same period has not been nearly so drastic. In the spring semester of 1975, the average G.P.A. was 2.86; in 2001 it had risen to only 3.02.

Still, we don't grade all that toughly. English departments have basically worked on the A/B binary system for some time: A's and A-minuses for the best students, B's for everyone else and C's, D's and F's for students who miss half the classes or threaten their teachers with bodily harm. At Penn State, A's accounted for 47 percent of the grades in English in 2002. The numbers are similar for sociology, comparative literature and psychology—and indeed for the College of Liberal Arts as a whole. The sciences and engineering, notoriously, are stingier.

What to do? If we so desired, we could recalibrate grades at Penn State, at Princeton or at any college in the country. The principle is simple enough, and it's crucial to every diving competition: we would merely need to account for each course's degree of difficulty.

Every professor, and every department, produces an average grade—an average for the professor over her career and an average for the discipline over the decades. And if colleges really wanted to clamp down on grade inflation, they could whisk it away statistically, simply by factoring those averages into each student's G.P.A. Imagine that G.P.A.'s were calculated on a scale of 10 with the average grade, be it a B-minus or an A-minus, counted as a 5. The B-plus in chemical engineering, where the average grade is, say, C-plus, would be rewarded accordingly and assigned a value of 8; the B-plus in psychology, where the average grade might be just over B-plus, would be graded like an easy dive, adequately executed, and given a 4.7.

After all, colleges keep all the necessary statistics—by year, by course and by department. We know perfectly well which courses require a forward somersault with two and a half twists from the pike position for an A, and which courses will give B's for cannonballs. We could even encourage professors and entire departments to increase their prestige by lowering their average grade and thereby increasing their "degree of difficulty." Students who earn A's in difficult courses would benefit—as would students who earn B's.

Incorporating "degree of difficulty" into students' G.P.A.'s would turn campuses upside down; it would eliminate faculty capriciousness precisely by factoring it in; and it would involve nothing more than using the numbers we already have at our disposal. It would be confusing as hell. But it would yield a world in which the average grade was never anything more or less than the middle of the scale.

PROFESSIONAL WRITING

One Thing to Do About Food

Eric Schlosser, Marion Nestle, Michael Pollan, Troy Duster and Elizabeth Ransom, Peter Singer, and Jim Hightower

It is well known that the United States faces an epidemic of problems related to food: childhood obesity, type II diabetes in adults, junk food advertising to children, unhealthy eating by adults, exploitative farm legislation, unsafe working conditions for agricultural laborers, factory farm cruelty to animals, and overall ignorance on the part of the American public about how food is produced. In a forum edited by Alice Waters for The Nation *magazine, the following seven authors were among a group of twelve writers contributing short responses about reforming food production, regulation, and consumption in the United States.*

Following each short response, Alice Waters provides a brief biographical sketch of the author. As you read each selection, consider how each author's proposal relates to his or her professional expertise and how all these potential solutions relate to each other and to an overall solution to the problem.

Eric Schlosser

Every year the fast-food chains, soda companies and processed-food manufacturers spend billions marketing their products. You see their ads all the time. They tend to feature a lot of attractive, happy, skinny people having fun. But you rarely see what's most important about the food: where it comes from, how it's made and what it contains. Tyson ads don't show chickens crammed together at the company's factory farms, and Oscar Mayer ads don't reveal what really goes into those wieners. There's a good reason for this. Once you learn how our modern industrial food system has transformed what most Americans eat, you become highly motivated to eat something else.

The National Uniformity for Food Act of 2005, passed by the House and now before the Senate, is a fine example of how food companies and their allies work hard to keep consumers in the dark. Backed by the American Beverage Association, the American Frozen Food Association, the Coca-Cola Company, ConAgra Foods, the National Restaurant Association, the International Food Additives Council, Kraft Foods, the National Cattlemen's Beef Association and the US Chamber of Commerce, among many others, the new law would prevent states from having food safety or labeling requirements stricter than those of the federal government. In the name of "uniformity," it would impose rules that are uniformly bad. State laws that keep lead out of children's candy and warn pregnant women about dangerous ingredients would be wiped off the books.

What single thing could change the US food system, practically overnight? Widespread public awareness—of how this system operates and whom it benefits, how it harms consumers, how it mistreats animals and pollutes the land, how it corrupts public officials and intimidates the press, and most of all, how its power ultimately depends on a series of cheerful and ingenious lies. The modern environmental movement began forty-four years ago when *Silent Spring* exposed the deceptions behind the idea of "better living through chemistry." A similar movement is now gaining momentum on behalf of sustainable agriculture and real food. We must not allow the fast-food industry, agribusiness and Congress to deceive us. "We urgently need an end to these false assurances, to the sugar-coating of unpalatable facts," Rachel Carson famously argued. "In the words of Jean Rostand, 'The obligation to endure gives us the right to know.'"

Eric Schlosser is the author of Fast Food Nation: The Dark Side of the All-American Meal *and, with Charles Wilson,* Chew on This: Everything You Don't Want to Know About Fast Food *(both Houghton Mifflin).*

Marion Nestle

From a public health perspective, obesity is the most serious nutrition problem among children as well as adults in the United States. The roots of this problem can be traced to farm policies and Wall Street. Farm subsidies, tariffs and trade agreements support a food supply that provides 3,900 calories per day per capita, roughly twice the average need, and 700 calories a day higher than in 1980, at the dawn of the obesity epidemic. In this overabundant food economy, companies must compete fiercely for sales, not least because of Wall Street's expectations for quarterly growth. These pressures induce companies to make highly profitable "junk" foods, market them directly to children and advertise such foods as appropriate for consumption at all times, in large amounts, by children of all ages. In this business environment, childhood obesity is just collateral damage. 1

Adults may be fair game for marketers, but children are not. Children cannot distinguish sales pitches from information unless taught to do so. Food companies spend at least $10 billion annually enticing children to desire food brands and to pester parents to buy them. The result: American children consume more than one-third of their daily calories from soft drinks, sweets, salty snacks and fast food. Worse, food marketing subverts parental authority by making children believe they are supposed to be eating such foods and they—not their parents—know what is best for them to eat. 2

Today's marketing methods extend beyond television to include Internet games, product placements, character licensing and word-of-mouth campaigns—stealth methods likely to be invisible to parents. When restrictions have been called for, the food industry has resisted, invoking parental responsibility and First Amendment rights, and proposing self-regulation instead. But because companies cannot be expected to act against corporate self-interest, government regulations are essential. Industry pressures killed attempts to regulate television advertising to children in the late 1970s, but obesity is a more serious problem now. 3

It is time to try again, this time to stop all forms of marketing foods   *4*
to kids—both visible and stealth. Countries in Europe and elsewhere are
taking such actions, and we could too. Controls on marketing may not be
sufficient to prevent childhood obesity, but they would make it easier for
parents to help children to eat more healthfully.

*Marion Nestle, Paulette Goddard Professor of Nutrition, Food Studies and Public Health at New
York University, is the author of* Food Politics (*California) and* What to Eat (*North Point*).

ˣ Michael Pollan

Every five years or so the President of the United States signs an obscure   *1*
piece of legislation that determines what happens on a couple of hundred
million acres of private land in America, what sort of food Americans eat
(and how much it costs) and, as a result, the health of our population. In a
nation consecrated to the idea of private property and free enterprise, you
would not think any piece of legislation could have such far-reaching effects, especially one about which so few of us—even the most politically
aware—know anything. But in fact the American food system is a game
played according to a precise set of rules that are written by the federal government with virtually no input from anyone beyond a handful of farm-
state legislators. Nothing could do more to reform America's food
system—and by doing so improve the condition of America's environment
and public health—than if the rest of us were suddenly to weigh in.

The farm bill determines what our kids eat for lunch in school every   *2*
day. Right now, the school lunch program is designed not around the goal
of children's health but to help dispose of surplus agricultural commodi-
ties, especially cheap feedlot beef and dairy products, both high in fat.

The farm bill writes the regulatory rules governing the production of   *3*
meat in this country, determining whether the meat we eat comes from
sprawling, brutal, polluting factory farms and the big four meatpackers
(which control 80 percent of the market) or from local farms.

Most important, the farm bill determines what crops the government   *4*
will support—and in turn what kinds of foods will be plentiful and cheap.
Today that means, by and large, corn and soybeans. These two crops are
the building blocks of the fast-food nation: A McDonald's meal (and most
of the processed food in your supermarket) consists of clever arrangements
of corn and soybeans—the corn providing the added sugars, the soy providing the added fat, and both providing the feed for the animals. These

crop subsidies (which are designed to encourage overproduction rather than to help farmers by supporting prices) are the reason that the cheapest calories in an American supermarket are precisely the unhealthiest. An American shopping for food on a budget soon discovers that a dollar buys hundreds more calories in the snack food or soda aisle than it does in the produce section. Why? Because the farm bill supports the growing of corn but not the growing of fresh carrots. In the midst of a national epidemic of diabetes and obesity our government is, in effect, subsidizing the production of high-fructose corn syrup.

This absurdity would not persist if more voters realized that the farm bill is not a parochial piece of legislation concerning only the interests of farmers. Today, because so few of us realize we have a dog in this fight, our legislators feel free to leave deliberations over the farm bill to the farm states, very often trading away their votes on agricultural policy for votes on issues that matter more to their constituents. But what could matter more than the health of our children and the health of our land?

Perhaps the problem begins with the fact that this legislation is commonly called "the farm bill"—how many people these days even know a farmer or care about agriculture? Yet we all eat. So perhaps that's where we should start, now that the debate over the 2007 farm bill is about to be joined. This time around let's call it "the food bill" and put our legislators on notice that this is about us and we're paying attention.

Michael Pollan, Knight Professor of Journalism at the University of California, Berkeley, is the author of The Omnivore's Dilemma: A Natural History of Four Meals *(Penguin).*

Troy Duster and Elizabeth Ransom

Strong preferences for the kinds of food we eat are deeply rooted in the unexamined practices of the families, communities and cultural groups in which we grow up. From more than a half-century of social science research, we know that changing people's habitual behavior—from smoking to alcohol consumption, from drugs to junk food—is a mighty task. Individuals rarely listen to health messages and then change their ways.

If we as a nation are to alter our eating habits so that we make a notable dent in the coming health crisis around the pandemic of childhood obesity and Type II diabetes, it will be the result of long-term planning that will include going into the schools to change the way we learn about food. With less than 2 percent of the US population engaged with agriculture, a whole generation of people has lost valuable knowledge that comes from growing, preserving and preparing one's own food. A recent initiative by the City of Berkeley, California, represents a promising national model to fill this void. The city's Unified School District has approved a school lunch program that is far more than just a project to change what students eat at the noon hour. It is a daring attempt to change the institutional environment in which children learn about food at an early age, a comprehensive approach that has them planting and growing the food in a garden, learning biology through an engaged process, with some then cooking the food that they grow. If all goes well, they will learn about the complex relationship between nutrition and physiology so that it is an integrated experience—not a decontextualized, abstract, rote process.

But this is a major undertaking, and it will need close monitoring and fine-tuning. Rather than assuming that one size fits all in the school, we will need to find out what menu resonates with schools that are embedded within local cultures and climatic conditions—for example, teaching a health-mindful approach to Mexican, Chinese, Italian, Puerto Rican, Caribbean and Midwestern cuisine. Finally, we need to regulate the kinds of food sold in and around the school site—much as we now do with smoking, alcohol and drugs. The transition from agrarian to modern society has created unforeseen health challenges. Adopting an engaged learning approach through agricultural production and consumption will help future generations learn what it means to eat healthy food and five healthy lives. *3*

Troy Duster, director of the Institute for the History of Production of Knowledge at New York University, holds an appointment as Chancellor's Professor at the University of California, Berkeley. Elizabeth Ransom is a sociologist at the University of Richmond whose work focuses on globalization, food and the changing structure of agriculture.

Peter Singer

There is one very simple thing that everyone can do to fix the food system. Don't buy factory-farm products. *1*

Once, the animals we raised went out and gathered things we could not or would not eat. Cows ate grass, chickens pecked at worms or seeds. Now the animals are brought together and we grow food for them. We use synthetic fertilizers and oil-powered tractors to grow corn or soybeans. Then we truck it to the animals so they can eat it. *2*

When we feed grains and soybeans to animals, we lose most of their nutritional value. The animals use it to keep their bodies warm and to de- *3* velop bones and other body parts that we cannot eat. Pig farms use six pounds of grain for every pound of boneless meat we get from them. For cattle in feedlots, the ratio is 13:1. Even for chickens, the least inefficient factory-farmed meat, the ratio is 3:1.

Most Americans think the best thing they could do to cut their per-   4
sonal contributions to global warming is to swap their family car for a fuel-efficient hybrid like the Toyota Prius. Gidon Eshel and Pamela Martin of the University of Chicago have calculated that typical meat-eating Americans would reduce their emissions even more if they switched to a vegan diet. Factory farming is not sustainable. It is also the biggest system of cruelty to animals ever devised. In the United States alone, every year nearly 10 billion animals live out their entire lives confined indoors. Hens are jammed into wire cages, five or six of them in a space that would be too small for even one hen to be able to spread her wings. Twenty thousand chickens are raised in a single shed, completely covering its floor. Pregnant sows are kept in crates too narrow for them to turn around, and too small for them to walk a few steps. Veal calves are similarly confined, and deliberately kept anemic.

This is not an ethically defensible system of food production. But in   5
the United States—unlike in Europe—the political process seems powerless to constrain it. The best way to fight back is to stop buying its products. Going vegetarian is a good option, and going vegan, better still. But if you continue to eat animal products, at least boycott factory farms.

Peter Singer is a professor of bioethics at Princeton University. His most recent book, co-written with Jim Mason, is The Way We Eat: Why Our Food Choices Matter *(Rodale).*

Jim Hightower

In the very short span of about fifty years, we've allowed our politicians to   1
do something remarkably stupid: turn America's food-policy decisions over to corporate lobbyists, lawyers and economists. These are people who could not run a watermelon stand if we gave them the melons and had the Highway Patrol flag down the customers for them—yet, they have taken charge of the decisions that direct everything from how and where food is grown to what our children eat in school.

As a result, America's food system (and much of the world's) has been   2
industrialized, conglomeratized and globalized. This is food we're talking about, not widgets! Food, by its very nature, is meant to be agrarian, small-scale and local.

...*continued* One Thing to Do About Food, **Jim Hightower**

But the Powers That Be have turned the production of our edibles *3*
away from the high art of cooperating with nature into a high-cost system
of always trying to overwhelm nature. They actually torture food—
applying massive doses of pesticides, sex hormones, antibiotics, genetically
manipulated organisms, artificial flavorings and color, chemical preservatives, ripening gas, irradiation . . . and so awfully much more. The attitude
of agribusiness is that if brute force isn't working, you're probably just not
using enough of it.

More fundamentally, these short-cut con artists have perverted the *4*
very concept of food. Rather than being both a process and product that
nurtures us (in body and spirit) and nurtures our communities, food is approached by agribusiness as just another commodity that has no higher
purpose than to fatten corporate profits.

There's our challenge. It's not a particular policy or agency that must be *5*
changed but the most basic attitude of policy-makers. And the only way
we're going to get that done is for you and me to become the policy-makers,
taking charge of every aspect of our food system—from farm to fork.

The good news is that this "good food" movement is already well un- *6*
der way and gaining strength every day. It receives little media coverage, but
consumers in practically every city, town and neighborhood across America are reconnecting with local farmers and artisans to de-industrialize,
de-conglomeratize, de-globalize—de-Wal-Martize—their food systems.

Of course, the Powers That Be sneer at these efforts, saying they can't *7*
succeed. But, as a friend of mine who is one of the successful pioneers in
this burgeoning movement puts it: "Those who say it can't be done should
not interrupt those who are doing it."

Look around wherever you are and you'll find local farmers, con- *8*
sumers, chefs, marketers, gardeners, environmentalists, workers, churches,
co-ops, community organizers and just plain folks who are doing it. These
are the Powers That Ought to Be—and I think they will be. Join them!

Jim Hightower (www.jimhightower.com) *is a syndicated newspaper columnist, a radio commenta-
tor and the author of six books including* Thieves in High Places (*Plume*).

vo·cab·u·lar·y

In your journal, write the meaning of the italicized words in the following phrases.

Eric Schlosser

- series of cheerful and *ingenious* lies **(3)**
- *sustainable* agriculture **(3)**
- sugar-coating of *unpalatable* facts **(3)**

Marion Nestle

- food marketing *subverts* parental authority **(2)**
- *product placements* **(3)**
- *stealth* methods **(3)**

Michael Pollan

- a nation *consecrated* to the idea of private property **(1)**
- *subsidizing* the production **(4)**
- not a *parochial* piece of legislation **(5)**

Troy Duster and Elizabeth Ransom

- the *pandemic* of childhood obesity **(2)**
- not a *decontextualized*, abstract, *rote* process **(2)**
- what menu *resonates* with schools **(3)**
- transition from *agrarian* to modern society **(3)**

Peter Singer

- use *synthetic* fertilizers **(2)**
- switched to a *vegan* diet **(4)**
- factory farming is not *sustainable* **(4)**
- deliberately kept *anemic* **(4)**
- not an *ethically* defensible system **(5)**

Jim Hightower

- has been industrialized, *conglomeratized* and globalized **(2)**
- attitude of *agribusiness* **(3)**
- pioneers in this *burgeoning* movement **(7)**

QUESTIONS FOR WRITING AND DISCUSSION

1. Choose one of the short essays and annotate it for the analysis of the problem and then for the proposed solution. For this author, how much discussion is about the problem and how much about the solution? Which part—the discussion of the problem or the explanation of the solution—is more specific, detailed, and supported? What parts could be explained further to make the author's recommendations more effective or more persuasive? Be prepared to present your findings in class.

2. Find and underline each author's claim statement. What "one thing" does each author recommend should be done to address the problem? What reasons and evidence does each author offer in support of his or her claim? Explain.

3. Do your own library or Web research on issues related to the topics in these responses. Check out an award-winning cartoon critiquing factory farms at www.themeatrix.com. A popular Web site for issues related to animal rights and vegetarianism is People for the Ethical Treatment of Animals (PETA) at http://www.peta.org. For an overview of effective farming practices, visit Polyface Farms at http://polyface.com. Finally, Michael Pollan's book *The Omnivore's Dilemma* addresses many of the issues raised in these authors' responses. Write up your research notes in a short investigative report to the members of your class.

4. Assume that Alice Waters has asked you to contribute a short essay to this forum. Write an essay that explains your position about food production and eating habits, and offer your best suggestion for resolving the problems presented in these essays.

PROFESSIONAL WRITING

The Argument Culture

Deborah Tannen

A professor of linguistics at Georgetown University, Deborah Tannen is also a best-selling author of many books on discourse and gender, including You Just Don't Understand: Women and Men in Conversation *(1990),* Talking from 9 to 5 *(1994),* The Argument Culture: Moving from Debate to Dialogue *(1998), and* I Only Say This Because I Love You *(2001). Throughout her career, Tannen has focused on how men and women have different conversational habits and assumptions, whether they talk on the job or at home. In the following essay, taken from* The Argument Culture, *Tannen tries to convince her readers that adversarial debates—which typically represent only two sides of an issue and thus promote antagonism— create problems in communication. As a culture, Tannen believes, we would be much more successful if we didn't always think of argument as a war or a fight but as a dialogue among a variety of different positions. As you read her essay, does Tannen persuade you that our "argument culture" really is a problem and that her solutions will help solve that problem?*

Balance. Debate. Listening to both sides. Who could question these noble American traditions? Yet today, these principles have been distorted. Without thinking, we have plunged headfirst into what I call the "argument culture." 1

The argument culture urges us to approach the world, and the people in it, in an adversarial frame of mind. It rests on the assumption that opposition is the best way to get anything done: The best way to discuss an idea is to set up a debate; the best way to cover news is to find spokespeople who express the most extreme, polarized views and present them as "both sides"; the best way to settle disputes is litigation that pits one party against the other; the best way to begin an essay is to attack someone; and the best way to show you're really thinking is to criticize. 2

More and more, our public interactions have become like arguing with a spouse. Conflict can't be avoided in our public lives any more than we can avoid conflict with people we love. One of the great strengths of our society is that we can express these conflicts openly. But just as spouses have to learn ways of settling their differences without inflicting real damage, so we, as a society, have to find constructive ways of resolving disputes and differences. 3

The war on drugs, the war on cancer, the battle of the sexes, politicians' turf battles—in the argument culture, war metaphors pervade our talk and shape our thinking. The cover headlines of both *Time* and *Newsweek* one recent week are a case in point: "The Secret Sex Wars," proclaims *Newsweek*. "Starr at War," declares *Time*. Nearly everything is framed as a battle or game in which winning or losing is the main concern. 4

The argument culture pervades every aspect of our lives today. Issues from global warming to abortion are depicted as two-sided arguments, when in fact most Americans' views lie somewhere in the middle. Partisanship makes gridlock in Washington the norm. Even in our personal 5

. . . continued The Argument Culture, **Deborah Tannen**

relationships, a "let it all hang out" philosophy emphasizes people expressing their anger without giving them constructive ways of settling differences.

Sometimes You Have to Fight

There are times when it is necessary and right to fight—to defend your country or yourself, to argue for your rights or against offensive or dangerous ideas or actions. What's wrong with the argument culture is the ubiquity, the knee-jerk nature of approaching any issue, problem or public person in an adversarial way.

6

Our determination to pursue truth by setting up a fight between two sides leads us to assume that every issue has two sides—no more, no less. But if you always assume there must be an "other side," you may end up scouring the margins of science or the fringes of lunacy to find it.

7

This accounts, in part, for the bizarre phenomenon of Holocaust denial. Deniers, as Emory University professor Deborah Lipstadt shows, have been successful in gaining TV air time and campus newspaper coverage by masquerading as "the other side" in a "debate." Continual reference to "the other side" results in a conviction that everything has another side—and people begin to doubt the existence of any facts at all.

8

The power of words to shape perception has been proved by researchers in controlled experiments. Psychologists Elizabeth Loftus and John Palmer, for example, found that the terms in which people are asked to recall something affect what they recall. The researchers showed subjects a film of two cars colliding, then asked how fast the cars were going; one week later they asked whether there had been any broken glass. Some subjects were asked, "How fast were the cars going when they bumped into each other?" Others were asked, "How fast were the cars going when they smashed into each other?"

9

Those who read the question with "smashed" tended to "remember" that the cars were going faster. They were also more likely to "remember" having seen broken glass. (There wasn't any.) This is how language works. It invisibly molds our way of thinking about people, actions and the world around us.

10

In the argument culture, "critical" thinking is synonymous with criticizing. In many classrooms, students are encouraged to read someone's life work, then rip it to shreds.

11

"What about here? This looks like a good spot for an argument."

When debates and fighting predominate, those who enjoy verbal spar- *12* ring are likely to take part—by calling in to talk shows or writing letters to the editor. Those who aren't comfortable with oppositional discourse are likely to opt out.

How High-Tech Communication Pulls Us Apart

One of the most effective ways to defuse antagonism between two groups *13* is to provide a forum for individuals from those groups to get to know each other personally. What is happening in our lives, however, is just the opposite. More and more of our communication is not face to face, and not with people we know. The proliferation and increasing portability of technology isolates people in a bubble.

Along with the voices of family members and friends, phone lines *14* bring into our homes the annoying voices of solicitors who want to sell something—generally at dinnertime. (My father-in-law startles phone solicitors by saying, "We're eating dinner, but I'll call you back. What's your

...continued The Argument Culture, **Deborah Tannen**

home phone number?" To the nonplused caller, he explains, "Well, you're calling me at home; I thought I'd call you at home, too.")

It is common for families to have more than one TV, so the adults can 15 watch what they like in one room and the kids can watch their choice in another—or maybe each child has a private TV.

E-mail, and now the Internet, are creating networks of human con- 16 nection unthinkable even a few years ago. Though e-mail has enhanced communication with family and friends, it also ratchets up the anonymity of both sender and receiver, resulting in stranger-to-stranger "flaming."

"Road rage" shows how dangerous the argument culture—and espe- 17 cially today's technologically enhanced aggression—can be. Two men who engage in a shouting match may not come to blows, but if they express their anger while driving down a public highway, the risk to themselves and others soars.

The Argument Culture Shapes Who We Are

The argument culture has a defining impact on our lives and on our culture. 18

- **It makes us distort facts,** as in the Nancy Kerrigan-Tonya Harding story. After the original attack on Kerrigan's knee, news stories focused on the rivalry between the two skaters instead of portraying Kerrigan as the victim of an attack. Just last month, *Time* magazine called the event a "contretemps" between Kerrigan and Harding. And a recent joint TV interview of the two skaters reinforced that skewed image by putting the two on equal footing, rather than as victim and accused.

- **It makes us waste valuable time,** as in the case of scientist Robert Gallo, who co-discovered the AIDS virus. Gallo was the object of a groundless four-year investigation into allegations he had stolen the virus from another scientist. He was ultimately exonerated, but the toll was enormous. Never mind that, in his words, "These were the most painful and horrible years of my life." Gallo spent four years fighting accusations instead of fight-ing AIDS.

- **It limits our thinking.** Headlines are intentionally devised to attract attention, but the language of extremes actually shapes, and misshapes, the way we think about things. Military metaphors train us to think about, and see, everything in terms of fighting, conflict and war. Adversarial rhetoric is a kind of verbal inflation—a rhetorical boy-who-cried-wolf.

- **It encourages us to lie.** If you fight to win, the temptation is great to deny facts that support your opponent's views and say only what supports your side. It encourages people to misrepresent and, in the extreme, to lie.

End the Argument Culture by Looking at All Sides

How can we overcome our classically American habit of seeing issues in *19* absolutes? We must expand our notion of "debate" to include more dialogue. To do this, we can make special efforts not to think in twos. Mary Catherine Bateson, an anthropologist at Virginia's George Mason University, makes a point of having her class compare three cultures, not two. Then, students are more likely to think about each on its own terms, rather than as opposites.

In the public arena, television and radio producers can try to avoid, *20* whenever possible, structuring public discussions as debates. This means avoiding the format of having two guests discuss an issue. Invite three guests—or one. Perhaps it is time to re-examine the assumption that audiences always prefer a fight.

Instead of asking, "What's the other side?" we might ask, "What are *21* the other sides?" Instead of insisting on hearing "both sides," let's insist on hearing "all sides."

We need to find metaphors other than sports and war. Smashing *22* heads does not open minds. We need to use our imaginations and ingenuity to find different ways to seek truth and gain knowledge through intellectual interchange, and add them to our arsenal—or, should I say, to the ingredients for our stew. It will take creativity for each of us to find ways to change the argument culture to a dialogue culture. It's an effort we have to make, because our public and private lives are at stake.

■　■　■

vo·cab·u·lar·y

In your journal, write the meanings of the italicized words in the following phrases.

- in an *adversarial* frame of mind **(2)**
- the *ubiquity* **(6)**
- *synonymous* with criticizing **(11)**

- with *oppositional* discourse **(12)**
- the *proliferation* **(13)**
- a *contretemps* between Kerrigan and Harding **(18)**
- he was ultimately *exonerated* **(18)**
- imaginations and *ingenuity* **(22)**

QUESTIONS FOR WRITING AND DISCUSSION

1. List three controversial topics currently in the news. Then choose one of those topics and explain the two "sides" of this argument. Now, imagine a third point of view. How is it different from the first two positions? Does coming up with a third position help you think creatively about how to resolve this dispute? Explain.

2. As she writes her essay, Tannen initially outlines the nature of the problem with the "argument culture" before she gives her solution. Which paragraphs most clearly demonstrate the problem? Which paragraphs explain her solution? Does she ignore any aspects of the problem? Would her solution really solve the problem she describes? Why or why not?

3. Critically analyzing the social, political, or cultural context is an important strategy for solving a problem. Where does Tannen explain the context(s) for the problem? Where does she argue that her solution will help resolve social, political, or cultural problems? Are there contexts where her solution might not work? Explain.

4. Read Tannen's advice in the final four paragraphs of her essay. Does she follow her own advice in writing this essay? Which pieces of advice does she follow and which does she ignore? Cite examples from the essay to support your analysis. Would her essay be more effective if she followed her own advice? Explain.

5. As a professor of linguistics, Tannen can write in a formal, academic style, but she can also write in an informal style for general audiences. In this essay, is Tannen writing for academics or for anyone interested in culture and communication? Find examples of Tannen's "academic" style as well as her informal style. Does she successfully integrate the two or is she too informal or too academic? Explain.

6. According to Tannen, the language we choose and the metaphors we use affect our perceptions of the world. Where does Tannen discuss how words

or metaphors shape our perceptions? What examples does she give? In her own argument, does Tannen herself avoid language or metaphors referring to war, violence, or conflict?

7. The *New Yorker* cartoon by BEK, "This looks like a good spot for an argument," did not originally appear with Tannen's essay. Evaluate the appropriateness of this visual image for Tannen's essay. Does the cartoon support Tannen's thesis? Does it contribute to the essay's appeal, or does it distract from Tannen's argument? Citing details from the cartoon and passages from Tannen's essay, explain your response.

8. On the Internet, log on to the Web site of a national news magazine such as *Newsweek* or *Utne* magazine and read their e-mail letters in response to an essay on a controversial topic such as stem cell research, global warming, public transportation, educational testing, and so forth. Read several letters or responses. Can you find at least *three* positions on that issue—rather than just the standard "pro" and "con"? Explain the controversial topic and then write out at least three different positions or points of view which you discover in the responses.

TECHNIQUES   PROCESS

Problem Solving: The Writing Process

ASSIGNMENT FOR PROBLEM SOLVING

Select a problem that you believe needs a solution. Narrow and focus the problem and choose an appropriate audience. Describe the problem and, if necessary, demonstrate for your audience that it needs a solution. State your solution, and justify it with reasons and evidence. Where appropriate, weigh alternative solutions, examine the feasibility of your own solution, and answer objections to your solution.

The problem-solving assignment leads naturally to the genre of a proposal. Some proposals are long, formal documents addressed to knowledgeable readers, while others are short and informal, intended more for general audiences. Review your assignment and your intended audience to help determine the amount of analysis and research you need for your essay.

| CHOOSING | COLLECTING | SHAPING | DRAFTING | REVISING |

CHOOSING A SUBJECT

If one of your journal entries suggests a possible subject, try the collecting and shaping strategies below. If none of these leads to a workable subject, consider the following suggestions:

- Evaluating leads naturally into problem solving. Reread your journal entries and topic ideas for "evaluating." If your evaluation of your subject was negative, consider what would make your evaluation more positive. Based on your evaluation, write a proposal, addressed to the proper audience, explaining the problem and offering your solution.

- Organized groups are already trying to solve a number of national and international problems: homelessness, illegal immigrants, the slaughter of whales, acid rain, abuse of animals in scientific experiments, drug and alcohol abuse, toxic-waste disposal, and so forth. Read several current articles on one of these topics. Then narrow the problem to one aspect that students or residents of your town could help to resolve. Write an essay outlining the problem and proposing some *specific and limited* actions that citizens could take.

"I can't think of anything I have no problem with."

© The New Yorker Collection (1987) (Stevenson) from cartoonbank.com.
All Rights Reserved.

- An important part of any community-service-learning project is collaborating with the agency to assess problems and propose possible solutions. If you have a community-service-learning project in one of your classes, work collaboratively with the agency to assess the community's and/or the agency's needs as well as the knowledge and skills you might bring to the agency to contribute to a possible solution. Working with the agency, decide on a purpose, audience, and genre for your proposal.

- Every day, the news media features images that seem to suggest a problem that needs a solution. Choose one image that you have found in the media and investigate the issue. What problem does the image suggest? What does your research and investigation reveal about the rhetorical situation and cultural context surrounding this image and this issue? Choose a possible audience, genre, and context, and write your own problem-solving essay based on the issue raised by this image.

CHOOSING **COLLECTING** SHAPING DRAFTING REVISING

COLLECTING

With a possible subject and audience in mind, write out answers for each of the following topics. Remember that not all of these approaches will apply to your subject; some topics will suggest very little, while others may prompt you to generate ideas or specific examples appropriate to your problem and solution. A hypothetical problem—large classes that hinder learning—illustrates how these topics may help you focus on your subject and collect relevant ideas and information.

IDENTIFY AND FOCUS ON THE SPECIFIC PROBLEM   Answer the first four "Wh" questions:

WHO: A Psychology I professor; the Psychology Department

WHAT: Psychology I class

WHEN: Spring semester (the structure of this class may be slightly different from previous semesters)

WHERE: University of Illinois (large lecture classes at one school may be different from those at another)

You may want to generalize about large lecture classes everywhere, but begin by identifying the specific problem at hand.

■ **DEMONSTRATE THAT THE PROBLEM NEEDS A SOLUTION** Map out the *effects* of a problem. (See the diagram.)

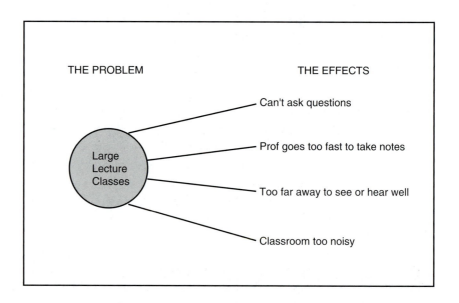

You may want to map out both *short-term effects* and *long-term effects.* Over the short term, large lecture classes prevent you from asking questions; over the long term, you may do poorly on examinations, get a lower grade in the class, lose interest in the subject, be unable to cope with your own and others' psychological problems, or end up in a different career or job.

■ **DISCOVER POSSIBLE SOLUTIONS** One strategy is to map out the history or the causes of the problem. If you can discover what caused the problem in the first place, you may have a possible solution. (See the diagram.)

A second strategy takes the imaginative approach. Brainstorm hypothetical cases by asking, "What if. . . ."

"What if students petitioned the president of the university to abolish all lecture classes with enrollments over 100 students?" Would that work?

"What if students invited the professor to answer questions at a weekly study session?" Would the professor attend? Would students attend?

"What if students taught each other in a psychology class?" How would that work?

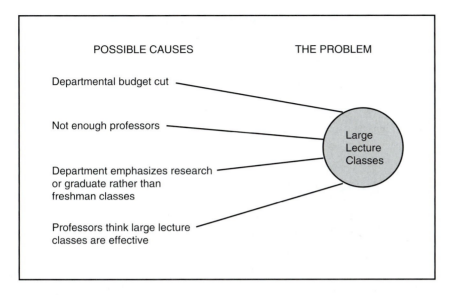

POSSIBLE CAUSES   THE PROBLEM

Departmental budget cut

Not enough professors

Department emphasizes research
or graduate rather than
freshman classes

Professors think large lecture
classes are effective

Large Lecture Classes

EVALUATE POSSIBLE SOLUTIONS   Apply the "If . . . then . . ." test on each possible solution: Consider whether each proposal would:

A. actually solve the problem;

B. meet certain criteria, such as cost-effectiveness, practicality, ethicality, legality;

C. not create new problems.

"*If* classes were smaller, *then* students would learn more":

If classes were smaller, students might learn more, but a small class size does not necessarily guarantee greater learning.

Although students might learn more, do smaller classes meet other criteria? While they are legal and ethical, are they practical and cost-effective?

Would smaller classes create new problems? Smaller classes might mean fewer upper-level course offerings. Is that a serious new problem?

CONVINCE YOUR READERS   Support your proposed solutions by stating *reasons* and finding supporting *evidence*.

Reason: Smaller classes are worth the additional expense because students actually engage the material rather than just memorizing for exams.

Evidence: Data from studies comparing large and small classes; personal testimony by students, interviews, or questionnaires; testimony or evidence from authorities on teaching.

▮ ANSWER POSSIBLE OBJECTIONS TO YOUR PROPOSAL Every
solution has a down side or possible drawbacks. You need to respond to the most
important objections.

List Drawbacks

Small classes cost more.

Small classes might reduce course offerings.

Small classes might mean less money for research.

List Your Responses

Good education does cost more. The University of Illinois has a reputation
as an excellent undergraduate institution, and small classes would help it
maintain quality education.

Perhaps some classes with low demand could be cut, but the necessary funds
should not be taken out of upper-division classes for psychology majors or
research projects.

▮ LIST POSSIBLE STEPS FOR IMPLEMENTATION   If appropriate, indi-
cate the key steps or chronological sequence of your proposal.

1. Poll students and teachers in large lecture classes to confirm that the problem
   warrants attention.
2. Gather evidence from other colleges or universities to show how they reduced
   class sizes.
3. Present results of polls and other evidence to the state legislature to request
   more funds.

> ❝ The best time for planning . . . is when you're doing the dishes. ❞
> —AGATHA CHRISTIE, MYSTERY WRITER

▮ OBSERVING   As you gather evidence and examples, use your observation
skills. If the problem is large lecture classes, attend classes and *observe* the behavior
of students and professors. Are students distracted by noise? Can they ask questions? Does the professor talk too softly to be heard in the back row? Remember
that *repeated* observation is essential. If necessary, observe your subject over a period
of several days or weeks.

▮ REMEMBERING   Use *freewriting*, *looping*, or *clustering* to help you remember
examples from your experience of the problem or of possible solutions. Brainstorm

Research Tips

As you begin researching your problem, don't spend all your time on the Internet or on the library's databases. Remember to interview people who may know about your problem. Use your investigating skills to locate local authorities and interview them in person, via e-mail, or on the telephone (see Chapter 7). Find out what other people think about this problem. How do they explain or define the problem? What are they already doing to solve the problem? Why are current solutions not working or not working effectively enough? Interview a teacher who knows about the problem, a student who has firsthand experience with the problem, an owner of a local business, or the coordinator of a community service or agency. Combining your online and library research with interviews makes your research more interesting, more local and current, and more effective.

or freewrite about previous class sessions in Psychology I. Do looping or mapping on other small-enrollment classes: What made these classes effective or ineffective? What teaching strategies, projects, or small-group activities were possible in these classes that would not be possible in a class of 250 students?

▪ **READING AND INVESTIGATING**   *Use the library* to find books or articles about the particular problem. Other writers have no doubt offered solutions to your problem that you could consider. Articles may even suggest objections to your proposed solution that you need to answer.

Interview participants or authorities on the problem. The professor who is teaching your Psychology I class may have some ideas about a solution. Administration—department chairs, deans, even the president—may agree to answer your questions and react to your possible solutions.

Design a questionnaire that addresses aspects of your problem. Responses to questionnaires provide evidence that a problem is serious, immediate, and in need of a solution. If the results of a questionnaire show that 175 of the 200 people in Psychology I who returned it favor smaller sections, you can include those data in your letter to the head of the department and the dean of the college.

SHAPING

■ **GENRES FOR PROBLEM SOLVING**   Initially, you must consider possible genres appropriate for your issue and your particular rhetorical situation. Typical genres used for proposals include articles in magazines, letters to the editor, academic essays, self-help essays, political essays, and business proposals. Depending on the genre and audience you choose, proposals often do the following.

- Identify, analyze, and demonstrate the problem
- Describe and evaluate alternative solutions
- Make proposals
- Give reasons and evidence to support the proposal
- Answer objections; discuss feasibility problems
- Indicate implementation and call for action

Of course, not all problem-solving essays have all six elements. Some do not discuss feasibility in detail or do not describe and evaluate alternative solutions. Michael Bérubé's proposal to end grade inflation, for example, presents only one possible solution and acknowledges that the feasibility problems might be confusing. Reconsidering your rhetorical situation and genre helps you decide how to shape your proposal.

■ **OUTLINES FOR PROBLEM SOLVING**   The following patterns indicate four possible ways to organize a problem-solving essay. One of these patterns may help you organize your proposal.

Problem-Solving Pattern
  I. Introduction
 II. The problem: Identify and demonstrate
III. The solution(s)
 IV. Answering possible objections, costs, drawbacks
  V. Conclusion: Implementation plan; call to action

Point-by-Point Pattern
  I. Introduction
 II. The overall problem: Identify and demonstrate

III. One part of the problem, solution, evidence, answers to possible objections, feasibility

IV. Second part of the problem, solution, evidence, answers to possible objections, feasibility

V. Third part of the problem, solution, evidence, and so on

VI. Conclusion: Implementation; call to action

Alternative Pattern

I. Introduction

II. The problem: Identify and demonstrate

III. Alternative Solution 1; why it's not satisfactory

IV. Alternative Solution 2; why it's not satisfactory

V. Alternative Solution 3; why it works best: Evidence, objections, feasibility

VI. Conclusion: Implementation; call to action

Step-by-Step Pattern

I. Introduction

II. The problem: Identify and demonstrate

III. Plan for implementing the solution or how solution has worked in the past:

    A. Step 1: Reasons and evidence showing why this step is necessary and feasible

    B. Step 2: Reasons and evidence showing why this step is necessary and feasible

    C. Step 3: Reasons and evidence showing why this step is necessary and feasible

IV. Conclusion

CAUSAL ANALYSIS   Causal analysis can be used to organize some paragraphs of a proposal. In arguing the benefits or advantages of a proposed solution, you are actually explaining the *effects* of your solution.

- The effects or advantages of smaller class sections in Psychology I would be greater student participation, fewer distractions, more discussion during lectures, and more individual or small-group learning.

- Shortening the work week to thirty-two hours would increase the number of jobs, reduce tensions for working parents, and give employees time to learn new skills.

In each of these cases, each effect or advantage can become a separate point and, sometimes, a separate body paragraph.

▮ **CRITERIA ANALYSIS**   In some cases, the *criteria* for a good solution are quite clear. For example, cost-effectiveness, feasibility, and worker morale might be important criteria for a business-related proposal. If you work in a fast-food restaurant and are concerned about the increasing number of crimes, for example, you might propose that your manager add a video surveillance system. In order to overcome the manager's resistance to spending the needed funds, you could defend your proposal (and answer possible objections) by discussing relevant criteria.

> **Proposal:** To reduce theft and protect the employees of the restaurant by installing a video surveillance system.
>
> - **Cost-effectiveness.** Citing evidence from other stores that have video cameras, you could prove that the equipment would pay for itself in less than a year. In addition, you could argue that if the life of just one employee—or possibly one manager—were saved, the cost would be worth it.
> - **Feasibility.** Installing a security system would not require any extensive remodeling or any significant training time for employees to learn how to operate the system.
> - **Employee morale.** The benefits to employee morale would be significant: Workers would feel more secure, they would feel that the management cares about them, and they would work more productively.

▮ **CHRONOLOGICAL ORDER**   If your proposal stresses the means of implementing your solution to a problem, you may organize several paragraphs or even an entire essay using a chronological order or step-by-step pattern.

A proposal to improve the reading skills of children might be justified by a series of coordinated steps, beginning by organizing seminars for teachers and PTA meetings to discuss possible solutions; establishing minimal reading requirements in grades K–6 that teachers and parents agree on; offering reading prizes; and organizing media coverage of students who participate in reading programs.

CHOOSING	COLLECTING	SHAPING	DRAFTING	REVISING

DRAFTING

Using your examples, recorded observations, reading, interviews, results from questionnaires, or your own experience, make a sketch outline and begin writing. As you write, let your own proposal and your intended audience guide you. In your first draft, get as much as possible on paper. Don't worry about spelling or awkward sentences. If you hit a snag, stop and read what you have written so far or reread your collecting and shaping notes.

PEER RESPONSE

Writer: Provide the following information about your essay before you exchange drafts with a peer reader.

1. a. Audience and genre
   b. Statement of problem and context of problem
   c. Possible or alternative solutions
   d. Your recommended solution(s)
2. Write out one or two questions about your draft that you want your reader to answer.

Reader: Read the writer's entire draft. As you *reread* the draft, do the following.

1. Without looking at the writer's responses, describe (a) the essay's intended audience, (b) the main problem that the essay identifies, (c) the possible or alternative solutions, and (d) the writer's recommended solution. What feasibility problems or additional solutions should the writer consider? Why?
2. Indicate one paragraph in which the writer's evidence is strong. Then find one paragraph in which the writer needs more evidence. What additional *kinds* of evidence (personal experience, testimony from authorities, statistics, specific examples, etc.) might the writer use in this paragraph? Explain.
3. Number the paragraphs in the writer's essay and then describe, briefly, the purpose or main idea of each paragraph: paragraph 1 introduces the problem, paragraph 2 gives the writer's personal experience with the problem, and so on. When you finish, explain how the writer might improve the organization of the essay.
4. List the three most important things that the writer should focus on during revision.
5. Respond to the writer's questions in number 2.

Writer: When your essay is returned, read the comments by your peer reader(s) and do the following.

1. Compare your description of the audience, the problem, and the solutions with your reader's description. Where there are differences, try to clarify your essay.
2. Reconsider and revise your recommended solution(s).
3. What additional kinds of evidence will make your recommendations stronger?
4. Make a revision plan. List, in order, the three most important things that you need to do as you revise your essay.

REVISING

When you have a completed draft and are ready to start revising your essay, get another member of your class to read and respond to your essay. Use the peer response guidelines that follow to get—and give—constructive advice on your draft.

Use the following revising guidelines to identify areas for improving your draft. Even at this point, don't hesitate to collect additional information, if necessary, or reorganize your material. If a reader makes suggestions, reread your draft to see if those changes will improve your essay.

GUIDELINES FOR REVISION

- **Review your rhetorical situation.** How can you revise your selected genre to make it more effectively communicate your purpose to your intended audience?
- **Review to make sure you critically analyze the problem.** Don't just assume that everyone will agree with your definition or representation of the problem. Investigate and describe the groups of people who are affected by the problem.
- **Have a classmate or someone who might understand your audience read your draft and play devil's advocate.** Have your reader pretend to be hostile to your solution and ask questions about alternative solutions or weaknesses in your own solution. Revise your proposal so that it answers any important objections.
- **Review your proposal for key elements.** If you are missing one of the following, would adding it make your proposal more effective for your audience? *Remember:* Proposals do not necessarily have to have all of these elements.

   Develop the items that are most applicable to your proposal.

   Show that a problem exists and needs attention.

   Evaluate alternative solutions.

   Propose your solution.

   Show that your solution meets certain criteria: feasibility, cost-effectiveness, legality.

   Answer possible objections.

   Suggest implementation or call for action.
- **Be sure that you *show* what you mean, using specific examples, facts, details, statistics, quotations from interviews or articles.** Don't rely on general assertions.

- **Signal the major parts of your proposal with key words and transitions.**
- **Avoid the following errors in logic and generalization.**

  Don't commit an "either-or" fallacy. For example, don't say that "*either* we reduce class sizes *or* students will drop out of the university." There are more than two possible alternatives.

  Don't commit an "ad hominem" fallacy by arguing "to the man" or "to the woman" rather than to the issue. Don't say, for example, that Deborah Tannen is wrong about argument because she is just another pushy woman who should stick to teaching linguistics.

  Test your proposal for "If . . . then . . ." statements. Does it really follow that "if we reduce class size, teaching will be more effective"?

  Avoid overgeneralizing your solution. If all your research applies to solving problems in large lecture classes in psychology, don't assume that your solution will apply to, say, classes in physics or physical education.

- **If you are citing data or quoting sources, make sure that your material is accurately cited.**
- **Read your proposal aloud for flabby, wordy, or awkward sentences.** Revise your sentences for clarity, precision, and forcefulness.
- **Edit your proposal for spelling, appropriate word choice, punctuation, usage, mechanics, and grammar.** Remember that, in part, your form and audience help determine what are appropriate usage and mechanics.

POSTSCRIPT ON THE WRITING PROCESS

Before you turn in your essay, answer the following questions in your journal.

1. As you worked on your essay, what elements of the rhetorical situation did you revise? How did you change the purpose, audience, or genre elements as you drafted your essay? Cite specific sentences or paragraphs from your essay as examples.

2. List the skills you used in writing this paper: observing people, places, or events; remembering personal experience; using questionnaires and interviews; reading written material; explaining ideas; evaluating solutions. Which of these skills was most useful to you in writing this essay?

3. What was your most difficult problem to solve while writing this paper? Were you able to solve it yourself, or did your readers suggest a solution?

Continued

4. In one sentence, describe the most important thing you learned about writing while working on this essay.

5. What were the most successful parts of your essay?

KRISTY BUSCH, STEVE KRAUSE, AND KEITH WRIGHT   x

No Parking

Kristy Busch, Steve Krause, and Keith Wright worked together on a proposal to solve the parking problem at their university. They met several times to discuss the topic, select questions for the survey and interview, divide the research responsibilities, and determine who was going to draft each section. They agreed that Keith Wright would interview the director of parking management, and that Kristy Busch and Steve Krause would survey students about the parking problem. After they collected their information, Wright drafted a first version of the section on the multilevel garage, Busch worked on the shuttle bus proposal, and Krause wrote out the introduction and the rezoning proposal. Then they worked together to combine and revise their drafts, adding new information, reorganizing the paragraphs, and editing the final draft. Shown below are the questions for the interview, the results of the survey, the first draft of the introduction and rezoning proposal, and the revised draft of the entire proposal.

INTERVIEW

Interview Questions for Wes Westfall, Director of Parking Management

1. Do you perceive a serious parking problem at CSU?
2. Do you think that students' arguments about lack of "X" parking spaces along the dorms on the north side of the campus are valid?
3. How many stickers for each zone are issued each year? Do these numbers fluctuate?
4. Are you in favor of building a multilevel parking facility?
   Where would you build such a structure?
   What would it cost? Is it feasible?
   How long would it take to build?
5. Have you considered a shuttle bus system between Moby Gym and the central campus?
   What would it cost? Is it feasible?
6. Is rezoning possible? Is it currently under consideration? Would it solve the problem? Is it feasible? What would it cost?

PARKING SURVEY RESULTS

1. Do you drive to CSU?
   Yes: 36
   Occasionally: 53
   No: 11
2. Does CSU need more parking for students?
   Yes: 62
   No: 38
3. Would rezoning close-in lots to eliminate dorm parking help?
   Yes: 78
   No: 22
4. Class (Fr., Soph., Jr., Sr., Other)
   Fr: 33
   Soph: 20
   Jr: 22
   Sr: 13
   Other: 12

FIRST DRAFT

If you drive to CSU, you may already know how hard it can be to find a parking place. If not, then now would be a good time to make the changes necessary to accommodate more cars (before you start driving). Not only is the parking inadequate for the number of cars, but it is also poorly organized and poorly distributed among the groups who use it. A very common occurrence is being forced to park very far from the building where you need to go. Not only students are affected; faculty, staff, and visitors also have problems finding somewhere to park. For a visitor, this is very distressing and certainly doesn't present an attractive first impression of CSU. It is clear that something will have to be done; what is unclear is exactly what would be the most practical and cost-effective solution. First, and probably the most effective for the immediate future, would be to rezone the existing parking to better accommodate the users. A shuttle bus system could also be used; however, this could be costly and would have to be used a lot to make it a practical investment. The ominous "multilevel parking facility" is a drastic last measure that we would have a lot of trouble paying for. [add closing sentence]

The most cost-effective and probably the most immediately effective would be a partial rezoning of existing parking. This year, the office of parking management sold 7,641 parking stickers for an available 6,238 spaces, a difference of 1,403. This means that there are a lot more stickers than places to park. Granted, all these people do not drive at the same time, but enough do to cause a problem. In a poll taken this March,

78 percent of the people said that they would like to see the parking re-zoned. In rezoning, we should first look at the parking areas which are not full and determine why and then shift the zones in a way in which they will help. For example, the western sections of the "Z" lot at Moby Gym could be changed to "X" for those dorm dwellers. Then the close-in lots could be changed to "Z" for the commuting students. Or we could eliminate the metered parking and put "Z" parking in its place. Rezoning the lots would seem to be the easiest solution to the problem, but it cannot be permanent, since if this school survives it will inevitably grow.

REVISED VERSION

No Parking

On Monday morning, Jennifer Martin left her apartment at 8:30 to drive to the Colorado State University campus, hoping to arrive on time for a test in her 9 A.M. sociology class. When she arrived at the student parking lot west of Aylesworth Hall, there were no parking spots. So she began cruising up and down the lot, hoping that someone would soon pull out. As she drove slowly up and down the lanes, she muttered to herself and clenched her hands on the steering wheel. She did have a permit to park in the lot, but there were obviously more permits than spaces. About five minutes before class, a car pulled out of a place at the far end of the lot. She accelerated down the next lane, driving as fast as she could without running over other students, but just as she arrived, a green Ford Focus cut in front of her and darted into the vacant space. She honked her horn and waved her fist, but the person quickly got out of the car and walked away. At this point, she realized that she had no choice. She wheeled into the area marked for motorcycles, parked her car, and raced for class. She was angry because she knew she was going to get a ticket even though she had a legal permit. *1*

If you drive to the CSU campus for classes, you have probably had a similar experience. But students are not the only ones who have parking problems on campus: Faculty, staff, and visitors also have problems finding places to park. Especially for visitors, the overcrowded conditions don't present an attractive first impression of the campus. Clearly, something has to be done to improve parking facilities. After studying the problem, interviewing the director of parking management, and polling 100 students, we believe that there are three alternatives that the CSU administration should consider: building a multilevel parking facility, starting a shuttle bus from remote lots, and rezoning the existing parking lots to better serve the users. *2*

A first possible solution to CSU's parking problem would be to build a *3* multilevel parking facility. This sounds like a promising idea because it would allow more students, faculty, and staff to park over the same amount of ground space. CSU could build this facility at any of several locations. One place is on the west side of the Morgan Library, where the "A" parking zone—for faculty—is now. This location would provide parking convenient to classes, faculty offices, and the library. A second site would be the open parking lot west of Moby Gym. Although this location is farther from classes, it would also be used during basketball games and concerts. A third location might be the large parking lot north of the Student Center. This, too, like the library lot, would be close to classrooms and faculty offices.

While these sites are all promising, we discovered that a multilevel *4* parking facility has some serious drawbacks. Wes Westfall, manager of CSU parking, explained that there are several problems with these garages that most people don't consider. A first drawback to the parking garage is the expense. Westfall said that a multilevel garage would cost a minimum of $6,000 per parking space, raising the price of a parking permit from $30 to over $300. And that would be for a sticky piece of paper that still wouldn't guarantee a parking space for every car. Perhaps the president of the university could pay $300 a year, but most students can barely afford $30.

A second drawback to a parking garage is that it doesn't last forever, *5* and the maintenance costs can be considerable. Mr. Westfall has some frightening photographs of sections of strong, stable-looking concrete that has collapsed for no visible reason at all. One picture shows a whole garage leveled as though a good-sized bomb had hit it—nothing was left standing except for a pillar here and there. Unless garages are carefully maintained, Westfall stated, they may not last over twenty years. The problem, he explained, lies in the rebar (steel rods inside the concrete) that reinforces the concrete. Gas, oil, and antifreeze from cars are gradually absorbed into the concrete, a condition causing the rebar to deteriorate and weaken the whole structure. The only way to check for this kind of damage, Westfall noted, is to use an expensive concrete X-ray machine. So even the maintenance of a garage can be an expensive proposition.

The third and most serious problem, Westfall claims, is security. *6* Parking garages can become just another place for sexual assault, drug trafficking, vandalism, and theft. Westfall commented that most garages have a monitor system and guards, but those precautions are not totally effective. By the time the guard detects a theft over the security system and arrives at the location, the thief has usually fled. In addition, any security system adds to the already high costs of a parking facility. Clearly, the problems connected with a multilevel garage make it a last resort for solving the parking problems on campus.

A second alternative for solving the parking problems on the CSU campus is to use a bus shuttle service from the outlying "Z" lot at Moby Gym to the central campus. Many of the students who responded to our survey said that the lots on the perimeter of the campus were nearly empty, but they were too far away from the library and the classrooms. The shuttle would solve this problem by taking the following route: Beginning at the Lory Student Center, the bus would head west down North Drive (along the residence halls) to the Moby Gym lot and then stop and pick up drivers at both the north and the south ends of the lot. It would then turn south onto Shields at the stoplight and turn east on South Drive, returning to central campus. This system would allow easier access to the core of the campus and, in return, put to full use the 539 parking spaces available in the Moby Gym parking lot. Of course, the shuttle, driver, and maintenance would cost money, so this solution would require a commitment from the university administration.

The most cost-effective solution would be a partial rezoning of the parking lots. This past year, the office of parking management sold 7,461 parking stickers for an available 6,238 spaces, a difference of 1,403. This means that they sold 1,403 more stickers than there are places to park. Not all people need to park at the same time, but enough do to cause a problem. Of the 100 students that we polled, 78 percent said that they would like to see the central campus lots rezoned. In this scheme, students parking their cars for long periods of time would use the outlying lots, and commuting students, faculty, and staff would use the closer lots. For example, if we changed the western section of the outlying "Z" lot to "X" for those students living in the dorms, the parking spaces near the dorms along South Drive could be made available to those who have to drive every day to campus to attend classes. Such rezoning seems to be the easiest and least expensive solution.

One main obstacle to overcoming CSU's parking problem is money. A multilevel parking facility would accommodate more cars per acre of ground space, yet it is the most expensive solution. The shuttle bus system—which could still be implemented—is more economical, but it would require raising additional revenue, most likely by raising the price of parking stickers. We certainly recommend that the university try a shuttle system on an experimental basis to determine the exact costs and to see whether the number of riders justifies the expense. Rezoning the lots, however, is clearly the least complicated and most economical solution. Signs could be changed during the summer months, and new maps and brochures printed in time for the beginning of fall semester. Our group proposes that the university rezone the lots at the end of this academic year and start planning for a shuttle bus and a garage to meet the need in future years. With more careful management of the close-in lots, the new parking stickers might be more than just a hunting license. A person with a permit might actually be able to arrive at a lot at 8:45 and still make that nine o'clock class.

QUESTIONS FOR WRITING AND DISCUSSION

1. After reading the revised version, look again at the questions for the interview and the survey. How would you advise the authors to modify either set of questions? What questions would you add? What questions would you change or delete? Explain.

2. Compare the introduction in the first draft with the introduction in the revised version. Which is more effective? Jot down an idea for a third introduction that the authors might consider.

3. Reread the revised version and outline the major parts of the proposal. Then compare your outline with the authors' initial outline, given here:

   I. Introduction
   II. Rezoning proposal
   III. Shuttle bus proposal
   IV. Multilevel garage proposal
   V. Conclusion

   Do you think that their revised plan for organizing the paper was an improvement? Explain.

4. Who is the intended audience for this proposal? What revisions would make this proposal appeal even more strongly to that audience? (During the planning stages of this essay, the authors decided to send this proposal to Wes Westfall, director of parking management. How do you think Westfall would react to this proposal as it stands?)

JESSICA COOK

New Regulations and You

For her problem-solving essay, Jessica Cook decided to write about current solutions for solving a recent outbreak of mad cow disease. Her purpose was "to persuade cattle ranchers that the new regulations and changes in policy that arose in the wake of the discovery of mad cow disease (BSE) in the U.S. are necessary and can even be beneficial." Her audience was beef producers and ranchers, and she chose Beef *magazine as a target publication. After reviewing current issues of* Beef *magazine, she modeled her essay on the genre features of their articles: a personal voice combined with current research, short paragraphs with headings and bullets, a two-column format, and graphics to illustrate her point. Cook also wrote a Works Cited page, but did not use in-text citation because that was not the format used by* Beef *magazine. As you read her essay, decide how successful she is at arguing for the recommended policies, addressing her target audience, and meeting the genre requirements.*

NEW REGULATIONS AND YOU

When I was growing up, my mother always told me that I was just one small pebble on a very large beach, meaning that I was just an insignificant part of the world, and as a single person, I couldn't bring about any huge changes.

It may sound demeaning, but the truth is, most people will never change the world.

However, after seeing how much of an impact one dairy cow in Washington can have on American agriculture and world trade, I am beginning to think my mother might have been wrong.

In case you hadn't already guessed, the infamous cow I am referring to is the Holstein that tested positive for mad cow disease, or bovine spongiform encephalopathy (BSE), on December 23, 2003.

According to a special report in *Cattle-Fax,* this discovery caused nearly all of our trading partners to ban the import of U.S. beef, a plunge in beef prices, and a recall of 10,400 pounds of beef associated with the cow. Consumer confidence in beef and bovine-derived products also plummeted. In addition, this cow spawned several new government-issued regulations and changes to procedures.

THE NEW RULES

In two articles in the *New York Times*, Denise Grady and Donald G. McNeil, Jr., the two writers following mad cow disease, discuss the new regulations, including bans on the following:

- Feeding cattle blood to calves as a milk replacer
- Allowing chicken litter—feathers, spilled feed, bedding, and feces—in cattle feed
- Using the same equipment that makes feed containing bone meal for making cattle feed
- Allowing dead or downer cattle to be used for human food or products, including dietary supplements, cosmetics or soups
- Feeding "plate waste" or table scraps to cattle
- Air-injection stunning

Also, carcasses that are tested for BSE must be held until the results are known.

Even more changes are being considered for the future, including testing more cattle, mandatory identification and tracking systems, and banning all animal protein from cattle feed.

WHAT THIS MEANS TO YOU

By now, beef producers have realized how these new rules will affect them, and most have already implemented the government-mandated changes.

Although many producers share the opinion that these new regulations just increase the time, effort and money it takes to produce beef, I disagree.

I believe that the new regulations and changes in policy that arose in the wake of the discovery of BSE in the U.S. are necessary and can even be beneficial to the cattle industry.

Although I realize that these changes will be expensive and tedious to implement, I believe that the advantages will outweigh the disadvantages. These regulations will increase food safety, open opportunities in niche markets, facilitate exportation, and boost consumer confidence and demand.

Because I was raised in a small town by the name of Burns, Wyoming, and grew up in an agricultural community, I know what it takes to produce our nation's food supply. I am familiar with the "blood, sweat and tears" that go hand-in-hand with raising cattle, or any other species of livestock.

...*continued* New Regulations and You, **Jessica Cook**

THE DOWNSIDE

Anyone who has been around agriculture and cattle knows that the new regulations will be expensive and time consuming to implement, and I acknowledge this.

Many ranchers feel that changing the way things have always been done is pointless; the current methods were passed down from our successful elders, and "if it isn't broke, why fix it?" Another argument against the new rules is that changing the way a ranch operates takes an exorbitant effort.

A group of government officials, many of whom have no idea what goes into raising cattle, have made several new rules that ranchers must follow. As Wes Ishmael phrased it in the February 1, 2004, issue of *Beef* magazine, "How many laws would a lawmaker make if a lawmaker could make laws without pause or cause?"

Despite all of those negative side effects, there are some redeeming features to the new regulations.

INCREASED FOOD SAFETY

Although the beef industry is quick to claim that the beef supply is safe (after all, there has only been one case of mad cow disease out of the nearly 36 million cattle slaughtered per year in the U.S.), there is evidence to the contrary.

Dave Louthan (as recorded by McNeil of the *New York Times*), the man who killed the infected cow at the slaughterhouse in Moses Lake, WA, warns of the danger.

Louthan claims that the infected cow was not a downer when it was killed, which contradicts the official reports from the federal Department of Agriculture, and would thus make the discovery of it just a fluke. Because the guidelines only mandate testing for downer cattle, this could mean BSE-infected cattle are slipping through the testing procedures and into the food chain.

According to another of McNeil's articles, last year only about 20,000 cattle were tested for BSE, which is only 0.06% of those slaughtered. New testing protocol calls for doubling the number tested, which is an improvement whose worth is easily demonstrated.

Even if only one cow slips by the testing, which is statistically insignificant, I sure don't want to be the person innocently consuming that meat and risking a fatal disease. Do you want to be the rancher responsi-

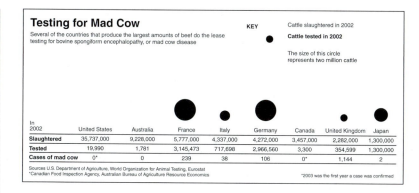

Testing for Mad Cow

Several of the countries that produce the largest amounts of beef do the lease testing for bovine spongiform encephalopathy, or mad cow disease

KEY — Cattle slaughtered in 2002

Cattle tested in 2002

The size of this circle represents two million cattle

In 2002	United States	Australia	France	Italy	Germany	Canada	United Kingdom	Japan
Slaughtered	35,737,000	9,228,000	5,777,000	4,337,000	4,272,000	3,457,000	2,282,000	1,300,000
Tested	19,990	1,781	3,145,473	717,698	2,966,560	3,300	354,599	1,300,000
Cases of mad cow	0*	0	239	38	106	0*	1,144	2

Sources U.S. Department of Agriculture, World Organization for Animal Testing, Eurostat
*Canadian Food Inspection Agency, Australian Bureau of Agriculture Resource Economics
*2003 was the first year a case was confirmed

ble for creating another disaster because you didn't implement the changes to move your enterprise into the future?

Louthan also claims that the carcass splitting process is unsafe as well. When the carcass is split the blade cleaves the spinal column while jets of water blast away the fat and bone dust.

The "slurry" containing spinal column matter, a portion of the carcass that can transmit BSE, "runs all over the beef." Obviously, this poses a risk, and if a way to change this process is feasible, it should be implemented.

NICHE MARKET OPPORTUNITIES

Another potential benefit of the new regulations is the opportunity to move into niche markets. Currently, raising beef is a commodity market, where one rancher's beef is basically the same as the next rancher's.

There have been some recent changes to help ranchers differentiate their products, like the Certified Angus Beef campaign.

In theory, the kind of packaging and label on a product shouldn't play a part in consumer's decisions, yet in reality, it does. In the text book *Scientific Farm Animal Production,* Drs. Taylor and Field, professors at Colorado State University, state that the five main factors used to determine value of meat products are palatability, fat composition, presentation, price, and convenience.

As the producers who can place the sticker that says "Certified Angus Beef" on their packages in the supermarket have found out, making your product just a little different so that it stands out from the crowd can be an effective marketing technique.

Although labeling of products, mandatory identification, and traceability are not yet required, I believe that the implementation of these procedures now—before they are deemed necessary—could benefit a producer in the same way.

According to Dr. Field during a lecture in Introduction to Animal Science, some Japanese producers can already testify to its effectiveness.

One ranch decided to raise all of its beef cattle from birth to slaughter on their family-owned ranch, and advertise their beef in that way. They stated that all of their beef was raised solely on that farm. Consumers liked knowing that they only had to trust one ranch instead of several places and businesses.

Another ranch put a picture of their family on the beef packaging, making it more personal. When the consumers saw the nice, honest-looking family on the package of steak, it made them choose it over the standard package beside it.

When marketing beef, producers must consider opportunities like these in order to move into niche markets and leave the commodity market in the past. Implementing things like identification and traceability before they are required can give producers a jump on the market and a chance to become more profitable.

EXPORTATION

As American agriculturalists, we know the importance of exportation. When BSE was discovered, our export markets were drastically affected.

According to an article from Mexico City on AOLNews, "U.S. beef exports came to a virtual halt after the Dec. 23 announcement that mad cow had been found." This is a major concern; last year alone, the U.S. exported $3.8 billion worth of beef products.

Many of the new regulations were essential in convincing our major trading partners, namely Mexico, Japan and South Korea, into reopening borders.

In a market where we are such a big player, we cannot afford to allow the borders to remain closed for long. Some of the regulations that might seem like they go beyond what is actually necessary for food safety are vital in meeting the requirements of other countries.

CONSUMER CONFIDENCE

Boosting consumer confidence is the most important advantage of the new rules and regulations. In a consumer-driven market, the importance of consumer confidence in the product cannot be overstated.

If confidence sinks, so will demand and prices. However, if we come up with a way to buoy their belief in the product, we can save the market from disaster during the mad cow crisis.

Many of the new regulations serve this purpose. While some of the rules may seem like they are more restricting than absolutely necessary for food safety, if they put the consumer's mind at ease, then they are indispensable.

For example, consider the rule that bans feeding cow blood to calves as a milk replacer. So far, there has been no conclusive evidence that BSE can be transmitted through blood, but once the topic had been brought up and consumers heard about this common practice, measures had to be taken.

Grady writes in the *New York Times,* consumers "imagine bucolic scenes of nursing calves and cows munching on grass."

Realistically, this isn't productive, but we must cater to the more delicate nature of consumers wherever possible to insure that they will buy the product.

According to one of Dr. Field's lectures in my animal science class, when you are producing a product for consumers, you have to produce it in a way that consumers want to buy it, not just in a way that you want to produce it.

An example of this is producing a product in a way that is inexpensive and easy, but yields a poor quality product that won't sell or bring a good price, so you are better off not producing anything at all.

If you produce *for* the consumers, giving them what they want, it will be worth the extra effort and money required.

That is why the new regulations are crucial. They force producers to yield to consumer desires on specific things, increasing the consumer's confidence in the product and therefore the demand for the product.

WHY THE GOVERNMENT?

Finally, I would like to discuss why it actually makes sense that the government is making these rules, when they really don't know much about cows. From their city dwellings, government officials might not know the exact nutrients that a lactating cow requires, but they have a much more comprehensive understanding of the economics of production.

They have the knowledge of other countries requirements and what is necessary to facilitate exportation. They understand the effects that the rules will have on consumer confidence and demand. Government officials also have scientific information that isn't available to the general public to help them make their decisions.

...continued New Regulations and You, **Jessica Cook**

And the last critical piece to the puzzle is the fact that they don't have a vested interest. They can attempt to satisfy all groups without favoring any.

THE DECISION

It's incredible to think that all of these issues stemmed from one cow, one incidence of a disease. However, now that it has occurred, we must accept and flow with the changes if we hope to be productive in the future.

The government's regulations have already been passed and ranchers are forced to comply. Although the changes will be expensive and a pain-in-the-round to implement they do have benefits.

It is up to each rancher to decide if they will plant their feet in resistance, hoping to hold on to the ways of the past, or embrace the changes and the increased food safety, niche market opportunities, export markets, and boosted consumer confidence that they will bring. If ranchers choose the latter, they will have the opportunity to profit and grow with the future of beef and make their product stand out from the rest of the herd.

Before you make your decision about how to react to these new regulations, consider all of the benefits. I'm sure they will tip the scale in favor of being proactive and optimistic.

Works Cited

Field, Thomas G., and Robert E. Taylor. *Scientific Farm Animal Production.* Ed. Debbie Yarnell. 8th ed. Upper Saddle River, NJ: Pearson, 2003.

Grady, Denise. "Mad Cow Quandary: Making Animal Feed." *New York Times* 6 Feb. 2004: A20.

Grady, Denise, and Donald G. McNeil, Jr. "Rules Issued on Animal Feed and Use of Disabled Cattle." *New York Times* 27 Jan. 2004: A12.

Ismael, Wes. "Raining Regulations." *Beef* Feb. 2004. 3 Mar. 2004 <http://beef-mag.com/ar/beef_raining_regulations/index.htm>.

McNeil, Donald G., Jr. "Doubling Tests for Mad Cow Doesn't Quiet Program Critics." *New York Times* 9 Feb. 2004: A8.

McNeil, Donald G., Jr. "Man Who Killed the Mad Cow Has Questions of His Own." *New York Times* 3 Feb. 2004: D2.

"Mexico to Ban U.S. Beef Until Mad Cow Controlled." *Reuters* 10 Feb. 2004. 10 Feb 2004 <http:aolsvc.news.aol.com/news/>.

"Time for Perspective." *Cattle-Fax* 36 (2004): 1.

QUESTIONS FOR WRITING AND DISCUSSION

1. In her essay, Cook takes a slightly different approach to her problem-solving essay. Instead of trying to prove that a problem exists, she assumes that her readers are aware of the problem and argues for accepting a solution already in place. List the reasons she gives in arguing that the advantages of this policy outweigh the disadvantages. What evidence or support does she provide for each reason? Will the readers of *Beef* magazine find her reasons and evidence persuasive? Why or why not?

2. In addressing her target audience, Cook uses a personal voice and an appeal to character (*ethos*). Voice is the personality of the writer as revealed through her language and personal experience. The appeal to character or *ethos* (see Chapter 11, p. 518) is based on the writer's character as honest, fair-minded, ethical, and knowledgeable about the key issues. Find examples in which Cook uses a personal voice and makes appeals based on her character. For each example, evaluate the effectiveness of her appeal. Overall, does her personal approach make her argument more effective or less effective for her target audience? Explain.

3. In the library, find a copy of *Beef* magazine and read one or two sample articles. What are the key genre features of articles that appear in this magazine? Pay attention to audience, reference to sources, voice, style, article length, use of pictures and graphics, organization and use of headings, and paragraph length. Then find examples where Cook successfully models these genre features. Are there genre features that Cook does not imitate? Explain why you believe that Cook has or has not effectively modeled the genre features of her target publication.

4. For your own problem-solving essay, choose a target magazine or newspaper where you might publish your essay. Analyze the genre features of articles that appear in that publication. Write out your own plan for revising your essay to meet the requirements of that publication. Specifically, list and explain the genre features that you would include in your essay.

For twelve swelteringly hot days in July 1925, the famous Scopes "Monkey Trial" in Dayton, Tennessee, tested a state law banning the teaching of evolution. The original debate between Clarence Darrow and William Jennings Bryan is recreated in this film version of the play *Inherit the Wind*. Written arguments sometimes recreate the pro–con debate style of a trial, but frequently, they represent multiple points of view, just as parents, teachers, administrators, and students might gather to recommend policy changes at a school or citizens get together to solve problems in the community. This chapter encourages you to imagine multiple images for written argument as you adapt to different audiences, genres, and social contexts.

Arguing

As a recent high school graduate, you decide to write about the increasing number of standardized tests currently required of primary and secondary school students. The question you want to investigate is whether schools are teaching students important skills and making them better members of society or whether schools are just teaching them how to do well on tests. After reading current articles on standardized tests and interviewing your classmates, you decide to write to politicians who are in favor of standardized tests and argue that, while the tests should not be thrown out, they should be changed in order to solve several serious problems they have created for students, teachers, and parents.

After being cited for not wearing a seat belt while operating a motor vehicle, you decide that your rights have been violated. In order to write a convincing argument to your representative that seat belt laws are unfair, you research current articles about the law and interview a law professor on the issue. You decide to claim that the seat belt laws should be repealed because they are a fundamental violation of individual liberty. You believe that the opposing argument— that seat belts save lives and reduce insurance rates for everyone—is not relevant to the issue of individual liberty. Because your representative has supported seat belt laws, you present both sides of the issue but stress the arguments supporting your viewpoint.

> ❝ Give me liberty to know, to utter, and to argue freely according to conscience, above all liberties. ❞
> —JOHN MILTON, POET

> ❝ Freedom of speech is established to achieve its essential purpose only when different opinions are expounded in the same hall to the same audience.... The opposition is indispensable. ❞
> —WALTER LIPPMANN, JOURNALIST

509

WHEN PEOPLE ARGUE WITH EACH OTHER, THEY OFTEN BECOME HIGHLY EMOTIONAL OR CONFRONTATIONAL. REMEMBER THE LAST HEATED ARGUMENT YOU HAD WITH A FRIEND OR FAMILY MEMBER: AT THE END OF THE ARGUMENT, one person stomped out of the room, slammed the door, and didn't speak to the other for days. In the aftermath of such a scene, you felt angry at the other person and angry at yourself. Nothing was accomplished. Neither of you came close to achieving what you wanted when you began the argument. Rather than understanding each other's point of view and working out your differences, you effectively closed the lines of communication.

When writers construct arguments, however, they try to avoid the emotional outbursts that often turn arguments into displays of temper. Strong feelings may energize an argument—few of us make the effort to argue without emotional investment in the subject—but written argument stresses a fair presentation of opposing or alternative arguments. Because written arguments are public, they take on a civilized manner. They implicitly say, "Let's be reasonable about this. Let's look at the evidence on all sides. Before we argue for our position, let's put all the reasons and evidence on the table so everyone involved can see what's at stake."

As writers construct written arguments, they carefully consider the rhetorical situation:

- What is the social or cultural context for this issue?
- Where might this written argument appear or be published?
- Who is the audience, and what do they already know or believe?
- Do readers hold an opposing or alternative viewpoint, or are they more neutral and likely to listen to both sides before deciding what to believe?

A written argument creates an atmosphere of reason, which encourages readers to examine their own views clearly and dispassionately. When successful, such argument convinces rather than alienates an audience. It changes people's minds or persuades them to adopt a recommended course of action.

> ❝ All writing . . . is propaganda for something. ❞
> —ELIZABETH DREW, WRITER AND CRITIC

TECHNIQUES   **CASEBOOK**   **PROCESS**

Techniques for Writing: Argument

A written argument is similar to a public debate—between attorneys in a court of law or between members of Congress who represent different political parties. It begins with a debatable issue: Is this a good bill? Should we vote for it? In such debates, one person argues for a position or proposal, while the other argues against it. The onlookers (the judge, the members of Congress, the jury, or the public) then decide what to believe or what to do. The chapter opening art, which shows a scene from *Inherit the Wind,* pictures the debate about evolution between Clarence Darrow and William Jennings Bryan during the 1925 Scopes trial. The judge in the picture makes sure the trial follows certain rules, and the audience (not in the picture) decides what or whom to believe.

Written argument, however, is not identical to a debate. *In a written argument, the writer must play all the different roles.* The writer is first of all the person arguing for the claim. But the writer must also represent what the opposition might say. In addition, the writer must think like the judge and make sure the argument follows appropriate rules. Perhaps certain arguments and evidence are inadmissible or inappropriate in this case. Finally, the writer often anticipates the responses of the audience and responds to them as well.

Written argument, then, represents several different points of view, responds to them reasonably and fairly, and gives reasons and evidence that support the writer's claim. An effective written argument uses the following techniques.

- **Analyzing the *rhetorical situation.*** Reviewing your purpose, audience, occasion, genre, and cultural context helps you understand how to write your essay. Pay particular attention to your *audience.* Knowing what your audience already knows and believes helps you convince or persuade them.

- **Focusing on a *debatable* proposition or claim.** This claim becomes your thesis.

- **Representing and evaluating the *opposing points of view* on the issue fairly and accurately.** The key to a successful arguing paper is anticipating and responding to the most important opposing positions.

- **Arguing reasonably *against opposing arguments* and *for your claim.*** State and refute opposing arguments. Present the best arguments supporting your claim. Argue reasonably and fairly.

- **Supporting your claims with *sufficient* evidence.** Use firsthand observations; examples from personal experience; statistics, facts, and quotations from your reading; and results of surveys and interviews.

In an article titled "Active and Passive Euthanasia," James Rachels claims that active euthanasia may be defensible for patients with incurable and painful diseases. The following paragraphs from that article illustrate the key features of argument.

The distinction between active and passive euthanasia is thought to be crucial for medical ethics. The idea is that it is permissible, at least in some

Opposing position

Claim

Audience

Argument for claim

Example

Example

Argument against opposition

cases, to withhold treatment and allow a patient to die, but it is never permissible to take any direct action designed to kill the patient. This doctrine seems to be accepted by most doctors. . . .

However, a strong case can be made against this doctrine. In what follows I will set out some of the relevant arguments, and urge doctors to reconsider their views on this matter.

To begin with a familiar type of situation, a patient who is dying of incurable cancer of the throat is in terrible pain, which can no longer be satisfactorily alleviated. He is certain to die within a few days, even if present treatment is continued, but he does not want to go on living for those days, since the pain is unbearable. So he asks the doctor for an end to it, and his family joins in the request.

Suppose the doctor agrees to withhold treatment, as the conventional doctrine says he may. The justification for his doing so is that the patient is in terrible agony, and since he is going to die anyway, it would be wrong to prolong his suffering needlessly. But now notice this. If one simply withholds treatment, it may take the patient longer to die, and so he may suffer more than he would if more direct action were taken and a lethal injection given. This fact provides strong reason for thinking that, once the initial decision not to prolong his agony has been made, active euthanasia is actually preferable to passive euthanasia, rather than the reverse. To say otherwise is to endorse the option that leads to more suffering rather than less, and is contrary to the humanitarian impulse that prompts the decision not to prolong his life in the first place.

| CLAIMS | APPEALS | ROGERIAN | TOULMIN |

CLAIMS FOR WRITTEN ARGUMENT

The thesis of your argument is a *debatable claim*. Opinions on both sides of the issue must have some merit. Claims for a written argument usually fall into one of four categories: claims of fact, claims about cause and effect, claims about value, and claims about solutions and policies. A claim may occasionally fall into several categories or may even overlap categories.

■ CLAIMS OF FACT OR DEFINITION   These claims are about facts that are not easily determined or about definitions that are debatable. If I claim that a Lhasa apso was an ancient Chinese ruler, you can check a dictionary and find out that I am wrong. A Lhasa apso is, in fact, a small Tibetan dog. There is no argument. But people do disagree about some supposed "facts": Are polygraph tests accurate? Do grades measure achievement? People also disagree about definitions: Gender discrimination exists in the marketplace, but is it "serious"? What is discrimination, anyway? And what constitutes "serious" discrimination? Does the fact that women currently earn only seventy-three cents for every dollar that men earn qualify as serious discrimination?

In an excerpt from a *Newsweek* column titled "A Case of Severe Bias," Patricia Raybon makes claims of both fact and definition when she argues that the news media's portrayal of black America is inaccurate, biased, and stereotyped.

> This is who I am not. I am not a crack addict. I am not a welfare mother. I am not illiterate. I am not a prostitute. I have never been in jail. My children are not in gangs. My husband doesn't beat me. My home is not a tenement. None of these things defines who I am, nor do they describe the other black people I've known and worked with and loved and befriended over these 40 years of my life.
>
> Nor does it describe most of black America, period.
>
> Yet in the eyes of the American news media, this is what black America is: poor, criminal, addicted and dysfunctional. Indeed, media coverage of black America is so one-sided, so imbalanced that the most victimized and hurting segment of the black community—a small segment, at best— is presented not as the exception but as the norm. It is an insidious practice, all the uglier for its blatancy.
>
> In recent months, oftentimes in this very magazine, I have observed a steady offering of media reports on crack babies, gang warfare, violent youth, poverty and homelessness—and in most cases, the people featured in the photos and stories were black. At the same time, articles that discuss other aspects of American life—from home buying to medicine to technology to nutrition—rarely, if ever, show blacks playing a positive role, or for that matter, any role at all.
>
> Day after day, week after week, this message—that black America is dysfunctional and unwhole—gets transmitted across the American landscape. Sadly, as a result, America never learns the truth about what is actually a wonderful, vibrant, creative community of people.

CLAIMS ABOUT CAUSE AND EFFECT

- Testing in the schools improves the quality of education.
- Secondhand smoke causes lung cancer.
- Capital punishment does not deter violent crime.

Unlike the claim that grades affect admission to college—which few people would deny—the above claims about cause and effect are debatable. Most states require tests in order to evaluate individual schools. But do these tests ultimately improve students' education, or do they just make students better test-takers? The claim that secondhand smoke causes cancer is behind the rush to make all public and commercial spaces smoke-free. But what scientific evidence demonstrates a cause-and-effect link? Finally, the deterring effect of capital punishment is still an arguable proposition with reasonable arguments on both sides.

In a selection from her book *The Plug-In Drug: Television, Children, and the Family,* Marie Winn argues that television has a negative effect on family life. In her opening paragraphs, she sets forth both sides of the controversy and then argues that the overall effect is negative.

> Television's contribution to family life has been an equivocal one. For while it has, indeed, kept the members of the family from dispersing, it has not served to bring them *together.* By its domination of the time families spend together, it destroys the special quality that depends to a great extent on what a family does, what special rituals, games, recurrent jokes, familiar songs, and shared activities it accumulates.
>
> "Like the sorcerer of old," writes Urie Bronfenbrenner, "the television set casts its magic spell, freezing speech and action, turning the living into silent statues so long as the enchantment lasts. The primary danger of the television screen lies not so much in the behavior it produces—although there is danger there—as in the behavior it prevents: the talks, the games, the family festivities and arguments through which much of the child's learning takes place and through which his character is formed. Turning on the television set can turn off the process that transforms children into people."
>
> Yet parents have accepted a television-dominated family life so completely that they cannot see how the medium is involved in whatever problems they might be having.

CLAIMS ABOUT VALUE

- Boxing is a dehumanizing sport.
- Internet pornography degrades children's sense of human dignity.
- Toni Morrison is a great American novelist.

Claims about value typically lead to evaluative essays. All the strategies discussed in Chapter 9 apply here, with the additional requirement that you must anticipate and respond to alternate or opposing arguments. The essay that claims that boxing is dehumanizing must respond to the argument that boxing is merely another form of competition that promotes athletic excellence. The claim that pornography degrades children's sense of dignity must respond to the claim that restricting free speech on the Internet would cause greater harm. Arguing that Morrison is a great American novelist requires setting criteria for great American novels and then responding to critics who argue that Morrison's work does not reach those standards.

In "College Is a Waste of Time and Money," teacher and journalist Caroline Bird argues that many students go to college simply because it is the "thing to do." For those students, Bird claims, college is not a good idea.

> Nowadays, says one sociologist, you don't have to have a reason for going to college; it's an institution. His definition of an institution is an arrangement everyone accepts without question; the burden of proof is not on why you go, but why anyone thinks there might be a reason for not going. The implication is that an 18-year-old . . . should listen to those who know best and go to college.
>
> I don't agree. I believe that college has to be judged not on what other people think is good for students, but on how good it feels to the students themselves.
>
> I believe that people have an inside view of what's good for them. If a child doesn't want to go to school some morning, better let him stay at home, at least until you find out why. Maybe he knows something you don't. It's the same with college. If high-school graduates don't want to go, or if they don't want to go right away, they may perceive more clearly than their elders that college is not for them. It is no longer obvious that adolescents are best off studying a core curriculum that was constructed when all educated men could agree on what made them educated, or that professors, advisors, or parents can be of any particular help to young people in choosing a major or a career. High-school graduates see college graduates driving cabs and decide it's not worth going. College students find no intellectual stimulation in their studies and drop out.

❙ CLAIMS ABOUT SOLUTIONS OR POLICIES

- Pornography on the Internet should be censored.
- The penalty for drunk driving should be a mandatory jail sentence and loss of driver's license.
- To reduce exploitation and sensationalism, the news media should not be allowed to interview victims of crime or disaster.

Claims about solutions or policies sometimes occur *along with* claims of fact or definition, cause and effect, or value. Because grades do not measure achievement (argue that this is a fact), they should be abolished (argue for this policy). Boxing is a dehumanizing sport (argue this claim of value); therefore, boxing should be banned (argue for this solution). Claims about solutions or policies involve all the strategies used for problem solving (see Chapter 10), but with special emphasis on countering opposing arguments: "Although advocates of freedom of speech suggest that we cannot suppress pornography on the Internet, in fact, we already have self-monitoring devices in other media that could help reduce pornography on the Internet."

In *When Society Becomes an Addict*, psychotherapist Anne Wilson Schaef argues that our society has become an "Addictive System" that has many characteristics in common with alcoholism and other addictions. Advertising becomes addictive, causing us to behave dishonestly; the social pressure to be "nice" can become addictive, causing us to lie to ourselves. Schaef argues that the solution for our social addictions begins when we face the reality of our dependency.

> We cannot recover from an addiction unless we first admit that we have it. Naming our reality is essential to recovery. Unless we admit that we are indeed functioning in an addictive process in an Addictive System, we shall never have the option of recovery. Once we name something, we own it. . . . Remember, to name the system as addict is not to condemn it: It is to offer it the possibility of recovery.
>
> Paradoxically, the only way to reclaim our personal power is by admitting our powerlessness. The first part of Step One of the AA [Alcoholics Anonymous] Twelve-Step Program reads, "We admitted we were powerless over alcohol." It is important to recognize that admitting to powerlessness over an addiction is not the same as admitting powerlessness as a person. In fact, it can be very powerful to recognize the futility of the illusion of control.

CLAIMS	APPEALS	ROGERIAN	TOULMIN

APPEALS FOR WRITTEN ARGUMENT

To support claims and respond to opposing arguments, writers use *appeals* to the audience. Argument uses three important types of appeals: to *reason* (logic and evidence support the claim), to *character* (the writer's good character itself supports the claim), and to *emotion* (the writer's expression of feelings about the issue may support the claim). Effective arguments emphasize the appeal to reason but may also appeal to character or emotion.

66 Mere knowledge of the truth will not give you the art of persuasion. **99**
—PLATO,
PHAEDRUS

▮ **APPEAL TO REASON** An appeal to reason depends most frequently on *inductive logic*, which is sometimes called the *scientific method*. Inductive logic draws a general conclusion from personal observation or experience, specific facts, reports, statistics, testimony of authorities, and other bits of data.

Experience is the best teacher, we always say, and experience teaches inductively. Suppose, using biologist Thomas Huxley's famous example, you pick a green apple from a tree and take a bite. Halfway through the bite you discover that the apple is sour and quickly spit it out. But, you think, perhaps the next green apple will be ripe and will taste better. You pick a second green apple, take a bite, and realize that it is just as sour as the first. However, you know that some apples—like the Granny Smith—look green even when they're ripe, so you take a bite out of a third apple. It is also sour. You're beginning to draw a conclusion. In fact, if you taste a fourth or fifth apple, other people may begin to question your intelligence. How many green apples from this tree must you taste before you get the idea that all of these green apples are sour?

Experience, however, may lead to wrong conclusions. You've tasted enough of these apples to convince *you* that all these apples are sour, but will others think that these apples are sour? Perhaps you have funny taste buds. You may need to ask several friends to taste the apples. Or perhaps you are dealing with a slightly weird tree—in fact, some apple trees are hybrids, with several different kinds of apples grafted onto one tree. Before you draw a conclusion, you may need to consult an expert in order to be certain that your tree is a standard, single-variety apple tree. If your friends and the expert also agree that all of these green apples are sour, you may use your experience *and* their testimony to reach a conclusion—and to provide evidence to make your argument more convincing to others.

In inductive logic, a reasonable conclusion is based on a *sufficient* quantity of accurate and reliable evidence that is selected in a *random* manner to reduce human bias or to take into account variation in the sample. The definition of *sufficient* varies, but generally the number must be large enough to convince your audience that your sample fairly represents the whole subject.

Let's take an example to illustrate inductive reasoning. Suppose you ask a student, one of fifty in a Psychology I class, a question of value: "Is Professor X a good teacher?" If this student says, "Professor X is the worst teacher I've ever had!" what conclusion can you draw? If you avoid taking the class based on a sample of one, you may miss an excellent class. So you decide to gather a *sufficient sample* by polling twenty of the fifty students in the class. But which twenty do you interview? If you ask the first student for a list of students, you may receive the names of twenty other students who also hate the professor. To reduce human or accidental bias, then, you choose a random method for collecting your evidence: As the students leave the class, you give a questionnaire to two out of every five students. If they all fill out the questionnaires, you probably have a *sufficient* and *random* sample.

Finally, if the responses to your questionnaire show that fifteen out of twenty students rate Professor X as an excellent teacher, what *valid conclusion* should you draw? You should not say, categorically, "X is an excellent teacher." Your conclusion must be restricted by your evidence and the method of gathering it: "Seventy-five percent of the students polled in Psychology I believe that Professor X is an excellent teacher."

Most arguments use a shorthand version of the inductive method of reasoning. A writer makes a claim and then supports it with *reasons* and representative *examples* or *data:*

Claim: Professor X is an excellent psychology teacher.

Reason #1:   Professor X is an excellent teacher because she gives stimulating lectures that students rarely miss.

Evidence: Sixty percent of the students polled said that they rarely missed a lecture. Three students cited Professor X's lecture on "assertiveness" as the best lecture they'd ever heard.

Reason #2:   Professor X is an excellent teacher because she gives tests that encourage learning rather than sheer memorization.

Evidence: Seventy percent of the students polled said that Professor X's essay tests required thinking and learning rather than memorization. One student said that Professor X's tests always made her think about what she'd read. Another student said he always liked to discuss Professor X's test questions with his classmates and friends.

APPEAL TO CHARACTER   An appeal based on your good character as a writer can also be important in argument. (The appeal to character is frequently called the *ethical appeal* because readers make a value judgment about the writer's character.) In a written argument, you show your audience—through your reasonable persona, voice, and tone—that you are a person who abides by moral standards that your audience shares: You have a good reputation, you are honest and trustworthy, and you argue "fairly."

A person's reputation often affects how we react to a claim, but *the argument itself* should also establish the writer's trustworthiness. You don't have to be a Mahatma Gandhi or a Mother Teresa to generate a strong ethical appeal for your claim. Even if your readers have never heard your name before, they will feel confident about your character if you are knowledgeable about your subject, present opposing arguments fairly, and support your own claim with sufficient, reliable evidence.

If your readers have reason to suspect your motives or think that you may have something personal to gain from your argument, you may need to bend over backward to be fair. If you do have something to gain, lay your cards on the table. Declare your vested interest but explain, for example, how your solution would benefit everyone equally. Similarly, don't try to cover up or distort the opponents' arguments; acknowledge the opposition's strong arguments and refute the weak ones.

At the most basic level, your interest in the topic and willingness to work hard can improve your ethical appeal. Readers can sense when a writer cares about his or her subject, when a writer knows something about the topic, about the rhetorical or cultural context, and about the various viewpoints on a topic. Show your readers that you care about the subject, and they will find your arguments more convincing.

- Show you care by using sufficient details and specific, vivid examples.
- Show you care by including any relevant personal experience you have on the topic.
- Show you care by including other people's ideas and points of view and by responding to their views with fairness and tact.
- Show you care by organizing your essay so your main points are easy to find and transitions between ideas are clear and logical.
- Show you care by revising and proofreading your essay.

Readers know when writers care about their subjects, and they are more willing to listen to new ideas when the writer has worked hard and is personally invested in the topic.

APPEAL TO EMOTION   Appeals to emotion can be tricky because, as we have seen, when emotions come in through the door, reasonableness may fly out the window. Argument emphasizes reason, not emotion. We know, for example, how advertising plays on emotions, by means of loaded or exaggerated language or through images of famous or sexy people. Emotional appeals designed to *deceive* or *frighten* people or to *misrepresent* the virtues of a person, place, or object have no place in rational argument. But emotional appeals that illustrate a truth or movingly depict a reality are legitimate and effective means of convincing readers.

COMBINED APPEALS   Appeals may be used in combination. Writers may appeal to reason and, at the same time, establish trustworthy characters and use legitimate emotional appeals. The following excerpt from Martin Luther King, Jr.'s "Letter from Birmingham Jail" illustrates all three appeals. He appeals to reason, arguing that, historically, civil rights reforms are rarely made without political pressure. He establishes his integrity and good character by treating the opposition (in this case, the Birmingham clergy) with respect and by showing moderation and restraint. Finally, he uses emotional appeals, describing his six-year-old daughter in tears and recalling his own humiliation at being refused a place to sleep. King uses these emotional appeals legitimately; he is not misrepresenting reality or trying to deceive his readers.

> One of the basic points in [the statement by the Birmingham clergy] is that the action that I and my associates have taken in Birmingham is untimely. Some have asked: "Why didn't you give the new city administration time to

Appeal to character and appeal to reason

act?" The only answer that I can give to this query is that the new Birmingham administration must be prodded about as much as the outgoing one, before it will act. We are sadly mistaken if we feel that the election of Albert Boutwell as mayor will bring the millennium to Birmingham. While Mr. Boutwell is a much more gentle person than Mr. Connor, they are both segregationists, dedicated to the maintenance of the status quo. I have hoped that Mr. Boutwell will be reasonable enough to see the futility of massive resistance to desegregation. But he will not see this without pressure from devotees of civil rights.

Appeal to reason

My friends, I must say to you that we have not made a single gain in civil rights without determined legal and nonviolent pressure.

Evidence

Lamentably, it is an historical fact that privileged groups seldom give up their privileges voluntarily. Individuals may see the moral light and voluntarily give up their unjust posture; but, as Reinhold Niebuhr has reminded us, groups tend to be more immoral than individuals.

We know through painful experience that freedom is never voluntarily given by the oppressor; it must be demanded by the oppressed.

Appeal to character and reason

Frankly, I have yet to engage in a direct-action campaign that was "well timed" in the view of those who have not suffered unduly from the disease of segregation. For years now I have heard the word "Wait!" It rings in the ear of every Negro with piercing familiarity. This "Wait" has almost always meant "Never." We must come to see, with one of our distinguished jurists, that "justice too long delayed is justice denied."

We have waited for more than 340 years for our constitutional and God-given rights. . . . Perhaps it is easy for those who have never felt the stinging darts of segregation to say, "Wait."

Appeal to emotion

Evidence

But when you have seen vicious mobs lynch your mothers and fathers at will and drown your sisters and brothers at whim; when you have seen hate-filled policemen curse, kick, and even kill your black brothers and sisters;

Appeal to emotion

Evidence

when you see the vast majority of your twenty million Negro brothers smothering in an airtight cage of poverty in the midst of an affluent society; when you suddenly find your tongue twisted and your speech stammering as you seek to explain to your six-year-old daughter why she can't go to the public amusement park that has just been advertised on television, and see tears welling up in her eyes when she is told that Funtown is closed to colored children . . .

Appeal to emotion

Evidence

when you take a cross-country drive and find it necessary to sleep night after night in the uncomfortable corners of your automobile because no motel will accept you; when you are humiliated day in and day out by nagging signs reading "white" and "colored"; when your first name becomes "nigger," your middle name becomes "boy" (however old you are) and your last name becomes "John" . . . —then you will understand why we find it difficult to wait. There comes a time when the cup of endurance runs over, and men are no longer willing to be plunged into the abyss of despair.

Appeal to character

I hope, sirs, you can understand our legitimate and unavoidable impatience.

CLAIMS	APPEALS	ROGERIAN	TOULMIN

ROGERIAN ARGUMENT

Traditional argument assumes that people are most readily convinced or persuaded by a confrontational "debate" on the issue. In a traditional argument, the writer argues reasonably and fairly, but the argument becomes a kind of struggle or "war" as the writer attempts to "defeat" the arguments of the opposition. The purpose of a traditional argument is thus to convince an undecided audience that the writer has "won a fight" and emerged "victorious" over the opposition.

In fact, however, there are many situations in which a less confrontational and less adversarial approach to argument is more effective. Particularly when the issues are highly charged or when the audience that we are trying to persuade is the opposition, writers may more effectively use negotiation rather than confrontation. *Rogerian argument*—named after psychologist Carl Rogers—is a kind of negotiated argument where understanding and compromise replace the traditional, adversarial approach. Rogerian, or *nonthreatening,* argument opens the lines of communication by reducing conflict. When people's beliefs are attacked, they instinctively become defensive and strike back. As a result, the argument becomes polarized: The writer argues for a claim, the reader digs in to defend his or her position, and no one budges.

Crucial to Rogerian argument is the fact that convictions and beliefs are not abstract but reside in people. If people are to agree, they must be sensitive to each other's beliefs. Rogerian argument, therefore, contains a clear appeal to character. While Rogerian argument uses reason and logic, its primary goal is not to "win" the argument but to open the lines of communication. To do that, the writer must be sympathetic to different points of view and willing to modify his or her claims in response to people who hold different viewpoints. Once the reader sees that the writer is open to change, the reader may become more flexible.

Once both sides are more flexible, a compromise position or solution becomes possible. As Rogers says, "This procedure gradually achieves a mutual communication. Mutual communication tends to be pointed toward solving a problem rather than toward attacking a person or group." Rogerian argument, then, imitates not a courtroom debate but the mutual communication that may take place between two people. Whereas traditional argument intends to change the actions or the beliefs of the opposition, Rogerian argument works toward changes *in both sides* as a means of establishing common ground and reaching a solution.

If you choose Rogerian argument, remember that you must actually be willing to change your beliefs. Often, in fact, when you need to use Rogerian argument most, you may be least inclined to use it—simply because you are inflexible on an issue. If you are unwilling to modify your own position, your reader will probably sense your basic insincerity and realize that you are just playing a trick of rhetoric.

Rogerian argument is appropriate in a variety of sensitive or highly controversial situations. You may want to choose Rogerian argument if you are an employer requesting union members to accept a pay cut in order to help the company avoid bankruptcy. Similarly, if you argue to husbands that they should assume responsibility for half the housework, or if you argue to Anglo-Americans that Spanish language and culture should play a larger role in public education, you may want to use a Rogerian strategy. By showing that you empathize with the opposition's position and are willing to compromise, you create a climate for mutual communication.

Rogerian argument makes a claim, considers the opposition, and presents evidence to support your claim, but in addition, it avoids threatening or adversarial language and promotes mutual communication and learning. A Rogerian argument uses the following strategies.

- **Avoiding** *a confrontational stance.* Confrontation threatens your audience and increases their defensiveness. Threat hinders communication.
- **Presenting your** *character* **as someone who understands and can empathize with the opposition.** Show that you understand by restating the opposing position accurately.
- **Establishing** *common ground* **with the opposition.** Indicate the beliefs and values that you share.
- **Being willing** *to change your views.* Show where your position is not reasonable and could be modified.
- **Directing your argument toward** *a compromise or workable solution.*

Note: An argument does not have to be either entirely adversarial or entirely Rogerian. You may use Rogerian techniques for the most sensitive points in an argument that is otherwise traditional or confrontational.

In his essay "Animal Rights Versus Human Health," biology professor Albert Rosenfeld illustrates several features of Rogerian argument. Rosenfeld argues that animals should be used for medical experiments, but he is aware that the issues are emotional and that his audience is likely to be antagonistic. In these paragraphs, Rosenfeld avoids threatening language, represents the opposition fairly, grants that he is guilty of *speciesism,* and says that he sympathizes with the demand to look for alternatives. He indicates that his position is flexible: Most researchers, he says, are delighted when they can use alternatives. He grants that there is some room for compromise, but he is firm in his position that some animal experimentation is necessary for advancements in medicine.

States opposing position fairly and sympathetically

It is fair to say that millions of animals—probably more rats and mice than any other species—are subjected to experiments that cause them pain, discomfort, and distress, sometimes lots of it over long periods of time.... All new forms of medication or surgery are tried out on animals first. Every new substance that is released into the environment, or put on the market, is tested on animals. . . .

In 1975, Australian philosopher Peter Singer wrote his influential book called *Animal Liberation,* in which he accuses us all of "speciesism"— as reprehensible, to him, as racism or sexism. He freely describes the "pain and suffering" inflicted in the "tyranny of human over nonhuman animals" and sharply challenges our biblical license to exercise "dominion over the fish of the sea, and over the fowl of the air, and over every living thing that moveth upon the Earth." *States opposing position fairly*

Well, certainly we are guilty of speciesism. We do act as if we had do-minion over other living creatures. But domination also entails some cus-todial responsibility. And the questions continue to be raised: Do we have the right to abuse animals? To eat them? To hunt them for sport? To keep them imprisoned in zoos—or, for that matter, in our households? Espe-cially to do experiments on these creatures who can't fight back? *Acknowledges common ground*

Sympathetic to opposing position

Hardly any advance in either human or veterinary medicine—cure, vaccine, operation, drug, therapy—has come about without experiments on animals. . . . I certainly sympathize with the demand that we look for ways to get the information we want without using animals. Most investi-gators are delighted when they can get their data by means of tissue cul-tures or computer simulations. But as we look for alternative ways to get information, do we meanwhile just do without? *Suggests compromise position*

CLAIMS	APPEALS	ROGERIAN	TOULMIN

THE TOULMIN METHOD OF ARGUMENT

In *The Uses of Argument* (1958), British philosopher Stephen Toulmin argued against applying formal logic and the concepts of deduction and induction to writ-ten arguments. Instead, he suggested, the laws of logic are not universal but depend upon the knowledge of each specific field. Thus, the rules for argument vary from economics to philosophy or from political science to biology. What counts as evi-dence and a good argument is not the same in human nutrition as it is in literature. The following six concepts that Toulmin identified are not universal rules but merely guidelines that can be helpful as we analyze the logic of an argument.

- **Data:** The evidence gathered to support a particular claim.
- **Claim:** The overall thesis the writer hopes to prove. This thesis may be a claim of fact or definition, of cause and effect, of value, or of policy.
- **Warrant:** The statement that explains why or how the data support the writer's claim.

- **Backing:** The additional logic or reasoning that, when necessary, supports the warrant.
- **Qualifier:** The short phrases that limit the scope of the claim, such as "typically," "usually," or "on the whole."
- **Exceptions:** Those particular situations in which the writer does not or would not insist on the claim.

We can illustrate each of these six concepts using Cathleen A. Cleaver's argument against Internet pornography in her essay, "The Internet: A Clear and Present Danger?" that appears later in this chapter. The relationship of the data, warrant, and claim may be illustrated in the following diagram.

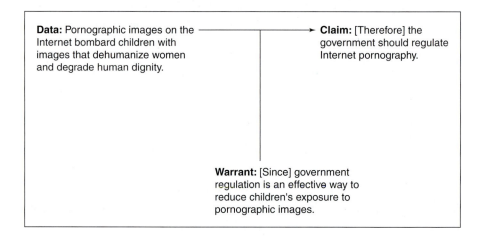

Data: Pornographic images on the Internet bombard children with images that dehumanize women and degrade human dignity.

Claim: [Therefore] the government should regulate Internet pornography.

Warrant: [Since] government regulation is an effective way to reduce children's exposure to pornographic images.

- **Backing:** Government regulation already exists in print, radio, and television media, so it should be extended to the Internet.
- **Qualifier:** *In most cases,* the government should regulate pornography on the Internet. (Cleaver does not actually use a qualifier for her claim. This is a qualifier she might use.)
- **Exceptions:** Government regulations must protect children, but *where children are not involved, regulation may not be as urgent.* (Cleaver implies this exception, since she focuses her argument only on pornography's effect on children.)

Applying the Toulmin model of argument to written texts can help us as readers and writers if we follow a few guidelines. First, the Toulmin model is especially helpful as we critically read texts for their logical strengths and weaknesses. As we become better critical readers, we are likely to make our own arguments more logical and thus more persuasive. Second, as we critically read texts, not all of us find the same warrant statements, because there can be several ways of explaining a logical connection between the data and the stated claim. Third, applying the Toulmin model and using warrants, backing, qualifiers, and exceptions becomes more important when our readers are likely to disagree with the claim. Just as Rogerian argument tries to reduce conflict in adversarial situations through mutual communication and a strong appeal to character, the Toulmin model helps communicate in adversarial contexts by being especially reasonable and logical. If our readers already agree that pornography on the Internet is a bad thing, we need to give only a few examples and go straight to our claim. But if readers are members of the ACLU or have a strong belief in free speech on the Internet, we need to qualify our claim and make our warrants—the connections between the data and the claim—as explicit and logical as possible. We may also need to state backing for the warrant and note the exceptions where we don't want to press our case. The more antagonistic our readers are, the more we need to be as logical as possible. The Toulmin model is just one approach that can help bolster the logic of our argument.

▌ **WARMING UP:** Journal Exercises

The following exercises will help you practice arguing. Read all of the following exercises and then write on the three that interest you most. If another idea occurs to you, write about it.

1. From the following list of "should" statements, choose one that relates to your experience and freewrite for ten minutes. When you finish your freewriting, state a claim and list arguments on both sides of the issue.

   - Bicyclists should be subject to regular traffic laws, including DWI.
   - The sale of all handguns should be illegal.
   - NCAA football should have playoffs.
   - High-quality child care should be available to all working parents at public expense.
   - Computer literacy courses should be required at the college level.
   - Police should live in the neighborhoods they serve.
   - Fraternities and sororities should be forbidden to serve alcoholic beverages.
   - Students should work for one year between high school and college.
   - Businesses should be required to provide free health insurance for all employees.
   - Nonmajor courses should be graded pass/fail.

> ❝ A society which is clamoring for choice [is] filled with many articulate groups, each arguing its own brand of salvation. ❞
> —MARGARET MEAD, ANTHROPOLOGIST

ANALYZING STATISTICS

Whether you are evaluating statistical sources in an essay that you are reading or choosing statistical data to use as evidence for a claim in your own essay, use the following questions to help you determine the relevance, validity, and bias of the statistics.

- Who is the author or the group responsible for gathering or presenting the information? Do they have a bias or point of view?
- What is the date of the study or survey? Are the data still relevant?
- For a survey or poll, what is the sample size (number of respondents) and sample selection (demographic group selected)? Is the sample large enough to give reliable results?
- Is the group randomly selected? Are certain key groups not included?
- Analyze the wording of the questions asked in the poll or survey. Are the questions relatively neutral? Do the questions lead respondents to a certain conclusion?
- Are the conclusions drawn justified by the data? Are the conclusions exaggerated or overgeneralized?

2. Controversial subjects depend as much on the audience as they do on the issue itself. Make a quick list of things you do every day: the kind of clothes you wear, the food you eat, the books you read, the friends you have, the ideas you discuss. For one of these activities, imagine people who might find what you do immoral, illogical, unjust, or unhealthy. What claim might they make about your activity? What reasons or evidence might they use to argue that your activity should be abolished, outlawed, or changed? Write for five minutes arguing *their* point of view.

3. Television and television advertising are often the subject of much criticism, such as in Marie Winn's excerpt from "The Plug-In Drug." Write a letter to Marie Winn, to your local or college newspaper, or to members of the PTA in your city defending the *positive* effects or value of television. Cite one particular program or commercial as an example.

4. Grades are important, but in some courses, they get in the way of learning. Choose an actual course that you have taken and write an open letter to the school administration, arguing for credit/no-credit grading in that

particular course. Assume that you intend to submit your letter to the campus news paper.

5. News items often contain incidents that spark arguments about morality or justice. Choose a recent controversial news story and write out the arguments for or against the action taken in the case.

PROFESSIONAL WRITING

The Internet: A Clear and Present Danger?

Cathleen A. Cleaver

Cathleen Cleaver is a former director of legal studies at the Family Research Council, an organization based in Washington, D.C. She has published extensively on issues relating to children and the Internet, in newspaper and magazines such as USA Today, Newsday, *and the* Congressional Quarterly Researcher. *The following essay was originally a speech given at Boston University as part of a College of Communication Great Debate. In this speech, she argues that some industry and government regulation of the Internet is necessary.*

- Someone breaks through your firewall and steals proprietary information from your computer systems. You find out and contact a lawyer who says, "Man, you shouldn't have had your stuff online." The thief becomes a millionaire using your ideas, and you go broke, if laws against copyright violation don't protect material on the Internet.   1

- You visit the Antiques Anonymous Web site and decide to pay their hefty subscription fee for a year's worth of exclusive estate sale previews in their private online monthly magazine. They never deliver and, in fact, never intended to—they don't even have a magazine. You have no recourse, if laws against fraud don't apply to online transactions.   2

- Bob Guccione decides to branch out into the lucrative child porn market and creates a Teen Hustler Web site featuring nude adolescents and preteens. You find out and complain, but nothing can be done, if child pornography distribution laws don't apply to computer transmissions.   3

... continued The Internet: A Clear and Present Danger?, **Cathleen A. Cleaver**

- A major computer software vendor who dominates the market *4*
  develops his popular office software so that it works only with his
  browser. You're a small browser manufacturer who is completely
  squeezed out of the market, but you have to find a new line of
  work, if antitrust laws don't apply online.
- Finally, a pedophile e-mails your son, misrepresenting himself *5*
  as a twelve-year-old named Jenny. They develop an online
  relationship and one day arrange to meet after school, where he
  intends to rape your son. Thankfully, you learn in advance about
  the meeting and go there yourself, where you find a forty-year-
  old man instead of Jenny. You flee to the police, who'll tell you
  there's nothing they can do, if child-stalking laws don't apply to
  the Internet.

The awesome advances in interactive telecommunication that we've *6*
witnessed in just the last few years have changed the way in which many
Americans communicate and interact. No one can doubt that the Internet
is a technological revolution of enormous proportion, with outstanding
possibilities for human advancement.

As lead speaker for the affirmative, I'm asked to argue that the Inter- *7*
net poses a "clear and present danger," but the Internet, as a whole, isn't
dangerous. In fact, it continues to be a positive and highly beneficial tool,
which will undoubtedly improve education, information exchange, and
commerce in years to come. In other words, the Internet will enrich many
aspects of our daily life. Thus, instead of defending this rather apocalyptic
view of the Internet, I'll attempt to explain why some industry and government regulation of certain aspects of the Internet is necessary—or, stated
another way, why people who use the Internet should not be exempt from
many of the laws and regulations that govern their conduct elsewhere. My
opening illustrations were meant to give examples of some illegal conduct
which should not become legal simply because someone uses the Internet.
In looking at whether Internet regulation is a good idea, I believe we
should consider whether regulation is in the public interest. In order to do
that, we have to ask the question: Who is the public? More specifically,
does the "public" whose interests we care about tonight include children?

Children and the Internet

Dave Barry describes the Internet as a "worldwide network of university, *8*
government, business, and private computer systems, run by a thirteen-

year-old named Jason." This description draws a smile precisely because we acknowledge the highly advanced computer literacy of our children. Most children demonstrate computer proficiency that far surpasses that of their parents, and many parents know only what their children have taught them about the Internet, which gives new relevance to Wordsworth's insight: "The child is father of the man." In fact, one could go so far as to say that the Internet is as accessible to many children as it is inaccessible to many adults. This technological evolution is new in many ways, not the least of which is its accessibility to children, wholly independent of their parents.

When considering what's in the public interest, we must consider the whole public, including children, as individual participants in this new medium.   9

Pornography and the Internet

This new medium is unique in another way. It provides, through a single avenue, the full spectrum of pornographic depictions, from the more familiar convenience store fare to pornography of such violence and depravity that it surpasses the worst excesses of the normal human imagination. Sites displaying this material are easily accessible, making pornography far more freely available via the Internet than from any other communications medium in the United States. Pornography is the third largest sector of sales on the Internet, generating $1 billion annually. There are an estimated seventy-two thousand pornographic sites on the World Wide Web alone, with approximately thirty-nine new explicit sex sites every day. Indeed, the *Washington Post* has called the Internet the largest pornography store in the history of mankind.   10

There is little restriction of pornography-related activity in cyberspace. While there are some porn-related laws, the specter of those laws does not loom large in cyberspace. There's an implicit license there that exists nowhere else with regard to pornography—an environment where people are free to exploit others for profit and be virtually untroubled by legal deterrent. Indeed, if we consider cyberspace to be a little world of its own, it's the type of world for which groups like the ACLU have long fought but, so far, fought in vain.   11

I believe it will not remain this way, but until it changes, we should take the opportunity to see what this world looks like, if for no other reason than to reassure ourselves that our decades-old decisions to control pornography were good ones.   12

With a few clicks of the mouse, anyone, any child, can get graphic and often violent sexual images—the kind of stuff it used to be difficult to find   13 without exceptional effort and some significant personal risk. Anyone with a computer and a modem can set up public sites featuring the perversion of their choice, whether it's mutilation of female genitals, eroticized urination and defecation, bestiality, or sites featuring depictions of incest. These pictures can be sold for profit, they can be sent to harass others, or posted to shock people. Anyone can describe the fantasy rape and murder of a specific person and display it for all to read. Anyone can meet children in chat rooms or via e-mail and send them pornography and find out where they live. An adult who signs onto an AOL chat room as a thirteen-year-old girl is hit on thirty times within the first half hour.

All this can be done from the seclusion of the home, with the feeling 14 of near anonymity and with the comfort of knowing that there's little risk of legal sanction.

The phenomenon of this kind of pornography finding such a welcome 15 home in this new medium presents abundant opportunities for social commentary. What does Internet pornography tell us about human sexuality? Photographs, videos, and virtual games that depict rape and the dehumanization of women in sexual scenes send powerful messages about human dignity and equality. Much of the pornography freely available without restriction on the Internet celebrates unhealthy and antisocial kinds of sexual activity, such as sadomasochism, abuse, and degradation. Of course, by its very nature, pornography encourages voyeurism.

Beyond the troubling social aspects of unrestricted porn, we face the 16 reality that children are accessing it and that predators are accessing children. We have got to start considering what kind of society we'll have when the next generation learns about human sexuality from what the Internet teaches. What does unrestricted Internet pornography teach children about relationships, about the equality of women? What does it teach little girls about themselves and their worth?

Opponents of restrictions are fond of saying that it's up to the parents 17 to deal with the issue of children's exposure. Well, of course it is, but placing the burden solely on parents is illogical and ineffective. It's far easier for a distributor of pornography to control his material than it is for parents, who must, with the help of software, search for and find the pornographic sites, which change daily, and then attempt to block them. Any pornographer who wants to can easily subvert these efforts, and a recent Internet posting from a teenager wanting to know how to disable the filtering software on his computer received several effective answers. Moreover, it goes without saying that the most sophisticated software can only be effective where it's installed, and children will have access to many computers that don't have filtering software, such as those in libraries, schools, and at neighbors' houses.

Internet Transactions Should Not Be Exempt

Opponents of legal restrictions often argue simply that the laws just cannot apply in this new medium, but the argument that old laws can't apply to changing technology just doesn't hold. We saw this argument last in the early '80s with the advent of the videotape. Then, certain groups tried to argue that, since you can't view videotapes without a VCR, you can't make the sale of child porn videos illegal, because, after all, they're just plastic boxes with magnetic tape inside. Technological change mandates legal change only insofar as it affects the justification for a law. It just doesn't make sense that the government may take steps to restrict illegal material in *every* medium—video, television, radio, the private telephone, *and* print—but that it may do nothing where people distribute the material by the Internet. While old laws might need redefinition, the old principles generally stand firm.   18

The question of enforcement usually is raised here, and it often comes in the form of: "How are you going to stop people from doing it?" Well, no law stops people from doing things—a red light at an intersection doesn't force you to stop but tells you that you should stop and that there could be legal consequences if you don't. Not everyone who runs a red light is caught, but that doesn't mean the law is futile. The same concept holds true for Internet laws. Government efforts to temper harmful conduct online will never be perfect, but that doesn't mean they shouldn't undertake the effort at all.   19

There's clearly a role for industry to play here. Search engines don't have to run ads for porn sites or prioritize search results to highlight porn. One new search engine even has sex as the default search term. Internet service providers can do something about unsolicited e-mail with hotlinks to porn, and they can and should carefully monitor any chat rooms designed for kids.   20

Some charge that industry standards or regulations that restrict explicit pornography will hinder the development of Internet technology. But that is to say that its advancement depends upon unrestricted exhibition of this   21

... *continued*   The Internet: A Clear and Present Danger?,   **Cathleen A. Cleaver**

material, and this cannot be true. The Internet does not belong to pornographers, and it's clearly in the public interest to see that they don't usurp this great new technology. We don't live in a perfect society, and the Internet is merely a reflection of the larger social community. Without some mitigating influences, the strong will exploit the weak, whether a Bill Gates or a child predator.

Conclusion: Technology Must Serve Man

To argue that the strength of the Internet is chaos or that our liberty 22 depends upon chaos is to misunderstand not only the Internet but also the fundamental nature of our liberty. It's an illusion to claim social or moral neutrality in the application of technology, even if its development may be neutral. It can be a valuable resource only when placed at the service of humanity and when it promotes our integral development for the benefit of all.

Guiding principles simply cannot be inferred from mere technical 23 efficiency or from the usefulness accruing to some at the expense of others. Technology by its very nature requires unconditional respect for the fundamental interests of society.

Internet technology must be at the service of humanity and of our 24 inalienable rights. It must respect the prerogatives of a civil society, among which is the protection of children.

■ ■ ■

vo·cab·u·lar·y

In your journal, write the meaning of the italicized words in the following phrases.

- steals *proprietary* information **(1)**
- rather *apocalyptic* view **(7)**
- legal *deterrent* **(11)**
- don't have *filtering* software **(17)**
- the law is *futile* **(19)**
- cannot be *inferred* **(23)**
- usefulness *accruing* to some **(23)**
- respect the *prerogatives* **(24)**

QUESTIONS FOR WRITING AND DISCUSSION

1. Before you read or reread Cleaver's essay, write down your own thoughts and experiences about pornography on the Internet. Have you run into sites that you find offensive? Should access to such sites be made more difficult? Do you think children should be protected from accessing such sites—either by accident or on purpose? What do you think are the best method(s) for such regulation: Internet software programs, parental regulation, governmental regulation? Explain.

2. Cleaver begins her essay with several scenarios describing potential abuses and crimes that occur online. Did you find these scenarios effective as a lead-in to her argument? Did they help you focus on her thesis? Should she use fewer scenarios? Why do you think she used all of these examples when only two dealt with child pornography on the Internet?

3. The rhetorical occasion for Cleaver's argument is a debate sponsored by the College of Communication at Boston University. In her essay, can you find evidences (word choice, vocabulary, sentence length, tone, use of evidence, use of appeals) that suggest that her original *genre* was a speech and that her *audience* was college students, college faculty, and members of the community? Cite evidence from the essay showing where Cleaver uses debate elements appropriate for this genre and makes appeals to this audience.

4. Cleaver states her case for government regulation of pornography on the Internet, but who is against regulation, and what are their arguments? What arguments opposing Internet regulation does Cleaver cite? (Are there other opposing arguments that Cleaver does not consider?) How well does Cleaver answer these opposing arguments?

5. Arguing essays make appeals to reason, to character, and to emotion. Find examples of each type of appeal in Cleaver's essay. Which type of appeal does she use most frequently? Which appeals are most or least effective? Does she rely too much on her emotional appeals (see paragraph 13, for example)? For her audience and her context (a debate), should she bolster her rational appeals with more evidence and statistics? Why or why not?

6. Imagine that you are at this debate on the Internet and that your side believes that there should be no or very little regulation of the Internet. What arguments might you make in response to Cleaver? Make a list of the possible pro–con arguments on this topic and explain which ones you will focus on as you respond to Cleaver.

PROFESSIONAL WRITING

Death and Justice

Edward I. Koch

As a lifelong public servant and former mayor of New York City, Edward I. Koch has written several books on political issues, including Mayor *(1984),* Politics *(1985), and* Ed Koch on Everything *(1994). "Death and Justice," which appeared originally in* The New Republic, *is a classically organized essay arguing for the death penalty for convicted murderers. Although the state of New York now has instituted the death penalty, Koch's arguments still apply to many states where the debate on the death penalty still continues. In his argument, Koch represents opposing positions, uses appeals to reason, character, and emotion responsibly, and provides a variety of supporting evidence. This does not mean, of course, that you should necessarily be persuaded by his arguments or that his appeals, reasons, and evidence are flawless. Before you read Koch's essay, be sure to review the discussions of techniques, claims, and appeals for written argument in the opening sections of this chapter. Be prepared to evaluate Koch's argument. Where is his argument most or least persuasive?*

Last December a man named Robert Lee Willie, who had been convicted   1
of raping and murdering an 18-year-old woman, was executed in the Louisiana state prison. In a statement issued several minutes before his death, Mr. Willie said: "Killing people is wrong. . . . It makes no difference whether it's citizens, countries, or governments. Killing is wrong." Two weeks later in South Carolina, an admitted killer named Joseph Carl Shaw was put to death for murdering two teenagers. In an appeal to the governor for clemency, Mr. Shaw wrote: "Killing is wrong when I did it. Killing is wrong when you do it. I hope you have the courage and moral strength to stop the killing."

It is a curiosity of modern life that we find ourselves being lectured on   2
morality by cold-blooded killers. Mr. Willie previously had been convicted of aggravated rape, aggravated kidnapping, and the murders of a Louisiana deputy and a man from Missouri. Mr. Shaw committed another murder a week before the two for which he was executed, and admitted mutilating the body of the 14-year-old girl he killed. I can't help wondering what prompted these murderers to speak out against killing as they entered the death-house door. Did their newfound reverence for life stem from the realization that they were about to lose their own?

Life is indeed precious, and I believe the death penalty helps to affirm   *3*
this fact. Had the death penalty been a real possibility in the minds of these
murderers, they might well have stayed their hand. They might have shown
moral awareness before their victims died, and not after. Consider the
tragic death of Rosa Velez, who happened to be home when a man named
Luis Vera burglarized her apartment in Brooklyn. "Yeah, I shot her," Vera
admitted. "She knew me, and I knew I wouldn't go to the chair."

During my 22 years in public service, I have heard the pros and cons   *4*
of capital punishment expressed with special intensity. As a district leader,
councilman, congressman, and mayor, I have represented constituencies
generally thought of as liberal. Because I support the death penalty for
heinous crimes of murder, I have sometimes been the subject of emotional
and outraged attacks by voters who find my position reprehensible
or worse. I have listened to their ideas. I have weighed their objections
carefully. I still support the death penalty. The reasons I maintained my position can be best understood by examining the arguments most frequently
heard in opposition.

1. *The death penalty is "barbaric."* Sometimes opponents of capital   *5*
punishment horrify with tales of lingering death on the gallows, of faulty
electric chairs, or of agony in the gas chamber. Partly in response to such
protests, several states such as North Carolina and Texas switched to execution by lethal injection. The condemned person is put to death pain-
lessly, without ropes, voltage, bullets, or gas. Did this answer the objections
of death penalty opponents? Of course not. On June 22, 1984, *The New
York Times* published an editorial that sarcastically attacked the new
"hygienic" method of death by injection, and stated that "execution can
never be made humane through science." So it's not the method that
really troubles opponents. It's the death itself they consider barbaric.

Admittedly capital punishment is not a pleasant topic. However, one   *6*
does not have to like the death penalty in order to support it any more than
one must like radical surgery, radiation, or chemotherapy in order to find
necessary these attempts at curing cancer. Ultimately we may learn how to
cure cancer with a simple pill. Unfortunately, that day has not yet arrived.
Today we are faced with the choice of letting the cancer spread or trying
to cure it with the methods available, methods that one day will almost
certainly be considered barbaric and would certainly delay the discovery of
an eventual cure. The analogy between cancer and murder is imperfect,
because murder is not the "disease" we are trying to cure. The disease is
injustice. We may not like the death penalty, but it must be available to

---

...*continued* Death and Justice, **Edward I. Koch**

punish crimes of cold-blooded murder, cases in which any other form of punishment would be inadequate and, therefore, unjust. If we create a society in which injustice is not tolerated, incidents of murder—the most flagrant form of injustice—will diminish.

2. *No other major democracy uses the death penalty.* No other major democracy—in fact, few other countries of any description—are plagued by a murder rate such as that in the United States. Fewer and fewer Americans can remember the days when unlocked doors were the norm and murder was a rare and terrible offense. In America the murder rate climbed 122 percent between 1963 and 1980. During that same period, the murder rate in New York City increased by almost 400 percent, and the statistics are even worse in many other cities. A study at M.I.T. showed that based on 1970 homicide rates a person who lived in a large American city ran a greater risk of being murdered than an American soldier in World War II ran of being killed in combat. It is not surprising that the laws of each country differ according to differing conditions and traditions. If other countries had our murder problem, the cry for capital punishment would be just as loud as it is here. And I daresay that any other major democracy where 75 percent of the people supported the death penalty would soon enact it into law.

3. *An innocent person might be executed by mistake.* Consider the work of Adam Bedau, one of the most implacable foes of capital punishment in this country. According to Mr. Bedau, it is "false sentimentality to argue that the death penalty should be abolished because of the abstract possibility that an innocent person might be executed." He cites a study of the 7,000 executions in this country from 1893 to 1971, and concludes that the record fails to show that such cases occur. The main point, however, is this. If government functioned only when the possibility of error didn't exist, government wouldn't function at all. Human life deserves special protection, and one of the best ways to guarantee that protection is to assure that convicted murderers do not kill again. Only the death penalty can accomplish this end. In a recent case in New Jersey, a man named Richard Biegenwald was freed from prison after serving 18 years for murder; since his release he has been convicted of committing four murders. A prisoner named Lemuel Smith, who, while serving four life sentences for murder (plus two life sentences for kidnapping and robbery) in New York's Green Haven Prison, lured a woman corrections officer into the chaplain's office and strangled her. He then mutilated and dismembered her body. An

additional life sentence for Smith is meaningless. Because New York has no death penalty statute, Smith has effectively been given a license to kill.

But the problem of multiple murder is not confined to the nation's penitentiaries. In 1981, 91 police officers were killed in the line of duty in this country. Seven percent of those arrested in the cases that have been solved had a previous arrest for murder. In New York City in 1976 and 1977, 85 persons arrested for homicide had a previous arrest for murder. Six of these individuals had two previous arrests for murder, and one had four previous murder arrests. During those two years the New York police were arresting for murder persons with a previous arrest for murder on the average of one every 8.5 days. This is not surprising when we learn that in 1975, for example, the median time served in Massachusetts for homicide was less than two-and-a-half years. In 1976 a study sponsored by the Twentieth Century Fund found that the average time served in the United States for first-degree murder is ten years. The median time served may be considerably lower.

4. *Capital punishment cheapens the value of human life.* On the contrary, it can be easily demonstrated that the death penalty strengthens the value of human life. If the penalty for rape were lowered, clearly it would signal a lessened regard for the victims' suffering, humiliation, and personal integrity. It would cheapen their horrible experience, and expose them to an increased danger of recurrence. When we lower the penalty for murder, it signals a lessened regard for the value of the victim's life. Some critics of capital punishment, such as columnist Jimmy Breslin, have suggested that a life sentence is actually a harsher penalty for murder than death. This is sophistic nonsense. A few killers may decide not to appeal a death sentence, but the overwhelming majority make every effort to stay alive. It is by exacting the highest penalty for the taking of human life that we affirm the highest value of human life.

5. *The death penalty is applied in a discriminatory manner.* This factor no longer seems to be the problem it once was. The appeals process for a condemned prisoner is lengthy and painstaking. Every effort is made to see that the verdict and sentence were fairly arrived at. However, assertions of discrimination are not an argument for ending the death penalty but for extending it. It is not justice to exclude everyone from the penalty of the law if a few are found to be so favored. Justice requires that the law be applied equally to all.

6. *Thou shalt not kill.* The Bible is our greatest source of moral inspiration. Opponents of the death penalty frequently cite the sixth of the Ten

---

...*continued* Death and Justice, **Edward I. Koch**

Commandments in an attempt to prove that capital punishment is divinely proscribed. In the original Hebrew, however, the Sixth Commandment reads, "Thou Shalt Not Commit Murder," and the Torah specifies capital punishment for a variety of offenses. The biblical viewpoint has been upheld by philosophers throughout history. The greatest thinkers of the 19th century—Kant, Locke, Hobbes, Rousseau, Montesquieu, and Mill—agreed that natural law properly authorizes the sovereign to take life in order to vindicate justice. Only Jeremy Bentham was ambivalent. Washington, Jefferson, and Franklin endorsed it. Abraham Lincoln authorized executions for deserters in wartime. Alexis de Tocqueville, who expressed profound respect for American institutions, believed that the death penalty was indispensable to the support of social order. The United States Constitution, widely admired as one of the seminal achievements in the history of humanity, condemns cruel and inhuman punishment, but does not condemn capital punishment.

7. *The death penalty is state-sanctioned murder.* This is the defense with which Messrs. Willie and Shaw hoped to soften the resolve of those who sentenced them to death. By saying in effect, "You're no better than I am," the murderer seeks to bring his accusers down to his own level. It is also a popular argument among opponents of capital punishment, but a transparently false one. Simply put, the state has rights that the private individual does not. In a democracy, those rights are given to the state by the electorate. The execution of a lawfully condemned killer is no more an act of murder than is legal imprisonment an act of kidnapping. If an individual forces a neighbor to pay him money under threat of punishment, it's called extortion. If the state does it, it's called taxation. Rights and responsibilities surrendered by the individual are what give the state its power to govern. This contract is the foundation of civilization itself.   13

Everyone wants his or her rights, and will defend them jealously. Not everyone, however, wants responsibilities, especially the painful responsibilities that come with law enforcement. Twenty-one years ago a woman named Kitty Genovese was assaulted and murdered on a street in New York. Dozens of neighbors heard her cries for help but did nothing to assist her. They didn't even call the police. In such a climate the criminal understandably grows bolder. In the presence of moral cowardice, he lectures us on our supposed failings and tries to equate his crimes with our quest for justice.   14

The death of anyone—even a convicted killer—diminishes us all. But we are diminished even more by a justice system that fails to function. It is   15 an illusion to let ourselves believe that doing away with capital punishment removes the murderer's deed from our conscience. The rights of society are paramount. When we protect guilty lives, we give up innocent lives in exchange. When opponents of capital punishment say to the state: "I will not let you kill in my name," they are also saying to murderers: "You can kill in your *own* name as long as I have an excuse for not getting involved."

It is hard to imagine anything worse than being murdered while neigh-   16
bors do nothing. But something worse exists. When those same neighbors shrink back from justly punishing the murderer, the victim dies twice.

■ ■ ■

vo·cab·u·lar·y

In your journal, write the meaning of the italicized words in the following phrases.

- I have represented *constituencies* **(4)**
- find my position *reprehensible* **(4)**
- the most *flagrant* form of injustice **(6)**
- the most *implacable* foes **(8)**
- this is *sophistic* nonsense **(10)**
- capital punishment is divinely *proscribed* **(12)**
- one of the *seminal* achievements **(12)**

QUESTIONS FOR WRITING AND DISCUSSION

1. What exactly is Koch's thesis or overall claim? Find one or two sentences from Koch's essay that clearly express his thesis. In paragraph 13, Koch says that "the state has rights that the private individual does not." Why is this statement important for Koch's thesis? Explain.

2. What are Koch's purposes in this essay? Is he making a claim of fact, value, cause and effect, or policy? Does he aim to convince us of a belief or persuade us to take some action? Cite specific passages from the essay to support your answer.

3. Koch's essay follows a classical argumentative organization. Review the six-part classical structure in the "Shaping" section of this chapter. Does Koch's essay follow the sequence outlined there (Introduction, Narration, Partition, Argument, Refutation, and Conclusion)? How does he revise or adapt this structure?

4. For supporting evidence, Koch uses statistics, specific examples of criminals, and analogies. In the essay, find examples of each of these kinds of support.

Evaluate his evidence. Are his specific examples appropriate and persuasive? Are his statistics timely and relevant? Are his comparisons or analogies effective? If you were giving Koch advice about revising and improving the evidence in his essay, what changes would you suggest?

5. Consider the arguing essay that you are currently writing. Keeping your own particular purpose and audience in mind, should you use Koch's classical organization? How do you intend to respond to opposing or alternative viewpoints? Should you use all three kinds of appeals (to reason, to character, and to emotion), as Koch does? What personal experiences, specific examples, statistics, and quotations from authorities could you use? Which of Koch's strategies can you use, and which do you need to revise?

TECHNIQUES   CASEBOOK   PROCESS

Multigenre Casebook on Immigration Reform

Dudley Erskine Devlin, **"Immigration Reform in America"** [Essay]

Barry Newman, **"Employers Have a Lot to Lose"** [Newspaper article]

Ruben Navarrette, Jr., **"Do Americans *Really* Want Jobs?"** [Editorial]

Khalil Bendib, **"The Problem with Immigrants"** [Cartoon]

Bruce Finley, **"Raid Leaves Families Fractured"** [Newspaper article]

Responses to **"Raid Leaves Families Fractured"** [Online comments]

BBC News, **"Viewpoints: U.S. Illegal Immigration"** [Web site posting]

Tom Briscoe, **"Who to Blame for Illegals"** [Cartoon]

SpeakOut.com, **"Immigration Forum"** [Online comments]

"IllegalAliens.US" [Webpage]

"United Food and Commercial Workers (UFCW)" [Webpage]

Photographs of demonstrations

The multiple-genre texts in this casebook represent a snapshot of the ongoing conversation and debate about reforming immigration laws in the United States. These arguments represent many of the multiple perspectives from people who influence and are influenced by current laws and cultural practices. They appear in a variety of contexts and genres, from formal arguments to editorials, letters to the editor, blogs, Web sites, news reports, and even photographs and other visuals. Sometimes these arguments have all the formal features of academic arguments, with strong appeals to reason and logic, an appeal to character through careful research, fair representations of alternative positions, and use of noninflammatory language. At other times, arguments on Web sites and blogs may contain highly emotional and biased language, a refusal to consider alternate or opposing positions, and obvious emotional and even racist appeals. The documents that follow illustrate a wide range of opinions, argument strategies, rhetorical appeals to the audience, and use of language, but taken together they represent many of the voices in the conversation and debate about immigration reform in the United States.

As you read these documents, consider how each writer uses—or does not use—the *argumentative strategies* discussed in this chapter. Careful appeals to reason and character may be followed by emotional appeals, fallacies in logic, inflammatory and biased language, or partial truths. Consider also how these writers construct their *audience:* Who do they think their reader is? What do they believe that their readers already know or believe? What strategies do they think will convince or persuade their readers?

Finally, after you have read all the documents, reread them and think about how the *genre* of the document—article, essay, editorial, news report, Web site, blog, letter, cartoon, or photograph—helps to shape the writer's argumentative strategies. What strategies are accepted, appropriate, and expected in a blog that are not appropriate in a news report? How do letters to the editor typically differ from essays or editorials? Can a news article cross genre boundaries and really be an editorial in disguise? What impact do photographs or visuals have on this ongoing conversation?

If your own assignment is to produce a multigenre document that makes an argument for a specific audience or if you simply want to integrate visuals and sidebars in your document, use the examples in this multigenre casebook to help you brainstorm ways to make your own argument more creative and effective for your selected audience.

PROFESSIONAL WRITING

Immigration Reform in America

Dudley Erskine Devlin

"Give me your tired, your poor, /Your huddled masses yearning to breathe free, The wretched refuse of your teeming shore, /Send these, the homeless, tempest-tost to me, I lift my lamp beside the golden door!"

—*Emma Lazarus, inscribed at the base of The Statue of Liberty*

...*continued* Immigration Reform in America, **Dudley Erskine Devlin**

America is a nation of immigrants. Native Americans were here first. Then 1
came waves of English, French, Irish, Germans, Italians, and Asians. And
most recently, millions of Latin Americans. America has thrived on immigrants for centuries, so what is the difference now? The problem is the
overwhelming numbers of Latin American immigrants, entering the
country illegally and taking mainly low-paying jobs.

The solution to the problem may lie in an immigration law recently 2
considered by the U.S. Congress. This bill would legalize the 10–12 million illegal immigrants currently in the United States but at the same time
increase border security. The legalization process would not be an
"amnesty" but a set of requirements allowing current workers to earn permanent legal status. First, they would need to pay a $2,000 fine. Next, they
would need to learn English. Third, after completing a background check,
they would wait for several years before applying for a green card and then
for U.S. citizenship. These requirements aim to appeal to conservative citizens who do not want to reward law breaking, to liberals and church
groups who argue that no human being should be "illegal" in America, and
to businesses who still want a plentiful supply of cheap labor.

The participants in this national debate include virtually every citi- 3
zen and every group in America. The government wants tighter security
to keep out terrorists. Schools and welfare agencies need money to fund
the extra load on their programs created by undocumented workers and
their children. Businesses want cheap labor. Most Americans want affordable housing, inexpensive food, and cheap labor for house cleaners,
cooks, and nannies. Immigrants themselves just want a chance at a better job; they don't want to be called criminals just because they work to
earn a living.

Finding reliable data to support specific immigration reforms is it- 4
self a difficult task. Most of the figures about numbers of illegal workers,
dollars spent for schools and public services, and the worker's overall effect on the economy are either unavailable or contested. Exactly how
many illegal immigrant workers are there in the United States? In agricultural or construction industries, experts estimate that a third of the
workers are illegal immigrants. Do these workers take jobs away from
American citizens? Andrew Sum, Director of the Center for Labor Market Studies at Northeastern University believes that this influx of undocumented workers has in fact taken jobs from some citizens, particularly
high school dropouts.

Many people think that illegal immigrants are a drain on public education and public services but the actual costs cannot be accurately determined. When Colorado passed a law requiring legal identification before workers could receive public services, the state's public service agencies themselves could not provide records suggesting the true costs of services for illegal workers. Economists at Rand have found wide variances in analyses of costs to taxpayers of providing services to immigrants, from a surplus of $1400 per immigrant to a deficit of $1600.

Finally, illegal workers keep the economy going both through their cheap labor and through the taxes they pay. A recent University of North Carolina study found that Hispanic residents, 45% of whom were undocumented, contributed $9.2 billion in spending to North Carolina's economy in 2004. In addition, illegal immigrants paid an estimated $463 billion into Social Security but did not take funds out. No matter what bill the U.S. Congress eventually passes, however, the benefits and drawbacks to undocumented workers will continue to be debated.

A recent sampling of letters to the editor in response to an article in a national magazine illustrates the range of voices and opinions. Any law considered by Congress needs to respond to these voices.

Letters to the Editor

The key problem is making felons out of everyone who is here without documents. What people miss is that includes 1.6 million children. If this House bill passed, I would be a criminal. I would be one of the first people arrested. This is no longer just an immigration issue. It is a civil rights movement now. People forget that less than 170 years ago, the whole West was part of Mexico. Who do you think named Los Angeles, San Francisco and San Antonio? It wasn't the people who came through Ellis Island. It was us. We didn't cross any borders. The borders crossed us.

—Baldemar Velasquez, President Farm
Labor Organizing Committee, AFL-CIO

As an immigrant myself, I am of two minds about the present situation. My husband, my daughter—then 4 years old—and I came to this country 53 years ago. Not only did we have to wait patiently for years before finally receiving our immigration visas, but we also needed to provide affidavits from relatives and friends stating that they would guarantee that we would never become a financial

...*continued* Immigration Reform in America, **Dudley Erskine Devlin**

burden on the United States. We also had to learn English. We did, and we have been supporting ourselves and paying taxes ever since. Why, at a minimum, have we never insisted on any of this for those who come here illegally? We need to deal with immigration in a fair but legal way.

—*Steffi B. Rath, Woburn, Massachusetts*

As a legal immigrant, I am astounded at the naiveté of the native born. No country south of the border would ever be as absurdly generous as the United States is toward those who break its immigration laws. And I would rather pay $10 for a head of lettuce than have my quality of life as severely affected as it already is here in Los Angeles, where we sometimes have 40 kids to a classroom, choke on our clogged freeways, and have our health-care systems completely overwhelmed. 10

—*Marcia Del Mar, Calabasas, California*

The fault lies with employers that hire, transport and house illegal immigrants. Penalize the employers if you must, not the workers who need the jobs so desperately. If you penalize the workers, you penalize agriculture in California and many other states that depend upon Mexican labor to harvest what we buy in the supermarkets. Let's not ignore the needs of so many different spheres in our vast country by keeping out the very folks who have helped to build it. 11

—*Ellen Wildfeuer, Carmichael, California*

One myth that needs to be laid to rest is that undocumented workers do jobs that Americans don't want to do. That's complete bunk. The issue revolves around money. If you are a building contractor, farm owner, or restaurant manager with an eye on your bottom line, you can hire an illegal immigrant for a fraction of what you'd have to pay an American citizen, and with no worries about lawsuits for injuries or complaints about job conditions or low pay. Large corporations do it by outsourcing jobs overseas. Its capitalism, pure and simple: the lowest bidder gets the work. 12

—*David Zartman, Seattle, Washington*

PROFESSIONAL WRITING

Employers Have a Lot to Lose

Barry Newman

The Wall Street Journal

Balding and weathered, wearing a work shirt, Dave Penry stands in a park while men in windbreakers rake grass behind him in a television commercial that casts him as the unlikely—and lonely—front man for employers who rely on immigrant laborers. 1

"My partner and I own a landscaping company in California that employs 60 people, and two-thirds of them are immigrants," Mr. Penry tells the camera in a 30-second spot now running nationally. "They have as much pride in America as you or me. We need to fix our laws so they can work in this country legally and get the respect and dignity they've earned." 2

The camera closes in on Hispanic-looking men pruning trees. As music rises, a caption appears: "Building the American Dream." 3

Immigrants are protesting from Los Angeles to New York, lawmakers are haggling over new bills and President Bush talks of bringing millions of workers out of the "shadows." The voice largely missing from the tense debate so far has been the bosses who hire illegal immigrants, leaving their lobbyists to speak for them. 4

"We don't press our members to come out and talk," says John Gay, who co-chairs the Essential Worker Immigration Coalition. Its 45 members range from the Society of American Florists to the Outdoor Amusement Business Association. "We make the case," he says, "rather than having individuals stick their necks out." 5

Mr. Penry was speaking out for a bill that, in sterner form than he would prefer, got bottled up in the Senate last week. If it sees the light again after Congress returns from its Easter recess—and then overcomes powerful opposition in the House—at least a portion of the country's undocumented population of more than 11 million could gain legal status and eventual citizenship. 6

But any new regime would also jack up workplace enforcement and impose severe punishment—including jail time—on employers who give jobs to people who don't have the proper documents. It is a sign of the issue's history of dangers and delicacies for business that, when asked the direct question—Do you, in fact, employ illegal immigrants?—even Mr. Penry stops short. He says, "I don't know." 7

...continued Employers Have a Lot to Lose, **Barry Newman**

Unauthorized immigrants may live 8 in the shadows, but they don't all work in them. The Migration Policy Institute, an independent think tank in Washington, reports that at least half the seven million thought to be illegally employed have aboveground bosses who check credentials and fill out forms, deduct taxes and pay Social Security.

Of the hotel industry's 1.5 million 9 employees, 150,000 aren't supposed to be here, according to statistics gathered by the Pew Hispanic Center. In food manufacturing, also with 1.5 million,

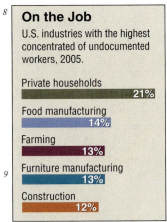

On the Job

U.S. industries with the highest concentrated of undocumented workers, 2005.

Private households — 21%
Food manufacturing — 14%
Farming — 13%
Furniture manufacturing — 13%
Construction — 12%

Source: Pew Hispanic Center

210,000 have no right to work. Landscaping, Mr. Penry's line, has 1.2 million workers, 300,000 of them illegally in the country.

"Most of the undocumented workers in America are working for 10 good, reputable, law-abiding employers," he says.

In 1986, Congress compromised on an immigration bill that gave 11 legal residence to three million foreign workers while giving the federal government greater powers to police work sites. Since then, employers have been asked to inspect an assortment of documents from job applicants as proof of work authorization, but, apart from blatant forgeries, they aren't expected to be judges of authenticity.

Even in such businesses as roofing, where one in three workers is 12 thought to be undocumented, "don't know" is the standard answer employers give when asked if any illegals are on their payrolls.

"I wouldn't be telling the truth if I tried to say that I'm 100% sure that 13 everybody we have is documented," says Rick Birkman, a commercial-roofing contractor in Austin, Texas. "Is there plausible deniability in what we do? Sure, there is."

Employers say it is possible to ask too many questions, leading job 14 seekers with the proper documents to feel as if they are being unfairly targeted because of their ethnicity. They say the rules were written that way to mollify civil-rights groups.

But others say the law gave bosses an intentional out. Adopted during 15 the antiregulation Reagan years, it was nevertheless the biggest leap in work-site monitoring since the Occupational Health and Safety Administration was created 15 years earlier.

The rules were further eased in recent years. Inspectors now need 16 written permission from supervisors before entering a work site. Employers get credit for "good faith attempts" to live up to the law. Since 1996, when the focus of enforcement began to move away from work sites to the borders, the number of fines collected have dropped to nearly zero from a high of about 8,000.

What crystallized the business lobby's support for immigration 17 reform today wasn't fear of enforcement; it was fear of losing workers. Its argument is for a new system that maintains the work force and also allows an employee's status to be authenticated instantly, with something like a swipe card at a grocery store.

The outpouring of illegal workers that continued yesterday didn't 18 bring many bosses onto the streets. But Dave Penry is thinking about it.

Ten years ago, when the landscaper had 250 employees, a raid cost him 19 more than 50 of them. "A couple of those men named their kids after me," he says. Now, he feels the atmosphere of protest "is strangely familiar to the '60s and '70s, when it was all about Vietnam."

"Sure employers are running scared," says Mr. Penry. "But a lot of 20 Hispanics have helped my company become successful. It was time for an employer to stand up." That is why he went on television. And why, on May 5—the Cinco de Mayo holiday—he has given his workers a day off for a protest "to show America how important they are."

"I'm willing to go march with these guys," he says. "These men are my 21 family. We owe them something. We owe them the good fight."

■ ■ ■

PROFESSIONAL WRITING

Do Americans *Really* Want Jobs?

Ruben Navarrette, Jr.

San Diego Union-Tribune

It's the big lie of the immigration debate: namely, that Americans would 1 eagerly and gladly do the jobs being done by illegal immigrants if only wages were higher.

It started out as a rebuttal to President Bush's insistence that illegal   *2*
immigrants "do jobs that Americans won't do." Anti-illegal immigrant cru-
saders responded that these are actually "jobs that Americans won't do . . .
for the wages offered." There are actually people out there who like to believe that there's some magical hourly or daily wage that an employer could
offer at which a slew of Americans would leave their desk jobs and line up
for a chance to do some of the hardest, dirtiest and crummiest jobs our
society has to offer. In many cases there is no such wage.

Still, *someone* has to do these types of jobs. And when employers try to   *3*
fill them with illegal immigrants, they get crossways with native-born
workers who are suddenly eager to do the very jobs that they and their families have shunned for a generation.

A recently filed class-action lawsuit against Tyson Foods Inc. insists   *4*
that the world's largest meat-processing company has kept wages low by
hiring illegal immigrants. The suit by former and current employees alleges
that the company violated federal racketeering laws, and that wages have
dropped between 10 percent and 30 percent since the company began hiring large numbers of illegal immigrants. If the claim is successful, the alleged damages could exceed $150 million.

Tyson has been in the headlines before. In 2003, the company was   *5*
acquitted in federal court of charges that it conspired to run an employee-
recruitment initiative that resembled a smuggling operation.

The government alleged that Tyson managers hired intermediaries to   *6*
transport hundreds of illegal immigrants across the U.S.-Mexico border
and place them in more than a dozen Tyson plants.

Meanwhile, two months ago, federal immigration agents raided a   *7*
number of Swift & Co. meatpacking plants (including one nearby in Greeley) and arrested hundreds of illegal immigrants, some of whom were
charged with identity theft.

We're told that employers hire illegal immigrants because they're will-   *8*
ing to work for less than American workers. But it's more complicated. The
issue is also how immigrants, illegal or not, approach the very institution
of work. While many native-born Americans have come to consider labor
a nuisance—especially if it is low-skilled, physical labor—immigrants have
tended to see work as an opportunity to get ahead in America and fulfill
the promise that brought them here.

Think about your own immigrant parents or grandparents, and what   *9*
they were willing to do for a dollar. Then think about what you would do.

Of course, employers shouldn't knowingly hire illegal immigrants, and   *10*
those who do so should be punished. But, as I've come to realize over the
years, the fact that employers are hiring illegal immigrants doesn't necessarily amount to exploitation. And, from what I gather, many employers
resent the accusation.

I've heard from employers who say that, when they try to hire Amer-   *11*
icans, all they get are headaches and demands and complaints and demands and attitude and more demands. Once on the job, the employers
say, many of these employees don't want to work; in fact, they spend their
energy trying to find creative ways *not* to work and still get paid. Some quit
after only a few weeks on the job—but not before making the employer feel
as if they're doing him a favor instead of the other way around. In some
cases, even the low-skilled are demanding high salaries because they value
their time as much as the high-skilled workers do.

This might include the workers at a construction firm in Denver that   *12*
was recently the subject of a report by Tom Brokaw of NBC. In the segment, the owner of the firm complained that some of the American workers he hired for as much as $15 an hour would quit after only a few weeks
on the job. What was the problem there? Certainly not the wages.

One employer told me that, when she hired the native-born, she got   *13*
a barrage of questions: "How much does this job pay? What are the benefits? How much vacation time do I get?" But when she hired immigrants,
some of whom may have been illegal, she got only one question: "How
much work can you give me?" Now, which one would you rather have
working for you? I still don't condone the hiring of illegal immigrants, but
I'm beginning to understand it.

■ ■ ■

PROFESSIONAL WRITING

The Problem with Immigrants

Khalil Bendib

—Khalil Bendib, *The Sun*

■ ■ ■

PROFESSIONAL WRITING

Raid Leaves Families Fractured

"Unblinking reality" dizzying for spouses, kids of detainees

Bruce Finley

Denver Post Staff Writer

Greeley—Isabel Ramirez wept as she clutched her 18-month-old daughter, Brenda, in the ramshackle trailer park where she lives.

Her husband, Juan, had been detained in the Immigration and Customs Enforcement raid on the Swift & Co. meatpacking plant where he worked, and she didn't know where he was.

Isabel Ramirez stands outside her Greeley home Wednesday with daughter Brenda and son Juanito. Her husband was detained in Tuesday's raid at Swift. (Post/Karl Gehring)

"He was the only one working. He paid for everything, the bills, rent. I have three kids," 33-year-old Isabel Ramirez said.   *3*

As she spoke, her 7-year-old daughter, Laura, was at school, and her 3-year-old son, Juanito, kicking muddy snow by the trailer, was having a very bad day.   *4*

His father "is in jail," Juanito said. He threw a stick angrily down at the snow and turned and banged his head against the side of a broken trampoline.   *5*

As authorities began deporting workers rounded up in raids at meat-packing plants here and in five other states, this city, which for decades has run on illegal labor from Mexico, confronted an unexpected challenge: what to do about kids left behind.   *6*

The raids left more than 100 children with no parents present, church officials and community organizers said. Hundreds more struggled in newly broken families, asking questions such as "Where is my daddy?" and "Why does immigration exist?"   *7*

A niece and cousin whose deported husbands had phoned from Mexico tried to console Juanito Ramirez and his mother. One drove to a regional immigration jail east of Denver and begged for information, to no avail.   *8*

Isabel Ramirez acknowledged that her son and 18-month-old daughter are the only ones in her immediate family legally entitled to be in the U.S.   *9*

This was the hard side of the sudden pressure ICE agents brought to 10 bear on Swift here and in Texas, Utah, Minnesota, Nebraska and Iowa.

The agents who conducted simultaneous raids Tuesday tried their best 11 when interviewing detainees to determine whether they had children, said ICE spokesman Carl Rusnok. "We do everything in our power to avoid having children left home alone or at school," he said.

Still, "violating federal law can lead to tragic consequences, sometimes 12 affecting a great many people. That's the unblinking reality," U.S. Attorney Troy Eid said in Denver.

Meanwhile, few if any relatives of detained workers turned to govern- 13 ment social-services agencies for help—mistrusting any authorities.

Under new state and federal laws, "we can only provide assistance to 14 citizens—citizens only—and qualified aliens who have been here for five years," said John Kruse, assistant payments administrator for Weld County Social Services.

Instead, friends and relatives worked their cell phones busily trying to 15 bypass government, keeping children whose parents weren't present in hiding, fearing that social-services agents would snatch them away.

Naturalized U.S. citizen David Silva, an oil-field worker who used 16 to work at the meatpacking plant, said he was able to retrieve his wife, Marisela, from a federal immigration detention center in Denver late Tuesday by driving to the center and presenting her legal residency papers.

Now with wrists bruised from handcuffs, Marisela was taking the day 17 off "trying to build up her confidence." She joined others from Mexico volunteering to take care of children whose parents were gone.

Inside the meatpacking plant, "there was a lady crying because she 18 didn't have anybody else here," Silva said. "She asked my wife if she wanted to adopt her child. Then she was taken away."

Anglo citizens came forward offering to do the same around noon at 19 Our Lady of Peace Catholic Church. "We are all affected deeply. But our most immediate concerns are for families that are suddenly separated and for children who have no understanding of what is happening in their lives," the Rev. Bernie Schmitz said.

Temporarily adopting children of detained or deported workers "is 20 why we came here," said Kris Kessinger, 45, a city traffic worker whose wife is from Mexico.

Weld County school officials who saw attendance drop to 75 percent *21* during Tuesday's raids, when Greeley residents flocked to the meatpacking factory, said classrooms were about 90 percent full Wednesday. But they had no way of knowing which children might be without their parents. "We've asked ICE to provide a list (of people arrested)," principal Paul Urioste said at Billie Martinez Elementary School. "ICE hasn't provided us with anything."

Separately, the United Way of Weld County set up a fund for affected *22* families. The agency is accepting donations at P.O. Box 1944, Greeley, CO 80632, or donors can call 970-353-4300.

For Isabel Ramirez at her trailer, crying regularly gave her relief as she, *23* with borrowed cell phone in hand, waited for word from her husband. Heading back to the family farm in central Mexico looked likely, she said.

She tried to persuade her troubled little boy to cry instead of banging *24* his head.

"It's OK to cry," she told him.   *25*

"No. I'm embarrassed," the 3-year-old said.   *26*

"If you feel sad, you should cry."   *27*

"It hurts my heart," Juanito said, delicately pointing to his chest.   *28*

■ ■ ■

PROFESSIONAL WRITING

Responses to "Raid Leaves Families Fractured"

Denverpost.com

Posted By: Gerry

Comment: I have no sympathy for these families that have repeatedly thumbed their nose at our laws. This family had a farm in Mexico and obviously has a place to return to. Any reasonable parent would not be conflicted about taking their children with them back to their home-land where they would have been bom anyway had they not broken our laws, shown up at our hospitals for free medical care and subsidies and basically stole the American dream from others waiting in line. Shame on these sinful people. This is why the idea of "comprehensive reform" is a joke. What kind of guest worker is this woman who is unemployed, living in a trailer and having babies she can not afford to feed. Send back the parasites. Stealing, cheating and lying to stay in someone else's country is WRONG. And tell that to the Catholic Church . . . who needs to take another look at the Ten Commandments.

Posted By: Chris

Comment: WHO hired these workers? WHO accepted the documentation for employment? WHO set the hiring policies? I have not read of arrests of management. The children are innocent victims of Swift's management!

Posted By: Emily

Comment: I am sad to hear such a complete lack of humanity coming from the readers—you are supposed to feel for the individuals and families affected by the raids because you are a human and others are hurting right now. Do your research, understand how migration works, understand the history of immigration, know about the role of our government in immigration past and present—don't resort to an inflamed political position when you don't understand the complexity. I don't care what your "position" is on immigration reform—we are all humans and can imagine the pain that many individuals are going through right now—having sympathy does not mean that you condone illegal acts but that you are a human. I hope that the families affected gain strength from their communities, churches, and know that people do care. And that our larger community can see the injustice in punishing individuals but leaving the corporation be.

Posted By: Burke

Comment: Whether you think the immigrants are wrong or right, the failure to plan for this eventuality (kids left parentless) is the fault of the ICE administration. Like FEMA in New Orleans, ICE failed to think past their immediate objective to subsequent possibilities.

PROFESSIONAL WRITING

Viewpoints: US Illegal Immigration

BBC News

President George W Bush plans to deploy up to 6,000 reserve soldiers of the US National Guard on the border with Mexico, as part of his plan to counter the flow of illegal migrants entering the United States.

Mexicans peer through a fence on the border in Tijuana, Mexico

The president has also spoken *1* of creating a legalised system that would allow foreigners to work temporarily in the US.

Many people, however, including a good part of the president's *2* Republican party, believe Mr Bush should be taking a harder line and criminalizing illegal immigrants.

Four people with a stake in the debate give their views. *3*

Click on the following links to read what they have to say.

"Illegal immigration has a negative effect on the country's economic security."

—Tom Tancredo, US House group for immigration reform

"The immigrant worker creates a value far and above what a native worker creates."

—Nativo Lopez, national president of Mexican–American Political Association

"We would see significant reduction in numbers if we enforce the laws."
—Marrian S Davies, You Don't Speak For Me Coalition

"There is so much hypocrisy—many businesses thrive on the back of undocumented workers."

—Felipe Aguirre, dep mayor of "sanctuary" town Maywood

... *continued* Viewpoints: US Illegal Immigration, **BBC News**

Congressman Tom Tancredo has campaigned throughout the US in support of tighter border controls and immigration reduction.

Americans are rightly outraged by our broken immigration system: there are roughly 12 to 15 million illegal aliens in the US, and hundreds of thousands sneak across our borders each year.

Mexican citizens waiting to cross the border illegally

Our porous borders pose a major national security threat because not all of the illegal aliens are coming to "do the job that no American will do," as President Bush often says. For example, in 2004, the US Border Patrol apprehended Iranians, Syrians, and Iraqis who tried to cross our southern border illegally.

Why are Iranians, Syrians or Iraqis trying to get into the US, traveling a great distance and at a great cost? Certainly, it's not to work at minimum wage jobs.

Illegal immigration also has a negative effect on the US's economic security. It doesn't take a degree in economics to realize that a massive flow of low-skilled labour puts downward pressure on the wages of native-born Americans.

These low-wage workers—who are largely paid off the books and without benefits—meanwhile cost the American taxpayer in terms of social services. Illegal aliens rarely pay taxes, yet they send their children to our schools free of charge, they receive welfare benefits, and they get free medical treatment.

The best solution to our illegal immigration problem is to begin enforcing our laws. That means the federal government needs to get serious about prosecuting employers who lure illegal aliens into the US with jobs. The threat of hefty fines and possible jail time will chasten employers' desire to hire cheap, illegal workers.

We also need to recommit to guarding our borders with more personnel, more technology and more money for physical infrastructure. And, we need to enable local police departments to aid the federal government in finding and deporting illegal aliens.

Over time, as it becomes more difficult to come here illegally, fewer *8* will try. And, as it becomes harder to stay illegally, more will leave over time. That's a workable solution to our broken borders.

Nativo Lopez is national president of Mexican-American Political Association, which campaigns for the Latino community

With a wink and a nod, the United States government essentially *1* allowed millions of people into the country to be employed in vital strategic industries.

These workers produce value and that value is appropriated by busi- *2* ness owners. The worker is never remunerated fairly for the value he creates and the immigrant worker creates a value far and above what a native worker creates because he works for a lower wage, does not have paid holidays, a pension plan or sick pay.

They make an incredible economic contribution to the economy. A *3* fair exchange would be a streamlined procedure allowing them to legalise their status.

The current legislation being debated by the Senate, the Hagel- *4* Martinez compromise, would not be satisfactory for the immigrant communities.

The three-tier legalisation procedure includes onerous conditions that *5* would preclude from citizenship the people it is supposed to help.

For example, anyone who has used fraudulent documents is disquali- *6* fied but in order to obtain employment, a driver's licence or emergency benefit, they would have had to have used false documentation.

Anyone who has been caught for illegal entry, was issued an order to *7* leave and has not done so would be disqualified. That is estimated to be 350,000 people.

There are a number of other provisions that eliminate the right for *8* judicial review and appeal for all immigrants. Instead of strengthening the rights of immigrants, Hagel-Martinez codifies the elimination of those rights.

And the president's militarisation proposal—to send National *9* Guard troops to the border and construct a border wall—essentially constitutes weakening of the rights for all Americans, not just for immigrants.

More appropriate legislation would be as close as possible to the *10* Immigration Reform and Control Act of 1986—a generally simple, streamlined, not cost-prohibitive procedure that successfully legalised 3.3 million individuals, most of whom have become citizens.

But considering the current composition of the Senate, I am not con- 11 fident that anything good will come from this Congress.

Mariann S Davies is with the You Don't Speak For Me Coalition, a group made up of US citizens of Hispanic heritage

My parents came to the United 1 States more than 45 years ago from Ecuador. My father served our military in Korea. They are proud, law-abiding citizens who taught us to respect the laws, customs and traditions of our country—America—with the expectation that all people do the same, no matter what their country of origin.

Passions have run high at the many recent marches on illegal immigration

I first noticed the magnitude of the illegal immigration crisis when I 2 worked as a college volunteer during the chaotic implementation of the Immigration and Control Act of 1986 which gave some 3.1 million people legal status. I witnessed chaotic and inconsistent paperwork for people with no documentation. It was a mess, and we now know that much of the information provided by illegal immigrants was fraudulent.

I was amazed that on September 12, 2001, our borders were not 3 secure, and here we are five years later with borders so porous that we now have the huge problem of 12–20 million illegal aliens in our country, many of whom came in since that dreadful day.

Our president and our lawmakers know that we would see a signifi- 4 cant reduction in numbers if we enforce the laws we have on the books, cut off the job magnet by punishing employers, and stop the social services and benefits for illegals and their families. Then and only then would we start to see people self-repatriating. Americans need to know the real cost of illegal immigration and tell our lawmakers that enough is enough.

Felipe Aguirre is deputy mayor of Maywood, California. The town, which is 97% Hispanic, is a self-declared sanctuary for 'undocumented' immigrants.

We believe that no human be- 1 ing can be described as illegal.

These are people who 2 work hard, pay taxes, buy houses and keep on the right side of the law for fear of being deported—they are part of the fabric of America.

Many have families and 3 have been contributing members of community for years. But the debate is now affecting

The town of Maywood has declared itself a "sanctuary" for illegal immigrants

family units. Many people who do not have the right documents have children who are US citizens. These families need to stay united.

That is why we have seen so many young people taking part in the 4 demonstrations, fighting for the rights of their parents.

These are people pay their taxes through the payroll system, but do not 5 qualify to receive any benefits at the end of the work week. And, while they pay sales taxes and property taxes, they do not qualify for any of the benefits that are associated with this, such as healthcare.

There is a tremendous amount of hypocrisy surrounding the debate. So 6 many businesses are doing well on the back of undocumented workers—from the oranges that are picked in Florida to the tomatoes harvested in Illinois.

Yet, their basic rights, such as the right to a safe workplace and fair 7 treatment, are not protected. Undocumented workers never file complaints for injuries sustained at work for fear of being sacked.

Rich families in Los Angeles employ undocumented nannies to look 8 after their children. They also employ undocumented housekeepers, cleaners and gardeners—many of whom have keys to their houses.

How can we be called criminals when we hold the keys to the houses 9 of some of the richest people in the state?

PROFESSIONAL WRITING

Who to Blame for Illegals

Tom Biscoe

PROFESSIONAL WRITING

Immigration Forum

SpeakOut.com

I, as a legal immigrant, spent years waiting patiently in queue, paying all the fees, filled out all of the forms, took English classes, traveled 800 miles to get interviewed at the US Consulate before coming to the states.

These illegals just walk across the border and want amnesty?

Giving amnesty to these illegals is a slap in the face to every legal immigrant.

I want to see congress grant green cards to skilled foreign workers and scholars. We should be stapling green cards to diplomas of foreign students who graduated from our universities. We need a more skilled work force for our economy, not a bunch of Mexicans with an 8th grade education.

I see rallies across U.S. call for illegal immigrant rights. I am sure that there are rallies for burglar rights, tax evader rights, and drunk driver rights to follow . . .

—*Naturalized Citizen*

Comment by Dave G

I believe that we need to work with the illegal immigrants that are already residing in our country to try to make them legal and have them make a contribution to our economy. By making them legal after they pass certain requirements such as paying back taxes and learning English, then we are making them a vital part of our country. Aren't we the country referred to as a melting pot? I think we need to work with the people who are here to better themselves as well as their families to make them legal and deport the people who are leeching off the country. We can do this by having the people who have been working for 5 years or longer and those who are not have them deported. If we tried to round them up and deport them all then we would just be adding to our already extremely large country deficit.

Comment by Moira Clarke

I'm not sure I favor an open boarder with Mexico, but you have to admit that there is a sort of poetic justice in the indigenous peoples of this continent expanding their presence. We don't refer to Mexicans and other Hispanics as "American Indians," but that's what they are (with just a smattering of Spanish among some of them). I'm part Cherokee myself.

Comment by Steve

I think the answer to immigration lies in a compromise between the two extremes we hear most often. I believe in tall walls with large gates. Let me emphasize this point more clearly.

Immigration is what made this country develop so quickly. The diversity this country enjoys as a result of massive immigration is the primary reason we have become the powerful country we are today. We should embrace this issue, and welcome our neighbors to the south. However, we should employ a far more efficient system to control this immigration without the bureaucratic, and often overly complex, system currently under scrutiny. Here is a proposition that should be considered.

Implement a system that will only be applied to North American Countries . . . Canada, and Mexico. Force companies to abide by the current system of immigration. However, require all companies to report to the government the number of illegal immigrants that are currently employed, and the government will agree to allow them to continue working in their current employment as long as they register with the government, allow fingerprinted identification cards, and document employment status monthly.

As long as employment remains constant, citizenship should be acceptable after a significant period of time. If our economy benefits from the labors of your back, your citizenship will be an option after a number of years. However, if you lose your employment, and cannot find subsequent employment elsewhere, you must return home. Biometric fingerprint devices are increasingly cost efficient methods of documenting a persons identification. Each employer found employing someone that is currently unregistered will face maximum punishment under the current law. However, all illegal aliens currently employed must be registered, contain a guest worker identification card/number, and have a biometric fingerprint on file subsequent to that number.

If aliens are convicted of multiple misdemeanors, or a single felony, they will immediately be deported following punishment. Re-entry will not be an option for repeat offenders or felons. However, deportation due to a lack of employment will result in the opportunity to return should we need them for jobs in our economy. This need should be advertised nationally, and in Mexico. This will reduce the number of people flooding into this country. It will also provide incentive for those already here to seek registration. Offices representing the U.S. Employment services should be in Mexico advertising needed employment. Open a big gate with a sign that says REGISTER HERE!!

Tell them it is O.K. to be here, but we need to know that you are, and that you are here to work. Give them requirements to strive for and meet in order to gain citizenship. Advertise jobs in Mexico that can only be filled with proper registration, and prosecute employers that don't require the same. I DON'T CARE IF EVERYONE CURRENTLY HERE STAYS, JUST MAKE THEM REGISTER AND PAY TAXES. REQUIRE EMPLOYERS TO PUT THEM IN THE SYSTEM.

WELCOME TO AMERICA . . . WORK HARD, LIVE LONG, AND BUY AN SUV.

■ ■ ■

PROFESSIONAL WRITING

IllegalAliens.US

This site, besides mocking the term undocumented, is an illegal immigration primer whose goal is to provide information on illegal immigration prevention, enforcement, and attrition.

IllegalAliens.US

AMNESTY means never having immigration enforcement!

Those 'undocumented' are actually 'highly documented' with fraudulent documents our government readily accepts.

If fences don't work then take down those around the White House.

The Statue of Liberty is a monument dedicated to freedom and liberty. She never meant that foreigners have the right to violate America's immigration laws. *Statue of Liberty*

Home★	Amnesties	Action	Articles	Attrition★
Aztlan	Blogs ★	Concepts	Contact Us	Crime
Disconnect★	Distortion	Economics★	Employment Verification★	Euphemisms
Facts/Myths	Illegal Alien ID Cards	Illegal Illegals Song	Forums ★	Impacts
Law	Merchandise★	Most Wanted	National Sites★	News ★
Non-discrimination	Numbers	Pictures★	Poem	Politics
Polls	Quiz	Quotes	Report Illegals★★	Rights
Sanctions	Search	Solutions	State Organizations★	Statue of Liberty
The Denver Post	Videos	Visas	Vote Fraud	Webmasters

■ ■ ■

PROFESSIONAL WRITING

United Food and Commercial Workers

PROFESSIONAL WRITING

Photographs of Demonstrations

Jean-Francois Brulotte, Barraclou.com
1 de Mayo dia de accion
Immigration rally, Chicago, IL May 1st, 2006

04/09/2007. Dallas, Texas. After marching through Dallas, an estimated half-million protesters with flags rally at Dallas City Hall to peacefully protest proposed changes in U.S. federal immigration laws that would make illegal aliens into felons.
PHOTO: Paul Chaplo

...continued Photographs of Demonstrations

A protester faces an immigrants rights rally in front of the city hall in Farmers Branch, Texas, Aug. 26, 2006.
L.M. OTERO/AP http://img.timeinc.net/time/daily/2006/0611/texas_immigration1117.jpg

In Denver, protestors rallied for the rights of immigrants.
http://www.thekibitzer.info/gallery/main.php?g2_itemId=202

Questions for Writing and Discussion

1. Dudley Devlin's essay explains the background information, but it also has a thesis and an argumentative claim. Where is the claim most evident? Most of the letters to the editor also construct short arguments. Choose two of them and explain the writers' claims, reasons, and supporting evidence. What kinds of appeals to emotion or character do they make?

2. The article by Barry Newman, which appeared in *The Wall Street Journal*, is primarily informational. By humanizing Dave Penry, however, the article encourages readers to view employers of illegal immigrants sympathetically. Where in the article is this emotional appeal most evident? Is this argument appropriate for *The Wall Street Journal* and for its readers? Explain.

3. In his editorial, Ruben Navarrette picks up the theme of employers and employees explored by Newman, but with a new twist. Where does Navarrette most explicitly state his thesis? In support of this thesis, does Navarrette's argument use appeals to reason, to character, to emotion, or to all three? Explain your response by referring to specific sentences from Navarrette's article.

4. Analyze the two cartoons by Khalil Bendib ("The Problem with Immigrants") and Tom Briscoe ("Who to Blame for Illegals"). What argument does each cartoon make? How do the visual elements and the writing support the argument in each cartoon? How does each cartoonist use satire or irony to help make his point?

5. Bruce Finley's article on the Immigration and Customs Enforcement (ICE) raids in Greeley, Colorado, reports the event and also constructs an argument. What is Finley's position, attitude, or argument? Where do you see him using highly emotional appeals to persuade his readers? (Should a newspaper article just report the key facts or may it also argue for a particular point of view?)

6. The online comments in response to the Denver *Post* article and the comments posted on the Speakout forum range from emotional rants and personal statements of opinion to carefully constructed arguments. Which of the responses are only emotional ranting? Which contain the clearest arguments backed up by convincing reasons and evidence?

7. In the short pieces cited by the BBC News article, which articles were most informative and persuasive? Do you think these excerpts would give British people an accurate picture of the conversation and debate here in the United States? Why or why not?

8. Using your computer, examine the Web sites for the UFCW and IllegalAliens.US. What is each site's position or argument? Does the site use mostly appeals to logic and reason, or to emotion and prejudice? Explain.

9. Analyze the photographs in the portfolio of pictures taken of the immigration rallies across the United States. Consider the composition of the photographs, the caption of the photograph, and the location as you analyze each photograph's argument. What argument does each picture make? How are the photographs similar or different? Which writers in the casebook might use one or more of these photographs to help make his or her point? Explain.

TECHNIQUES   CASEBOOK   **PROCESS**

Arguing: The Writing Process

ASSIGNMENT FOR ARGUING

For this assignment, choose a subject that interests you or relates to your own experience. You may even choose a subject that you have already written about for this class. Then examine the subject for a debatable claim of fact or definition, value, cause and effect, or policy that you could make about it. If the claim is arguable, you have a focus for your arguing paper. Analyze your probable audience to guide your argumentative strategy. (Avoid ready-made pro–con subjects such as abortion, drinking age, drugs, and euthanasia *unless* you have clear beliefs based on your own experience.)

Arguments can appear in a wide range of genres, depending on your purpose and audience. Letters to the editor, essays for a college class, postings to an Internet forum, scripts for a debate, and political documents use the strategies of argument. As you select your topic, consider what audience and genre would most effectively meet the assignment, purpose, and audience.

> ❝ You can write about anything, and if you write well enough, even the reader with no intrinsic interest in the subject will become involved. ❞
> —TRACY KIDDER, NOVELIST

CHOOSING   COLLECTING   SHAPING   DRAFTING   REVISING

CHOOSING A SUBJECT

If a journal entry suggested a possible subject, do the collecting and shaping strategies. Otherwise, consider the following ideas.

- Review your journal entries from previous chapters and the papers that you have already written for this class. Test these subjects for an arguable claim that you could make, opposing arguments you could consider, and an appropriate audience for an argumentative piece of writing.

- Brainstorm possible ideas for argumentative subjects from the other courses you are currently taking or have taken. What controversial issues in psychology, art, philosophy, journalism, biology, nutrition, engineering, physical education, or literature have you discussed in your classes? Ask current or past instructors for possible controversial topics relating to their courses.

- Newspapers and magazines are full of controversial subjects in sports, medicine, law, business, and family. Browse through current issues or online magazines looking for possible subjects. Check news items, editorials, and cartoons. Look for subjects related to your own interests, your job, your leisure activities, or your experiences.

- Interview your friends, family, or classmates. What controversial issues are affecting their lives most directly? What would they most like to change about their lives? What has irritated or angered them most in the recent past?

- If you are doing a community-service-learning project, consider one of the following possible topics: (1) Which of the agency's activities best meet the goals of the agency? Write an essay to the agency coordinator recommending a reallocation of resources to the most effective activities. (2) How might agency volunteers more usefully serve the agency in future projects? Write to your project coordinator recommending improvements that would better meet the dual goals of academic learning and agency service.

CHOOSING	COLLECTING	SHAPING	DRAFTING	REVISING

COLLECTING

▪ NARROWING AND FOCUSING YOUR CLAIM   Narrow your subject to a specific topic, and sharpen your focus by applying the "Wh" questions. If your subject is "grades," your responses might be as follows.

SUBJECT: GRADES

- **Who:** College students
- **What:** Letter grades
- **When:** In freshman and sophomore years
- **Where:** Especially in nonmajor courses
- **Why:** What purpose do grades serve in nonmajor courses?

Determine what claim or claims you want to make. Make sure that your claim is *arguable*. (Remember that claims can overlap; an argument may combine several related claims.)

CLAIM OF FACT OR DEFINITION

- Letter grades exist. (not arguable)
- Employers consider grades when hiring. (slightly more arguable, but not very controversial)
- Grades do not measure learning. (very arguable)

CLAIM ABOUT CAUSE OR EFFECT

- Grades create anxiety for students. (not very arguable)
- Grades actually prevent discovery and learning. (arguable)

CLAIM ABOUT VALUE

- Grades are not fair. (not very arguable: "fairness" can usually be determined)
- Grades are bad because they discourage individual initiative. (arguable)
- Grades are good because they give students an incentive to learn. (arguable)

CLAIM ABOUT A SOLUTION OR POLICY

- Grades should be eliminated altogether. (arguable—but difficult)
- Grades should be eliminated in humanities courses. (arguable)
- Grades should change to pass/fail in nonmajor courses. (arguable—and more practical)

Focusing and narrowing your *claim* helps determine what evidence you need to collect. Use your observing, remembering, reading, and investigative skills to gather the evidence. *Note:* An argumentative essay should not be a mathematical equation that uses only abstract and impersonal evidence. *Your experience* can be crucial to a successful argumentative essay. Start by doing the *remembering* exercises. Your audience wants to know not only why you are writing on this particular *topic,* but also why the subject is of interest to *you.*

■ **REMEMBERING**   Use *freewriting, looping, branching,* or *clustering* to recall experiences, ideas, events, and people who are relevant to your claim. If you are writing about grades, brainstorm about how *your* teachers used grades, how you reacted to specific grades in one specific class, how your friends or parents reacted, and what you felt or thought. These prewriting exercises will help you understand your claim and give you specific examples that you can use for evidence.

■ **OBSERVING**   If possible for your topic, collect data and evidence by observing, firsthand, the facts, values, effects, or possible solutions related to your claim. *Repeated* observation will give you good inductive evidence to support your argument.

■ **INVESTIGATING**   For most argumentative essays, some research or investigation is essential. Because it is difficult to imagine all the valid counterarguments, interview friends, classmates, family, coworkers, and authorities on your topic. From the library, gather books and articles that contain arguments in support of your claim. *Note:* As you do research in the library, print out articles or make photocopies of key passages from relevant sources to hand in with your essay. If you cite sources from your research, list them on a Works Cited page following your essay. (See Chapter 13 for the proper format.)

CHOOSING	COLLECTING	SHAPING	DRAFTING	REVISING

SHAPING

As you plan your organization, reconsider your rhetorical situation. Will the *genre* you have selected (letter, essay, Web site, brochure, PowerPoint presentation) help carry out your *purpose* for your intended audience? Is there a relevant *occasion*

" No one can write decently who is distrustful of the reader's intelligence, or whose attitude is patronizing. "

—E. B. WHITE,
ESSAYIST

(meeting, anniversary, or response to news item) that your writing might focus on? What is the *cultural, social,* or *political context* for your writing? Finally, reconsider your *audience.* Try imagining one real person who might be among your readers. Is this person open-minded and likely to be convinced by your evidence? Does this person represent the opposing position? If you have several alternative positions, are there individual people who might represent, in your mind, each of these positions? After reconsidering your rhetorical situation, try the shaping strategies that follow.

■ **LIST OF "PRO" AND "CON" ARGUMENTS**   Either on paper or in a computer file, write out your *claim,* and then list the arguments for your position (pro) and the arguments for the opposing positions (con). After you have made the list, match up arguments by drawing lines, as indicated. (On the computer file, move "Con" column arguments so they appear directly opposite the corresponding "Pro" column arguments.)

If some pro and con arguments "match," you will be able to argue against the con and for your claim at the same time. If some arguments do not "match," you will need to consider them separately.

Claim: Grades should be changed to pass/fail in nonmajor courses.

PRO	CON
Grades inhibit learning by putting too much emphasis on competition.	Grades actually promote learning by setting students to study as hard as possible.
Pass/fail grading encourages students to explore nonmajor fields.	Students should be encouraged to compete with majors. They may want to change majors and need to know if they can compete.
Grade competition with majors in the field can be discouraging.	If students don't have traditional grading, they won't take nonmajor courses seriously.
Some students do better without the pressure of grades; they need to find out if they can motivate themselves without grades, but they shouldn't have to risk grades in their major field to discover that.	

■ **DRAW CIRCLE OF ALTERNATIVE POSITIONS**   If you are considering multiple alternative positions, put your claim in the middle of a circle and indicate the various positions or stakeholders on the outside of the circle. This diagram will help you identify the most important positions in the debate and will help you organize your writing. The following example is based on the claim that standardized testing in schools should put the students' needs first.

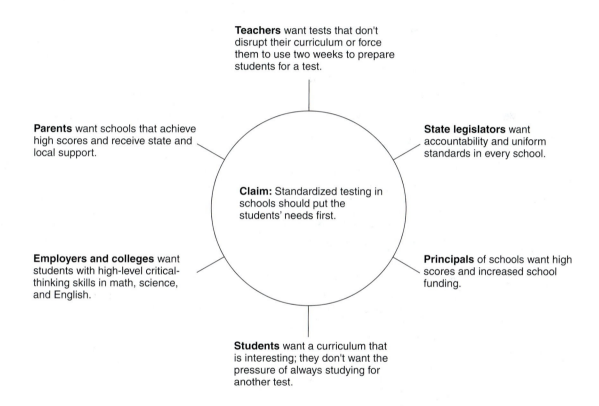

Once you have a diagram for all the major alternative positions or stakeholders, decide the focus of your argument. For your purpose, audience, and context, you may want to focus just on the different goals of teachers, students, and parents. Or you may want to suggest how teachers, students, and parents should organize and force legislators to change the standardized tests or change how schools are funded based on test results.

▮ **OUTLINES FOR ARGUMENTS**   For more than two thousand years, writers and speakers have been trying to determine the most effective means to persuade audiences. One of the oldest outlines for a successful argument comes from classical rhetoric. The following six-part outline is intended as a guideline rather than a rigid list. Test this outline; see if it will work for *your* argument.

Introduction:	Announces subject; *gets audience's interest and attention;* establishes a trustworthy character for the writer
Narration:	Gives *background,* context, statement of problem, or definition
Partition:	States thesis or *claim,* outlines or *maps* arguments
Argument:	Makes *arguments* and gives *evidence* for the claim or thesis
Refutation:	Shows why *opposing arguments* are not true or valid
Conclusion:	Summarizes arguments, suggests solution, *ties into the introduction or background*

Most arguments have these features, but not necessarily in this order. Some writers prefer to respond to or refute opposing arguments before giving the arguments in support of their claims. When con and pro arguments match, refuting an argument followed by the argument for your claim may work best. As you organize your own arguments, put your strongest argument last and your weakest argument either first or in the middle.

Because most short argumentative essays contain the introduction, narration, and partition all in a few introductory paragraphs, you may use the following abbreviated outlines for argument.

Outline 1	Introduction (attention getter, background, claim or thesis, map)
	Your arguments
	Refutation of opposing arguments
	Conclusion
Outline 2	Introduction
	Refutation of opposing arguments
	Your arguments
	Conclusion
Outline 3	Introduction
	Refutation of first opposing argument that matches your first argument
	Refutation of second opposing argument that matches your second argument, and so on
	Additional arguments
	Conclusion

For Rogerian arguments, you can follow one of the above outlines, but the emphasis, tone, and attitude are different.

Introduction	Attention getter, background Claim (often downplayed to reduce threat) Map (often omitted) Appeal to character (crucial to Rogerian argument)
Opposing arguments	State opposing arguments fairly Show where, how, or when those arguments may be valid; establish common ground
Your arguments	State your position fairly Show where, how, or when your arguments are valid
Resolution	Present compromise position State your solution to the problem, and show its advantages to both sides

▌ DEVELOPING ARGUMENTS   Think of your argument as a series of *because* statements, each supported by evidence, statistics, testimony, expert opinion, data, specific examples from your experience, or a combination of these.

> ### *THESIS OR CLAIM: Grades should be abolished in nonmajor courses.*

Reason 1	Because they may keep a student from attempting a difficult nonmajor course *Statistics, testimony, data, and examples*
Reason 2	Because competition with majors in the field can be discouraging *Statistics, testimony, data, and examples*
Reason 3	Because grades inhibit students' learning in nonmajor fields *Statistics, testimony, data, and examples*

You can develop each reason using a variety of strategies. The following strategies may help you generate additional reasons and examples.

Definition	Define the crucial terms or ideas. (What do you mean by *learning?*)
Comparison	Compare the background, situation, and context with another similar context. (What other schools have tried pass/fail grading for nonmajor courses? How has it worked?)
Process	How does or should a change occur? (How do nonmajors become discouraged? How should a school implement pass/fail in grading?)

Research Tips

When you draft your arguing essay, don't let your citations or direct quotations overpower your own argument. Two tactics will keep you in control of your argument:

First, always avoid "unidentified flying quotations" by *sandwiching* your quotations. *Introduce* quotations by referring to the author, the source, and/or the author's study. *Follow* quotations with a sentence explaining how the author's evidence supports your argument. For examples, see paragraphs 4 and 5 in the essay by student writer Crystal Sabatke at the end of this chapter.

Second, keep your direct quotations *short*. If possible, reduce a long passage to one sentence and incorporate the quoted material in the flow of your own language. For example, in her essay at the end of this chapter, Sabatke writes,

> According to Ruth Conniff, author of "Big Bad Welfare: Welfare Reform, Politics, and Children," the welfare reform discussion "indicates that what happens to children doesn't matter to Americans, so long as mothers are forced to work" (8).

These strategies may help you develop an argument coherently and effectively. If several strategies are possible, consider which would be most effective for your audience.

CHOOSING	COLLECTING	SHAPING	DRAFTING	REVISING

DRAFTING

You will never really know "enough" about your subject or have "enough" evidence. At some point, however, you must stop collecting and start your draft. The most frequent problem in drafting an argumentative essay is delaying the actual writing too long, until the deadline is too close.

For argumentative essays, start with a working order or sequence and sketch an outline on paper or in your head. Additional examples and appeals to reason, character, or emotion may occur to you as you develop your argument or refute opposing arguments. In addition, if you have done some research, have your notes, photocopies of key data, statistics, quotations, and citations of authorities close at hand. As you write, you will discover that some information or arguments simply don't fit into the flow of your essay. Don't force arguments into your draft if they no longer seem to belong.

CHOOSING	COLLECTING	SHAPING	DRAFTING	REVISING

REVISING

Argumentation is the most public of the purposes for writing. The rhetorical situation (purpose, audience, genre, occasion, and cultural context) plays a crucial role. As you revise, look at this larger context, not just at phrasing, words, or sentences. Test your argument by having friends or classmates read it. Explain your claim, your focus, and your intended audience, genre, and context. Ask them to look for counterarguments that you have omitted or for weaknesses, omissions, or fallacies in logic. But don't automatically change your draft. Take the advice that makes your overall purpose more effective for your audience.

GUIDELINES FOR REVISION

- **When you finish your draft, reconsider the elements of the rhetorical situation** (writer, purpose, audience, genre, occasion, cultural context). Look at the big picture. What needs changing? What needs to be added? What parts are repetitious or not effective?

- **Ask a class member or friend to read your draft to determine the intended audience for your argument.** See which arguments your reader thinks would not be effective for your audience.

- **Use the Toulmin model to evaluate your essay.** Is your claim clearly stated? Does your claim have a qualifier? Do you note exceptions to your claim? Do you have warrant statements explaining how your data support your reasons and claim?

- **Which of your *because* arguments are most effective?** Least effective? Should you change the outline or structure that you initially chose?

- **Revise your draft to avoid fallacies or errors in reasoning.** Errors in logic create two problems: They can destroy your rational appeal and open your argument to a logical rebuttal, and they lessen your credibility—and thus reduce your appeal to your character. (Review the list of fallacies below.)

- **Support your reasons with evidence: *data, facts, statistics, quotations, observations, testimony, statistics, or specific examples from your experience.*** Check your collecting notes once again for additional evidence to add to your weakest argument. Is there a weak or unsupported argument that you should simply omit?

- **Signal the major arguments and counterarguments in your partition or map.** Between paragraphs, use clear transitions and paragraph hooks.

PEER RESPONSE

Writer: Before you exchange drafts with a peer reader, provide the following information about your essay.

1. a. Intended audience and genre
    b. Primary claim or thesis
    c. Opposing arguments that you refute
    d. Arguments supporting your claim
2. Write out one or two questions about your draft that you want your reader to answer.

Reader: Read the writer's entire draft. As you reread, answer the following questions.

1. **Arguments.** Without looking at the writer's responses above, describe the essay's (a) target audience, (b) primary claim, (c) opposing arguments that are refuted, (d) arguments supporting the claim. Which of these did you have trouble identifying? What additional pro or con arguments should the writer consider?
2. **Organization.** Identify the following parts of the writer's draft: introduction, narration, partition, argument, refutation, and conclusion. Does the writer need all of these for his or her particular subject and audience? Why or why not? Where could the writer clarify transitions between sections? Explain.
3. **Appeals.** Identify places where the writer appeals to reason, to character, and to emotion. Where could these appeals be stronger? Identify sentences where the writer is overly emotional or illogical (see the section "Revising Fallacies in Logic").
4. **Evidence.** Identify at least one paragraph in which the supporting evidence is strong. Then identify at least one paragraph in which the writer makes assertions without sufficient supporting evidence. What kind of evidence might the writer use—first-hand observation, personal examples, testimony from experts, interviews, statistics, or other? Explain.
5. **Revision plan.** List three key changes that the writer should make during the revision.
6. Answer the writer's questions.

Writer: When your essay is returned, read the comments by your peer reader(s) and do the following.

1. Compare your descriptions of the audience, genre, claim, and pro and con arguments with your reader's descriptions. Where there are differences, clarify your essay.
2. Read all of your peer reader's responses. List revisions that you intend to make in each of the following areas: *audience, genre, arguments, organization, appeals,* and *supporting evidence.*

- **Could your essay be improved by visuals or special formatting?** Reconsider your genre and audience. If visuals might make your essay more effective, do a search on the computer. If you need help formatting your essay, check with a peer, a computer lab assistant, or your instructor.
- **If you cite sources in your essay, check the *accuracy* of your statistics, quotations, and source references.** (See Chapter 12 for the proper format of in-text documentation and the Works Cited page.)
- **Revise sentences to improve conciseness and clarity.**
- **Edit sentences for grammar, punctuation, and spelling.**

■ REVISING FALLACIES IN LOGIC   Listed below are common fallacies in logic. Reread your draft or your peer's draft and revise as appropriate to eliminate these logical errors.

- **Hasty generalization:** Conclusion not logically justified by sufficient or unbiased evidence. If your friend Mary tells you that Professor Paramecium is a hard grader because he gave her a 36 percent on the first biology test, she is making a hasty generalization. It may be *true*—Prof P. may *be* a difficult grader—but Mary's logic is not valid. She cannot logically draw that conclusion from a sample of one; the rest of the class may have received grades of between 80 and 100.
- **Post hoc ergo propter hoc:** Literally, "after this, therefore because of this." Just because Event B *occurred after* Event A does not mean that A *necessarily caused* B. You washed your car in the morning, and it rained in the afternoon. Though we joke about how it always rains after we wash the

car, there is, of course, no causal relationship between the two events. "I forgot to leave the porch light on when I went out last night, and someone robbed my house": Without further evidence, we cannot assume that the lack of light contributed to the robbery. A more obvious cause might be the back door left unlocked.

- **Genetic fallacy:** Arguing that the origins of a person, object, or institution determine its character, nature, or worth. Like the post hoc fallacy, the genetic fallacy is an error in causal relationships.

  This automobile was made in Detroit. It'll probably fall apart after 10,000 miles.
  He speaks with a funny German accent. He's really stupid, you know.
  He started Celestial Seasonings Herb Teas just to make a quick buck; it's just another phony yuppie product.

  The second half of each statement *may* or *may not* be true; the logical error is in assuming that the origin of something will necessarily determine its worth or quality. Stereotyping is frequently caused by a genetic fallacy.

- **Begging the question:** Loading the conclusion in the claim. Arguing that "pornography should be banned because it corrupts our youth" is a logical claim. However, saying that "filthy and corrupting pornography should be banned" is begging the question: The conclusion that the writer should *prove* (that pornography corrupts) is assumed in the claim. Other examples: "Those useless psychology classes should be dropped from the curriculum"; "Senator Swingle's sexist behavior should be censured by Congress"; "Everyone knows that our ineffective drug control program is a miserable failure." The writers must *prove* that the psychology classes are useless, that Senator Swingle is sexist, and that the drug program is a failure.

- **Circular argument:** A sentence or argument that restates rather than proves. Thus, it goes in a circle: "President Reagan was a great communicator because he had that knack of talking effectively to the people." The terms in the beginning of the sentence (*great communicator*) and the end of the sentence (*talking effectively*) are interchangeable. The sentence ends where it started.

- **Either/or:** An oversimplification that reduces alternatives to only two choices, thereby creating a false dilemma. Statements such as "Love it or leave it" attempt to reduce the alternatives to two. If you don't love your school, your town, or your country, you don't have to leave: A third choice is to change it and make it better. Proposed solutions frequently have an either/or fallacy: "Either we ban boxing or hundreds of young men will be senselessly killed." A third alternative is to change boxing's rules or equipment. "If we don't provide farmers with low-interest loans, they will go bankrupt." Increasing prices for farm products might be a better alternative.

- **Faulty comparison or analogy:** Basing an argument on a comparison of two things, ideas, events, or situations that are similar but not identical. Although comparisons or analogies are often effective in argument, they can hide logical problems. "We can solve the meth problem the same way we reduced the DWI problem: Attack it with increased enforcement and mandatory jail sentences." Although the situations are similar, they are not identical. The DWI solution will not necessarily work for drugs. An analogy is an extended comparison that uses something simple or familiar to explain something complex or less familiar. "Solving a mathematics problem is like baking a cake: You have to take it one step at a time. First, you assemble your ingredients or your known data. . . ." Like baking, solving a problem does involve a process; unlike baking, however, mathematics is more exact. Changing the amount of flour in a recipe by 1 percent will not make the cake fall; changing a numeric value by 1 percent, however, may ruin the whole problem. The point, however, is not to avoid comparisons or analogies. Simply make sure that your conclusions are qualified; acknowledge the *differences* between the two things compared as well as the similarities.

- **Ad hominem (literally, "to the man"):** An attack on the character of the individual or the opponent rather than his or her actual opinions, arguments, or qualifications: "Susan Davidson, the prosecuting attorney, drinks heavily. There's no way she can present an effective case." This is an attack on Ms. Davidson's character rather than an analysis of her legal talents. Her record in court may be excellent.

- **Ad populum (literally, "to the people"):** An emotional appeal to positive concepts (God, mother, country, liberty, democracy, apple pie) or negative concepts (fascism, atheism) rather than a direct discussion of the real issue: "Those senators voting to increase the defense budget are really war-mongers at heart." "If you are a true American, you should be for tariffs to protect the garment industry."

- **Red herring and straw man:** Diversionary tactics designed to avoid confronting the key issue. *Red herring* refers to the practice of dragging a smelly fish across the trail to divert tracking dogs away from the real quarry.

A red herring occurs when writers avoid countering an opposing argument directly: "Of course equal pay for women is an important issue, but I wonder whether women really want to take the responsibility that comes with higher paying jobs. Do they really want the additional stress?" This writer diverts attention away from the argument about equal pay to another issue, stress—thus, a red herring. In the *straw man* diversion, the writer sets up an artificially easy argument to refute in place of the real issue. Former President Richard Nixon's famous "Checkers" speech is a good example. Accused of spending $18,000 in campaign gifts for personal use, Nixon described how he received Checkers, a little black-and-white spotted cocker spaniel dog. Because his daughter Tricia loved this dog, Nixon decided to keep it. Surely, there's nothing wrong with that, is there? The "Checkers" argument is a "straw man" diversion: Justifying his personal use of this gift was much easier than explaining how and why he spent the $18,000. Avoid red herring and straw man tactics by either refuting an argument directly or acknowledging that it has some merit. Don't just change the subject.

POSTSCRIPT ON THE WRITING PROCESS

In your journal, answer the following questions.

1. Describe how your beliefs about your subject changed from the time you decided on your claim to when you revised your essay. What caused the change in your views?

2. What opposing argument was most difficult to counter? Explain how you handled it.

3. Which was your strongest argument? Did you use logical appeals and evidence, or did you rely more on appeals to character or emotion? Explain.

4. How did your writing process for the argumentative essay change from the process for your previous essays? What steps or stages took longer? What stages did you have to go back and rework?

Welfare Is Still Necessary
for Women and Children in the U.S.

Crystal Sabatke decided to write her arguing essay about changes in the welfare system that require women to work in order to receive certain welfare payments. She decided to focus particularly on readers who believe that welfare mothers will simply become lazy if they don't have to work for the money to support their families. She hopes that "by showing examples of positive welfare stories, I can show that mothers and their children are more important than saving a few cents per dollar." Reproduced below are Sabatke's notes for her audience analysis, her rough draft, the responses to her peer review workshop, and her final, revised draft.

AUDIENCE ANALYSIS: READERS' BELIEFS

My readers will assume that women on welfare who have children can go out and get jobs. That they should get jobs for the betterment of themselves and their children. That when they do get a job, their financial problems will be solved and that welfare will be a thing of the past. In order to shake these assumptions, I believe that emotional appeals should be used. Examples of factual women on welfare in negative situations that prevent them from getting jobs—children, low-income wage jobs, etc.

My readers also believe in the principle of a strong work ethic, the idea that if you work hard, you can achieve the "American Dream." I do feel that I should show how this principle is not applicable in certain situations—ones that my readers probably do not take into strong consideration.

Finally, I feel that my readers blindly value getting jobs more than taking care of children (even though these are the same people who hypocritically focus on family values). I think that family values should be focused on because this is something that is held in high regard by nearly every human being.

Welfare in the United States—
Necessity Without Programming

FIRST DRAFT

What defines an American woman? Women in the United States play numerous roles; many are successful executives, mothers, wives, and scholars. Women have broken many barriers throughout U.S. history and have become, in general, a very successful group in society. But what about the women who haven't broken the barriers? What about the women who had children at a young age with a boyfriend or husband who left them alone soon after? What about the women who can't find a job because their education level hinders their prosperity? What about the women who can't seem to find their way above the poverty level and have to seek help from the government?

Throughout the United States, poverty is not abnormal—especially for women and children. With "44.6 percent of the children who lived in [female-headed households] poor in 1994, and almost half of all children who are poor living in female-headed households," (A) doesn't it seem ironic that the government is cutting welfare expenditures for women and children? Many government officials believe that "the welfare system and its recipients are the cause of the problem." (B) What the lawmakers aren't considering, however, is that poverty is essentially the catalyst in a circle of controversy, and that the only way out of the problems is to provide adequate educational opportunities for welfare recipients, along with ample child care programs and options and a sufficient minimum wage for all citizens. The answer is not ending welfare, but dealing with the problems of poverty in a realistic manner.

In contrast to opposing arguments, most women aren't poor and having children because they want more welfare money or because they are lazy, but because they don't have a sufficient education. As Nicholas Zill, a writer for *Public Health Reports,* states, "Girls and boys who become parents while they are still of school age are . . . predominantly those with low test scores and grades, who are disengaged from school or in active conflict with parents, teachers, or school authorities." (C) The government needs to provide for all Americans an education system that works not only for the successful student, but also for the students that are not doing well. Female students, especially, should be educated about birth control and negative outcomes of having children at younger ages. We should not be punishing and impeding children for the mistakes of their parents and the deficiencies of our education system. Welfare is indispensable for uneducated women and their children until a system of education and support can be initiated and proven successful.

For people opposing government assistance of the poor, another popular argument is that welfare needs to be ended in all forms, and women with children need to get jobs. According to Charles Murray, a strong oppressor of the welfare system in America and an advocate of family values, a "strict job program" needs to be established that will force women to "drop out of a welfare program altogether." (D) Essentially, to the opposition, "the welfare-reform discussion indicates that what happens to children doesn't matter to Americans, so long as mothers are forced to work." (E) Unfortunately, however, for women with children who either decide to go into or are forced into the job market, there isn't a child care system that works with mothers to make a "strict job program" successful. The truth is, there is a scarcity of child care options in this country, and the ones that are available are generally out of the price range of a welfare mother. Shouldn't children be put foremost in this debate? If our country is really focused on family values, shouldn't women have the option to stay home and give their children good care even if it means keeping them on welfare? Welfare is essential in providing a means for women to provide not only adequate care for their children, but positive values for their future.

Another category of women on welfare who are quite often overlooked are those mothers who have minimum-wage jobs and who still need government assistance. The current method of getting women into the workplace is the Job Training Partnership Act, or "the Government's biggest training program." (E) According to *The Wall Street Journal,* however, this program, which offers low-wage jobs such as fast food "is a sham" (E) and "actually led to lower wages for poor young women compared with a control group." (E) Once a woman is in the workplace, it is easy to assume that she will be removed from welfare and become an effective member of society. What is not taken into consideration, however, is that a minimum wage can hardly keep up with the needs of a single mother. "The average [welfare] recipient who gets a full-time job . . . makes $6.74 an hour—about $14,000 a year. Daycare for two children can easily cost $12,000." (E) It is obvious that after subtracting child care, this equation leaves a mother with virtually nothing left to provide herself and her children with necessities such as food, clothing, and shelter. The answer is clearly not to simply put women in low-wage-earning jobs. Until Washington can come up with a solution that involves education and child care assistance and has raised the minimum wage enough to support a mother with children, a welfare system still needs to be provided.

The answer is not ending welfare, but providing supplemental programs that can realistically assist a single mother. With the minimum wage being too low, child care costs being impractical, and education programs virtually nonexistent, it is not fair to assume that welfare can be abolished. Of course, there are problems with the current welfare system, but supplemental programming is the only way to effectively change these glitches.

ARGUING ESSAY: PEER-RESPONSE WORKSHEET

To the Writer: Briefly describe the audience for this paper. (Be sure to include your audience's position on the issue you're writing about.) Also note what you want your readers to focus on as they read.

My audience is white, conservative males who are against any welfare. Please comment on my development—and I kind of gave up on my conclusion. How can I make it better?

To the Reader: Answer the following questions.

1. Underline the *claim/thesis*. Is it clear? Make suggestions for improvement.

    Bev: Good thesis. It is clear and placed in a good spot, just after enough background and before the bulk of the paper. However, I would elaborate more on the "realistic manner" either in your thesis sentence or a separate sentence.

    Amy: *The thesis is very clear—however, the sentence after it confused me.*

2. Is the claim adequately *focused*—narrow within manageable/defensible limits? Why or why not? Explain.

    Bev: The claim is well focused and clear.

    Amy: *Possibly even too focused. Reads more like an essay map than a thesis.*

3. Do you feel the writer needs to add any *qualifiers* or exceptions in order to avoid overgeneralizing? If yes, explain.

    Bev: You sort of overgeneralize about women on welfare, but not too noticeably. Maybe some statistics concerning these women would help.

    Amy: *Possibly qualify for 2 parent and singles—see paragraph #5.*

4. Does the paper deal with *opposing arguments?* How successful do you feel the paper is in conceding and/or refuting opposing arguments? Explain.

Bev: *Good job of laying out the opposing sides of the argument.*

Amy: *Opposition clearly stated each time and then refuted. No work needed on the ones you have stated. Does not take into consideration two-parent welfare families or singles. Will some of your claims work for them as well?*

5. Does the *evidence* support the reasons? Where is more evidence needed? What kind of evidence is needed?

Bev: *Your use of evidence is effective. However, I would suggest more evidence in the first body paragraph. You only have one quotation—maybe throw another one in there.*

Amy: *More statistics would be helpful, for example, test scores as related to teen pregnancy.*

6. What are *one* or *two* areas that you feel the writer should address *first* in revising this paper? What suggestions can you make for conducting those revisions?

Bev: *Good organization of the paper. You follow a clear layout and it is easy to follow. I would develop your quotations more in paragraph 2. You use good evidence. Just develop it more. In your conclusion, maybe if you tied it into the intro, it would help you out. Restate arguments that you made in the introduction.*

Amy: *The lead paragraph seems to give an essay map but doesn't. Possibly phrase some of the questions to relate to the paragraphs? Conclusion: Instead of summing up what you said, try an analysis of the problem and its solutions.*

7. Return the paper to the writer and discuss your comments.

FINAL DRAFT
Welfare Is Still Necessary for Women and Children in the U.S.

What defines an American woman? Women in the United States play *1* numerous roles; many are successful executives, mothers, wives, and scholars. Women have broken many barriers throughout U.S. history and have become, in general, a very successful group in society. But what about the women who haven't broken the barriers? What about the women who had children at a young age with a boyfriend or husband who left them soon after? What about the women who can't find a job because their education level hinders their prosperity? What about the women who can't seem to find their way above the poverty level and have to seek help from the government?

In the United States, poverty is not abnormal—especially for women *2* and children. With "44.6 percent of the children who lived in [female-headed households] in 1994, and almost half of all children who are poor living in female-headed households," doesn't it seem ironic that the government continues to cut welfare expenditures for women and children? (Wellstone 1). Many government officials believe that "the welfare system and its recipients are the cause of the problem" (Rank 1). What these lawmakers aren't considering, however, is that poverty is essentially the catalyst in a circle of controversy, and that the only way out of the problem is to provide adequate educational opportunities for welfare recipients, ample child care programs and options, and a sufficient minimum wage for all citizens. Until methods such as these are instituted, it is necessary for the government to maintain a supportive welfare system for the women and children of our country.

In refutation of opposing arguments, most women aren't poor and *3* having children because they want more welfare money or because they are lazy, but because they don't have a sufficient education. As Nicholas Zill, a writer for *Public Health Reports,* states, "Girls and boys who become parents while they are still of school age are . . . predominantly those with low test scores and grades, who are disengaged from school or in active conflict with parents, teachers, or school authorities" (6). Recent studies by the National Center for Health Statistics show that "nearly one in every four children in the U.S. is born to a mother who has not finished high school" (Zill 2). The government needs to provide an educational system that focuses not only on the successful student, but also on the student who is performing poorly. Because "parent education is linked to children's economic well-being," positive programs need to be created that provide support and alternatives to mainstream education for students who are "high risk" or are not college-bound (Zill 3). Female students, specifically, should be educated about birth control and the negative consequences of having children at younger ages. Until our nation takes active measures to improve the educational system, welfare is necessary to support the children who are born because of the inadequacies of our schools. America should not be punishing and impeding children for the mistakes of their parents and the deficiencies of our school system. Welfare is indispensable for uneducated women and their children until a better system of education and support can be initiated and proven successful.

Another popular argument given by people who oppose welfare is that single women with children should be working, not accepting welfare. According to Charles Murray, a strong critic of the welfare system, we need to institute a "strict job program" that will force women to "drop out of welfare altogether" (285). According to Ruth Conniff, author of "Big Bad Welfare: Welfare Reform Politics and Children," the welfare reform discussion "indicates that what happens to children doesn't matter to Americans, so long as mothers are forced to work" (8). Unfortunately, however, for single women with children who either decide to work or are forced into the job market, there isn't a child care system that could make a "strict job program" successful (Murray 285). With child care costing "about $116 a week for a toddler and $122 for an infant," not only is American day care economically insensitive, but day care options are limited as well (Conniff 8). According to Mark Robert Rank, author of "Winners and Losers in the Welfare Game," the "scarcity of affordable child care for low-income families" makes the current welfare system in this country a "losing game" (1). How can women be expected to get jobs when there aren't sufficient means to care for their children? Ruth Conniff wonders that if our country "is so concerned about family values, wouldn't it make sense to let mothers stay home with their young children?" (8). Welfare is essential to provide means for women to supply not only adequate care for their children but also positive values for their children's future.

Another category of women on welfare who are quite often overlooked are those mothers who have minimum-wage jobs and who still need government assistance. The current method of getting women into the work place is the Job Training Partnership Act, or "the Government's biggest training program" (Conniff 5). According to *The Wall Street Journal*, however, this program—which offers low-wage jobs such as fast-food work—has "actually led to lower wages for poor young women compared with a control group" (Conniff 5). Once a woman is in the workplace, many people assume that she will be removed from welfare and become an independent member of society. What is not considered, however, is that the minimum wage can scarcely keep up with the needs of a single mother. According to a survey done of welfare recipients in Dane County, Wisconsin, "the average [welfare] recipient who gets a full-time job . . . makes $6.74 an hour—about $14,000 a year. Day care for two children can easily cost $12,000" (Conniff 7). It is obvious that after subtracting child care costs, this equation leaves a mother with virtually nothing left to provide herself and her children with necessities such as food, clothing, and shelter—making it necessary to stay on government assistance. Until the minimum wage has been raised to keep up with these strenuous living situations, Washington needs to continue providing welfare to help single mothers and their children survive.

One of the many roles that American women assume is often 6 that of a poverty-stricken single mother. With current education programs that are not effective for "high-risk" women students, with child care costs that are overwhelming, and with a minimum wage so low that it can't keep up with the needs of single mothers, it is not fair to assume that welfare can be abolished. As Michelle Tingling Clement of National Public Radio states, "What [women] truly need is . . . education, skills development . . . and not just any job but jobs that pay living wages with family health benefits and child care" (2). Until programs that can realistically assist women and children are created, welfare is still a definite necessity.

Works Cited

Clement, Michelle T. "Republicans Finalize Welfare Reform Package." *All Things Considered*. National Public Radio. 15 Nov. 1998. Transcript.

Conniff, Ruth. "Big Bad Welfare: Welfare Reform Politics and Children." *The Progressive* 84 (1994): 1–10.

Murray, Charles. "Keeping Priorities Straight on Welfare Reform." *The Aims of Argument*. Ed. Timothy W. Crucius and Carolyn E. Channell. Mountain View, CA: Mayfield, 1998. 285–88.

Rank, Mark Robert. "Winners and Losers in the Welfare Game." Editorial. *St. Louis Post-Dispatch* 15 Sept. 1994: 1–2.

Wellstone, Paul. "If Poverty Is the Question." *The Nation Digital Edition* 4 Apr. 1997. 10 Oct. 1998 <*http://www.thenation.com*>.

Zill, Nicholas. "Parental Schooling and Children's Health." *Public Health Reports* 111 (1996): 1–10.

QUESTIONS FOR WRITING AND DISCUSSION

1. Sabatke says that her audience consists of white, conservative males who believe that everyone should have a job and no one should be on welfare. Where in her essay does she address this audience? Could she revise her essay to focus on this audience even more specifically? Explain.

2. Read Sabatke's first draft and then the responses by Bev and Amy on the peer-response sheet. Which of Bev's and/or Amy's suggestions do you agree with? What other suggestions might you give Sabatke? Which of the peer-response suggestions does Sabatke take or ignore in her final draft? How might Sabatke have improved her final version even more? Explain.

3. What opposing arguments does Sabatke consider? Choose one of her responses, and explain why you think the counterargument is or is not effective. Think of one additional counterargument that she might consider. Should she address that argument? Why or why not?

4. At what points in her essay should Sabatke give additional evidence? Should she use more statistics about welfare mothers? Should she give a more specific description of the current welfare system? Should she give evidence from case studies of welfare recipients? Explain your choices.

STUDENT WRITING   ☒

ERIC BOESE   x

Standardized Tests: Shouldn't We Be Helping Our Students

As standardized testing has increased in the nation's high schools in recent years, so have the attacks against these tests. Several universities have followed the University of California's lead and deemphasized the SAT test. High school tests, such as the Texas TAAS, California's Stanford 9, Minnesota's MJCA, or Colorado's CSAP, have come under fire because they seem to punish the poorer school districts mainly for having insufficient funds to compete with the wealthy suburban schools. Eric Boese, a student at Colorado State University, decided to write about the problems created by these standardized tests. His purpose, he explains, is to persuade his readers—primarily politicians who set testing policies—that "the use of standardized tests in the education system has to be changed."

Over the past few decades our nation's school systems have progressed 1
with leaps and bounds. We have seen improvements in textbooks, technology, teacher resources, and so much more. The opportunities for children to excel going through primary education are enormous, greater
now than they have ever been. Still we see so many children being held
back. Funds are being used inefficiently, and our priorities have become
a little mixed up. I'm talking about what it is that we actually teach in primary schools. Are we teaching students skills and giving them knowledge
that will make them better members of society or have we decided that it
is more important to teach kids how to do well on tests? The answer to
this question you may not like, but it is an answer that we can do something about.

To begin working on a solution, we should first locate the source of 2
the problem. As I have said, everything in the world of education is
changing, and I have seen that there is one change in particular that can
go a long way towards explaining, and solving, our problem. This change
is in the use of standardized tests. They have become a more important
and more destructive component of our schools. Of course I'm not suggesting that we throw the tests out, for they can be a vital part of education. I hope to show how the current use of these tests is harming the
educational process and show how we can use them in a more productive
manner in the future.

Over the last ten years in Texas some interesting things have hap- 3
pened. The first was that, in 1990, an exam called the Texas Assessment
of Academic Skills (TAAS) was administered for the first time in a number of schools (Weisman). The test was given in grades three through
eight and was used as an exit exam early in school. A lot of stress was
placed on this test because it was used to determine the longevity of the
careers of teachers and administrators. Their jobs depended on the success of their students in taking the exam. In 1994 George W. Bush, the
test's biggest supporter, mandated that it be administered statewide. Over
six years, the pass rate of the test increased in all student populations
(Weisman). The test appeared to be a huge success.

George W. Bush credited the better scores to the test challenging 4
students to do better. I, however, credit it to how the test changed the way
the schools function. An alarming article by Jonathan Weisman reviews
just this case. He shows how improvements on the TAAS are not corre-
lated to improvements on other standardized tests that were given to the

same students. While the TAAS scores went up, the other scores did nothing. The biggest revelation in his article is when he explains why students raised their test scores on that exam and not on others. What he found was that teachers were teaching them how to take the exam. Student learning was compromised because too much stress was put on teachers to make sure their students scored well. Jonathan Weisman knows this to be true:

> In a study published by the Harvard Civil Rights Project in January, Professors Linda McNeil of Rice University and Angela Valenzuela of the University of Texas delivered a scathing assessment of the TAAS's impact on Texas classrooms, asserting that "behind the rhetoric of the test scores are a growing set of classroom practices in which test-prep activities are usurping a substantive curriculum."

Of course it didn't really take experts to figure this out. Anyone involved in the classrooms of these schools knew that was going on:

> Teachers protested that they were spending eight to ten hours a week in test-preparation drills and that their principals were pressuring them to spend even more. Only 27 percent said they believed the rising TAAS scores reflected increased learning and higher-quality teaching; half said the scores indicated nothing of the sort. (Weisman)

This is a situation that is simply unacceptable. Endorsing tests that have these kinds of side effects is pumping out graduating classes of test takers. It's causing students to become less capable of meeting challenges that will face them in college and in the future. Texas isn't the only place this is taking place, but it is a great example of the way our nation's schools will turn out if we allow the use of these tests to continue to spread.

In Texas there are still other factors that cause the test scores to 5 be misleading. There was legislation that allowed schools to exempt special-ed students from taking the test. The number of exemptions increased during the years that the test was administered (Weisman). From this we see that the students aren't even improving as much on the tests as the figures show.

The fact that students score better on this kind of exam reveals noth- 6 ing about their personal improvements. If used differently, however, the exams could be much more effective in meeting students' needs and less destructive of their education. We could eliminate undue stress on teachers and create better evaluations of students' abilities.

In other places than Texas, standardized tests are being used in coun-   7
terproductive ways. The biggest problem seems to be that the tests have
too much riding on them. In her article "Test Case: Now the Principal's
Cheating," Carolyn Kleiner gives some examples of how the stakes of
standardized tests have been raised:

> Twenty-eight states now use standard exams to determine gradua-
> tion and 19 to govern student promotion; a growing number also
> dole out performance-based bonuses for schools that show progress
> and threaten intervention, even closure, for those that don't.

Kleiner links the growing importance of the tests to an inevitable side
effect, cheating. Of course there are more ways that tests have grown in
importance, and yes, more downfalls. The results of standardized tests
can have impacts on the jobs of teachers and principals, the money they
will make, the reputation of a school or district, and the high school graduation rates. The scores can also affect school funding and various different community issues. People would rather send their children to school
somewhere that has a reputation for scoring well on exams and that
doesn't have funding problems. In extreme cases, test results can have effects on the property values of residents in a district. George Madaus
notes that the test results "don't provide a full picture of a child's—or a
school's—accomplishments" and says that "You can't use these tests by
themselves to make any decisions" (Kantrowitz et al.). The tests have,
however, been used to determine a number of the things above, and as a
result, some drawbacks of the tests are that they affect student learning in
the classroom, and they cause great stress to students and teachers.

In "Schools for Scandal," Thomas Toch and Betsy Wagner discuss   8
how standardized tests have ultimately led to a problem of educators
cheating. The problem of cheating has been one that, until recently, involved students breaking the rules. The new problem we are seeing is that
teachers and even principals have started to help their students cheat on
some tests. Why would they do this, you ask? It's similar to the situation
in Texas—high stakes tests put pressure on them. They are pressured by
administrators, principals, and parents alike, all of whom want to see the
students get good scores for their own benefit. For parents, good scores
are expected, and they see them as being equivalent to their students' doing well in school. In other words, if they see that a school has scored
poorly on any given test, they see it as a failure on the part of the school,
a further incentive for schools to improve their scores.

It's not something many of us want to hear, but the need for high   *9*
scores has caused many school officials to encourage cheating as well as
raise their school's score by any means possible. "In a national survey of
educators in 1990, 1 in 11 teachers reported pressure from administrators
to cheat on standardized tests" (Toch and Wagner). On top of the pressures of cheating, there is almost nothing stopping teachers from giving
out answers. In most common standardized tests, security monitoring is
minimal, answers are available to test givers (who are usually the teachers), and tests are used multiple times. This makes it easy for teachers not
only to cheat, but to teach the material that they know will be covered on
any given test. Researchers in Colorado found that tests scores dropped
dramatically from a first test that teachers had the time to prepare their
students for and a very similar test given only a few weeks later. University of Colorado testing expert Lorrie Shepard said, "Teachers are not
teaching students skills and concepts. . . . They are teaching specific examples by rote memorization" (Toch and Wagner).

Due to cheating and various other issues, standardized tests reveal   *10*
less accurate scores each year. In other words, tests are getting worse at
what they were designed to do: measure skill levels of students. The reason, Toch and Wagner mention, is that people want high scores. Many
tests that challenge students are not being used by schools simply because they yield low scores. The basic skills covered by these tests are in-
flating scores and forcing teachers to focus on teaching remedial skills
and not on the needs of the individual students. In "Education: Is That
Your Final Answer?" Jodie Morse gives an example in which the problem is even worse:

> Educators say they have had to dumb down their lessons to teach the
> often picayune factoids covered by the exams. A study released last
> month by the University of Virginia found that while some schools
> had boosted their performance on Virginia's exam, teachers had
> to curtail field trips, elective courses and even student visits to the
> bathroom—all in an effort to cram more test prep into the school
> day. Says the study's author, education professor Daniel Duke:
> "These schools have become battlefield units."

Causing practices like these to occur in our nation's schools is unjustifi-
able. The inflation of scores doesn't stop there; tests are being reused to
a point where most schools can manage to do very well on them. This
creates a false impression of students' skills. The U.S. Department of

Education agreed that "with respect to national averages, [school] districts and states are presenting inflated results and misleading the public." How can somebody defend a policy that diminishes the education of students for tests that don't accurately reflect student achievement or, in some cases, even challenge them to think on their own?

So far we have considered some of the many effects of our current *11* testing system. It is equally important to review exactly what materials the tests cover and whether or not they are testing the right things. First of all, 80 percent of standardized tests used in America are produced by corporations (Toch and Wagner). Who says corporations know what should be on these tests in the first place? The relevancy and difficulty of tests are determined by people who have little or no concern for their effects on schools. They are not held accountable for the material covered on their exams and do not feel that security is their concern. Often-times, the corporations will make the materials on their tests easier because more schools will buy tests that make themselves look good. In other cases, the corporations simply don't know what to include in their tests for different grade levels. A side effect of corporations writing tests is that they usually recycle their tests and so they rarely "allow schools to return copies of their graded exams to students so they, and their teachers, might learn from their mistakes" (Toch and Wagner). Of the students I surveyed, none claimed that they had ever even learned their own scores on school-mandated standardized tests, and none claimed that they learned anything substantial from the exams that they had taken. On many exams, questions relating to students' advanced-thinking skills are almost nonexistent. Corporations are just not giving tests that are beneficial to students. This is the first change we need to make: either make the corporations answer to a selected group of educational officials or have somebody make tests that have the student in mind.

Along the same lines as above, we need to throw out the tests that *12* are too difficult for students of any particular age group. Only a few people actually oppose this argument. New York State Education Commissioner Richard Mills said that "subjecting 9-year-olds to tests they can't pass is one of the strategies to change things for the better" (Ohanian). I wish somebody would explain this to me. Is this supposed to make students want to work harder because they failed miserably or is it going to discourage them? This may not be an opinion that is held by too many people, but it sure seems to be in some cases. In some states, like Massachusetts for example, students are required to take tests that can last up to 18 hours in order to graduate from high school. We can't expect this much of students who are only 18 years old; not many of them would be able to pass such a test if their classes weren't so focused on preparing them for it, and as we have seen, test preparation often adversely affects student learning.

A level of testing has to be found such that students will be chal- *13* lenged and yet they will not be overwhelmed. Standardized tests should include materials relevant to a student's grade level, some materials that would require the student to explore new ideas, and some questions de- signed to test a student's advanced-thinking skills. This test would cover materials that would be included in a normal school curriculum and therefore would take up less class time. A teacher could concentrate on students' needs again, and classes could cover more material, explore sub- jects more deeply and give students the education they deserve. There would be time to do more of what one student claims to love most about school, "getting into great conversations and developing ideas" (Selzer). A test that fits these criteria would give a more accurate evaluation of the student's skills and of the student's potential to succeed in higher-level and college courses. Such a test may not be easy to make, but it would definitely be worth the effort.

It's getting harder and harder to see the positive side of using today's *14* standardized tests. Not only are the tests giving inaccurate evaluations of students' skills, but they are causing corruption in our schools and dimin- ishing the opportunities for educational excellence of our students. I've discussed ideas for new tests that could be used, but that is not enough to make up for the disturbances involved with the importance of the tests. It is my opinion that we cannot allow these tests to undermine the cur- rent system. First of all, funding should not be determined by scores; it should be determined by need. Taxpayers in any given region would also be able to vote to increase funding for the schools that they support. I mentioned that, in Texas, for teachers and administrators the tests held an additional, personal importance. Determining who holds these posi- tions needs a more personal evaluation than looking at test scores. We need to look at how their students are really improving and the effort they put into their students' education.

I'm sure that the public will still have the bias that their students *15* should be getting the best scores, but this is an issue that will have to be faced. They need to be shown that the test scores are a sign for teachers to read to determine the extra attention that some students may require, and this is what the test should be used for. There is no greater purpose for having these tests than for improving education. Many of the problems of the current system will prove to be very difficult to resolve, but any steps towards a new system are ones for the better.

It may all sound difficult now, but the state of our schools is in desperate need of change. Pushing for more tests as so many people are doing is not the answer. I urge you to consider how bright children are being discouraged by an unproductive testing system and to be the person who puts the needs of the children first. *16*

Works Cited

Kantrowitz, Barbara, Daniel McGinn, Ellise Pierce, and Erika Check. "When Teachers Are Cheaters." *Newsweek* 19 June 2000. 15 Apr. 2001 <*http://www.elibrary.com*>.

Kleiner, Carolyn. "Test Case: Now the Principal's Cheating." *U.S. News and World Report* 12 June 2000. 10 Apr. 2001 <*http://www.elibrary.com*>.

Morse, Jodie. "Education: Is That Your Final Answer?" *Time* 19 June 2000. 15 Apr. 2001 <*http://www.elibrary.com*>.

Ohanian, Susan. "Editorials: Standardized Schools." *The Nation* 18 Sep. 1999. 10 Apr. 2001 <*http://www.elibrary.com*>.

Selzer, Adam. "High-Stakes Testing: It's Backlash Time." *U.S. News & World Report* 3 Apr. 2000. 15 Apr. 2001 <*http://www.usnews.com/usnews/issue/000403/education.htm*>.

Toch, Thomas, and Betsy Wagner. "Schools for Scandal." *U.S. News & World Report* 27 Apr. 1992. 10 Apr. 2001 <*http://www.elibrary.com*>.

Weisman, Jonathan. "Only a Test." *The New Republic* 10 Apr. 2000. 15 Apr. 2001 <*http://www.thenewrepublic.com/041000/weisman041000.html*>.

vo·cab·u·lar·y

In your journal, write the meaning of the italicized words in the following phrases.

- determine the *longevity* of the careers of teachers **(3)**
- test-prep activities are *usurping a substantive* curriculum **(4)**
- a further *incentive* **(8)**
- teach the often *picayune factoids* **(10)**
- preparation often *adversely* affects student learning **(12)**

QUESTIONS FOR WRITING AND DISCUSSION

1. In your journal, write three short paragraphs explaining your own experience with standardized tests. First, which tests have you taken, and when did you take them? Next, what was the purpose of the tests—to evaluate you or your school? Finally, describe the effect of these tests on your own education. Did they detract from the regular curriculum? Did they give you motivation and incentive to learn? Did they help you get into college?

2. Eric Boese uses a problem-solving format for his arguing essay. Which paragraphs describe the problems with standardized tests? List these problems. Which paragraphs indicate his solutions? What are his solutions? Is his essay clear or would you give him suggestions for improving his organization? Explain.

3. Boese writes that the intended audience for his essay is politicians who are in favor of increased use of standardized tests. Where does Boese address this audience? Where and how could he make his appeal to this audience even stronger? Write out actual sentences Boese could add to his essay.

4. On the Internet, read more recent articles on standardized testing. Has testing in high schools changed since Boese wrote his essay in 2001? Do more or fewer high schools give mandated tests? Has the quality of the tests improved? Do students and teachers like or dislike these tests? Explain.

Pieter Brueghel
The Fall of Icarus (c. 1558)
Oil-tempera
Museum of Fine Arts, Brussels

Works of art—poetry, stories, and paintings—often choose earlier myths, stories, and legends for their subject. In *The Fall of Icarus,* Brueghel draws on the Greek myth of Daedalus and his son, Icarus, as told by the Roman poet Ovid. Several modern poets, including W. H. Auden and William Carlos Williams, have written poems inspired by both the myth and Brueghel's painting (see highlight on page 607). To see how painting inspires poetry—and vice versa—see W. H. Auden's poem, "Musée des Beaux Arts" on page 607 as well as the journal exercises on page 610.

Responding to Literature

12

In Introduction to Literature class, you and a friend are assigned to work collaboratively on an essay about Eudora Welty's "A Worn Path." You are both interested in how Phoenix Jackson's journey contains images of the phoenix—a mythological bird said to live for five hundred years, after which it burns itself to death and then rises from its ashes to become youthful and beautiful again. You draft your essays separately and then read each other's drafts. At that point, you collaborate on a single essay, combining the best ideas and evidence from your separate drafts. Your collaborative essay shows how Phoenix Jackson is characterized by birdlike images, how she calmly faces images of fire and death on her journey, and how her grandson represents her rebirth.

In a film class, you watch Roman Polanski's *Tess,* an adaptation of Thomas Hardy's novel *Tess of the D'Urbervilles.* You decide to compare the film with the novel, focusing on four key episodes: the "strawberry scene," in which Tess meets Alec; the rape scene at night; the harvesting scene; and the final scene at Stonehenge. On the basis of your comparison, you argue that Polanski's interpretation (and the acting of Nastassia Kinski) retains Hardy's view of Tess as a victim of social and sexist repression.

> **❝** I hungered for new books, new ways of looking and seeing. It was not a matter of believing or disbelieving what I read, but of feeling something new, of being affected by something that made the look of the world different. **❞**
> —RICHARD WRIGHT
> AUTHOR OF *BLACK BOY*

> **❝** No one else can read a literary work for us. The benefits of literature can emerge only from creative activity on the part of the reader. **❞**
> —LOUISE ROSENBLATT
> AUTHOR OF *LITERATURE AS EXPLORATION*

RESPONDING TO POEMS AND SHORT STORIES REQUIRES BOTH IMAGI-
NATION AND CRITICAL-READING SKILL. AS READERS, WE ANTICI-
PATE, IMAGINE, FEEL, WORRY, ANALYZE, AND QUESTION. A STORY OR
POEM IS LIKE AN EMPTY BALLOON THAT WE INFLATE WITH THE
warm breath of our imagination and experience. Our participation makes us
partners with the author in the artistic recreation.

First, readers must *imagine* and recreate that special world described by the
writer. The first sentences of a short story, for example, throw open a door to a world
that—attractive or repulsive—tempts our curiosity and imagination. Like Alice in
Alice in Wonderland, we cannot resist following a white rabbit with pink eyes who
mutters to himself, checks his watch, and then zips down a rabbit hole and into an
imaginary world.

Here are three opening sentences of three very different short stories.

Young Goodman Brown came forth at sunset into the street at Salem
village; but put his head back, after crossing the threshold, to exchange a
parting kiss with his young wife.

> —Nathaniel Hawthorne, "Young Goodman Brown"

As Gregor Samsa awoke one morning from uneasy dreams he found himself transformed in his bed into a gigantic insect.

> —Franz Kafka, "The Metamorphosis"

The morning of June 27th was clear and sunny, with the fresh warmth of
a full-summer day; the flowers were blossoming profusely and the grass
was green.

> —Shirley Jackson, "The Lottery"

Whether our imaginations construct the disturbing image of a "gigantic
insect" or the seemingly peaceful picture of a perfect summer day, we actively recreate each story.

In a similar way, poems invite the reader to participate in actively creating characters, images, places, feelings, and reflections. Below are lines from several poems,
each creating its own characters, places, images, and themes.

Because I could not stop for Death—
He kindly stopped for me—
The Carriage held but just Ourselves—
And Immortality.

> —Emily Dickinson, "Because I could not stop for Death"

anyone lived in a pretty how town
(with up so floating many bells down)
spring summer autumn winter
he sang his didn't he danced his did.
      —e.e. cummings, "anyone lived in a pretty how town"

Tyger! Tyger! burning bright
In the forests of the night,
What immortal hand or eye
Could frame thy fearful symmetry?
      —William Blake, "The Tyger"

Two roads diverged in a yellow wood,
And sorry I could not travel both
And be one traveler, long I stood
And looked down one as far as I could
To where it bent in the undergrowth
      —Robert Frost, "The Road Not Taken"

Responding to literature also requires that readers *reread*. First, you should reread for yourself—that is, reread to write down your ideas, questions, feelings, and reactions. To heighten your role in re-creating a story or poem, you should note in the margins your questions and responses to main characters, places, metaphors and images, and themes that catch your attention: "Are the names of Hawthorne's characters significant? Is Young Goodman Brown really good? Is his wife, Faith, really faithful?" "Why does Emily Dickinson have her speaker personify Death as the driver of a carriage? Why does her speaker say that 'he *kindly* stopped for me'? What action is taking place?" Don't just underline or highlight passages. Actually *write* your questions and responses in the margins.

Second, you should reread with a writer's eye. In fiction, identify the major and minor characters. Look for conflicts between characters. Mark passages that contain foreshadowing. Pinpoint sentences that reveal the narrative point of view. Use the appropriate critical terms (*character, plot, conflict, point of view, setting, style,* and *theme*) to help you reread with a writer's eye and see how the parts of a story relate to the whole. Similarly, in poetry, look for character, key events, and setting, and *always* pay attention to images and metaphors, to voice and tone, to word choice, and to rhythm and rhyme. Each critical term is a tool—a magnifying glass that helps you understand and interpret the literary work more clearly.

In addition to rereading, responding to literature requires that readers *share* ideas, reactions, and interpretations. Sharing usually begins in small-group or class discussions, but it continues as you explain your interpretation in writing. A work of literature is not a mathematical equation with a single answer. Great literature is worth interpreting precisely because each reader responds differently. The purpose of literature is to encourage you to reflect on your life and the lives of others—to look for new ways of seeing and understanding your world—and ultimately to expand your world. Sharing is crucial to appreciating literature.

> Hawthorne doesn't come right out and say that people become disillusioned by experiencing evil. He shows how it actually happens in the life of young Goodman Brown.

> Shirley Jackson's "The Lottery" helps me see that the notion of human sacrifice and the idea of the human scapegoat still exist in our culture today.

> In "Because I could not stop for Death," Emily Dickinson uses personification and metaphors as vehicles for her own reflection and introspection.

Writing about your responses and sharing them with other readers helps you "reread" your own ideas in order to explain them fully and clearly to other readers.

RESPONDING TO A SHORT STORY

Read and respond to Kate Chopin's "The Story of an Hour." Use your imagination to help create the story as you read. Then *reread* the story, noting in the margin your questions and responses. When you finish rereading and annotating your reactions, write your interpretation of the last line of the story.

PROFESSIONAL WRITING

The Story of an Hour

Kate Chopin

Kate O'Flaherty Chopin (1851–1904) was an American writer whose mother was French and Creole and whose father was Irish. In 1870, she moved from St. Louis to New Orleans with her husband, Oscar Chopin, and over the next ten years she gave birth to five sons. After her husband died in 1882, Chopin returned to St. Louis to begin a new life as a writer. Many of her best stories are about Louisiana people and places, and her most famous novel, The Awakening, *tells the story of Edna, a woman who leaves her marriage and her children to fulfill herself through an artistic career.*

Knowing that Mrs. Mallard was afflicted with a heart trouble, great care *1*
was taken to break to her as gently as possible the news of her husband's
death.

It was her sister Josephine who told her, in broken sentences, veiled *2*
hints that revealed in half concealing. Her husband's friend Richards was
there, too, near her. It was he who had been in the newspaper office when
intelligence of the railroad disaster was received, with Brently Mallard's
name leading the list of "killed." He had only taken the time to assure himself of its truth by a second telegram, and had hastened to forestall any less
careful, less tender friend in bearing the sad message.

She did not hear the story as many women have heard the same, with *3*
a paralyzed inability to accept its significance. She wept at once, with sudden, wild abandonment, in her sister's arms. When the storm of grief had
spent itself she went away to her room alone. She would have no one follow her.

There stood, facing the open window, a comfortable, roomy armchair. *4*
Into this she sank, pressed down by a physical exhaustion that haunted her
body and seemed to reach into her soul.

She could see in the open square before her house the tops of trees that *5*
were all aquiver with the new spring life. The delicious breath of rain was
in the air. In the street below a peddler was crying his wares. The notes of
a distant song which someone was singing reached her faintly, and countless sparrows were twittering in the eaves.

There were patches of blue sky showing here and there through the *6*
clouds that had met and piled one above the other in the west facing her
window.

She sat with her head thrown back upon the cushion of the chair quite *7*
motionless, except when a sob came up into her throat and shook her, as a
child who has cried itself to sleep continues to sob in its dreams.

She was young, with a fair, calm face, whose lines bespoke repression *8*
and even a certain strength. But now there was a dull stare in her eyes,
whose gaze was fixed away off yonder on one of those patches of blue sky.
It was not a glance of reflection, but rather indicated a suspension of intelligent thought.

There was something coming to her and she was waiting for it, fear- *9*
fully. What was it? She did not know; it was too subtle and elusive to name.
But she felt it, creeping out of the sky, reaching toward her through the
sounds, the scents, the color that filled the air.

Now her bosom rose and fell tumultuously. She was beginning to rec- *10*
ognize this thing that was approaching to possess her, and she was striving

. . . continued The Story of an Hour, **Kate Chopin**

to beat it back with her will—as powerless as her two white slender hands would have been.

When she abandoned herself a little whispered word escaped her 11 slightly parted lips. She said it over and over under her breath: "Free, free, free!" The vacant stare and the look of terror that had followed it went from her eyes. They stayed keen and bright. Her pulses beat fast, and the coursing blood warmed and relaxed every inch of her body.

She did not stop to ask if it were not a monstrous joy that held her. A 12 clear and exalted perception enabled her to dismiss the suggestion as trivial.

She knew that she would weep again when she saw the kind, tender 13 hands folded in death; the face that had never looked save with love upon her, fixed and gray and dead. But she saw beyond that bitter moment a long procession of years to come that would belong to her absolutely. And she opened and spread her arms out to them in welcome.

There would be no one to live for during those coming years; she 14 would live for herself. There would be no powerful will bending her in that blind persistence with which men and women believe they have a right to impose a private will upon a fellow creature. A kind intention or a cruel intention made the act seem no less a crime as she looked upon it in that brief moment of illumination.

And yet she had loved him—sometimes. Often she had not. What did 15 it matter! What could love, the unsolved mystery, count for in face of this possession of self-assertion which she suddenly recognized as the strongest impulse of her being.

"Free! Body and soul free!" she kept whispering. 16

Josephine was kneeling before the closed door with her lips to the key- 17 hole, imploring for admission. "Louise, open the door! I beg; open the door—you will make yourself ill. What are you doing, Louise? For heaven's sake open the door."

"Go away. I am not making myself ill." No; she was drinking in a very 18 elixir of life through that open window.

Her fancy was running riot along those days ahead of her. Spring days, 19 and summer days, and all sorts of days that would be her own. She breathed a quick prayer that life might be long. It was only yesterday she had thought with a shudder that life might be long.

She arose at length and opened the door to her sister's importunities. 20 There was a feverish triumph in her eyes, and she carried herself unwittingly like a goddess of Victory. She clasped her sister's waist, and together they descended the stairs. Richards stood waiting for them at the bottom.

Someone was opening the front door with a latchkey. It was Brently   21
Mallard who entered, a little travel-stained, composedly carrying his grip-sack and umbrella. He had been far from the scene of accident, and did not even know there had been one. He stood amazed at Josephine's piercing cry; at Richards's quick motion to screen him from the view of his wife.

But Richards was too late.   22

When the doctors came they said she had died of heart disease—of   23
joy that kills.

■ ■ ■

RESPONDING TO A POEM

Read and respond to W. H. Auden's "Musée des Beaux Arts." Begin by examining the painting by Pieter Brueghel, *Landscape with the Fall of Icarus,* reproduced at the beginning of this chapter. Carefully read and reread the poem, comparing it with details in the painting. Then go on-line to find the description of Daedalus and Icarus described in the Roman poet Ovid's *Metamorphoses.* As you reread Auden's poem, pay particular attention to the detail in the description, to Auden's references to scenes not depicted in the painting, and to the language and word choice.

PROFESSIONAL WRITING

Musée des Beaux Arts

W. H. Auden

In the following poem, W. H. Auden reflects on the art and the theme of Pieter Brueghel's famous painting, Landscape with the Fall of Icarus *(c. 1558). Auden (1907–1973) was born in England, went to school at Oxford, and eventually moved to the United States. Auden describes and interprets Brueghel's vision of the Fall of Icarus, and Brueghel in turn visualizes and interprets the Roman poet Ovid's version of the story of Daedalus and his son, Icarus. In this Greek myth, according to Ovid, Daedalus fashions wings made out of feathers and wax in order to help them escape the island of Crete. Daedalus cautions his son not to fly too near the heat of the sun, but Icarus ignores his father's advice.*

...continued Musée des Beaux Arts, **W. H. Auden**

When Icarus soars too high, the sun melts the wax in his wings, and he plunges into the ocean. In Brueghel's painting, only the white legs of Icarus are visible (in the lower right-hand corner of the painting) as he disappears into the water.

About suffering they were never wrong,
The old Masters: how well they understood
Its human position: how it takes place
While someone else is eating or opening a window or just
    walking dully along;
How, when the aged are reverently, passionately waiting   5
For the miraculous birth, there always must be
Children who did not specially want it to happen, skating
On a pond at the edge of the wood:
They never forgot
That even the dreadful martyrdom must run its course   10
Anyhow in a corner, some untidy spot
Where the dogs go on with their doggy life and the torturer's
    horse
Scratches its innocent behind on a tree.
In Brueghel's Icarus, for instance: how everything turns away
Quite leisurely from the disaster; the ploughman may   15
Have heard the splash, the forsaken cry,
But for him it was not an important failure; the sun shone
As it had to on the white legs disappearing into the green
Water, and the expensive delicate ship that must have seen
Something amazing, a boy falling out of the sky,   20
Had somewhere to get to and sailed calmly on.

TECHNIQUES   PURPOSES   SHORT FICTION   POETRY   PROCESS

Techniques for Responding to Literature

As you read and respond to a work of literature, keep the following techniques in mind.

- **Understanding the assignment and selecting a possible purpose and audience.** Unless stated otherwise in your assignment, your purpose is to *interpret* a work of literature. Your audience will be other members of your class, including the teacher.

- **Actively reading, annotating, and discussing the literary work.** Remember that literature often contains *highly condensed experiences.* In order to give imaginative life to literature, you need to reread patiently both the major events and the seemingly insignificant passages. In discussions, look for the differences between your responses and other readers' ideas.

- **Focusing your essay on a single, clearly defined interpretation.** In your essay, clearly state your main idea or thesis, focusing on a *single* idea or aspect of the piece of literature. Your thesis should *not be a statement of fact.* Whether you are explaining, evaluating, or arguing, your interpretation must be clearly stated.

- **Supporting your interpretation with evidence.** Because your readers will probably have different interpretations, you must show which specific characters, events, scenes, conflicts, images, metaphors, or themes prompted your response, and you must use these details to support your interpretation. *Do not merely **retell** the major events of the story or **describe** the main images in the poem*—your readers have already read your story or poem.

▮ WARMING UP: Journal Exercises

Read all of the following questions and then write for five minutes on two or three. These questions should help clarify your perceptions about literature or develop your specific responses to "The Story of an Hour" or to "Musée des Beaux Arts."

1. On your bookshelves or in the library, find a short story or poem that you read at least six months ago. Before you reread it, write down the name of the author and the title of the work. Note when you read it last and describe what you remember about it. Then reread the story or poem. When you finish, write for five minutes, describing what you noticed that you did not notice the last time you read it.

2. Write out the *question* that "The Story of an Hour" seems to ask. What is your answer to this question? What might have been Kate Chopin's answer?

3. The words *heart, joy, free, life,* and *death* appear several times in "The Story of an Hour." Underline these words (or synonyms) each time they appear. Explain how the meaning of each of these words seems to change during the story. Is each word used ironically?

4. Write out a dictionary definition of the word *feminism.* Then write out your own definition. Is Mrs. Mallard a feminist? Is Kate Chopin a feminist? What evidence in the story supports your answers?

5. Kate Chopin's biographer, Per Seyersted, says that Chopin saw that "truth is manifold" and thus preferred not to "take sides or point a moral." Explain how "The Story of an Hour" does or does not illustrate Seyersted's observations.

6. In Ovid's account of the myth of Daedalus and Icarus, the fisherman, shepherd, and plowman are "astonished" as they observe Icarus flying, and Ovid suggests that they might worship Icarus and Daedalus as gods. In what way does Brueghel revise Ovid's account? Explain how and why Brueghel changes this part of the myth.

7. Auden suggests that one theme of Brueghel's painting is that suffering is largely ignored by the general populace. Study Brueghel's painting again. What other themes or ideas are present in the painting that Auden does not mention? Explain another possible interpretation of the painting based on specific images or points of focus in the painting.

8. Auden says that the theme of Brueghel's painting is about suffering, but he also includes a description of "the miraculous birth" and children who "did not specially want it to happen." Does this image distract from Auden's main point, or is the idea of the miraculous birth related to Auden's theme? Explain.

9. Literature often expresses common themes or tensions, such as the conflict between generations, the individual versus society, appearance versus reality, self-knowledge versus self-deception, and civilization versus nature. Which of these themes are most apparent in "The Story of an Hour" or in "Musée des Beaux Arts"? Explain your choices.

TECHNIQUES **PURPOSES** SHORT FICTION POETRY PROCESS

Purposes for Responding to Literature

In responding to literature, you should be guided by the purposes that you have already practiced in previous chapters. As you read a piece of literature and respond in the margin, begin by writing *for yourself.* Your purposes are to observe, feel, remember, understand, and relate the work of literature to your own life: What is happening? What memories does it trigger? How does it make you feel? Why is this passage confusing? Why do you like or dislike this character? Literature has special, personal value. You should write about literature initially in order to discover and understand its importance in your life.

When you write an interpretive essay, however, you are writing *for others*. You are sharing your experience in working with the author as imaginative partners in recreating the work. Your purposes will often be mixed, but an interpretive essay often contains elements of *explaining, evaluating, problem solving,* and *arguing.*

- **Explaining.** Interpretive essays about literature explain the *what, why,* and *how* of a piece of literature. What is the key subject? What is the most important line, event, or character? What are the major conflicts or the key images? What motivates a character? How does a character's world build or unravel? How does a story on poem meet or fail to meet our expectations? How did our interpretations develop? Each of these questions might lead to an interpretive essay that explains the *what, why,* and *how* of your response.

- **Evaluating.** Readers and writers often talk about "appreciating" a work of literature. *Appreciating* means establishing its value or worth. It may mean praising the work's literary virtues; it may mean finding faults or weaknesses. Usually, evaluating essays measure *both strengths and weaknesses,* according to specific criteria. What important standards for literature do you wish to apply? How does the work in question measure up? What kinds of readers might find this story worth reading? An evaluative essay cites evidence to show why a story is exciting, boring, dramatic, puzzling, vivid, relevant, or memorable.

- **Problem solving.** Writers of interpretive essays occasionally take a problem-solving approach, focusing on how the reader overcomes obstacles in understanding the story or poem, or on how the author solved problems in writing key scenes, choosing images and language, developing character, and creating and resolving conflicts. Particularly if you like to write fiction or poetry yourself, you may wish to take the writer's point of view: how did the writer solve (or fail to solve) problems of image, metaphor, character, setting, plot, or theme?

- **Arguing.** As readers share responses, they may discover that their interpretations diverge sharply from the ideas of other readers. Does "The Story of an Hour" have a feminist theme? Is it about women or about human nature in general? Is the main character admirable, or is she selfish? Is Auden's interpretation of Brueghel's painting faithful to Brueghel's conception, or does Auden impose his interpretation? Is Auden's the only way to interpret Bureghel's painting? In interpretive essays, writers sometimes argue for their beliefs. They present evidence that refutes an opposing or alternate interpretation and supports their own reading.

Most interpretive essays about literature are focused by these purposes, whether used singly or in combination. Writers should *select* the purpose(s) that are most appropriate for the work of literature and their own responses.

TECHNIQUES   PURPOSES   **SHORT FICTION**   POETRY   PROCESS

Responding to Short Fiction

Begin by noting in the margins your reactions at key points. *Summarize* in your own words what is happening in the story. Write down your *observations* or *reactions* to striking or surprising passages. Ask yourself *questions* about ambiguous or confusing passages.

After you respond initially and make your marginal annotations, use the following basic elements of fiction to help you *analyze how the parts of a short story relate to the whole.* Pay attention to how setting or plot affects the character, or how style and setting affect the theme. Because analysis artificially separates plot, character, and theme, look for ways to *synthesize* the parts: Seeing how these parts relate to each other should suggest an idea, focus, or angle to use in your interpretation.

▌ CHARACTER   A short story usually focuses on a *major character*—particularly on how that character faces conflicts, undergoes changes, or reveals himself or herself. *Minor characters* may be flat (one-dimensional), static (unchanging), or stereotyped. To get a start on analyzing character, diagram the *conflicts* between or among characters. Examine characters for motivation: What causes them to behave as they do? Is their behavior affected by *internal* or *external* forces? Do the major characters reveal themselves *directly* (through their thoughts, dialogue, and actions) or *indirectly* (through what other people say, think, or do)?

▌ PLOT   *Plot* is the sequence of events in a story, but it is also the cause-and-effect relationship of one event to another. As you study a story's plot, pay attention to *exposition, foreshadowing, conflict, climax,* and *denouement.* To clarify elements of the plot, draw a time line for the story, listing in chronological order every event—including events that occur before the story opens. *Exposition* describes the initial circumstances and reveals what has happened before the story opens. *Foreshadowing* is an author's hint of what will occur before it happens. *Conflicts* within characters, between characters, and between characters and their environment may explain why one event leads to the next. The *climax* is the high point, the point of no return, or the most dramatic moment in a story. At the climax of a story, readers discover something important about the main character. *Denouement* literally means the "unraveling" of the complications and conflicts at the end of the story. In "The Story of an Hour," climax and denouement occur almost at the same time, in the last lines of the story.

▪ NARRATIVE POINT OF VIEW

Fiction is usually narrated from either the first-person or the third-person point of view.

A *first-person narrator* is a character who tells the story from his or her point of view. A first-person narrator may be a minor or a major character. This character may be relatively *reliable* (trustworthy) or *unreliable* (naive or misleading). Although reliable first-person narrators may invite the reader to identify with their perspectives or predicaments, unreliable narrators may cause readers to be wary of the narrator's naive judgments or unbalanced states of mind.

A *third-person omniscient narrator* is not a character or participant in the story. Omniscient narrators are assumed to know everything about the characters and events. They move through space and time, giving readers necessary information at any point in the story. A *selective omniscient narrator* usually limits his or her focus to a single character's experiences and thoughts, as Kate Chopin focuses on Mrs. Mallard in "The Story of an Hour." One kind of selective omniscient point of view is *stream-of-consciousness narration,* in which the author presents the thoughts, memories, and associations of one character in the story. Omniscient narrators may be *intrusive,* jumping into the story to give their editorial judgments, or they may be *objective,* removing themselves from the action and the minds of the characters. An objective point of view creates the impression that events are being recorded by a camera or acted on a stage.

Reminder: As you reread a story, do not stop with analysis. Do not quit, for example, after you have identified and labeled the point of view. Determine how the point of view affects your reaction to the central character or to your understanding of the theme. How would a different narrative point of view change the story? If a different character told the story, how would that affect the theme?

▪ SETTING

Setting is the physical place, scene, and time of the story. It also includes the social or historical context of the story. The setting in "The Story of an Hour" is the house and the room in which Mrs. Mallard waits, but it is also the social and historical time frame. *Setting is usually important for what it reveals about the characters, the plot, or the theme of the story.* Does the setting reflect a character's state of mind? Is the environment a source of tension or conflict in the story? Do changes in setting reflect changes in key characters? Do sensory details of sight, touch, smell, hearing, or taste affect or reflect the characters or events? Does the author's portrait of the setting contain images and symbols that help you interpret the story?

■ **STYLE**   *Style* is a general term that may refer to sentence structure and to figurative language and symbols, as well as to the author's tone or use of irony. *Sentence structure* may be long and complicated or relatively short and simple. Authors may use *figurative language* (Mrs. Mallard is described in "The Story of an Hour" as sobbing, "as a child who has cried itself to sleep continues to sob in its dreams"). A *symbol* is a person, place, thing, or event that suggests or signifies something beyond itself. In "The Story of an Hour," the open window and the new spring life suggest or represent Mrs. Mallard's new freedom. *Tone* is the author's attitude toward the characters, setting, or plot. Tone may be sympathetic, humorous, serious, detached, or critical. *Irony* suggests a double meaning. It occurs when the author or a character says or does one thing but means the opposite or something altogether different. The ending of "The Story of an Hour" is ironic: The doctors say Mrs. Mallard has died "of joy that kills." In fact, she has died of killed joy.

■ **THEME**   The focus of an interpretive essay is often on the *theme* of a story. In arriving at a theme, ask how the characters, plot, point of view, setting, and style *contribute* to the main ideas or point of the story. The theme of a story depends, within limits, on your reactions as a reader. "The Story of an Hour" is *not* about relationships between sisters, nor is it about medical malpractice. It is an ironic story about love, personal freedom, and death, but what precisely is the *theme*? Does "The Story of an Hour" carry a feminist message, or is it more universally about the repressive power of love? Is Mrs. Mallard to be admired or criticized for her impulse to free herself? Do not trivialize the theme of a story by looking for some simple "moral." In describing the theme, deal with the complexity of life recreated in the story.

PROFESSIONAL WRITING

A Worn Path

Eudora Welty

Eudora Welty was born in Jackson, Mississippi, in 1909 and studied at Mississippi State College, the University of Wisconsin, and Columbia University. While she was writing short stories during the early 1930s, Welty held jobs with the

Works Progress Administration, a Jackson radio station, and local newspapers. Like Flannery O'Connor and William Faulkner, Eudora Welty wrote stories and novels set in the American South. Her first major publication, A Curtain of Green and Other Stories, *appeared in 1941 and was followed by three more collections of short stories. Her novels include* Delta Wedding *(1946) and* The Optimist's Daughter *(1972), which won a Pulitzer Prize. Welty's collection of reviews and essays,* The Eye of the Story *(1978), and her brief autobiography,* One Writer's Beginnings *(1984), provide insight into her fiction and her life. Welty died in 2001.*

It was December—a bright frozen day in the early morning. Far out in the country there was an old Negro woman with her head tied in a red rag, coming along a path through the pinewoods. Her name was Phoenix Jackson. She was very old and small and she walked slowly in the dark pine shadows, moving a little from side to side in her steps, with the balanced heaviness and lightness of a pendulum in a grandfather clock. She carried a thin, small cane made from an umbrella, and with this she kept tapping the frozen earth in front of her. This made a grave and persistent noise in the still air, that seemed meditative like the chirping of a solitary little bird.

She wore a dark striped dress reaching down to her shoe tops, and an equally long apron of bleached sugar sacks, with a full pocket: all neat and tidy, but every time she took a step she might have fallen over her shoelaces, which dragged from her unlaced shoes. She looked straight ahead. Her eyes were blue with age. Her skin had a pattern all its own of numberless branching wrinkles and as though a whole little tree stood in the middle of her forehead, but a golden color ran underneath, and the two knobs of her cheeks were illuminated by a yellow burning under the dark. Under the red rag her hair came down on her neck in the frailest of ringlets, still black, and with an odor like copper.

Now and then there was a quivering in the thicket. Old Phoenix said, "Out of my way, all you foxes, owls, beetles, jack rabbits, coons, and wild animals! . . . Keep out from under these feet, little bob-whites. . . . Keep the big wild hogs out of my path. Don't let none of those come running my direction. I got a long way." Under her small black-freckled hand her cane, limber as a buggy whip, would switch at the brush as if to rouse up any hiding things.

On she went. The woods were deep and still. The sun made the pine needles almost too bright to look at, up where the wind rocked. The cones dropped as light as feathers. Down in the hollow was the mourning dove—it was not too late for him.

...continued   A Worn Path, **Eudora Welty**

The path ran up a hill. "Seem like there is chains about my feet, time *5* I get this far," she said, in the voice of argument old people keep to use with themselves. "Something always take a hold of me on this hill—pleads I should stay."

After she got to the top she turned and gave a full, severe look behind *6* her where she had come. "Up through pines," she said at length. "Now down through oaks."

Her eyes opened their widest, and she started down gently. But before *7* she got to the bottom of the hill a bush caught her dress.

Her fingers were busy and intent, but her skirts were full and long, so *8* that before she could pull them free in one place they were caught in another. It was not possible to allow the dress to tear. "I in the thorny bush," she said. "Thorns, you doing your appointed work. Never want to let folks pass—no sir. Old eyes thought you was a pretty little green bush."

Finally, trembling all over, she stood free, and after a moment dared to *9* stoop for her cane.

"Sun so high!" she cried, leaning back and looking, while the thick *10* tears went over her eyes. "The time getting all gone here."

At the foot of this hill was a place where a log was laid across the creek. *11*

"Now comes the trial," said Phoenix. *12*

Putting her right foot out, she mounted the log and shut her eyes. *13* Lifting her skirt, leveling her cane fiercely before her, like a festival figure in some parade, she began to march across. Then she opened her eyes and she was safe on the other side.

"I wasn't as old as I thought," she said. *14*

But she sat down to rest. She spread her skirts on the bank around her *15* and folded her hands over her knees. Up above her was a tree in a pearly cloud of mistletoe. She did not dare to close her eyes, and when a little boy brought her a little plate with a slice of marblecake on it she spoke to him. "That would be acceptable," she said. But when she went to take it there was just her own hand in the air.

So she left that tree, and had to go through a barbed-wire fence. There *16* she had to creep and crawl, spreading her knees and stretching her fingers like a baby trying to climb the steps. But she talked loudly to herself: she could not let her dress be torn now, so late in the day, and she could not pay for having her arm or her leg sawed off if she got caught fast where she was.

At last she was safe through the fence and risen up out in the clearing. *17* Big dead trees, like black men with one arm, were standing in the purple stalks of the withered cotton field. There sat a buzzard.

"Who you watching?"   *18*

In the furrow she made her way along.   *19*

"Glad this not the season for bulls," she said, looking sideways, "and   *20* the good Lord made his snakes to curl up and sleep in the winter. A pleasure I don't see no two-headed snake coming around that tree, where it come once. It took a while to get by him, back in the summer."

She passed through the old cotton and went into a field of dead corn.   *21* It whispered and shook and was taller than her head. "Through the maze now," she said, for there was no path.

Then there was something tall, black, and skinny there, moving be-   *22* fore her.

At first she took it for a man. It could have been a man dancing in the   *23* field. But she stood still and listened, and it did not make a sound. It was as silent as a ghost.

"Ghost," she said sharply, "who be you the ghost of? For I have heard   *24* of nary death close by."

But there was no answer—only the ragged dancing in the wind.   *25*

She shut her eyes, reached out her hand, and touched a sleeve. She   *26* found a coat and inside that an emptiness, cold as ice.

"You scarecrow," she said. Her face lighted. "I ought to be shut up for   *27* good," she said with laughter. "My senses is gone, I too old. I the oldest people I ever know. Dance, old scarecrow," she said, "while I dancing with you." She kicked her foot over the furrow, and with mouth drawn down, shook her head once or twice in a little strutting way. Some husks blew down and whirled in streamers about her skirts.

Then she went on, parting her way from side to side with the cane,   *28* through the whispering field. At last she came to the end, to a wagon track where the silver grass blew between the red ruts. The quail were walking around like pullets, seeming all dainty and unseen.

"Walk pretty," she said. "This the easy place. This the easy going."   *29*

She followed the track, swaying through the quiet bare fields, through the   *30* little strings of trees silver in their dead leaves, past cabins silver from weather, with the doors and windows boarded shut, all like old women under a spell sitting there. "I walking in their sleep," she said, nodding her head vigorously.

In a ravine she went where a spring was silently flowing through a hol-   *31* low log. Old Phoenix bent and drank. "Sweet-gum makes the water sweet," she said, and drank more. "Nobody know who made this well, for it was here when I was born."

The track crossed a swampy part where the moss hung as white as lace   *32* from every limb. "Sleep on, alligators, and blow your bubbles." Then the track went into the road.

...*continued* A Worn Path, **Eudora Welty**

Deep, deep the road went down between the high green-colored 33
banks. Overhead the live-oaks met, and it was as dark as a cave.

A black dog with a lolling tongue came up out of the weeds by the 34
ditch. She was meditating, and not ready, and when he came at her she only
hit him a little with her cane. Over she went in the ditch, like a little puff
of milkweed.

Down there, her senses drifted away. A dream visited her, and she 35
reached her hand up, but nothing reached down and gave her a pull. So she
lay there and presently went to talking. "Old woman," she said to herself,
"that black dog come up out of the weeds to stall you off, and now there he
sitting on his fine tail, smiling at you."

A white man finally came along and found her—a hunter, a young 36
man, with his dog on a chain.

"Well, Granny!" he laughed, "what are you doing there?" 37

"Lying on my back like a June-bug waiting to be turned over, mister," 38
she said, reaching up her hand.

He lifted her up, gave her a swing in the air, and set her down. "Any- 39
thing broken, Granny?"

"No sir, them old dead weeds is springy enough," said Phoenix, when 40
she had got her breath. "I thank you for your trouble."

"Where do you live, Granny?" he asked, while the two dogs were 41
growling at each other.

"Away back yonder, sir, behind the ridge. You can't even see it from here." 42

"On your way home?" 43

"No, sir, I going to town." 44

"Why, that's too far! That's as far as I walk when I come out myself, 45
and I get something for my trouble." He patted the stuffed bag he carried,
and there hung down a little closed claw. It was one of the bob-whites, with
its beak hooked bitterly to show it was dead. "Now you go on home,
Granny!"

"I bound to go to town, mister," said Phoenix. "The time come 46
around."

He gave another laugh, filling the whole landscape. "I know you old 47
colored people! Wouldn't miss going to town to see Santa Claus!"

But something held Old Phoenix very still. The deep lines in her face 48
went into a fierce and different radiation. Without warning, she had seen
with her own eyes a flashing nickel fall out of the man's pocket onto the
ground.

"How old are you, Granny?" he was saying.   *49*

"There is no telling, mister," she said, "no telling."   *50*

Then she gave a little cry and clapped her hands and said, "Git on away   *51*
from here, dog! Look! Look at that dog!" She laughed as if in admiration.
"He ain't scared of nobody. He a big black dog." She whispered, "Sic him!"

"Watch me get rid of that cur," said the man. "Sic him, Pete! Sic him!"   *52*

Phoenix heard the dogs fighting, and heard the man running and   *53*
throwing sticks. She even heard a gunshot. But she was slowly bending forward by that time, further and further forward, the lids stretched down
over her eyes, as if she were doing this in her sleep. Her chin was lowered
almost to her knees. The yellow palm of her hand came out from the fold
of her apron. Her fingers slid down and along the ground under the piece
of money with the grace and care they would have in lifting an egg from
under a sitting hen. Then she slowly straightened up, she stood erect, and
the nickel was in her apron pocket. A bird flew by. Her lips moved. "God
watching me the whole time, I come to stealing."

The man came back, and his own dog panted about them. "Well, I   *54*
scared him off that time," he said, and then he laughed and lifted his gun
and pointed it at Phoenix.

She stood straight and faced him.   *55*

"Doesn't the gun scare you?" he said, still pointing it.   *56*

"No, sir, I seen plenty go off closer by, in my day, and for less than what   *57*
I done," she said, holding utterly still.

He smiled, and shouldered the gun. "Well, Granny," he said, "You   *58*
must be a hundred years old, and scared of nothing. I'd give you a dime if
I had any money with me. But you take my advice and stay home, and
nothing will happen to you."

"I bound to go on my way, mister," said Phoenix. She inclined her head   *59*
in the red rag. Then they went in different directions, but she could hear
the gun shooting again and again over the hill.

She walked on. The shadows hung from the oak trees to the road like   *60*
curtains. Then she smelled wood-smoke, and smelled the river, and she saw
a steeple and the cabins on their steep steps. Dozens of little black children
whirled around her. There ahead was Natchez shining. Bells were ringing.
She walked on.

In the paved city it was Christmas time. There were red and green   *61*
electric lights strung and crisscrossed everywhere, and all turned on in the
daytime. Old Phoenix would have been lost if she had not distrusted her
eyesight and depended on her feet to know where to take her.

She paused quietly on the sidewalk where people were passing by. A *62* lady came along in the crowd, carrying an armful of red-, green-, and silver-wrapped presents; she gave off perfume like the red roses in hot summer, and Phoenix stopped her.

"Please, missy, will you lace up my shoe?" She held up her foot. *63*

"What do you want, Grandma?" *64*

"See my shoe," said Phoenix. "Do all right for out in the country, but *65* wouldn't look right to go in a big building."

"Stand still then, Grandma," said the lady. She put her packages down *66* on the sidewalk beside her and laced and tied both shoes tightly.

"Can't lace 'em with a cane," said Phoenix. "Thank you, missy. I doesn't *67* mind asking a nice lady to tie up my shoe, when I gets out on the street."

Moving slowly and from side to side, she went into the big building *68* and into a tower of steps, where she walked up and around and around until her feet knew to stop.

She entered a door, and there she saw nailed up on the wall the docu- *69* ment that had been stamped with the gold seal and framed in the gold frame, which matched the dream that was hung up in her head.

"Here I be," she said. There was a fixed and ceremonial stiffness over *70* her body.

"A charity case, I suppose," said an attendant who sat at the desk *71* before her.

But Phoenix only looked above her head. There was sweat on her face, *72* the wrinkles in her skin shone like a bright net.

"Speak up, Grandma," the woman said: "What's your name? We must *73* have your history, you know. Have you been here before? What seems to be the trouble with you?"

Old Phoenix only gave a twitch to her face as if a fly were bothering her. *74*

"Are you deaf?" cried the attendant. *75*

But then the nurse came in. *76*

"Oh, that's just old Aunt Phoenix," she said. "She doesn't come for *77* herself—she has a little grandson. She makes these trips just as regular as clockwork. She lives away back off the old Natchez Trace." She bent down. "Well, Aunt Phoenix, why don't you just take a seat? We won't keep you standing after your long trip." She pointed.

The old woman sat down, bolt upright in the chair. *78*

"Now, how is the boy?" asked the nurse. *79*

Old Phoenix did not speak. *80*

"I said, how is the boy?"   81

But Phoenix only waited and stared straight ahead, her face very   82
solemn and withdrawn into rigidity.

"Is his throat any better?" asked the nurse. "Aunt Phoenix, don't you   83
hear me? Is your grandson's throat any better since the last time you came
for the medicine?"

With her hands on her knees, the old woman waited, silent, erect and   84
motionless, just as if she were in armor.

"You mustn't take up our time this way, Aunt Phoenix," the nurse said.   85
"Tell us quickly about your grandson, and get it over. He isn't dead, is he?"

At last there came a flicker and then a flame of comprehension across   86
her face, and she spoke.

"My grandson. It was my memory had left me. There I sat and forgot   87
why I made my long trip."

"Forgot?" The nurse frowned. "After you came so far?"   88

Then Phoenix was like an old woman begging a dignified forgiveness   89
for waking up frightened in the night. "I never did go to school, I was too
old at the Surrender," she said in a soft voice. "I'm an old woman without
an education. It was my memory fail me. My little grandson, he is just the
same, and I forgot it in the coming."

"Throat never heals, does it?" said the nurse, speaking in a loud, sure   90
voice to Old Phoenix. By now she had a card with something written on
it, a little list. "Yes. Swallowed lye. When was it—January—two-three
years ago—"

Phoenix spoke unasked now. "No, missy, he not dead, he just the same.   91
Every little while his throat begin to close up again, and he not able to
swallow. He not get his breath. He not able to help himself. So the time
come around, and I go on another trip for the soothing medicine."

"All right. The doctor said as long as you came to get it, you could have   92
it," said the nurse. "But it's an obstinate case."

"My little grandson, he sit up there in the house all wrapped up, wait-   93
ing by himself," Phoenix went on. "We is the only two left in the world.
He suffer and it don't seem to put him back at all. He got a sweet look. He
going to last. He wear a little patch quilt and peep out holding his mouth
open like a little bird. I remembers so plain now. I not going to forget him
again, no, the whole enduring time. I could tell him from all the others in
creation."

"All right." The nurse was trying to hush her now. She brought her a   94
bottle of medicine. "Charity," she said, making a check mark in a book.

...continued A Worn Path, **Eudora Welty**

Old Phoenix held the bottle close to her eyes and then carefully put it 95 into her pocket.

"I thank you," she said. 96

"It's Christmas time, Grandma," said the attendant. "Could I give you 97 a few pennies out of my purse?"

"Five pennies is a nickel," said Phoenix stiffly. 98

"Here's a nickel," said the attendant. 99

Phoenix rose carefully and held out her hand. She received the nickel 100 and then fished the other nickel out of her pocket and laid it beside the new one. She stared at her palm closely, with her head on one side.

Then she gave a tap with her cane on the floor. 101

"This is what come to me to do," she said. "I going to the store and 102 buy my child a little windmill they sells, made out of paper. He going to find it hard to believe there such a thing in the world. I'll march myself back where he waiting, holding it straight up in this hand."

She lifted her free hand, gave a little nod, turned round, and walked out 103 of the doctor's office. Then her slow step began on the stairs, going down.

■ ■ ■

QUESTIONS FOR WRITING AND DISCUSSION

1. Which of the following approximates your response(s) to the character of Phoenix Jackson: Surprise that she should be the subject of a story? Anger that no one helps her on her journey? Boredom that you just read a story in which nothing seems to happen? Puzzlement at her apparently senile behavior? Amazement at her determination and courage? Describe any other responses you may have.

2. According to legend, the Phoenix is a mythological bird that lives for five hundred years, burns itself to death, and then rises from its ashes in the freshness of youth to live through another life cycle. What *events, references,* and *images* in the story suggest that Welty's Phoenix Jackson is like the mythological bird?

3. One reader has suggested that during her journey, Phoenix encounters twelve obstacles (internal and external) that represent tests, or trials, of her faith and courage. How many of these tests can you find? Does she "pass" each test? What do these tests reveal about her character?

4. In an essay entitled "Is Phoenix Jackson's Grandson Really Dead?" Eudora Welty says, "The story is told through Phoenix's mind as she undertakes her errand. As the author is at one with the character as I tell it, I must assume that the boy is alive. As the reader, you are free to think as you like, of course: the story invites you to believe that no matter what happens, Phoenix for as long as she is able to walk and can hold to her purpose will make her journey." Explain how the boy's actual condition might affect your interpretation of the story.

5. Kate Chopin's "The Story of an Hour" and Eudora Welty's "A Worn Path" are both stories about love. By way of contrast, what do the character and behavior of Mrs. Mallard tell you about Phoenix? What do the character and behavior of Phoenix reveal about Mrs. Mallard?

PROFESSIONAL WRITING

The Lesson

Toni Cade Bambara

Toni Cade Bambara (1939-1995) was an activist for the African-American community on many fronts: political, cultural, and literary. She worked for political and social causes in urban communities, taught African-American studies at half a dozen different colleges and universities, and is the author of several collections of short stories and novels, including Gorilla, My Love *(1972),* The Sea Birds Are Still Alive *(1977),* The Salt Eaters *(1980), and* If Blessing Comes *(1987). "The Lesson," which appears in* Gorilla, My Love, *dramatizes the gradual awakening of several children to the political and economic realities of contemporary urban life. As you read the story, pay attention to the narrator, Sylvia. What is the lesson, and what does Sylvia learn?*

Back in the days when everyone was old and stupid or young and foolish and me and Sugar were the only ones just right, this lady moved on our block with nappy hair and proper speech and no makeup. And quite naturally we laughed at her, laughed the way we did at the junk man who went about his business like he was some big-time president and his sorry-ass horse his secretary. And we kinda hated her too, hated the way we did the winos who cluttered up our parks and pissed on our handball walls and stank up our hallways and stairs so you couldn't halfway play hide-and-seek without a goddamn gas mask. Miss Moore was her name. The only woman

1

...*continued* The Lesson, **Toni Cade Bambara**

on the block with no first name. And she was black as hell, cept for her feet, which were fish-white and spooky. And she was always planning these boring-ass things for us to do, us being my cousins, mostly, who lived on the block cause we all moved North the same time and to the same apartment then spread out gradual to breathe. And our parents would yank our heads into some kinda shape and crisp up our clothes so we'd be presentable for travel with Miss Moore, who always looked like she was going to church, though she never did. Which is just one of the things the grownups talked about when they talked behind her back like a dog. But when she came calling with some sachet she'd sewed up or some gingerbread she'd made or some book, why then they'd all be too embarrassed to turn her down and we'd get handed over all spruced up. She'd been to college and said it was only right that she should take responsibility for the young ones' education, and she not even related by marriage or blood. So they'd go for it. Specially Aunt Gretchen. She was the main gofer in the family. You got some ole dumb shit foolishness you want somebody to go for, you send for Aunt Gretchen. She been screwed into the go-along for so long, it's a blood-deep natural thing with her. Which is how she got saddled with me and Sugar and Junior in the first place while our mothers were in a la-de-da apartment up the block having a good ole time.

So this one day Miss Moore rounds us all up at the mailbox and it's   *2*
puredee hot and she's knockin herself out about arithmetic. And school suppose to let up in summer I heard, but she don't never let up. And the starch in my pinafore scratching the shit outta me and I'm really hating this nappy-head bitch and her goddamn college degree. I'd much rather go to the pool or to the show where it's cool. So me and Sugar leaning on the mailbox being surly, which is a Miss Moore word. And Flyboy checking out what everybody brought for lunch. And Fat Butt already wasting his peanut-butter-and-jelly sandwich like the pig he is. And Junebug punchin on Q.T.'s arm for potato chips. And Rosie Giraffe shifting from one hip to the other waiting for somebody to step on her foot or ask her if she from Georgia so she can kick ass, preferably Mercedes's. And Miss Moore asking us do we know what money is, like we a bunch of retards. I mean real money, she say, like it's only poker chips or monopoly papers we lay on the grocer. So right away I'm tired of this and say so. And would much rather snatch Sugar and go to the Sunset and terrorize the West Indian kids and take their hair ribbons and their money too. And Miss Moore files that remark away for next week's lesson on brotherhood, I can tell. And finally I

say we oughta get to the subway cause it's cooler and besides we might meet some cute boys. Sugar done swiped her mama's lipstick, so we ready.

So we heading down the street and she's boring us silly about what *3* things cost and what our parents make and how much goes for rent and how money ain't divided up right in this country. And then she gets to the part about we all poor and live in the slums, which I don't feature. And I'm ready to speak on that, but she steps out in the street and hails two cabs just like that. Then she hustles half the crew in with her and hands me a five-dollar bill and tells me to calculate 10 percent tip for the driver. And we're off. Me and Sugar and Junebug and Flyboy hangin out the window and hollering to everybody, putting lipstick on each other cause Flyboy a faggot anyway, and making farts with our sweaty armpits. But I'm mostly trying to figure how to spend this money. But they all fascinated with the meter ticking and Junebug starts laying bets as to how much it'll read when Flyboy can't hold his breath no more. Then Sugar lays bets as to how much it'll be when we get there. So I'm stuck. Don't nobody want to go for my plan, which is to jump out at the next light and run off to the first bar-b-que we can find. Then the driver tells us to get the hell out cause we there already. And the meter reads eighty-five cents. And I'm stalling to figure out the tip and Sugar say give him a dime. And I decide he don't need it bad as I do, so later for him. But then he tries to take off with Junebug foot still in the door so we talk about his mama something ferocious. Then we check out that we on Fifth Avenue and everybody dressed up in stockings. One lady in a fur coat, hot as it is. White folks crazy.

"This is the place," Miss Moore say, presenting it to us in the voice she *4* uses at the museum. "Let's look in the windows before we go in."

"Can we steal?" Sugar asks very serious like she's getting the ground *5* rules squared away before she plays. "I beg your pardon," say Miss Moore, and we fall out. So she leads us around the windows of the toy store and me and Sugar screamin, "This is mine, that's mine, I gotta have that, that was made for me, I was born for that," till Big Butt drowns us out.

"Hey, I'm goin to buy that there." *6*

"That there? You don't even know what it is, stupid." *7*

"I do so," he say punchin on Rosie Giraffe. "It's a microscope." *8*

"Whatcha gonna do with a microscope, fool?" *9*

"Look at things." *10*

"Like what, Ronald?" ask Miss Moore. And Big Butt ain't got the first *11* notion. So here go Miss Moore gabbing about the thousands of bacteria in a drop of water and the somethinorother in a speck of blood and the million and one living things in the air around us is invisible to the naked eye. And what she say that for? Junebug go to town on that "naked" and we rolling. Then Miss Moore ask what it cost. So we all jam into the window smudgin it up and the price tag say $300. So then she ask how long'd take for Big Butt and Junebug to save up their allowances. "Too long," I say. "Yeh," adds Sugar, "outgrown it by that time." And Miss Moore say no, you never outgrow learning instruments. "Why, even medical students and interns and," blah, blah, blah. And we ready to choke Big Butt for bringing it up in the first damn place.

"This here costs four hundred eighty dollars," say Rosie Giraffe. So we 12 pile up all over her to see what she pointin out. My eyes tell me it's a chunk of glass cracked with something heavy, and different-color inks dripped into the splits, then the whole thing put into a oven or something. But for $480 it don't make sense.

"That's a paperweight made of semi-precious stones fused together 13 under tremendous pressure," she explains slowly, with her hands doing the mining and all the factory work.

"So what's a paperweight?" asks Rosie Giraffe. 14

"To weigh paper with, dumbbell," say Flyboy, the wise man from 15 the East.

"Not exactly," say Miss Moore, which is what she say when you warm 16 or way off too. "It's to weigh paper down so it won't scatter and make your desk untidy." So right away me and Sugar curtsy to each other and then to Mercedes who is more the tidy type.

"We don't keep paper on top of the desk in my class," say Junebug, fig- 17 uring Miss Moore crazy or lyin one.

"At home, then," she say. "Don't you have a calendar and a pencil case 18 and a blotter and a letter-opener on your desk at home where you do your homework?" And she know damn well what our homes look like cause she nosys around in them every chance she gets.

"I don't even have a desk," say Junebug. "Do we?" 19

"No. And I don't get no homework neither," says Big Butt. 20

"And I don't even have a home," say Flyboy like he do at school to keep 21 the white folks off his back and sorry for him. Send this poor kid to camp posters, is his specialty.

"I do," says Mercedes. "I have a box of stationery on my desk and a pic- 22 ture of my cat. My godmother bought the stationery and the desk. There's a big rose on each sheet and the envelopes smell like roses."

"Who wants to know about your smelly-ass stationery," say Rosie *23*
Giraffe fore I can get my two cents in.

"It's important to have a work area all your own so that. . . ." *24*

"Will you look at this sailboat, please," say Flyboy, cuttin her off and *25*
pointin to the thing like it was his. So once again we tumble all over each
other to gaze at this magnificent thing in the toy store which is just big
enough to maybe sail two kittens across the pond if you strap them to the
posts tight. We all start reciting the price tag like we in assembly. "Hand-
crafted sailboat of fiberglass at one thousand one hundred ninety-five
dollars."

"Unbelievable," I hear myself say and am really stunned. I read it again *26*
for myself just in case the group recitation put me in a trance. Same thing.
For some reason this pisses me off. We look at Miss Moore and she lookin
at us, waiting for I dunno what.

"Who'd pay all that when you can buy a sailboat set for a quarter at *27*
Pop's, a tube of glue for a dime, and a ball of string for eight cents? It must
have a motor and a whole lot else besides," I say. "My sailboat cost me about
fifty cents."

"But will it take water?" say Mercedes with her smart ass. *28*

"Took mine to Alley Pond Park once," say Flyboy. "String broke. Lost *29*
it. Pity."

"Sailed mine in Central Park and it keeled over and sank. Had to ask *30*
my father for another dollar."

"And you got the strap," laugh Big Butt. "The jerk didn't even have a *31*
string on it. My old man wailed on his behind."

Little Q.T. was staring hard at the sailboat and you could see he *32*
wanted it bad. But he too little and somebody'd just take it from him. So
what the hell. "This boat for kids, Miss Moore?"

"Parents silly to buy something like that just to get all broke up," say *33*
Rosie Giraffe.

"That much money it should last forever," I figure. *34*

"My father'd buy it for me if I wanted it." *35*

"Your father, my ass," say Rosie Giraffe getting a chance to finally push *36*
Mercedes.

"Must be rich people shop here," say Q.T. *37*

"You are a very bright boy," say Flyboy. "What was your first clue?" *38*
And he rap him on the head with the back of his knuckles, since Q.T. the
only one he could get away with. Though Q.T. liable to come up behind
you years later and get his licks in when you half expect it.

"What I want to know is," I says to Miss Moore though I never talk 39 to her, I wouldn't give the bitch that satisfaction, "is how much a real boat costs? I figure a thousand'd get you a yacht any day."

"Why don't you check that out," she says, "and report back to the 40 group?" Which really pains my ass. If you gonna mess up a perfectly good swim day least you could do is have some answers. "Let's go in," she say like she got something up her sleeve. Only she don't lead the way. So me and Sugar turn the corner to where the entrance is, but when we get there I kinda hang back. Not that I'm scared, what's there to be afraid of, just a toy store. But I feel funny, shame. But what I got to be shamed about? Got as much right to go in as anybody. But somehow I can't seem to get hold of the door, so I step away for Sugar to lead. But she hangs back too. And I look at her and she looks at me and this is ridiculous. I mean, damn, I have never ever been shy about doing nothing or going nowhere. But then Mercedes steps up and then Rosie Giraffe and Big Butt crowd in behind and shove, and next thing we all stuffed into the doorway with only Mercedes squeezing past us, smoothing out her jumper and walking right down the aisle. Then the rest of us tumble in like a glued-together jigsaw done all wrong. And people lookin at us. And it's like the time me and Sugar crashed into the Catholic church on a dare. But once we got in there and everything so hushed and holy and the candles and the bowin and the hand-kerchiefs on all the drooping heads, I just couldn't go through with the plan. Which was for me to run up to the altar and do a tap dance while Sugar played the nose flute and messed around in the holy water. And Sugar kept givin me the elbow. Then later teased me so bad I tied her up in the shower and turned it on and locked her in. And she'd be there till this day if Aunt Gretchen hadn't finally figured I was lyin about the boarder takin a shower.

Same thing in the store. We all walkin on tiptoe and hardly touch-in 41 the games and puzzles and things. And I watched Miss Moore who is steady watchin us like she waitin for a sign. Like Mama Drewery watches the sky and sniffs the air and takes note of just how much slant is in the bird formation. Then me and Sugar bump smack into each other, so busy gazing at the toys, 'specially the sailboat. But we don't laugh and go into our fat-lady bump-stomach routine. We just stare at that price tag. Then Sugar run a finger over the whole boat. And I'm jealous and want to hit her. Maybe not her, but I sure want to punch somebody in the mouth.

"Watcha bring us here for, Miss Moore?" 42

"You sound angry, Sylvia. Are you mad about something?" Givin me *43*
one of them grins like she tellin a grown-up joke that never turns out to be
funny. And she's lookin very closely at me like maybe she plannin to do my
portrait from memory. I'm mad, but I won't give her that satisfaction. So I
slouch around the store bein very bored and say, "Let's go."

Me and Sugar at the back of the train watchin the tracks whizzin by *44*
large then small then gettin gobbled up in the dark. I'm thinkin about this
tricky toy I saw in the store. A clown that somersaults on a bar then does
chin-ups just cause you yank lightly at his leg. Cost $35. I could see me
askin my mother for a $35 birthday clown. "You wanna who that costs
what?" she'd say, cocking her head to the side to get a better view of the
hole in my head. Thirty-five dollars could buy new bunk beds for Junior
and Gretchen's boy. Thirty-five dollars and the whole household could go
visit Granddaddy Nelson in the country. Thirty-five dollars would pay for
the rent and the piano bill too. Who are these people that spend that much
for performing clowns and $1,000 for toy sailboats? What kinda work they
do and how they live and how come we ain't in on it? Where we are is who
we are, Miss Moore always pointin out. But it don't necessarily have to be
that way, she always adds then waits for somebody to say that poor people
have to wake up and demand their share of the pie and don't none of us
know what kind of pie she talkin about in the first damn place. But she ain't
so smart cause I still got her four dollars from the taxi and she sure ain't
gettin it. Messin up my day with this shit. Sugar nudges me in my pocket
and winks.

Miss Moore lines us up in front of the mailbox where we started from, *45*
seem like years ago, and I got a headache for thinkin so hard. And we lean
all over each other so we can hold up under the draggy-ass lecture she
always finishes us off with at the end before we thank her for borin us to
tears. But she just looks at us like she readin tea leaves. Finally she say,
"Well, what did you think of F. A. O. Schwarz?"

Rosie Giraffe mumbles, "White folks crazy." *46*

"I'd like to go there again when I get my birthday money," says Mer- *47*
cedes, and we shove her out the pack so she has to lean on the mailbox by
herself.

"I'd like a shower. Tiring day," say Flyboy. *48*

Then Sugar surprises me by sayin, "You know, Miss Moore, I don't *49*
think all of us here put together eat in a year what that sailboat costs." And
Miss Moore lights up like somebody goosed her. "And?" she say, urging
Sugar on. Only I'm standin on her foot so she don't continue.

. . . continued The Lesson, **Toni Cade Bambara**

"Imagine for a minute what kind of society it is in which some people 50
can spend on a toy what it would cost to feed a family of six or seven. What
do you think?"

"I think," say Sugar pushing me off her feet like she never done before, 51
cause I whip her ass in a minute, "that this is not much of a democracy if
you ask me. Equal chance to pursue happiness means an equal crack at the
dough, don't it?" Miss Moore is besides herself and I am disgusted with
Sugar's treachery. So I stand on her foot one more time to see if she'll shove
me. She shuts up, and Miss Moore looks at me, sorrowfully I'm thinkin.
And somethin weird is goin on, I can feel it in my chest.

"Anybody else learn anything today?" lookin dead at me. I walk away 52
and Sugar has to run to catch up and don't even seem to notice when I
shrug her arm off my shoulder.

"Well, we got four dollars anyway," she says.   53

"Uh hunh."   54

"We could go to Hascombs and get half a chocolate layer and then go 55
to the Sunset and still have plenty money for potato chips and ice cream
sodas."

"Uh hunh."   56

"Race you to Hascombs," she say.   57

We start down the block and she gets ahead which is O.K. by me cause 58
I'm going to the West End and then over to the Drive to think this day
through. She can run if she want to and even run faster. But ain't nobody
gonna beat me at nuthin.

■ ■ ■

Questions for Writing and Discussion

1. Describe one incident when a parent, friend, or family member tried to get
    you to do something that you didn't want to do. How did you react? How
    was your behavior similar to or different from the reaction of Sylvia, the
    narrator in "The Lesson"?

2. Reread the opening sentence of the story. What does the first half of that
    sentence reveal about the character of the narrator? Does the rest of the story
    confirm that initial impression? Explain.

3. Locate at least one sentence or passage describing the reactions of each of
    the following children to the merchandise at F. A. O. Schwarz: Sylvia (the

narrator), Sugar, Flyboy, Mercedes, Big Butt, Junebug, Rosie Giraffe, and Q.T. How do their reactions to the toys and their prices affect the narrator? Why does Bambara include all of these children in the story rather than tell it using just Miss Moore, Sylvia, and Sugar?

4. Miss Moore is the "teacher" for this "lesson," but what kind of teacher is she, and how do her students react to her? What strategies does she use to help the children learn? Are her methods effective? How do the children react to each other's learning? Does Miss Moore make some mistakes?

5. What evidence (cite specific sentences) suggests that Sylvia is learning more from this lesson than she wants to? What exactly is she learning? Describe what she might do in the future as a result of what she learns.

6. Explain how each of the following quotations from Sylvia's thoughts relates to the theme or main idea of "The Lesson":

   White folks crazy.
   I mean, damn, I have never ever been shy about doing nothing or going nowhere.
   If you gonna mess up a perfectly good swim day least you could do is have some answers.
   But ain't nobody gonna beat me at nuthin.

7. Write two paragraphs comparing and contrasting the "awakenings" of Mrs. Mallard in "The Story of an Hour" and Sylvia in "The Lesson." What—and how—does each character learn? How do they react to what they learn? What do we, as readers, learn?

TECHNIQUES   PURPOSES   SHORT FICTION   **POETRY**   PROCESS

Responding to Poetry

Poems often have characters, setting, and point of view, but they also have other features that are important to reading imaginatively and critically. Use the following literary terms to help focus your reading and response to poems.

VOICE AND TONE.   The speaker in a poem is not necessarily the same as the author of the poem. When Robert Frost says in "The Road Not Taken," "Two roads diverged in a yellow wood, /And sorry I could not travel both," the "I" in the poem is not directly equivalent to Robert Frost. The "I" represents a speaker faced with this particular choice. *Tone,* the speaker's attitude toward the subject matter, is also important in the poem. A speaker's tone might be happy or sad, delighted or angry, serious or humorous, spontaneous or reflective, straightforward or ironic. In Frost's poem, the speaker's tone is serious and reflective when he says, in conclusion, "I took the one less traveled by, / And that has made all the difference." In Auden's poem, the speaker is a person explaining or interpreting a painting. Phrases such as "how well they understood its human position" or "In Brueghel's Icarus, for instance" reveal the speaker as knowledgeable and perhaps slightly academic. The speaker's tone is serious and reflective: he is praising the virtues of a painting by one of the Old Masters.

Word Choice.   In poetry, diction and word choice are especially important. A poet might use academic language and formal phrasing or might use street language or slang. A poet might use short, emphatic words, or longer, more flowing language. Sometimes a poem juxtaposes formal and informal language. Auden deliberately contrasts a more formal diction ("About suffering they were never wrong, / The Old Masters") with more informal and colloquial (spoken) language ("Anyhow in a corner, some untidy spot / Where the dogs go on with their doggy life and the torturer's horse / Scratches its innocent behind on a tree").

Figures of Speech: Similes, Metaphors, Symbols, Personification. Figures of speech enable poets to compress experience, to add emotional impact, or to make an experience vivid, dramatic, or memorable. *Simile* is a comparison using *like* or *as:* "My love is like a red, red rose." A *metaphor* creates a direct equivalency without using *like* or *as:* "My love is a red, red rose." William Blake uses metaphor when he writes, "Tyger! Tyger! burning bright / In the forests of the night." The tiger is not literally a burning fire, but the colors of his coat and his potentially violent spirit are directly compared to a fire. A word becomes a *symbol* when it represents something larger or more abstract than its literal meaning. The tiger in Blake's poem becomes a symbol because it represents something larger than itself: the potential for violence and perhaps natural evil in the world. Similarly, readers might argue that Auden uses Icarus to symbolize human suffering in the world. Finally, in *personification,* an abstraction or an inanimate object is given human qualities. Death, in Emily Dickinson's poem, is personified: like the driver of a carriage, it stops to pick up the speaker and carry her on toward eternity.

Sound, Rhyme, and Rhythm.   Poets often use repetitions of sounds, of rhyming words, and of patterns of stressed (long) and unstressed (short) syllables. Emily Dickinson's poem, "Because I could not stop for death" uses an *iambic* pattern (one short syllable followed by one long syllable) to create a regular rhythm: "Because I could not stop for death— / He kindly stopped for me." Every second and fourth lines end with a rhyming word. William Blake rhymes the first and second lines and uses the *trochaic* pattern (one long syllable followed by one short syllable): "Tyger! Tyger! burning bright / In the forests of the night." In contrast, W. H. Auden uses an open form, without a set rhythm of rhyme. Poets also use patterns or combinations of sounds to reflect the meaning of the poem. *Alliteration* is the repetition of consonant sounds, and *assonance* is the repetition of vowel sounds. "Tyger! Tyger! burning bright" uses the alliteration of the t's and g's in "Tyger! Tyger!" and the repeated b's and r's in "burning bright" to give emphasis and power to the lines. In e. e. cummings's poem, "anyone lived in a pretty how town," cummings repeats the /o/ sound in several successive words to give a smooth, easy flow to the language.

PROFESSIONAL WRITING

Five Contemporary Poems

Aurora Levins Morales

Born in Puerto Rico in 1954 to a Jewish father and a Puerto Rican mother, Aurora Levins Morales moved with her family to the United States in 1967. She has published a collection of short stories and collaboratively written with her mother, Rosario Morales, a book containing short stories, essays, and poetry, Getting Home Alive *(1986). She currently lives near San Francisco.*

Child of the Americas

I am a child of the Americas,
a light-skinned mestiza of the Caribbean,
a child of many diaspora,[1] born into this continent at a crossroads.

I am a U.S. Puerto Rican Jew   5
a product of the ghettos of New York I have never known.
An immigrant and the daughter and granddaughter of
   immigrants.
I speak English with passion: it's the tongue of my
   consciousness,
a flashing knife blade of crystal, my tool, my craft.

I am Caribeña,[2] island grown. Spanish is in my flesh,   10
ripples from my tongue, lodges in my hips:
the language of garlic and mangoes,
the singing in my poetry, the flying gestures of my hands.

I am of Latinoamerica, rooted in the history of my continent:
I speak from that body.

...continued Child of the Americas, **Aurora Levins Morales**

I am not african. Africa is in me, but I cannot return.   15

I am not taína.[3] Taíno is in me, but there is no way back.

I am not european. Europe lives in me, but I have no home there.

I am new. History made me. My first language was spanglish.[4]

I was born at the crossroads

and I am whole.   20

---

[1] **diaspora** "a scattering," referring to the dispersion of Jews from Israel.
[2] **Caribeña** Carribean woman
[3] **taína** a native Indian tribe in Puerto Rico
[4] **spanglish** a mixture of Spanish and English

Gary Soto

Gary Soto was born in Fresno, California, in 1952. Soto is the author of many books of fiction and poetry, including Black Hair *(1985),* Who Will Know Us? *(1990), and* Canto Familiar/Familiar Song *(1994). He currently lives in northern California.*

Black Hair

At eight I was brilliant with my body.

In July, that ring of heat

We all jumped through, I sat in the bleachers

Of Romain Playground, in the lengthening

Shade that rose from our dirty feet.   5

The game before us was more than baseball.

It was a figure—Hector Moreno

Quick and hard with turned muscles,

His crouch the one I assumed before an altar

Of worn baseball cards, in my room.   10

I came here because I was Mexican, a stick

Of brown light in love with those

Who could do it—the triple and hard slide,

The gloves eating balls into double plays.

What could I do with 50 pounds, my shyness,   15

My black torch of hair, about to go out?

Father was dead, his face no longer

Hanging over the table or our sleep,

And mother was the terror of mouths

Twisting hurt by butter knives.   *20*
In the bleachers I was brilliant with my body,
Waving players in and stomping my feet,
Growing sweaty in the presence of white shirts.
I chewed sunflower seeds. I drank water   *25*
And bit my arm through the late innings.
When Hector lined balls into deep
Center, in my mind I rounded the bases
With him, my face flared, my hair lifting
Beautifully, because we were coming home
To the arms of brown people.

Joy Harjo

A prolific writer of poems and songs, Joy Harjo was born in Tulsa, Oklahoma, in 1951. Her books of poetry include She Had Some Horses *(1983),* The Woman Who Fell From the Sky *(1994), and* How We Became Human: New and Selected Poems *(2002). She has received the Josephine Miles poetry award and the American Indian Distinguished Achievement in the Arts award. She has lived in Colorado, California, and Hawaii.*

Perhaps the World Ends Here

The world begins at a kitchen table. No matter what, we must eat to live.

The gifts of earth are brought and prepared, set on the table. So it has been since creation, and it will go on.

We chase chickens or dogs away from it. Babies teethe   *5*
at the corners. They scrape their knees under it.

It is here that children are given instructions on what it means to be human. We make men at it, we make women.

At this table we gossip, recall enemies and the ghosts   *10*
of lovers.

Our dreams drink coffee with us as they put their arms around our children. They laugh with us at our poor falling-down selves and as we put ourselves back together once again at the table.   *15*

...*continued* Perhaps the World Ends Here, **Joy Harjo**

This table has been a house in the rain, an umbrella
in the sun.

Wars have begun and ended at this table. It is a place
to hide in the shadow of terror. A place to celebrate
the terrible victory.   *20*

We have given birth on this table, and have prepared
our parents for burial here.

At this table we sing with joy, with sorrow.
We pray of suffering and remorse.
We give thanks.   *25*

Perhaps the world will end at the kitchen table,
while we are laughing and crying,
eating of the last sweet bite.

Wislawa Szymborska

Wislawa Szymborska was born in Poland in 1923. She is the author of many books of poetry, including two that are translated into English: Sounds, Feelings, Thoughts: Seventy Poems by Wislawa Szymborska *(1981) and* View with a Grain of Sand: Selected Poems *(1995). She won the Nobel Prize in Literature in 1996. She currently lives in Cracow.*

End and Beginning Translated by Joseph Brodsky

After each war
somebody has to clear up
put things in order
by itself it won't happen.

Somebody's got to push   *5*
rubble to the highway shoulder
making way
for the carts filled up with corpses.

Someone might trudge
through muck and ashes,   *10*
sofa springs,
splintered glass
and blood-soaked rugs.

Somebody has to haul
beams for propping a wall,   15
another put glass in a window
and hang the door on hinges.

This is not photogenic
and takes years.
All the cameras have left already   20
for another war.

Bridges are needed
also new railroad stations.
Tatters turn into sleeves
for rolling up.   25

Somebody, broom in hand,
still recalls how it was,
Someone whose head was not
torn away listens nodding.
But nearby already   30
begin to bustle those
who'll need persuasion.

Somebody still at times
digs up from under the bushes
some rusty quibble   35
to add it to burning refuse.

Those who knew
what this was all about
must yield to those
who know little   40
or less than little
essentially nothing.

In the grass that has covered
effects in causes
somebody must recline,   45
a stalk of rye in the teeth,
ogling the clouds.

. . . continued

Yusef Komunyakaa

Born in 1947 in Bogalusa, Louisiana, Yusef Komunyakaa served in Vietnam before returning to earn degrees at the University of Colorado, Colorado State University, and the University of California, Irvine. He has published many books of poetry, including Thieves of Paradise *(1998),* Pleasure Dome: New & Collected Poems, 1975–1999 *(2001), and* Dien Cai Dau *(1988), in which the poem "Facing It" appears. The photograph of the Vietnam Veterans Memorial was selected to appear with this poem. After you read the poem, consider how effectively this photograph illustrates the themes and images in the poem.*

Facing It

My black face fades,
hiding inside the black granite.
I said I wouldn't,
dammit: No tears.
I'm stone. I'm flesh.   5
My clouded reflection eyes me
like a bird of prey, the profile of night
slanted against morning. I turn
this way—the stone lets me go.
I turn that way—I'm inside   10
the Vietnam Veterans Memorial
again, depending on the light
to make a difference.
I go down the 58,022 names,
half-expecting to find   15
my own in letters like smoke.
I touch the name Andrew Johnson;
I see the booby trap's white flash.
Names shimmer on a woman's blouse
but when she walks away   20
the names stay on the wall.
Brushstrokes flash, a red bird's
wings cutting across my stare.
The sky. A plane in the sky.
A white vet's image floats   25

closer to me, then his pale eyes
look through mine. I'm a window.
He's lost his right arm
inside the stone. In the black mirror
a woman's trying to erase names: *30*
No, she's brushing a boy's hair.

Paul Merideth, photographer
USA, Washington DC, man touching Vietnam Veterans Memorial.

QUESTIONS FOR WRITING AND DISCUSSION

1. In "Child of the Americas," Aurora Levins Morales compares the mixture of
   languages and cultures within her to geographical mixtures and crossroads.
   Find several places in the poem where Levins Morales makes this comparison. What kinds of figurative language does she use (simile, metaphor, or
   image)? Explain how these images help construct one of Levins Morales's
   themes in the poem.

2. In Greek mythology, Hector was a great Trojan warrior. Hector was killed by
   Achilles in the Trojan War, but his death was avenged by his brother, Paris.
   In "Black Hair," how does Gary Soto use the legend of Hector? Which lines
   suggest references to Hector, and how do these references relate to a theme in
   the poem?

3. Although Joy Harjo titles her poem, "Perhaps the World Ends Here," the poem is about both beginnings and endings. What images or examples of figurative language illustrate the beginnings, and which refer to endings? In your own words, explain how Harjo does or does not resolve the conflicts between beginnings and endings.

4. Wislawa Szymborska's poem, "End and Beginning," echoes Harjo's theme of beginnings and endings in a poem about the aftermath of war. The end of war, Szymborska says, "is not photogenic / and takes years. / All the cameras have left already / for another war." What images in the poem suggest the hard, dirty, and thankless work required to rebuild a civilization? How do these images fit into Szymborska's overall theme in the poem?

5. In "Facing It," Yusef Komunyakaa contrasts the realities outside the memorial wall with the reflections and images inside the wall. What does Komunyakaa describe that is outside the wall? What does he see in the wall or in the reflections of the wall? What do you think Komunyakaa means when he says of a white vet, "He's lost his right arm / inside the stone"? Explain how these images or reality and reflection help explain a major theme of the poem.

6. Do a comparison and contrast of two of the poems in this chapter. Your purpose is to compare lines, images, figures of speech, and themes in order to show how one poem relates to the other. How do the similarities and differences enhance your reading of one or both of the poems? Possibilities for comparison include the poems by Aurora Levins Morales and Gary Soto, by Harjo and Szymborska, and by Szymborska and Komunyakaa.

TECHNIQUES   PURPOSES   SHORT FICTION   POETRY   **PROCESS**

Responding to Literature: The Writing Process

ASSIGNMENT FOR RESPONDING TO LITERATURE

Choose one of the poems or short stories from this chapter (or a work of literature assigned in your class), reread and annotate the work, and share your responses with others in the class. Then write an interpretative essay. Assume that you are writing for other members of your class (including your instructor) who have read the work but who may not understand or agree with your interpretation.

COLLECTING	SHAPING	DRAFTING	REVISING

COLLECTING

In addition to reading, rereading, annotating, and sharing your responses, try the following collecting strategies. Illustrations below are based on an interpretive essay about "The Story of an Hour."

- **Collaborative annotation.** In small groups, choose a work of literature or select a passage that you have already annotated. In the group, read each other's annotations. Then discuss each annotation. Which annotations does your group agree are the best? Have a group recorder record the best annotations.

- **Elements of poetry analysis.** Reread the paragraphs earlier in the chapter on voice and tone, word choice, figures of speech, and sound, rhyme, and rhythm. Focus on the elements that seem most important for the poem you have selected. After you have finished annotating, freewrite a paragraph explaining how these elements work together to create the theme or overall effect of the poem.

- **Elements of fiction analysis.** Reread the paragraphs defining *character, plot, point of view, setting*, and *style*. Choose three of these elements that seem most important in the story that you are reading. Reread the story, annotating for these three elements. Then freewrite a paragraph explaining how these three elements are interrelated or how they explain the theme.

- **Time line.** In your journal, draw a time line for the story. List above the line everything that happens in the story. Below the line, indicate where the story opens, when the major conflicts occur, and where the climax and the denouement occur. For "The Story of an Hour," student writer Karen Ehrhardt drew the following time line.

TIME LINE FOR "THE STORY OF AN HOUR"

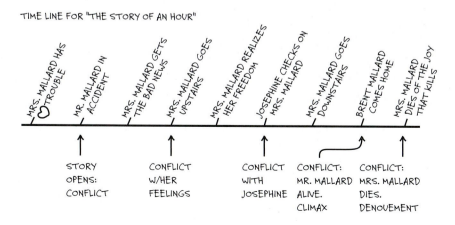

- **Feature list.** Choose a character trait, repeated image, or idea that you wish to investigate in the poem or story. List, in order of appearance, every word, image, or reference that you find.

- **Scene vision or revision.** Write a scene for this story in which you change some part of it. You may *add* a scene to the beginning, middle, or end of the story. You may *change* a scene in the story. You may write a scene in the story from a different character's point of view. You may change the style of the story for your scene. How, for example, might Eudora Welty have described the opening scene of "The Story of an Hour"?

- **Draw a picture.** For your poem or short story, draw a picture based on images, characters, conflicts, or themes in the work of literature. Student writer Lori Van Sike drew the following picture for "The Story of an Hour" that shows how the rising and falling action of the plot parallels Mrs. Mallard's ascent and descent of the stairs.

- **Character conflict map.** Start with a full page of paper. Draw a main character in the center of the page. Locate the other major characters, internal forces, and external forces (including social, economic, and environmental pressures) in a circle around the main character. Draw a line between each of these peripheral characters or forces and the main character. For his character conflict map for "The Story of an Hour," student writer Darren Marshall used images from his computer program to surround his picture of Mrs. Mallard.

"The Story of an Hour"

Story Picture: The Rising/Falling Action

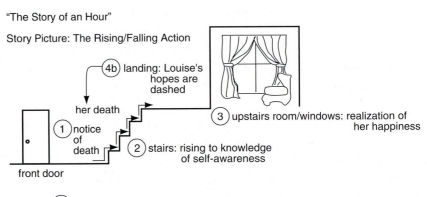

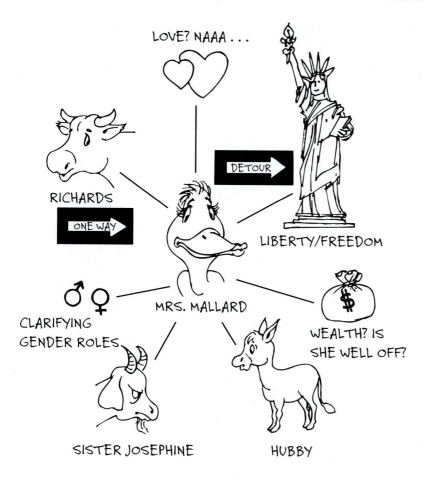

- **Background investigation.** Investigate the biographical, social, or historical context of the poem or story. Go online or to your library databases to find biographical information or other stories or poems by the same author. How does this background information increase your understanding or appreciation of the poem or story?

- **Reconsideration of purposes.** What idea, theme, or approach most interests you? Will you be explaining, evaluating, problem solving, or arguing? Are you combining purposes? Do these purposes suggest what kinds of information you might collect?

COLLECTING	SHAPING	DRAFTING	REVISING

SHAPING

Test each of the following possible shapes against your ideas for your essay. Use or adapt the shape or shapes that are most appropriate for your own interpretation.

▪ **EXPLAINING RELATIONSHIPS**   Interpretative essays often analyze how the parts of a poem or story relate to the whole. As you explain these relationships, you should show how key images, lines, or scenes contribute to the overall theme or idea of the poem or story.

Introduction and thesis:	The details and images in the work reveal that the theme is X.
First scene, stanza, or group of lines:	How details and images establish the theme.
Second scene or group of lines:	How details and images relate to or build on previous images and contribute to the theme.
Third scene or group of lines:	How details and images continue building the theme.
Conclusion:	How the author highlights the key images or themes.

▪ **EVALUATING**   If your response suggests an evaluating purpose, you may wish to set up criteria for an effective poem or short story and then provide evidence showing how this poem or story does or does not measure up to your standards. Using criteria for a story, your essay might use the following outline.

Introduction and thesis:	Story X is highly dramatic.
Criterion 1:	A dramatic short story should focus on a character who changes his or her behavior or beliefs. Judgment and evidence for Criterion 1.
Criterion 2:	A dramatic story must have striking conflicts that lead to a crisis or a predicament. Judgment and evidence for Criterion 2.
Criterion 3:	A dramatic story should have a theme that makes a controversial point. Judgment and evidence for Criterion 3.
Conclusion:	Reinforces thesis.

▌**ARGUING**   During class discussion, you may disagree with another person's response. Your thesis may then take the form, "Although some readers believe this poem or story is about X, the poem or story can also be about Y."

Introduction and thesis:	Although some readers suggest the poem or story is about X, it is really about Y.
Body paragraphs:	State the opposing interpretation and give evidence for that interpretation. Then state your interpretation and give evidence (images, characters, events, points of conflict) supporting your interpretation.
Conclusion:	Clarify and reinforce thesis.

▌**INVESTIGATING CHANGES IN INTERPRETATION**   Often, readers *change* interpretations during the course of responding to a piece of literature. Thus, your main point might be, "Although I initially believed X about the poem or story, I gradually realized the theme of the poem or story is Y." If that sentence expresses your main idea, you may wish to organize your essay following the chronology or the steps in the changes in your interpretation.

Introduction and thesis:	Although I initially thought X, I now believe Y.
Body paragraphs:	First step (your original interpretation of the story or poem and supporting evidence).
	Second step (additional or contradictory ideas and evidence that forced you to reconsider your interpretation).
	Third step (your final interpretation and supporting evidence).
Conclusion:	Show how steps lead to thesis.

Note: One strategy you should not use is to simply retell the key parts of a poem or the plot of the story. Your audience has already read the poem or story. They want you to state your interpretation and then use details to show how and why your interpretation is credible. Although you will cite key characters, images, or events in the poem or story, you must explain how or why each of these details support your interpretation.

DRAFTING

To prepare to draft your essay, read through your annotations and gather your collecting and shaping notes. Some writers prefer to write one-sentence statements of their main ideas at the top of the page to keep them focused as they write. Other writers prefer to make rough outlines to follow, based on their adaptations of one of the preceding shaping strategies. When you begin drafting, you may wish to skip your introduction and start with the body of your essay. You can fill in the introduction after you have written a draft.

Once you start writing, keep your momentum going. If you draw a blank, reread what you have already written or look at your notes. If you cannot think of a particular word or are unsure about a spelling, draw a line _____ and keep on writing.

REVISING

Use the following guidelines as you read your classmates' drafts and revise your own essay. Be prepared to make changes in your ideas, organization, and evidence, as well as to fix problems in sentences and word choice.

GUIDELINES FOR REVISIONS

- **Clarify your main idea or interpretation.** Ask your readers to write, in one sentence, the main point of your interpretation. If their statements do not exactly match your main point, clarify your thesis. Your interpretation (not a statement of fact) should be clearly stated early in your essay.

- **Do not just summarize the poem or story.** Your readers have read the story or poem. Start with your interpretation; cite key images, metaphors, or lines that support your interpretation; and then explain why these images or key words are important.

- **Support each part of your interpretation with references to specific passages from the text.** Do not be satisfied with one piece of evidence. Find as many bits of evidence as possible. The case for your interpretation grows stronger with each additional piece of evidence.

- **Explain how each piece of evidence supports your interpretation.** Do not just cite several pieces of evidence and go on to your next point. Explain for your readers *how* the evidence supports your interpretation.

- **Define key terms in your essay.** If you are writing about the hero in a story, define what you mean by *hero* or *heroine*. If you are arguing that "The Story of an Hour" has a *feminist* theme, define *feminism*.

- **Signal the major parts of your interpretation.** Let your readers know when you shift to a new point. Use transitions and paragraph hooks at the beginning of body paragraphs.

- **Use the present tense as you describe the events in the story.** If you are describing the end of "The Story of an Hour," write, for example, "Mrs. Mallard descends the stairs and learns the 'good news' about her husband."

- **Quote accurately and cite page numbers for each reference.** Double-check your quotations to make sure they are accurate, word-for-word transcriptions. Following each direct quotation, cite page references as follows:

  In the first sentence, Kate Chopin says, "Mrs. Mallard was afflicted with a heart trouble" (479).

  In "Child of the Americas," the author states the central idea of the poem when she says, "I am of Latinoamerica, rooted in the history of my continent" (line 13).

  Note: The period goes outside the parentheses. See Chapter 12 for correct documentation style.

- **Revise your essay for sentence clarity and conciseness.** Read your essay aloud or have a classmate read it. Reduce unnecessary repetition. Use active verbs. Rework awkward or confusing sentences.

- **Edit your essay.** Check your essay for correct spelling, word choice, punctuation, and grammar.

POSTSCRIPT ON THE WRITING PROCESS

Before you turn in your essay, answer the following questions in your journal.

1. Explain what part of this essay (collecting ideas and evidence, focusing on your interpretation, shaping your essay, drafting, or revising) was most difficult for you. How did you work around the problems?

2. What do you like best about your essay? Refer to specific places in the essay (lead-in, thesis, pieces of evidence, ideas, conclusion). Which specific paragraphs do you like best? Why?

Continued

3. What did you learn about the story by writing your interpretation? What do you realize now that you did not understand when you first read the story?

4. If you had two more hours to work on this essay, what would you change? Why?

STUDENT WRITING

JULIA MACMILLAN AND BRETT MACFADDEN

A Worn Path

Julia MacMillan and Brett MacFadden collaboratively wrote their essay on the Phoenix imagery in Eudora Welty's "A Worn Path." They drafted their own essays separately and then collaborated on a revision that shared their interpretations and their best textual evidence. The following are their original separate notes and drafts, their plans for their collaborative revision, and their final revised interpretation. Read their separate versions first, and then see how they collaborated to produce their revised essay.

ROUGH DRAFTS

JULIA MACMILLAN

The journey that Phoenix Jackson makes in Eudora Welty's "A Worn Path" is very similar to that made by the mythological phoenix on its way to rebirth. Much of the symbolism and figurative language throughout the story shows the succession of events that parallel a Phoenix-like ending to the old woman.

We can feel, almost from the beginning, that Phoenix's long life is coming to an end. She is described with "the two knots of her cheeks illuminated by a yellow burning under the dark" (289). In only a few more sentences, however, we hear the mourning dove, apparently mourning for Phoenix. The yellow burning under the dark is almost a desperate, final fiery burst in the face of oncoming death.

Her death is also foreshadowed in the mention of a buzzard, watching her from the tall, dead trees. She asks of him, "Who you watching?" as if she knows it is herself. Further in her journey, upon meeting the white hunter, her impending death as well as her expectation of it are shown. The little bob-white, "its beak hooked bitterly to show it was dead" (262), that the hunter is carrying on his bag quite forcefully shows us her death. The fact that she does not fear but expects this death is shown when the hunter points his gun at Phoenix, and she "stood straight and faced him" quite fearlessly (263). In not fearing this death and seeming to understand its nearness, Phoenix Jackson becomes more like the bird she is named for.

It is most clearly seen that the author intended her reader to see the Phoenix imagery when the grandson is introduced near the end of the story. On page 264, she "entered a door, and there she saw the document that had been stamped with the gold seal and framed in the gold frame, which matched the dream that was hung up in her head." The gold in this passage seems to represent flame—the flame of her funeral pyre and the dream in her head of perpetuation and reincarnation through her grandson's life. It is even more clearly stated when, once in the doctor's office, she goes into a strange trance, becoming unable to answer the agitated nurse's questions. When finally asked, "He isn't dead, is he?," "a flicker and then a flame of comprehension" come across her face (265). These flames are symbolic of her death, yet they are caused by her remembering the importance of her grandson's life to her. This life is most precious to her, because it is through her grandson that Phoenix, like the mythological bird, will live again.

BRETT MACFADDEN

In many ways Phoenix Jackson is like the mythical bird she is named after; her physical characteristics, her purpose in life, and her extreme age and nearness to death all support her likeness to the mythological phoenix.

The phoenix is a bird of myth that lives for five hundred years and then burns itself to death, rising from its ashes renewed and beautiful. Phoenix Jackson in the story "A Worn Path" by Eudora Welty is a very old black woman near the end of her life cycle who takes a long walk through the woods to town in order to get medicine for her ailing grandson. The core story is very simple, and it is because of this simplicity that the reader is forced to look beyond the core for a more complex tale. One of the first clues to the inner story is the name of the main character, Phoenix. With the knowledge of what a Phoenix is, we can find many clues supporting the idea of the old woman living her life as a Phoenix.

Throughout the short story, words and phrases that describe the old woman might also describe the mythological bird. Her skin is black with a "golden color underneath" (259) and the "two knobs of her cheeks were illuminated by a yellow burning under the dark" (259). Both the golden color and especially the yellow burning are colors of fire, symbolizing the bird's fiery death. A red rag that she wears on top of her head is also another color of flame. Her black, wrinkled skin can be thought of as looking quite like ashes, and assuming that her grandson is a blood relative, his skin should also be the color of charred ash. She is like a fire that is almost out. It is mostly black, but there is the small flicker of flame to show you it is not yet extinguished.

Assuming the reader chooses to believe that Phoenix does in fact have a grandson and he is in fact sick, then the main purpose of her trip is to get the boy his medicine. This idea goes along nicely with the phoenix theme because she is giving everything she has left for the benefit of her grandson. She is essentially burning herself up so that the new person can exist. We can assume from the physical appearance and actions of Phoenix that she is pretty nearly burnt out. Phoenix knows her grandson is the one with the potential now, and so she gives all the effort she has to get him his medicine. Her only wish is to see him rise from his sick bed.

There are many hints of Phoenix's extreme age. At one time she tells herself, "I is the oldest person I ever know" (261), indicating that she has lived longer than most. Another time the hunter that she comes across estimates that she is "a hundred years old" (263). Much of the imagery in the story symbolizes her oncoming death. The fact that it is winter can be seen as the winter of her life. Other death images include the big dead trees, the buzzard, the scarecrow she mistakes for a ghost, and the black dog that knocks her into the ditch.

REVISED DRAFT
A Singular Perpetuation

BRETT MACFADDEN AND JULIA MACMILLAN

Phoenix Jackson, in the story "A Worn Path," by Eudora Welty, is in many ways like the mythological bird she is named after. Her purpose in life, bird-like characteristics, and nearness to death all support a clear parallel between the character and her namesake. The story is very simple, and because of this simplicity the reader is forced to search for a more meaningful tale. One of the first clues to the inner story is the name of the main character, Phoenix. With the knowledge of what a phoenix is, it is possible to find many clues supporting the idea of the old woman living her life as a phoenix, burning herself out for the benefit of the new bird, her grandson.

The phoenix is a mythological bird who, after living for five hundred years, burns itself to ashes on a pyre and rises renewed to live another cycle. Phoenix Jackson journeys through the woods to town to get medicine for her ailing grandson. This idea parallels the phoenix theme, because she is making what appears to be her final journey, in order that her grandson may rise from his sickbed. The legend of the phoenix is one of singular perpetuation; only one exists in the world. This is shown when she tells the nurses that "We is the only two left in the world" (Welty 265). Phoenix is concerned because if both of them were to die, then it would result in the extinction of the species. As much as she worries about him surviving, she is confident that he, like the immortal bird, will survive. Speaking to the nurses again, she says, "He suffer and it don't seem to put him back at all. . . . He going to last" (265–66). As well as his immortality, his birdlike characteristics and dependence on Phoenix for his perseverance are shown when he peeps out of his quilt "holding his mouth open like a little bird" (266). He is her reincarnation, and she is devoted to his successful ascension.

Throughout the story many words and phrases that describe the old *3* woman might also describe the mythological bird. Her skin is described as black with "a golden color underneath," and the "two knobs of her cheeks were illuminated by a yellow burning under the dark" (259). She wears on top of her head a red rag. Both the "golden color" and the "yellow burning," as well as the red of her rag, are colors of fire, symbolizing her approaching death. As she walks, the tapping of her umbrella sounds like "the chirping of a solitary little bird" (259). Her likeness to a bird is evidenced when, in passing a scarecrow in a field, she is frightened, as a bird would be. When startled by a dog, she falls into a ditch "like a little puff of milk-weed" (262). This gives the appearance that she is a light creature, mostly flame and feather. These birdlike characteristics of Phoenix seem to imply that the author intended her to represent the mythical bird.

The myth of the phoenix holds that when "its eyes begin to grow *4* dim, it knows that the time of death has come" (Oswalt 239). When we are first introduced to the main character, as well as being old, she is described as having "eyes . . . blue with age" (259). Many images of death, some quite vivid, link Phoenix Jackson's impending death to that of the phoenix of myth. At one point in her journey she stoops and looks upward, exclaiming, "Sun so high! Time getting all gone here" (260). This clearly indicates her knowledge of her approaching death. Her death is also foreshadowed by the mention of several images that bombard us from the dawn of the story. Early on she reflects on the call of a mourning dove—mourning being something done in the wake of death. Later she comes upon a buzzard sitting in a dead tree. She asks of him, "Who

. . . continued A Worn Path, **Julia MacMillan and Brett MacFadden**

you watching?" (261), as if she knows it is herself. Her death is foreshadowed further when walking through a cornfield she happens upon what she perceives to be a ghost. Upon closer inspection, the ghost turns out to be a scarecrow. However, she shows no fear approaching what she thinks is a ghost, which demonstrates that she is comfortable with dying. The black dog that knocks her into a ditch is another vivid image of death. Further in her journey, upon meeting a white hunter, her impending death as well as her expectation of it are shown. The little bob-white, "its beak hooked bitterly to show that it was dead" (262), that the hunter is carrying in his bag quite forcefully shows us her anticipated death. The fact that she does not fear but expects this death is shown when the hunter points his gun at Phoenix, and she "stood straight and faced him" quite fearlessly (263). In not fearing this death and seeming to understand its nearness, Phoenix Jackson becomes more like the bird she is named for.

A carefully wrought story, "A Worn Path" is more than a tale of an   5 old woman's formidable journey. It is the rebirth of an age-old myth wrapped in the cloak of conventionality. In examining some of the symbols, allusions, and the underlying legend, we find a well-hidden but evident parallel between the lives of the main character and her namesake, the phoenix.

Works Cited

Oswalt, Sabine G. "Phoenix." *Concise Encyclopedia of Greek and Roman Mythology.* Chicago: Follett, 1969.

Welty, Eudora. "A Worn Path." *The Collected Stories of Eudora Welty.* New York: Harcourt, 1980. 258–66.

POSTSCRIPT ON THE COLLABORATIVE REVISION

We began this collaboration by reading each other's papers and rereading our own in order to find the strengths and weaknesses of each paper. Then together we combed through each paper, pulling out what we both agreed were our strongest points, and compiled these into a thesis. For our thesis, we used the second sentence in the first paragraph: "Her [Phoenix's] purpose in life, bird-like characteristics, and nearness to death all support a clear parallel between the character and her namesake."

Having decided on a thesis and a rough plan of action, we then went to the computer lab and began writing. At this point, the paper became more difficult because we had to narrow two papers into one and decide what we should omit. For example, Julia's paper discussed the emblem on the doctor's office wall as another symbol of Phoenix's fiery death. After discussing this scene, we decided that the symbolism was not strong enough and should be left out. We knew each other before deciding to write the collaborative essay, so we were both comfortable around each other and were able to say what we really thought about each other's writing. We knew also that our basic writing styles are opposing. Brett's is concise, and Julia's is more flowing. Our different writing styles had to be combined into one smooth style. We did this by having one person dictate and the other type, which caused an intertwining of our styles by the time the words hit the screen. We had fun working on this paper and learned quite a bit about collaboration in the process. For example, we found it challenging because we had to work on one sentence at a time, making sure each sentence was right before we went on to the next one. This process made the revision take far longer to complete than if it had been done by one person.

QUESTIONS FOR WRITING AND DISCUSSION

1. What are the best ideas or evidence in this essay? Explain the points at which you might disagree with the writers' interpretation.

2. Compare MacMillan's and MacFadden's drafts with the final version of their essay. Explain how their interpretation changed as they worked collaboratively on the final version. What did they add to their final version? What did they omit from the earlier drafts?

3. In the final version, MacMillan and MacFadden do not cite evidence from the final part of the story. Explain why the events in town support or do not support the Phoenix parallels.

4. Review the "Guidelines for Revisions." In the authors' essay, underline sentences that contain the *main idea*, that *define key terms*, that contain *evidence* or support, that *explain* how the evidence supports the thesis, that *signal* major parts of the interpretation, and that contain *accurate quotations*. Based on your annotations, what suggestions for further revision do you have for the authors?

STUDENT WRITING

PAT RUSSELL

Death: The Final Freedom

Following a class discussion of the feminist theme in Kate Chopin's "The Story of an Hour," Pat Russell wrote in his journal, "Is the story a feminist one? No. It is not just about feminism but about how people stifle their own needs and desires to accommodate those of their mate." In his essay, Russell argues that the traditional feminist reading limits the universal theme of the story. As you read his essay, see if you are persuaded by his argument.

The poor treatment of women and their struggle for an individual identity make up a major underlying theme of Kate Chopin's stories. Although many regard Chopin's "The Story of an Hour" as a feminist story, today a more universal interpretation is appropriate. This story is not about the oppression of a woman, but about how people strive to maintain the normality and security of their relationships by suppressing their own individual wants and needs.

Evidence in favor of the feminist argument begins with the period the story was written in, sometime around the turn of the century. Society prevented women from coming out of the household. Most women weren't allowed to run a business, and for that matter, they couldn't even vote. Their most important jobs were wife and mother. This background sets the tone for the main character's life. In the beginning we are told Mrs. Mallard has a "fair, calm face whose lines be-spoke repression" (Chopin 414). There is also evidence that suggests her husband is ignorant of her ideas and forceful with his own. Chopin writes: "There would be no powerful will bending her in that blind persistence with which men and women believe they have a right to impose a private will upon a fellow creature" (415). In addition, Mrs. Mallard is described early as fearful and powerless, and later as a triumphant "goddess of Victory," indicating her rebirth. These citations suggest that this is a feminist story, but this label limits the meaning behind the story.

Many people who are unhappy with their marriages either fail to recognize their unhappiness or refuse to accept responsibility for it. I feel sorry for those who don't recognize their unhappiness. However, it is pathetic to see someone such as Mrs. Mallard hold onto a relationship simply because she doesn't know how to let go. "And yet she had loved him—sometimes. Often she had not" (415). She continuously fell in and out of love with her husband until he "died," at which point she told herself that love didn't matter compared to the self-assertion "which she suddenly recognized as the strongest impulse of her being" (415). It is as if she has waited for all of her life for this moment; she prays for a long life, when only the day before she dreaded it. She weeps for him but at the same time compares her husband to a criminal, a man whom she has lived her life for, never once thinking of herself. But now "there would be no one to live for during those coming years; she would live for herself" (415). She is lucky in that she feels "free." Her emotional suppression is over, and she will no longer have anyone to blame for her unhappiness.

It is important not only to try to interpret the author's intended *4* meaning of the story, but also to think about what message "The Story of an Hour" has for us today. As a feminist story, the lesson "The Story of an Hour" teaches is one-dimensional. Interpreting it as a story about the struggle of all people opens up the possibility of teaching others that selfishness and selflessness are both good, when used in moderation. In Mrs. Mallard's case, correcting this balance becomes a matter of life and death. In the face of her suppressor, her desperation for freedom forces her to choose death.

Work Cited

Chopin, Kate. "The Story of an Hour." *The Awakening and Selected Stories.* New York: Penguin, 1984. 413–16.

QUESTIONS FOR WRITING AND DISCUSSION

1. With what parts of Russell's interpretation do you agree? What additional evidence from the story might Russell cite in support of his interpretation? What ideas or sentences might you challenge? What evidence from the story might refute those statements?

2. Write out your definition of *feminism*. Where does or should Russell explain his definition? How should Russell clarify his definition?

3. Write out Russell's main idea or thesis. Explain why his thesis is an interpretation and not just a statement of fact.

4. What shaping strategy does Russell use to organize his essay?

5. Write out two other possible titles for Russell's essay. Explain why your alternate titles are (or are not) better than Russell's title.

Franz Marc, a German expressionist painter, is noted for his vivid and colorful paintings of horses and deer. His works contain recognizable figures but also expressionist and cubist elements that invite the viewer to tease out the meaning of his works. In addition, Marc's life and untimely death during World War I suggest parallels between his personal experiences and the subjects and styles of his paintings. A journal exercise on page 665 suggests using the art of Franz Marc to practice using library databases and evaluating the accuracy, reliability, and usefulness of sources found there.

Writing a
Research Paper

13

While taking an art class, you become interested in the work of German artist Franz Marc and decide to examine how animals in his paintings help convey the central meaning of his work. You research key elements in the artist's life, his philosophy as a German expressionist, and his founding of Der Blaue Reiter (The Blue Rider). Focusing on *Deer in the Forest II,* you notice that Marc presents animals in harmony with their natural world, which seems threatened by external forces shattering this peaceful scene. Writing for other students who are interested in twentieth-century art, you argue that Marc condemns people's inhumanity as he anticipates the devastating effects of World War I. The fact that he was killed in action near Verdun, France, in World War I helps highlight, you believe, the antiwar message of Franz Marc's work.

After spending two months in France living with a family and trying to understand their dinner conversation, you wonder why you—and other Americans— know so little about foreign languages. After reflecting on your inadequate background in French language and culture, you decide to investigate the current state of foreign-language studies in the United States. During your research, you discover that Americans know very little about foreign languages and cultures simply because foreign languages are rarely required of students either in high school or in college. You decide to write a research paper that documents the current state of foreign-language studies and demonstrates a need for a mandatory foreign-language requirement for secondary schools. You hope that it will persuade more students to study foreign languages and encourage some schools to revise their requirements.

> " Research is formalized curiosity. It is poking and prying with a purpose. "
> —ZORA NEALE HURSTON, NOVELIST AND FOLKLORE RESEARCHER

> " You know when you think about writing a book, you think it is overwhelming. But, actually, you break it down into tiny little tasks any moron could do. "
> —ANNIE DILLARD, NATURALIST, AUTHOR *PILGRIM AT TINKER CREEK*

LTHOUGH STARTING A RESEARCH PROJECT SOUNDS DIFFICULT AND COMPLICATED, RESEARCH IS REALLY A NATURAL AND ENJOYABLE PART OF OUR EVERYDAY EXPERIENCE, BOTH OUTSIDE AND INSIDE COLLEGE CLASSROOMS. WE PRIDE OURSELVES ON BEING GOOD detectives—whether it's window-shopping for a good bargain, finding the best used car, asking coworkers for tips on the best new restaurant in town, or reading up on a new diet. Even in college classes, curiosity leads us to explore new topics. Whenever we wonder about how global warming is affecting our weather, what makes the Internet work, how artists turn clay into beautiful pottery, or how the psychological fight-or-flight mechanism works, the seed for a research idea is planted in our minds.

At some point, the idea becomes a research question that we want to pursue by reading a variety of sources or doing field research. A *research question* sets forth the topic or controversy that we want to explore. What meanings or messages are behind the animal paintings of Franz Marc? What ethical problems arise when we test people for genetically based diseases? Should students in high school have a foreign language requirement? The research question then serves as a guide to start the research process. As we read and research further, we may need to revise our research question based on what we learn about the subject.

Like any other kind of writing, research-based writing takes place in a rhetorical situation. As a writer, you may start with your own research question, or you may have an occasion (an assignment in class or on the job) to write with a specific audience and genre already designated. As always, your purpose, the intended audience, the genre, and the social or cultural context are key factors in helping you focus and shape your research project.

Writing a source-based essay requires four specific skills that this chapter explains. First, you need to learn how to *access ideas and information* in the library, on the Internet, and from field research. Most school libraries have orientation sessions to help you learn which databases are most appropriate for your project. Second, you need to learn to *critically evaluate* your sources. While many Internet Web sites are reliable, some are not. Even reputable, published sources often have a specific bias or point of view that affects the accuracy or reliability of the ideas and information. Third, you must learn to *smoothly integrate* your sources by introducing the author and source, citing the relevant information, and indicating how or why the source is relevant to your point. Finally, you must learn how to *document your sources* in the text and in a Works Cited page.

This chapter outlines the key steps in the process of writing a source-based paper—preparing, locating, and evaluating sources; taking notes; collecting and shaping information; revising; and documenting your sources. As in other writing assignments presented in this text, the process is recursive. Often, you need to stop and retrace your steps, revise your research question, collect new information, or revise parts of your paper during the writing process. At the end of this chapter, student writer Kate McNerny's paper, "Foreign Language Study: An American Necessity," illustrates the important features of a source-based paper. Interspersed in the chapter, samples from her research log, her notes and drafts, and her documentation illustrate various stages in one writer's process of writing a research paper.

TECHNIQUES   **RESEARCH PROCESS**   **WRITING PROCESS**

Techniques for Writing a Research Paper

> **❝** Criticism [is] a disinterested endeavor to learn and propagate the best that is known and thought in the world. **❞**
> —MATTHEW ARNOLD, POET AND ESSAYIST

Like other kinds of writing, a research paper requires that you assess your purpose, audience, and possible genre, and then focus on a particular subject, develop your thesis, and support your position with convincing evidence: background information, facts, statistics, descriptions, and other results of interviews and research. The evidence that you present in a research paper, however, is more detailed than in a typical essay, and the sources are usually cited in the text and documented at the end of the paper.

In a sense, a research paper is like a scientific experiment. **Your readers should be able to trace your whole experiment—to see what ideas and evidence you worked with, where you found them, and how you used them in your paper.** If readers have any questions about the information you've presented or the conclusions you've reached, they can start with your sources and recreate or check the "experiment" for themselves. If they want to investigate your subject further, your sources will guide their reading. As you write your research paper, keep the following techniques in mind.

- **Use purpose, occasion, audience, genre, and context as your guides for writing.** Research is just a method of collecting and documenting ideas and evidence. The rhetorical situation still directs your writing.
- **Find the best that has been written or said about your subject.** Instead of trying to reinvent the wheel, discover what other people or writers know and then build on what they have learned.
- **Critically evaluate your sources for accuracy, reliability, and bias.** Internet sources can be reliable, but they often represent people or organizations with a pronounced bias or give inaccurate or misleading information.

- **Use sources to make *your* point.** As you gather information, you may revise your thesis in light of what you learn, but don't let the tail wag the dog: don't allow your sources to control you or your paper.

- **Document your sources, both in the text and at the end of the paper.** Avoid *plagiarism* by carefully and accurately acknowledging all ideas, information, paraphrases, or actual language that you find in your sources.

GUIDES   FINDING   EVALUATING   USING   DOCUMENTING

USING PURPOSE, AUDIENCE, AND GENRE AS GUIDES

Like any other kind of writing, research papers have a *purpose*. Reporting, explaining, evaluating, problem solving, and arguing are all purposes for research papers. Purposes may appear in combinations, as in a paper that summarizes current research and then proposes a solution to a problem. Research papers, however, are not just reports of other people's ideas or evidence. What you, the researcher, observe and remember and learn is important, too. Most subjects are not interesting until writers make them so. Your curiosity, your interest in the subject, your reason and intuition establish why the subject is worth researching in the first place—and why a reader would want to read the paper once it is finished.

Research papers have a defined *audience,* too. The subject you choose, the kind of research you do, the documentation format, the vocabulary and style you use— all should be appropriate for your selected audience. If you write a senior research paper in your major, you will write for a professor and for a community of people knowledgeable about your field. If you are a legal assistant or a junior attorney in a law firm, a superior may ask you to research a specific legal precedent. If you work for a manufacturer, a manager may assign you a research report on the sales and strategies of a competitor. Although your classmates and teacher will probably read the research paper that you write for this class, you will ask them to role-play your audience. They will try to read your paper from the point of view of a defined audience—an employer, a politician, a nutritionist, an artist, an astronomer, or a senior law partner. In fact, your instructor may ask you to send your paper to some person or persons who actually are part of your audience.

Finally, your research paper must follow a *genre* that fits your purpose and meets the expectations and needs of your audience. If you are researching advances in sports medicine for an audience of experts, you need to use the genre (article, pamphlet, thesis) used by experts in the field. If your paper is an academic article, you may have an abstract at the beginning, a section reviewing and evaluating current research, subsections for each of your main points, diagrams and charts for illustration, and an appendix with supplementary materials. If, however, you are writing primarily for jogging enthusiasts, your research-based paper may look more like an informal essay. Magazines and journals in the field illustrate a variety of appropriate forms for source-based papers. The student essay by Kate McNerny at the end of this chapter illustrates one typical genre.

| GUIDES | FINDING | EVALUATING | USING | DOCUMENTING |

FINDING THE BEST SOURCES

Accessing information from published sources, field sources, and Web sites is central to all research. To find good sources, you need to hone your detective skills. Unfortunately, Hollywood has promoted the myth that good detectives follow their suspects in high-speed car chases or through glamorous affairs. Of course, that's just fantasy. Detectives must do actual research—computer searches, paperwork, and legwork—to track down leads. Writers are, in a real sense, also detectives, constantly searching for key information from the best possible sources. For your own research project, be sure to take your library's orientation session to learn how to access the most useful catalogs, indexes, and databases for your topic. Full-text databases such as *LexisNexis Academic, EBSCO Academic Search Premier, Contemporary Authors, InfoTrac,* and the *CQ Researcher* are just a few of the many indexes and databases that can help you with your research.

Research combines careful planning with good luck, mindless drudgery, moments of inspiration, many dead ends, and a few rare discoveries. As coaches sometimes say, those who prepare and work hard make their own luck. The following excerpt from the introduction to Pauli Murray's *Proud Shoes: The Story of an American Family* recounts her research into her family genealogy, which included slaves, free blacks, some racially mixed family members, and other relatives who were white and socially prominent. Although her detective work took several years and involved both library and field research, her account reflects the problems and successes that all researchers experience.

> My field research had the thrill of detection when the clues panned out.
> Rigorous discipline was needed for the drudgery of sifting through masses
> of documentary material in search of one relevant fact or one confirmation
> of a family legend. The trail of the Fitzgerald family led me into nearly a
> dozen localities in several states. It took me into musty basements of old
> courthouses to pore over dust-silted and sometimes indecipherable hand-
> written entries in old volumes. I found that each locality had its own cap-
> tivating legends preserved in family papers; its traditions recorded in

pamphlets and privately published little books; its stories printed in almanacs, newspapers, business directories. Almost every place had "the oldest living inhabitants" and their recollections. Most important, almost every locality had its own regional-history enthusiasts, who welcomed me into a fellowship of digging into the past. Some of them gave me expert guidance which improved the efficiency of my research and shortened my labors.

GUIDES   FINDING   **EVALUATING**   USING   DOCUMENTING

CRITICALLY EVALUATING YOUR SOURCES

With a computer and the Internet, it is easy to find books, articles, and Web sites that relate to your topic. It can be difficult, however, to find sources that are appropriate for your audience and purpose and are also accurate and reliable. If you are writing for an academic or professional audience, look for books and articles on the topic appropriate for your audience. Some databases, such as *InfoTrac*, search popular newspapers and magazines. However, if you are writing for an academic or professional audience, you may want databases and indexes such as LexisNexis and subject indexes such as *Architectural Index, AGRICOLA, Art Abstracts, Biological Abstracts, ERIC, MEDLINE, PsycINFO*, or *Sociological Abstracts*.

Once you have found a source, learn to critically evaluate the source for accuracy, reliability, and bias. An article from a professional or academic journal such as *Science* or *The New England Journal of Medicine* will probably give accurate, up-to-date information. However, information from a popular magazine, a newspaper, or a Web site may not have accurate or reliable information or may have a personal or commercial bias. Read the sections later in this chapter on evaluating Internet and library sources. Examine your sources carefully. Who or what organization is the author or authors? Are they selling something? What is their point of view or bias? How recent, accurate, or reliable is their information? Failing to critically evaluate your sources may ruin all of your research efforts, so don't forget this important step!

GUIDES   FINDING   EVALUATING   **USING**   DOCUMENTING

USING SOURCES TO MAKE YOUR POINT

The effective use of sources is a critical part of writing any research paper. What sources you choose to cite depends in part on what you assume about the reader's knowledge and viewpoint. Just be sure that you use your sources to make *your* point and that *your* voice still emerges in your writing.

Even writing that is merely intended to convey information makes a point about the subject. It answers the implied question all readers ask: "So what?" To show that you are informed on the subject, you will want to include sources that offer background information and summarize what people are (or are not) saying on the subject to capture the various points of view. You might cite a source to distinguish your position from that of another writer, point to a gap in the discussion of the issue, or draw a connection between two or more sources.

Using sources effectively is especially important if your assignment is to write an argumentative essay. An argument necessarily involves disagreements and different perspectives, and your instructor will expect you to take a clear position on the controversy, in part by discussing sources that support your point of view. Your sources should not only help you to align yourself with others, however. To make a credible argument and present yourself as reasonable, you will also want to include sources that represent perspectives on the subject other than your own. When you include such views, you should be prepared to counter them, conceding some of their points if necessary, but explaining why you disagree with the view they support.

A smooth weaving of your sources into your text will help your readability. Therefore, you will need to decide how to work with your sources—that is, when it is best to quote, paraphrase, or summarize a source and what options are available to you for effectively integrating them into your writing. (For more on quotation, paraphrase, and summary, see Chapter 5, Reading.)

A note of caution: When your hard work does yield sources that have good information and ideas about your subject, don't be tempted to let those sources take over your paper. Remember: *You* are the author of your paper; you are using your sources for support to help you make your points. If you start stringing together passages from your sources, you'll be summarizing rather than doing research. You'll be letting the sources tell you what to think, what information is important, or what conclusions to reach. Write your own paper; don't let your sources write it for you.

Remember that, in some fashion, all writing involves a transaction between the writer and the reader. Writing allows you to enter into active discussion on a subject with that reader. Understanding this will help you to develop a better plan for your writing, and it will make your writing more purposeful—more interesting to read and more interesting for you to produce.

GUIDES   FINDING   EVALUATING   USING   **DOCUMENTING**

DOCUMENTING YOUR SOURCES

Documenting your sources is an important part of writing a research paper. Documentation takes place in two stages: First, in the body or text of your paper, you give credit for any material that you have taken from your sources. Then, at the end of the paper, you include a list of Works Cited or Works Consulted that gives fuller information about these sources for your readers. If your readers doubt a fact or statistic, they can check your sources for themselves. If your readers want more information, your documentation enables them to track down the sources.

Note: Decide on the documentation format (usually MLA or APA style) before you begin your research. You need to know what relevant bibliographical information you need to record in your notes.

TECHNIQUES   RESEARCH PROCESS   WRITING PROCESS

Preparing Yourself for the Research Process

Writing a research paper involves the same process that you used in writing essays. The major difference is that each stage or dimension of the process takes longer. You may spend two weeks just collecting sources, reading articles and books, jotting down ideas, testing your ideas on classmates and friends, and narrowing and focusing your subject. And because you gather so much material, the shaping and organizing processes are also more demanding. Sometimes you may feel as if you're trying to put forty frogs in a dishpan: By the time you arrange ten, the first four have already jumped out. The revising also takes longer, partly because you have to include your documentation, but partly because the sections of the paper may not fit together as smoothly as you had hoped. There is really no way to rush research. If writing an ordinary paper is like fixing your lunch, then writing a research paper is like preparing Thanksgiving dinner. You can't microwave a research paper. Good things take time.

The first step in writing a research paper is to *readjust your inner clock.* Initially, you'll think that you're not making much progress. You'll think that you're in a slow-motion movie or that you're trying to jog through butter. However, once you readjust your inner clock, set more modest goals, and content yourself with a slower but more persistent pace, you've won half the battle. By reducing the pressure on yourself, you'll feel less frustrated when you reach a dead end and also readier to appreciate valuable information when you discover it.

To help you adjust mentally and physically to a new pace and an extended writing process, begin your preparation by making a research notebook, outlining a realistic timetable for the paper, and selecting a documentation format.

▌ WARMING UP: Journal Exercises

Do at least one of the following journal exercises to help get yourself into a research frame of mind or to discover a possible research subject.

1. Look again at the painting by Franz Marc reproduced at the beginning of this chapter. Assume that paintings by Franz Marc are the subject of your research paper for your art class. First, do a search on Google for information about the author and some of his famous paintings. Print the first page of any sites that contain useful information about the author and his works. You should find Internet sites from the WebMuseum, from the Guggenheim Museum, and from the Franz Marc museum, among others. Then, using EBSCO Academic Search Premier, enter "Franz Marc" in the search box and print out or e-mail yourself articles cited there from the *Art Journal*. Compare the length, detail, and usefulness of the articles you have found. Which of these sites or sources seem most or least reliable, and why? Which sources might be most or least useful for your paper, and why?

2. In the library, look in the computer catalog for books on a topic that you might select for your research paper. Go to the shelves where books on that topic are located. Choose one or two books and see if they refer to or cite other books in their *index* or *bibliography* at the end of the book. Take one book that has references to other works, go back to the library computer, and see if you can find any of those books or articles cited in the bibliography. Practicing this technique may suggest other *key words* for a search or other interesting and relevant sources that your computer search in the library did not initially cite. Be prepared to explain in class what other relevant books or articles you found using this research method.

3. In the library, find an issue of a magazine or newspaper published on or near the date and year of your birth. The issue may be on microfilm. Record the date and title of the newspaper or magazine. Browse through the issue, looking at headlines, articles, advertisements, editorials, comics, weather, sports, local news, and so forth. As you look through the issue, record any items, facts, or historical incidents that interest you. Photocopy one page that you find especially interesting. Explain why that page captured your attention.

4. Sit down with a family member, friend, or classmate. On a sheet of paper, write down the subject of the most interesting course that you are currently taking. Hand the sheet of paper to that person and ask him or her to write

down questions for an interview designed to find out *why* you like this course and *what* you like best about it. Then have that person interview you and record your responses. At the end of the interview, discuss your responses. What ideas could you research in order to explain to your interviewer what is interesting about this subject?

NOTEBOOK	TIMETABLE	DOCUMENT FORMAT

RESEARCH NOTEBOOK

Although some researchers still recommend using index cards for recording bibliographical entries and notes, for most shorter research projects (up to twenty pages), a notebook computer, a loose-leaf notebook, or a spiral notebook with pockets for additional papers and photocopies may be more functional. Divide your notebook into four sections: research log, bibliography, notes from sources (including photocopies), and drafts and ideas.

The *research log* section of your notebook serves as a scratch pad and log of your research progress. In it, you will record what you accomplish during each research session, potential references you need to check, reminders to yourself, questions to ask a librarian or your instructor, and notes about your problems, progress, and intended next steps. As you work, jot down what you did and what you still need to do. These notes about your problems, progress, questions, and next steps will help you maintain momentum on your research project. Each time you return to the library or to your research, you can check your notes to see what you need to do next.

4/26

4:30–6:00 p.m.

Still working on finding articles. EBSCO Academic Search Premier had several good articles. I tried using several search terms including "Foreign Language Study," "Foreign Language Requirements," and

"Foreign Language Education." Each gave me different results. When I tried searching in the ERIC database and put in "Foreign Language Study" I got 7,000 articles! I need to narrow the search terms. LexisNexis had some good articles but not as many. I need to stop by the reference desk and ask about the best search terms.

April issue of <u>Education Digest</u> missing from the shelves. UGH—I hate that.

Question: Do I want to survey students to find out about typical attitudes toward taking foreign languages? What questions should I ask? Maybe I can try out some sample questions on some of my classmates.

Another question: Is this going to be an arguing paper? Is there a controversy? Are there multiple points of view about the problem or the best solution?

Remember that 5-6 p.m. is a good time to work in the library. Everyone clears out, so I don't have to fight over the Internet computers or the

In the *bibliography* section of your notebook, keep a list of every source that you consult, with complete information about each source. If your library's online catalog system shows the status of every source, be sure to print out every source you want to check. If you cannot print the source, you'll need to copy it in your notebook. Leave space between entries for additional information, such as call numbers. This list becomes *your working bibliography.* McNerny's bibliography included the following entries.

Hines, Marion E. "Foreign Language Curriculum Concerns in Times of Conflict." <u>Delta Kappa Gamma Bulletin</u> 70(2003): 15-22.

I retrieved this from the EBSCO Academic Search Premier, so I need to cite the database I found it in:

Hines, Marion E. "Foreign Language Curriculum Concerns in Times of Conflict." <u>Delta Kappa Gamma Bulletin</u> 70(Fall 2003): 15-22. <u>Academic Search Premier.</u> EBSCO. Colorado State U Lib. 23 May 2004 <http://o-web2.epnet.com.catalog.library.colostate.edu>.

Lambert, Richard D. "Some Issues in Language Policy for Higher Education" <u>The Annals of the American Academy of Political and Social Science</u> 532 (1994): 123:37.

H1.A4 Current issues in Current Periodicals Room: Older issues in

In the *source notes* section, leave plenty of pages to record direct quotations, paraphrases of key ideas, and facts from the sources in your bibliography list. Introduce each section with a reference to the author and a short version of the title. After each note, indicate the page number or numbers. One page of McNerny's notes contained the following entries.

Lambert, "Some Issues in Language Policy"

Lambert explains how the lack of coordination between secondary schools and higher education causes problems. As Lambert notes, "The result of this strong tradition of university autonomy is that in the United States, foreign language planning for higher education must take place one institution at a time and implementation of change must occur in house-to-house, hand-to-hand combat" (125).

Ranwez and Rogers, "Status of Foreign Languages"

91% of the 536 Colorado secondary schools responding to the questionnaire offered foreign languages, but 91% of schools responding didn't require any foreign language credits for graduation (pp. 99-100).

For your source notes section, make *photocopies* of any valuable source materials. Write author, title, and page numbers on each photocopied source.

In the *drafts and ideas* section of the notebook, jot down brainstorms, looping or clustering exercises, sketch outlines, trial drafts, and examples from your own experience. During a research project, ideas can come to you at any time. When they do, take time to write them down. This section of your notebook serves as a journal devoted solely to your research paper. One example from McNerny's drafts and ideas section records her personal experience with foreign languages.

4/29

I can remember my mom always telling me, "Take French classes, learn how to speak French so that you can go visit your cousins in France some day." At the time (junior high school) though, learning a foreign language was low on my priority list. I did take French classes for two years – but dropped out after my sophomore year and immediately lost any basic competency I might have acquired.

In college, I'd like to take a language again, but it never seems to fit with my schedule. But last year, as my mom had promised, I got the opportunity to visit my cousins in France. For some reason, the fact that I couldn't speak French didn't seem to me like it would be a big problem. That was until I stepped off the train at Gare du Nord in Paris and couldn't find the relative who was supposed to meet me. After frantically searching the entire station several times, I had to break down and ask for help. At the information desk a few completely butchered French phrases escaped my lips – only to be received by an unimpressed, unresponsive station attendant. He muttered something about dumb Americans and then pointed me off toward some unknown destination. Well I survived that ordeal – but at the same time swore to myself that I would never make another trip to France until I could speak the language.

<table>
<tr><td>NOTEBOOK</td><td>TIMETABLE</td><td>DOCUMENT FORMAT</td></tr>
</table>

RESEARCH TIMETABLE

Before you begin your research, write out a tentative schedule. Your instructor may assign due dates for specific parts of the paper (invention exercises, topic selection, working bibliography, rough draft), but you should make a schedule that fits your work habits and your weekly schedule.

The following schedule assumes that you have at least a month to work on your research paper. The amount of time required by each part depends on the amount of time you can work each day. On some days, you may have only thirty minutes. On other days, you may have several hours. The key is to do a little bit every day to keep your momentum going.

Prepare for research. Buy and organize a research notebook; set up a timetable; select a documentation format.	1–2 days
Choose a subject. Begin the narrowing and focusing process.	2–3 days
Collect sources. Find library sources; identify and find unpublished sources; do interviews or surveys; record personal experiences; browse sites on the Internet. *Evaluate* source materials; take *notes* on selected sources; *photocopy* sources.	12–14 days
Shape and outline ideas; *reread* notes and photocopies; *draft* sections of the essay. Continue to *focus* the thesis while rereading, planning, and drafting.	6–10 days
Revise the draft. Get peer response; collect additional information; sharpen the thesis; reshape or revise the outline; cite sources in the text and in the bibliographical list; edit and proofread the paper.	6–8 days

Tailor your schedule to your own temperament and work habits. If you like to work exactly to a schedule or even finish early, design your schedule so you can finish a day or two before the due date. If you are like most writers—you love to procrastinate or you are often up all night just before an assignment is due—then use your schedule to set early target dates, to get your momentum going. When you finish drafting your schedule, put a copy in the *research log* section of your notebook so that you can check your progress as you work.

NOTEBOOK   TIMETABLE   DOCUMENT FORMAT

DOCUMENTATION FORMAT: MLA AND APA STYLES

A final step in preparing for the research paper is to select a documentation style. This chapter illustrates both the MLA and APA styles. If you are writing a paper for the humanities, follow the Modern Language Association (MLA) style set forth in the *MLA Handbook for Writers of Research Papers* (6th ed., 2003). If you are writing a paper in the behavioral sciences, use the American Psychological Association (APA) style as described in the *Publication Manual of the American Psychological Association* (5th ed., 2001).

Leading academic and professional journals also illustrate the documentation styles customary in specialized fields. You may want to consult issues of those journals to determine the exact format for footnotes or in-text citation of sources. *Before you begin doing research, however, select a documentation style* that is appropriate for your subject, purpose, and audience. Then practice that style as you compile your working bibliography.

TECHNIQUES   RESEARCH PROCESS   WRITING PROCESS

Research Paper: The Writing Process

ASSIGNMENT FOR THE RESEARCH PAPER

Choose a subject that strongly interests you and about which you would like to learn more. It may be a subject that you have already written about in this course. Research this subject in a library and, as appropriate, supplement your library research with questionnaires, interviews, Internet research, or other unpublished sources of information. Check with your instructor for suggested length, appropriate number or kinds of sources, and additional format requirements. Use a documentation style appropriate for your subject, purpose, and audience.

CHOOSING	COLLECTING	GLOSSARY	EVALUATING	PLAGIARISM
SHAPING	DRAFTING	GRAPHICS	REVISING	MLA/APA

CHOOSING A SUBJECT

For this research paper, choose a subject in which you already have personal interest or experience. Start by rereading your journal entries for possible research subjects. Even a personal entry may suggest an idea. If you wrote about how you fainted in the gym during aerobics or weight training, you might research the potential dangers of exercising in high heat and humidity or sitting in a sauna after hard exercise. If you wrote a journal entry about a friend's drinking problem, you might like to read more about the causes and treatments of alcoholism.

In addition, reread the essays that you have written to see whether one of them refers to a possible research subject. If your observing essay, for example, was about a tattoo parlor that you visited, use that essay as the starting point for further investigation and research. Whom could you interview to find out more about tattooing? What is the history of tattooing? Why is it becoming more popular? What controversies surround its use? What resources does your library have? What sites can you find on the Internet? You might also use a topic from your remembering, reading, or investigating essays as starting places for additional reading and research. *Build on what you already know and what already interests you rather than launching into an entirely unknown subject.*

■ **NARROWING AND FOCUSING YOUR SUBJECT** Once you have a tentative idea, remember that you'll need to narrow it, focus it, or otherwise limit the subject to make it appropriate for your audience and context. The topic of alcoholism is too general. Focus on a particular research question: "Do beer commercials on television contribute to alcoholism?" "Are there really positive effects of drinking moderate amounts of alcohol?" "What methods does Alcoholics Anonymous use to help people?" "Have DWI laws actually reduced the number of fatal automobile accidents?" Your research question may lead to a *thesis statement* that you will demonstrate in your research essay: "Although some studies show a definite link between consuming moderate amounts of red wine and reduced incidence of heart disease, the negative effects of alcohol consumption far outweigh the potential benefits."

Only after you've started your research, however, will you know whether your research question is still too broad (you can't begin to read everything about it in just two weeks) or too narrow (in two weeks, you can't find enough information about that question).

Two techniques may help narrow and focus your subject. You may wish to try these now, wait until you have done some initial reading, or do them several times during your collecting and shaping.

The first strategy is simply to think about your *purpose* and *audience*. The best way to focus your paper is to reflect on your purpose: What kinds of claims do you want to make about your topic? (If necessary, review the claims of fact, cause and effect, value, and policy outlined in Chapter 11, "Arguing.") As you collect articles, think about the kinds of claims you might want to make about your topic.

CLAIMS OF FACT: Are makers of hard liquor being discriminated against by not being allowed to advertise on TV? Is alcoholism a disease or just an addiction?

CLAIMS OF CAUSE AND EFFECT: Does TV advertising increase alcohol consumption or just affect the brands that are consumed? Can students who are "recreational" drinkers become alcoholics? Do recovery programs like Alcoholics Anonymous really work?

CLAIMS OF VALUE: Does beer have any nutritional value? Are microbrews really made better or are they fresher than beers from larger breweries?

CLAIMS OF POLICY: Do age-based drinking laws really work? Should liquor consumption be banned at campus sporting events? At dorms, fraternities, and sororities? At any campus function? Should makers of hard liquor be allowed to advertise on television?

Asking questions about your potential audience may also help you find a focus for your essay. If you are writing for a local audience, consider what they believe and what they might be interested in. Is the topic of alcohol regulation controversial? Who are your readers? What are they likely to believe about this issue? Profile your audience and brainstorm how you can connect your research question to those particular readers.

Question analysis is a second narrowing and focusing strategy. The who, what, when, where, and why questions that you use to focus your topic are the same questions that reference librarians use to help you focus your research in the library.

Who: What group of people is interested or affected?

What: How are key terms defined? What academic discipline is involved?

When: What is the period or time span?

Where: What continent, country, state, or town is involved?

Why: What are possible effects or implications?

Answering these questions—by yourself, in a group, or with a reference librarian—may suggest new angles, new avenues for research, or subtopics that could lead to a focus for your research paper. As you narrow your topic, you are narrowing and focusing the range of your research in the library. Student writer Kate McNerny, brainstorming with another class member, applied these questions to her subject about foreign-language study and came up with the following possibilities.

Foreign Language Study

Who?   Ans: I am interested in Americans. Specifically, I want to focus on why Americans should begin learning a foreign language early in school, in grade school, secondary school, and college. Learning a foreign language would affect how foreigners see us.

What?   Ans: Key terms defined – perhaps what "learning" means. Does it mean just basic speaking competency? Probably. If I could have asked a few simple questions in the Gare du Nord, I wouldn't have felt so stupid. Academic discipline – learning the foreign language is important, but <u>culture</u> is part of it, too. History should teach us about foreign cultures. So should psychology – do the Japanese think differently from the Spanish? Why did the French seem rude and Italians friendly? Do I want to research the psychology of languages? I don't think so.

When?   Ans: I really want to know why foreign language studies are currently not emphasized. But what about trends – is it getting better or worse? Are more people learning foreign languages than a few years ago? I don't know.

Where? Ans: In the United States. In my home town. Why is it that in the French schools, children as a matter of course learn several languages while we aren't required to learn any?

       Supposedly, we are the "melting pot" for many different languages and cultures, but we don't know each other's languages.

Why?   Ans. I can make a long list of the effects
    – We can't communicate when we're tourists.
    – We can't read anything printed in their
       language.
    – We don't understand their culture.
    – We don't even understand the cultures of
       the millions of Americans from other
       cultures.
    – We isolate ourselves in business, too.

      To avoid these effects, I want to argue
for stronger foreign language requirements
in secondary schools and colleges.

As a result of her question analysis, McNerny decided to discuss both language and culture, to focus on the current conditions, and to recommend that secondary schools require foreign languages. *In any research, however, what you look for and what you find are always different. You will need to modify your focus as you read and learn.*

CHOOSING	COLLECTING	GLOSSARY	EVALUATING	PLAGIARISM
SHAPING	DRAFTING	GRAPHICS	REVISING	MLA/APA

COLLECTING

With ideas for a tentative subject, a possible purpose, and an audience, you can focus on collecting information. Collecting data for your research paper will require identifying and locating published and unpublished sources, evaluating your sources and choosing those that are the most appropriate for your needs, and then taking notes on your selected sources. *Remember, however, that finding sources—like writing itself—is an ongoing and recursive process.* You often identify new sources after you have taken notes on others. Although you may begin your search in the online catalog, in the reference section, or on the Internet, as you narrow and focus your topic or draft sections of your paper, you may come back and recheck the online catalog, basic references, periodical indexes, or bibliographies.

Use *informal contacts* with friends or acquaintances as an integral part of your collecting process. Friends, family members, business associates, or teachers may be able to suggest key questions or give you some sources: relevant books and magazine articles, television programs that are available in transcript, or local experts on your subject.

■ **UNPUBLISHED SOURCES** Although the library may be your main source of information, other sources can be important, too. You may *interview* authorities on your subject or design a *questionnaire* to measure people's responses. (Interviews and questionnaires are discussed in Chapter 7.) *Phone calls* and *letters* to experts, government agencies, or businesses may yield background information, statistics, or quotations. *Notes from classes, public lectures,* or *television programs* are useful sources. Use a tape recorder to ensure that you transcribe your information accurately. A *scientific experiment* may even be appropriate. *Unpublished public documents,* such as deeds, wills, surveyors' maps, and environmental impact statements, may contain gold mines of information. Finally, don't ignore the most obvious sources: your room, the attic in your home, or your relatives may have repositories of valuable unpublished data—private letters, diaries, old bills, or check stubs.

For her research paper, Kate McNerny decided to conduct an informal survey of attitudes toward foreign languages. She recorded the responses in the *drafts and ideas* section of her research notebook. When she drafted her paper, she used some of these responses in her introduction.

Q: Should foreign languages be required in Junior and Senior High?

A: (Mindy, 21, student) Yes, I think its a good idea – It would have been more valuable to me than some of the other required classes I took – like P.E.

A: (Jodi, 22, student) No, I had a hard enough time with English. Besides, I don't think I'd ever need to use it.

A: (Roger, 23, carpenter) Yes, I was in Europe last year and missed out on a lot because I couldn't speak any other language. Europeans don't speak English as much as we hear they do, but most of the people I met there spoke at least two languages.

A: (Jim, 49, contractor) No, I've never gone to Europe and never needed to speak another language for any other reason. I had enough trouble getting through other classes.

A: (Carolyn, 59, teacher) Yes, when I was teaching there were few language classes available. But as a reading teacher I can see many ways in which language studies would have enhanced our program.

▌ PRIMARY AND SECONDARY SOURCES   Some sources—accounts of scientific experiments, transcripts of speeches or lectures, questionnaires, interviews, private documents—are known as *primary sources*. They are original, firsthand information, "straight from the horse's mouth." Secondhand reports, analyses, and descriptions based on primary sources are known as *secondary sources*. Secondary sources may contain the same information, but they are once-removed. For example, a lecture or experiment by an expert in food irradiation is a primary source; the newspaper report of that lecture or experiment is a secondary source.

The distinction between primary and secondary sources is important for two related reasons. First, secondary sources may contain errors. The newspaper account, for example, may misquote the expert or misrepresent the experiment. If possible, therefore, find the primary source—a copy of the actual lecture or a published article about the experiment. Second, finding the primary sources may make your research document more persuasive through an appeal to character (see Chapter 11, "Arguing"). If you can cite the original source—or even show how some secondary accounts distorted the original experiment—you will gain your readers' trust and faith. Not only does uncovering the primary data make your research more accurate, but your additional effort makes all your data and arguments appear more credible.

▌ LIBRARY SOURCES   Before you begin collecting information, acquaint yourself with the library itself. If you have not already done so, inquire at the information desk about library tours, or walk through the library with a friend or classmate. Locate the *reference section;* the *online catalog* for books and articles; the *indexes* for newspapers, journals, and magazines; the *microfilm room;* the *stacks;* and the *government documents* section. Don't assume that because you've used one library, you can immediately start your research in a new library. Remember: *Librarians* themselves are valuable sources of information. Use their expertise early in your research.

▮ BACKGROUND INFORMATION AND GENERAL REFERENCE

Before you consult the online catalog, you may need a *general overview* of your subject. Start with an encyclopedia, dictionary, almanac, or biography for background information. Many people associate encyclopedias with their grade-school "research"—when they copied passages out of *The World Book* or *Collier's Encyclopedia*. But encyclopedias are an excellent source of basic information and terminology that may help you focus, narrow, and define your subject. *Use them as background reading, however, not as major sources.*

In addition to the general encyclopedias, there are hundreds of references—one or two might just save you hours of research in the library and lead you directly to key facts or important information on your topic. (You may wish to begin your collecting in the reference room or check there only after you have collected information from other books and articles. Often these references are more valuable *after* you have done some reading on your subject.) Beyond the standard college dictionary or thesaurus, the *Oxford English Dictionary,* known as the *OED,* or *Webster's Third New International Dictionary of the English Language* may help you find key ideas or definitions.

There are also many specialized dictionaries for scientific terms, slang words, symbols, and a host of other specialized vocabularies. If you need facts, figures, or statistics, consult the *World Almanac,* the *Book of Facts,* or the *Statistical Abstracts of the United States.* If your subject is a person, look at *Who's Who in America,* or check one of the references that indexes collections of biographies. *Biography and Genealogy Master Index* and *Biographical Dictionaries* reference more than three million biographical sketches.

The *librarian* is still the most valuable resource for your research. At some point during your research in the library, probably after you have a focused topic and have collected some sources, talk to a reference librarian. For many writers, asking for help can be really intimidating. To make the process of asking for help as painless—and productive—as possible, try saying something like the following: "Hi, I'm Kate McNerny. I'm doing a research project for my college writing course. My topic is foreign-language study in the United States. I'm trying to find information about the current state of foreign-language study in the United States and collect some arguments for increasing requirements in secondary schools and colleges. Here's what I've found so far [explain what you've done]. What additional reference books, Web sites, indexes, dictionaries, or bibliographies might help me in my research?" The resulting conversation may be the most productive five minutes of your entire library research. After you've talked to the librarian once, it will be easier to return and ask a question when you hit a snag.

▌ THE ONLINE CATALOG

The good news for researchers in the twenty-first century is that computerized databases have revolutionized the whole process of library research. In most university libraries, a computer terminal can, in a few seconds, give you information that used to require hours of searching card catalogs or printed indexes. You can easily locate books, articles, and government documents relevant to your topic. You can find the library call numbers and locations of sources. You can determine if a source is available or checked out and get an abstract or a short description of a source. For some systems, you can print out the bibliographical information so that you don't have to take notes. Often, you can print out whole articles right there.

The only bad news is that nearly every online catalog system is different. Whatever you do, don't try to learn the system by yourself. Take a library orientation tour. Collect the library's handouts about its computerized databases. Ask the librarians for help. And don't wait until your research paper is assigned to walk into the library. If you have to learn a new computer system *and* write your paper at the same time, you will be inviting massive frustration.

You will likely find that your library provides access to many different bibliographic databases, which allow you to search efficiently and in many cases retrieve full text of periodical articles and other research materials. EBSCO Academic Search Premier, LexisNexis Academic, and InfoTrac are popular databases that span academic disciplines. Other databases such as ERIC, which focuses on education topics, or PsycINFO for psychology, specialize in materials from a particular discipline. FirstSearch and similar services allow you to search multiple databases at once for the information you need.

When McNerny started her search in her library's online databases, she chose EBSCO Academic Search Premier. After looking at the abstract and the full text of an article by Marion Hines, she decided to email them to herself. Once she had them in electronic form, she reasoned, she could refer to them whenever necessary, search them electronically, and retain an electronic record of the information necessary for completing her bibliographical entry. She could also print them out if she liked. A slightly edited version of the citation appears here.

> ❝ Knowledge is of two kinds. We know a subject ourselves, or we know where we can find information upon it. ❞
> —SAMUEL JOHNSON, FROM JAMES BOSWELL'S *LIFE OF JOHNSON*

Author: Hines, Marion E.

Source: *Delta Kappa Gamma Bulletin;* Fall 2003, Vol 70 Issue 1, p. 15, 7p.

Subject Terms: LINGUISTS; UNIVERSITIES & colleges; SCHOOLS; EDUCATION; LANGUAGE & languages; NATIONAL security; GLOBALIZATION

Reviews & Products: *Tongue-Tied American, The* (Book)

People: SIMON, Paul

Abstract: Argues that globalization and national security dictate the inclusion of foreign language study in the core curricula of American schools, colleges and universities. Statement from Paul Simon, former senator and author of the book, "The Tongue-Tied American: Confronting the Foreign Language Crisis"; Purpose of the National Virtual Translation Center; Fact which aggravates the shortages of U.S. linguists.

Persistent link to this record: http://0-search.epnet.com.catalog.library.colostate.edu:80/direct.asp?an=11264017&db=aph

Database: Academic Search Premier

Five pieces of information from this citation are especially helpful and worth noting. First, the **source line** gives the key bibliographic information needed for the citation: place and date of publication with volume and page numbers. Second, the **subject terms** (sometimes including **descriptors**) give other key words that might be helpful in searching databases. In addition to the key words *foreign language study,* this line suggests that the words *universities, schools, education,* or *globalization* might also be helpful search terms. Third, the **abstract** summarizes the main ideas or focus of the article. Fourth, the **persistent link** gives the URL at which McNerny could find this article if she didn't have her printed copy and needed to check a fact or quotation. Fifth, the **database** indicates that she found this article on Academic Search Premier. This information is necessary to include in the bibliographic entry on the Works Cited or References page. *Always print out this citation page so you have accurate information for your own citations.*

■ **SEARCH STRATEGY**   As you spend time with your library's online system, you'll discover that the *search strategy* you use and the *search terms* you enter become very critical. Should you use a *keyword, subject, author,* or *title* search? Generally, when starting research on a topic, you'll start either with keyword or subject searches. When performing a subject search, you need to use the categories defined in the online system. (These are often drawn from Library of Congress subject listings.) When performing a keyword search, you have more latitude, but you'll still need to pay careful attention to the words you enter. If you are writing an essay about teenagers' psychological problems, entering the word *teen* may get you nowhere, while entering the word *adolescent* or even *teenage* may hit the jackpot. However, one-word searches may turn up too many options. If so, entering multiple terms—*adolescent psychology,* for example—will usually help you narrow down your results. Depending on the system, connectors such as *and, or, not,* or *and not* can help you search even more efficiently, and , in many systems, putting an exact phrase in quotes (*"adolescent psychology"*) helps to narrow things.

To help with your search, try the following. First, make a list of all the possible terms that may relate to your subject. When you enter the terms, note any alternate terms or subject headings suggested by the system. When you find a source that looks promising, take a look at the subject categories assigned to it, and search those categories to find further sources.

If you are having trouble gathering information on your topic, be sure to consult a librarian and discuss your search strategy and the list of search terms you are using. Even in this age of technological wonders, the flesh-and-blood research librarian can be your most valuable resource.

INTERNET SOURCES Where should you start your search for relevant sources—in the library databases or on the Internet? The answer to that question depends on your topic, your purpose, and your audience. But the recent explosion of Web sites indicates that, for many writers and topics, the Internet may well be the place to start. The immense variety of sources makes the Internet a great place to do your browsing—especially if you're not quite sure exactly what your topic will be or what angle you wish to investigate. Other writers—especially those who are already sure of their focus—may wish to begin with an online search in their library and to save their Internet research for later, when they want to find sources they cannot locate in the library. Whatever choice you make, you will probably want to browse the Internet at some point during your research.

Especially if you are not an expert at Internet research, you should think about the strengths and weaknesses of Internet research. The strengths of Internet research are many:

- The Internet has a mind-boggling number of sources and Web pages.
- The Internet can have an amazing retrieval speed for sources from around the world.

- The Internet gives you the ability to chat with other people who share similar interests.
- The Internet gives you personal access—from your library or your home—to key information from libraries, businesses, organizations, and governments.

Unfortunately, doing research on the Internet does have drawbacks that are often related to its strengths. Internet enthusiasts often praise the Web for creating a democratic space where every person and site are equal. On the downside, however, librarians often shudder at doing research on the Internet simply because everything is so decentralized and disorganized. There are other problems as well:

- The sheer number of possible sources on the Internet may make finding the exact source you need very difficult.
- Browsing on the Web may be fun, but you may spend hours going from one site to the next without making any real progress.
- The increasing commercialization of Web sites may interfere with locating relevant information.
- Waiting for a source to download from a busy site can be tedious and frustrating.
- Sources on the Internet may not be accurate or reliable—and thus not appropriate for your paper.

With realistic estimations about the Internet's virtues and faults, however, you should be able to find relevant and even exciting sources that will help you learn about your topic and communicate your findings to your audience.

Note: As you continue to read in this section of the chapter, you may want to open a connection to the Internet so you can check out several of the sites. Also, remember to start making bookmarks for any sites you want to revisit later.

Internet Browsers and Search Engines   Once you have an idea for a possible topic, you can begin searching sites on the Internet for relevant information. If you need to review the basics of Internet research and terminology, refer to the Internet glossary on page 684. If you are sitting at a computer with a browser, such as Netscape or Internet Explorer, you can begin working on your topic right now by accessing one of the popular search engines described below. Of course, there are actually hundreds of such searching tools available on the Web, but the ones described here can get you started.

According to most industry reports, the most popular search engines on the Web today are owned by Google, Yahoo!, MSN, and Ask.com, in that order. Of the four, Google is far and away the most popular, accounting for over 60% of all searches. Because all search engines have their strengths and weaknesses, however, the best advice is to try more than one for your particular subject and use what works best.

> **Ask.com** *http://www.ask.com* Formerly known as AskJeeves, Ask.com was at first an entirely "natural language" search engine that required users to ask questions rather than entering keywords. It now allows for keyword searches as well.
>
> **Clusty** *http://clusty.com* A metasearch engine that returns results from a number of free search engines and directories. Clusty's unique feature is that it clusters search results into topics.
>
> **Dogpile** *http://www.dogpile.com* Dogpile, another metasearch engine, searches Google, Yahoo, LookSmart, Ask.com, Windows Live Search, and several other popular search engines.
>
> **Find Articles** *http://findarticles.com* Powered by LookSmart, this site allows you to search for articles from hundreds of magazines, journals, newspapers, and trade publications.
>
> **Google** *http://www.google.com* Google has quickly become the highest-rated Web search engine because of its huge index and the high relevancy of its responses.
>
> **Google Scholar** *http://scholar.google.com* Google Scholar indexes the full text of scholarly literature from a wide variety of disciplines.

Windows Live Search *http://www.live.com/?searchonly&tru&mkt=en-US* (formerly MSN Search) Microsoft's Web search engine was designed to compete with industry leaders Google and Yahoo! and shares many of their features.

Yahoo! Search *http://www.yahoo.com* Yahoo!, one of the oldest search engines on the Web, still provides excellent searches. Among other services, you can check Web sites that have been evaluated by a human editor.

Of course, Web sites and search engines are constantly changing. But the good news is that you can find comparative reviews and data about the various research tools and search engines on the Internet. Search Engine Watch at *http://searchenginewatch.com* is one good site for reviews and comparisons of popular and specialized search engines.

| CHOOSING | COLLECTING | **GLOSSARY** | EVALUATING | PLAGIARISM |
| SHAPING | DRAFTING | GRAPHICS | REVISING | MLA/APA |

BASIC INTERNET GLOSSARY

The URL (uniform resource locator) is the address that identifies each Internet site. In the address that follows, for example, **http** stands for "Hypertext Transfer Protocol," **www** stands for World Wide Web, **Yahoo!** is the manager of the Web site, and **.com** indicates a commercial site:

URL: http://www.yahoo.com

In addition to commercial (**.com**), you can access a variety of locations, including educational (**.edu**), governmental (**.gov**), noncommercial (**.org**), military (**.mil**), and networking (**.net**). Other URLs can access gopher sites (**gopher://**), ftp (**ftp://**), newsgroups (**news://**), and so forth.

Note: URLs have no spaces between any letters, periods, or slashes. URLs must be typed with complete accuracy—one missed slash or period or letter and your computer will not be able to find the correct address.

As you get started doing research on the Internet, acquaint yourself with the following key terms and definitions. If you know the basic language for navigating the Internet, you won't remain a newbie very long.

blog   A blog (short for Web log) is a journal available on the Web. Blogs are usually updated daily by the owner of the log. Updating a blog is called "blogging."

bookmark   Your computer's browser (see next page) enables you to record each URL that you want to remember, so the next time you want to visit that site, you merely have to click the right line in your bookmark rather than type out a complete URL string. Remember to bookmark sites that look promising as you do your research!

browser Your computer needs a browser such as Netscape or Internet Explorer to help you access Telnet, gopher, or Web sites on the Internet. (A browser is not the same as a search engine such as Yahoo! or Google.)

cyberspace The online world created in electronic space or on the Internet.

DOI (Digital Object Identifier) The DOI is an alpha-numeric string that allows for persistent identification of an electronic source. This is useful as such sources may change or move to different locations.

FTP The File Transfer Protocol is the set of commands that enables you to transfer files between two sites on the Internet.

home page The home page is usually the first page of any Web site, and it identifies the author of the page, the location or sponsor of the site, and the basic information about the site.

html Hypertext Markup Language is the computer code used to write pages on the Web.

hyperlink Often just called *links,* these are highlighted words, icons, or bits of graphic that you can click on to move to a related site. A hypertext is simply a collection of documents or graphics connected by these links.

listserv A listserv is a mail list that enables users to conduct an ongoing e-mail conversation about a particular topic.

MOO A multiuser domain, object-oriented, provides a space in which people can meet at a given time to discuss a particular topic.

MUD A multiuser domain (or dungeon) enables simultaneous communication, often by role-playing a certain character or persona.

newsgroup Any group of people who post messages on Usenet. Usenet is a network that gives access to an electronic discussion group.

search engine A program that enables Internet users to find relevant sites on the Internet. Popular search engines or search tools include Yahoo! and Google.

This short list is just the tip of the iceberg of Internet terminology. If you want to know about **ASCII, baud rates, bytes, cookies, flame wars, MIMEs, POPs, spam, Veronica, WYSIWYC,** or literally hundreds of other terms, visit one of the dozens of Internet glossaries available online, such as the Internet Literacy Consultants' Glossary of Internet Terms at http://matisse.net/files/glossary.html. Check out this site and make a bookmark so you can return whenever you have a question.

TIPS FOR DOING RESEARCH ON THE INTERNET

- If it takes more than a couple of minutes to get files from your site, click on the "Stop" button and try another source.

- Use the "bookmark" or "favorites list" to record your best sites. You may even want to organize your favorites or bookmarks into a folder designated specifically for the topic of this paper.
- Make sure your browser is set so that the location (URL), title, date, and page are recorded on the copies you print. If they do not appear, ask your laboratory monitor or teacher for assistance.
- The time of day you access the Internet may be crucial. Obviously, 3 A.M. is a good time for minimal Net traffic, but you do need your sleep. Log on at different times of the day to find out when is best for your location.
- Make sure you have enough information from your source (author, title, title of work, full URL address, and date of visit) so that you can write an in-text citation and a references citation in either MLA or APA format. (See the sections on MLA and APA citation of online sources later in this chapter.)

Useful Research Addresses   In some cases, instead of browsing through a search engine such as Google or Yahoo!, you may wish to go directly to a reliable and relevant site. Here are a few you may wish to visit as you research your topic. Each of these sites offers links to other relevant sites.

ERIC *http://www.eric.ed.gov/* ERIC (Educational Resources Information Center), sponsored by the U.S. Department of Education, provides access to more than 1.2 million bibliographic records of journal articles and other education-related materials and includes links to full text when available. Your library will probably have an ERIC database that you can conveniently search, but if you are not at a library, you can access the ERIC site at this URL. You may even order ready-made searches on popular topics such as "English Only/English Plus," "Teaching ESL Abroad," or "Peace Corps Language Teaching Materials."

FedStats *http://www.fedstats.gov* This site provides access to official statistical information produced by over 100 agencies of the U.S. Government.

The Library of Congress *http://www.lcweb.loc.gov/index.html* The Library of Congress site can give you direct access to an immense range of government and library resources.

News Index *http://www.newsindex.com* News Index, one of many news and newspaper indexes, searches the current issue and archives of over three hundred newspapers and news sources. You can also use Google and Yahoo! to find specific newspapers with searchable indexes.

The *New York Times* *http://www.nytimes.com* You will need to register with the *New York Times,* but then you can access the current paper or do a keyword search of the archives for relevant articles, editorials, and feature stories.

Online Writing Centers Check out the online writing centers at the following addresses for help with writing as well as with finding relevant research strategies and sites: Colorado State University's Writing@CSU at *http://writing.colostate.edu/* or Purdue University's OWL at *http://owl.english.purdue.edu/*

Popular Magazines Many magazines, such as *Mother Jones* and *Utne Reader,* have home pages that allow you to access articles and participate in online listservs or "salon" conversations on current issues. Use your search engine to find their URLs.

USA.gov *http://www.usa.gov* This site provides access to official information, services, and resources from the U.S. government.

U.S. Government Printing Office *http://www.gpoaccess.gov/index.html* The Government Printing Office (GPO) is the largest publisher in the world, and the GPO Access site allows you to find government publications on almost every topic imaginable.

The WWW Virtual Library *http://vlib.org* Organized by major subject area, the WWW Virtual Library (VL) is a nonprofit site compiled by volunteers who are expert in their fields. It is widely recognized for the quality of its offerings.

| CHOOSING | COLLECTING | GLOSSARY | EVALUATING | PLAGIARISM |
| SHAPING | DRAFTING | GRAPHICS | REVISING | MLA/APA |

EVALUATING INTERNET SOURCES

Evaluating sources on the Internet requires much more care and attention than judging print sources. Printed sources in the library have often been screened and filtered for accuracy and reliability, whereas often Web sources may represent simply one person's opinion, reaction, or point of view. Even more problematic is our inability to judge the context of the information. When we read an article in the *New York Times,* for example, we can expect a certain level of accuracy and reliability; conversely, when we read an article in a supermarket tabloid, we know we should expect very little accuracy. We know not to quote a tabloid article about diet supplements when we are writing an academic paper about health and nutrition. Even in the television media, we know when we're watching *CNN News* and when we're seeing an infomercial. On the Internet, however, we may have very few context cues to help us judge what we're reading.

Internet sources must be evaluated with a critical eye. Unless you critically appraise your sources, you don't know whether the site you are using was written by a sixth-grader doing research for a class assignment, a grandmother doing her first Web page, a wild-eyed radical, or a neighborhood dog. When we find a source, we need to ask some key questions: Who is the author? Is the author an expert, a salesperson, or a person with a reason to be biased? What organization is publishing this information? Where did the author find his or her sources? Can we verify the information in other reliable sources? How current is this information? As you read and download texts from the Internet, pay particular attention to the six criteria below. (These criteria are adapted from guidelines designed by Elizabeth E. Kirk, the Library Instruction Coordinator for the Milton S. Eisenhower Library at Johns Hopkins University, and are available at http://www.library.jhu.edu/researchhelp/general/evaluating.)

"On the Internet, nobody knows you're a dog."

- **Authorship.** Who is the author? Is the author well known? Are the author's credentials or biographical information available on the Internet or elsewhere? Does the author have a reason to be biased? The less you know about the author, the more cautious you need to be about using the source. *If you decide to use a document by a questionable authority, indicate exactly what you know or don't know about the author's credentials.*
- **Publishing organization.** Does the site indicate the organization responsible for the text? Is there information in the header or footer indicating the organization, Webmaster, or designer of the home page? Is this organization recognized in its field? Is the organization selling something? *If you know the source is not authoritative or has a commercial basis, indicate the organization's identity if you quote from the site.*

- **Point of view or bias.** Every document or text has a point of view or bias—but some biases may mean that the site's information is not reliable or accurate. Does the author or the organization have a commercial, political, philosophical, religious, environmental, or even "scientific" agenda? *When you use a source with highly selective or biased information or perspectives, indicate the author's probable bias or agenda when you cite the text.*

- **Knowledge of the literature.** Reliable sources refer to other texts available or published in that discipline or field. Look for documents that have in-text citation or reference to other sources, a fair and reasonable appraisal of alternative points of view, and a bibliography. *Any source that has no references to other key works may simply be one writer's opinion and/or may contain erroneous information.*

- **Accuracy and reliability.** Can the information in the text be verified for accuracy? Are the methods of gathering information indicated? Has this study been replicated elsewhere? *If you have reason to believe the source is not reliable or accurate, find another source.*

- **Currency.** Depending on your purpose and audience, currency may or may not be important. If you are writing about the reception of Shakespeare's plays, information from texts written in the seventeenth century may be more relevant than current ones. If you are writing about stem cell research or about censorship on the Internet, however, you need the most current available information. Can you determine the date the text was written? Can you find the date the information was posted on the site? Are cited statistics based on recent data? *You may use information from an older study, but acknowledge that it is dated and supplement it with more recent studies.*

As you gather sources from the Internet, be skeptical! Question the authority of the texts you find. If you think the source is not reliable, trust your judgment and don't use it. If the text seems accurate and reliable, but you cannot verify all of these criteria, indicate the problems in the source when you introduce your citation:

> Certainly Mind Extension University is in the business of selling online education, but they may be right when they claim that distance learning is the wave of the future.

> Karen Levine is a Spanish teacher at Thousand Oaks High School and has sponsored school-to-school exchange programs, but her testimonial for the International Education Forum's program—an exchange program for which she has worked—should be balanced against recommendations of other foreign-language exchange programs.

If you have a question about the reliability, relevance, or accuracy of any source, check with your instructor or a librarian. *If you decide to use any questionable or biased sources, you need to qualify their findings and data when you introduce the source.* Otherwise, your reader may believe that your argument is based on biased, inaccurate, or unreliable data.

▮ **EVALUATING LIBRARY SOURCES**   Even with published library sources, you should appraise your sources with a critical eye, just as you do for Internet and Web sources. Just because something is published or printed does not mean that it is relevant, current, accurate, or reliable. Some sources will not relate specifically to your topic; others will be too superficial or too technical. Some will be out of date; others will be biased or simply inaccurate. Evaluate your printed sources based on the following criteria.

- **Sources should be relevant.** The sources you select should be relevant to your subject, your purpose, and your intended audience. If your narrowed topic is still too general, all your sources will look relevant. In that case, narrow your subject even more. Sources must also be relevant to your purpose. If you are writing an argumentative research paper, for example, you need sources representing both sides of the issue. If you are proposing a solution to a problem, look for sources describing the problem or the solution. Finally, sources should be appropriate for your intended audience. The articles that Kate McNerny found in *Foreign Language Annals* were more appropriate for her academic audience than was a brief and superficial article she found in *Parents* magazine.

- **Sources should be current.** As a rule of thumb, look for the most current sources—especially those on scientific or technical subjects. Research and data on AIDS are more accurate and complete now than they were in 1990. Sometimes, however, older books and articles are important. If you are doing historical research about the Great Depression in the United States, you may want to read key documents from the 1930s. In every academic discipline, some sources remain authoritative for decades. When you find that many writers refer to a single source, it may be valuable regardless of its date of publication.

- **Sources should be reliable.** Check for possible biases in articles and books. Don't expect the National Rifle Association to give an unbiased report on gun-control legislation. Don't assume that representatives of right-to-life or prochoice groups will objectively represent the full range of facts about abortion. Because at least some bias is inevitable in any source, locate and use a variety of sources representing several points of view. If you are in doubt about an author's point of view or credibility, consult experts in the field or check book reviews. *Book Review Digest,* for example, contains references to reviews that may indicate the author's reputation or reliability.

| CHOOSING | COLLECTING | GLOSSARY | EVALUATING | **PLAGIARISM** |
| SHAPING | DRAFTING | GRAPHICS | REVISING | MLA/APA |

AVOIDING PLAGIARISM

As you collect your sources, make notes, and draft your essay, be sure to give credit to your sources. Plagiarism occurs when we use the language, ideas, or visual materials from another person or text without acknowledging the source. Use the following guidelines to avoid plagiarism.

- Do not use language, ideas, or graphics from any essay, text, or visual image that you find *online,* in the *library,* or from *commercial sources* without acknowledging the source.

- Do not use language, ideas, or visuals from *any other student's essay* without acknowledging the source.

Students who plagiarize typically fail the course and face disciplinary action by the university.

Sometimes, however, students create problems by rushing or by not knowing how to quote or paraphrase accurately and fairly. You can avoid this *inadvertent* plagiarism by quoting accurately from your sources, by paraphrasing using your own words, and by citing your sources accurately.

Let's assume that you are working with the following passage, taken from the opening paragraph of an article by Marion E. Hines, "Foreign Language Curriculum Concerns in Times of Conflict," which appeared in the *Delta Kappa Gamma Bulletin* in 2003:

The United States' chronically weak language resources and lack of linguistic preparedness are invariably exposed when events such as the war in Iraq and the September 11 terror strikes threaten the balance of power, peace or detente in global affairs. In order to regain or maintain a competitive edge, the government offers grants to encourage the restructuring of curriculum, to "retool" educators, and to infuse new technologies. The efforts have been heroic, but they have not succeeded in correcting the overall problem.

Plagiarism: Every college needs to require a foreign language, in part because we need to communicate better in times of crisis. *Events such as the war in Iraq and the terror strikes* of *September 11* have exposed our *lack of linguistic preparedness.* Better knowledge of foreign languages would help us communicate with people from different cultures or religions.

Explanation: This writer uses several phrases lifted directly from the source (see italics) without using quotation marks or acknowledging the source.

Proper Citation: Every college needs to require a foreign language in part because we need to communicate better in times of crisis. Marion E. Hines, an assistant professor in modern languages and linguistics at Howard University, argues that "the United States' chronically weak language resources and lack of linguistic preparedness" result in our inability to communicate with people from different cultures or religions (15).

Explanation: In this passage, the writer cites the author before introducing the quotation, uses quotation marks for words and phrases that appear in the article, and uses the proper citation format at the end of the sentence. This article by Marion E. Hines would also be cited in the Works Cited or References page at the end of the essay.

As you take notes and write your drafts, practice using proper citation practices. If at any point you have a question about how to cite your sources accurately, recheck the sections in this chapter or ask your instructor.

▌ TAKING NOTES Taking careful notes from both published and unpublished sources is, of course, fundamental to accurate documentation. When a source appears relevant and useful, do the following.

1. **Record complete bibliographical information in the bibliography section of your research notebook (or in your computer notebook).** For many online library systems, you will be able to print out the bibliographical information you need right from your computer terminal. For *books,* you need authors, editors, titles, volumes, publishers, places of publication, and years of publication.

    For *articles,* you need authors; article titles; magazine or journal titles; volume numbers or dates, months, and years of publication; and beginning and ending page numbers. As Kate McNerny did in her log, leave a space between each entry to record call numbers or locations of documents:

(Book): Freed, Barbara F., ed. <u>Second Language Acquisition in a Study Abroad Context.</u> Philadelphia: John Benjamins, 1995.

   HF5549.A2P38   Current Periodical Room

(Article): Brady, Robert I. "English-Only Rules Draw Controversy." <u>HR Focus</u> June 1996: 20.

   P118.2.S433   1995   First Floor East

If the source is unpublished—such as a telephone conversation, a letter, or a public document in the county courthouse—record all the information about it that your readers will need to identify and consult the source themselves. (See the "Documenting Sources" section in this chapter.)

2. **Record notes in the source notes section of your research notebook.** Identify each entry with the author's name and the title. If your notes fill two or more pages, put the author and title at the top of each page. Write on only one side of each page. Briefly *summarize* the main points made in the source, note specific information useful to you, paraphrase key ideas, transcribe interesting quotations, and jot down your own brief comments, questions, and memories. Place page numbers immediately following each paraphrase or quotation. Use direct quotation rather than paraphrase when the actual words in the source are more concise, authoritative, or persuasive than your paraphrase might be. *Be sure that direct quotations are accurate, word-for-word transcriptions from the original.*

3. **Photocopy important sources for later rereading and reference.** Make sure all photocopies clearly show authors, titles, and page numbers. (For some research projects, your instructor may request photocopies of every source you paraphrase or quote.) *Tip:* If you photocopy several pages, *copy title pages or the magazines' covers,* and staple the copies together. Then you will have all the necessary bibliographical information, and you can underline key passages or make notes on the photocopies themselves.

4. **As you read sources and take notes, record your own reactions and ideas in the drafts-and-ideas section of your research or computer notebook.** Be an active reader of your sources. When you agree or disagree with what you are reading, stop for a minute and jot down your ideas. When you think of a comparison, a process, a way to analyze or evaluate something, possible causes and effects, or examples from your own experience, *write out your ideas as completely as you can, right then, while they're fresh in your mind.* Don't get so absorbed in taking notes that you forget to record your own ideas. You don't have to collect twenty sources and *then* do a draft; instead, draft ideas *as* you collect information.

| CHOOSING | COLLECTING | GLOSSARY | EVALUATING | PLAGIARISM |
| SHAPING | DRAFTING | GRAPHICS | REVISING | MLA/APA |

SHAPING

Once you've collected information for your research paper, you may feel overwhelmed by the task of shaping it into a coherent form. You can assert control over your data, however, and shape them into coherent form by reconsidering your purpose and thesis. *Reread your own notes and especially your draft sections from your research notebook.* Then, in the draft section of your notebook, answer the following questions.

Subject:	What is your general subject?
Narrowed topic or question:	What aspect of your subject is most interesting to you now? What question will you answer or explain?
Purpose:	Is your purpose primarily to inform, explain, evaluate, describe a problem and propose a solution, or argue a claim?
Working thesis:	What thesis, claim, or proposal do you want to impress upon your readers?
Audience:	Analyze your audience. How can you interest them in your subject? What aspects of your collected data are most appropriate for your audience?
Genre:	What genre will work best for your assignment or your purpose and audience? Find a sample of your genre and analyze its features. Will graphics and images be appropriate for this genre and audience?

Asking these questions will allow you to evaluate your progress, an essential step in the research process. Reread your answers to the questions above, and then ask the following questions in order to gauge whether you have a viable plan.

* Do you have enough interest in your subject at this point? Will you be able to sustain your motivation?
* Is your claim arguable? If not, should you adjust it?
* Do you have enough research to help you support your claim? If not, how will you search for it?
* Does your research display a variety of perspectives and types of sources?

These questions will help you to pinpoint problems you may be having with the project, help you identify solutions, and increase the likelihood of your success. As you shape, draft, and revise your research paper, you may continue to refocus your topic and question, refine your thesis, or revise your sense of audience.

CHOOSING	COLLECTING	GLOSSARY	EVALUATING	PLAGIARISM
SHAPING	DRAFTING	GRAPHICS	REVISING	MLA/APA

SHAPING STRATEGIES

Your goal now is to design some order, sequence, plan, or outline for your research paper. Forcing yourself to write an outline, however, simply may not work. You should have an idea from your previous papers about how your writing process works best, but if you're stuck, feeling frustrated, or overwhelmed, try several of the following strategies.

- *Review strategies for shaping* that are appropriate for your particular purpose. If you are arguing for a certain claim, reread the shaping strategies discussed in Chapter 11. If you are evaluating something or analyzing a problem and proposing a solution, review the strategies discussed in Chapter 9 or 10.
- *Explain to a friend or classmate your purpose, audience, and working thesis.* Then try to explain how you might proceed.
- *Try freewriting, looping, or clustering* to develop a plan.
- *Reread your notes and drafts* from your research notebook.
- *Take a break.* Let your ideas simmer for a while. Go for a walk. Work on assignments for another course. Go jogging or swimming. Let your mind run on automatic pilot for a while—the information and ideas in your mind may begin organizing themselves into an initial "sketch outline" without your conscious effort.
- *Try branching or treeing your main ideas.* On paper or at the chalkboard, begin with your topic and draw the trunk and main branches of your topics. Try to explain your sketch or chalkboard drawing to someone.

Think of these activities as a circle: Begin at any point, work in either direction, and repeat them as necessary. When something starts to work, stay with it for a while. If you start to block or become frustrated, go on to the next activity.

WORKING OUTLINE   If the shaping activities helped you discover a basic design or plan, translate it into a working outline. If not, you may need to begin drafting in order to discover an outline. Kate McNerny decided to follow a pattern for writing an argument. Although she modified it considerably to change her purpose to problem solving, the sketch outline helped her organize her ideas and source material so she could begin drafting.

I. Introduction: Comments—quotations from informal survey—why people feel they don't need to know a foreign language.

Mention study on misconceptions of school-aged children about Russian children.

II. Narration: Foreign-language studies' position in other countries as opposed to U.S.

Mention "Official English" here?

Include example of European requirements?

Statistics on how many Americans are actually competent in another language.

Mention bills to require a state language?

U.S. position in world as far as power, trade.

III. Partition: American students should be required to study a foreign language throughout the six years of junior and senior high school. To increase number of students studying foreign language, we need changes in administrators and teachers, changes in students, and changes in state and national policies.

IV. Arguments: An increase in number of students studying foreign languages would:

Help to improve diplomatic relations with other countries—peace cannot be achieved without this.

Change Americans' attitudes toward foreigners and change foreigners' attitudes toward Americans.

Facilitate international trade and other business.

Increase jobs for students abroad and at home.

Without requirement, no incentive for many students.

V. Refutation: Not necessary because other countries can speak English. (This is more an argument against learning a language, not against a requirement.)

Not essential for quality education.

As requirement, would detract from other important subjects.

Not enough federal, state, or local money to change number of foreign-language courses offered.

VI. Conclusion: Call for action on part of federal government.

Contrary to popular belief, we are not an isolated country.

A required study of languages will bring us one step closer to global understanding and peace.

▌ **ORGANIZING YOUR NOTES**   With a rough outline as a guide, reread your draft ideas, notes, and photocopies, and label them according to headings and subheadings in your working outline (for instance, I: Intro; II: Background and History; III: Required Changes; IV: Advantages of Changes; and V: Conclusion). Before you remove pages from the source notes section of your notebook or unstaple photocopied articles or sections of books, *make sure each entry or photocopy contains the author, title, and page numbers.* Now you are ready to arrange your notes and copies for use during drafting. Organize your notes into groups according to each section of your working outline. Reread each group, deciding which information should come first, in the middle, or last.

CHOOSING	COLLECTING	GLOSSARY	EVALUATING	PLAGIARISM
SHAPING	**DRAFTING**	GRAPHICS	REVISING	MLA/APA

DRAFTING

At this point, some of the most difficult work is behind you. Congratulate yourself—there aren't many people who know as much as you do right now about your subject. You are an authority: You have information, statistics, statements, ideas from other writers and researchers, and your own experiences and observations at your fingertips. As you write, remember your purpose and audience. What is your purpose—to inform, explain, evaluate, offer a solution, or argue? Who exactly is your audience? What arguments and evidence will convince them? Your sources will become the evidence and support for *your ideas.* Remember that your voice and point of view should unify the information for your reader.

Many writers prefer to start a draft with the first main idea, leaving the introduction until later. As you write, you may discover a quotation, example, or narrative that doesn't fit anywhere else but that would be a perfect lead-in. Or you may already know how you want to start, using an idea that will help organize and direct your thoughts. As you draft, be guided by your working outline and your notes. Avoid copying passages verbatim from your own notebook ideas; instead, reread your notes and express those ideas in language that fits the idea you're working on.

If you get stuck, go back and reread what you have drafted so far or reread the source notes and ideas that you have assembled from your notebook and photocopies. Try to maintain your momentum by writing as quickly as possible. Don't be upset if the natural flow of your writing suggests a slightly different order or deviates from your working outline. Consider the new possibility. You may have discovered a better way to shape your material. If you are missing some fact or quotation, just leave a long line and keep writing. Later you can find the source and add the material you need.

USING GRAPHICS

As you draft your essay, you may need to decide whether to include data and statistics in your sentences or add graphics, charts, or other visuals to emphasize your point. Writing on foreign-language requirements, for example, imagine that you have photocopied pages from an article by the Department of Modern and Classical Languages at the University of Connecticut, "A National Study on Secondary to Postsecondary Foreign Language Articulation." You have photocopied the following two paragraphs and accompanying figures.

Reason for Studying a Foreign Language

When administrators and teachers were asked to state the main reason students study a foreign language, the overwhelming majority (82% and

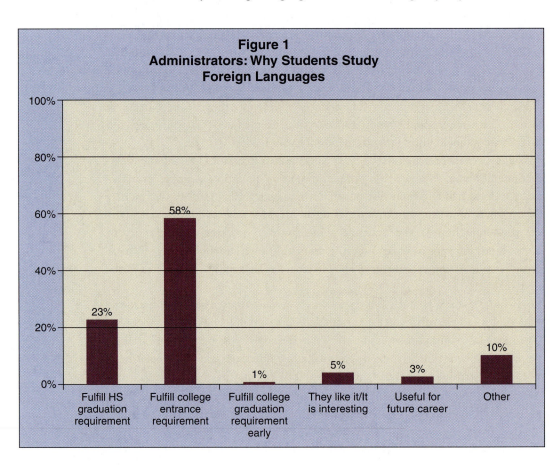

Figure 1
Administrators: Why Students Study
Foreign Languages

84% respectively) felt it was to fulfill a requirement. Only 5% of administrators and 8% of teachers believed students learn a foreign language for enjoyment or interest [Figure 1]. Students were also asked the main reason they studied foreign languages. For more than half (56%) of the students, the stated reason was to fulfill a requirement. About one out of four (24%) students studied a language because they find it interesting or they like it.

However, when given the opportunity to list all the reasons they studied a foreign language, students selected the following: 52% to fulfill a high school graduation requirement, 44% to fulfill a college entrance requirement, 43% due to interest or enjoyment, 15% for traveling, 13% for a future career, 8% to learn the language of ethnic heritage, and 7% to fulfill a college graduation requirement early. An additional 6% gave other reasons for learning a foreign language [Figure 2].

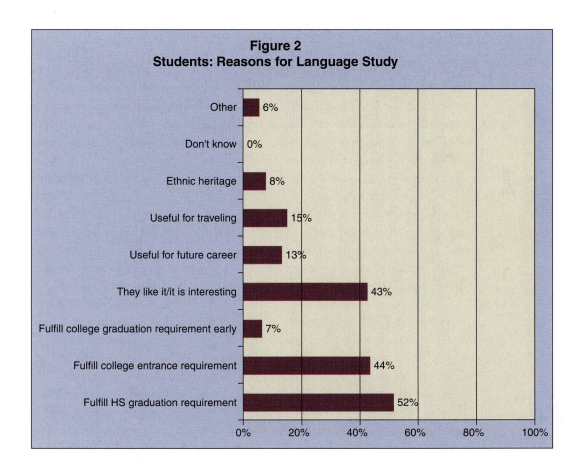

Figure 2
Students: Reasons for Language Study

As you draft, decide when you want to make your point by using data in your sentences and when you want to add a graph for illustration. In this example, you might want to cite the statistic in the first sentence of the first paragraph. ("According to this study, approximately 82% of administrators indicated that students took a foreign language primarily because of high school or college requirements.") The accompanying bar graph would help make the point, but might not be necessary. However, in the second paragraph, including all the percentages would make your argument too tedious and dry. Using the bar graph with a short introduction would make the point much more concisely.

■ **USING SOURCES** Proper use of sources requires both creativity and scrupulous honesty. On the one hand, you want to use other people's information and ideas when and where they serve *your* purpose and *your* ideas. A research paper is not simply a long string of quotations connected by a few transitions. On the other hand, the sources you cite or quote must be used *fairly* and *honestly*. You must give credit for other writers' ideas and information. You must quote accurately, cite your sources in your text, and document those sources accurately.

■ **WHAT SOURCES TO CITE** You must cite a source for any fact or bit of information that is not *general knowledge*. Obviously, what is "general knowledge" varies from one writer and audience to another. **As a rule, however, document any information or fact that you did not know before you began your research.** You may know, for example, that America spends more money on defense than it does on education. However, if you state that the defense budget for the previous year is greater than the total amount spent on education for the past forty years, then cite the source for that fact.

Knowing when you must cite a source for an idea, however, can be tricky. You do not need to indicate a source for *your* ideas, of course. But if you find a source that agrees with your idea, or if you suspect that your idea may be related to ideas from a particular source, cite that source. A citation gives your idea additional credibility: You show your reader that another authority shares your perception.

■ **HOW TO CITE SOURCES** In the text of your research paper, you will need to cite your sources according to either the Modern Language Association (MLA) style or the American Psychological Association (APA) style. Remember: Choose either the MLA style or the APA style and stick with it. Don't mix styles.

According to the MLA style, the in-text citation contains the author and page number of your source (Torres 50). No comma appears between author and page number. (If the author is unknown, identify the title and page number of your source. Underline or italicize book titles; place quotation marks around article titles.)

According to the APA style, the in-text citation contains author and date (Torres, 1996). Use a comma between author and date. If you refer to a page number, it should appear after the author and date (Torres, 1996, p. 50). Use a *p.* (or *pp.* for more than one page) before the page number(s).

The in-text citation (either MLA or APA) refers readers to the end of your paper, where you give complete information about each source in a "Works Cited" (MLA) or "References" (APA) list. For illustration purposes, the following examples use MLA style. See the "Documenting Sources" section (pp. 706–729) for examples of both APA and MLA styles.

▌ IDENTIFY CITED REFERENCES (MLA STYLE)   Once you have

decided that a fact, a paraphrase, or a direct quotation contributes to your thesis and will make a strong impression on your reader, use the following guidelines for in-text citation.

- **Identify in the text the persons or source for the fact, paraphrased idea, or quotation.**

As two foreign-language teachers noted, "Like it or not, we are members of a world community consisting of hundreds of nations, and our fates are closely intertwined" (Long and Long 366).

Note: The parentheses and the period *follow* the final quotation marks.

- **If you cite the author in your sentence, the parentheses will contain only the page reference.**

According to Paul Simon, former member of the President's Commission on Foreign Language, the United States should erect a sign at each port of entry that reads, "WELCOME TO THE UNITED STATES—WE CANNOT SPEAK YOUR LANGUAGE" (1).

- **Use block format (beginning on a new line, indented one inch from the left margin, and double-spaced) for quotations of five lines or more.**

Educator Gerald Unks points out two instances in which a lack of language proficiency caused companies to initiate fatal marketing programs.

> When Pepsi-Cola went after the Chinese market, "Come Alive with Pepsi" was translated into Chinese in Taiwan as "Pepsi Brings Your Ancestors Back from the Dead." No Sale! General Motors sought to sell its Nova in South America, oblivious to the fact that "No va" in Spanish means "It doesn't go." (24)

Note: In block quotations, the final punctuation mark comes *before* the parentheses, and no quotation marks are used to set off the cited material.

CITING A BOOK

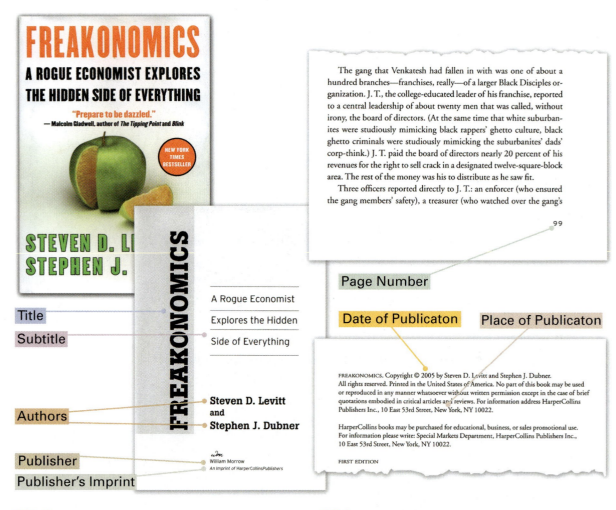

MLA

Works Cited Format

Levitt, Steven D., and Stephen J. Dubner. Freakonomics: A Rogue Economist Explores the Hidden Side of Everything. New York: William Morrow-Harper, 2005.

In-Text Citation

The authors of one recent bestseller claim that "if you were to hold a McDonald's organizational chart and a Black Disciples org chart side by side, you could hardly tell the difference" (Levitt and Dubner 99).

APA

Reference Page Format

Levitt, S. D., & Dubner, S. J. (2005). *Freakonomics: A rogue economist explores the hidden side of every-thing.* New York: William Morrow-Harper.

In-Text Citation

The authors of one recent bestseller claim that "if you were to hold a McDonald's organizational chart and a Black Disciples org chart side by side, you could hardly tell the difference" (Levitt & Dubner, 2005, p. 99).

CITING A PERIODICAL

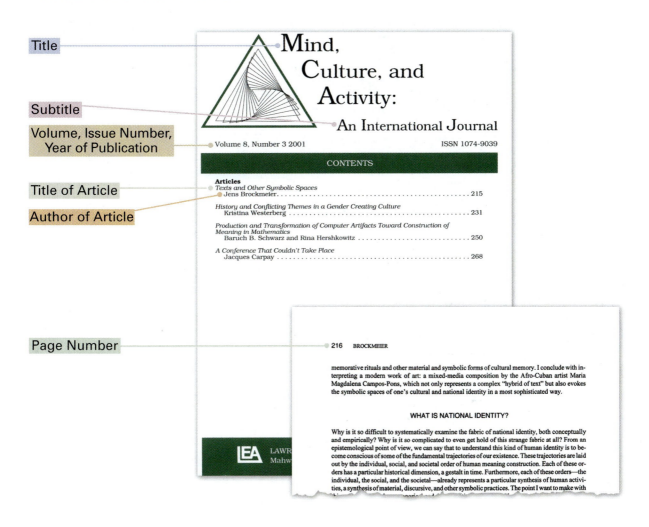

Title

Subtitle

Volume, Issue Number, Year of Publication

Title of Article

Author of Article

Page Number

Mind, Culture, and Activity:
An International Journal

Volume 8, Number 3 2001   ISSN 1074-9039

CONTENTS

Articles
Texts and Other Symbolic Spaces
   Jens Brockmeier. 215

History and Conflicting Themes in a Gender Creating Culture
   Kristina Westerberg 231

*Production and Transformation of Computer Artifacts Toward Construction of
Meaning in Mathematics*
   Baruch B. Schwarz and Rina Hershkowitz 250

A Conference That Couldn't Take Place
   Jacques Carpay 268

LEA   LAWR
Mahw

216   BROCKMEIER

memorative rituals and other material and symbolic forms of cultural memory. I conclude with interpreting a modern work of art: a mixed-media composition by the Afro-Cuban artist Maria Magdalena Campos-Pons, which not only represents a complex "hybrid of text" but also evokes the symbolic spaces of one's cultural and national identity in a most sophisticated way.

WHAT IS NATIONAL IDENTITY?

Why is it so difficult to systematically examine the fabric of national identity, both conceptually and empirically? Why is it so complicated to even get hold of this strange fabric at all? From an epistemological point of view, we can say that to understand this kind of human identity is to become conscious of some of the fundamental trajectories of our existence. These trajectories are laid out by the individual, social, and societal order of human meaning construction. Each of these orders has a particular historical dimension, a gestalt in time. Furthermore, each of these orders—the individual, the social, and the societal—already represents a particular synthesis of human activities, a synthesis of material, discursive, and other symbolic practices. The point I want to make with

MLA

Works Cited Format

Brockmeier, Jens. "Texts and Other Symbolic Spaces." Mind, Culture, and Activity: An International Journal 8 (2001): 215-30.

In-Text Citation

Educational psychologist Jens Brockmeier defines national identity as "a synthesis of material, discursive, and other symbolic practices" (216).

APA

Reference Page Format

Brockmeier, J. (2001). Texts and other symbolic spaces. *Mind, Culture, and Activity: An International Journal, 8,* 215-230.

In-Text Citation

Educational psychologist Jens Brockmeier (2001) defines national identity as "a synthesis of material, discursive, and other symbolic practices" (p. 216).

CITING A WORK FROM AN ONLINE SUBSCRIPTION DATABASE

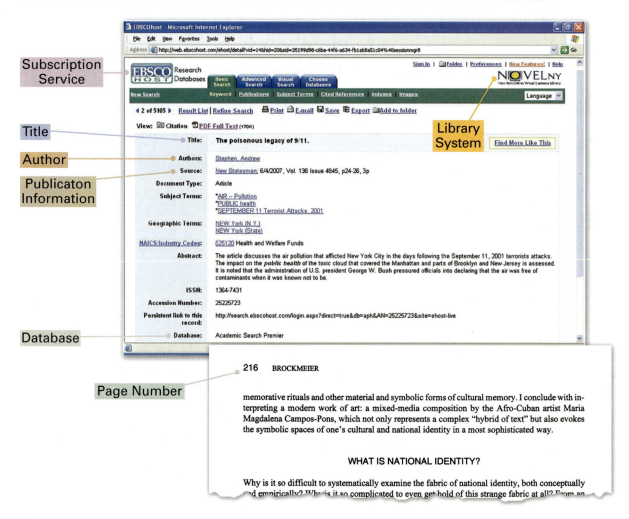

MLA

Works Cited Format

Stephen, Andrew. "The Poisonous Legacy of 9/11." *New Statesman* 24 June 2007: 24–26. Academic Search Premier. EBSCO. New York Public Library. 20 June 2007. <http://www.epnet.com/>.

In-Text Citation

Journalist Andrew Stephen reports that 10,000 people have so far filed court claims alleging that they were exposed to toxic substances after the attack on the World Trade Center (24).

APA

Reference Page Format

Stephen, A. (2007). The poisonous legacy of 9/11. *New Statesman:* 24–26. Retrieved June 20, 2007, from Academic Search Premier database.

In-Text Citation

Journalist Andrew Stephen (2007) reports that 10,000 people have so far filed court claims alleging that they were exposed to toxic substances after the attack on the World Trade Center (p. 24).

- **Vary your introductions to quotations.**

Educator Gerald Unks claims that "only 15 percent of American high school students study a foreign language. Only 8 percent of our colleges require credit in a foreign language for admission (down from 34 percent in 1966)" (24).

The problem is that high school students are not taking foreign languages, and most colleges no longer require a foreign language for admission: "Only 15 percent of American high school students study a foreign language. Only 8 percent of our colleges require credit in a foreign language for admission (down from 34 percent in 1966)" (Unks 24).

- **Edit quotations when necessary to condense or clarify.** Use ellipsis marks, which are three points preceded and followed by a space (. . .), if you omit words from the middle of a quoted sentence.

As two foreign language teachers noted, "We are members of a world community . . . and our fates are closely intertwined" (Long and Long 366).

> If you omit words from the end of a quoted sentence or omit sentences from a long quoted passage, place a period after the last word quoted before the omission; follow it with ellipsis marks—for a total of four periods. Be sure that you have a complete sentence both before and after the four points.

Paul Simon advises us that our nation's lack of language proficiency may have been a partial cause of our disastrous policies in Vietnam:

> Vietnam and the Middle East have taught us that our security position is not solely a matter of dealing with the Warsaw Pact countries or the giants among the nations. Before our heavy intervention in Vietnam, fewer than five American-born experts on Vietnam, Cambodia, or Laos . . . could speak with ease one of the languages of that area. . . . What if—a big if—we had had . . . a mere twenty Americans who spoke Vietnamese fluently, who understood their culture, aspirations, and political history? Maybe, just maybe, we would have avoided that conflict. (9)

Note: The first line is indented an additional half-inch because in the source the quotation begins a new paragraph.

> In some cases you may want to change the wording of a quotation or add explanatory words of your own to clarify your quotation. If you do so, clearly indicate your changes or additions by placing them within square brackets.

As Simon suggests, if only a few Americans knew Vietnamese, then "maybe, just maybe, we would have avoided [the Vietnam War]" (9).

CHOOSING   COLLECTING   GLOSSARY   EVALUATING   PLAGIARISM
SHAPING   DRAFTING   GRAPHICS   **REVISING**   MLA/APA

REVISING

You have been revising your research essay since the first day of the project. You thought about several subjects, for example, but you chose only one. You started with a focus but revised it as you thought, read, and wrote more. You initially tested your ideas in the draft section of your research notebook, but you revised those ideas as you drafted. At this point, you are just continuing your revising; now, however, you have a complete draft to revise.

> **❝** What makes me happy is rewriting. . . . It's like cleaning house, getting rid of all the junk, getting things in the right order, tightening things up. **❞**
> —ELLEN GOODMAN, JOURNALIST

Start the revision of your complete draft by taking a break. Fix your schedule so that you can do something else for a couple of days. When you return and reread your draft, be prepared to be flexible. If there is something missing in your data, prepare yourself to track down the information. If a favorite source or quotation no longer seems relevant, have the courage to delete it. If an example on page 4 would work better as a lead-in for the whole paper, reorder your material accordingly. If the evidence for one side of an argument appears stronger than you initially thought, change your position and your thesis. *Being willing to make such changes is not a sign of poor research and writing. Often, in fact, it demonstrates that you have become more knowledgeable and sophisticated about your subject.*

After you have finished your rough draft, ask friends or classmates to give you their responses. Accept their criticism gracefully, but ask them to explain *why* they think certain changes would help. Would they help to make your purposes clearer? Would they be more appropriate for your audience? Don't be intimidated and feel that you must make every change that readers suggest. You must make the final decisions.

CHOOSING   COLLECTING   GLOSSARY   EVALUATING   PLAGIARISM
SHAPING   DRAFTING   GRAPHICS   REVISING   **MLA/APA**

DOCUMENTING SOURCES

Both the MLA and APA documentation styles require citation of sources in the text of your paper, followed by a Works Cited (MLA style) or References list (APA style) at the end of your paper. Use footnotes only for content or supplementary notes that explain a point covered in the text or offer additional information. *Note:* MLA in-text documentation and Works Cited documentation are explained here. See pages 720–729 for APA in-text documentation and References format.

In-Text Documentation: MLA Style   In the MLA style, give the author's name and the page numbers in parentheses following your use of a fact, paraphrase, or direct quotation from a source. These in-text citations then refer your readers to the complete documentation of the source in a Works Cited or Works Consulted list at the end of the paper.

As you cite your sources in the text, use the following guidelines.

If you cite the author in the text, indicate only the page number in parentheses.

According to Vicki Galloway, Project Director for the American Council on the Teaching of Foreign Languages, a student's horizons will not be broadened by "grammar lectures and manipulative classroom exercises" (33).

If the author is unknown, use a short version of the title in the parentheses.

Most students in the United States would be surprised to learn that the Communist Party in Russia actually sponsors rock concerts (A Day in the Life 68).

If the source is unpublished, cite the name or title used in your Works Cited.

In an informal interview, one university administrator noted that funding of foreign-language study has steadily decreased over the past ten years (Meyers).

If the source is from the Internet or the Web, use the author, or if there is no author, use the title. Include page or paragraph numbers if provided (as, for example, in a PDF document):

Many Web sites now provide detailed information about how to plan a study-abroad semester or year (Foreign Language).

If your bibliography contains more than one work by an author, cite the author, a short title, and page numbers. The following examples show various ways of citing a reference to Paul Simon, *The Tongue-Tied American.*

In The Tongue-Tied American, Simon explains that students can earn a doctorate degree in the United States without ever studying a foreign language (2).

As Simon notes, "It is even possible to earn a doctorate here without studying any foreign language" (Tongue-Tied 2).

In the United States, one can earn a doctorate degree without studying a single foreign language (Simon, Tongue-Tied 2).

Note: Use a comma between author and title, but not between title and page number.

If a source has two or three authors, cite all authors' names in the text or in the parentheses.

A recent study sampling 536 secondary schools revealed that 91 percent did not require foreign-language credits for graduation (Ranwez and Rodgers 98).

Note: If there are three authors, use commas to separate them, e.g., (Ranwez, Rogers, and Smith 98).

If a source has more than three authors, you may either list all authors' names, separated by commas, or simply give the name of the author listed first followed by the abbreviation *et al.,* meaning "and others."

> Teachers should integrate the study of history, culture, politics, literature, and religion of a particular region with the study of language (Berryman et al. 96).

If you cite several volumes from the same source, precede the page number with the volume number and a colon, as indicated.

> Language and grammar can be taught with real-life contexts or scenarios (Valdman 3:82).

Note: If you cite only one volume of a multivolume work, you need not list the volume number in your in-text citation, but you must list it in your Works Cited.

If you are citing a quotation or information that is itself cited in another source, use the abbreviation *qtd. in* for "quoted in" to indicate that you have used an indirect source for your information or quotation. (If possible, however, check the original source.)

> As Sue Berryman and her colleagues explain, "The course is developed as a world tour during which time the students take a vicarious trip . . . to become saturated in every aspect of a particular area of the globe" (qtd. in Simon 96).

If you cite two or more authors as sources for a fact, idea, or plan, separate the citations with a semicolon, as follows.

> Most recently, two prominent foreign language educators have published plans to coordinate foreign-language studies (Lambert 9–19; Lange 70–96).

Content or Supplementary Notes

You may include footnotes or endnotes in your paper if you have an important idea, a comment on your text, or additional information or sources *that would interrupt the flow of your ideas in the text.* During her research, for example, McNerny read about the movement to make English the "official language" of the United States. She didn't want to digress in her paper, so she described the controversy in a supplementary endnote. Here is a first draft of that note.

> [1]Several states currently have bills before their legislatures to make English the "official language." Proponents of these bills argue that immigrants need incentives to learn English. Many opponents from ethnic and civil rights

groups believe these bills are racist (McBee 64). If Americans were all educated in foreign languages, these bills would be unnecessary. Americans'
ignorance and fear of foreign languages are probably a reason that these bills
are so popular.

Works Cited List: MLA Style   After you have revised your essay and are
certain that you will not change any in-text documentation, you are ready to write
your list of sources. Depending on what you include, it will be one of the following:

- A Works Cited list (only those works actually cited in your essay)
- A Works Consulted list (works cited and works you read)
- A Selected Bibliography (works cited and the most important other works)
- An Annotated List of Works Cited (works cited, followed by a short
  description and evaluation of each source)

A Works Cited list alphabetically orders, by author's last name, all published
and unpublished sources cited in your research paper. If the author is unknown, alphabetize by the first word (excluding *A, An,* or *The*) of the title. Use the following
abbreviations for missing information other than an unknown author: n.p. (no place
of publication given), n.p. (no publisher given), n.d. (no date of publication given),
or n. pag. (no pagination in source). The first line of each citation begins at the left
margin, and succeeding lines are indented one-half inch. Double-space the entire
Works Cited list.

Following are examples of MLA-style entries in a Works Cited list, organized
by kind of source: books, articles, and unpublished sources. Use these as models for
your own Works Cited list. For additional information and examples, see *MLA
Handbook for Writers of Research Papers* (6th ed., 2003).

Note: In your essay or manuscript, citations of titles of articles, poems, and short
stories should be surrounded by quotation marks ("The Story of an Hour"). Titles
of books, plays, novels, magazines, journals, or collections should be underlined
(<u>Caramelo</u>, <u>National Geographic</u>). Underlining indicates to a publisher that a title
should be placed in italics. When your essay or manuscript is published, underlining is then replaced by italics (*Caramelo, National Geographic*). If you wish to use italics in your Works Cited list to indicate underlining, check with your instructor.

BOOKS: MLA STYLE

Order the information as follows, omitting information that does not apply.

Author's Last Name, First Name. "Title of Article or Part of Book." <u>Title of Book</u>.

Ed. or Trans. Name. Edition. Number of volumes. Place of Publication: Name
of Publisher, date of publication.

A Book by One Author

Cisneros, Sandra. <u>Caramelo</u>. New York: Random, 2002.

IN-TEXT CITATION: (Cisneros 24), or simply (24) if the author's name is mentioned in the text.

(The names of well-known publishers are often shortened to the first key word. Thus, "Houghton Mifflin Co." becomes "Houghton," and "Harcourt Brace Jovanovich, Inc." becomes simply "Harcourt.")

Two or More Works by Same Author

Morrison, Toni. <u>Song of Solomon</u>. New York: Knopf, 1977.

IN-TEXT CITATION: (Morrison, <u>Song of Solomon</u> 64)

——. <u>Jazz</u>. New York: Knopf, 1992.

IN-TEXT CITATION: (Morrison, <u>Jazz</u> 52)

A Book with Two or Three Authors

Conklin, Nancy F., and Margaret A. Lourie. <u>A Host of Tongues: Language Communities in the United States</u>. New York: Free Press, 1983.

IN-TEXT CITATION: (Conklin and Lourie 67)

Padilla, Amando M., Halford H. Fairchild, and Concepcion M. Valadez. <u>Foreign Language Education</u>. Newbury Park, CA: Sage, 1990.

IN-TEXT CITATION: (Padilla, Fairchild, and Valdez 87)

A Book with More Than Three Authors

Abrams, M. H., et al. <u>The Norton Anthology of English Literature</u>. 7th ed. New York: Norton, 2000.

IN-TEXT CITATION: (Abrams et al. 168)

An Unknown or Anonymous Author

<u>Encyclopedia of White-Collar Crime</u>. Westport, CT: Greenwood, 2007.

IN-TEXT CITATION: (<u>Encyclopedia</u> 304)

A Book with an Author and an Editor

Austen, Jane. <u>Pride and Prejudice</u>. Ed. Mark Schorer. Boston: Houghton, 1956.

IN-TEXT CITATION: (Austen 49)

An Edited Book

Myers, Linda, ed. <u>Approaches to Computer Writing Classrooms</u>. Albany: State U of
New York P, 1993.

IN-TEXT CITATION: (Myers 12)

(The words *University* and *Press* are commonly shortened to *U* and *P* wherever they
appear in citations.)

A Translation

Allende, Isabel. <u>Paula</u>. Trans. Margaret Sayers Peden. New York: Harper, 1996.

IN-TEXT CITATION: (Allende 20)

An Article or Chapter in an Edited Book

Sophocles. <u>Electra</u>. Trans. David Grene. <u>Greek Tragedies</u>. Ed. David Grene and
Richmond Lattimore. Vol 2. Chicago: U of Chicago P, 1960. 2 vols. 45–109.

IN-TEXT CITATION: (Sophocles 346)

A Work in More Than One Volume

Morrison, Samuel Eliot, and Henry Steele Commager. <u>The Growth of the American
Republic</u>. 2 vols. New York: Oxford UP, 1941.

IN-TEXT CITATION: (Morrison and Commanger 1:2)

A Work in an Anthology

Chopin, Kate. "The Awakening." <u>The Harper Single-Volume American Literature</u>.
Ed. Donald McQuade, et al. 3rd ed. New York: Longman, 1999.

IN-TEXT CITATION: (Chopin 247)

An Encyclopedia or Dictionary Entry

"Don Giovanni." <u>The Encyclopedia Americana</u>. 2004 ed.

IN-TEXT CITATION: ("Don Giovanni" 409)

A Government Document: Known Author

Juhnke, Gerald A. <u>Addressing School Violence: Practical Strategies &
Interventions</u>. ERIC Counseling and Student Services Clearinghouse.
Greensboro, NC: GPO, 2001.

IN-TEXT CITATION: (Juhnke 112-138)

(*GPO* stands for "Government Printing Office.")

A Government Document: Unknown Author

United States. Maternal and Child Health Bureau. <u>Babies Sleep Safest on Their</u>
<u>Backs: Reduce the Risk of Sudden Infant Death Syndrome (SIDS)</u>. Bethesda,
MD: GPO, 2001.

IN-TEXT CITATION: (United States, Maternal and Child Health Bureau 55–78)

An Unpublished Dissertation

Burnham, William A. "Peregrine Falcon Egg Variation, Incubation, and Population
Recovery Strategy." Diss. Colorado State U, 1984.

IN-TEXT CITATION: (Burnham 79)

A Pamphlet

<u>Guide to Raptors</u>. Denver: Center for Raptor Research, 2003.

IN-TEXT CITATION: (<u>Guide</u> 43)

PERIODICALS: MLA STYLE

For all articles published in periodicals, give the author's name, the title of the
article, and the name of the publication. For newspapers and magazines, add complete dates and inclusive page numbers. Use the first page number and a plus sign
if an article is not printed on consecutive pages. For most professional journals, add
volume numbers, issue numbers if appropriate, years of publication, and inclusive
page numbers.

An Article in a Weekly or Biweekly Magazine

Hersh, Seymour M. "Chain of Command." <u>The New Yorker</u> 17 May 2004: 38–43.

IN-TEXT CITATION: (Hersh 38)

An Article in a Monthly or Bimonthly Magazine

Appenzeller, Tim. "The End of Cheap Oil." <u>National Geographic</u> June 2004:
80–109.

IN-TEXT CITATION: (Appenzeller 80)

Morrison, Ann M., Randall P. White, and Ellen Van Velsor. "Executive Women:
Substance Plus Style." <u>Psychology Today</u> Aug. 1987: 18+.

IN-TEXT CITATION: (Morrison, White, and Van Velsor 18)

An Unsigned Article in a Magazine

"E-Commerce Takes Off." <u>Economist</u> 15–21 May 2004: 9.

IN-TEXT CITATION: ("E-Commerce")

An Article in a Professional Journal

Many professional journals have continuous page numbers throughout the year. The first issue of the year begins with page 1, but every issue after that begins with the number following the last page number of the previous issue. For such journals, give volume followed by the year.

Swope, Christopher. "Panel OKs Bill to Make English Official Government

Language." <u>Congressional Quarterly Weekly Report</u> 54 (1996): 2128–29.

IN-TEXT CITATION: (Swope 2128)

(For page numbers over 100, use only two digits for the final page citation: 2128–29.)

If each issue of a professional journal begins with page 1, cite the volume number followed by a period, then the issue number and year. In the following example, the article is in Volume 9, Issue 1, published in January 1987.

Brodkey, Linda. "Writing Ethnographic Narratives." <u>Written Communication</u> 9.1

(1987): 25–50.

IN-TEXT CITATION: (Brodkey 25)

An Article in a Newspaper

Omit the introductory article (*New York Times* instead of *The New York Times*). If the masthead indicates an edition (late ed.), include it in your entry. Newspaper articles do not usually appear on consecutive pages, so indicate the page number on which the article begins and then put a plus sign + to indicate that the article continues on later pages. Indicate section numbers (A, B, C) when appropriate.

Harmon, Amy. "In New Tests for Fetal Defects, Agonizing Choices for Parents."

<u>New York Times</u> 20 June 2004, late natl. ed.: A1+.

IN-TEXT CITATION: (Harmon A1)

An Unsigned Article in a Newspaper

"A Jet Crash That Defies Resolution." <u>Los Angeles Times</u> 5 Sept. 2001: A1.

IN-TEXT CITATION: ("Jet Crash")

An Editorial

Fish, Stanley. "When Principles Get in the Way." Editorial. <u>New York Times</u>

26 Dec. 1996, late ed.: A27.

IN-TEXT CITATION: (Fish)

A Published Interview

Lamm, Richard D. "Governments Face Tough Times." With Robert Baun.

<u>Coloradoan</u> [Ft. Collins, CO] 30 Nov. 1995: B9.

IN-TEXT CITATION: (Lamm)

An Unsigned Editorial in a Newspaper

"A Primary Choice: Mark Green." <u>New York Times</u> 2 Sept. 2001, sec. 5: 8.

IN-TEXT CITATION: ("Primary Choice")

A Review

Iovine, Julie V. "Hi, Honey, I'm at the Airport." Rev. of <u>The Terminal</u>, dir. Steven
      Spielberg. <u>New York Times</u> 9 May 2004, late ed.: A36.

IN-TEXT CITATION: (Iovine)

Rosen, Charles, and Henri Zerner. "Scenes from the American Dream." Rev. of
      <u>Norman Rockwell: Pictures for the American People</u> by Maureen Hart
      Hennessey and Anne Knutson. <u>New York Review of Books</u> 8 Oct. 2000: 16–20.

IN-TEXT CITATION: (Rosen and Zerner 16)

ELECTRONIC AND INTERNET SOURCES: MLA STYLE

The World Wide Web and the Internet are still changing, so MLA guidelines, the latest of which are available in the sixth edition of the *MLA Handbook for Writers of Research Papers* (2003), will continue to change. The current abbreviated basic features of an electronic or Internet citation, given below, appear in complete form on the MLA home page at http://www.mla.org. Use the specific citations following this list as models for your own citations. For additional examples, consult the MLA home page or the most recent edition of the *MLA Handbook for Writers of Research Papers.*

1. Name of author (if known)
2. Title of article, short story, poem, or short work within a book, periodical, or database
3. Title of book (underlined)
4. Name of the editor or translator (if relevant), preceded by appropriate abbreviation, such as *Ed.* or *Trans.*
5. Publication information for any print version of the source
6. Title of periodical, database, scholarly project, or site (underlined), or for a site with no title, a description such as *home page*
7. Name of the editor of the project or database (if available)
8. The volume number, issue number, or other version number of the source
9. Date of electronic publication, update, or posting
10. Name of the subscription service and—if the library is a subscriber—the name and city (and state abbreviation, if necessary) of the library

11. For a posting to a discussion list or forum, the name of the list or forum

12. The number of pages, paragraphs, or sections, if they are numbered

13. The name of any organization sponsoring the Web site

14. Date when researcher accessed the source or site

15. Electronic address or URL of the source in angle brackets. *Note:* If a URL must be divided between two lines, break it only after a slash. Do not use a hyphen.

A Scholarly Project

<u>Labyrinth: Resources for Medieval Studies</u>. 2005. Georgetown U. 20 June 2007
        <http://www8.georgetown.edu/departments/medieval/labyrinth/>.

IN-TEXT CITATION: (<u>Labyrinth</u>)

A Book

Hawthorne, Nathaniel. <u>The Scarlet Letter: A Romance</u>. Boston: Ticknor and Fields,
        1850. <u>Eldritch Press</u>. 1999. 14 Mar. 2007 <http://www.eldritchpress.org/
        nh/sl.html#toc>.

IN-TEXT CITATION: (Hawthorne, ch. 15: pars. 22–25)

(If the online source includes paragraph numbers instead of page numbers, use *par.* with the number.)

A Poem

Wheatley, Phillis. "On Being Brought from Africa to America." <u>Poems on Various</u>
        <u>Subjects, Religious and Moral</u>. Philadelphia, 1786. <u>Electronic Text Center</u>.
        Nov. 2006. U. of Virginia Library. 4 June 2007 <http://etext.lib.virginia.edu/
        toc/modeng/public/WhePoem.html>.

IN-TEXT CITATION: (Wheatley 13)

A Web Site

American Medical Association. Home page. April 2007. 12 May 2007 <http://www.
        ama-assn.org>.

IN-TEXT CITATION: (American)

A Page from a Web Site

American Medical Association. "Principles of Medical Ethics." 30 April 2007
        <http://www.ama-assn.org/ama/pub/category/2512.html>.

IN-TEXT CITATION: (American)

An Article in a Scholarly Journal

Mossman, Mark. "Acts of Becoming: Autobiography, Frankenstein, and the
Postmodern Body." <u>Postmodern Culture</u> 11.3 (2001). 10 Sept. 2006
<http://www3.iath.virginia.edu/pmc/text-only/issue.501/11.3mossman.txt>.

IN-TEXT CITATION: (Mossman, par. 28)

An Article in a Magazine

Smith, Dakota. "Black Women Ignore Many of Media's Beauty Ideals. <u>Women's</u>
<u>E-News</u> 17 June 2004. 4 June 2007 <http://www.womensenews.org/article.
cfm/dyn/aid/1865>.

IN-TEXT CITATION: (Smith)

An Anonymous Article in a Magazine

"The First Private Rocket Ship Soars into Space." <u>USNews.com</u> 22 June 2004.
6 June 2007 <http://www.usnews.com/usnews/tech/nextnews/archive/
next040622.htm>.

IN-TEXT CITATION: ("First Private")

An Article in a Newspaper

Safire, William. "The Great Cash Cow." <u>NYTimes.com</u> 23 June 2004. 25 June 2004
<http://www.nytimes.com/2004/06/23/opinion/23SAFI.html>.

IN-TEXT CITATION: (Safire)

An Editorial

Regan, Tom. "The New Political Correctness and the GOP." Editorial. <u>Christian</u>
<u>Science Monitor</u> 2 Feb. 1999. 3 Feb. 1999 <http://www.csmonitor.com/
atcmonitor/commop/regan/>.

IN-TEXT CITATION: (Regan)

A Letter to the Editor

Fuld, Leonard. Letter. <u>NYTimes.com</u> 4 Sept. 2001. 6 Sept. 2001 <http://www.
nytimes.com/2001/09/05/opinion/LOCELL.html>.

IN-TEXT: (Fuld)

A Work from an Online Subscription Database

To cite online material from a database to which a library subscribes, complete the
citation by giving the name of the database (underlined), the name of the service (if

available), the name of the library, and the date of access, followed by the URL of the service's home page, in angle brackets.

Hines, Marion E. "Foreign Language Curriculum Concerns in Times of Conflict."
Delta Kappa Gamma Bulletin 70 (Fall 2003): 15–22. Academic Search Premier.
EBSCO. Colorado State U Lib. 23 May 2004 <http://0-web2.epnet.com>.

IN-TEXT CITATION: (Hines 15)

Jost, Kenneth. "Could the Terrorist Attacks Have Been Prevented?" CQ
Researcher 4 June 2004. CQ Researcher. Colorado State U Lib. 26 June 2004
<http://0-library.cqpress.com>.

IN-TEXT CITATION: (Jost)

A Blog

Baron, Dennis. "Semantic State of the Union." Blog posting. 24 Jan. 2007. The Web
of Language. 6 May 2007 <http://webtools.uiuc.edu/blog/view?blogId=25>.

IN-TEXT CITATION: (Baron)

An Archived Posting

Anson, Chris. "Plagiarism Essay." 27 Feb. 2007. Council of Writing Program
Administrators. 13 May 2007 <http://lists.asu.edu/archives.wpa-l.html>.

IN-TEXT CITATION: (Anson)

A Usenet Posting

Benenson, Fred. "Free Thesis Project Released Today." Online posting. 5 May
2007. 15 May 2007 <discuss@freeculture.org>.

IN-TEXT CITATION: (Benenson)

A Podcast

Brody, Jane. "Health Update." Podcast. 4 June 2007. NYTimes.com. 14 May 2007
<http://www.nytimes.com/ref/multimedia/podcasts.html>.

IN-TEXT CITATION: (Brody)

Posting to a Discussion List

Mitchell, Kerri. "Composition Philosophies and Rhetoric." Online posting. 24 Sept.
2003. Syllabase Discussion Group. 17 Jan. 2004 <http//writing.colostate.edu/
Syllabase/classroom/communication/discussion/display_
message.asp?MessageID=23726>.

IN-TEXT CITATION: (Mitchell)

Synchronous Communications (MOOs, MUDs)

Grigar, Dene. Online defense of dissertation "Penelopeia: The Making of Penelope in Homer's Story and Beyond." 25 July 1995. LinguaMOO. 25 July 1995 <telnet://lingua.utdallas.edu:8888>.

IN-TEXT CITATION: (Grigar)

A Publication on CD-ROM, Diskette, or Magnetic Tape

"World War II." Encarta. CD-ROM. Seattle: Microsoft, 1999.

IN-TEXT CITATION: ("World War II")

Godwin, M. E. "An Obituary to Affirmative Action and a Call for Self-Reliance." ERIC. CD-ROM. SilverPlatter. Oct. 1992.

IN-TEXT CITATION: (Godwin)

An E-Mail Communication

Gogela, Anne. "RE: Teaching British Literature Survey." E-mail to the author. 30 May 2004.

IN-TEXT CITATION: (Gogela)

A Map

Map of the Battlefield of Gettysburg. Map. New York: H. H. Lloyd, 1864. Map Collections 1500–2004. 2 May 2007. American Memory. Lib. of Congress. 15 May 2007 <http://hdl.loc.gov/loc.gmd/g3824g.cw0333000>.

IN-TEXT CITATION: (Map)

OTHER SOURCES: MLA STYLE

Computer Software

Microsoft Word. Computer Software. Microsoft, 2004.

IN-TEXT CITATION: (Microsoft)

A Film

The Terminal. Dir. Steven Spielberg. Perf. Tom Hanks and Catherine Zeta-Jones. Dreamworks, 2004.

IN-TEXT CITATION: (Terminal)

A Recording

Carey, Mariah. "Hero." Music Box. Columbia, 1993.

IN-TEXT CITATION: (Carey)

A Television or Radio Program

"Not Quite Dead." Narr. Mike Wallace. <u>Sixty Minutes</u>. CBS. WCBS, New York. 13
   Apr. 1997.

IN-TEXT CITATION: ("Not Quite")

A Performance

Clapton, Eric. Live performance. EnergySolutions Arena, Salt Lake City. 8 Mar. 2007.

IN-TEXT CITATION: (Clapton)

A Letter

McCarthy, Cormac. Letter to the author. 22 Feb. 2003.

IN-TEXT CITATION: (McCarthy)

A Lecture or Speech

Evans, Pierre. Lecture on Colorado Raptors. U of Colorado, Boulder. 17 Sept. 2003.

(In this case, it is best to avoid using the in-text citation by mentioning the speaker's
name in the text. If the title is unknown, list the type of oral presentation such as
Reading, Speech, or *Lecture.*)

A Personal Interview

Miller, J. Philip. Personal interview. 19 Mar. 2004.

IN-TEXT CITATION: (Miller)

A Personal Survey

Morgan Library Interlibrary Loan Questionnaire. Personal survey. 15 March 2000.

IN-TEXT CITATION: (Morgan Library)

A Cartoon

Roberts, Victoria. Cartoon. <u>New York</u> 13 Jan. 1997: 47.

IN-TEXT CITATION: (Roberts)

An Advertisement

Give the name of the product or company followed by the label *Advertisement,* not
underlined or in italics. Follow with the usual publication information.

Escape Hybrid by Ford. Advertisement. <u>National Geographic</u> May 2004: 2.

IN-TEXT CITATION: (Escape Hybrid)

A Painting, Sculpture, or Photograph

Indicate the artist's name first, followed by the title, the museum or collection, the owner if indicated, and the city.

> Marc, Franz. <u>Deer in the Forest II</u>. Staatliche Kunsthalle, Karlsruhe.
>
> IN-TEXT CITATION: (Marc)

> Vermeer van Delft, Jan. <u>The Astronomer</u>. Musée du Louvre, Paris.
>
> IN-TEXT CITATION: (Vermeer)

In-Text Documentation: APA Style

In APA style, give the author's name and date when you use a summary or paraphrase. If you quote material directly, give the author's name, the date, and the page number. (Use *p.* for one page and *pp.* for more than one page.) These citations will direct your reader to your References list, where you give complete bibliographical information. As you cite your sources, use the following guidelines.

If you do not cite the author in the text, give the author and date in parentheses at the end of the citation. If you are specifically citing a quotation or a part of a source, indicate the page with *p.* (for one page) or *pp.* (for more than one page).

> A recent study of elementary school students studying a foreign language showed that participants from bilingual households "invariably scored higher than participants from English-speaking only households" (Cortes, 2002, p. 320).

If you cite the author in the text, indicate the date in parentheses immediately following the author's name, and cite the page number in parentheses following the quotation.

> According to Vicki Galloway (1984), a student's horizons will not be broadened by "grammar lectures and manipulative classroom exercises" (p. 33).

If you cite a long direct quotation (40 or more words), indent the passage one-half inch from the left margin. Omit the enclosing direct quotation marks. Place the period at the end of the passage, not after the parentheses that include the page reference.

> In an article explaining the strategic value of foreign language study, Hines (2003) argues that our response has been inadequate:
>
> > The United States' chronically weak language resources and lack of linguistic preparedness are invariably exposed when events such as the war in Iraq and the September 11 terror strikes threaten the balance of power, peace or détente in global affairs. (15)

If you are paraphrasing or summarizing material (no direct quotations), you may omit the page number.

> According to Coxe (1984), many top American businesspeople agree that students who combine some business or economics training with fluency in Japanese have unlimited job possibilities.

Note: Although the APA style manual says that writers may omit page citation for summaries and paraphrases, check with your instructor before you omit page references.

If you have previously cited the author and date of a study, you may omit the date.

> In addition, Coxe points out that many top American businesspeople agree that students who combine some business or economics training with fluency in Japanese have unlimited job possibilities.

If the work has two to five authors, cite all authors in your text or in parentheses in the first reference.

Note: In your text, write "Frith and Mueller"; in a parenthetical citation, use an ampersand "(Frith & Mueller)."

> Frith and Mueller (2003) cite another recent example of foreign-language ignorance in marketing. When the California Milk Processor Board wanted an ad agency to translate the "Got Milk?" campaign into Spanish, the unfortunate translation came out as "Are you lactating?" (p. 33).

> Two researchers cited another recent example of foreign language ignorance in marketing. When the California Milk Processor Board wanted an ad agency to translate the "Got Milk?" campaign into Spanish, the unfortunate translation came out as "Are you lactating?" (Frith & Mueller, 2003, p. 33).

For subsequent citations, cite both names each time if a work has two authors. If a work has three to five authors, give the last name of the first author followed by *et al.* Include the year for the first citation within a paragraph.

> Shedivy et al. (2004) found similar results. . . .

If a work has six or more authors, use only the last name of the first author and the abbreviation *et al.* followed by the date.

> Teachers should integrate the study of history, culture, politics, literature, and religion of a particular region with the study of language (Berryman et al., 1988).

If a work has no author, give the first few words of the title (italicized, if a book or report, or in quotes, if an article or chapter) and the year.

> Most students in the United States would be surprised to learn that the Russian government sponsored rock concerts (*A Day in the Life*, 1988).

If the source is from the Internet or the Web, use the author, or if there is no author, use the title.

> Many Web sites now provide detailed information about how to plan a study-abroad semester or year (*Foreign Language*, 2004).

If the author is a corporation, cite the full name of the company in the first reference.

> Foreign-language study must be accompanied by in-depth understanding and experience of culture (University of Maryland, 1990).

If the source is an unpublished personal communication (e-mail, letter, memo, interview, phone conversation), provide an in-text citation, but do not include the source in your "References" list.

> As Professor Devlin explained, "Foreign-language study encourages students to see their own language and culture from a fresh perspective" (personal interview, September 21, 2003).

If you are citing a government document, give the originating agency, its abbreviation (if any), the year of publication, and (if you include a direct quotation) the page number.

> Newcomers to a foreign culture should "pay attention to their health as well as their grammar. What the natives regularly eat may be dangerous to a foreigner's constitution" (Department of Health and Human Services [DHHS], 1989, p. 64).

If your citation refers to several sources, list the authors and dates in alphabetical order.

> Several studies (Frith & Mueller, 2003; Hines, 2002; Simon, 1980) have documented severe deficiencies in Americans' foreign-language preparation.

References List: APA Style
If you are using APA style, you should make a separate list, titled References (no underlining or quotation marks), that

appears after your text but before any appendixes. Include only sources actually used in preparing your essay. List the sources cited in your text *alphabetically,* by author's last name. Use only *initials* for authors' first and middle names. If the author is unknown, alphabetize by the first word in the title (but not *A, An,* or *The*). In titles, capitalize only the first word, proper names, and the first word following a colon. As in MLA reference style, begin first line of each reference flush left and indent subsequent lines one-half inch. Double-space the entire References list. ***Note:*** The APA recommends using italics—not underlining—for titles of books, journals, and other documents.

Following are samples of APA-style reference list entries. For additional information and examples, consult the *Publication Manual of the American Psychological Association* (5th ed., 2001).

Books: APA Style

A Book by One Author

Cisneros, S. (2002). *Caramelo*. New York: Random.

IN-TEXT CITATION: (Cisneros, 2002, p. 123)

A Book by Several Authors

For books with up to six authors, use last names followed by initials and an ampersand (&) before the name of the last author. For books with more than six authors, use last name and initial of the first author followed by "et al."

Conklin, N. F., & Lourie, M. A. (1983). *A host of tongues: Language communities in the United States*. New York: Free Press.

IN-TEXT CITATION: (Conklin & Lourie, 1983)

Corbett, P. J., Myers, N., & Tate, G. (2000). *The writing teacher's sourcebook* (4th ed.) New York: McGraw-Hill.

IN-TEXT CITATION: (Corbett et al., 2000, p. 56)

Additional Books by Same Author

List the author's name for all entries. Note that in-text citations are distinguished by copyright year. In the case of two works by the same author with the same copyright date, assign the dates letters *a, b* according to their alphabetical arrangement.

Morrison, T. (1977). *Song of Solomon*. New York: Knopf.

IN-TEXT CITATION: (Morrison, 1977, p. 10)

Morrison, T. (1992). *Jazz*. New York: Knopf

IN-TEXT CITATION: (Morrison, 1992, p. 254)

An Unknown or Anonymous Author

Encyclopedia of white-collar crime. (2007). Westport, CT: Greenwood Publishing
     Group.

IN-TEXT CITATION: (*Encyclopedia*, 2007, p. 304)

A Book with an Author and an Editor

Austen, J. (1956). *Pride and prejudice* (M. Schorer, Ed.). Boston: Houghton Mifflin.

IN-TEXT CITATION: (Austen, 1956, p. 341)

Note: APA style usually uses the full name of publishing companies.

A Work in an Anthology

Chopin, K. (1989). The story of an hour. In E. V. Roberts & H. E. Jacobs (Eds.),
     Literature: An introduction to reading and writing (pp. 304–306). Englewood
     Cliffs, NJ: Prentice Hall.

IN-TEXT CITATION: (Chopin, 1989, p. 305)

Note: Titles of poems, short stories, essays, or articles in a book are not underlined
or italicized or put in quotation marks. Only the title of the anthology is underlined
or italicized.

A Translation

Lefranc, J. R. (1976). *A treatise on probability* (R. W. Mateau & D. Trilling, Trans.).
     New York: Macmillan. (Original work published 1952.)

IN-TEXT CITATION: (Lefranc, 1976, p. 201)

An Article or Chapter in an Edited Book

Sophocles. (1960). *Electra* (D. Grene, Trans.). In D. Grene & R. Lattimore (Eds.),
     Greek tragedies (Vol. 2, pp. 45–109). Chicago: University of Chicago Press.

IN-TEXT CITATION: (Sophocles, 1960, p. 46)

A Government Document: Known Author

Machenthun, K. M. (1973). *Toward a cleaner aquatic environment.* Environmental
     Protection Agency. Office of Air and Water Programs. Washington, DC: U.S.
     Government Printing Office.

IN-TEXT CITATION: (Machenthun, 1973, p. 12)

A Government Document: Unknown Author

Maternal and Child Health Bureau. (2001). *Babies sleep safest on their backs:
     Reduce the risk of sudden infant death syndrome (SIDS).* Bethesda, MD: U.S.
     Government Printing Office.

IN-TEXT CITATION: (Maternal and Child Health Bureau, 2001, p. 1)

Dissertation (Published)

Wagner, E. (1988). On-board automatic aid and advisory for pilots of control-
impaired aircraft. *Dissertation Abstracts International, 49*(8), 3310. (UMI
No. AAd88-21885)

IN-TEXT CITATION: (Wagner, 1988)

PERIODICALS: APA STYLE

The following examples illustrate how to list articles in magazines and periodicals
according to APA style.

Note: Do *not* underline or italicize or put quotation marks around titles of articles. Do italicize titles of magazines or periodicals. Italicize the volume number for
magazines, if there is one, and omit the *p.* or *pp.* before any page numbers. If an article is not printed on continuous pages, give all page numbers, separated by commas.

An Article in a Weekly or Biweekly Magazine

Hersh, S. M. (2004, May 17). Chain of command. *The New Yorker,* 38–43.

IN-TEXT CITATION: (Hersh, 2004, p. 38)

An Article in a Monthly or Bimonthly Magazine

Dunbar, D. (1997, February). White noise. *Travel and Leisure, 27*, 106–110, 150–158.

IN-TEXT CITATION: (Dunbar, 1997, p. 150)

An Unsigned Article in a Magazine

E-commerce takes off. (2004, 15–21 May). *Economist, 371*, 9.

IN-TEXT CITATION: ("E-Commerce," 2004)

An Article in a Journal with Continuous Pagination

Italicize the volume number and do not include *pp.* Also, APA style requires repeating all number digits: Write 2552–2555.

Sady, S. P. (1986). Prolonged exercise augments plasma triglyceride clearance.
Journal of the American Medical Association, 256, 2552–2555.

IN-TEXT CITATION: (Sady, 1986, p. 2552)

An Article in a Journal That Paginates Each Issue Separately

Italicize the volume number followed by the issue number (not italicized) in
parentheses.

Brodkey, L. (1987). Writing ethnographic narratives. *Written Communication,
9*(1), 25–50.

IN-TEXT CITATION: (Brodkey, 1987, p. 31)

An Article in a Newspaper

Use *p.* or *pp.* before newspaper section and page numbers.

> Harmon, A. (2004, June 20). In new tests for fetal defects, agonizing choices for
> parents. *New York Times,* p. A1.

> IN-TEXT CITATION: (Harmon, 2004)

An Unsigned Article in a Newspaper

> A jet crash that defies resolution. (2001, September 5). *Los Angeles Times,*
> pp. A1, A7.

> IN-TEXT CITATION: ("Jet Crash," 2001, p. A1)

An Editorial

> Fish, S. (1996, December 26). When principles get in the way [Editorial]. *New York
> Times,* p. A27.

> IN-TEXT CITATION: (Fish, 1996)

An Unsigned Editorial

> European summit of uncertainty. (1994, January 7). [Editorial]. *Los Angeles
> Times,* p. B6.

> IN-TEXT CITATION: ("European Summit," 1994)

ELECTRONIC AND INTERNET SOURCES: APA STYLE

The World Wide Web and the Internet are still changing, so even the latest APA guidelines, available in the fifth edition of the *Publication Manual of the American Psychological Association* (2001), will continue to change. See revised and updated version of section 4.16 of the APA manual for the latest information on citing electronic sources. The basic features of an electronic or Internet citation, given in abbreviated form below, are available for downloading from the APA home page at http://www.apa.org/journals/webref.html. Use the specific citations following this list as models for your own citations.

1. Name of author (if given)
2. Title of article (with APA capitalization rules)
3. Title of periodical or electronic text (italicized)
4. Volume number and/or pages (if any)
5. If information is retrieved from an electronic database (e.g., ABI/FORM, PsychINFO, Electric Library, Academic Universe), give the name of the database. (No library address or URL needed.)

6. When information is retrieved from an electronic database and a DOI is available, include it instead of the URL.

7. Use the words "Retrieved" (include date here) "from" (give the URL or DOI here). (Use the words "Available from" to indicate that the URL leads to information on how to obtain the cited material rather than the complete address of the material itself.)

8. Do not use angle brackets around URL.

9. If citation ends with the URL, do not end URL with a period.
   Note: APA style does not cite personal communications such as e-mail in a reference list. Cite such references in the text only. Also, you may vary the in-text citation by mentioning the name of the author(s) or the work in your text, in which case you need only cite the date parenthetically.

An Article in a Journal with DOI Assigned

Jackson, B., et al. (2007, May). Does harboring hostility hurt? *Health Psychology, 26*(3), 333–340. doi: 10.1037/0278-6133.26.3.333

IN-TEXT CITATION: (Jackson et al., 2007, p. 338)

An Article in a Journal with No DOI Assigned

Jackson, B., et al. (2007, May). Does harboring hostility hurt? *Health Psychology, 26*(3), 333–340. Retrieved from http://www.apa.org/journals/releases/ hea263333.pdf

IN-TEXT CITATION: (Jackson et al., 2007, p. 338)

An Article in an Internet-Only Journal

Twyman, M., Harries, C., & Harvey, N. (2006, January). Learning to use and assess advice about risk. *Forum: Qualitative Social Research, 7*(1), Article 22. Retrieved from http://www.qualitative-research.net/fqs-texte/1-06/ 06-1-22-e.htm

IN-TEXT CITATION: (Twyman, Harries, & Harvey, 2006, para. 16)

An Article in a Newspaper

Greenhouse, L. (2004, June 25). Justices, in 5–4 vote, raise doubts on sentencing rules. *New York Times*. Retrieved June 27, 2004, from http://www. nytimes.com

IN-TEXT CITATION: (Greenhouse, 2004)

A Work from an Online Database

Hines, M. E. (2003, Fall). Foreign language curriculum concerns in times of conflict. *Delta Kappa Gamma Bulletin, 70,* 15–22. Retrieved May 23, 2004.

IN-TEXT CITATION: (Hines, 2003, p. 15)

Message Posted to an Online Forum

Etter, B. (2001, August 24). Composition, philosophies, and rhetoric. Message posted to http://writing.colostate.edu/SyllaBase/classroom/communication/discussion/display_message.asp?MessageID=16232

IN-TEXT CITATION: (Etter, 2001)

A Blog

Cambridge, B. (2007, April 24). ACT survey conclusion-more grammar instruction. *NCTE Literacy Educationzs Updates*. Retrieved May 6, 2007, from http://ncteblog.blogspot.com

IN-TEXT CITATION: (Cambridge)

OTHER SOURCES: APA STYLE

In the APA system, unpublished personal communications (e-mail, letter, interview, memo, etc.) do not appear in the References list. Do, however, cite personal communications in your text. (See "In-Text Documentation: APA Style.")

A Review

Rosen, C., & Zerner, H. (2000, October 8). Scenes from the American dream [Review of the book *Norman Rockwell: Pictures for the American people*]. *New York Review of Books,* 16–20.

IN-TEXT CITATION: (Rosen & Zerner, 2000, p. 16)

A Published Interview

Lamm, R. (1995, November 30). Governments face tough times [Interview with Baun, R.]. *Coloradoan,* p. B9.

IN-TEXT CITATION: (Lamm, 1995)

A Film

Producer, A. (Producer), Spielberg, S. (Director). (2004). *The terminal* [Motion Picture]. USA: Dreamworks.

IN-TEXT CITATION: (Spielberg, 2004)

A Recording

Carey, M. (1993). Hero. On *Music box* [CD]. New York: Columbia Records.

IN-TEXT CITATION: (Carey, 1993)

A Television or Radio Program

Bogdonich, R. (Producer). (1997, April 13). *Sixty minutes.* New York: WCBS.

IN-TEXT CITATION: (Bogdonich, 1997)

EDITING AND PROOFREADING   Edit your paper for conciseness, clarity, and accuracy of grammar, spelling, and punctuation. See your handbook for assistance in revising errors and improving usage. Check your direct quotations to make sure they are *accurate, word-for-word transcriptions* of the originals. Make sure that your in-text citation of sources is accurate. Proofread both the text *and* the Works Cited or References section. Finally, have someone else proofread your research paper for typos, spelling errors, missing words, or confusing sentences.

POSTSCRIPT ON THE WRITING PROCESS

You have completed your research paper, navigating a long and involved process and encountering both challenges and successes. Reflecting on this process and its end result (your paper) can tell you a great deal about the way you learn. In considering the choices you made along the way and the thinking behind those choices, you offer an account of yourself as a learner and writer to your instructors, and, perhaps more important, to yourself.

One of the main benefits of reflective writing is that it can help you discover new ways to solve challenges you encountered. It also offers you a greater say in how you will be evaluated. In a reflective essay, you can discuss what you have learned about your subject. Also, such writing may allow you to highlight the learning that may not be immediately evident to you or your instructor. Reflective writing can lead to more integrative or "deep" learning, which is the kind of understanding normally credited to experts.

As your final entry in your research notebook, then, answer the following questions.

1. Reread your research log section. Compare your initial schedule with your actual progress. What parts of the research paper took longer than you anticipated? What took less time?

Continued

2. Describe your intended *audience* for this essay. Where in the essay do you indicate or address this audience?

3. What *genre* did you select for your writing? Describe the main features of this genre. Where might this genre be published? Does it typically contain visuals or graphics? Refer to several passages that you felt you were successful at imitating the key features of this genre.

4. Describe your overall *purpose* or purposes for your essay. Were you narrating, informing, explaining, evaluating, problem solving, or arguing? Did you have different purposes at different parts of your essay? Cite several passages from your essay to illustrate your purpose(s).

5. What was the most difficult problem you encountered while writing the research paper? How did you try to solve that problem?

6. What do you like best about the final version of your paper? Why? What do you like least? What would you change if you had two more days to work on your paper?

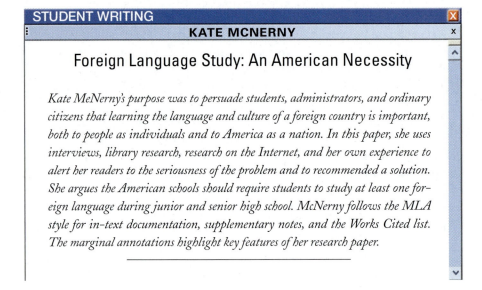

STUDENT WRITING

KATE MCNERNY

Foreign Language Study: An American Necessity

Kate McNerny's purpose was to persuade students, administrators, and ordinary citizens that learning the language and culture of a foreign country is important, both to people as individuals and to America as a nation. In this paper, she uses interviews, library research, research on the Internet, and her own experience to alert her readers to the seriousness of the problem and to recommended a solution. She argues the American schools should require students to study at least one foreign language during junior and senior high school. McNerny follows the MLA style for in-text documentation, supplementary notes, and the Works Cited list. The marginal annotations highlight key features of her research paper.

↕ **1"**   ↓ ½"
McNerny 1

Kate McNerny

Professor Thomas   */double space*

English 101   */double space*

Foreign-Language Study: */double space*

An American Necessity

"Why should I learn a foreign language—everyone speaks
English!" "I would never use another language—I never plan to
leave the United States." "I had a hard enough time learning
English!" These are only a few of the excuses people have given for
opposing foreign-language studies, and unfortunately they represent
the ideas of more than a few American citizens. In possibly the most
multicultural nation in the world, it is ironic that so many people—
who themselves have come from foreign cultures and foreign
languages—should want to remain isolated from international
languages and cultures. A recent indication of the backlash against
foreign languages came when the House of Representatives passed
legislation recommending that English should be the official
language of the U.S. Government.[1] In addition, twenty-three states
already have Official English laws on the books (Swope 2128; Torres
51). Because these attitudes are so widespread, we need a national
policy supporting foreign-language study in elementary and
secondary schools. If we are to continue to develop as a people and a
nation, we must be able to communicate with and understand the
cultures of people from countries around the globe.

Historically, Americans' attitudes toward foreign languages
have swayed from positive to negative, depending on current

↕ **1"**

←→ **1"** (left margin)   **1"** →← (right margin)

*For her lead-in, McNerny
uses quotations she
collected in her informal
survey.*

*McNerny gives first
version of her **thesis** for
her problem-solving
essay: "We need a national
policy supporting foreign-
language study."
McNerny presents
historical background on
the problem.*

↑ 1" ↓ ½"

McNerny 2

events around the world. Theodore Huebener's study <u>Why Johnny Should Learn Foreign Languages</u> shows how attitudes reflect the times. In 1940, in an isolationist period before World War II, a committee of the American Youth Commission issued a report labeling foreign-language studies as "useless and time-consuming" (Huebener 13). An even more appalling statement came from a group of Harvard scholars. They suggested that "foreign language study is useful primarily in strengthening the student's English. . . . For the average student, there is no real need at all to learn a foreign language" (Huebener 14). With such attitudes, it is no wonder that students and administrators ignored foreign language programs during the 1940s and 1950s.[2] Through the years, each international crisis has brought a renewed interest in foreign languages. Just as the advent of Sputnik in the late 1950s was followed by a surge of interest in learning foreign languages, the terrorist attacks of September 11, 2001 have created more interest in languages less commonly taught in the United States (Hines 20).

Despite some occasional surges of interest, however, foreign-language study still holds the weakest position of any major subject in American secondary schools. A recent study of foreign-language programs reports that "only 15 percent of American high school students study a foreign language. Only 8 percent of [American] colleges require credit in a foreign language for admission (down from 34 percent in 1966)" (Unks 24). Because available programs at the junior and senior high school level are generally limited in variety

1"   1"

↑ 1"

Ellipsis points indicate material omitted from the source.

The superscript number refers the reader to the "Notes" page for McNerny's comment on the history of the problem.

Square brackets in quoted material indicate a word added by McNerny to clarify the sentence.

McNerny 3

and scope, only a small percentage of those students who take a foreign language ever become fluent in it. A 1984

"Let me put this in terms you'll understand. First, you'll have to tell me what language you're speaking."

www.CartoonStock.com

study that sampled 536 secondary schools revealed that most offered a foreign language, but 91 percent did not require foreign-language credits for graduation (Ranwez and Rodgers 98). In contrast, most European countries require all students to learn at least one and often two foreign languages. Norway, Spain, France, Sweden, Italy, England, Germany, and Finland all require at least one foreign language. According to Rune Bergentoft, currently a Mellon Fellow at the National Foreign Language Center, "Several [European] countries require knowledge of two foreign languages for entry to the upper

McNerny included the cartoon at this point to illustrate Americans' stubborn ignorance of foreign language.

In-text citation for a source with two authors.

secondary school; in the Netherlands, the requirement is three foreign languages" (18).

The United States cannot continue to lag behind other countries in language capability. As two foreign-language researchers noted, "We are members of a world community consisting of hundreds of nations, and our fates are closely intertwined" (Long and Long 366). It is time to change attitudes and to recognize that in order to successfully interact with its "world community," the United States must drastically change its foreign-language practices and policies. American students should be encouraged to start their language studies in elementary school and required to study at least one foreign language during their six years of junior and senior high school.

How do we encourage more students to study a foreign language in our elementary and secondary schools? The solution requires changes on the part of administrators and teachers, changes in the attitudes and experiences of students themselves, and changes in our state and national foreign language policies.

School administrators across the country often oppose the idea of requiring foreign languages because they cannot see the contribution these studies make to the overall goals of the schools' curriculum. In a recent survey, New Jersey secondary school administrators "rated social studies objectives as contributing most to the attainment of high priority goals, and foreign language as contributing least" (Koppel 437). These administrators fail to realize that language studies can add a valuable dimension to a social studies program. Educators can use a combined program to

McNerny restates her thesis, using more specific language: "American students should be . . . required to study at least one foreign language during . . . junior and senior high school."

*McNerny's **essay map**: The solution requires changes by administrators, by students, and by national policymakers.*

*Notice **punctuation** for in-text citation: Source appears in parentheses after the quotation marks but before the period.*

McNerny 5

emphasize a global perspective in language and cultural studies. "The world looks and sounds different when one is 'standing in the shoes' of another, speaking another language, or recognizing another's point of view based on an alternative set of values" (Bragaw 37). This global awareness is crucial in our increasingly interdependent world.

Likewise, teachers need to continue to make changes in their foreign-language courses to attract more students. More and more primary and secondary language courses already focus on cultural issues more than grammar, but now they need to use all the computer, on-line, and Internet resources currently available to attract and motivate their students. Linguist Mark Warschauer, in a preface to papers collected at a conference on Global Networking in Foreign Language Learning, asserts that "foreign language learners can communicate rapidly and inexpensively with other learners or speakers of the target language around the world. With the World Wide Web, learners can access a broad array of authentic foreign language materials . . . or they can develop and publish their own materials to share with others across the classroom or across the globe" (ix). Teachers need to make use of the Internet communication possibilities to help motivate and interest their students.

Of course, students themselves need motivation in order to enroll in foreign-language classes. Many students simply fail to see why they will ever need to use a foreign language. I used to belong to that group. I remember my mom always telling me, "Take French classes. Learn how to speak French so you can visit your cousins in

*McNerny uses **personal experience** in her research paper. Her experience provides a great example of why students can benefit from studying a foreign language.*

McNerny 6

France someday." At the time, during junior high, I did take French classes for a while, but then dropped them when my schedule became "too busy." Then, as my mom had promised, I got the opportunity to visit my cousins in France. For some reason, the fact that I couldn't speak French didn't really hit me—until I stepped off the train at Gare du Nord in Paris and couldn't find the relative who was supposed to meet me. After frantically searching the entire station several times, I had to break down and ask for help. At the information desk, a few completely butchered French phrases escaped my lips—only to be received by an unimpressed, unresponsive station attendant. He muttered something about dumb Americans. Then, with a wave of his hand, he gestured toward some unknown destination. I did survive that painful ordeal, but I vowed I wouldn't embarrass myself—and other Americans—again.

Another way to change students' attitudes is to encourage them to participate in exchange programs or study-abroad programs.[3] Again, the Internet and the World Wide Web offer students and their teachers immediate access to a variety of exchange and study-abroad programs. The World Wide Web has hundreds of sites related to foreign-language study that can help both teachers and students. The International House World Organization, at http://www. international-house.org, is "a worldwide network of language schools sharing a common commitment to the highest standards of teaching and training" (International). Students wishing to find out about exchange and study-abroad programs should browse the Web, perhaps

beginning at a site such as the Foreign Language Study Abroad
Service at http://www.netpoint.net/~flsas. The Foreign Language
Study Abroad Service was started in 1971 and is, according to
its home page, "the oldest study abroad service in the U.S."
(Foreign).

Study-abroad programs and exchange programs help students
learn the language, but just as important, they enable students to
learn about different cultures. In his resource book, Teaching Culture,
H. Ned Seelye, Director of Bilingual-Bicultural Education for the State
of Illinois, cites just one of many cultural lessons that American
students—and tourists—need to learn:

> At a New Year's Eve celebration in an exclusive
> Guatemalan hotel, one American was overheard telling
> another, "You see all these people? They're all my wife's
> relatives. And every damn one of them has kissed me
> tonight. If another Guatemalan man hugs and kisses me
> I'll punch him right in the face!" The irritated American
> was disturbed by two things: the extended kinship
> patterns of the group and the *abrazo de ano neuvo* as
> executed by the men (he did not complain of the female
> abrazos). Both customs—close family ties that extend to
> distant relatives and the abrazo given as a greeting or
> sign of affection devoid of sexual overtures—elicited
> hostility in the American who was bored by unintelligible
> language and depressed by nostalgia and alcohol. (85)

In order to prevent such linguistic and cultural misunderstandings,
more and more Americans should take advantage of study-abroad

*McNerny introduces the
author, the title of the
book, and the author's
credentials to lend
authority to the quoted
passage.*

*At the end of the
quotation, McNerny cites
only the page number,
since she has already
introduced the author.
The page number follows
the period in indented
block quotations.*

*McNerny does not end
her paragraph with a
quotation; instead, she
shows how this evidence
supports her point.*

McNerny 8

and exchange programs that will acquaint them with a variety of cultures and languages.

Finally, in order to coordinate our schools' foreign-language studies, America needs changes in our state and national foreign-language policies to ensure that every child will receive some basic instruction in foreign languages and culture. Changes in our foreign-language requirements would not only promote cultural understanding but also would strengthen U. S. international relations in business and diplomacy. International trade is continually increasing in the United States and has created a demand for businesspeople competent in foreign languages. Many top American businesspeople agree that students who combine some business or economics training with fluency in Japanese have unlimited job possibilities (Coxe 194). Company executives simply cannot expect to make efficient, sound decisions in their international markets without understanding and speaking the language of the country they are dealing with (Huebener 45). Educator Gerald Unks points out two instances in which a lack of language proficiency caused companies to initiate fatal marketing programs:

> When Pepsi-Cola went after the Chinese market, "Come Alive With Pepsi" was translated into Chinese in Taiwan as "Pepsi Brings Your Ancestors Back from the Dead." No Sale! General Motors sought to sell its Nova in South America oblivious to the fact that "No va" in Spanish means "It doesn't go." (24)

Another recent example of foreign-language ignorance in marketing occurred when the California Milk

McNerny 9

wanted an ad agency to translate the "Got Milk?" campaign into Spanish. The unfortunate translation initially came out as "Are you lactating?" (Frith & Mueller 33). These examples illustrate that business people need thorough competence in, not just a rudimentary knowledge of, foreign languages.

Finally, proficiency in foreign languages and cultures is important not only for business and trade overseas, but also for jobs in America. Required foreign-language study would help our future citizens understand and appreciate our multicultural heritage—and help them become employable. Verada Bluford, writing in Occupational Outlook Quarterly, argues that as our country "becomes more involved in foreign trade, tourism, and international cooperative ventures, the number of jobs open to fluent speakers of a foreign language increases" (25). Bluford explains that there are "language-centered jobs" such as teaching, translating, and interpreting, but there are also "language-related jobs," such as jobs in marketing and finance, engineering, airlines, banking, and government, where language skills are necessary. These "language-related jobs" will go to students who have language skills in addition to some other skill (Bluford 26). A foreign-language requirement, whether mandated by each state or by Congress, would make all Americans better citizens of the world and their own country.

The need for required language study in the United States is urgent. Some states already require schools to introduce children to some foreign language during their grade school years (Kuo 2). For example, North Carolina, Arkansas, Louisiana, Arizona, and Oklahoma already have laws, and Oregon has a proposed law that

Before quoting from Bluford, McNerny names the author and the journal from which the article is taken.

McNerny begins her conclusion, citing precedents and calling for state and federal administrators to support a foreign-language requirement.

will require all tenth-graders to know a language other than English (Kuo 2). Since some individual schools and states realize the benefits of foreign-language requirements, Congress should guide all the states and formulate a national foreign-language policy that would make all our schools more like the European model.

Although the ideas and the plans for a national policy exist, often the funds do not. Some funds can be diverted from within school districts, but the federal government must take some initiative. The current administration spends endless time and money subsidizing business interests and propping up weak foreign economies. Since foreign-language knowledge contributes strongly to success in both these areas, however, it would be practical for the administration also to support expansion of language studies. Instead, it continues to reduce funding for special programs, including language studies centers and international teaching facilities (Unks 25). Realistically, a foreign-language requirement in junior and senior high school cannot be initiated without the support of both local school districts and the federal government. Americans must acknowledge the fact that they are not isolated from the rest of the world. Successful interaction in the "world community" depends on our ability, as a nation, to effectively communicate with and understand people from other countries. Understanding, communication, and world peace cannot be achieved without cultural awareness and foreign-language proficiency.

1"
Notes

[1]Americans not only hesitate to take a foreign language but also seem bent on keeping foreign languages officially "out of sight." The debate over "official English" has spilled over into the workplace, in the form of "English-only" rules in business. Robert Brady, writing in HR Focus, reviews the two sides of the English-only debate: "Advocates of English-only rules argue that a single language promotes good organizational communications, ensures workplace safety, improves service to the English-speaking customer base, and avoids discrimination" (20). On the other side, Brady says, opponents believe that requiring employees to speak English goes against the melting-pot heritage of our country—and may violate Title VII of the Civil Rights Act (20). Many opponents from ethnic and civil rights groups believe these bills and rules are racist (McBee 64). Americans' ignorance of foreign languages (and the fear that ignorance breeds) is an important cause of the popularity of both the "official English" laws and the "English-only" rules.

[2]One of the most disturbing facts is that although Huebener's study was done in 1961, very little has changed in over forty years. Except for slight changes in statistics, dates, and names of wars, Americans have remained strikingly insular in their attitudes toward foreign languages and foreigners.

[3]Recent figures on study-abroad programs illustrate the huge gap between the number of foreign students who study in the United States and U.S. students who study abroad. In an article on language learning and study abroad, Barbara Freed gives the following figures: "Close to half a million international students

1"

Content notes are placed on a separate page and double-spaced. Use raised footnote numbers and indent the first line five spaces.

In her notes, McNerny includes her ideas about "English-only" and "official English," which would have been digressive in the text of her paper.

In this footnote, McNerny puts statistics that didn't seem to fit in the flow of her paragraph but are relevant to study-abroad programs.

1"

McNerny 12

came to the United States to study in 1993–94 [while] approximately 71,000 American undergraduates participated in study abroad programs" (3). That means that nearly ten times more foreign students study English in the United States than American students study foreign languages abroad.

1"

1"

1"

1"
Works Cited

½"
McNerny 13

Bergentoft, Rune. "Foreign Language Instruction: A Comparative Perspective." <u>The Annals of the American Academy of Political and Social Science</u> 532 (1994): 8–34.

Bluford, Verada. "Working with Foreign Languages." <u>Occupational Outlook Quarterly</u> 38.4 (1994): 25–28.

Brady, Robert I. "English-Only Rules Draw Controversy." <u>HR Focus</u> June 1996: 20.

Bragaw, Donald H., and Helene Zimmer-Loew. "Social Studies and Foreign Language: A Partnership." <u>Education Digest</u> Dec. 1985: 36–39.

Coxe, Donald. "The Back Page." <u>Canadian Business</u> Feb. 1984: 194.

<u>Foreign Language Study Abroad Service.</u> 21 Feb. 2003 <http://www.netpoint.net/flas.>

Freed, Barbara F. "Language Learning and Study Abroad." <u>Second Language Acquisition in a Study Abroad Context.</u> Ed. Barbara F. Freed. Philadelphia: John Benjamins, 1995, 3–33.

Frith, Katherine T., and Barbara Mueller. <u>Advertising and Societies: Global Issues.</u> New York: P. Lang, 2003.

Hines, Marion E. "Foreign Language Curriculum Concerns in Times of Conflict." <u>Delta Kappa Gamma Bulletin</u> 70 (Fall 2003): 15–22. <u>Academic Search Premier.</u> EBSCO. Colorado State U Lib. 3 Dec. 2003 <http://0-web2.epnet.com>.

Huebener, Theodore. <u>Why Johnny Should Learn Foreign Languages.</u> New York: Chilton, 1961.

<u>International House: The Worldwide Language Teaching Organization.</u> Jan. 2003. 2 Mar. 2003 <http://www.international-house.org>.

1"

1"

1"

The "Works Cited" list begins a new page. List the entries alphabetically by the author's last name. If no author is given, list by the first word in the title. Double-space all lines.

Indent five spaces after first line of each entry.

Book

Internet Web page

Article from a journal with contiguous pagination

For inclusive page numbers over 100, use only the last two digits in the second number (366–68).

Article from a monthly magazine

McNerny 14

Works Cited

Koppel, Irene E. "The Perceived Contribution of Foreign Language to High Priority Education Goals." Foreign Language Annals 15 (1982): 435–37.

Kuo, Fidelius. "Foreign Language Proposal in Washington State Worthy." Northwest Asian Weekly 9 Dec. 1994: 4.

Long, Delbert H., and Roberta A. Long. "Toward the Promotion of Foreign Language Study and Global Understanding." Education 105 (1985): 366–68.

McBee Susanna. "A War over Words." U.S. News and World Report 6 Oct. 1986: 64.

Ranwez, Alain D., and Judy Rodgers. "The Status of Foreign Languages and International Studies: An Assessment in Colorado." Foreign Language Annals 17 (1984): 97–102.

Seelye, H. Ned. Teaching Culture: Strategies for Foreign Language Educators. Skokie, IL: National Textbook, 1974.

Swope, Christopher. "Panel OKs Bill to Make English Official Government Language." Congressional Quarterly Weekly Report 54 (1996): 2128–29.

Torres, Joseph. "The Language Crusade." Hispanic 9.6 (1996): 50–54.

Unks, Gerald. "The Perils of Our Single-Language Policy." Education Digest Mar. 1985: 24–27.

Warschauer, Mark. Preface. Telecollaboration in Foreign Language Learning. By Warschauer. Ed. Mark Warschauer. Honolulu: Second Language Teaching & Curriculum Center, 1996.

Appendix: Writing Under Pressure

The main chapters of this text describe purposes for writing and strategies for collecting, shaping, drafting, and revising an essay. These chapters assume that you have several days or even weeks to write your paper. They work on the premise that you have time to read model essays, time to think about ideas for your topic, and time to prewrite, write several drafts, and receive feedback from other members of your class. Much college writing, however, occurs on midterm or final examinations, when you may have only fifteen to twenty minutes to complete the whole process of writing. When you must produce a "final" draft in a few short minutes, your writing process may need drastic modification.

A typical examination has some objective questions (true/false, multiple-choice, definition, short-answer) followed by an essay question or two. For example, with just twenty-five minutes left in your Western Civilization midterm, you might finish the last multiple-choice question, turn the page, and read the following essay question.

> Erich Maria Remarque's *All Quiet on the Western Front* has been hailed by critics the world over as the "twentieth century's definitive novel on war." What does Remarque's novel tell us about the historical, ideological, national, social, and human significance of twentieth-century warfare? Draw on specific illustrations from the novel, but base your observations on your wider perspective on Western civilization. Good luck!

Overwhelmed by panic, you find the blood drains from your face and your fingers feel icy. You now have twenty-two minutes to write on the "historical, ideological, national, social, and human significance of twentieth-century warfare." Do you have to explain everything about modern warfare? Must you use specific examples from the novel? Good luck, indeed! Everything you remembered about the novel has now vanished. Bravely, you pick up your pen and start recounting the main events of the novel, hoping to show the instructor at least that you read it.

You can survive such an essay examination, but you need to prepare yourself emotionally and intellectually. Following is some advice from senior English majors who have taken dozens of essay examinations in their four years of college. These seniors answer the question, "What advice would you give to students who are preparing to take an essay examination?"

> Even though I'm an English major, I'm perfectly petrified of writing impromptu essays. My advice is to calm yourself. Read the question. Study key

words and concepts. Before beginning an essay question, write a brief, informal outline. This will organize your ideas and help you remember them as well. Take a deep breath and write. I would also recommend *rereading* the question while you are writing, to keep you on track.

The first step is to know the material. Then, before you begin, read the instructions. Know what the teacher expects. Then try to organize your thoughts into a small list—preferably a list that will become your main paragraphs. Don't babble to fill space. Teachers hate reading nonsense. Reread what you've written often. This will ensure that you won't repeat yourself. Proofread at the end.

Organization is important but difficult in a pressure situation. Well-organized essays do have a tendency to impress the professor, sometimes more than information-packed essays. Organize your notes and thoughts about those notes as you study (not necessarily in a chronological order, but rather in a comprehensible order). Good luck.

Read the question carefully.

Get your thoughts in order.

Write what the question asks, not what you wish it asked.

Don't ramble.

Give textual facts or specific examples.

Summarize with a clear, understandable closing.

Proofread.

Keep calm. Your life doesn't depend on one test.

My advice would be first to learn how to consciously relax and practice writing frequently. *Practice!!!* It's important to practice writing as much as possible in any place possible, because the more writing you do, the better and easier it becomes. Also, your belief that it *can* be done is critical!

Know the information that you will be tested on well enough so that you can ask yourself tough and well-formed questions in preparation. You should be able to predict what essay questions your professor will ask, at least generally. I always go to the test file or ask friends for sample essay questions that I can practice on. Then I practice writing on different areas of the material.

The common threads in these excerpts of advice are to know your audience, analyze key terms in the question, make a sketch outline, know the material, practice writing before the test, and proofread when you finish writing. Knowing how to read the question and practicing your writing before the test will help you relax and do your best.

KNOW YOUR AUDIENCE

Teachers expect you to answer a question exactly as it is asked, not just to give the information that you know. Because teachers must read dozens of essays, they are impressed by clear organization and specific detail. As one senior says, teachers hate babble because they cannot follow the thread of your argument. Although they demand specific examples and facts from the text, they want you to explain how these examples *relate* to the overall question. In a pile of two hundred history exams graded by one professor, margins featured comments like "Reread the question. This doesn't answer the question." "What is your main point? State your main point clearly." "Give more specific illustrations and examples." Keep this teacher in mind as you write your next essay response.

ANALYZE KEY TERMS

Understanding the key terms in the question is crucial to writing an essay under pressure. Teachers expect you to respond to *their* specific question, not just to write down information. They want you to use your writing to *think* about the topic—to analyze and synthesize the information. In short, they want you to make sense of the information. Following are key terms that indicate teachers' expectations and suggest how to organize your answer.

> **DISCUSS:** A general instruction that means "write about." If the question says *discuss,* look for other key words to focus your response.
>
> **DESCRIBE:** Give sensory details or particulars about a topic. Often, however, this general instruction simply means "discuss."
>
> **ANALYZE:** Divide a topic into its parts, and show how the parts are related to each other and to the topic as a whole.
>
> **SYNTHESIZE:** Show how the parts relate to the whole or how the parts make sense together.
>
> **EXPLAIN:** Show relationships between specific examples and general principles. Explain what (define), explain why (causes/effects), and/or explain how (analyze process).
>
> **DEFINE:** Explain what something is. As appropriate, give a formal definition, describe it, analyze its parts or function, describe what it is not, and/or compare and contrast it with similar events or ideas.
>
> **COMPARE:** Explain similarities and (often) differences. Draw conclusions from the observed similarities and differences.

CONTRAST: Explain key differences. Draw conclusions from the observed differences.

ILLUSTRATE: Provide specific examples of an idea or process.

TRACE: Give the sequence or chronological order of key events or ideas.

EVALUATE: Determine the value or worth of an idea, thing, process, person, or event. Set up criteria and provide evidence to support your judgments.

SOLVE: Explain your solution; show how it fixes the problem, why it is better than other alternatives, and why it is feasible.

ARGUE: Present both sides of a controversial issue, showing why the opposing position should not be believed or accepted and why your position should be accepted. Give evidence to support your position.

INTERPRET: Offer your understanding of the meaning and significance of an idea, event, person, process, or work of art. Support your understanding with specific examples or details.

MAKE A SKETCH OUTLINE

The key terms in a question should not only focus your thinking but also suggest how to organize your response. Use the key terms to make a sketch outline of your response. You may not regularly use an outline when you have more time to write an essay, but the time pressure requires that you revise your normal writing process.

Assume that you have twenty-five minutes to read and respond to the following question from a history examination. Read the instructions carefully, note the key terms, and make a brief outline to guide your writing. Answer *one* of the following. Draw on the reading for your answer. (25 pts)

1. Define globalization, then explain both the advantages and disadvantages of globalization for both modern and third-world countries. Based on your explanation, argue for or against globalization as a means of improving the standard of living in both modern and third-world countries.

2. Explain the arguments that the United Nations does and does not play a positive role in international relations (discuss and illustrate both sides of the argument). Then take a stand—citing the evidence for your position.

Let's assume that because you know more about the United Nations, you choose the second question. First, you should identify and underline key words in the question. The subject for your essay is the *United Nations* and its role in *international relations*. You need to *explain* the reasons why the UN does or does not have a positive effect on international relations. You will need to *discuss* and *illustrate* (give specific examples of) both sides of the controversy. Finally, you need to *take a stand* (argue) for your belief, citing *evidence* (specific examples from recent history) of how the UN has or has not helped to resolve international tensions.

Based on your rereading and annotation of the key words of the question, make a quick outline or list, perhaps as follows.

   I. Reasons (with examples) why some believe the UN is effective

      A. Reason 1 + example

      B. Reason 2 + example

  II. Reasons (with examples) why some believe the UN is not effective

      A. Reason 1 + example

      B. Reason 2 + example

 III. Reasons why you believe the UN is effective

      Refer to reasons and examples cited in I, above, but explain why these reasons and examples outweigh the reasons cited in II, above.

With this sketch outline as your guide, jot down reasons and examples that you intend to use, and then start writing. Your outline will make sure that you cover all the main points of the question, and it will keep your essay organized as you concentrate on remembering specific reasons and examples.

▌ WARMING UP: Journal Exercise

For practice, analyze at least one question from two of the following subject areas. First, underline key terms. Then, in your journal explain what these terms ask you to do. Finally, sketch an outline to help organize your response. If you are not familiar with the topics, check a dictionary or encyclopedia. (Do not write the essay.)

BIOLOGY

- Describe the process by which artificial insulin was first produced.
- What is reverse transcriptase and how was it used in genetic engineering?
- Humans—at least most of us—walk on two legs as opposed to four. How might you account for this using a Darwinian, Lamarckian, and Theistic model?

HISTORY

- Discuss the significant political developments in the English colonies in the first half of the eighteenth century.
- Account for the end of the Salem witchcraft delusion, and discuss the consequences of the outbreak for Salem Village.

HUMAN DEVELOPMENT

- Discuss evidence for nature versus nurture effects in human development.
- Contrast Piaget's Vygotsky's, and Whorf's ideas on connections between language and thought.

HUMANITIES

- How and why did early Christian culture dominate the Roman Empire? In terms of art and architecture, discuss specific ways in which the early Christians transformed or abolished the Greco-Roman legacy.

LITERATURE

- Aristotle wrote that a tragedy must contain certain elements, such as a protagonist of high estate, recognition, and reversal, and should also evoke pity and fear in the audience. Which of the following best fits Aristotle's definition: *Hamlet, Death of a Salesman,* or *The Old Man and the Sea?* Explain your choice.

PHILOSOPHY

- On the basis of what we have studied in this class, define *philosophy*. Taking your major subject of study (for example, biology, history, literature), discuss three philosophical problems that arise in this field.
- Write an essay explaining the following statement. Be clear in your explanation and use specific examples. "Egoism allows for prudent altruism."

POLITICAL SCIENCE

- Evaluate the achievements of the current administration's policy in Africa.
- Analyze the role of force in the contemporary international system.

PSYCHOLOGY

- Contrast Freud's and Erikson's stage theories of personality.
- What is meant by triangulation of measurement (multiple methodology)?

KNOW THE MATERIAL

It goes without saying that you must know the material in order to explain the concepts and give specific examples or facts from the text. But what is the best way to review the material so that you can recall examples under pressure? The following three study tactics will improve your recall.

First, read your text actively. Do not just mark key passages in yellow high lighter. Write marginal notes to yourself. Write key concepts in the margin. Ask questions. Make connections between an idea in one paragraph and something you read earlier. Make connections between what you read in the text and what you heard in class.

Second, do not depend only on your reading and class discussion. Join or form a study group that meets regularly to review course material. Each person in the group should prepare some question for review. Explaining key ideas to a friend is an excellent way to learn the material yourself.

Finally, use your writing to help you remember. Do not just read the book and your notes and head off for the test. Instead, review your notes, *close* your notebook, and write down as much as you can remember. Review the assigned chapters in the text, close the book, and write out what you remember. If you can write answers to questions with the book closed, you know you're ready for an essay examination.

WARMING UP: Journal Exercise

Get out the class notes and textbook for a course that you are currently taking. Annotate your notes with summary comments and questions. In the margins, write out the key ideas that the lecture covered. Then write out questions that you still have about the material. Open your textbook for that class. Annotate the margins of the chapter that you are currently reading. Write summary comments about important material. Write questions in the margins about material that you do not understand. Note places in the text that the instructor also covered in class.

PRACTICE WRITING

As several of the senior English majors suggested, practicing short essays *before* an examination will make you feel comfortable with the material and reduce your panic. A coach once noted that while every athlete wants to win, only the true winners are willing to *prepare* to win. The same is true of writing an examination. Successful writers have already completed 80 percent of the writing process *before* they walk into an examination. They have written notes in the margins of their notebooks and textbooks. They have discussed the subject with other students. They have closed the book and written out key definitions. They have prepared questions and practiced answering them. Once they read a question, they are prepared to write out their "final" drafts.

WARMING UP: Journal Exercise

For an upcoming examination in one of your other courses, write out three possible essay questions that your instructor might ask. For each question, underline the key words, and make a sketch outline of your response. Set your watch or timer for fifteen minutes, and actually write out your response to *one* of your questions.

PROOFREAD AND EDIT

In your normal writing process, you can put aside your draft for several days and proofread and edit it later. When you are writing under pressure, however, you need to save three or four minutes at the end to review what you have written. Often, you may be out of time before you have finished writing what you wanted to say about the question. At this point, one effective strategy is to draw a line at the end of what you have written, write "Out of Time," and then write one or two quick sentences explaining what you planned to say: "If I had more time, I would explain how the UN's image has become more positive following the crises in Israel and Iraq." Then use your remaining two or three minutes to reread what you have written, making sure that your ideas are clear and that you have written in complete sentences and used correct spelling and punctuation. If you don't know how to spell a word, at least write "sp?" next to a word to show that you think it is spelled incorrectly.

SAMPLE ESSAY QUESTIONS AND RESPONSES

The following are sample essay questions, students' responses, and instructors' comments and grades.

HISTORY 100: WESTERN CIVILIZATION
Examination II over Chapter 12, class lectures, and Victor Hugo's *The Hunchback of Notre Dame*

Essay I (25 Points)

What was the fifteenth-century view of "science" as described in *The Hunchback?* How did this view tend to inhibit Claud Frollo in his experiments in his closet in the cathedral?

ANSWER 1

An excellent response. Your focus an superstition and heresy along with the specific examples of the roasted mouse, the "Philosopher's Stone," and La Esmeralda's goat illustrate the fifteenth-century view of science and its inhibiting effect. Grade: A

The fifteenth-century view of "science" was characterized by superstition and heresy. In *The Hunchback of Notre Dame,* for example, we see superstition operating when the king's physician states that a gunshot wound can be cured by the application of a roasted mouse. Claud Frollo, a high-ranking church official, has a thirst for knowledge, but unfortunately it pushes beyond the limits of knowledge permitted by the church. When he works in his closet on the art of alchemy and searches for the "Philosopher's Stone" (gold), he is guilty of heresy. Frollo has read and mastered the arts and sciences of the university and of the church, and he wants to know more. He knows that if he presses into the "Black Arts," the Devil will take his soul. And indeed, the "Devil" of passion does. Frollo feels inhibited because many of the experiments he has performed have made him guilty of heresy and witchcraft in the eyes of the church. And this seems to be the case in almost anything "new" or out of the ordinary. La Esmeralda, for instance, is declared "guilty" of witchcraft for the training of her goat. Her goat appears to have been possessed by the Devil himself, when, in fact, all the girl is guilty of is training the goat to do a few simple tricks. All in all, the fifteenth-century view of "science" was one not of favor, but of oppression and fear. Thankfully, the Renaissance came along!

ANSWER 2

The fifteenth-century view of science was that according to the Bible, God was the creator of all, and as to scientific theory, the subject was moot. No one was a believer in the scientific method—however, we do find some science going on in Claud Frollo's closet, alchemy. At that time he was trying to create gold by mixing different elements together. Though alchemy seems to be the only science of that time period, people who practiced it kept it to themselves. We even find King Louis IX coming to Frollo, disguised, to dabble in a little of the science himself. At this time people were rejecting the theory of the Earth revolving around the sun because, as a religious ordeal, God created the Earth and man, and they are the center of all things, so there were no questions to be answered by science, because the answer was God.

Give more examples from the novel and show how the fifteenth-century view actually inhibited Frollo. Otherwise, generally good response. (Why was creating the Earth such a religious "ordeal"?) Grade: B

ANSWER 3

According to *The Hunchback of Notre Dame*, the view of "science" in the fifteenth century was basically alchemy, that is, being able to turn base metals into gold. Everything else that we would regard as scientific today was regarded as sorcery or magic in the fifteenth century. What inhibited Claud Frollo in his experiments of turning base metals into gold was that, according to the laws of alchemy, one needed "The Philosopher's Stone" to complete the experiment, and Claud Frollo was unable to find this particular stone.

Needs more specific illustrations from the novel. Frollo is inhibited by his lack of scientific method and the censure of the church. Underline title of novel: The Hunchback of Notre Dame. Grade: C

ANSWER 4

During the period that the *Hunchback* took place, the attitude toward science was one of fear. Because the setting was in the medieval world, the people were afraid to admit to doing some things that were not being done by a majority of people. The overall view during that period was to keep one's own self out of trouble. The fright may be the result of the public executions which were perhaps Claud Frollo's deterrent in admitting to performing acts of science which others are uneducated in.

Claud Frollo was outnumbered in the area of wanting to be "educated" and he kept to himself because he feared the people. He was in a position that didn't give him the power to try and overcome people's attitude of fear toward science. If he tried, he risked his life.

BIOLOGY 220: ECOLOGY
FINAL EXAMINATION

Essay II (20 Points)

Water running down a mountainside erodes its channel and carries with it considerable material. What is the basic source of the energy used by the water to do this work? How is the energy used by water to do this work related to the energy used by life in the stream ecosystem?

ANSWER 1

The process begins with the hydrologic cycle. The sun radiates down and forces evaporation. This H_2O gas condenses and forms rain or snow, which precipitates back to earth. If the precipitation falls on a mountain, it will eventually run down the hillside and erode its channel. (Some water will evaporate without running down the hill.) The energy used by water to do its work relates directly to the energy used by life in the stream system. The sun is an energy input. It is the source of energy for stream life just as it is the source of energy for the water. Through photosynthesis, the energy absorbed by the stream is used by higher and higher trophic levels. So the sun is the energy source for both running water and the life in the stream. It all starts with solar energy.

ANSWER 2

Ultimately, the sun is the basic source of energy that allows water to do the work it does. Solar power runs the hydrologic cycle, which is where water gets its energy. Heat evaporates water and allows molecules to rise in the atmosphere, where it condenses in clouds. Above the ground, but still under the effects of gravity, water has potential energy at this point. When enough condensation occurs, water drops back to the ground, changing potential energy to kinetic energy, which is how water works on mountainsides to move materials. As water moves materials, it brings into streams a great deal of organic matter, which is utilized by a number of heterotrophic organisms. That is the original source of energy for the ecosystems and also how energy used by water is related to the energy that is used by life in streams.

ANSWER 3

The actual energy to move the water down the mountains is gravitational pull from the center of the earth. The stream's "growth" from the beginning of the mountain-top to the base starts out with being a heterotrophic system. This is because usually there is not enough light to bring about photosynthesis for the plants and in turn help other organisms' survival, so the streams use outside resources for energy. Once the stream gets bigger (by meeting up with another stream), it is autotrophic. It can produce its own energy sources. When the water reaches the base and becomes very large, it falls back to a heterotrophic system because the water has become too deep for light to penetrate and help with photosynthesis.

Reread the question. The basic source of energy is solar power. You almost discover the answer when you discuss photosynthesis, but after that, you get off track again. Grade: C—

Handbook

SECTION 1
REVIEW OF BASIC SENTENCE ELEMENTS

If you are unfamiliar with grammatical terms, parts of speech, or basic sentence elements, check the definitions and examples in this section.

1A Sentence Structure
1B Nouns and Pronouns
1C Adjectives and Adverbs
1D Verbs
1E Phrases and Clauses
1F Articles, Prepositions, Interjections

SECTION 2
SENTENCE STRUCTURE AND GRAMMAR

This section shows you how to revise such common problems as sentence fragments, faulty parallelism, unnecessary use of passive voice, and lack of subject-verb agreement.

2A Fragments
2B Mixed Constructions and Faulty Predication
2C Dangling Modifiers and Misplaced Modifiers
2D Faulty Parallelism
2E Active and Passive Voice
2F Nominals and *Be* Verbs
2G Subject-Verb Agreement
2H Verb Tense
2I Pronoun Agreement
2J Pronoun Reference

SECTION 3
DICTION AND STYLE

This section contains tips on making your writing more precise, concise, and effective. You will learn to recognize and eliminate vague words, needless words, clichés, and jargon. At the end of this section, the Usage Glossary explains distinctions between confusing pairs of words such as *affect/effect*, *advise/advice*, and *amount/number*.

3A Vague Words
3B Wordiness

> " A piece of writing is never finished. It is delivered to a deadline, torn out of a typewriter on demand, and sent off with a sense of accomplishment and shame and pride and frustration. If only there were a couple more days, time for just another run at it, perhaps then . . . "
>
> —DONALD MURRAY, TEACHER AND WRITER

SECTION 4
PUNCTUATION AND MECHANICS

If you have problems using commas, semicolons, colons, or dashes, this section will help you pinpoint errors and fix them. The examples show you how to revise comma splices and fused sentences, how to punctuate dialogue, and how to use numbers, apostrophes, italics, and capitals.

The information in this Handbook will help you with the final stages of the revising process: editing and proofreading. Most writers and researchers agree that editing and proofreading should wait until the end of the writing process, when you are least likely to interrupt the flow of your ideas. During this final stage, you should clarify your sentences and correct any errors in grammar, usage, diction, spelling, and mechanics. As you edit, concentrate on polishing the surface blemishes in your writing, but don't get so locked in on punctuation or grammar that you ignore the meaning, organization, or development of your essay. Even when you are proofreading, you may find an occasional spot to add another bit of detail, take out a repetitious phrase, or sharpen a transition.

To be a good editor, you need to understand the *conventions* of language and the *expectations* of the reader instead of memorizing rules. In fact, the "rules" of grammar, punctuation, and usage may vary from one occasion to the next. A sentence fragment or a substandard usage such as "ain't" may be appropriate in one situation but not in another. Moreover, the notion of "rules" tends to suggest that language is static or unchanging. In fact, the opposite is true: vocabulary, acceptable usage, even grammatical choices depend on current conventions and expectations. What is acceptable for one occasion or audience may be totally inappropriate for another. If you are not aware of these conventions, all your hard work in collecting, shaping, drafting, and revising may be wasted. A sloppy job of editing can ruin the best of essays.

This chapter describes standard conventions of editing in formal American English usage. As you edit your writing, however, remember that your purpose and audience should be your final guide.

Why Edit and Proofread?

Most writers and readers agree that grammar, usage, spelling, and mechanics are less important than content and ideas. But writers should realize that readers react not only to the ideas in an essay but also to the clarity, accuracy, and even the surface appearance of the writing. Often, writers will say, rather defensively, "Of course, there are a few typos and grammar problems in my essay, but readers can still get the message. After all, it's my *ideas* that count." Unfortunately, ideas count only if the reader *gets* them. If the reader becomes irritated by unclear sentences and errors in spelling or usage, your good ideas may never reach their destination.

> " Easy writing's curst hard reading. "
> —RICHARD BRINSLEY SHERIDAN, DRAMATIST

Writers who say that surface errors are unimportant are either rationalizing or living in a fantasy world. In the real world, most readers react negatively if writing is not neat, accurate, and readable. If your friend or roommate leaves a scrawled note that says, "I borried your shert for too day—hope you do'nt mind!" you may worry about the "shert"—and look for a new roommate. If your bank statement has misspellings, crossed-out numbers, or penciled-in debits, you may change banks in a hurry. If your doctor writes a note saying, "In my opinnion you should have bone serjury immediately!" you may rush to get another "opinnion" before agreeing to "serjury." The medium may communicate the real message: If the medium—your language—is flawed by surface errors, readers often suspect that the message is flawed, too.

> " The man snoozing in his chair with an unfinished magazine open on his lap is a man who was being given too much unnecessary trouble by the writer. "
> —WILLIAM ZINSSER, WRITER AND TEACHER

Some readers believe that writers who do not edit or proofread are just lazy. Although you need time to polish your writing, effective editing and proofreading are not just matters of effort or willpower. Rereading your essay ten times will not necessarily resolve all the problems. Editing is often difficult because many of your errors really don't look like mistakes—primarily because *you already know what you are trying to say.* When you reread what you have written, you tend to recall the idea already in your mind instead of reading the words exactly as they are written on the page.

If you live with a friend or roommate, try this experiment. Sit in a neutral corner of the room and look at your desk. It looks relatively clean, right? A few books, papers, and pencils are scattered here and there, but you know where everything is. It has an order. It makes sense. The math book is on the corner of the desk—under the notebook, the sock, and the coffee—just where you left it last night. The psychology book is open to Chapter 4, right underneath the sweatshirt and the lecture notes that you're going to study after dinner. Stuff is kind of stacked up, but not really messy. Now look at your friend's desk. Everything looks disorganized, as if it were dumped upside down from a backpack. You count four books, two spiral notebooks, four dog-eared sheets of paper, one cup of stale coffee, a broken ballpoint pen, and a T-shirt. It's a mess, right? And sometimes it really irritates you. *How can your roommate stand to live in such chaos?* But wait. Your roommate's desk has some order to it, too, just as yours does. You just can't see the order for the mess.

Unfortunately, the same is true of writing: In your *own* writing, all you see is the meaning—the order that is in your mind. In other people's writing, you see the errors first and then, only after careful reading, the meaning. The bedrock truth is that readers will more easily see your mess than your meaning. Your writing will be more effective if your readers aren't irritated about the mess that they have had to read through. Errors or surface distractions may even undermine your credibility as a writer. For some kinds of writing—letters of application or essays for classes—the result of a few errors may be more than irritation; you simply may not be admitted, get the job, or get a passing grade.

How to Edit and Proofread

The purpose of editing is, of course, to keep language problems from interfering with the ideas or message—to make language work for your purpose rather than against it. Editing usually requires that you read over your work several times, checking for errors and anticipating problems that your readers might have. However, because you literally may not see many "obvious" errors, have friends or classmates look over your draft for problems or mistakes. When you use other readers, however, explain your purpose and audience. Then ask them to use conventional proofreading and editing marks to indicate their suggestions. *Remember: Your editors' marks are suggestions.* If they mark errors you've simply overlooked, make the correction. But if they mark something that you don't understand, check the appropriate section in this Handbook. If you disagree with their marks or suggestions, ask them to explain why they are suggesting the change. *You are responsible for deciding whether and how to make the change.*

Begin your editing and proofreading process for each essay by *reviewing your previous essays.* What problems and errors did your peer readers notice or your teacher mark? If you are keeping a log in your journal of your problems in grammar, usage, punctuation, or mechanics, review your entries. If you typically have punctuation problems and wordy sentences, reread those sections in this Handbook and focus on those specific items as you edit.

To improve your editing and proofreading skills, learn the following proofreading marks and correction symbols.

PROOFREADING MARKS

⋀	Insert comma
embaŗassing	Insert letter or word
hot tub.	Insert quotation marks
south‿bound	Close up
¶	Begin a new paragraph
NO ¶	Do not begin a new paragraph
down his face⊙	Add period
hop#back	Add space
peice of pie	Transpose letters
left/will/that/	Transpose words
in a ~~large~~ sweat	Delete words
encounter͵is	Delete punctuation
Los Angelᵉs	Replace a letter
deep ~~inhilations~~ breaths	Replace a word
Manure	Use lowercase
friday	Capitalize

The following paragraph by student writer Kenneth Clause illustrates how to use these proofreading marks.

My Home Town, LA Style

It is 11:00 p.m. on a chilly friday night. We are traveling South on the 405 freeway and have just entered Los Angeles city limits. A thick, damp fog rolls in from the ocean to blanket the city. Visibility is low. The vehicle descends through a sharp, banked turn and the headlights reveal the first glimpse of "it" looming in the distance. What my weary traveling companion from New York is about to encounter, is the most embarrassing and horrifying beast known to residents of Los Angeles. I break out in a ~~large~~ sweat, realizing there are no exits left will that detour this formation. In a moment of desperation, I step on the accelerator. Perhaps I can speed by this ~~depraved~~ ugly monument so my friend will not notice. Unfortunately, I'm too late. In that instant, he begins howling with laughter. We are suddenly upon it. The headlights reveal a heaping pile of Manure ~~appears~~ with a sign posted on the pinnacle that says, "Welcome to Los Angeles! A town where the grass is greener . . . on the other side of the hot tub." Well, no use in trying to hide any longer. I hit the brakes and pull the car over to the side of the road. Immediately, my jovial friend from New York opens the door and falls to the pavement with tears of laughter streaming down his face. The last thing he expected to see among the palm trees of California was a huge dungheap. The laughter of my merry schoolmate quickly ceases after a few deep ~~inhilations.~~ breaths The foul stench of this revolting glob of dung is enough to make even his pollution-hardened lungs feel weak. Upon my request, we hop back in the car and head for home. After recieving such a shock to his senses, his only hope for revival is a long shower and a peice of my dad's hot apple pie.

Editing Symbols

As you edit someone else's draft, use the following symbols to refer the writer to problems discussed in this Handbook. Your instructor may also use these correction marks to guide your own editing. Listed here are some of the most common symbols, with an explanation and reference to the section number in this Handbook.

adj	use adjective, 1C
adv	use adverb, 1C

cs	comma splice, 4B
d	revise diction (word choice)
dm	dangling modifier, 2C
frag	sentence fragment, 2A
fs	fused sentence, 4B
mm	misplaced modifier, 2C
//	revise faulty parallelism, 2D
p	punctuation needed, 4A–J
pn	agr make pronoun agree with antecedent, 2I
ref	pronoun referent problem, 2J
sp	spelling error
sv	agr subject-verb agreement error, 2G
sxt	sexist language, 3E
t	verb tense error, 1D, 2H
trans	needs transition
v	verb form problem, 1D
wdy	wordy—omit needless words, 2F, 3A, 3B
wc	revise word choice

TIPS FOR EDITING AND PROOFREADING

1. Review sections of this chapter just before you begin editing. If you need to review basic grammatical terms, begin with Section 1. Otherwise, review appropriate parts of Sections 2, 3, or 4.

2. Practice your editing and proofreading skills first on others' essays. You will see others' problems much more readily than you will see your own. Becoming a good editor of their writing will, in turn, help you recognize your own problems more easily.

3. As you edit, look for one problem at a time. Concentrate, for example, just on punctuation, or just on subject-verb agreement, or just on diction or word choice.

4. Have a friend or classmate read your essay aloud. Listen as the person reads. If you notice something that is not clear, stop and revise the sentence. If the reader does not understand what he or she is reading, stop and revise.

5. If you are writing on a computer, reformat and print out your essay, double-spaced, in narrow columns, forty to forty-five spaces wide. Many obvious errors will jump out at you as you reread your writing in a new format.

6. For proofreading, place a ruler or a blank piece of paper underneath the line you are checking. If you are proofreading for typos, try reading backward, one word at a time, from the bottom of the page to the top.

SECTION 1
REVIEW OF BASIC SENTENCE ELEMENTS

This section reviews the names and definitions of basic sentence elements. Other sections in this Handbook use the terms defined and illustrated in this section.

1A Sentence Structure

A sentence is a group of words beginning with a capital letter and ending with a period or other end mark; it has a subject and a predicate and expresses a complete thought. The *subject* is the word or group of words that is the topic or focus of the sentence. It acts, is acted upon, or is described. The *predicate* gives information about the subject: what the subject is, what it is doing, or what is done to it.

SUBJECT	PREDICATE
Piranhas	bite!
The McNeils	dig clams at the seashore.
Bubble gum	can cause cancer in rats.

Sentences may contain the following elements: subject (S), verb (V), direct object (DO), indirect object (IO), subject complement (SC), object complement (OC), modifier (M), and conjunction (+).

    S   V
Piranhas bite.

    S   V   DO + DO   M
Piranhas attack fish or animals in their waters.

    S   V   IO   M   DO
Andrea gave Carlos two piranhas.

    S   V   DO   OC
Carlos considers Andrea a prankster.

    S   V   SC
Andrea is a prankster.

Subjects may be nouns, pronouns, noun phrases, or noun clauses.

Verbs may be single words (*bite*) or verb phrases (*will have bitten*). Verbs may be transitive or intransitive; verbs have tense, voice, and mood.

Direct objects can be nouns, pronouns, noun phrases, or noun clauses. A direct object receives the action of a transitive verb. Direct objects usually answer the question "What?" or "Whom?" about the subject and verb.

Piranhas bit [whom?] people.

Indirect objects can be nouns, pronouns, noun phrases, or noun clauses. The indirect object answers the question "To whom?" or "For whom?" about the subject and verb.

Andrea gave [to whom?] Carlos two piranhas.

Complements occur in the predicate of the sentence following a *to be* or other linking verb. Subject complements rename or describe the subject. Object complements rename or describe the object.

SC

Carlos is *upset*.

OC

Carlos named one piranha *Bucktooth*.

Modifiers describe or limit a subject, verb, object, or complement. They may be single words, groups of words, or entire clauses:

M

Piranhas have a nasty disposition.

Conjunctions are words that link words, phrases, clauses, or sentences. The word *conjunction* means "a joining together." (See Section 4a for additional examples of conjunctions.)

- *Coordinating conjunctions (and, but, or, yet, for, nor, so)* join equal sentence elements:
  Carlos is angry, *but* Andrea is laughing.

- *Correlative conjunctions (both . . . and, either . . . or)* also join equal sentence elements:
  Neither Carlos nor his aquarium fish are particularly happy about the piranhas.

- *Subordinating conjunctions (because, since, although, if, until, while,* and others) begin many dependent clauses:
  If Andrea plays another joke on Carlos, she may lose a good friend.

1A struc

1B Nouns and Pronouns

A *noun* names a person, place, object, or idea. Nouns may be grouped in several classes.

- *Proper nouns* name specific people, places, or things.
  Abraham Lincoln, Cape Hatteras, Buick

- *Common nouns* name all nouns that are not proper nouns.
  cat, ocean, helicopter

- *Concrete nouns* name things that can be sensed.
  table, waves, coat

- *Abstract nouns* name things not knowable by the senses.
  justice, pity, freedom

- *Collective nouns* name groups.
  family, committee, team

- *Compound nouns* are several words joined by hyphens to form a noun.
  brother-in-law, commander-in-chief

A *pronoun* takes the place of a noun. Pronouns must meet three requirements.

- *Reference:* A pronoun must refer to a specific, identifiable word, phrase, or clause. This referent or antecedent occurs within the sentence or in a preceding sentence. (See Section 2J for examples of how to solve problems in pronoun reference.)
  Evelyn has the flu. *She* has missed two classes. [*Evelyn* is the referent for *she*.]

- *Agreement:* A pronoun must agree with or correspond to the noun that it replaces. A pronoun must agree in *person* (first, second, or third person), *number* (singular or plural), and *gender* (he, she, it). (See Section 2I for examples of how to solve problems in pronoun agreement.)
  Each girl should check on *her friend.* [*Her* agrees in person (third person), in number (singular), and gender (feminine) with the referent, *girl*.]

- *Case:* Pronouns must take the appropriate case (subjective, objective, possessive): *Subjective pronouns (I, you, he, she, it, we, they, who)* should be the subject or the complement in a sentence.
  They have the flu. [Subject]

  Who is sleeping there? It is she. [Complement]

  Objective pronouns *(me, you, her, him, whom, us, you, them)* should act as objects in a sentence.
  Evelyn gave *me* the flu. [Indirect object]

Possessive pronouns *(my, mine, your, yours, his, her, hers, its, our, ours, their, theirs, whose)* show possession.

I am sick as a dog with *her* flu virus.

Pronouns may be grouped in several classes.

- *Personal pronouns (I, me, mine, we, us, our, ours, you, yours, she, her, hers, he, him, his, it, its, they, them, theirs)* refer to people or things.
  She bought a cat for *him*.

- *Relative pronouns (that, who, whom, which, what, whose, whoever)* introduce clauses.
  Whoever fed the cat made a mistake.

- *Interrogative pronouns (who, whose, what, which, whom)* introduce a question.
  Which cat is the mother?

- *Reflexive* and *intensive pronouns (myself, yourself, herself, ourselves,* and so on) refer back to a pronoun or antecedent or intensify the antecedent.
  She says she paid for the cat *herself.* I *myself* suspect she just found it.

- *Indefinite pronouns (all, anyone, another, anybody, both, each, few, most, some, several, none, someone, something, such,* and so on) refer to nonspecific persons or things.
  Someone will turn up and claim the cat.

- *Demonstrative pronouns (this, that, these, those)* refer to an antecedent.
  On Tuesday morning, I must pay my bill. *That* will be a painful moment.

1C Adjectives and Adverbs

Adjectives are modifiers that limit, describe, or add information about nouns and pronouns.

Secretariat was my *favorite* horse. [modifies noun, *horse*]
Even standing still, he looked *dynamic.* [modifies pronoun, *he*]

Adverbs limit, describe, or add information about verbs, adjectives, or other adverbs, and they complete sentences.

He won *overwhelmingly.* [modifies verb, *won*]
The Kentucky Derby was a *very* important victory. [modifies adjective, *important*]
On that day, he ran *extremely* fast. [modifies adverb, *fast*]
Fortunately, he won the Triple Crown. [modifies whole sentence]

1D Verbs

The *verb* is the heart of most sentences. Verbs can set up equations or definitions ("A flotilla *is* a small fleet of ships"). They can describe states of being ("Fear and confusion *exist* in Lebanon"). They can explain occurrences ("The players *became* angry at the referee's call") or describe actions ("The candidate *defeated* her opponent"). When sentences communicate clearly, verbs often deserve the credit.

The great variety of verb forms creates a richness in the language. This richness, however, can create confusion. Some verbs are regular; others, irregular. In some cases, combinations of verb tense, voice, and mood may entangle sentences. The following explanations and examples will help you resolve problems in verb forms so that you can communicate precisely and vividly.

PRINCIPAL PARTS OF VERBS

Verbs have three principal parts: simple form, past tense, and past participle.

SIMPLE FORM (INFINITIVE)	PAST TENSE	PAST PARTICIPLE
live (to live)	lived	lived
go (to go)	went	gone

REGULAR AND IRREGULAR VERBS   *Regular verbs* form the past tense and past participle by adding *-ed* or *-d* to the simple form.

SIMPLE FORM	PAST TENSE	PAST PARTICIPLE
count	counted	counted
dance	danced	danced
create	created	created

Irregular verbs can cause problems because they form the past tense and past participle by changing letters, sounds, or entire words. Check your dictionary to determine if a verb is irregular. If the dictionary gives only two forms *(catch, caught)*, the past participle is the same as the past tense *(caught)*. Following are some examples of the nearly two hundred irregular English verbs.

SIMPLE FORM	PAST TENSE	PAST PARTICIPLE
sing	sang	sung
begin	began	begun
break	broke	broken
drive	drove	driven
sink	sank, sunk	sunk
sleep	slept	slept
read	read	read
eat	ate	eaten
see	saw	seen
slide	slid	slid

LINKING VERBS *Linking verbs (is, becomes, seems, looks,* and so on) equate subjects with predicates, so that the word or words in the predicate rename or describe the subject. A linking verb creates a subject complement (SC)—a word or words that complete the equation.

> s v sc m
>
> Lillian was president of the company. [Lillian = president]

> s v sc
>
> The storm seemed threatening. [Storm = threatening]

AUXILIARY VERBS *Auxiliary verbs,* also called *helping verbs,* combine with main verbs to show tense, voice, or mood. The verbs *be, do,* and *have* are common auxiliary verbs.

> She is running a marathon. [auxiliary verb = *is*]
>
> They did enjoy the dinner. [auxiliary verb = *did*]
>
> He had left before she arrived. [auxiliary verb = *had*]

TENSE *Tense* tells *when* a verb's action, occurrence, or state of being takes place. The six verb tenses in English are illustrated here with the regular verb *create.* The parentheses contain the *progressive* form *(-ing)* to show continual or ongoing action, occurrence, or state of being.

Present	I create (I am creating)
Past	I created (I was creating)
Future	I will create (I will be creating)
Present Perfect	I have created (I have been creating)

The present perfect tense describes actions occurring or conditions existing at an unspecified time in the past and continuing into the present: *I have created several award-winning recipes for chili.*

Past Perfect	I had created (I had been creating)

The past perfect tense describes actions occurring or conditions existing before a specific time in the past: *I had created three different recipes for extra-hot chili before I won my first award.*

Future Perfect	I will have created (I will have been creating)

The future perfect tense describes actions that have already occurred or conditions that will exist by a specific future time: *I will have created a new salsa recipe before the county fair begins.*

TRANSITIVE AND INTRANSITIVE   Many verbs in English can be either transitive or intransitive, depending on the sentence. *Transitive* verbs take objects. As the prefix *trans-* suggests, they carry the action across to the object:

S   V   DO

Myrna developed the film.

S   V   DO

Michael sees the oncoming car.

Intransitive verbs do not take objects.

S   V   M

Myrna developed early. [*Early* is not a direct object; it describes when Myrna developed.]

S   V   M

Michael sees in the dark. [*In the dark* is not a direct object.]

VOICE   Verbs have *active* and *passive* voice. *Active voice* means that the subject of the sentence performs the action. *Passive voice* means that the subject is acted upon. A passive-voice sentence uses a form of *be* plus a past participle. (For additional discussion of active and passive voice, see Section 2e.)

Active Voice   Inuits *build* stone and peat houses.
Passive Voice   Stone and peat houses *are built* by Inuits. [Contains a form of *be* + past participle: *are* + *built*]

MOOD   Verbs have three moods that indicate a writer's attitude toward a statement. *Indicative mood* expresses a statement of fact or asks a question. *Imperative mood* expresses commands or directives. *Subjunctive mood* expresses a wish or condition contrary to fact:

Indicative   She has perfect pitch. [fact]
Why does she sing opera? [question]
Imperative   Pay attention to the music. [command]
Turn and face the spotlight. [directive]
Subjunctive   I wish that I were more talented. [wish]
If she were to catch a cold, she would not sing on opening night. [condition contrary to fact]

1E Phrases and Clauses

PHRASES

A *phrase* is a group of related words that does not contain a subject or a predicate.

Prepositional Phrase	He wrote *on the computer.*
Noun Phrase	*A notebook computer* is handy.
Appositive Phrase	The Apple II, *the first popular school computer,* is the Model T of home computers. [An appositive phrase identifies or provides more information about the preceding noun or pronoun.]

A *verbal phrase* is a group of related words that contains a verbal: an infinitive *(to talk),* a present participle *(talking),* or a past participle *(talked).* There are three kinds of verbals.

- *Infinitives* usually use *to + simple verb;* they function as nouns, adjectives, or adverbs.

Infinitive	*To talk*
Infinitive Phrase	He planned to *talk for three minutes.* [infinitive phrase = direct object]
	To listen carefully was his first objective. [infinitive phrase = subject]

- *Gerunds* are nouns made from the *-ing* or present participle form of the verb.

Gerund	*Talking* got her into trouble. [*Talking* is a gerund; gerund = subject]
Gerund Phrase	*Talking during the lecture* got her into trouble. [gerund phrase = subject]

- *Participles* are adjectives made from verb forms. As adjectives, they modify nouns or pronouns. They can use either the *-ing* (present participle) or the *-ed* (past participle) verb form.

Participle	*Coughing* students may bother the teacher. [Participle modifies *students.*]
	Whispered conversations may distract students. [Participle modifies *conversations.*]
Participial Phrases	*Rustling their papers and snapping their notebooks closed,* they prepare to leave the lecture hall. [Participial phrase modifies *they.*]
	Several students, *entranced by the final scene in the film,* wrote quietly for a few moments. [Participial phrase modifies *students.*]

1F art

CLAUSES

A *clause* is a group of words containing a subject and a verb. It need not be an entire sentence or a complete thought. Clauses can be independent (main) or dependent (subordinate).

- *Independent* or *main clause:* A group of words containing a subject and a verb that can stand by itself as a complete thought.
  We drank decaffeinated coffee.

- *Dependent clause:* A group of words that contains a subject and verb but cannot stand by itself as a complete thought.
  Because we drank decaffeinated coffee

- *Subordinate clauses* (sometimes called *adverb clauses*): Dependent clauses that begin with a subordinating conjunction, such as *because, if, although, unless, when, while, since, as until, before,* and *after.*
  Although I drank coffee, everyone else drank tea.

- *Relative clauses* (also called *adjective clauses*): Dependent clauses that begin with *when, where,* or *why,* or with relative pronouns *(who, that, which, whom, whoever, whomever, whatever).*
  Driving when you are under the influence of alcohol may result in a mandatory jail sentence. [Adjective clause modifies *driving.*]

  Free coffee, which the bar serves after midnight, is part of a campaign for responsible drinking. [Adjective clause modifies *coffee.*]

  The police officer gave a ticket to the woman who was driving the red pickup truck. [Adjective clause modifies *woman.*]

1F Articles, Prepositions, Interjections

ARTICLES

Articles (a, an, the) often appear before nouns. They are modifiers that limit a noun. *A* and *an* are less limiting than *the.*

I have a plan to solve our problems.

I have the plan to solve our problems. [*The* suggests that the plan is more definitive.]

The article *a* appears before words that begin with a *consonant sound* (not necessarily a consonant): *a* kite, *a* hammer, *a* university, *a* one-sided victory.

The article *an* appears before words that begin with a *vowel sound* (not necessarily a vowel): *an* opening, *an* egg, *an* old shirt, *an* honor, *an* E.

PREPOSITIONS

Prepositions (*in, on, up, to, after, by, for, across, within,* and others) usually occur in prepositional phrases with a noun or pronoun that is the object of the preposition.

> *In* the hot sun *by* the edge *of* the water, a small turtle lay perfectly still.

Note that some words can function as either prepositions or conjunctions.

> We will row home *after* lunch. [preposition]

> *After* you finish your sandwich, we will row home. [conjunction]

INTERJECTIONS

Interjections (*oh, alas, yea, damn, hooray, ouch,* and others) are words conveying strong feeling or surprise. Interjections occasionally appear in informal writing or in a dialogue.

> The Cardinals won the pennant *(yea!)* but lost the World Series *(boo, hiss).*

> *Alas,* their hitting was anemic.

> *"Oh,* she moped about it for days."

SECTION 2
....
SENTENCE STRUCTURE AND GRAMMAR

When sentences don't follow standard American English conventions, readers may become aggravated, confused, or simply lost. While some deviations from established conventions barely distract the reader, others totally scramble meaning. If "sickening grammar" detracts from your meaning, your readers may react uncharitably. If you write a confusing sentence fragment, some readers will think, "This writer doesn't know what a sentence is." If you have a problem in subject-verb agreement, readers may think, "This writer didn't reread the sentence or doesn't know what the subject of the sentence is." If you write a sentence with a dangling modifier, the reader may think, "The writer doesn't know how comical this sounds." This section will help you avoid those embarrassing problems that confuse readers or invite them to think about your grammar rather than your meaning.

2A Fragments

Use sentence fragments only for special emphasis. A *fragment* is an incomplete sentence. A fragment may lack a subject or verb, or it may be only a dependent clause.

2A
frag

> ❝ I've noticed a good deal, and there's no bird, or cow, or anything that uses as good grammar as a bluejay. You may say a cat uses good grammar. Well, a cat does—but you let a cat get excited once; you let a cat get to pulling fur with another cat on a shed, nights, and you'll hear grammar that will give you the lockjaw. Ignorant people think it's the noise which fighting cats make that is so aggravating, but it ain't so; it's the sickening grammar they use. ❞
> —MARK TWAIN,
> FROM "BAKER'S BLUEJAY YARN"

Test for sentence fragments by taking the group of words out of context. If the group of words cannot stand by itself as a complete thought, it is a fragment.

Revise sentence fragments by adding a subject or verb or by combining the fragment with the preceding sentence:

Fragment   I still remember the championship basketball game when I scored forty points. *Breaking the existing conference record.* ["Breaking the existing conference record" is not a complete sentence. It cannot stand by itself as a complete thought. Combine with previous sentence.]

Revision   I still remember the championship basketball game when I broke the existing conference record by scoring forty points.

Fragment   At home I enjoy many water sports. *Waterskiing and sailing, which are my two favorites.* ["Waterskiing and sailing, which are my two favorites" cannot stand by itself as a complete thought. Revise to make one complete sentence.]

Revision   At home, I enjoy my two favorite water sports: waterskiing and sailing.

Fragment   She stood in line for four hours in the freezing rain. *To get tickets for the rock concert.* ["To get tickets for the rock concert" cannot stand by itself as a complete thought. Combine with previous sentence.]

Revision   To get tickets for the rock concert, she stood in line for four hours in the freezing rain.

Fragment   After a tough class, I took a long shower, dried my hair, and put on my underwear. Then I walked into the living room. *Because I thought no one was home.* Was I surprised to discover my mother talking to Reverend Jones! ["Because I thought no one was home" cannot stand by itself as a complete thought. It is a dependent clause or fragment.]

Revision   After a tough class, I took a long shower, dried my hair, and put on my underwear. Because I thought no one was home, I walked into the living room. Was I surprised to discover my mother talking to Reverend Jones!

Fragment   At the end of the game, the frustrated fans began to throw snowballs on the field. *The score being 42–0.* ["The score being 42–0" is not a complete sentence. Change *being* to *is* or *was*.]

Revision   At the end of the game, the frustrated fans began to throw snowballs on the field because the score was 42–0.

For special emphasis, however, sparingly used sentence fragments can be effective. In context, the following are examples of effective sentence fragments.

> When the river was dammed almost all of these things were lost. Crowded out—or drowned and buried under mud.
>
> —Edward Abbey

> Head off? Decapitation cases are rather routinely handled.
>
> —Jessica Mitford

> When I finally did fall asleep, I had that same hideous nightmare in which a woodchuck is trying to claim my prize at a raffle. Despair.
>
> —Woody Allen

EXERCISE

In the following passage, identify all sentence fragments. Then revise the passage to eliminate inappropriate fragments.

(1) Most people think that a library is as quiet as growing grass, but often it is the noisiest place on campus to study. (2) The worst time being finals week. (3) Some of the chatter is from people who come to the library just to visit: "How did you like the party Saturday night?" (4) "Did you get the notes from chemistry?" (5) The chatter goes on continually, punctuated by coughs, gasps, and giggles. (6) Just when I start to panic about my calculus examination. (7) Someone across the table tells a joke, and they all start laughing. (8) They try to cover their laughter with their hands, but the sound explodes out anyway. (9) Irritating ten other students who are trying to study. (10) Sometimes I wish the library had its own police force. (11) To arrest those gabby, discourteous "party people." (12) I would sit there smiling as they handcuffed these party people and dragged them out of the library. (13) Ah, the sweet revenge of daydreams.

2B Mixed Constructions and Faulty Predication

MIXED CONSTRUCTIONS

Occasionally, writers begin sentences with one structure and then switch, right in the middle, to another. Revise sentences with mixed constructions by choosing one structure and sticking to it.

Mixed	Because the repairs were so expensive is why I ended up selling the car.
Revised	Because the repairs were so expensive, I sold the car.
Mixed	By getting behind in math classes is a quick way to flunk out.
Revised	Getting behind in math classes is a quick way to flunk out.

FAULTY PREDICATION

Sometimes the predicate does not *logically* fit with the subject. Remember that the verb *to be* is an *equals* sign. Revise faulty predication by changing either the subject or the predicate.

Faulty	Freestyle ski jumping is where skiers take crazy chances in midair.
	Note: "Ski jumping" is an activity, not a place. It is illogical to say, "Ski jumping is where . . ."
Revised	Freestyle ski jumping is a sport that encourages skiers to take crazy chances in midair.
Faulty	My dog Noodles is the reason I'm feeling depressed.
	Note: "My dog Noodles" is a specific animal, not a "reason." Missing Noodles, however, could be a cause for depression.
Revised	I'm feeling depressed because I miss my dog Noodles.
Faulty	Real intelligence is when you can say no to that third piece of chocolate cream pie.
	Note: "Intelligence" is or equals a mental condition, not a "when."
Revised	Saying no to that third piece of chocolate cream pie requires real intelligence.

EXERCISE

In the following passage, identify sentences with mixed constructions, faulty predication, or both, and then revise them.

(1) After my sophomore year, I intend to transfer to Boston College. (2) Basically, I want to attend a school that has a city environment and a diverse population of students. (3) I suppose my sister Nadine is a big reason I want to transfer. (4) She wants me to move closer to home. (5) Also, by attending a city school will enable me to see plays, to visit museums occasionally, and to eat out at good restaurants. (6) Finally, I'd like to meet all sorts of students. (7) A good university is when a student

can meet people from all walks of life. (8) Because Boston College has diversity is really why I intend to transfer.

2C Dangling Modifiers and Misplaced Modifiers

DANGLING MODIFIERS

Modifying phrases must clearly describe, qualify, or limit some word in the sentence. When the modifying phrase occurs at the beginning of a sentence, the word that is modified must appear *immediately* following the phrase. Otherwise, the modifying phrase "dangles" or is logically "unattached" to the sentence. Such sentences are confusing and often comical:

Faulty	Rushing to get to class on time, my shoelace broke. [*Who* was rushing to get to class? The shoelace? Revise by indicating the person immediately after the comma.]
Revised	Rushing to get to class, I broke a shoelace.
Faulty	Flying at five thousand feet, the cars looked like tiny toys. [*Who* is flying at five thousand feet? The cars? Revise by indicating that person immediately after the comma.]
Revised	Flying at five thousand feet, I saw cars that looked like tiny toys.
Faulty	From birth until the first grade, one parent should be home with the children. [Does the opening phrase, "From birth until the first grade," modify *parent* or *children?* Revise by placing the appropriate word immediately after the introductory phrase.]
Revised	From birth until the first grade, children should have one parent at home.
Faulty	Sue practiced her freestyle stroke until she knew she could swim faster than Flipper, being a fanatical swimmer. [Who is the fanatical swimmer—*Sue* or *Flipper?* When modifying phrases "dangle" from the *end* of a sentence, revise by placing the phrase next to the word it modifies.]
Revised	Being a fanatical swimmer, Sue practiced her freestyle stroke until she knew she could swim faster than Flipper.

MISPLACED MODIFIERS

Place a modifying word, phrase, or clause immediately before or after the word it modifies. In the following sentences, notice how changing the placement of the word *only* changes the meaning of the sentence.

Only I tasted grandfather's pumpkin pie. [I was the only one who tasted it.]

I only tasted grandfather's pumpkin pie. [I only tasted it; Pete actually ate it.]

I tasted only grandfather's pumpkin pie. [I didn't taste anything else; I didn't even taste Aunt Margaret's pecan pie.]

I tasted grandfather's only pumpkin pie. [Grandfather made only one pumpkin pie, and I tasted it.]

2C
dm /
mm

Confusing	He borrowed a computer from his professor with a faulty memory. [*Who* or *what* has the faulty memory? Place the phrase "with a faulty memory" next to the word it modifies *(computer).*]
Revised	He borrowed a computer with a faulty memory from his professor.
Confusing	The hamburgers have been horrible in the fast-food restaurants that I've eaten. [Did the writer eat restaurants or hamburgers? Revise by placing the clause "that I've eaten" next to the word it should modify *(hamburgers).*]
Revised	The hamburgers that I've eaten in fast-food restaurants have been horrible.

Exercise

In the following passage, identify sentences with dangling modifiers and misplaced modifiers, and then revise each faulty sentence.

(1) SP302, History of Film, is a worthwhile class to take. (2) Occurring on Tuesday night from 7:00 P.M. to 9:45 P.M., Professor Hancock teaches the class so that it coincides with dollar movie night at the campus theater. (3) Normally, a long class would be boring because of the Nod Factor. (4) However, Professor Hancock keeps everyone awake and entertains the students, being very energetic. (5) Her lecture on *Citizen Kane* was a particularly good example. (6) Unfortunately, the film began before she finished her lecture. (7) Rushing across the stage just as the film was beginning, an electrical cord tripped her up, causing her to lose her balance and fall. (8) She regained her composure in time to remind us that Orson Welles also wrote and performed the famous broadcast about the invasion of the Martians on the radio. (9) We certainly were relieved to get that important information!

2D Faulty Parallelism

Repeated elements in a sentence that are similar in meaning or function should be *parallel* in grammatical form. The parallel form should, in turn, help to emphasize the meaning. Any repeated sentence elements, from subjects and verbs to prepositional phrases, may occur in parallel form.

Parallel Clauses	*I came, I saw, I conquered.*
Parallel Adverbs	He read *slowly* and *thoroughly*.
Parallel Prepositional Phrases	She walked *through the archway, across the quadrangle,* and *into the library*.

Identifying and numbering the repeated elements may help you see the parallel elements in a sentence.

She walked	(1) through the archway, (2) across the quadrangle, and (3) into the library.

Faulty   Walking, biking, and automobiles are the three most popular modes of transportation.
[Identify and number elements that should be parallel. "(1) *Walking*, (2) *biking*, and (3) *automobiles* are the three most popular modes of transportation." Revise, choosing one pattern for all three elements.]

Revised   Walking, biking, and driving are the three most popular modes of transportation.

Faulty   Traveling abroad last summer, John increased his social awareness, his cultural knowledge, and overall sophistication.
[Identify and number elements that should be parallel. "Traveling abroad last summer, John increased (1) *his social awareness*, (2) *his cultural knowledge*, and (3) _____ *overall sophistication*." Then revise, choosing one grammatical pattern for all three elements.]

Revised   Traveling abroad last summer, John increased his social awareness, his cultural knowledge, and his overall sophistication.
[OR]

Revised   Traveling abroad last summer, John increased his social awareness, cultural knowledge, and overall sophistication.

Faulty   There are three commandments for college students: Thou shalt go to class; thou shalt read the text; and be sure to borrow your neighbor's notes.

2E
act

[Identify and number elements that should be parallel. Since the first and second "commandments" set the grammatical pattern, the reader expects the third commandment to take the same "thou shalt" form.]

Revised   There are three commandments for college students: Thou shalt go to class; thou shalt read the text; and thou shalt borrow thy neighbor's notes.

Faulty   She was angry not only because he was late but also he forgot the tickets.
Note: Compared or contrasted sentence elements introduced by "either . . . or," "both . . . and," or "not only . . . but also" must be parallel.
[Identify and number elements that should be parallel. "She was angry not only (1) because he was late but also (2) _____ he forgot the tickets." Revise to make (1) and (2) parallel.]

Revised   She was angry not only because he was late but also because he forgot the tickets.

EXERCISE

In the following passage, identify and revise any sentences with faulty parallelism.

(1) Alcohol abuse is a primary cause of spectator violence at college football games. (2) On average, the police department makes between five and ten arrests at each home football game. (3) These arrests are for property destruction, public intoxication, and occasionally when students conduct themselves in a disorderly manner. (4) When spectators consume too much alcohol not only do they hurt themselves but also act obnoxiously toward others. (5) Following a recent fight, ambulance attendants said that some drunken spectators or "animals" actually pelted them with sod while they tried to assist an injured man. (6) The attendants tried pleading, reason, and shouting, but to no avail. (7) To reduce these ugly incidents and restoring the enjoyment of the game, alcohol should not be sold at football games after the beginning of the second half.

2E Active and Passive Voice

Verbs that can have direct objects (transitive verbs) are in the *active voice* when the subject of the sentence *acts upon the object.*

The wolfhound bit Perry.

Wolfhound, the subject of the sentence, *acts upon the object, Perry.* The arrow shows that in the active voice, the action of the verb *bit* goes forward, toward the object, *Perry.*

Verbs that can have objects (transitive verbs) are in the *passive voice* when the *subject is acted upon.* The passive voice uses a form of *be (is, am, are, was, were, been, being)* followed by the past participle of the main verb (in this case, *bitten*).

Perry was bitten by the wolfhound.

The verb *was bitten* is transitive, but *Perry,* now the subject of the sentence, is acted upon. The arrow shows that the action of the verb goes backward, so that *Perry* receives the action.

Notice the following *differences* between active and passive voice.

The active-voice sentence, "The wolfhound bit Perry," uses two fewer words than the passive version, its action moves in a normal forward direction, and it clearly identifies the actor.

The passive-voice sentence, "Perry was bitten by the wolfhound," uses two more words, and it inverts the direction of the action in the sentence. In some cases, the passive voice may omit the actor altogether: "Perry was bitten on Friday." In that case, the reader does not know who or what bit Perry.

ACTIVE VOICE

Usually, *active voice* is preferable because it is more direct, vivid, and concise than passive voice. Remember, however, that sentences must be judged *in the context* of the writer's purpose, audience, and focus.

Following are examples of passive-voice constructions that, in context, may be more effective in the active voice. To change from passive to active, move the actor (often identified in the *by* phrase) to become the subject of the sentence.

Passive	Children's unruly behavior cannot be accepted by their parents.
	Note: The actor in the *by* phrase is *parents.* Change to active voice by making *parents* the subject of the sentence.
Active	Parents cannot accept their children's unruly behavior. [The active-voice version makes the actor the subject of the sentence and has two fewer words.]
Passive	It is argued by the members of our class that the teacher grades too hard.

Note: The *actor* in the *by* phrase is *members*. Change to the active voice by making *members* the subject of the sentence.

Active   Members of our class argue that the teacher grades too hard. [This active-voice version is more direct and has four fewer words.]

Passive   Under the current proposal, property taxes will be raised $1,000 dollars over the next two years.

Note: The *actor* is not identified in a *by* phrase; however, the *governor* actually proposed the tax increase. Change to active voice by making *governor* the subject of the sentence.

Active   The governor currently proposes to raise property taxes by $1,000 over the next two years. [The active-voice version reveals who, in fact, is responsible. It adds information without increasing the length of the sentence.]

PASSIVE VOICE

The *passive voice* is appropriate when the actor is unknown or is less important than the action or the receiver of the action. Use the passive voice in the following situations.

When the actor is unknown:

When her sports car swerved off the road and into the river, Carolyn was killed. [We don't know who or what actually killed her.]

When you want to emphasize that person or thing is helpless or is a victim:

The small Kansas town was leveled by the tornado.

Our football team was mauled by the Bears, 42–0.

The bag lady was mugged in broad daylight.

When the scientific experiment and the results should be the focus of the sentence or the passage (scientific writing typically uses the passive voice to lend objectivity to the findings):

The first recordings of humpback whales were obtained in 1952 from a U.S. Navy hydrophone installation.

The titration experiment was performed under careful laboratory conditions.

One typical *abuse of the passive voice* occurs when writers omit the actor in order to conceal responsibility:

The tuition for nonresident students was increased by $500 for the upcoming academic year.

This sentence, which was written by university officials, omits the actor or the agency responsible for the change. Because tuition increases are unpopular with students, university officials may have deliberately omitted the responsible actor or agency to avoid confrontation or blame. Careful readers should recognize such deceptive uses of the passive voice.

Caution: Don't assume that all verbs that follow the pattern, *be* verb form = past participle ["was ed"], are necessarily in the passive voice. In the sentence "I was scared," for example, the verb *scared* can be either transitive or intransitive, depending on the context. Only *transitive verbs* can be in either the active or the passive voice.

Transitive Active	A horrible Halloween mask scared me.
Transitive Passive	I was scared by a horrible Halloween mask.
Intransitive	At the Cave of Horrors, I was upset and scared.
Transitive Active	The boss fired me.
Transitive Passive	I was fired.
Intransitive	I was tired.

Test: To distinguish between intransitive and transitive passive, try adding the word *very*. If *very* cannot logically be used, the construction is passive voice.

> I was [very] tired. [*Very* works; *tired* is intransitive.]

> I was [very] fired. [*Very* doesn't work; *fired* is transitive passive.]

In addition, a good dictionary will indicate whether a verb is transitive, intransitive, or both.

EXERCISES

Identify sentences containing the passive voice. Change passive-voice sentences into the active voice.

1. People communicate using body movements.
2. A nod, a gesture, or a glance can be interpreted by people in several ways.
3. A wave and a smile mean one thing, but a wave and a tear can be interpreted to mean something else.
4. In addition, some people may be irritated by a continual or intense stare.
5. We may also be intimidated by a person who talks to us at very close range.

Read the following passage and identify sentences that are in the active or passive voice. Then determine which sentences should be in the active voice and which should be in the passive voice. Revise the passage, leaving sentences as they are,

2E
act

changing active-voice sentences to passive, or changing passive-voice sentences to active—as appropriate for the context.

(1) Writing on a computer can transform the act of writing, but only if the writer has some rudimentary typing skills. (2) Unfortunately, many men have a sexist hang-up about typing, so that their writing on a computer is inhibited. (3) Traditionally, it has been felt by most men that only females (i.e., secretaries) should type. (4) Only the macho Hemingways and Mailers of the world actually type their own novels and stories. (5) Now, however, many male business executives are caught by conflicting role images. (6) It is socially acceptable for them to be computer-literate, but it is still somehow demeaning to sit at a keyboard and practice the "female" skill of typing. (7) One more example of how notions about sexist roles can hurt men as well as women is thus provided by computers.

2F Nominals and *Be* Verbs

NOMINALS

Nominals (also called *nominalizations*) are *nouns* created from verbs. Nominals often make sentences less dynamic because they disguise or eliminate the action in a sentence. Frequently, nominals are nouns ending in *-ment, -ance, -ence, -ion,* and *-ing.* Each of the following nominals "contains" a verb: *expectation (expect), description (describe), solution (solve), resistance (resist), government (govern), preference (prefer), meeting (meet).* For many purposes and audiences, you can make your writing more vigorous, dynamic, and readable by changing nominals into verbs.

Nominal	Bill's *expectation* was to win the marathon.
Revised	Bill *expected* to win the marathon.
Nominal	The owner's manual contains a *description* of how to adjust the timing.
Revised	The owner's manual *describes* how to adjust the timing.
Nominal	On this campus, there exists some *resistance* among students to tuition increases.
Revised	On this campus, students *resist* tuition increases.
Nominal	*Dissatisfaction* with drinking-policy *decisions* is likely to be a major *contribution* to student *objections.* *Note:* When repeated nominals obscure the meaning, rewrite the whole sentence, making the primary *actor* the subject of the sentence.
Revised	Students object to the drinking policy.

Be Verbs

Be verbs *(is, am, are, was, were, been, being)* are effective in stating conditions, definitions, or concepts:

> Edgar Allan Poe's "The Raven" is a literary classic.

> An iconoclast is one who destroys sacred images or seeks to overthrow popular ideas or institutions.

Often, however, *be* verbs create static, flat, or lifeless sentences. Where appropriate, make your writing more dynamic by replacing *be* verbs with action verbs.

Eliminate *be* verbs by changing passive voice to active voice, by changing nominals or adjectives into verbs, by selecting a more vigorous verb, or by combining sentences.

Be Verb	The classical mythology course that *is* offered by the English department *is* fascinating.
Revised	The English department *offers* a fascinating course in classical mythology.
Be Verb	The driving force for many workaholics *is* their fear of failure.
Revised	Fear of failure *drives* many workaholics.
Be Verb	AIDS *is* a simple but sometimes lethal malfunction of the immune system. AIDS *is* a disease that can lead to the physical and mental destruction of its victim.
Revised	AIDS, a simple but sometimes lethal malfunction of the immune system, can *destroy* its victim physically and mentally.

Exercise

In the following passage, identify *nominals* and *be* verbs. Then revise the passage to make it more vivid, energetic, and concise by eliminating inappropriate nominals and be verbs.

(1) As parents, we know that many young people love to ride motorcycles, motorbikes, and motorscooters. (2) Today, however, our ten-year-old kids have some attraction to those off-road three-wheelers.
(3) Although kids get enjoyment from riding three-wheelers in the hills, these vehicles can be the cause of serious injury. (4) Unfortunately, these young drivers—and their parents—do not receive sufficient education from salespeople about the potential dangers. (5) As a result, some activist groups are in opposition to the sales of all three-wheelers. (6) These groups want regulations for the industry in order to make riding safer for children and adults. (7) The efforts of these groups to reform the industry are commendable to every responsible parent.

**2F
nom**

2G Subject-Verb Agreement

A verb must agree *in number* with its subject. Remember: *-s* or *-es* added to a noun makes it plural: *whale, whales.* Adding *-s* to a present-tense verb makes it singular: *whales sing; whale sings.*

1. Many agreement problems occur when plural words come between a singular subject and its verb. To correct a subject-verb error, first identify the actual subject, and then use the correct verb ending for that subject.

    Faulty A list of campaign promises often hurt the candidate.
    [Put brackets around any prepositional phrases. The subject of the sentence is never in a prepositional phrase. "A list [of campaign promises] often hurt the candidate." *List* is the subject and *hurt* is the verb. Read without the words inside the brackets and revise the verb.]
    Revised A *list* of campaign promises often *hurts* the candidate.

    Faulty This company, with few skilled mechanics and electricians, do not guarantee any repairs.
    [Put brackets around the prepositional phrase. "This company [with few skilled mechanics and electricians], do not guarantee any repairs." Read the sentence without the words in brackets and revise the verb.]
    Revised This company, with few skilled mechanics and electricians, *does* not guarantee any repairs.

2. Two subjects connected by *and* take a plural verb. "The sergeant and his recruits march double-time across the grounds." When two subjects are connected by *or* or *nor,* however, the verb agrees with the closer subject.

    Faulty Neither the recruits nor the sergeant know how to march.
    Revised Neither the recruits nor the sergeant *knows* how to march.
    [or]
    Revised Neither the sergeant nor the recruits *know* how to march.

3. Indefinite pronouns *(each, one, either, everyone, neither, everybody, nobody, no one, none, somebody, someone)* usually take a singular verb.

    Faulty Each of the books cost twenty dollars.
    [Remove the prepositional phrase: "Each [of the books] cost twenty dollars." *Each* is singular, so the verb should be *costs.*]
    Revised Each of the books *costs* twenty dollars.

Faulty	Everybody in all three classes are going to see the film. [Remove the prepositional phrase: "Everybody [in all three classes] are going to see the film." *Everybody* is singular, so the verb should be *is.*]
Revised	Everybody in all three classes *is* going to see the film.

4. A collective noun as a subject usually takes a singular verb. Collective nouns *(family, committee, audience, class, crowd,* and *army)* usually refer to a single *unit* or *group* of several individuals or elements, and thus they take a singular verb.

Faulty	The audience at the concert whistle its approval.
Revised	The audience at the concert *whistles* its approval.
	Note: When referring to the action or condition of *several individuals* within a group, use the phrase *the members of* or the phrase *a number of* followed by the plural verb: The members of the committee *argue* about the policy.

5. Even when the normal subject-verb order is reversed, the verb should agree in number with the subject.

Faulty	For such a small dormitory, there is far too many students. [Put the subject and verb in their normal order: Too many students are in the small dormitory. (*Students* is the subject, so the verb is plural: *are.*)]
Revised	For such a small dormitory, there *are* far too many students.

2G
sv agr

EXERCISE

In the following passage, revise all errors in subject-verb agreement.

(1) If you have friends or a family member who smoke, I have some suggestions to help this person quit. (2) First, if the family are supportive, try talking openly about the facts. (3) There is a few public service agencies that will provide evidence demonstrating the link between smoking and cancer. (4) Next, investigate this person's behavior: What does this person do just before he or she smokes? (5) To quit smoking, the smoker must disrupt the patterns of behavior that leads to smoking. (6) An inventory of the activities and places that cause a person to smoke provide key information. (7) For example, if the person always smokes after dinner, suggest eating snacks over a two-hour period instead of having a sit-down meal. (8) If he or she always smoke in a certain chair in the living room, change the furniture. (9) Breaking any habit is always easier if you break the entire behavior pattern. (10) Of course, each of these smokers need to want to stop smoking.

2H Verb Tense

Avoid unnecessary shifts in verb tense.

Shift	After they *ate* ice cream and cake for dessert, they *are* ready to relax.
Revised	After they *ate* ice cream and cake for dessert, they *were* ready to relax.
Shift	Peter *ate* dinner before you *had offered* to cook tacos.
Revised	Peter *ate* dinner before you *offered* to cook tacos.
Shift	At one point in this film, Gandhi *gathered* his followers together to discuss strategy. Suddenly, a British general *gave* an order to fire upon them. People then *scurry* around and *try* to protect themselves and their children from the hail of bullets. *Note:* For summaries or accounts of artistic works, films, literary works, or historical documents, use the present tense.
Revised	At one point in this film, Gandhi *gathers* his followers together to discuss strategy. Suddenly, a British general *gives* an order to fire upon them. People then *scurry* around and *try* to protect themselves and their children from the hail of bullets.

EXERCISE

In the following passage, revise any unnecessary shifts in tense.

(1) In Sophocles' play *Antigone*, two characters are tragic figures: Antigone and Creon. (2) In the play, Antigone faced a choice of conscience. (3) Should she be loyal to her family and bury her brother, or should she have been loyal to the state and obeyed the edict of Creon, the king of Thebes? (4) She assumes that she knew the best way to handle the situation and willfully chooses her own death. (5) Creon also faced a choice of conscience. (6) Should he punish someone who has betrayed the state, even if that person is a member of his family? (7) Like Napoleon and General Custer, Creon thought primarily about himself and his public image. (8) In Creon's case, ego or "hubris" leads to tragic results for the people around him.

21 Pronoun Agreement

A pronoun must agree in number and person with the noun to which it refers.

Faulty	One of the scientists signed their name to the report. [Because the subject is never in the prepositional phrase, put parentheses around the prepositional phrase ("of the

scientists"). Now look for another noun that could be the subject of the sentence. *One* is the subject of the sentence, and it is a singular noun. Change *their* to the singular form, *his* or *her*.]

Revised   One of the scientists signed *her* name to the report.

Faulty   Each of the students felt cheated on their test.
Note: Each is singular: *their* is plural.
Revised   The *students* felt cheated on *their* tests.

Faulty   Everyone brought their gift to the party.
Revised   Everyone brought *his* or *her* gift to the party.
Note: Avoiding sexist language by using *his or her* can be wordy or awkward in some contexts. Rewrite the sentence with a plural subject and a plural pronoun.
Revised   The *guests* brought *their* gifts to the party.

Avoid shifts in person. Avoid shifting between third person *(people, one, they, he, she)* and second person *(you)*.

Faulty   When you come to the party, everyone should bring a friend.
Note: You is second person; *everyone* is third person. Revise the sentence, using either second or third person throughout.
Revised   When *you* come to the party, bring a friend.

Faulty   A good party should make *people* feel at ease, so *you can* make new friends.
Revised   A good party should make *people* feel at ease, so *they can* make new friends.
Revised   A good party should make *you* feel at ease, so *you* can make new friends.

2J Pronoun Reference

A pronoun should refer clearly and unambiguously to its antecedent.

Unclear   Joan told Bev that her bank account was overdrawn.
[Whose bank account was overdrawn?]
Revised   When Joan discovered that her bank account was overdrawn, she told Bev.

Unclear   If people do not take care of their cats, we should turn them in to the humane society.
[Who should be turned in—the cats or their owners?]
Revised   If people do not take care of their cats, we should report the owners to the humane society.

EXERCISE

In the following passage, correct problems in pronoun agreement and reference.

(1) People use the term *best friend* to describe a person who has a special warmth and friendliness. (2) I still remember when Michelle Martin, one of my best friends, said that they really like me, too. (3) I called her my best friend; we stood by each other. (4) One time at a party, I saw her talking angrily to another woman. (5) It turned out that she had dated Tom, the guy she was going with at the time. (6) Each of them felt cheated by their boyfriend. (7) Before I knew what was happening, they were screaming at each other. (8) When I tried to stick up for her, she took a swing at me, and so I swung back with my best left hook, popping her in the right eye. (9) As a result, I was suspended from school for a week. (10) It just goes to show that when you have a best friend, everyone expects that you'll help them if you can.

3A
wdy

SECTION 3

DICTION AND STYLE

Effective writing hides a curious paradox. On the one hand, good writing contains vivid detail. Good writing does not merely assert that thus-and-so is true; it supports a claim or assertion with evidence. It recreates an experience, shows exactly how the writer feels, or communicates precisely what the writer thinks. To accomplish this, writers *add* specific details, examples, facts, or other data. On the other hand, good writing is also concise. Good writers *take out* vague words, weak verbs, and empty language. Their writing is as lean and sinewy as a long-distance runner. As you edit your writing for diction (choice of words) and clarity of style, you should *add* specific examples but *remove* vague, imprecise language. Your details should be ample; your diction and style, spare.

> "Vigorous writing is concise. A sentence should contain no unnecessary words, a paragraph no unnecessary sentences, for the same reason that a drawing should have no unnecessary lines and a machine no unnecessary parts. This requires not that the writer make all his sentences short, or that he avoid all detail . . . but that every word tell."
>
> —WILL STRUNK, JR., COAUTHOR OF ELEMENTS OF STYLE

3A Vague Words

Replace vague words with more specific or concrete language.

1. The following *nouns* are vague or unspecific. Vague nouns encourage writers to *tell* rather than to *show* with specific details or examples. Vague nouns may also lead to wordy and imprecise sentences. In most cases, *replace* the following nouns with more specific words, details, or examples.

thing	situation	difficulty
something	type	feeling
anything	way	beauty
someone	fun	people
some	trouble	deal
area	problem	place
case	field	character
manner	nature	appearance
factor	aspect	

Vague   During their freshman year, students worry about all sorts of *things*. [Be specific: What things?]

Revised   During their freshman year, students worry about leaving their families, making new friends, and passing their courses.

Vague   I have taken courses in the *field* of statistics for two years, and it has changed my *feeling* toward studying in the *area* of mathematics.

Revised   After taking statistics courses for two years, I no longer hate studying mathematics.

Vague   Meteorologists occasionally have a *great deal of trouble in forecasting a situation* where an upper-level disturbance becomes a *factor* in local weather. [Be specific: What kind of trouble? Be concise: Omit unnecessary, vague words.]

Revised   When an upper-level disturbance affects local weather, meteorologists occasionally miss a forecast.

2. The following *modifiers* are weak, vague, or unspecific. Replace them with stronger modifiers or add specific details.

very	a lot	pretty
really	good	bad
a few	certain	happy
many	nice	much
regular	similar	soon

Vague   I *really* liked certain classes in high school very much, but I just couldn't stand a *lot* of the *really boring* courses. [Be specific: What *certain classes?* Be specific: How or why were they *really boring?*]

Revised   I really looked forward to learning about the turtles, snakes, and birds in the biology lab, but I couldn't stand just sitting still and practicing grammar hour after hour in French class.

3A wdy

3A
wdy

Vague	Overall, *The Cosby Show* is *pretty good,* but sometimes it gets somewhat *unreal.* [Be specific: What makes it pretty good? What makes it unreal?]
Revised	*The Cosby Show* has entertaining stories about family problems—I still remember the episode when Theo decides he just has to join the Blue Angels—but in many episodes, the family seems to resolve the conflict too easily and simply.

3. The following *verbs* are weak, vague, or unspecific. Where appropriate, replace them with more active, energetic, or vivid verbs. When these verbs occur with nominals or the passive voice, change to active verbs or the active voice. Always test your revision: In your context, is the change more effective, concise, or vivid?

deals with	take	get
gets involved with	relate to	go
has to do with	make	give

Vague	He *gets* some enjoyment from sky diving.
Revised	He *enjoys* sky diving.

Vague	Her job *deals with* collecting rare species of lizards.
Revised	She *collects* rare species of lizards.

Vague	Jogging along the path, she *got involved* with a rattlesnake in a serious way. [How exactly was she "involved" with this rattlesnake?]
Revised	Jogging along the path, she was seriously bitten by a rattlesnake.

EXERCISE

In the following passage, substitute specific and vivid words or phrases for all vague nouns, verbs, and modifiers.

(1) When I was separated from my girlfriend, I missed her a lot. (2) Being alone sometimes gave me a pretty empty-type feeling. (3) When I called her on the phone, we talked about all the nice times we spent together, not about all the very big fights we used to have. (4) Since there was no stress to deal with, we had a fun-filled, long-distance relationship. (5) I know that one aspect of this relationship will improve the way we get along, now that we're back together. (6) We

always had difficulty talking in a serious manner about our future.
(7) Now we are more involved with each other and can really talk about
all sorts of things. (8) For anyone who is having troubles, I recommend
this kind of separate situation because, in the long run, the relationship
will be much happier.

3B Wordiness

1. The following wordy phrases can be made more concise.

WORDY	CONCISE
due to the fact that	because
despite the fact that	though
regardless of the fact that	although
at this point in time	now
at the present time	now
until such time as	until
in the event that	if, when
at all times	always
there is no doubt that	doubtless
in a deliberate manner	deliberately
by means of	by
the reason is that	[omit]

2. The following phrases are redundant; they say the same thing twice or repeat unnecessarily.

REDUNDANT	CONCISE
new innovation	innovation
disappear from view	disappear
repeat again	repeat
reflected back	reflected
circle around	circle
few in number	few
cheaper in cost	cheaper
oblong in shape	oblong
blue in color	blue
consensus of opinion	consensus
important essentials	essentials
resulting effect	effect
cooperate together	cooperate

**3B
wdy**

3. Where appropriate, make your writing more concise by omitting *there is, there are, it is,* and *this is* constructions.

Wordy	There are seven people living in that apartment.
Revised	Seven people live in that apartment.
Wordy	This is the step that is crucial for getting a job.
Revised	This step is crucial for getting a job.

4. Some *who, which,* and *that* clauses can be changed into modifying words or phrases.

Wordy	Cheryl Stickfinger, who is the mayor, is accused of embezzling city funds.
Revised	Mayor Cheryl Stickfinger is accused of embezzling city funds.
Wordy	Then they each wolfed down a banana split that contained five-hundred calories.
Revised	Then they each wolfed down a five-hundred-calorie banana split.
Wordy	The police officer, who was frustrated about missing his promotion, started taking kickbacks.
Revised	The police officer, frustrated about missing his promotion, started taking kickbacks.

**3B
wdy**

EXERCISE

Revise the following passage to reduce wordiness.

(1) One of the most recent new discoveries in medicine is the so-called diving reflex. (2) When people fall into water that is icy, their circulation slows down due to the fact that the water is so cold. (3) In addition, the metabolism of every cell that is in the body slows down, conserving oxygen. (4) In a recent case, Alvaro Garza, who is eleven years old, disappeared from view underneath the ice for forty-five minutes. (5) When rescuers finally pulled him at long last from beneath the ice, he was unconscious, his body temperature was cold and below normal, and his skin was grayish-blue in color. (6) Regardless of the fact that rescuers could find no pulse or heartbeat, they began CPR (cardiopulmonary resuscitation) immediately. (7) Within a few days, Alvaro began to recover in a steady manner, and soon he was asking for a hamburger and french fries. (8) Although he may have some lingering effects from his ordeal that do not go away in a short period of time, the unexplainable miracle is that he survived.

3C Colloquial Language and Slang

Your audience and purpose should determine whether conversational language is appropriate. In informal or expressive writing, colloquial language (spoken language), slang, or trendy expressions may be vivid and effective. In conversation or informal writing, we may say that something is *cool, hip, gross, weak, sweet,* or *too much.* We may call a friend *dude,* a skateboarder a *thrasher,* or someone we don't like a *wimp* or *geek.*

In formal writing, however, you should avoid colloquial expressions and slang. Your readers may not know the expressions, they may find some slang offensive, or they may think *gross* is simply too vague to describe what really happened. Slang, in fact, tends to become a shorthand for a whole experience and thus invites *telling* ("This guy was a real geek") rather than *showing* ("Rudolph had messy hair, wore adhesive tape on his glasses, and always had one green and one orange sock sticking out of his polyester pants. He lived out of a forty-pound bookpack, watched *Dr. Who* on TV every day, and spoke like William F. Buckley").

3D Clichés and Jargon

3D wdy

CLICHÉS

Some expressions are so commonly used that they have become automatic, predictable, trite, or hackneyed. The phrases in the left-hand column, for example, may have been fresh and original once, but now they are as stale as dirty dishwater and about as exciting as a secondhand sock. The expressions in the right-hand column, for example, are so predictable that we can easily guess the missing word.

tried and true	strong as an _____
needle in a haystack	dark as _____
easier said than done	heavy as _____
burning the midnight oil	cold as _____
didn't sleep a wink	busy as a _____
crack of dawn	happy as a _____
dead of night	white as _____
last but not least	quick as a _____
birds of a feather	blind as a _____
hit the nail on the head	sober as a _____
face the music	tough as _____
straw that broke the camel's back	gentle as a _____

JARGON

Jargon is the technical vocabulary of any specialized occupation, field, or profession. In technical or specialized writing, writers should use the vocabulary of their field. In the following passage, the specialized vocabulary (*homeotic, mutant, rudimentary,* and *thoracic*) is entirely appropriate.

> In the cockroach *Bletella germanica,* a homeotic mutant produces rudimentary wings on the first thoracic segment. No modern insect normally bears wings on its first thoracic segment, but the earliest winged fossil insects did!
>
> —Stephen J. Gould, *Hen's Teeth and Horse's Toes*

Jargon, however, is also a generic label for impressive words used for their own sake. Any specialized vocabulary is inappropriate when used not to *inform* but to *impress* an audience with the writer's intelligence. When writers use jargon inappropriately, they are not communicating—they're showing off.

Below is a jargon-filled parody, in legalese, of the simple, clear sentence, "Have an orange." This passage, by the editors of *Labor Magazine,* appears in Stuart Chase's essay "Gobbledygook":

> I hereby give and convey to you, all singular, my estate and right, title, claim and advantages of and in said orange, together with all rind, juice, pulp and pits, and all rights and advantages therein . . . anything hereinbefore or hereinafter or in any other deed or deeds, instrument or instruments of whatever nature or kind whatsoever, to the contrary, in any wise, notwithstanding.

Sometimes writers use jargon not to make themselves sound impressive but to promote the *subject* they're writing about. We commonly call the result *advertising.* Here is a sample of a Nike advertisement for a walking shoe.

> Walking. To you, it's a simple matter of putting one foot in front of another. To Nike, it's an entire science.

> In fact, we have studied walking in one of the world's leading biomechanical labs. Our own. And as a result, we've designed a technically advanced shoe specifically for the walking motion. The EXW. We built it close to the ground for stability. With a tri-density midsole that supports and centers your foot. A vented toe area for cool comfort. Flex grooves that bend with your foot. And a Nike-Air cushioning system that makes you feel, literally, like you're walking on air.

**3D
wdy**

Now, all this technology may seem a bit much. But try on a pair. You'll see that the EXW doesn't make walking more complicated. It just takes it one step further.

Nike hopes the inflated language and technical jargon in this passage will make you feel better about spending eighty dollars for a walking shoe. "World's leading bio-mechanical labs," "advanced shoe specifically for the walking motion," "tri-density midsole," "vented toe area," and "flex grooves"—all this jargon does seem a bit much. We may ridicule such language, but remember that if the advertisement causes us to buy the shoe, the language is appropriate for the audience.

EXERCISE

In the following passage, replace clichés with fresh, figurative language, and eliminate or replace inappropriate jargon.

(1) The television news media in America need to be reformed. (2) The bottom line is that serious news has been lost as stations rush to entertain the viewer. (3) Trying to find an informative story on the evening news is like looking for a needle in a haystack. (4) The station executives who finalize the programmatic output for the evening news believe that the average American is dumber than an ox. (5) As a result, viewers see in-depth stories about a sex scandal involving a local politician, but only a few seconds explaining why the stock market is scraping the bottom of the barrel. (6) Newscasters attempt to maximize their humor by telling jokes that go over like a lead balloon rather than informing the viewer about the latest decision-making process on armament restrictions. (7) If station programmers actually interfaced with the public occasionally, they would recognize the error of their ways.

3E Sexist Language

Do not use language that unfairly stereotypes people or discriminates against either women or men. Just as you would avoid racist terms, you should avoid language that stereotypes people's roles, occupations, or behavior by gender. Sentences such as "A doctor always cares for his patient" or "A secretary should always help her boss" imply that all doctors are men and all secretaries are women. Phrases such as *female logic, male ego, emotional woman,* or *typical male brutality* imply that all women are excessively emotional and all men are egotistical brutes. In fact, those stereotypes are not true. If you use sexist language, you will offend your readers. Even more important, your language should not encourage you or your reader to see the world in sexist stereotypes.

3E
sxt

1. Avoid words that suggest sexist roles.

SEXIST	REVISED
man	people, person
chairman	chair, head
businessman	businessperson
policeman	police officer
mankind	humanity
congressman	representative
statesman	politician, diplomat
lady lawyer	lawyer
career girl	professional woman

SEXIST	REVISED
coed	student
mailman	letter carrier
old wives' tale	superstition

Note, however, that some words that link occupation with gender are still appropriate. Most writers still use *actor* and *waiter* for men and *actress* and *waitress* for women. Other words, however, such as *stewardess* or *seamstress,* are often replaced with *flight attendant* or *garment worker.*

2. Be consistent in your use of people's names. If you write *Ernest Hemingway,* then write *Emily Dickinson,* not *Miss Dickinson.* If you write Lennon instead of *John Lennon,* then write *Parton,* not *Dolly Parton* or *Dolly.*

3. Avoid using the pronouns *he, his,* or *him* when you are referring to activities, roles, or behavior that could describe either sex.

Sexist	A doctor should listen carefully to his patient.
	Note: Use a plural if it does not alter your meaning.
Revised	Doctors should listen carefully to their patients.
Sexist	An effective teacher knows each of her students.
	Note: You may use *his or her* sparingly, but avoid using the construction *s/he.*
Revised	An effective teacher knows each of his or her students.
Sexist	Everyone hopes that he will survive the first year of college.
	Note: Often, you can revise the sentence by using first or second person or by omitting the pronoun.
Revised	I hope to survive the first year of college.
Revised	All of us hope to survive the first year of college.
Revised	You hope to survive the first year of college.
Revised	Everyone hopes to survive the first year of college.
	Note: Do *not* mix singular and plural by saying, "Everyone hopes *they* will survive the first year of college."

EXERCISE

Revise the following passage to eliminate sexist language.

(1) Everyone in college now is looking for that special job that will match his talents and yet bring him sufficient income. (2) Teaching is a low-paying but good career if you don't mind being a professor who spends his life reading papers, getting grants, and serving on committees. (3) A secretary or stewardess can begin her career with minimal training, but a nurse must dedicate herself to rigorous medical schooling. (4) In business and entertainment, girls can work right alongside the men. (5) In the entertainment field, many people dream of being a Bruce Springsteen or a Tina Turner, although most singers don't have Springsteen's talent or Tina's perseverance. (6) A businessman often works his way up the ladder and becomes chairman of the company. (7) Even staying at home and raising a family is a respectable career for either a man or his wife, though most men simply don't have the temperament to raise children. (8) Whatever your chosen career, from mailman to congressman, hard work and dedication are the keys to landing and keeping that important job.

3F dn/cn

3F Denotation and Connotation

The *denotation* of a word is its literal or dictionary definition. Both *house* and *home* refer, denotatively, to a structure in which people live. Many words have, in addition, a *connotation* or emotional association that can be negative, neutral, or positive. *House* has, for most people, a *neutral* or sterile connotation, whereas *home,* for most people, has a *positive* connotation, suggesting warmth, comfort, security, and family.

Choose words appropriately for their connotative value.

Inappropriate	Dr. Aileen Brown, a *notorious* scientist, just received the Nobel Prize for her work with superconductors. [*Notorious* people are usually famous for their *misconduct.*]
Revised	Dr. Aileen Brown, a *famous* scientist, just received the Nobel Prize for her work with superconductors.
Inappropriate	Beverly looked at her friend Steve and said, "Why don't you finish your dinner? You need the food—you're already a bit *scrawny* looking." [Steve prefers to think of himself as *thin* or *slim* rather than scrawny.]
Revised	Beverly looked at her friend Steve and said, "Why don't you finish your dinner? You need the food—you're already a bit *thin.*"

Inappropriate	Lynn's father told Paul that the apartment was decorated cheaply but tastefully. [Paul's feelings may be hurt. He does have good taste in furnishings, and he did the best he could on his tight budget.]
Revised	Lynn's father told Paul that the apartment was decorated tastefully but inexpensively.

EXERCISE

The following groups of words have similar denotative meanings but vary widely in their emotional associations or connotative meanings. Rank the words in each group from most negative, to neutral, to most positive.

- social drinker, wino, lush, reveler, alcoholic, sot, party animal, elbow bender, inebriate, problem drinker, booze hound, bar hopper
- scholar, intellectual, four-eyes, walking encyclopedia, geek, savant, bookworm, genius, pedant, bibliophile
- thrifty, penny-pinching, frugal, miserly, tight-fisted, cheap, economical, prudent, stingy
- steady, loyal, stubborn, firm, unyielding, dedicated, obstinate, devoted

3G Usage Glossary

This glossary lists alphabetically words and phrases that frequently cause problems for writers. In many cases, writers disagree about the preferred usage in formal writing. If you are in doubt, check a dictionary, such as *The American Heritage Dictionary*, *The Random House Dictionary*, or a guide, such as Margaret Bryant's *Current American Usage*.

Because this glossary references only the most obvious usage errors, refer to a standard or unabridged dictionary for items not included.

a, an: Use *a* when the following word begins with a *consonant sound:* a book, a clever saying, a hat. Use *an* when the following word begins with a *vowel sound:* an apple, an old building, an honor.

accept, except: *Accept* is a verb meaning "to receive": "I accept the gift." *Except* is a preposition meaning "other than" or "excluding": "Everyone received a gift except John." Rarely, *except* is a verb meaning "to exclude": "The editor excepted the footnote from the article."

advise, advice: *Advise* is a verb: "I advise you to exercise regularly." *Advice* is a noun: "Please take this advice."

affect, effect: *Affect* is usually a verb: "The flying beer cups did not affect the outfielder's concentration." *Effect* is a noun: "His obvious poise had a calming effect on the crowd." ***Remember:*** If you can say, "The effect," then you are correctly using the noun form. Less often, *effect* is also a verb: "His behavior effected a change in the crowd's attitude."

all right, alright: *All right,* two words, is the accepted spelling. *Alright* is nonstandard in the opinion of most experts.

a lot: *A lot* is always two words that mean "many." Wherever possible, however, *avoid* using *a lot.* Replace with a more specific description. See Section 3A.

already, all ready: *Already* means "by now" or "previously": "The essay was already completed." *All ready* means "completely prepared": "The paragraphs were all ready to be printed."

among, between: Use *among* for *three or more* people or things: "We should distribute the winnings among all the players." ***Note:*** *Between* is used for three or more items when location or a reciprocal relationship is indicated: "They found the treasure at a point equidistant between the three trees." "Through careful negotiations, a nonaggression treaty was reached between the four nations."

amount, number: *Amount* refers to quantity: "He saved a large amount of food for the winter months." *Number* refers to countable items: "She owned a large number of expensive sports cars."

anyone, any one: *Anyone* is a pronoun: "Anyone who likes Mayan art should hear the lecture." *Any one* is an adjective phrase modifying a noun: "He owns more Mayan art than any one person could possibly appreciate."

bad, badly: *Bad* is an adjective used in the predicate ("After a week of the flu, she looked bad") or before a noun ("She caught my cold at a bad time"): "She felt bad because she had a bad cold." *Badly* is an adverb: "He wrote badly because he had a high fever."

being, being that: *Being* cannot be used as a complete verb. "The seat being taken" is not a complete sentence. *Being that* is nonstandard: "Being that the bus was late, we missed the show." Use *because* or *since:* "Because the bus was late, we missed the show."

beside, besides: *Beside* is a preposition meaning "next to" or "by the side of ": "Peggi sat beside the senator." *Besides* is a preposition meaning "moreover" or "in addition to": "Besides, the senator likes several people besides George."

can, may: In formal writing, use *can* for ability: "I can take out the garbage." Use *may* for permission: "May I have the honor of taking out the garbage?" Also use *may* for possibility: "If I have time, I may take out the garbage."

center around: Illogical: One can "circle around" but not "center around." Replace with "center on" or "focus on": "The controversy focused on the right of the worker to a safe, smoke-free environment."

3G gls

cite, site: *Cite* is a verb meaning "to quote as an authority" or "to mention": "She cited Newcastle's blue law, which forbade card playing on Sunday." *Site* is a noun meaning a "place" or "location": "The church basement was, in fact, the site of Newcastle's first bingo game."

continual, continuous: *Continual* means "frequently repeated": "Most soap operas have continual interruptions for commercials." *Continuous* means "unceasing": "Throughout the broadcast, we heard a continuous buzzing sound."

could of, should of: Nonstandard. Use *could have* or *should have.*

data, media, criteria: The singular forms are *datum, medium,* and *criterion.* In formal writing, use plural verbs and pronouns with the plural noun. "Our data reveal a sharp increase in rapes and assaults since last year." "The media use their own criteria for sex and violence."

different from, different than: For prepositional phrases, use *different from:* "His chili recipe is different from yours." Although *different from* is preferred, sometimes *different than* results in a more concise sentence. "She is a different player than she used to be" is less wordy than "She is a different player from the player she used to be."

disinterested, uninterested: *Disinterested* means "objective or impartial": "As a disinterested third party, Marji resolved our dispute." *Uninterested* means "not interested": "We were uninterested in the outcome of the fall elections."

farther, further: *Farther* usually refers to distance: "How much farther are we going to jog?" *Further* refers to additional time, amount, or degree: "Furthermore, if you cannot hire me, I will go further into debt."

fewer, less: *Fewer* refers to numbers or countable items: "Fewer teenagers smoke than a decade ago." *Less* refers to amount ("less sugar") or degree ("less important"): "Teenagers spend less money on cigarettes than they did a decade ago."

hopefully: *Hopefully* means "with hope," or "in a hopeful manner": "Charlene waited hopefully for a letter from home." Most good writers still object to the colloquial usage of *hopefully* (meaning, "I hope," or "it is to be hoped"): "Hopefully, Charlene will get her letter from home." Change to: "I hope Charlene gets her letter from home."

imply, infer: *Imply* means to suggest without directly stating: "The news report implied that the president was seriously ill." *Infer* means to draw a conclusion: "I inferred from the news report that the president was seriously ill." Writers and speakers *imply;* readers and listeners *infer.*

its, it's: *Its,* like *his* or *her,* is a possessive pronoun: "The tree is losing its leaves." *It's* is a contraction of *it is:* "It's your turn to rake the leaves."

lay, lie: *Lay* is the transitive verb *(lay, laid)*, *laid* meaning "put" or "place": "Please lay the book on the table." *Lie* is an intransitive verb *(lie, lay, lain)* meaning "recline" or "occupy a place": "The books lie on the table."

like, as, as if: *Like* is a preposition: "A great race driver is like an opera singer—vain and arrogant." *As* can be a preposition ("His mission as a driver was to demonstrate his grace and courage"), but it can also introduce a clause: "Even at the end of the race, he looked as if he had just stepped off the cover of a magazine."

lose, loose: *Lose* is a verb meaning "misplace" or "be deprived of": "Good detectives never lose their nerve." *Loose* is an adjective meaning "free" or "not tight": "The psychopath got loose by climbing through the ventilating system."

principal, principle: *Principal* as an adjective means "major" or "main"; as a noun, *principal* refers either to a "chief official" or to a "capital sum of money": "The principal of the high school listed as his principal debt the $50,000 he owed on the principal of his house mortgage." *Principle* is a noun meaning "basic truth," "rule," or "moral standard": "He learned the principles of accounting and finance."

quote, quotation: *Quote* is a verb: "I quoted the passage from Thoreau's *Walden*." Do not use *quote* as a noun ("The following quote from *Walden*"); instead, use *quotation, remark,* or *passage:* "The following passage from *Walden* illustrates Thoreau's politics."

that, which: *That* always introduces restrictive clauses; *which* introduces either restrictive or nonrestrictive clauses. Some writers prefer, however, to use *that* only for restrictive clauses and *which* only for nonrestrictive. "The hat that has the pheasant feather was a birthday present." The clause "that has the pheasant feather" restricts, limits, and identifies which hat was the present. "The hat, which is nearly ten years old, was a birthday present." The clause "which is nearly ten years old" is only incidental information; it does not specify which hat was the present.

their, they're, there: *Their* is a pronoun: "She is playing with their tennis balls." *They're* is a contraction: "They're really upset that she didn't even ask." *There* is an adverb or an expletive: "She's practicing over there. There are the tennis balls."

to, too, two: *To* is a preposition: "I am writing to Bev." *Too* is an adverb meaning "in addition" or "also": "You too can write her a letter." *Too* also is an intensifier meaning "very": "Dad expects me to write too often." *Two* is a number: "I have written two times this month."

used to, supposed to: Use the past tense ("used to") not ("use to"): "I used to go there every weekend." "I was supposed to be at swimming practice at 3:30 P.M."

**3G
gls**

SECTION 4
PUNCTUATION AND MECHANICS

The purpose of punctuation is to clarify meaning and promote communication. Commas, periods, semicolons, dashes, and other punctuation marks guide readers to meanings, just as traffic signals, double yellow lines, turning lanes, and one-way signs guide motorists to destinations. The conventions of punctuation create *expectations* in the reader. Just as you are surprised when a car runs a red light and nearly hits you, readers are surprised when writers fail to follow the conventions of punctuation.

Punctuation—or the lack of it—can change the entire meaning of a sentence. In actual conversation, pauses, inflections, intonation, gestures, and facial expressions do the work of punctuation. In writing, however, punctuation must provide these clues.

Read the following sentences. How many different ways can you find to punctuate each sentence? How does each version alter the meaning?

> Give the peanuts to my daughter Ella
>
> She said walk quietly
>
> Let's go see the lions eat Marcia.

Sometimes writers unintentionally create confusion by omitting important punctuation. Notice how the appropriate use of commas in the following sentences prevents a possible surprise and clarifies the meaning.

Confusing	To keep the pipes from freezing the plumber advised us to run the water all night. [How exactly did the pipes freeze the plumber?]
Revised	To keep the pipes from freezing, the plumber advised us to run the water all night.
Confusing	On the menu for lunch was ham and Sam was doing the cooking. [Is Sam on the menu?]
Revised	On the menu for lunch was ham, and Sam was doing the cooking.

The guidelines for punctuation and mechanics in this section will help you to avoid unintentional problems and to clarify your writing. Review these guidelines as you edit your own and other people's writing.

4

4A Sentence Punctuation

Much of the confusion about punctuation occurs because connecting words often have similar meanings but signal different punctuation conventions. A stop sign, a red light, and a blinking red light, for example, all mean that motorists must stop, but each signals a slightly different procedure. In English, *but*, *although*, and *however* mean that a contrast is coming, but each requires different punctuation:

> We won the volleyball game, *but* our best hitter broke her wrist.

> *Although* we won the game, our best hitter broke her wrist.

> We won the game; *however*, our best hitter broke her wrist.

"Sorry, but I'm going to have to issue you a summons for reckless grammar and driving without an apostrophe."

Using commas and semicolons to punctuate sentences and clauses requires knowing the three basic types of connecting or *conjunctive* words.

Coordinate conjunctions: Conjunction means "a joining together"; "coordinates" are "equals." A coordinate conjunction (coord. conj.) joins equals together. The acronym BOYFANS will help you remember the coordinate conjunctions:

b	o	y	f	a	n	s
but	or	yet	for	and	nor	so

Subordinating conjunctions: A subordinate conjunction (sub. conj.) joins a dependent or subordinate clause to an independent or main clause. The following are the most common subordinating conjunctions.

after	before	since	until
although	even if	so that	when
as	even though	than	whenever
as if	if	that	where
as though	in order that	though	wherever
because	rather than	unless	while

Adding a subordinating conjunction changes an independent clause (IC) to a dependent clause (DC).

                                                IC
Independent Clause He buys a newspaper.

                SUB
                CONJ   DC
Dependent Clause *If* he buys a newspaper

                            DC   IC
Complete Sentence If he buys a newspaper, he will see the story.

Conjunctive adverbs: A conjunctive adverb (conj. adv.) acts as a transitional phrase. Following are the most common conjunctive adverbs.

accordingly	however	meanwhile	still
also	incidentally	moreover	thereafter
consequently	indeed	nevertheless	therefore
furthermore	instead	otherwise	thus
hence	likewise	similarly	

If you are uncertain whether a connecting word is a conjunctive adverb, *test* by moving the connecting word to another place in the clause. Conjunctive adverbs can be moved; subordinating conjunctions (such as *if* or *because*) and coordinating conjunctions *(but, or, yet, for, and, nor, so)* cannot.

Conjunctive adverbs can be moved:

We won the game; *however,* our best hitter broke her wrist.

We won the game; our best hitter, *however,* broke her wrist.

We won the game; our best hitter broke her wrist, *however.*

Subordinating conjunctions cannot be moved:

Although our best hitter broke her wrist, we won the game.

Our best hitter, *although,* broke her wrist, we won the game.

[Obviously, *although* cannot be moved to another position in the clause.]

**4A
p**

Coordinating conjunctions cannot be moved.

> We won the game, *but* our best hitter broke her wrist.

> We won the game, our best hitter, *but,* broke her wrist.

[Moving a coordinating conjunction scrambles the sentence.]

Follow these rules for joining independent clauses (IC) and dependent clauses (DC).

1. Join two independent clauses with a *comma* and a *coordinating conjunction.*

```
              COORD
  IC,        CONJ      IC.
```

> The pizza is good, *but* the mystery meat is disgusting.

2. Join two independent clauses with a *semicolon* and a *conjunctive adverb.*

```
            CONJ
  IC;       ADV           IC.
```

> The pizza is good; *however,* the mystery meat is disgusting.

3. Join two independent clauses with a *semicolon.*

```
  IC;              IC.
```

> The pizza is good; the mystery meat is disgusting.

4. Join a dependent clause to an independent clause with a *comma.*

```
        DC,              IC.
```

> *Although* mystery meat tastes all right, it looks disgusting.

4B Comma Splices and Fused Sentences

Two common errors in joining independent clauses are the *comma splice* and the *fused sentence* (also called a *run-on sentence*). Revise by following one of the patterns in 1–3 in the rules just cited.

Comma Splice	[IC, IC.] I know that airplanes are safer than cars, I still have a fear of flying.
Revised	I know that airplanes are safer than cars, *but* I still have a fear of flying.
Comma Splice	[IC, Conj. Adv., IC.] I know that airplanes are safer than cars, however, I still have a fear of flying.
Revised	I know that airplanes are safer than cars; *however,* I still have a fear of flying.

**4B
cs/fs**

Fused Sentence   [IC IC.] I know that airplanes are safer than cars I still have a fear of flying.

Revised   *Although* I know that airplanes are safer than cars, I still have a fear of flying.

EXERCISE

In the following passage, correct all comma splices and fused sentences.

(1) For years, scientists have attempted to teach animals to communicate for the most part, their efforts have failed. (2) In the 1950s, psychologists failed to teach a chimpanzee to speak, the ape was able to grunt only a few words. (3) In the 1960s, however, a chimp named Washoe learned the sign language of the deaf. (4) Washoe came to understand hundreds of words, he used them to communicate and express original ideas. (5) As it turns out, the great apes have the capacity to learn language, but they cannot speak. (6) This research proved that humans are not the only animals capable of using language they are, however, the most sophisticated users of language.

4C Commas

COMMAS FOR INTRODUCTORY ELEMENTS

Use commas to set off most introductory elements.

Because I broke three flasks, I'm going to have a large bill for chemistry lab. [introductory dependent clause]

In the middle of finals week last semester, I became seriously depressed. [long introductory prepositional phrase]

Jogging home after classes, I see children playing in the schoolyard. [introductory participial phrase]

To save money, I often take the bus [introductory infinitive phrase]

Incidentally, I hope my roommate will be here this weekend. [introductory adverb]

ITEMS IN A SERIES

Use *commas* to separate items in a series (a, b, and c). Generally, use a comma before the *and*. In some cases, omitting the comma before the final item in the series may cause confusion.

Confusing	She rented an apartment with a convection oven, a microwave, a refrigerator with an icemaker and a garbage disposal. [Does the refrigerator have a built-in icemaker and garbage disposal?]
Revised	She rented an apartment with a convection oven, a microwave, a refrigerator with an icemaker, and a garbage disposal.

EXERCISE

Revise the punctuation in the following passage.

(1) Everyone can have fun outside in the wintertime by following some commonsense rules. (2) If you are going to be outside for several hours be sure to eat a nutritious meal before leaving. (3) On cold damp or windy days wear clothes that are warm and dry. (4) To stay warm protect yourself against moisture that builds up from the inside. (5) Most experts recommend dressing in layers. (6) The inner layer wicks moisture away from your body the middle layer provides thermal protection and the outer layer protects against rain or wind. (7) Curiously enough most people tend to put on too many clothes, underestimating their body's ability to exercise comfortably naturally and safely in cold weather.

NONRESTRICTIVE ELEMENTS

Nonrestrictive modifiers should be separated from the sentence by commas. Always *test* the phrase or clause. If it can be removed from the sentence without a change in the meaning, use commas.

Nonrestrictive	Coach Hall, who was invited to the party, celebrated the victory. [The clause "who was invited to the party" is incidental information. It does not restrict or specify which coach was celebrating. The two commas indicate that removing the clause from the sentence will not change the meaning: "Coach Hall celebrated the victory."]
Nonrestrictive	Seattle, which has a reputation as a rainy city, is actually drier than New Orleans. [Remove the clause, and the meaning of the sentence is not altered: "Seattle is actually drier than New Orleans."]
Nonrestrictive	Charles, the man in the gray suit, eats fried grasshoppers when no one is looking.

4C
,

	[The appositive "the man in the gray suit" can be removed from the sentence without an alteration in the meaning.]
Restrictive	Demonstrators who hurled bricks were arrested by the police. [The meaning is that *only those* demonstrators *who hurled bricks* were arrested by the police. The phrase *who hurled bricks* cannot be removed from the sentence without a change in meaning. Do *not* use commas to separate restrictive elements.]
Nonrestrictive	The class, which was taught by Anne Perkins, met at eight o'clock in the morning. *Note:* This sentence says that the class met at eight o'clock, and Anne Perkins was, incidentally, the teacher. (Usually use *which* for nonrestrictive clauses.)
Restrictive	The class that was taught by Anne Perkins met at eight o'clock in the morning. *Note:* This sentence says that the particular class taught by Professor Perkins met at eight o'clock. Other classes met at some other time. (Use *that* for restrictive clauses. Do not use commas.)

UNNECESSARY COMMAS

Do not use a comma to separate a subject and a verb.

| **Faulty** | My toughest class of the day, met at eight o'clock. |
| **Revised** | My toughest class of the day met at eight o'clock. |

Do not use a comma to separate compound subjects or predicates.

| **Faulty** | The dean of students, and the chancellor decided to cancel classes. [compound subject] |
| **Revised** | The dean of students and the chancellor decided to cancel classes. |

| **Faulty** | Because of the heavy snowfall, I stayed inside all afternoon, and popped popcorn. [compound predicate]
Note: When coordinate conjunctions do not join independent clauses or items in a series, a comma is usually not necessary (see Section 4A for appropriate use of commas with coordinate conjunctions). |
| **Revised** | Because of the heavy snowfall, I stayed inside all afternoon and popped popcorn. |

4C
,

COORDINATE ADJECTIVES

Use a comma to separate coordinate (equal) adjectives. Test for coordinate adjectives: (1) Insert an *and* between the adjectives and (2) reverse the order of the adjectives. If the meaning of the sentence remains unchanged, the adjectives are equal or coordinate.

Example	It was a dull dark day.
	[Insert *and;* reverse adjectives: *It was a dull and dark day. It was a dark and dull day.* Since the meaning of the sentence has not changed, these are coordinate or equal adjectives. Remove the *and* and add a comma.]
Revised	It was a dull, dark day.
Example	The car had studded snow tires.
	[Insert *and;* reverse adjectives: *The car had studded and snow tires. The car had snow and studded tires.* The meaning of the original sentence is changed; therefore, the adjectives are not coordinate. Do *not* separate with comma.]
Revised	The car had studded snow tires.

DIALOGUE

Use commas to set off a direct quotation or dialogue.

Direct Quotation

> The author points out, "One of the effects of embalming by chemical injection, however, has been to dispel fears of live burial."
>
> —Jessica Mitford

Dialogue

> "We'll try it," the professor said to me, grimly, "with every adjustment of the microscope known to man."
>
> —James Thurber

In fiction or nonfiction, indent (begin a new paragraph) when the dialogue shifts from one person to the next.

> A white man finally came along and found her—a hunter, a young man, with his dog on a chain.

> "Well, Granny!" he laughed, "what are you doing there?"

> "Lying on my back like a June-bug waiting to be turned over, mister," she said, reaching up her hand.

He lifted her up, gave her a swing in the air, and set her down. "Anything broken, Granny?"

"No sir, them old dead weeds is springy enough," said Phoenix, when she had got her breath. "I thank you for your trouble."

—Eudora Welty, "A Worn Path"

ADDRESSES, DATES, DEGREES

Use commas to set off addresses, dates, and degrees/titles.

Addresses	What Cheer, Iowa, is his hometown.
Dates	On December 7, 1941, the Japanese bombed Pearl Harbor.
Degrees	Randal Beaver, D.D.S., is my orthodontist.

EXERCISE

Revise the punctuation in the following passage.

(1) Dinosaurs which have been extinct for millions of years are making news again. (2) At a meeting of the Geological Society of America in November 1987 scientists announced a startling discovery. (3) Dinosaurs, that lived 80 million years ago, benefited from an atmosphere that contained nearly 50 percent more oxygen than it does now. (4) Gary Landis geochemist for the U.S. Geological Service and Robert Berner professor at Yale University reached that conclusion after analyzing, air bubbles trapped in bits of amber. (5) They found that the tiny, air bubbles contained 32 percent oxygen, compared with 21 percent in the modern atmosphere. (6) When asked whether a decreasing oxygen supply, could have caused the extinction of the dinosaurs, Berner explained "It was a very gradual change, and most organisms easily adapt." (7) "The large slow-moving dinosaurs probably became extinct" he said "following some cataclysmic, geological, event."

4D Periods and Semicolons

PERIODS

Use periods at the end of sentences, indirect questions, and commands.

Sentence	The Statue of Liberty was officially rededicated.
Indirect Question	I asked my friend when he was going to stop taking pictures.
Command	Wait until the ship moves into the picture.

4D
./;

SEMICOLONS

Use a semicolon to join related independent clauses. Remember to test for independent clauses by using a period. If you can use a period at the end of each independent clause, and if the sentences are related, you may wish to use a semicolon. Remember, however, that semicolons are usually more appropriate in formal writing.

> Nowadays, says one sociologist, you don't have to have a reason for going to college; it's an institution. His definition of an institution is an arrangement everyone accepts without question; the burden of proof is not on why you go, but why anyone thinks there might be a reason for not going.
>
> —Caroline Bird

> I take a dim view of dams; I find it hard to learn to love cement.
>
> —Edward Abbey

Use a semicolon to separate items in a series that already have internal punctuation.

> We quickly meet the "good guys" of *Star Wars:* Luke Skywalker, played by Mark Hamill; Ben "Obi-Wan" Kenobi, played by Alec Guinness; and Han Solo, played by Harrison Ford.
>
> —Judith Crist

Do *not* use a semicolon to join dependent with independent clauses.

> Harrison Ford played the leading role in *Raiders of the Lost Ark;* which made him an instant star.

4E :/—

4E Colons and Dashes

COLONS

Use a colon to introduce a list or an explanation. Colons often create formal, structured sentences.

> When you go to the grocery store, please get the following items: two boxes of frozen peas, five pounds of baking potatoes, and a package of stuffing for the turkey.

> There is only one guaranteed method to lose weight: eat less and exercise more.

Usually, a colon following a verb is unnecessary.

Unnecessary	The best way to lose weight is: eat less and exercise more.

Revised	The best way to lose weight is to eat less and exercise more.
Unnecessary	I need: peas, baking potatoes, and stuffing.
Revised	I need peas, baking potatoes, and stuffing.

DASHES

Use a single dash for an abrupt shift. Use a pair of dashes for an interrupting or parenthetical comment. Use a dash instead of a comma, colon, or parentheses when you want a sentence to have a more informal, colloquial flavor.

> At last a happy thought struck me—I would draw the fish.
>
> —Samuel Scudder

> Indeed, there are moments today—amid outlaw litter, tax cheating, illicit noise, and motorized anarchy—when it seems as though the scofflaw represents the wave of the future.
>
> —Frank Trippett

EXERCISE

In the following passage, insert semicolons, colons, or dashes at the appropriate places. In some cases, there are several ways to punctuate the sentences correctly, so be prepared to explain your choice.

> (1) Yo-yo dieting the process of repeatedly losing and gaining weight is common today. (2) Instead of changing eating habits and exercise patterns, the yo-yo dieter uses three common strategies to lose weight taking diet pills, drinking diet liquids, and fasting outright. (3) The yo-yo dieter, however, needs to know the truth about dieting diet cycles decrease the muscle-to-fat ratio in the body and decrease the body's ability to lose weight during the next dieting cycle. (4) Quick-fix diets, in other words, will lead to rapid weight losses however, they will be followed by an even faster weight gain. (5) Ultimately, crash diets do more harm than good the body just wasn't designed to be a yo-yo.

4F Exclamation Points and Question Marks

4F ¡/?

EXCLAMATION POINTS

Use exclamation points sparingly, for stylistic emphasis.

> I saw the sleek gray-haired manager standing near the dance floor, snapping his fingers and smiling. . . . I bet myself that he owned one of the few blow-

dryers in Moscow. . . . He was watching the growing success of the only Western-style club in town and thinking: These kids! Right on! Crazy, but I love 'em!

—Andrea Lee

Bicyclists often ride as though two-wheeled vehicles are exempt from all traffic laws. Litterbugs convert their communities into trash dumps. . . . And then there are (hello, Everybody!) the jaywalkers.

—Frank Trippett

QUESTION MARKS

Use a question mark after a direct question.

> What is your first childhood memory?

Do not combine question marks with commas or periods.

> "What is your earliest memory?" she asked me. [Do not use a comma and a question mark: "What is your earliest memory?," she asked me.]

4G Quotation and Ellipsis Marks

QUOTATION MARKS

Use quotation marks to indicate a writer's or speaker's exact words.

> Marya Mannes says, "Woman, in short, is consumer first and human being fourth."

Use quotation marks for titles of *essays, articles, short stories, poems, chapters,* and *songs*—any title that is part of a larger collection.

> "Television: The Splitting Image" is the title of an essay by Marya Mannes.

Use single quotation marks for quotations within a quotation.

> James said, "I know I heard her say, 'Meet me outside the east door.' "

ELLIPSIS MARKS

Use ellipsis marks (three *spaced* points) to indicate material omitted from a direct quotation.

> Marya Mannes said, "Woman . . . is consumer first and human being fourth." [The ellipses indicate that words are omitted from the middle of the sentence.]

4G
" / . . .

Use a period *plus* three spaced points to signal either omitted words at the end of a sentence or omitted intervening sentence(s).

> Marya Mannes said, "Woman, in short, is consumer first and human being fourth. . . . The conditioning starts very early. . . ."

PUNCTUATION WITH QUOTATION MARKS

The following guidelines will help you to punctuate sentences with quotation marks. Periods and commas go *inside* quotation marks.

> According to biologist Julie Earwig, "Penguins are more densely covered with feathers than any other bird—nearly 180 feathers per square inch."

Colons and semicolons go *outside* quotation marks.

> Recent data about the eagle's feathers may revise the old saying "light as a feather": The vaned feathers on a bald eagle weigh more than its entire skeleton.

Exclamation points and question marks go *inside* or *outside* quotation marks. They go *inside* if they are a part of the quoted material.

> The award for the highest number of feathers, according to Earwig, "goes to the whistling swan with a staggering 25,000 feathers!" [The original sentence ends with an exclamation point.]

They go *outside* if they are not a part of the quoted material.

> Is it true that, as Earwig claims, "the tiny ruby-throated hummingbird has 940 feathers"? [The original sentence ends with a period.]

4H
italic

4H Italics

Most word-processing programs allow you to *italicize* certain words for emphasis. When using a typewriter or writing by hand, use underlining to indicate words that should be set in italics.

Titles   "Down the River" is the most interesting chapter in Edward Abbey's *Desert Solitaire*.
[Underline (or italicize) titles of books, magazines, films, paintings, newspapers—any work published separately. Use quotation marks for titles of chapters, articles, or poems—any title that is part of some collection in a book or magazine.]

	Exceptions: Do not underline the Bible or titles of legal documents, such as the Deed of Trust or the U.S. Constitution.
Names	The most famous travel ships used to be the *Santa Maria,* the *Titanic,* and the *Queen Mary.* Now the great ones are the *Apollo* and the *Challenger.* [Underline (or italicize) names of ships, trains, aircraft, or spacecraft.]
Foreign Words	He graduated *cum laude,* while his friend, who barely passed freshman mathematics, graduated *magna cum laude.* "C'est la vie," he thought. [Note, however, that many foreign words (burrito, bourgeois, genre, cliché, junta, and many others) have been incorporated into the language and do not need italics. Consult your dictionary if you are in doubt.]
Words or Letters	*Suppose* to should have a *d: supposed to* [Quotation marks are also used to indicate italics in handwritten or typed manuscripts.] *Note:* Do not underline or put quotation marks around the title of your essay when it appears on a title page or the first page of your manuscript.

EXERCISE

Revise the following passage, underlining appropriate words and titles.

(1) Tom Wolfe, author of The Right Stuff, wrote a novel about a Wall Street broker, The Bonfire of the Vanities. (2) This novel first appeared in twenty-seven installments in Rolling Stone magazine. (3) Wolfe's style has always been au courant, and Bonfire is no exception. (4) This novel features New York characters who run the gamut from drug pushers to the cunning and ambitious young lions of the investment world. (5) It is not a cliché to say that this book is difficult to put down.

41 Parentheses and Brackets

PARENTHESES

Use parentheses ( ) to set off additional information, examples, or comments.

> Outside our lifeboat, let us imagine another 210 million people (say the combined populations of Colombia, Ecuador, Venezuela, Morocco, Pakistan, Thailand, and the Philippines), increasing at a rate of 3.3 percent per year.
>
> —Garrett Hardin

Writing a film review requires that you carefully examine the criteria for your judgment (see Chapter 8).

BRACKETS

Use brackets [ ] to set off editorial remarks in quoted material. Brackets indicate that you, as an editor, are adding comments to the original material.

Original	After you hear my arguement, you will reelect Eastwood.
Edited	After you hear my arguement [sic], you will reelect [Mayor Clint] Eastwood. [As editor, you add information about Eastwood and indicate by using *sic* ("thus it is") that the misspelling, grammatical mistake, or inappropriate usage occurs in the original source and is not your error.]

4J Apostrophes and Hyphens

APOSTROPHES

Use apostrophes for contractions, possession, and some plurals.

Contractions	It's too bad you don't agree.
Possession	The wind blew the student's notes across the front lawn. [The notes belonging to one student blew across the lawn.] The wind blew the students' notes across the front lawn. [The notes belonging to several students blew across the lawn.] Your sister-in-law's accident was someone else's fault. [In compounds, make the last word possessive.]
Plurals	The 1980's [or 1980s] were the Yuppie years. Eliminate unnecessary use of the word *which*.

HYPHENS

Use hyphens for compound words, compound adjectives before nouns, some prefixes, and some numbers. When in doubt, always check a good dictionary.

Compounds	cross-reference; president-elect
Adjectives	a twentieth-century writer; the slate-blue sea; the three-year-old child *Note:* When the compound adjectives follow a noun, omit the hyphen: He is a writer well known only in Vermont.

Prefixes	ex-President Reagan; self-motivation
Numbers	twenty-six; one hundred sixty-five; one-fifth

4K Capitals and Numbers

CAPITALS

Capitalize proper nouns and adjectives, professional titles, principal words in titles of books or articles, and regional locations.

Proper Names	Judson Smith, Atlanta, Los Angeles, Missouri River, English, Swahili, American, Labor Day, Christmas, Hanukkah, Wednesday, October [Do not capitalize seasons or terms: autumn, spring, summer, fall semester, freshman year.]
Titles	Senator Kennedy, President Lincoln, Professor Findlay, Associate Dean Natalie Renner, Uncle Don, Father [Do not capitalize family titles preceded by a pronoun: my mother, my uncle, our grandfather.]
Titles	*Gone with the Wind,* "The Short Happy Life of Francis Macomber," "The Triumph of the Wheel," *Star Wars* [Some style manuals suggest capitalizing only the first word in a title. If you are citing titles in a bibliography or list of works cited, check your style manual.]
Regions	the South, the Northwest, the Middle East [Do not capitalize directions: traveling east, walking due north.]

NUMBERS

Conventions regarding numbers vary. Generally, except in scientific or technical writing, spell out numbers of one hundred or less or numbers that require two words or less. If a passage requires many numbers, be consistent in your usage.

This stadium seats fifty thousand people, but adding the end-zone bleachers increases the seating to fifty-seven thousand. [Hyphenated words count as one word.]

Our chemistry lecture hall seats 425 students, but only 310 are enrolled this semester in Chemistry 201. [However, at the beginning of sentences, spell out numbers ("Three hundred and ten students are enrolled this semester") or rewrite the sentence ("In Chemistry 201, 310 students are enrolled").]

**4K
cap**

EXERCISE

Revise the following passage for proper use of apostrophes, hyphens, capitals, italics, and numbers. Use your dictionary to help you edit this passage.

(1) The advertisement shows a sky-diver floating down to earth, and the pictures caption says, "I take vitamin supplements every day, just to be on the safe side." (2) Self styled experts, from your local pharmacist to physicians from the mount Sinai school of Medicine in New York city, encourage the public to believe that vitamins are a cure all. (3) There are only thirteen known vitamin deficiencies (such as scurvy, which is a Vitamin C deficiency), but nearly sixty percent of the two hundred fifty two american's responding to our questionnaire believed in taking vitamin supplements. (4) These days, its almost patriotic to take vitamins—even your Mother says, "Don't forget to take your vitamins!" (5) During the 1980's, vitamins popularity rose an astonishing twenty nine percent, and revenue from vitamin sale's jumped to nearly three billion. (6) Although sales are generally higher in the west, some Eastern cities such as boston and Philadelphia have also shown dramatic increase's in sales. (7) If you want to learn more about vitamins, read The Vitamin-Pushers in a recent issue of Consumer Reports.

Credits

University of Wisconsin won the Rose Bowl in 1994. Layne Kennedy, Corbis/Bettmann. **Girl writing in notebook while sitting on a blanket,** Photos.com. **Stonehenge,** Adam Woolfitt, CORBIS-NY. **Monet, Claude** (1840-1926) - Impression, Sunrise. 1872. Oil on canvas, 48 x 63 cm. Painted in Le Havre, France. Critics called Monet and his circle - at first ironically - "Impressionists" after the title of this work, Erich Lessing, Art Resource, N.Y. **Japanese-American Internees Farming at Manzanar,** CORBIS-NY. **Sugar wafer,** Stephen Reid. **Fig Newton,** Stephen Reid. **Boccioni, Umberto** (1882-1916) - Dynamism of a Cyclist, Scala, Art Resource, N.Y. **A gray timber-wolf feeds on fresh caribou kill,** Ron Niebrugge, Niebrugge Images. **Cartoon - "Write about dogs!",** The Cartoon Bank. **Cliff Palace,** George H. H. Huey, CORBIS-NY. **John Gast** (Active 1870s), "American Progress," c. 1872, Christie's Images Inc. **Prism,** iStock Photo International/Royalty Free. **Cartoon** – "Sorry, but I'm going to have to issue you a summons for reckless grammar and driving without an apostrophe." The Cartoon Bank. **Memorial Day services at Manzanar,** 5/31/1942, Stewart, Francis Manzanar, The Bancroft Library. **Rendering of Cesar Chavez,** Image is conte crayon on black paper.   Garcia Bavi, Cesar_Chavez_Bavi_2. **Man on yellow couch with tv re-mote,** Photos.com. **Cartoon - Viuti - "Buenos Aires, Argentina,"** Viuti, Cartoonists & Writers Syndicate. **Day and Night,** by M.C. Escher, The M. C. Escher Company BV. **Diego Rivera** (1886-1957), "The Flower Carrier" (formerly 'The Flower Vendor'). 1935. Oil and tempera on Masonite. 48 in. x 47 3/4 in. (121.92 cm x 121.29 cm). Ben Blackwell, San Francisco Museum of Modern Art. **Man & woman sitting with their backs to each other on a picnic table,** man is holding flower out to woman, Photos.com. **Migrant agricultural worker's family.** Seven hungry children. Mother aged thirty-two. Father is native Californian. Nipomo, California. CREATED/PUBLISHED © 1936 Mar. Dorothea Lange, Library of Congress. **Cartoon** - "Dear Andy, How have you been? Your mother and I miss you. Please sign off your computer and come downstairs for something to eat. Love, Dad." Randy Glasbergen, Randy Glasbergen. **AP Wide World Photos,** This is an artist's rendering of a Mars Exploration Rover. A Delta II rocket is scheduled to launch the first of two Mars Exploration Rover (MER) Missions for NASA on Sunday June 8, 2003. **Join American Red Cross,** Recruitment Poster by Robert C. Kauffmann, CORBIS-NY. **USA. San Francisco. 1982.** "My dream was to become a skool teacher. Mrs. Stone is rich. I have talents but not opportunity. I am used to standing behind Mrs. Stone. I have been a servant for 40 years." Jim Goldberg, Magnum Photos, Inc. **AP Wide World Photos,** Actor Michael J. Fox listens to Josh Bowler, who suffered a severe spinal cord injury in a fall, speak as they join Tammy Duckworth, the Democratic candidate for the U.S. House in Illinois' 6th Congressional District, during a rally for stem cell re-search, Tuesday, Oct. 24, 2006, in Wheaton, Ill. Duckworth faces Republican opponent Peter Roskam in the Nov. 7 election. M. Spencer Green. **Cartoon** - The Far Side - "Ok, stranger...What's the circumference of the Earth?...Who wrote "The Odyssey" and "The Iliad?"...What's the average rainfall of the Amazon Basin?" Bart, you fool! you can't shoot first and ask questions later!" Gary Larson, Creators Syndicate, Inc., The Far Side® by Gary Larson ©1986 FarWorks, Inc. All Rights Reserved. Used with Permission. **NEW OR-LEANS - AUGUST 29:** Two residents wade through chest deep water after finding bread and soda from a local grocery store after Hurricane Katrina came through the area on August 29, 2005 in New Orleans, Louisiana. Katrina was downgraded to a category 4 storm as it approached New Orleans. Chris Graythen, Getty Images. **We Can Do It!** Poster by J. Howard Miller. A World War II color poster depicting "Rosie the Riveter" encourages American women to show their strength and go to work for the war effort. Corbis/Bettmann. **AP Wide World Photos,** World War II: U.S. Posters and Propaganda. **Are you a girl with star-spangled heart?** - Join the WAC now! Thousands of Army jobs need filling! Library of Congress. **U.S. Army Photo,** U.S. Army Col. Debra Lewis, the commanding officer of the U.S Army Corps of Engineers, Gulf Region Central District, and Hammiah Nahia council member Sheik O'rhaman Hama Raheem cut the ribbon of the new women's center in Assyria, Iraq, Aug. 2, 2006. The Assyrian women's center, constructed through the U.S. Army Corps of Engineers, is a place where women of all ages can go to use computers to take classes or increase their literacy as well as providing sewing machines and materials. MC2 ELI J. MEDELLIN. **PATRIOTISM MEANS SILENCE,** A message from the office of Homeland Security, Brad Roberts. **Absolut End,** Adbusters Media Foundation. **Big Mac Attack,** Adbusters Media Foundation. **"Well, then, it's unanimous."** The Cartoon Bank. **"Alfred Eisenstaedt, V-J Day: Sailor Kissing Girl(1945)."** Alfred Eisenstaedt, Getty Images/Time Life Pictures. **August 1942, Washington, DC, USA** — Mrs. Ella Watson, a charwoman employed in a federal office building in Washington, DC, stands in front of an American flag with her mop and broom in a pose reminiscent of Grant Wood's "American Gothic." Gordon Parks documented Mrs. Watson's daily life for the Farm Security Administration in 1942 as part of a nationwide photography project on America's poor. His photo-essay on Mrs. Watson brought special focus to the lives of poor African-Americans in an era of war, depression, recovery, and social segregation. Gordon Parks, CORBIS-NY. **Cartoon** - "I was distracted for a moment. Go on." The Cartoon Bank. **Human Skull in a Desert,** CHARLY FRANKLIN, Getty Images, Inc. - Taxi **Pair of industrial chimneys emitting smoke, sunset, silhouette,** Jermey Walker, Getty Images Inc. - Stone Allstock. **Sled dogs and pups relax on a rock overlooking Ilulissat glacier.** It is Greenlands fastest moving glacier and major contributor to the mass balance of the continental ice sheet. A UN heritage site, it is considered one of the wonders of the world. It has shrunk by over 10 kilometers in just a few years in one of the most alarming examples of global warming in the Arctic region. National Geographic Image Collection. **AP Wide World Photos,** Former Vice President Al Gore testifies on Capitol Hill in Washington, Wednesday, March 21, 2007, before a joint hearing of the House Energy and Commerce, and Science and Technology subcommittees on climate change. Susan Walsh. **Global warming projections,** Wikipedia Foundation, Inc. **Cesar Chavez, Robert F. Kennedy.** Robert F. Kennedy sitting next to Cesar Chavez (looking very weak after a prolonged hunger strike) during a rally in support of the United Farm Workers Union. Michael Rougier, Getty Images/Time Life Pictures. **Labor activist Cesar Chavez** (C) walking in field with grape pickers in support of the United Farm Workers Union. Arthur Schatz, Getty Images/Time Life Pictures. **AP Wide World Photos,** Released prisoner of war Lt. Col. Robert L. Stirm is greeted by his family at Travis Air Force Base in Fairfield, Calif., as he returns home from the Vietnam War, March 17, 1973. In the lead is Stirm's daughter Lori, 15, followed by son Robert, 14; daughter Cynthia, 11; wife Loretta and son Roger, 12. Sal Veder. **Close-up of back side of macaroni and cheese meal showing nutrition facts,** Susan Van Etten, PhotoEdit Inc. **Machaut, Guillaume de** (c.1300-1377): Christmas Carol dance. Manuscript illumination. Art Resource, N.Y. **Girl on exercise equipment with feet in the air,** iStock Photo International/Royalty Free. **A migrant agricultural worker's wife and children in a camp.** In Nipomo, California, March 1936. Dorothea Lange, Corbis/Stock Market. **Leonardo da Vinci** (1452-1519) - Mona Lisa. 1503-1506. Oil on wood. 77 x 53 cm. Erich Lessing, Art Resource, N.Y. **Marie-Louise-Elisabeth Vigee-Lebrun** (1755-1842), Portrait of Marie Antoinette with Her

Index

Alphabetical Reference to the Handbook